FRANZ LISZT

ERNST BURGER

FRANZ LISZT

A CHRONICLE OF HIS LIFE IN
PICTURES AND DOCUMENTS

TRANSLATED BY
STEWART SPENCER

FOREWORD BY
ALFRED BRENDEL

PRINCETON UNIVERSITY PRESS

Library of Congress Cataloging-in-Publication Data
Burger, Ernst, 1937-
[Franz Liszt, English]
Franz Liszt : a chronicle of his life in pictures and documents
Ernst Burger : translated by Stewart Spencer :
foreword by Alfred Brendel.
p.   cm.
Translation of Franz Liszt : eine Lebenschronik in
Bildern und Dokumenten.
Bibliography: p.
Includes indexes.
ISBN 0-691-09133-1 (alk. paper) :
1. Liszt, Franz, 1811-1866—Chronology. 2. Liszt, Franz,
1811-1886—Pictorial works. 3. Composers—
Pictorial works. I. Title.
ML410.L7B913   1989
780'.92'4—dc19
[B]   88-39348

This book has been composed in Linotron Times Roman

Clothbound editions of Princeton University Press books are
printed on acid-free paper, and binding materials are chosen for
strength and durability.
Paperbacks, although satisfactory for personal collections,
are not usually suitable for library rebinding

Printed in the Federal Republic of Germany

Originally published in German as
Franz Liszt. Eine Lebenschronik in Bildern und Dokumenten:
Copyright 1986 by Paul List Verlag in der
Südwest Verlag GmbH & Co., KG, Munich

CONTENTS

"My insignificant career in performing and writing music is divided up
unclassically, like a Classical tragedy, into five acts:
 1st = My childhood years until the death of my father, 1828*
 2nd = 1830 to 1838, desultory studies and creativity in Paris and, for a time,
         in Geneva and Italy, before my reappearance in Vienna in 1838, the
         success of which launched me on my career as a virtuoso
 3rd = Concert tours: Paris, London, Berlin, Petersburg etc.: fantasias, tran-
         scriptions, *living like a lord*
 4th = 1848 to 1861, self-composure and work in Weimar
 5th = Its logical continuation and conclusion, in Rome, Pest, Weimar from
         1861 to . . ."
                              (Franz Liszt to Lina Ramann, 30 August 1884)
                              * Liszt's father died in 1827

ACKNOWLEDGEMENTS

This book was produced with generous support from the piano firm of Carl Hirsch (as Munich representatives of the firm of Bösendorfer), the City of Bayreuth, Alfred Brendel, Margarita Höhenrieder, Ludwig Hoffmann, and Eleonore Recher.

The author wishes also to thank Dr Felix Raabe (Aachen); Winifred Wagner, Wolfgang Wagner, Dr Manfred Eger, Margot Ludwig, and Günter Fischer (Bayreuth); Dr Gertrud Marotz (Berchtesgaden); Hildegard Grob (Geneva); Professor Alan Walker (Hamilton, Ontario); Leslie Howard and Adrian Williams (London); Dr Robert Münster, Julian von Karolyi, Dr Ekkehard Reitter, Dr Hansjörg Graf, Eleonore Recher, and Heide Hohendahl (Munich); Mme Ollivier de Prevaux (Paris); Dr Otto Biba (Vienna); Dr Dieter Eckardt, Dr Willy Handrick, and Professor Gerhard Schmid (Weimar); and Clara von Koronghy (Zurich).

I am particularly grateful to Jean-René Bory (Château de Penthes, Geneva), Mrs Gerry Keeling (San Gabriel, California), Ernst Wieckenberg (Munich), and my good friend Wolfgang Dömling (Hamburg). My final debt is to Rudolf Miggisch for his kind assistance in designing the book.

– E.B.

The translator wishes to record his gratitude to Alfred Brendel, Ernst Burger, Eric Van Tassel, and Professor Alan Walker, and especially to Leslie Howard, who generously made available his unique knowledge of Liszt's works.

– S.S.

FOREWORD

By Alfred Brendel

On the Centenary of Liszt's Death

"The nineteenth century is repudiated with a sense of aversion such as only one's own past history can ever excite." What Carl Dahlhaus wrote in 1961 on the occasion of the sesquicentenary of Franz Liszt's birth is scarcely true of a quarter of a century later. Romanticism's central musical figure, as Liszt is increasingly recognized to be, is now so much more familiar to many people. Music is once more allowed to speak and paint pictures, to express and represent images, and is no longer obliged to be (as it has in any case scarcely ever been) "self-sufficient". The stages in our re-evaluation of Liszt have led us back from the discovery of his late piano pieces – works which point far in the direction of musical modernity and which attest to a radical liberation from tonality and classical expectations of form – to the rehabilitation of turn-of-the-century art (an art which owed so much to Liszt) and, finally, to that period when Liszt was the most famous man in Europe, when virtuosity bore strange fruits, and when music was at once as "absolute" and as literary as never previously.

None the less, Liszt's rehabilitation can by no means be deemed a foregone conclusion, and the argument whether his niche should be in the pantheon or in a bazaar of oddities and monstrosities may well drag on. "Thalberg is three-quarters feeling and one-quarter dexterity, while Liszt is three-quarters dexterity and one-quarter feeling." This *bon mot* of Rossini's was recently used as the epigraph to a successful book on the pianoforte, where it was clearly calculated to set the reader against the artist from the very outset. (Chopin and Schumann, at any rate, held a different opinion.) And in the same book we find a play on words to the effect that "the passion of his playing (which is exceedingly cold) affects his listeners in adverse fashion." The assumption that Liszt's passion was somehow cold would have left his contemporaries somewhat bemused.

What was it that stood (or stands) in the way of a better understanding of Liszt?

1. When Liszt died, he made the mistake of leaving behind an unusual legacy of envy. There is a relation between envy and posthumous fame. Liszt's early European success as virtuoso and improviser equalled that of Mozart; a few years later, his "genius of expression" (Schumann) and boundless pianistic skill made him, as a player, superior even to Chopin, Mendelssohn, or Clara Schumann. The combination of a lively mind, personal magnetism, masculine beauty, the social triumphs enjoyed by a privileged parvenu, and a love life bordering on scandal turned out to be, within one human being, barely forgivable. There was a conspicuous absence of mitigating circumstances such as Mozart's or Schubert's early death, Mozart's alleged impoverishment and unmarked "pauper's grave," Schubert's syphilis, Beethoven's deafness, Chopin's consumption, or Schumann's mental disorder – features that make the fame of a genius a great deal more gratifying, and guarantee its solidity. (Wagner's monstrous egotism and merciless promotion of his own ends, while not stimulating compassion or malicious glee, present a frame of mind which many people enjoy sharing.)

Arguably, Liszt and Haydn are the most frequently misunderstood among major composers; their biographers afford little food for pity. (The insufferable bigotry of Haydn's wife and the senility of his last years do not, it seems, sufficiently atone for his achievement in being the first great symphonist and the grand master of the string quartet.) In old age, Haydn reigned over the musical world as its undisputed leading light. For this, the nineteenth century punished him – as it punished Liszt for his undisputed supremacy as a performer. Haydn was branded the ingenuous classicist (something he rarely was), "the family friend who is always welcome but has nothing to say that is new" (Schumann). Liszt, in his compositions, was seen as a poseur and charlatan (which he only occasionally was), the embodiment of a superficial and bombastic romanticism. Not until our century did a greater number of composers – from Richard

Strauss, Ravel, and Busoni to Schoenberg, Bartók, and Boulez – appreciate Liszt by taking him seriously.

2. Where Liszt has been casual and uncritical, the player and listener must come to his rescue. After many a lesser piece is eliminated there still remains a rich harvest, at least within his piano music. It is bound to include his B minor Sonata, the *Années de Pèlerinage*, the *"Weinen, Klagen"* Variations, late pieces like *Mosonyi gyázmenete*, and a selection from the *Études* – works that can stand alongside the best of Chopin and Schumann.

3. It is difficult to find for Liszt's music a fitting national identity. In the end, not even Hungary laid claim to it after Liszt made the mistake of equating the native folklore of his country with gypsy music. Instead of "specializing in himself," Liszt presents a panorama of style. His skill in appropriation resembles that of his beloved gypsies. Already the intellectual poets of German Romanticism had half adopted, half created a manner of folk poetry; and later nineteenth-century architects made unhesitating use of past styles. Not until Stravinsky, however, did another composer emerge who elaborated on the most varied musical material without losing himself. Liszt's variety extends from the sacred to the utterly profane, from the lavishly sumptuous to the ascetic – and from the carefree to the masterly. His music was deemed lacking in "Germanity" as long as instrumental music was taken to be a German monopoly. For European purists of the twentieth century, on the other hand, until recently only original compositions were admissible, and preferably those which avoided rhetoric, apotheoses, and arpeggios. These days, arrangements have regained respectability. If Liszt, however, had left nothing but his Lied transcriptions and operatic paraphrases he would hardly be better remembered than his erstwhile rival Thalberg.

4. "Alas," wrote Lina Ramann in her *Lisztiana*, "none of our masters is so dependent on performances that make sense of their compositions . . . and only too few players manage to get through to the core of his music! There is a lack of either poetry, or intelligence, or wealth of feeling." Liszt must be protected against those of his interpreters who trivialize him, and against those of his admirers who admire that trivialization. Most leading pianists of the later nineteenth century had been, at least briefly, among Liszt's disciples, yet, despite all claims to the contrary, no convincing tradition of Liszt playing developed. Of course, Liszt, after his virtuoso years, hardly ever performed his own works himself and did very little to promote them. (Rather, he helped others, notably Wagner.) For Liszt, the much-maligned programme musician, music was fundamentally a tool of poetic expression, and the piano an object to be transformed into an orchestra, turned into the elements, lifted into the spheres. In lesser hands, his extraordinary pianistic demands risk becoming an end in themselves.

Liszt's music, unlike that of Mozart, projects the man. With rare immediacy, it gives away the character of the composer as well as the musical probity of his executant. Hans von Bülow, Liszt's favourite pupil and the first pianist to offer a complete Liszt recital, taught his students to distinguish between *Gefühl* (feeling) and *Dusel* (giddiness, sentimentality). Likewise, one might add, the Liszt player should keep pathos and *Schwulst* (pomposity) firmly apart. When playing Liszt's superb variations of Bach's *Weinen, Klagen, Sorgen, Zagen*, he or she should make the music weep, lament, worry, and despair without lapsing into howling or chattering of teeth and, at the work's conclusion, whether a believer or not, should prove capable of demonstrating certainty of faith without producing a wrong gesture. To a good mime, nothing is unattainable.

5. Modern chroniclers of the piano like to call Liszt a showman. That he was capable of behaving ostentatiously during the most hectic years of his virtuoso career, throwing his kid gloves to the floor of the stage and gazing at the ladies while playing, is undeniable. As a general characterization of his art and personality, however, the label is undeserved. Liszt was the first to depart from the salon. To the displeasure of some contemporaries, he democratized the concert by occasionally performing for an audience of thousands in large theatres like La Scala. This required a different projection of the music, one based on a physically freer and more demonstrative treatment of the piano that, when we take account of the feeble instruments of the 1830s and 1840s, may well have "used up" three pianos during one evening. He also inaugurated the "recital," a concert presented by one single player, and was promptly castigated for his self-sufficiency.

6. The personal life of Liszt, like that of Paganini, soon became the subject of myth and calumny. Neither his alleged noble origin nor the "evidence" of his unofficial children bears scrutiny. Liszt inhabited a world populated by women writers and fascinated by *romans à clef*. George Sand and Marie d'Agoult parted company over private indiscretions revealed in Balzac's *Béatrix*. The Comtesse d'Agoult, under the pen name of Daniel Stern, then gave vent to her resentments against Liszt in her novel *Nélida*; in the guise of a painter, Liszt is accused of being unable to produce works in a large format, a charge he once and for all refuted with his B minor Sonata a few years later. The pinnacle of malice was reached by Olga Janina, who was neither a countess nor a Cossack but a pathological impostor. It is significant that Ernest Newman was taken in by her books because they accord with his own view in representing Liszt as a feeble character. Newman's book on Liszt caused untold harm in the English-speaking world not least because it came from the pen of a Wagner scholar who prided himself on his own "objectivity." His distorted portrait rests on his musical scepticism: where access to Liszt's music is clouded by prejudice or lack of sympathy, the outline of Liszt's personality easily becomes shaped according to the writer's distrust. Eduard Hanslick, Vienna's ruling critic, was a remarkable exception: he esteemed Liszt highly as a man and as a performer, though he despised his compositions.

Of course Liszt was no saint. Yet there is no composer I would rather meet. His vanity was counterbalanced by his selflessness, his urge to dominate held in check by his humility. Has there been another musician as generously helpful, as magnanimously appreciative? Liszt bore the "bitterness of heart," the personal and artistic disappointments of his later years, with imposing self-control. He mustered the strength to react against the hysteria surrounding a triumphant virtuoso career by leaving the concert platform at the age of thirty-five; he did penance for a superabundance of notes by carrying music, in his uncompromising and spare late pieces, to the brink of silence.

To be sure, the excess of worship bestowed on him by blind admirers and the biographical semifiction fabricated by his mistress Carolyne Sayn-Wittgenstein in conjunction with Lina Ramann were bound to provoke criticism. Alongside the efforts of modern musicologists to rehabilitate Liszt and give the truth its due, Ernst Burger's important book provides a chronicle of the composer's life of the kind that he urgently needs. Its well-ordered wealth of documents, eyewitness accounts, and hitherto often unknown illustrations will allow its users to paint their own portrait of Liszt. Through the work of many years and at great personal cost, Ernst Burger – pianist, teacher and leading expert on Liszt's iconography – has assembled a unique Liszt archive from which this book draws the greater part of its contents. May it open the reader's eyes to Liszt, while encouraging the listener to open his ears to a composer whom Wagner described as "the most musical of all musicians."

1 Franz Liszt. Anonymous drawing, ca. 1824.

*"My childhood years
until the death of my father"*

2 Adam Liszt (1776–1827), Franz Liszt's father. Anonymous gouache, 1819.

On the back are the words ''Franz Liszt's father and teacher, seated at the spinet on which Franz learned to play. Raiding 1819.''

Franz Liszt's father, Adam Liszt, was born in Edelstal, a small village in the neighbourhood of Preßburg (modern Bratislava), on 16 December 1776. He attended primary school in the nearby town of Kittsee, where his father was the village schoolmaster. From 1790 to 1795 he studied at the Catholic Gymnasium in Preßburg and had music lessons there with a certain Paul Riegler. In September 1795 he entered the Order of St Francis as a novice in the monastery of Malacka (Slovakia) – the register of the Faculty of Philosophy describes him as ''Adam Matthäus Liszt, natio et locus natalis Germanus [German by nationality and birth]'' – but he left the order on 29 July 1797. After briefly studying philosophy at the University of Preßburg, he entered the service of Prince Nicholas Esterházy, working as a secretary on the Prince's estates at Forchtenau and offering his employer a *Te Deum for Chorus and Sixteen Instruments*, written in 1801. In 1805 the Prince, complying with Adam Liszt's wishes, transferred him to Eisenstadt, where he played the cello in the local orchestra and made the acquaintance of Hummel. He may also have met Beethoven when the latter conducted a concert in Eisenstadt on 13 September 1808. At around this date Adam Liszt was transferred to the nearby village of Raiding in the district of Ödenburg (Sopron). The following year he met Anna Lager, who became his wife in 1811. In 1823 he gave up his secure appointment in order to devote himself to his eleven-year-old son's education and career. He died in Boulogne-sur-mer on 28 August 1827.

3 Adam Liszt. Ivory miniature, 1826, signed C.F.P.

Although this portrait bears no similarity to the one reproduced in Illus. 2, it is generally considered a likeness of Franz Liszt's father. It is not impossible that the man depicted in Illus. 2 is wearing a wig, which would explain, at least in part, the striking dissimilarity between the two portraits.

4 The village of Raiding (Burgenland, Austria), where Franz Liszt was born. Anonymous painting, ca. 1900.

The long building with the pointed door pediments in front of the church is the house in which Liszt was born. The village (known in Hungarian as Doborján) was a part of Hungary at the time of Liszt's birth. His father was steward here.

The original of this painting is believed to be lost; it is reproduced here from an inferior copy.

Franz Liszt's mother, Anna Liszt, née Lager, came into the world on 9 May 1788 in the Lower Austrian town of Krems on the Danube. (Since 29 May 1924 the house in which she was born has displayed a commemorative plaque.) Her mother died when she was eight, and she lost her father on her ninth birthday. Shortly afterwards her parental home was sold, and she went to live with relatives in Krems. She then moved to Vienna and worked there as a chambermaid, but from December 1810 onwards she lived with her brother in the village of Mattersdorf, where the father of her future husband also lived. It was presumably here that she met Adam Liszt, who hailed from the neighbouring village of Raiding. She married him on 11 January 1811 in the parish church at Unterfrauenhaid. Franz Liszt was born on 22 October 1811. Anna Liszt accompanied her son to Paris in the autumn of 1823, returning to her native Austria in 1824 and living for the next three years with her sister in Graz. On her husband's death in 1827 she moved to Paris to be with her son, who supported her by giving concerts and piano lessons. More than a hundred affectionate letters have survived between Liszt and his mother, who later devoted herself to the task of bringing up Liszt's children. In Paris she came into contact with many of the leading musicians, painters, and writers of her day. Anna Liszt died in Paris on 6 February 1866 at the house of Liszt's son-in-law Émile Ollivier, who in 1870 was to become Prime Minister of France. She is buried in the cemetery at Montparnasse.

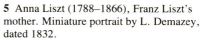

5 Anna Liszt (1788–1866), Franz Liszt's mother. Miniature portrait by L. Demazey, dated 1832.

The original is missing, but a copy survives in the Richard-Wagner-Museum, Eisenach.

6 Anna Liszt. Lithograph by Lemercier, dated ca. 1840 and based on a miniature by L. Sebbers.

This rare portrait is believed to be a likeness of Franz Liszt's mother.

7 Anna Liszt. Photograph, ca. 1860, by the Paris Studio of Sabatier-Blot.

8 Anna Liszt. A previously unpublished drawing, dated 1846 and signed ''Ingres''(!).

LIFE

22 October: Franz Liszt is born in Raiding (Hungarian Doborján), a small village about fifty kilometres to the south of the Austrian town of Eisenstadt (see Illus. 4). His father is employed as intendant of the sheep flocks on the Esterházy estates.

The uncertainty often encountered with regard to Liszt's national identity is understandable: his father was of German extraction and the family spoke almost exclusively German (in addition to which the official language at Court was German), but the village of Raiding was situated in Hungary. (Since 1921 the federal region of Burgenland in which Raiding is situated has been a part of Austria.) Franz Liszt cannot properly be described as either German or Austrian, so perhaps it would be best to describe him as from the ''German-speaking part of Hungary.''

The delicate, fined-boned child spends the first years of his life in the rustic idyll of his place of birth. According to an entry in his father's diary, ''A smallpox vaccination was followed by a period of illness in which the boy had to contend alternately with a nervous complaint and with feverishness, so that we often had cause to fear for his life. Once, when he was two or three, we thought he had died and so we had a coffin made for him. This unsettling situation lasted until he was six.''

The child's unusual musicality soon reveals itself. Adam Liszt writes in his diary, ''In his sixth year he heard me play a concerto by Ries in C sharp minor. He leaned against the piano, listening, all ears. In the evening, when he came in from the garden where he had gone for a walk, he sang the theme of the concerto. We made him repeat it; he did not know what he was singing: that was the first indication we had of his genius. He kept on begging me to let him begin playing the piano with me.''

His wish is fulfilled: Franz Liszt is taught to play the piano by his father and soon gains an astonishing fluency in improvisation and sight-reading.

9 The house in which Franz Liszt was born in Raiding, with the village church and stream. Lithograph by J. Stadler, based on a drawing by J. Grünes; ca. 1850.

It is not quite accurate to describe this building as Franz Liszt's birthplace, since the wing seen here (demolished in 1940) was the transverse section of a T-shaped building. The actual building in which Liszt was born lay behind the section shown here (see Illus. 27).

10 Font in which Franz Liszt was baptized.

The baptismal font and certificate of baptism (23 October 1811) have both survived. Raiding was not a separate parish at this time, so Liszt was baptized in the neighbouring village of Unterfrauenhaid.

11 Raiding Church organ. Photograph, ca. 1970.

When he visited Raiding in February 1840, Liszt gave the community some 100 ducats to purchase this organ. It is now in the house where the composer was born.

12 The sixteenth-century house where Liszt was born. Photograph, ca. 1970.

Above the gateway with its basket arch is a statue of the Virgin, with the inscription and coat of arms (1587) of the aristocratic Illésy family.

13 Georg Adam Liszt (List), Franz Liszt's grandfather. Anonymous oil painting, ca. 1820.

Georg Adam Liszt, a teacher, notary, choirmaster, and organist in the Esterházy chapel at Pottendorf (Austria), was born in Ragendorf (Hungarian Rajka) on 14 October 1755. He died in Pottendorf on 8 August 1844.

Liszt's grandfather signed his name ''List'' until around 1843, when he added the ''z'' – evidently in recognition of his grandson's European reputation. Liszt's father mostly signed himself ''Liszt,'' sometimes ''Lißt,'' but never ''List.''

14 The house in which Franz Liszt was born, ca. 1856. Painted on a portfolio owned by Liszt.

The Liszt Museum in Ödenburg owns a water-colour painted by Karl Steinacker on 26 August 1856 and identical in every detail (including the woman in the middle of the picture) to the painting reproduced here. It seems reasonable to assume that the picture on the portfolio is by the same artist or is a copy of Steinacker's water-colour.

Apart from the illustrations shown here, hardly any pictures of Raiding and the house where Liszt was born have survived from the early nineteenth century. In a letter to his mother of March 1846, Liszt mentions a small package which he has sent her containing ''two daguerre-otypes of Raiding.''[1]* These potentially highly interesting photographs, which must therefore have been taken before March 1846, unfortunately appear to have been lost.

* Superscript numbers in the main body of the text, together with those in the biography, work-lists and illustration captions, refer to the List of Sources on pp. 345–7.

LIFE

Adam Liszt wishes to give his son a better education. Various appeals to his employer, Prince Esterházy, to grant him financial support or to agree to his transfer to Vienna come to nothing (see pp. 14 and 16). Equally unsuccessful is his attempt to have young Franz taught piano by Johann Nepomuk Hummel.

The boy's talent and love of music are becoming increasingly apparent; when asked what he wanted to become, he is said to have replied, with a glance at a portrait of Beethoven, "Someone like him!"[2]

August/September: in all probability Liszt's first public appearance, in Baden near Vienna, dates from this time. Unfortunately, no press reports have survived.

August: Adam Liszt is given eight to ten days' leave of absence and probably takes the opportunity to travel to Vienna to introduce his son to the eminent piano teacher Carl Czerny (see Czerny's autobiographical report on p. 15).

September: Franz Liszt performs for a select audience at the castle in Eisenstadt, where he wins considerable recognition and applause; he can now hope for financial support.

CLEMENTI.

15 Muzio Clementi (1752–1832). Copper engraving, ca. 1800.
The keyboard sonatas and the *Gradus ad Parnassum* of this respected composer and keyboard virtuoso, whose pupils included Johann Baptist Cramer and John Field, were the daily bread of the young Franz Liszt. Clementi attended Liszt's concerts in London in 1824 and 1827.

16 Prince Nicholas Esterházy (1765–1833).
Copper engraving, 1820.

Adam Liszt's letter of 4 August 1819 to Prince Nicholas Esterházy:

Your Serene Highness has deigned to honour with his especial attention the musical talents of my 7½-year-old son, and has graciously advised me to submit in writing the most humble request for your august support which I addressed to you in person, together with the plan which might best lead to the realization of that goal. In all submissiveness I now make so bold as to obey that advice, and do so as follows:

In order to be trained in the inexhaustible art of music, and in order to discover and communicate the aesthetic sense and beauty or, rather, the soul of a piece of music, and finally to impart those qualities to new compositions, what my son needs, in addition to tireless theoretical and practical exercises, is a knowledge of the great masters; he must travel, learn languages, and study the science of nations, &c. To garner this knowledge and turn it to profit, it would therefore be necessary:

First, to send the boy to Vienna, which, being the home of music, will enable him to be well provided for and where, in addition to his receiving board, he may be given a solid moral education.

Secondly, to engage a good music teacher who would be enjoined to give him lessons at least three times a week, whereby it would be necessary, in order to derive the greatest benefit from those expensive lessons, to have some expert authority convince himself of the boy's progress or lack of it, inasmuch as this is all too often a matter of indifference to the teacher concerned, an indifference which may well also be found in the case of the boy's learning the French or Italian language, the latter especially being indispensable for the study of music.

Thirdly, in order to make more rapid progress and thus achieve his goal all the sooner, the boy would have to attend frequent performances of church music, operas, and public and private concerts; but for this a guardian would be necessary, since it is not advisable to leave a child to his own resources in so large a town.

Not including the clothes and the very expensive music scores and books which he will need, the foregoing and certain other similar items would require an annual outlay of at least 1300–1500 florins and perhaps even then not lead to the desired result, requiring a degree of support which I have even less right to claim in that I have done so little to earn it.

I therefore make so bold as to submit, in all humility, the following proposal for Your Highness's consideration, a proposal which is less expensive and which will certainly achieve the greatest success in the swiftest possible time: it is that Your Highness deign to appoint me to a position in Vienna consonant with my well-known abilities and character, and that Your Highness most graciously agree merely to lend the boy the sum to be disbursed on a music teacher; the rest, however large the sum involved, I shall gladly endeavour to meet from my own pocket, without ever becoming a burden to Your Highness . . .

„Im Jahre 1819, kurze Zeit, nachdem die Belleville (die 10jährige Ninetta Belleville, „eines der seltensten musikalischen Talente", hatte Czerny im Jahre 1816 zur musikalischen Ausbildung übernommen, und sie war bei den Eltern Czernys zugleich in Kost und Wohnung) uns verlassen hatte, kam eines Morgens ein Mann mit einem kleinen Knaben von ungefähr acht Jahren zu mir mit der Bitte, den Kleinen auf dem Fortepiano etwas vorspielen zu lassen. Es war ein bleiches, schwächlich aussehendes Kind, und beim Spielen wankte es am Stuhle wie betrunken herum, so daß ich oft dachte, es würde zu Boden fallen. Auch war sein Spiel ganz unregelmäßig, unrein, verworren, und von der Fingersetzung hatte er so wenig Begriff, daß er die Finger ganz willkürlich über die Tasten warf. Aber demungeachtet war ich über das Talent erstaunt, welches die Natur in ihn gelegt hatte. Er spielte einiges, das ich ihm vorlegte, a vista zwar als reiner Naturalist, aber eben darum um so mehr in einer Art, daß man sah, hier habe die Natur selber einen Clavierspieler gebildet. Ebenso war es, als ich auf den Wunsch seines Vaters ihm ein Thema zum Fantasiren gab. Ohne die geringste erlernte harmonische Kenntniß brachte er doch einen gewissen genialen Sinn in seinen Vortrag.

Der Vater erzählte mir, er heiße Liszt, sei ein untergeordneter fürstlich Esterhazyscher Beamter, habe bis jetzt seinen Sohn selber unterwiesen, bittet mich aber, ob ich mich seines kleinen Franzi annehmen wollte, wenn er ein Jahr später nach Wien kommen würde.

Ich sagte dieses natürlich gerne zu und gab ihm zugleich die Anweisung, auf welche Art er einstweilen den Kleinen selber weiter fortbilden solle, indem ich ihm die Scalenübungen u. s. w. zeigte. Ungefähr ein Jahr später kam Liszt mit seinem Sohne nach Wien, bezog in derselben Gasse, wo wir wohnten (in der Krugerstraße), eine Wohnung, und ich widmete dem Kleinen, da ich bei Tag wenig Zeit hatte, fast täglich jeden Abend.

Nie hatte ich einen so eifrigen, genievollen und fleißigen Schüler gehabt. Da ich aus mancher Erfahrung wußte, daß gerade solche Genies, wo die Geistesgaben der physischen Kraft vorauseilen, das gründlich Technische zu versäumen pflegen, so erschien es mir vor allem Andern nöthig, die ersten Monate dazu anzuwenden, seine mechanische Festigkeit dergestalt zu regeln und zu befestigen, daß sie in späteren Jahren auf keinen Abweg mehr gerathen könnte.

In kurzer Zeit spielte er die Scalen in allen Tonarten mit all der meisterhaften Geläufigkeit, welche seine zum Clavierspiel höchst günstig organisirten Finger möglich machten, und durch das ernste Studium der Clementischen Sonaten (welche stets für den Clavieristen die beste Schule bleiben werden, wenn man sie in seinem Sinne zu studiren weiß) gewöhnte ich ihm die bisher ganz mangelnde Taktfestigkeit, den schönen Anschlag und Ton, den richtigsten Fingersatz und richtige musikalische Declamation an, obwohl diese Compositionen dem lebhaften und stets höchst muntern Knaben anfangs ziemlich trocken vorkamen.

Diese Methode bewirkte, daß ich, als wir einige Monate später die Werke der Hummel, Ries, Moscheles, sodann Beethoven und Seb. Bach vornahmen, nicht mehr nöthig hatte, auf die mechanischen Regeln zu viel zu achten, sondern ihn gleich den Geist und Charakter dieser verschiedenen Autoren auffassen lassen konnte. Da er jedes Tonstück äußerst schnell einstudiren mußte, so eignete er sich das A-vista-Spielen endlich so an, daß er fähig war, selbst bedeutende schwierige Compositionen öffentlich vom Blatte wegzuspielen, als ob er sie lange studirt hätte. Ebenso bestrebte ich mich ihm das Fantasiren anzueignen, indem ich ihm häufig die Themas zum Improvisiren aufgab.

Die unveränderliche Munterkeit und gute Laune des kleinen Liszt nebst der so außerordentlichen Entwicklung seines Talents bewirkte, daß meine Eltern ihn wie ihren Sohn, ich wie einen Bruder liebte, und nicht nur daß ich ihn völlig unentgeltlich unterrichtete, sondern ich gab ihm auch alle nöthigen Musikalien, die so ziemlich in allem Guten und Brauchbaren bestanden, was bis zu jener Zeit existirte. Ein Jahr später konnte ich ihn schon öffentlich spielen lassen, und er erweckte in Wien einen Enthusiasmus, wie es wenigen Künstlern gelungen ist. Im nächstfolgenden Jahre gab sein Vater mit ihm öffentliche Concerte zu eigenem Vortheil, in welchen der Kleine Hummels damals ganz neue Concerte in A-moll und H-moll, Moscheles' Variationen, Hummels Septett, die Concerte von Ries, manche von meinen Compositionen vortrug, wie auch jedesmal vom Publikum gegebene Motive improvisirte, und die Welt hatte damals in der That nicht unrecht, wenn sie in ihm einen neuen Mozart entstehen zu sehen glaubte.

Leider wünschte sein Vater von ihm große pekuniäre Vortheile, und als der Kleine im besten Studieren war, als ich eben anfing, ihn zur Composition anzuleiten, ging er auf Reisen, zuerst nach Ungarn und zuletzt nach Paris und London 2c., wo er, wie alle damaligen Blätter bezeugen, das größte Aufsehen machte. In Paris, wo er sich mit seinen Eltern niederließ, gewann er allerdings viel Geld, verlor aber viele Jahre, indem sein Leben wie seine Kunst eine falsche Richtung nahmen. Als ich sechzehn Jahre später nach Paris kam (1837), fand ich sein Spiel in jeder Hinsicht ziemlich wüst und verworren bei aller ungeheuren Bravour. Ich glaubte ihm keinen bessern Rath geben zu können, als Reisen durch Europa zu machen, und als er ein Jahr später nach Wien kam, bekam sein Genie einen neuen Schwung. Unter dem grenzenlosen Beifall unseres feinfühlenden Publikums nahm sein Spiel bald jene glänzende und dabei doch klare Richtung, durch die er sich jetzt in der Welt so berühmt macht. Allein ich habe die Ueberzeugung, daß er, wenn er seine Jugendstudien in Wien noch einige Jahre fortgesetzt hätte, jetzt auch in der Composition alle die hohen Erwartungen rechtfertigen würde, die man damals mit Recht von ihm hegte.

18 Ludwig van Beethoven (1770–1827). Undated lithograph by Meissner based on a drawing by Becker.

Liszt revered Beethoven more than any other composer. The latter's original death mask (a gift of the painter Danhauser) and his Broadwood piano (presented by the publisher Spina) were both among Liszt's prized possessions.

17 Czerny's autobiographical report as originally published in the *Münchener Propyläen* of 1869.

It is not entirely out of the question that Czerny made a mistake over the year 1819, and that his first meeting with Liszt did not take place until two years later in 1821. This supposition receives support from Czerny's remark that "About a year later Liszt came to Vienna . . .". Liszt's move to the city is documented as having taken place in spring 1822. (For a translation of the text, see p. 335.)

19 Johann Nepomuk Hummel (1778–1837). Copper engraving by Fleischmann, based on a drawing by F. H. Müller; 1822.

Adam Liszt's wish to have his son taught by the famous pianist and composer Johann Nepomuk Hummel was frustrated by the latter's high fees. Hummel's keyboard concertos in B minor and A minor, to which the young Chopin was notably drawn, were also the young Liszt's showpieces. Hummel was until 1837 Court Kapellmeister in Weimar, a post which, as chance would have it, was later to be held by Liszt.

LIFE

April: Adam Liszt addresses a further appeal to Prince Esterházy, explaining his troubles and at the same time the enormous progress that his son has made. He finally receives permission "to go to Vienna for a year, at the end of the sheep-shearing, in order for his promising son to be taught to play the pianoforte, and to return to his former position if at the end of that period he and his son do not have the good fortune to prosper in their pursuit of music . . ." He is also provided with 200 forints towards his expenses. This offer appears insufficient to Adam Liszt, and he declines it "with tears in his eyes and with an oppressed father's heart."

October: Franz Liszt gives his first major concert. It takes place in the Casino in Ödenburg (modern Sopron, Hungary). He plays the E flat major Piano Concerto by Ferdinand Ries and improvises on given themes. The overwhelming success of the concert leads to a second appearance in Ödenburg a few weeks later.

26 November: Little Liszt gives a concert in the palace of Count Michael Esterházy in Preßburg (modern Bratislava, Czechoslovakia). A group of Hungarian aristocrats, including Counts Esterházy, Amadé, Apponyi, Erdödy, Viczay, and Szapáry, declare their readiness to donate an annual sum of 600 gulden over a period of six years. How far this promise was kept is not clear, but it appears that only a single payment was made and that the sum in question was small.

20 Ödenburg. Steel engraving, ca. 1845.
   In the period around 1820 Ödenburg was part of the same administrative area as Raiding, and it was here, in October 1820, that Liszt gave his first great public concert. He played Ferdinand Ries's E flat major Piano Concerto and also improvised on themes suggested by the audience.

21 Last page of the original autograph of Adam Liszt's letter to Prince Esterházy dated 13 April 1820.

22 The theatre in Ödenburg. Steel engraving, ca. 1845.
   The Ödenburg Theatre was rebuilt after a fire in 1834. It was here that the young Liszt gave his first major concerts. The building was later used as a casino and is now an arts centre. Liszt also performed here on 3 August 1846.

Extract from Adam Liszt's petition to Prince Esterházy of 13 April 1820:

Relying upon Your Highness's resolution of last year, No. 2957, I venture to repeat my most humble entreaty and beg leave to be granted an appointment in Vienna. At the same time I beg to notify Your Highness, in deepest veneration, not only of the tremendous progress which my son has made in playing the fortepiano, but also the sacrifices which I have made to date and, finally, the most recent sacrifice which I have performed for this purpose.

   To overcome, with ease and within the space of 22 months, all the difficulties inherent in a Bach, Mozart, Beethoven, Clementi, Hummel, Cramer etc; to play even the most difficult keyboard pieces at sight, without ever having seen them before; and to play them in the strictest tempo, correctly and accurately, represents, to my musical way of thinking, tremendous progress. Experts might perhaps be not entirely unjustified in doubting my word and in regarding my claim as a form of self-trumpeting; but I am confident that I can prove what I say not only by means of an appropriate test, but also by adding, most humbly, that if my son had not been prevented from working by frequent illness and a lack of teaching and music his art would already have reached an unheard-of degree of achievement. I say this not as something possible, but as something certain. [. . .]

   We should achieve our goal most inexpensively and speedily if I were to be granted an appointment in Vienna; but if such an appointment should be impossible, then, at the end of May and with Your Highness's gracious consent, I should resign my post for a year, and convert my furniture and cattle into ready money [. . .], but even this plan could not take root without your most gracious support, since, having made precise calculations, I now realize that the value of my disposable wealth would scarcely suffice to cover the cost of board and lodging for a year, and how then should I cover the cost of such expensive music and language lessons, or acquire sheet music and books? A servant in the employment of His Highness Prince Esterházy can scarcely go begging on this occasion . . ."

24 Report in the *Kaiserlich-Königliche privilegirte städtische Preßburger Zeitung* of 28 November 1820, describing Liszt's concert in Preßburg on 26 November. (For a translation of the text, see p. 335.)

23 Liszt Pavilion in Preßburg. Photograph, ca. 1980.

In this house, in the courtyard of Archduke Michael Esterházy's palace, the nine-year-old Liszt gave his first concert in Preßburg, in the presence of a select gathering of Hungarian aristocrats, on 26 November 1820. The building, in what was once the Venturgasse, now the Jiraschgasse, is currently used by the University of Slovenia as a music room.

25 Preßburg. Steel engraving, ca. 1845.

Liszt's successful concert appearance in Preßburg in 1820 prompted a number of Hungarian aristocrats to pledge a fund that would enable him to continue his studies abroad. On Liszt's visits to Preßburg, see p. 119.

LIFE

Liszt perfects his keyboard technique in his home town.

His encounter with gypsies, who frequently passed through the village or camped on the surrounding hills, is worth mentioning here since it may have contributed to his later predilection for rhapsodic music. His reasons for remarking that "I am half Franciscan, half gypsy" almost certainly date back to his childhood years.

It will be recalled in this context that Liszt's father was a member of the Order of St Francis for two years, and that Franz himself entered the order in 1857.

His first meeting with Carl Czerny may also date from this year (but see Czerny's autobiographical report on p. 335 and the commentary on p. 15).

26 The doors and commemorative plaques on the house in Raiding where Liszt was born. Photograph, 1970.

The inscription on the right-hand pediment is engraved in letters of gold on a grey marble tablet and reads, "Itt született Liszt Ferencz 1811-dik évi Október-dikén. Hódolata jeléül a soproni irodalmi és müvészeti kör 1881-ben" (Franz Liszt was born here on 22 October 1811. As a token of homage. The Sopron Association for Literature and Art. 1881). The plaque was unveiled on 7 April 1881 in the presence of the composer (see Illus. 558). The plaque on the left-hand pediment was erected in 1926 by the German Imperial Government, the Austrian Federal Government, and the Regional Government of Burgenland: in addition to a portrait relief, it carries the inscription "Hier wurde Franz Liszt 22. Okt. 1811 geboren. Diese Gedenktafel weiht dem deutschen Meister das deutsche Volk" (Franz Liszt was born here on 22 October 1811. This memorial plaque is dedicated to the German Master by the German people).

In contrast to 1820 (when Liszt gave concerts in Ödenburg and Preßburg) and 1822 (lessons with Czerny and Salieri, together with major concert appearances in Vienna), the year 1821 passed without any events outwardly of note. Liszt stayed in Raiding. His parents' house there is shown in detail on these two pages.

27 The house in which Liszt was born. Photograph, ca. 1890.

28 The house in which Liszt was born. Photograph, ca. 1980.

The illustration shows the building in its present condition. A small Liszt Museum is housed in the family's former living quarters. The house, which is of some architectural interest, is approached through an archway. Above the archway (see Illus. 12), which is crowned by a statue of the Virgin, is a coat of arms with the date 1587 and an inscription that runs, "I D ILLESY AULA REG FAM INT STATUS HUNG ORIENT SECRET ET INTERPRES HCNC," which may perhaps be read as "Illustris Dominus Illésy Aula Regiae Familiaris Intimus Status Hungariae Orientalis Secretarius et Interpres Hunc Castellum Novum Castellum." From this it may be gathered that "His Honour Herr Illésy, Privy Councillor, Secretary and Interpreter in Eastern Hungary, built this castle" in 1587. The building was laid out in the shape of a T and served as private residence for the aristocratic Illésy family. The transverse section consisted of six rooms, a kitchen-cum-pantry, and a room for pressing grapes, with a cellar beneath. Some of the rooms were vaulted, others decorated with stucco. The courtyard contained a shed and stables for horses and cows, while the sheep-sheds were diagonally opposite the main part of the building.

Prince Nicholas Esterházy acquired the estate at the beginning of the nineteenth century, turning it into a leasehold farm. Adam Liszt and his family lived here for almost fourteen years during his period as manager and accountant in charge of the Prince's flock of sheep.

Franz Liszt revisited his home village on several occasions in later life (see p. 261). On the occasion of the composer's seventieth birthday, Count Géza Zichy expressed a desire to acquire the house. Liszt turned down his request: "Your noble desire to acquire the modest farmhouse in Raiding where I was born does me much honour. But I must beg you to let the matter rest and agree, instead, to my proposal whereby one-third of the pecuniary proceeds of your splendid concerts in Hungary, which you had intended to donate to the Raiding farmhouse, should be used instead for a patriotic musical purpose, namely the Liszt Anniversary Scholarships generously established by the municipal authorities in Budapest in 1873. [. . .] I hope that more and more eligible artists will gradually emerge in our much-loved and fertile fatherland. This is my wish and endeavour. – Your most obedient servant F. Liszt."[3]

In the course of the years the Illésy mansion underwent numerous structural alterations. Doors and windows were moved, triangular pediments placed above the doors with commemorative tablets, and three rooms demolished in the main section of the building. The transverse section (clearly identifiable in Illus. 27, where the main section can also be seen in its original form) was demolished in 1940, when the dairy farming activities ceased and the surrounding plots of land were sold. Only the actual birthplace remained.

To mark the centenary of Liszt's birth in 1911 the then parish priest of Raiding set up a small museum devoted to Liszt. It was temporarily closed during the chaos of two world wars and was not reopened until 1951. In 1971 Prince Paul Esterházy donated the house to the parish of Raiding, which now maintains the building with affectionate respect. This simple structure, whose former inhabitant was one of the most cosmopolitan figures of the nineteenth century, is one of the major tourist attractions in the Austrian province of Burgenland.

LIFE

2 January: Franz Liszt appears on the same platform as the Viennese violinist Joseph Böhm at a concert in Preßburg.

April: Prince Nicholas Esterházy grants Adam Liszt a year's leave of absence to go to Vienna. Adam Liszt may take up his appointment in Raiding again, on condition that he returns within the specified period.

8 May: Liszt's family moves to 92 Stiftsgasse, off the Mariahilferstraße, "Zum Grünen Igel." Their first-floor flat (No. 1) looks out over the street. That same year, however, they move nearer Czerny, renting rooms at 1014 Krugerstraße, second staircase on the second floor, first door on the right.

Liszt has piano lessons with Czerny. Antonio Salieri (see Illus. 52) teaches him figured bass, score-reading, composition, and singing.

12 July: Adam Liszt addresses a renewed appeal for help to Prince Esterházy (see p. 24). He receives a small sum of money by way of a reply.

September/October: Franz Liszt appears in aristocratic circles in Vienna, performing at several private concerts.

1 December: Liszt gives a major public concert in the Landesständischer Saal in Vienna. He plays Hummel's A minor Piano Concerto and improvises on themes suggested by the audience.

9 December: Concert in Vienna's Kärntnerthortheater. He plays the rondo from a piano concerto by Ferdinand Ries with an improvised introduction.

29 Title page of the first edition of the *50 Variations on a Waltz by Diabelli*, 1824.

In around the year 1820 the publisher Anton Diabelli invited fifty composers to write one variation each on his waltz. Among the composers who accepted were Schubert, Moscheles, Hummel, and Kalkbrenner. Beethoven used the occasion to write his famous *Diabelli Variations*, thus ensuring the publisher's immortality.

The eleven-year-old Liszt was given the honour of writing the 24th variation. Composed in 1822, it was his first published work.

30 Liszt's variation in the first edition of 1824.

Variation on a Waltz Theme by Diabelli (for piano). See Illus. 30. Pub. 1824.
Tantum ergo (probably for *a cappella* chorus). Lost. When Lina Ramann asked Liszt about the whereabouts of this piece in 1874, he told her, ''Forgotten, but the same emotion probably recurs in the *Tantum ergo* published by Kahnt four years ago in his volume of nine motets.''[5]

31 Carl Czerny, Liszt's piano teacher in 1822–3. Lithograph by Josef Kriehuber, 1833.

According to Liszt's letter to D. Pruckner of 17 March 1856, ''In the twenties, when a large part of Beethoven's works were like a kind of sphinx for most musicians, Czerny played *nothing but* Beethoven with an excellent understanding matched only by his effective technique. [. . .] All the greater pity is it that excessive productivity necessarily left him debilitated and prevented him from making any further progress in the direction hinted at in his first Sonata (op. 6 in A flat major) and a few other works of this period, works which I value highly as significant, finely wrought compositions belonging to the noblest disposition.

''Unfortunately, the influences which dominated Viennese society and the city's publishing houses at that time were of a detrimental kind, and Czerny did not possess the necessary degree of brusqueness to escape from them and thus preserve his better self.''[4]

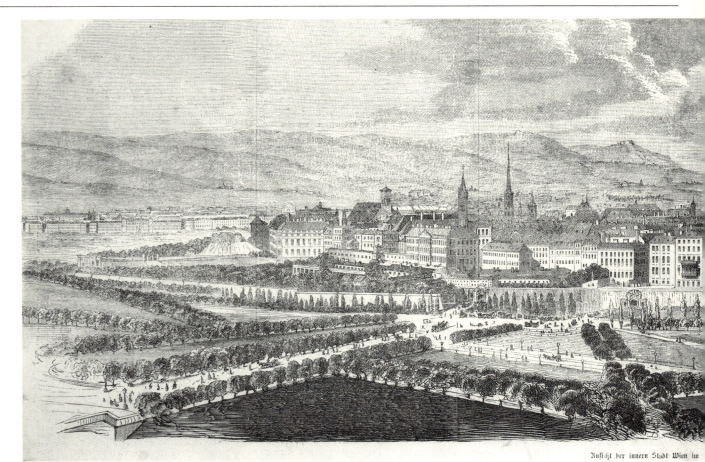

Auſicht der innern Stadt Wien im

32 Vienna. Wood engraving, mid-nineteenth century.

Accompanied by his parents, the young Franz Liszt moved to Vienna in 1822, remaining there for eighteen months and studying with Czerny and Salieri.

Der Karlskirche aufgenommen.

*re cose nella quali l'esercito in ogni lezione per introdurlo a poco
la volta alla composizione, e conservarlo così sempre nel buon gusto.*

*Nei giorni caldi però essendo venuto da me col Padre alle undi-
ci sempre sudatissimo e visto che, rilevai che alloggia a mariahilf
dissi al suo genitore che nei cattivi giorni è pericoloso questo viaggio
per la salute delicata del figlio; e che sarebbe necessario di farlo
alloggiare in Città. Egli mi rispose che avea fatto pregar l'A.V.
per tal fine, ma che non era ancora venuta risposta. Ultimamente
poi mi assicurò l'A.V. avea accettato un memoriale per lo stesso
oggetto. Per non tediar più a lungo V.A. con la presente lette-
ra questa non è che per unire a qual memoriale anche le mie
caldissime preghiere, promettendo all'A.V. ch'io vantaggierò di qu-
lo col farlo venire allora tutti li giorni da me, perché veramente
merita tutta l'attenzione per li talenti di musica da Dio a quel
Ragazzo concessi.*

*domandole umilmente perdono della libertà che mi sono presa,
ho l'alto onore di dirmi*

Ped'A.V.

*Umilissimo Dev.mo ed Obbl.mo
Servo. Antonio Salieri
Maestro di Cappella della Corte
Imp.le e Reale di Vienna.*

Vienna 25 Agosto 1822

33 Autograph letter from Antonio Salieri to
Prince Esterházy dated 25 August 1822 and re-
questing financial support for the young Liszt.
(A translation appears on p. 24).

Salieri taught Liszt figured bass and composition in 1822. Such was the eleven-year-old boy's
skill at sight-reading that Salieri often asked him
to accompany his singing pupils at the piano.

Left-hand column:
Antonio Salieri's letter of 25 August 1822 (Illus. 33, pp. 22–3).

Your Highness,

The undersigned humbly dares to beg a great favour of Your Highness's generous heart.

When I chanced to hear the young Francesco Liszi [!] at a private house, improvising on the piano and playing at sight, I was so amazed that I actually thought I was dreaming. When I then spoke with his father and expressed my sincerest congratulations, I learned that he is in Your Highness's service and that he has received permission to spend a year in Vienna in order that his son may study languages and perfect his skill on his instrument with one of the best masters in this field. He also said that he had found teachers for every discipline except for the study of figured bass and composition. As soon as I realized that he finally intended to ask *me*, I offered my services with the greatest of pleasure and purely out of friendship, as I have been wont to do these many years with indigent students. And so, since the middle of last month, the boy's father has been bringing his son to my house three times a week, and the young man is making astonishing progress, both in singing and in figured bass, in addition to deciphering full scores of the most varied kinds – three disciplines in which I drill him at every lesson in order to introduce him gradually to composition and to maintain his sense of good taste. On hot days he always arrives with his father at eleven, bathed in sweat and flushed with the heat, and thus I discovered that he lodges in Mariahilf. I told his father that on days when the weather was bad, this journey was hazardous to his son's delicate health and that he should allow him to live in the inner city. To this he replied that he had already addressed an entreaty to Your Highness in this regard, but that he had not yet been favoured with a reply. He assured me that only very recently Your Highness had received a memorandum on the subject. In order not to detain Your Highness unnecessarily with the present letter, I will say only that its purpose is to add my warmest entreaties to that memorandum, and I promise Your Highness that I shall redouble my efforts by having him come to my house every day, since I feel that his God-given talents are worthy of every attention.

Humbly begging forgiveness for the liberty which I have taken, I have the very great honour of signing myself Your Highness's

> most humble, devoted, and obedient servant Antonio Salieri,
> Kapellmeister to the Imperial and Royal Court of Vienna.

Vienna, 25 August 1822

Your Most Serene Highness and Right Honourable Prince of the Realm!

Most gracious and dread Lord! Sire!

To have to impose yet again on the great favour and generosity from which so many demonstrations of Your Highness's grace have already flowed is something I find most difficult and, indeed, all the more difficult in that I cannot lay claim to personal merit.

Like a wretched man borne along by a flood, I brood day and night upon ways of achieving deliverance, but, in spite of every effort to save myself from destruction, I can find no other means than, once again, to approach Your Serene Highness's throne, disclose my sad situation and entreat, in all humility, Your Highness's most gracious help.

By Michaelmas I shall no longer have anywhere to live, since I rented my present rooms for half a year and could in any case not stay in the suburbs during the winter, since the teachers who are instructing my son live in the town, and not only have we lost a good deal of time through having to travel to and fro, but many lessons have been missed through the increasingly inclement weather, so that on the whole the boy's education has been significantly affected. I cannot rent rooms in the city in future since I lack the means to pay for them, my entire wealth now consisting of 162 florins 30 kreutzers, together with 8 gold ducats which my son has received as individual gifts; of this I have to pay 100 florins in cash for my rent by the 26th of July, and what can I do with the insignificant sum that remains? God! Never before have I trembled so much for want of money as I do at present in this money-gobbling city of Vienna.

It is true that I brought a significant sum of money with me, but my expenses have not been insignificant: I first had to buy clothes for myself and my son, in order that we could at least be seen in respectable houses and not compromise the splendid reputation of Your Highness's household;

and what of the money spent on sheet music – books – music and language teachers – accommodation – wood – and food? How many sleepless nights has this cost me? indeed, I can admit in all conscience that my senses often forsake me utterly when I recall how happy was my former position, and how sad my present plight.

It is therefore with the deepest reverence that I make so bold as to entreat Your Serene Highness on bended knee, begging that Your Highness might most generously promote my son's continuing education /: since, according to the testimony of so many experts, he possesses no ordinary talents, and justifies the greatest expectations :/ and agree, most graciously, to my receiving accommodation in kind, together with cash support for the coming year, whereby it may please Your Highness to rescue me from what is at present so painfully difficult a situation.

> I am Your Serene Highness's
> most humble petitioner and servant
> Adam Liszt.
> Accountant on Your Highness's Sheep-Farm.

Vienna, 12 July 1822

Right-hand column:
Adam Liszt's letter of 12 July 1822 (Illus. 34), addressed to Prince Nicholas Esterházy from the "money-gobbling city of Vienna."

34 Autograph letter from Adam Liszt to Prince Esterházy of 12 July 1822. (Translation on facing page.)

Acta Musicalia, Nr. 3325

LIFE

12 January: Liszt takes part in a musical matinée in Vienna.

13 April: Grand concert in the small Redoutensaal in Vienna. Liszt plays Hummel's B minor Piano Concerto, Ignaz Moscheles's Variations for Piano and Orchestra, and improvisations on themes given to him by the audience (see Illus. 36).

Anton Schindler reports that the concert was attended by Beethoven, but he later withdraws this claim. Uncertainty continues to cloud the issue of a *Weihekuß* or "kiss of consecration" which Beethoven is said to have planted on Liszt's forehead. On the basis of Beethoven's Conversation Books, which contain his written correspondence with Schindler, it appears that Liszt visited Beethoven the day before the concert (i.e. on the 12th), in order to ask him for a theme, in a sealed envelope, which he could improvise at his concert. Liszt himself told his pupil Ilka Horowitz-Barney in 1875 that he played the first movement of the C major Concerto (op. 15) and transposed a Bach fugue for Beethoven to hear. The *Weihekuß* could have taken place on this occasion.

1 May: Concert in Pest, in the main hall of the Inn of the Seven Prince-Electors (Hét Választófejedelem).

10/17 and 24 May: Concerts in the Pest Municipal Theatre.

19 May: Liszt performs at a soirée in Pest.

27 May: Visit to Preßburg.[6]

June/July: Liszt studies piano and theory in Vienna.

August: Adam Liszt resigns his appointment in Raiding in order to devote himself full-time to his son's promising career.

20 September: Liszt and his family leave Vienna and set off for Paris.

26 September to 28 October: Liszt in Munich. Concerts at the Court Theatre on 17, 24, and 27 October (see pp. 28 and 29).

29 October (to early November): Liszt in Augsburg. Three concerts in four days, followed by two in Stuttgart.

3 and 6 December: Concerts in Strasbourg (in the Saal zum Geist and the Municipal Theatre: see p. 30).

11 December: Liszt and his parents arrive in Paris, where the piano maker Sébastien Erard assumes responsibility for the young pianist – no doubt also acting in his firm's interests. The family moves into rooms in the Hôtel d'Angleterre (No. 10), in the immediate neighbourhood of the Maison Erard.

12 December: As a foreigner Liszt is refused admission to the Paris Conservatoire (see p. 31).

35 Beethoven's famous "Weihekuß" or "kiss of consecration." Detail from a lithograph published in 1873 to celebrate the jubilee of Liszt's Vienna debut (see Illus. 512).

The scene depicted here appears to be a fabrication. Beethoven's Conversation Books and Liszt's own account make it clear that the kiss, if it took place at all, did so not at a public concert but in Beethoven's private rooms.

36 Concert billing for Liszt's recital on 13 April 1823 in the small Redoutensaal in Vienna.

37 Austrian mail-coach on the road from Vienna to Graz. Lithograph by F. von Maleck, 1824.

The tower-like structure to the right of the picture is the so-called "Spinnerin am Kreuz" outside Vienna on the main road to Trieste.

Liszt's father believed the time was ripe to bid farewell to Vienna. Paris – the stronghold of cultural life – awaited the young prodigy. His first tour followed the same itinerary as that undertaken by the young Mozart, with whom contemporaries were fond of comparing the young Franz Liszt. Indeed, it was perhaps this that prompted Adam Liszt to adopt the same route. Salzburg, Munich, Augsburg, Stuttgart, Strasbourg, and Paris were their ports of call.

Franz Liszt boarded the mail coach in Vienna on 20 September 1823. Twenty years later the musical world of Europe would lie at his feet.

WORKS

Vocal and keyboard pieces. Written late 1823 or early 1824, and mentioned by Liszt's father in a letter of 20 March 1824. Lost.

Waltz in A major (for piano). Written 1823 or earlier. Pub. in Vienna in 1825 and in *The Musical Gem* in 1832. A version for violin and piano from 1825 was published in the late 1820s.

LISZT FERENTZ

Im Verlage bei N. Meidingers Wwe in Preßburg.

38 Franz Liszt. Lithograph by Joseph Trentsensky of Vienna, based on a drawing (ca. 1823) by Baron Ferdinand von Lütgendorff.

As the first known portrait of Liszt this likeness deserves more than a passing glance. It is normally dated 1820 and linked to Liszt's first concert in Preßburg on 26 November 1820. This dating, however, is highly improbable. Lütgendorff (1785–1858) did not move to Preßburg until the autumn of 1824. He had previously lived in Prague and moved to Vienna on 13 May 1823, where he lived opposite the building that housed the Hungarian Guards. He was immediately commissioned to undertake a series of artists' portraits in the form of lithographs. Liszt was living in Vienna at this time and had recently become better known as a result of his concerts, so the present portrait may well have been made at this time. An earlier meeting between Liszt and the painter, although not out of the question, is most unlikely.

The lithograph was included in a volume of portraits published under the title *Magyar Pantheon* in 1825–6 by Meidinger's publishing house in Preßburg.

Lütgendorff met his subject for a second time on 19 December 1839, when Liszt gave a concert in Preßburg. Between 1841 and 1844 he lived in Munich, where he had a studio next to Ludwig von Schwanthaler in the Lerchenstraße (modern Schwanthalerstraße.) A banquet held in Munich in Liszt's honour on 31 October 1843 was the occasion for a further, and probably final, meeting between Lütgendorff and Liszt.

39 Programme for Moscheles's Munich concert on 10 October 1823.

Königliches Hof-Theater an der Residenz.

Mit allergnädigster Erlaubniß
wird
Morgen Freytag den 10. Oktober 1823
J. Moscheles
auf seiner Durchreise von England
bey beleuchtetem Hause
ein großes
Vokal- und Instrumental-Konzert
zu geben die Ehre haben.

Erste Abtheilung.
Ouvertüre von Cherubini.
Neues Piano-Forte-Konzert (in E dur), komponirt und vorgetragen von J. Moscheles.
Arie, gesungen von . . . . . Hrn. Mittermayr.
Phantasie für die Violine, komponirt und vorgetragen von . Hrn. Molique.

Zweyte Abtheilung.
(Auf Verlangen) Variationen über den Alexander-Marsch, komponirt
und vorgetragen von . . . . J. Moscheles.
Arie aus der Oper: Der Freyschütz, gesungen von . Dlle. Schechner.
Variationen für die Flöte, von Drouet, vorgetragen von . Hrn. Böhm.
Freye Phantasie auf dem Piano-Forte, von . . J. Moscheles.

Preise der Plätze:
Eine Loge auf 7 Personen im 1ten und 2ten Rang . . 16 fl. — fr.
Ein Logenplatz im 1ten und 2ten Rang . . . . 2 fl. 24 fr.
Eine Loge auf 7 Personen im 3ten Rang . . . 14 fl. — fr.
Ein Logenplatz im 3ten Rang . . . . . 2 fl. — fr.
Eine Loge auf 7 Personen im 4ten Rang . . . 11 fl. — fr.
Ein Logenplatz im 4ten Rang . . . . . 1 fl. 36 fr.
Ein gesperrter Sitz im Parterre . . . . 1 fl. — fr.
Parterre . . . . — fl. 48 fr.
Gallerie . . . . — fl. 30 fr.

Der Anfang ist um halb 7 Uhr, das Ende gegen 9 Uhr.

Auf die gefälligen Bestellungen der Titl. Logen-Abonnenten wird bis Freytag den 10.
Vormittags bis 10 Uhr im Königl. Hoftheater Nro. 3. gewartet, dann aber wie gewöhnlich über diejenigen Logen, welche nicht ganz beybehalten worden sind, disponirt.

Königliches Hof-Theater an der Residenz.

Mit allergnädigster Erlaubniß
wird
Freytag den 17. Oktober 1823
auf seiner Durchreise nach Paris und London, der aus Ungarn gebürtige
eilfjährige Knabe
Franz Liszt,
Sohn eines Beamten des regierenden Fürsten Nikolaus Esterhazy, und Schüler des rühmlich bekannten Tonsetzers und Clavierspielers Carl Czerny, sein in der österreichischen
Kaiserstadt Wien allgemein anerkanntes Musik-Talent am Piano-Forte
hören zu lassen, und zu dem Ende
ein großes
Vokal- und Instrumental-Konzert
zu geben die Ehre haben.

Erste Abtheilung.
Ouvertüre mit Orchester.
Grand Concerto aus H moll von J. N. Hummel, mit Orchester-
Begleitung, vorgetragen von . . . dem jungen Konzertgeber.
Herrn Löhle.
Vierstimmige Gesänge, gesungen von . . . Herrn Bayer.
Herrn Ebenauer.
Herrn Staudacher.
Concertino für Clarinette von Carl Maria Weber, vorgetragen von Herrn Schaden.

Zweyte Abtheilung.
Freyer Eingang und Variationen von Carl Czerny mit Orchester-Begleitung, vorgetragen von . . . dem Konzertgeber.
Aria aus der Oper: Algieri, von Rossini, gesungen von . Mademoiselle Pöstl.
Freye Phantasie am Piano-Forte von . . . dem Konzertgeber.
Um aber diesfalls nach dem strengsten Sinne der Ankündigung einer freyen Phantasie reali-
siren zu können, unterfanget sich der Knabe eine die pl. T. Zuhörer und Verehrer der edlen Tonkunst
ergebenst zu bitten, ihm hiezu ein zum phantasiren geeignetes schriftliches Thema, wenn es auch
nur aus 4 Takte bestehet, gütigst zu ertheilen.

Preise der Plätze:
Eine Loge auf 7 Personen im 1ten und 2ten Rang . 9 fl. — fr.
Eine Loge auf 7 Personen im 3ten Rang . . 7 fl. — fr.
Ein Logenplatz im 1ten, 2ten und 3ten Rang . 1 fl. — fr.
Eine Loge auf 7 Personen im 4ten Rang . . 5 fl. 36 fr.
Ein Logenplatz im 4ten Rang . . . . — fl. 48 fr.
Ein gesperrter Sitz im Parterre . . . 1 fl. — fr.
Parterre . . . . . . — fl. 24 fr.
Gallerie . . . . . . — fl. 15 fr.

Der Anfang ist um halb 7 Uhr, das Ende um halb 9 Uhr.

Auf die gefälligen Bestellungen der Titl. Logen-Abonnenten wird bis Freytag den 17.
Vormittags bis 10 Uhr im Königl. Hoftheater Nro. 3. gewartet, dann aber wie gewöhnlich über diejenigen Logen, welche nicht ganz beybehalten worden sind, disponirt.

Königliches Hof-Theater an der Residenz.

Mit allergnädigster Erlaubniß
wird
Freytag den 24. Oktober 1823
Franz Liszt,
auf Verlangen sein zweytes und letztes
Vokal- und Instrumental-Konzert
zu geben die Ehre haben.

Erste Abtheilung.
Ouvertüre.
Großes Konzert aus A moll von J. N. Hummel, für Piano-
Forte, vorgetragen von . . . dem jungen Konzertgeber.

Arie von Caraffa, gesungen von . . . Herrn Loehle.

Variationen für die Violine, componirt und vorgetragen von . Herrn Stahl.

Zweyte Abtheilung.
Variationen aus G dur für Piano-Forte, von Ignaz Moscheles,
vorgetragen von . . . . . dem Konzertgeber.

Arie von Rossini, gesungen von . . . Demois. Schechner.

Zum Beschluß freye Phantasie von . . . dem Konzertgeber.

Preise der Plätze:
Eine Loge auf 7 Personen im 1ten und 2ten Rang . 8 fl. — fr.
Ein Logen-Platz im 1ten und 2ten Rang . . 1 fl. 12 fr.
Eine Loge auf 7 Personen im 3ten Rang . . 7 fl. — fr.
Ein Logenplatz im 3ten Rang . . . . 1 fl. — fr.
Eine Loge auf 7 Personen im 4ten Rang . . 5 fl. 36 fr.
Ein Logenplatz im 4ten Rang . . . . — fl. 48 fr.
Ein gesperrter Sitz im Parterre . . . 1 fl. — fr.
Parterre . . . . . . — fl. 24 fr.

Die Kasse wird um 5 Uhr geöffnet.

Der Anfang ist um halb 7 Uhr, das Ende um halb 9 Uhr.

Auf die gefälligen Bestellungen der Titl. Logen-Abonnenten wird bis Freytag den 24.
Vormittags bis 10 Uhr im Königl. Hoftheater Nro. 3. gewartet, dann aber wie gewöhnlich über diejenigen Logen, welche nicht ganz beybehalten worden sind, disponirt.

Königliches Hof-Theater an der Residenz.

Mit allergnädigster Erlaubniß
werden
Mondtag den 27. Oktober 1823
die Gebrüder Karl und Anton Ebner,
ersterer 11 und letzterer 12 Jahre alt, Königl. Preußische Cammer-Musiker,
aus Ungarn gebürtig
ein
Vokal- und Instrumental-Konzert
zu geben die Ehre haben.

Erste Abtheilung.
Ouvertüre.
Variationen für die Violine, componirt von Mayseder, vorgetragen von Karl Ebner.

Arie von Rossini, gesungen von . . . Herrn Staudacher.

Freyer Eingang und Variationen von Karl Czerny, mit ganzer
Orchester-Begleitung, vorgetragen von . . . Herrn Franz Liszt.

Zweyte Abtheilung.
Concertante für zwey Violinen, von Eck, vorgetragen von . den Gebrüdern Ebner.

Arie von Pucitta, gesungen von . . . Mad. Vespermann.

Variationen für Piano-Forte und Violine, vorgetragen von . Herrn Franz Liszt.
Karl Ebner.

Freye Phantasie am Piano-Forte, vorgetragen von . . Herrn Franz Liszt.

Preise der Plätze:
Eine Loge auf 7 Personen im 1ten und 2ten Rang . 8 fl. — fr.
Ein Logen-Platz im 1ten und 2ten Rang . . 1 fl. 12 fr.
Eine Loge auf 7 Personen im 3ten Rang . . 7 fl. — fr.
Ein Logenplatz im 3ten Rang . . . . 1 fl. — fr.
Eine Loge auf 7 Personen im 4ten Rang . . 5 fl. 36 fr.
Ein Logenplatz im 4ten Rang . . . . — fl. 48 fr.
Ein gesperrter Sitz im Parterre . . . 1 fl. — fr.
Parterre . . . . . . — fl. 24 fr.
Gallerie . . . . . . — fl. 15 fr.

Die Kasse wird um 5 Uhr geöffnet.

Der Anfang ist um halb 7 Uhr, das Ende um halb 9 Uhr.

Auf die gefälligen Bestellungen der Titl. Logen-Abonnenten wird bis Mondtag den 27.
Vormittags bis 10 Uhr im Königl. Hoftheater Nro. 3. gewartet, dann aber wie gewöhnlich über diejenigen Logen, welche nicht ganz beybehalten worden sind, disponirt.

40, 41, 42 Programmes for the twelve-year-old Liszt's appearances in Munich on 17, 24, and 27 October 1823.

''And you, my little one, you dared to appear after Moscheles?'' King Maximilian I is alleged to have asked the young prodigy (see Adam Liszt's letter, p. 30).

Liszt and his family arrived in Munich on 26 September 1823 and remained in the city until 28 October. The Court and National Theatre had burned down at the beginning of the year and could not be used for concerts. Franz Liszt performed in the Cuvilliés Theatre, where the famous keyboard virtuoso Ignaz Moscheles had appeared the previous week. The Augsburg *Allgemeine Zeitung* carried the following report on Liszt's first concert:

'' 'A new Mozart has appeared among us,' Munich announces to the musical world. It is known that this child prodigy was only seven years old when he first began to attract the world's attention through his artistic talent. The young Liszt, it is true, is already four years older than Mozart was. But if we take account of the difference in time and in the demands that audiences now make of their artists, we are bound to admit that we are indeed well justified in declaring, 'A new Mozart has appeared among us!'

The young Liszt performed Hummel's Concerto in B [minor] with such ease and purity, with such precision and power, and with such profound and genuine feeling that not even the boldest imagination could have dared to expect anything comparable from a child of such tender years. We have heard Hummel and Moscheles, and we do not shrink from claiming that this child was by no means their inferior in his powers of execution. But what increased our admiration to the highest pitch was an improvisation on given themes. The young Liszt had already invited the audience, by way of the concert placard, to be so kind as to submit motifs to him; and he was given the theme of the variations which Molique had played at Moscheles's concert, together with the tune of *God save the King*. The boy began with Molique's theme and varied it with such consummate skill that we thought we were hearing a finished composition. He did the same thing later with the second theme, subsequently combining it with the first, so that the two themes were interwoven and merged together in the most brilliantly inspired of ways.

The reader will therefore not be surprised to learn that the packed and enthusiastic audience was scarcely able to contain its applause.''

43 Interior of the Royal Court Theatre in the Residenz, generally known as the Cuvilliés Theatre, Munich. Watercolour by Gustav Seeberger, 1867.

This is one of the few nineteenth-century illustrations to show the interior of the Cuvilliés Theatre, seen here during a performance.

Adam Liszt's letter to Carl Czerny of 2 November 1823, reporting on his son's successes in Munich.

Augsburg, 2 November 1823

Dear Sir,

We arrived safely in Munich on the evening of the 26th of September, and left the city on the 28th of October. The reason why we were there so long was first that Herr Moscheles had already arrived there before we did, secondly because the October Festival was then in full swing, and thirdly that Moscheles postponed his concert. You will gather from the enclosed with what acclaim the latter was met. We gave our first concert on the 17th of October, and since we were not known, the hall was somewhat thinly attended. But we had the good fortune that our most gracious King and the Princesses were there. The applause was tremendous, and I was immediately invited to give a second concert, which took place on the 24th. To put it briefly, it would have been preferable if as many people had been present on the first occasion as were turned away for lack of space on this latter occasion, so that in the end the box office had to be closed. I have subjoined a few enclosures to show the sort of applause that Zizy [Franz] reaped. Idle as we had been at the outset, we were now fully occupied after the first of our concerts and were honoured on all sides by the most flattering commissions. For a third time I responded to the most urgent entreaties on the part of the theatre directors and agreed to Franzl's appearance at a concert in the Royal Theatre given by the two Ebner violinists. Among other pieces which he was required by popular request to perform were the E flat major Variations with orchestra which you yourself possess, and although we had no share in the receipts we ensured our immortal fame, and even good King Max said how kind it was of us to support these other two performers.

We twice enjoyed the great good fortune of having an audience with this most kind-hearted of monarchs, and on both occasions were received with conspicuous grace and favour. On the first occasion the King said, "and you, my little one, you dared to appear after Moscheles?" – When we took our leave, the kind King said, "Come here, my boy, and let me kiss you," and so he did; there were tears in my eyes. Let-

ters of recommendation were immediately prepared on the King's instructions, and a number of them were entrusted to us to take to Strasbourg and Paris, so that we may look forward to a favourable reception there. I had the words "Pupil of Carl Czerny" inserted on the concert billing; everyone said how much they looked forward and hoped to make the acquaintance of this excellent mentor, and I was asked in many quarters whether Herr von Czerny had many more such pupils. To which I replied that if pupils are talented and hardworking they may well acquire this degree of virtuosity through the wise and thorough teaching of your own good self. [. . .]

The orchestra in Munich is exceptionally good, and I have never heard a better one, in addition to which the gentlemen there are most obliging. The B minor Concerto by Hummel was uniquely done and left nothing to be desired. What a pity that the theatre is too small.

Moscheles has outlived his reputation in Munich, and they no longer speak of him with the proper respect. For my own part, I must say that the way he performed his concerto was unsurpassable, but that the Fantasia was empty, so that I cannot really call it a Fantasia. If he has lost respect, it is especially because he charged double admission. [. . .]

I pray to God that what I have heard about Salieri is not true, and yet I should not like to remain in a state of uncertainty, so I would ask you to send me an explanation in Paris. [It was being reported at this time that, as his mind clouded over with age, Antonio Salieri was accusing himself of having poisoned Mozart. He died soon afterwards, on 7 May 1825, in his 75th year.] My family and I ask to be remembered to you, and I myself remain respectfully

Your eternally grateful
and obedient servant
Liszt.

From Munich Liszt travelled to Augsburg, Stuttgart, and Strasbourg. Only a few years later Frédéric Chopin was to follow the same itinerary to Paris, probably filled with the same expectations as Liszt was now.

The *Allgemeine Musikalische Zeitung* reviewed Liszt's concerts in Strasbourg. The original review is reproduced as Illus. 45 (a translation appears on p. 335).

44 The Strasbourg Theatre. Steel engraving by G. M. Kurz, based on a drawing by R. Höfle; ca. 1840.
Liszt performed here on 6 December 1823.

Am 3ten December im Saale zum Geist, und am 6ten im Theater, überraschte uns der eilfjährige Liszt mit seinem fertigen und ausdrucksvollen Klavierspiel; er erregte besonders in seinen freyen Phantasieen den ausserordentlichsten Beyfall. Er spielte unter andern ein Klavier-Concert von Hummel (nicht Himmel, wie angezeigt war) in H moll, ferner die Variationen über den *Alexander-Marsch* von Moscheles, mit bewunderungswürdiger Fertigkeit und mit Gefühl. Er begab sich von hier mit seinem Vater nach Paris. —

45 Review of Liszt's two concerts in Strasbourg in 1823, reproduced from the *Allgemeine Musikalische Zeitung*, 1824, no. 39. (For a translation see p. 335.)

46 Street scene in Paris at the time of Liszt's arrival in the city. Steel engraving by Westwood, based on a drawing by Batty; 1821.

world collapsed around his father, for the whole purpose of his journey had come to nothing. The director of the Conservatoire, Luigi Cherubini, upheld the regulation forbidding foreigners from entering the school. Liszt never held this against Cherubini (who, be it added, was himself a foreigner). His genius allowed him to seek and find his own way to success. Some twelve years later, Liszt recounted the fateful moment at the Conservatoire:

''The very next day after our arrival in Paris, we hurried to see Cherubini. [. . .] Scarcely had I passed through the entrance (or, more accurately, the hideous archway) in the Rue Faubourg-Poissonnière when I was overcome by a feeling of deep and reverential awe. 'So this,' I thought, 'is the fateful place. Here in this glorious sanctuary the tribunal sits whose sentence of life or death is eternally binding' – I almost sank to my knees before the crowd of people there, all of whom I took to be celebrities and yet whom, to my amazement, I could see walking to and fro like simple mortals.

Finally, after a quarter of an hour of agonizing waiting, the beadle opened the door to the director's office and beckoned me in. More dead than alive, but driven on by an overwhelming force, I rushed over to Cherubini to kiss his hand. [. . .] Happily, my torment did not last long. We had already been advised that difficulties might stand in the way of my admission to the Conservatoire, but until then we had not been aware of the institution's rule, which was clearly intended to exclude all foreigners from taking part in its teaching. Cherubini began by informing us of this rule. We were thunderstruck! I felt myself trembling in every limb. None the less, my father lingered and entreated; his voice restored my courage and I, too, tried to stammer a word or two. [. . .] But the rule was inexorable – and I unconsolable. All appeared to be lost, even our honour, and I no longer hoped for help from any quarter [. . .]''[7]

47 Luigi Cherubini (1760–1842). Lithograph from *Galerie de la Presse*, ca. 1830.

Cherubini – regarded by Beethoven as the leading composer of his age – was director of the Paris Conservatoire from 1821 to 1842. He refused to admit Liszt as a student when the latter presented himself in 1823, since the Conservatoire regulations prevented foreigners from registering there.

Liszt and his family arrived in Paris on 11 December 1823 and lodged at the Hôtel d'Angleterre, 10 Rue du Mail, next door to the piano firm of Erard. When the twelve-year-old Liszt was refused admission to the Paris Conservatoire, the

LIFE

1 January: Liszt plays for the Duchesse de Berry, and afterwards for the Duc d'Orléans (later the Citizen King Louis-Philippe.)

11 January: Liszt improvises at the piano during a meeting of the Société Académique des Enfants d'Apollon and is thereupon elected an honorary member.

He is taught composition by Ferdinando Paer (see Illus. 54), learns French, and appears at various *salons* (17 January and 21 February.)

7 March: Grand concert in the Théâtre-Italien. Accompanied by the opera-house orchestra, Liszt plays Hummel's B minor Piano Concerto and Czerny's Variations, and improvises on an aria from *Le Nozze di Figaro*. The press compares him with Mozart.

26 and 28 March: Takes part in charity concerts in Paris.

12 April: Concert at the Théâtre-Italien. "Le petit Litz" becomes the darling of Paris audiences.

May: Liszt's mother returns to Graz, while father and son travel to England accompanied by Sébastien Erard.

5 June: Concert in London's Argyll Rooms.

21 June: Grand concert in Argyll Rooms attended by Clementi, Cramer, Ries and Kalkbrenner.

29 June: Concert at the Theatre Royal, Drury Lane.

July: While in London, Liszt works on his opera *Don Sanche* and on several other compositions.

4 August: Concert in Manchester (Theatre-Royal); then back to France.

12 August: In Calais (see Illus. 59).

September to December: In Paris. Liszt continues to study piano and composition, and to work on the score of his opera.

Adam Liszt's letter to Carl Czerny of 17 March 1824:

Paris, 17 March 1824

Dear Sir,

It is true, is it not, that there is no intermission in music as long as there has been since I last wrote, yet until now it has been almost impossible for me to write a long letter, and when one is so far away and has so many things in mind which may be disclosed to you alone and which are of value only to you, one cannot be brief. I shall therefore begin without further ado. – We have been in Paris since the 11th of December, and since we were announced in advance by newspapers and by many private letters, we immediately found ourselves busy, after a few days' rest, and have been received with the greatest enthusiasm. Since we have been here, we have already accepted invitations to 36 soirées in the very best families, and these soirées never pay less than 100 francs, and often as much as 150. In order not to neglect my boy's peace and quiet or compromise his studies, I am obliged to decline many invitations.

On one occasion he played at the home of Madame la Duchesse de Berry, where the entire royal family was present and where he improvised four times on themes that were set him; likewise three times at the home of the Duc d'Orléans. The applause was so great that he was invited back on several occasions to both these leading households. On the 7th of March we gave our first public concert in the Royal Italian Opera House, which was made available to us, free of charge, together with the orchestra and lighting, for our own benefit. In consequence we had expenses of only 343 francs to defray, and we were left accordingly with a net income of 4,711 francs. It is a shame that the theatre is so small and that I did not wish to raise the prices to any conspicuous extent, otherwise we could certainly have doubled the receipts. The boxes had all been reserved a week beforehand by the subscribers, and so no one else could obtain a box. The applause which my boy earned for himself is indescribable, and I think I have said enough when I say that the general wish that a second concert be given was expressed on repeated occasions both in the theatre and in public journals. You will think and say that this is a wish that Liszt could easily meet, and of course you are right; but you must know that this was a special favour which we owe solely to the august patronage of the Duchesse de Berry and the royal minister Lauriston. Such a favour is granted to very few artists, not least in the way that we got the theatre. I do not believe you will find a single example in Vienna of a foreign artist who has been allowed free use of a theatre for his own benefit, in addition to having an act from an opera performed to support him. This single example may provide adequate proof of how far the French surpass other nations in the respect which they feel for the arts and in their generosity. I could tell you much more besides, but my diary will one day tell you all this in minute detail; I would ask you therefore to heed only this: anyone who has any ability must come to Paris, for here a love of art is paramount, here the artist is appreciated, honoured, and rewarded. Herr Pixis had little success with the instrument which Graf had made for him, and the enterprise caused

both men more harm than it profited them. There are good instruments here too, of which the latest invention by that most skilful technician Monsieur Erard is distinguished by its excellence. I believe that this man has performed a most essential service for the piano. I would not be capable of offering you a description, but shall tell you only one small characteristic about it: the touch is very light, and yet you can vary the sound (which is very good) in every way. You can play chords, soft or loud, as often as you like, without raising your hands after the initial touch: it really is most amazing. Only three examples of this kind of instrument are finished at present, but a fourth is now being made for my boy, and we shall send it to Vienna in due course; I am convinced that it will receive your approval.

[. . .] At many social gatherings people have expressed the liveliest wish to meet the teacher of this child prodigy (as my boy is generally called). Will he not come to Paris, they ask. This brings me to speak of you, you who are the dearest and most valued of friends to us, and I ask: will you never leave Vienna? If I am to provide an answer to this question, I would say that you should do so and come to Paris, armed with a supply of your compositions; we shall do everything possible to prepare for your reception here, and you will find an altogether unhoped-for welcome and earn the kind of remuneration that you can never dream of in Vienna. We shall probably not go to London until next year, since our prospects here continue to improve. And so if you would like to come to Paris (and it would have to be at the beginning of next autumn), please write and tell me; you can stay with us here free of charge, you'll have a beautiful room with a separate bedroom overlooking the street, in the centre of the town, on the second floor; we would still have a sitting-room and two bedrooms for our own use, and if you would make do with eating with us (we dine at home) you would redouble our pleasure.

There is something else I must tell you about Herr Pixis: this gentleman appears to be our enemy. The cause is a mystery even to me. We have spoken to him only on one occasion, when we happened to meet in the Palais Royal; since that time we have often seen him at his music publisher's, where Herr P. has never deigned so much as to look at us. Fortunately, this rival of ours is too ineffectual to be able to harm us, and his actions may perhaps bring down on him only the censure of others. Dearest and best Herr Czerny, we send you and your very dear parents our warmest good wishes, accompanied by our very great esteem and veneration, and look forward very much to receiving a letter from you soon. No doubt we shall also learn something of Vienna's musical world. There is still so much I could tell you, but my sheet of paper is coming to an end. Give our kind regards to Messrs Steiner, Haslinger, Abbé Stadler, Leidesdorf, Diabelli and Streicher, and if you would be so kind as to drop in on Countess Vincenz Bathiany in the Kärntnerstraße and mention how much we esteem her, I should forever be in your debt.

Your obedient servant
Liszt.

Address: Adam Liszt, Hotel d'Angleterre, 10 Rue du Mail.

Liszt,

Membre correspondant de la Société académique
des Enfans d'Apollon.

WORKS

Huit Variations (for piano). Written ca. 1824. Pub. 1824 or 1825 as op. 1.

Sept Variations brillantes sur un thème de Rossini (*Ermione*) (for piano). Written ca. 1824. Pub. ca. 1824 as op. 2.

Impromptu brillant sur des thèmes de Rossini et Spontini (for piano). Pub. 1824 as op. 3 (see Illus. 63). Introduction used in No. 7 of the 24 *Grandes Études* of 1837–38.

Deux Allegri di Bravura (for piano). Pub. 1825 as op. 4. Also pub. separately as *Rondo di Bravura* and *Allegro di Bravura* (see Illus. 62). On Liszt's opus numbers, see p. 46. An incomplete orchestral version of the *Allegro di Bravura* appears to date from around 1830. It is unpublished.

Fantasia (for piano). Mentioned by Liszt's father in a letter of 29 July 1824 (see p. 36). Lost.

Rondo (for piano). Mentioned in the same letter. Lost.

Don Sanche, ou Le Château d'Amour (opera in one act). Written 1824–25. Orchestration probably by Ferdinando Paer. Performed several times in 1825. (For years the full score was believed lost. Liszt himself assumed it had been destroyed in the fire at the Paris Opéra in 1873. However, the performing material used in 1825 was discovered in the Paris Opéra Library in 1903. There have been at least four productions of the work since 1825: in 1954 by the Berne conductor Luc Balmer, in 1977 by the Collegiate Theatre in London, and in 1986 by both the Musikhochschule Franz Liszt in Dresden and the 36th International Youth Festival in Bayreuth; a concert performance was given in Naples in May 1986, and a recording was made in Hungary in the same year.) A vocal score arranged by Guy Woolfenden was published in 1977.

48 Franz Liszt. Lithograph by François de Villain, based on a drawing by A. X. Leprince; 1824.

In January 1824 Liszt attended a concert in Paris organized by the Société Académique des Enfants d'Apollon. Having listened to a trio, he rushed onto the platform and performed a keyboard improvisation on the theme that had just been played. The Society spontaneously elected him an honorary member, and the present lithograph was produced to commemorate the event.

An account of Liszt's concert on 7 March 1824, written by Alphonse Louis Dieudonné Martainville and published on 9 March in the *Drapeau blanc*, a journal of extreme royalist views which Martainville himself edited and which appeared in Paris between 1819 and 1830, the year of Martainville's death.

The review is reproduced here almost in its entirety, since there are so few detailed reports of the young Liszt's playing. At the same time, this review is one of the earliest examples of a major piece of writing on music to appear in a daily newspaper.

ROYAL ITALIAN THEATRE
Concert by the Young Liszt

I cannot help it: since yesterday evening I am a believer in metempsychosis. I am convinced that the soul and spirit of Mozart have passed into the body of young Liszt, and never has an identity revealed itself by plainer signs. The same country, the same wonderful talent in childhood, and in the same art. I appeal to all who had the great good fortune to hear the wonderful little virtuoso. But in order to be better able to assess the parallel between the Mozart of yesterday and the Mozart of today, I should like to quote what Baron Grimm once said of the former; I mean that distinguished dilettante who became Mozart's enthusiastic admirer at the time of his first appearance in France in 1763.[a]

''True marvels are so rare that we must not fail to speak of it whenever the opportunity presents itself to witness such a marvel. A Kapellmeister from Salzburg by the name of Mozart arrived here recently with two wholly delightful children. His eleven-year-old daughter plays the clavier in a most brilliant manner; she performs the greatest and most difficult pieces with an astonishing degree of precision. Her brother, who is not yet quite seven, is so extraordinary a phenomenon that one can scarcely believe what one sees with one's eyes and hears with one's ears. It is the easiest thing in the world for this child to perform the most difficult pieces with the greatest exactness. [. . .]''

Not one of the wondrous things which Grimm relates surpasses those things which Liszt – or Mozart in his new incarnation – achieves today to the admiration of every artist and of all the capital's lovers of music. His little arms can scarcely stretch to the opposite ends of the keyboard; his little feet can barely reach the pedals – and yet this child is beyond compare; he is the foremost pianist in Europe: even Herr Moscheles would not feel offended by such an assertion.

In taking the name of Liszt, Mozart has lost none of that charming exterior which always enhances the interest which a child can inspire in us by dint of precocious talent. [. . .]

It is, as Grimm reports, the easiest thing in the world for this child to perform a concerto of exceptional difficulty with total precision, unfailing assurance and boldness, with brilliant freedom and a feeling which brings out every shade of musical nuance; in a word, with a degree of perfection which drives to distraction the most skilful performers who for thirty years have worked and practised at this most beautiful and most difficult instrument. To give an idea of the impression which he has been able to make on his listeners, I would mention only the effect of his playing on the orchestra at the Italian Opera, the best in France and Europe: eyes, ears, and soul were fixed on the young virtuoso's enchanted instrument, so that they forgot for a moment that they too were performing at this selfsame concert – so that all the instruments missed their entry. The audience showed by their laughter and clapping that they were very happy to

forgive a distraction which was perhaps the most flattering homage that has yet been paid to the little prodigy's talent.

The instrument had initially been placed, foolishly enough, with the end turned towards the audience as usual. Liszt was completely hidden behind its music stand. The audience expressed a wish to see the child whose playing had given them such great pleasure. The position of the instrument was therefore altered: it was turned around so that the performer had his back to the conductor. Without allowing himself to be discountenanced by this awkward arrangement, he played – with the same ascendancy that he had already shown in the earlier concerto – variations on a theme by Czerny, his teacher (if, indeed, it is true that he has ever had a teacher). Only in the rarest cases did he glance at the music: his eyes roamed round the hall, and he greeted the persons whom he recognized in the boxes with friendly smiles and nods.

Finally Liszt folded back the stand, put aside his music, and gave himself up to his genius in a free improvisation. Here words fail us to express the admiration which he excited. After an harmoniously structured introduction, he took as his theme Mozart's beautiful aria from *Le Nozze di Figaro*, ''Non più andrai.''[b] If, as I said, Liszt is merely a continuation of Mozart through some happy transmigration, it is he himself who provided the theme in question.

If you have ever seen how a child plays with an insect which he has bound with a silken thread or a hair, allowing it to flutter around as his unwitting captive, how he follows its flight and its rapid movements, releasing the thread and then drawing it back to himself, restraining the fugitive only to let it fly up again, then you have an idea of the way in which Liszt plays with his theme, abandoning it only to take it up again quickly, losing it a second time before snatching it up once again, leading it through every possible modulation, through the happiest and most unexpected transitions – and all this in the midst of the most astonishing difficulties which he seems to create while playing, purely in order to have the pleasure of triumphing over them. The liveliest applause and repeated appeals to return to the stage re-echoed throughout the hall; the demonstrations of pleasure and admiration were inexhaustible; even the delicate hands of the charming female listeners were untiring in their applause. The happy child returned his thanks with a smile.

I forgot to say that two vocal numbers allowed him a few moments' rest. Although Pellegrini[c] sang very beautifully and although Mlle Cinti[d] was better than usual, both formed no more than a minor episode within the concert itself. Liszt was the undisputed monarch. And I too admit that I believe this child will turn my head if I listen to him much more often; but I am happy to take that risk and have vowed to neglect no opportunity to repeat such lively and precious impressions as this concert has provided me with. All those members of the audience who had the good fortune to be present will no doubt agree with me in this.

A. MARTAINVILLE.

Notes on the text:
(a) Baron Friedrich Melchior Grimm (born Regensburg, 1723; died Gotha, 1807) was friendly with Mozart's family. The review mentioned here was dated 1 December 1763 and appeared in the form of an open letter to a German prince.
(b) Liszt later sketched a Fantasy on themes from *Le Nozze di Figaro* and played it in Berlin on 11 January 1843. It was believed lost until Ferruccio Busoni rediscovered and published it in 1912.
(c) Félix Pellegrini (1774–1832), bass singer and (from 1819 to 1826) a member of the Italian Opera in Paris.
(d) Laura-Cinthie Montalant-Damoreau (1801–1863), leading soprano and a member of the Italian Opera from 1819 to 1827.

49 The Italian Opera (Théâtre Royal Italien) in Paris. Copper engraving by Née, based on a drawing by Lallemand; ca. 1800.

Liszt performed here on 7 March 1824. The decisive success of this concert transformed ''le petit Litz'' into a Parisian celebrity.

50 Poster for the concert of 7 March 1824.

Liszt played Hummel's B minor Piano Concerto and Czerny's *Thème Varié à Grand Orchestre*, in addition to improvising on an aria from Mozart's opera *Le Nozze di Figaro*.

Adam Liszt's letter to Carl Czerny of 29 July 1824, in which he reports on his son's successes.

London, 29 July 1824.

Dear Sir,

Your valued letter of the 3rd of June reached me here; our joy at receiving it knew no bounds, and we wish for nothing more than to take possession of the music which you have most kindly made over to us, but this has not yet been possible. The reason for my long silence is simply that it has not until now been possible to tell you about everything in detail. When we arrived in London, we had many more difficulties to overcome than in Paris; one of the reasons was that we arrived too late, when the season was already well advanced and the soirées had all been arranged, and the second reason was that none of the artists here, with the honourable exception of Herr Ries, had done anything to help; Kalkbrenner in particular distinguished himself through his negligence. However, as you know, the good cannot be suppressed for long, and victory when it comes is all the more glorious. We gave our first concert on the 21st of June (a second was impossible, since too many other concerts had already been arranged), and I invited Messrs Clementi, Cramer, Ries, and Kalkbrenner, who duly all appeared, and I also invited London's leading artists, so that in spite of the fact that my boy is still little known and that on the very same evening another concert was being given in the theatre as a benefit performance for one of the leading Italian singers, and although we had enormous expenses, we nevertheless had a net income of 90 pounds, which is about 36 silver kreutzers. This concert had important consequences not only for Franzi's reputation but also for our financial position, since we were soon up to our ears in work and have earned 172 pounds in all for simple soirées (5 guineas for a soirée, sometimes more, and as much as 20 pounds from the French ambassador), making around 1,376 florins all told. The day before yesterday we were greatly honoured to be presented to His Majesty the King, an audience which took place at his summer residence at Windsor. It was a soirée arranged for only a handful of ladies and officers; Franzi played on his own and did so, moreover, for over two hours. He began by playing your Variations in E flat, a piece which was universally admired; even during the introduction, His Majesty deigned to remark that he had never heard anything like it before. At the conclusion His Majesty's acclaim was echoed on every side in the liveliest fashion. His Majesty then deigned to suggest the minuet from *Don Giovanni* as a theme for Franzi to improvise, and its execution aroused the highest degree of amazement on every side, so that His Majesty deigned to say repeatedly, in English, German, and French, that he had never heard anything like it before and that this boy surpassed Moscheles, Cramer, and Kalkbrenner [. . .]

Mr Ries has left London for good and gone to live with his father in the country not far from Bonn. Lessons here cost a guinea each, and although the greatest teachers live here it is rare to find a well-schooled pupil – there are more in Paris – and I can assure you that piano playing is still in its infancy in spite of the fact that the nation, and more especially the young women, are enthusiastic music lovers, and every house is overflowing with instruments and pieces of music. I may also say that one finds in every house in London what is nowhere else to be seen, namely wealth, order, cleanliness, collections of valuable pictures and books, etc. A cruise down the Thames surpasses everything; here one can see the wealth that England possesses by way of water. Wherever one sees a village, a city, or a small town, one encounters wealth, cleanliness, and order everywhere. Anyone who has not seen England has missed the world's greatest treasure. The people are very obliging, and the country is like a true Paradise. It is not cheap to live here, but money there is aplenty. I must just tell you what it normally costs to put on a concert: the hall costs 30 guineas, the orchestra 35, the printer 9, newspapers 26, and tickets 9½, making 109½ guineas in all, or some 916 gulden. From this you can see the total sum that our concert cost, and at the same time see that the expenses are greater than what we were left with; yet every day there are concerts here in abundance. The young Aspull, of whom I had already read extraordinary things in the Paris journals [George Aspull, then eight years old, showed an outstanding musical talent; but, as Liszt predicted, his fame was short-lived], gave his second concert of the season, playing your concerto adapted for piano: there was nothing about his playing to confirm the reports I had read, and even the applause was somewhat indifferent. Later Aspull paid us a visit and played some short variations, from which I concluded that the boy has plenty of talent but that he is being badly instructed, and that for this reason he will never achieve real greatness; I feel very sorry for him, since he is a dear little fellow and very well behaved, albeit somewhat timid. – Franzi is playing and scribbling busily away. His playing now would certainly win your approval; he plays cleanly and expressively, and his technique has reached a high level. I am still making him play scales and studies with a metronome and am not wavering from the principles which you yourself laid down, since it is clear from their success that they are the best. He has now achieved a high degree of competence in free improvisation: indeed, his proficiency is remarkable for his age. As for his compositions, he has already completed two Rondo di bravura (which the people here want to buy, but which I am not prepared to relinquish to them); one Rondo, one Fantasia; Variations on several themes; one *Amusement* or, rather, Quodlibet on various themes by Rossini and Spontini, which he played for His Majesty to great acclaim. But his principal work is a French opera, *Don Sanche ou Le Château d'amour*. The subject was adapted especially for him; apart from the recitatives, he has worked on all the rest here, and since he sang parts of it at a number of social gatherings here, His Majesty too learned about it and invited him to perform some of it. It won him the greatest applause. I am most eager to know what will happen when this work is completely finished. What is certain is that the opera is to be given in the large opera house in Paris, but I shall send you more details of this in advance of the event. There is so much else I should like to tell you, but, alas, there is no more space. We send you and your dear parents our most sincere good wishes, and deem ourselves fortunate to be able to sign ourselves

Your most grateful servant Liszt.

CARL CZERNY.

Top left:

51 Carl Czerny (1791–1857). Steel engraving by Carl Mayer, ca. 1840.
Liszt's piano teacher in Vienna in 1822–3. His famous pupil retained a lifelong devotion to him.

Top right:

52 Antonio Salieri (1750–1825). Copper engraving based on a drawing by F. Rehberg; 1821.
Liszt's composition teacher in Vienna in 1822–3. The fiction that Salieri poisoned Mozart continues to cling to him.

FRANZ LISZT'S TEACHERS

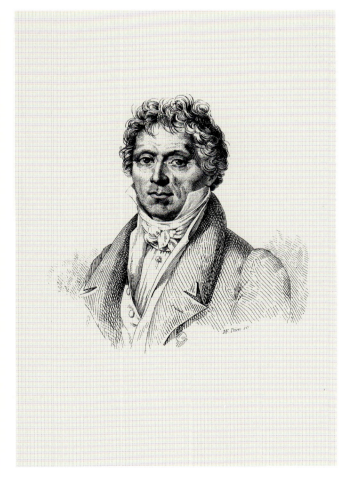

Paër
'76

Ferd. Paër

Bottom left:

53 Antonin Reicha (1770–1836). Lithograph by M. F. Dien, ca. 1840.
Liszt's teacher for theory and counterpoint around 1825, Reicha was professor at the Paris Conservatoire.

Bottom right:

54 Ferdinando Paer (1771–1839). Lithograph by Delpech, ca. 1830.
Director of the Théâtre-Italien and a significant figure in the musical life of Paris, Paer taught Liszt composition around the year 1825.

55 The Theatre Royal, Drury Lane, in London. Steel engraving by Hébert, based on a drawing by Marville; ca. 1830.

Liszt performed here in June 1824. A later performance in June 1825 was attended by King George IV.

Adam Liszt's letter to Carl Czerny of 3 September 1824, reporting his son's successes.

Paris, 3 September 1824

Dear Sir,

[. . .] We have been back in Paris for the last four weeks and are planning to remain here until March of next year, as I wrote to tell you from London; indeed, we may not leave Paris again so soon, apart from going to London in the spring: there is only *one* Paris for music in the whole of the world. The French have often been accused of frivolousness and inconstancy, but I am bound to maintain the opposite and say that never have I found such great and lasting enthusiasm for all that is good as I have done in Paris. Gluck's operas, for example, are frequently given here: the theatre is always packed to the rafters, and the enthusiasm reaches the highest pitch. With what respect the hallowed names of Mozart, Haydn, and Gluck are spoken here – I shall say only briefly that the French are great and thorough judges and practitioners of music, and generous patrons of art. I can say this from experience; anyone who says otherwise either does not know them, or else has taken worthless goods to market which of course are not bought here.

Little Putzi (though actually he is almost as tall as you) is working hard, and I can assure you that you would be totally satisfied with how conscientiously and how nicely he performs a sonata by Dussek, Steibelt, or Beethoven. We often receive visits from persons of the highest rank who ask to hear a sonata by Beethoven. We would have similar visits every day, were I no longer concerned for his education. His imagination is inexhaustible and incomprehensible to me. Permit me to give you an instance of his faithful memory: when we were in London, he played through full scores – mostly Gluck's operas – for an hour almost every day; a few days ago we were invited to a soirée at the minister's and

the conversation turned to Gluck's operas; my boy said that he knew them all by heart, which astonished everyone present. It was a well-attended evening, and a great many of those present were curious to know more; several urged themselves on him, this one quoting a chorus, that one another, this one a duet, that one another, this woman an aria, and so on. And – just imagine – he sang them all note for note; but what raised their astonishment to the highest pitch was that he also listed and named the different instruments for which the piece in question was written. His opera, on which he is hard at work, is bound to please you, and I hope it will be the culmination of our journey. [. . .]

Rossini is writing two operas here, one for the French theatre, the other for the Italian one. Paer is writing an opera too. Onslow has given his opera here a handful of times, but opinions are divided as to its merit; I have not heard it myself.

I wish I could write and tell you much more about art, but things have gone very quiet.

I dearly long to receive a letter from you very soon, more especially in reply to the contents of my letter from London.

Erard's pianos have reached such a degree of perfection that they are a century ahead of their time. It is impossible to describe them; you have to see and hear them, and play them yourself.

In extending our most sincere good wishes to you and your dear parents, we ask to be commended to your most valued friendship.

Your devoted servant Liszt.

56 Franz Liszt. Lithograph by François de Villain, based on a drawing by A. E. Roehn; 1824.

Although the text describes Liszt as "âgé de 11 ans," this cannot be correct. The lithograph was undoubtedly produced in Paris, where Liszt did not arrive until December 1823, by which date he was twelve years old. The accompanying lines might be rendered into English as:

Harmonious bond of genius and child,
Presentiment art thou of future state;
And at an age when hope is undefiled
By care, thou canst fond memories create.

57 The Maison Erard, overlooking the Rue du Mail in Paris. Photograph, ca. 1960.

The white plaque makes mention of the fact that Liszt was a frequent visitor to the house between 1823 and 1878. The complex of buildings included workshops where Erard pianos and harps were made, a concert hall, and the family's living accommodation in winter. (During the summer they lived in a private mansion called La Muette, which Sébastien Erard had bought in 1820, in the vicinity of what is now the Eiffel Tower.)

The Erard family made a fuss over the young virtuoso almost as soon as Liszt arrived in Paris, arranging concerts and concert tours, and ensuring that they received the best public-ity by announcing that the world's leading piano player preferred their instruments.

Liszt introduced Erard pianos, with their recently invented "double-escapement" action, everywhere he played, and the firm sent examples of their instruments to every town on his itinerary.

58 The Erard family home as it existed at the time of Liszt's arrival in Paris. Lithograph, ca. 1830.

The young boy was a regular visitor to the Erards, whom he later called his "adoptive family."

59 Letter of 12 August 1824 from the thirteen-year-old Franz Liszt to Pierre Erard, nephew of the piano builder Sébastien Erard.

One of the few surviving letters from Liszt's childhood.

60 The Salons Erard, Paris. Contemporary lithograph.

With few exceptions, all of Liszt's Paris concerts between 1824 and 1844 took place in the Théâtre-Italien or the Salons Erard. The Salons Erard were rebuilt in 1855 and have long since ceased to be used for concerts; although the splendid hall still exists, it is now scarcely recognizable, having been partitioned up to provide office space for a press agency.

61 Sébastien Erard (1752–1831). Lithograph by Hardivillier, ca. 1830.

Sébastien Erard (descended from a German family by the name of Erhard) was the leading piano builder of his day. He built the first pianoforte in France in 1777 and subsequently developed a type of hybrid piano-organ, as well as inventing the double-action pedal harp. Our modern grand pianos still use the double-escapement action invented by Erard around 1823.

LIFE

January/February: Intense composing activity in Paris.

13 March: Concert at the Théâtre-Italien in Paris.

20 March: Further concert appearance in Paris.

1 April: Liszt takes part in a concert at the Paris Opéra.

17 April: Concert at the Salons Erard.

22 April: Liszt takes part in a concert at the Salle Rue de Cléry.

June: Concerts in London and at Windsor Castle in the presence of King George IV, who also attends a concert given by Liszt at the Theatre Royal, Drury Lane.

16 June: Concert in Manchester (Theatre-Royal).

20 June: Concert in Manchester (Theatre-Royal). Liszt is described as the greatest living pianist.

July: Adam Liszt and his son leave England, spending several days in Boulogne-sur-mer before returning to Paris in mid-July.

August/September: Under the guidance of Ferdinando Paer, Liszt devotes himself to composition.

17 October: Liszt's opera *Don Sanche* receives its first performance at the Paris Opéra (see Illus. 65 and 66). The conductor is Rodolphe Kreutzer (the dedicatee of Beethoven's *Kreutzer* Sonata), and the title role is sung by Adolphe Nourrit, probably the most celebrated tenor of his day. (The only other child so to distinguish himself with an opera is Mozart with his *Bastien und Bastienne*.) The *Gazette de France* of 18 October 1825 reports, "The young Liltz [!] has been fortunate: his opera *Don Sanche, ou Le Château d'amour* contains several numbers which our most popular composers would not disclaim."

19, 21, and 26 October: Further performances of *Don Sanche*.

62 Title page of the first German edition of Liszt's *Allegro di Bravura*, written in 1824.

The work was published as early as 1825 by Erard of Paris and Diabelli of Vienna.

63 Opening bars of the first German edition of Liszt's *Impromptu on Themes by Rossini and Spontini*.

This piece was written in 1824 and published soon afterwards by Mechetti, Arnold, Fürstner, and Simrock. It is notable that fifteen years later Liszt was to reuse these opening bars, only slightly modified, at the beginning of his *Eroica Study*.

F. LISZT.

(Pianiste.)

WORKS

2 Piano Sonatas. Liszt mentions them in a conversation with Lina Ramann in October 1881. Lost. The first sixteen bars of one of these sonatas (in F minor) were noted down from memory on 10 October 1881 and published in *Lisztiana*, 1983, p. 179.

2 Piano Concertos. Liszt's father mentions them in a letter of 14 August 1825. Lost.

Quintet. Mentioned in the same letter. Lost.

Piano Sonata for Four Hands. Mentioned in the same letter. Lost.

Trio. Mentioned in the same letter. Lost.

Grande Ouverture (for orchestra). Mentioned as part of a programme performed in Manchester on 20 June 1825. Lost, or perhaps identical with the Overture to *Don Sanche*.

64 Franz Liszt. Lithograph by C. Motte, Paris, ca. 1825.

Around 1825 "le petit Litz" (as the French pronounced and wrote his name almost invariably) captured the hearts of all Parisians not only through his pianistic abilities but also through his enchanting appearance. At a later date his striking physical appearance, with its "profile d'ivoire" (his oft-reproduced ivory profile), was as much the subject of conversation as his musical talent. Foyatier chose the young Liszt as his model for a statue of Spartacus in the Tuileries, and Deveria and Ary Scheffer both painted romanticized portraits (see Illus. 98 and 166).

Paris, 14 August 1825

Dear Sir and most valued of friends,

You have every reason to be angry with me, for I have long been silent and would incur the justifiable charge of ingratitude, were I not able to adduce compelling counter-evidence in the form of a claim that a letter which I wrote to you in April was perfidiously purloined and the money I had paid for its postage pocketed by the messenger. [. . .]

We therefore returned to England for a second time, and although certain eminent families were away in Rheims for the coronation, we were just as satisfied as we had been last year, notwithstanding the fact that the greater part of the artists there worked against us. When I finally return to Vienna we shall need several days to talk about this, but in the meantime I shall dispense with all further detail. There is, however, one soirée in London which I really must tell you about and which took place in a very respectable house where all the leading artists were gathered: they included Herr Nicholson the flautist (the English Drouet), who had brought with him a Fantasy and Variations of his own composition with solo interludes for the piano. When his turn came, the pianoforte had unfortunately been tuned down a semitone, since Velutti was singing that evening, and for the sake of his voice he always has the instrument tuned down a semitone when he sings. Monsieur Potter (one of the four directors of the Philharmonic Society), who was sitting at the piano and who was accompanying Herr Nicholson, told the latter that his flute was too high. "Very well," said the other, "you must transpose the piece, for I cannot flatten my flute." "What – the piece is in C, and you expect me to play it in C sharp? I cannot risk that, it is out of the question." These gentlemen argued at length and finally drew attention to themselves, since the intermezzo had already lasted too long, but the argument always ended up with the words, "I cannot risk it." My lad was standing to one side, and heard their weaknesses; Herr Potter finally said to Franzi, "Do you also know how to transpose a little?" "Yes, a little," Franzi replied, "and I do not think it should be too hazardous to transpose this." "Very well, try it, for I will not risk it before so distinguished a gathering," Herr Potter replied. Franzi hurried over to the piano and transposed the piece better than if he had written it himself. Forgive me if I do not describe the enthusiasm and the astonishment which this trifle aroused among both the artists who were present and the rest of the distinguished gathering. [. . .]

We returned to Paris and hoped to remain incognito for a couple of weeks in order to arrange our affairs and little by little visit all our good friends; but we had been back in Paris only five days when our plan was upset by a letter from the Ministry of Arts commanding us to have Franzi's opera (*Don Sancho ou Le Château d'amour*) ready within eight days for scrutiny by its jury. Well, you can imagine the dilemma we were in. Nothing was copied, not a single singer was warned; I requested a postponement of fourteen days, which, however, was not forthcoming; but they granted us a few days' grace. The jury or tribunal (consisting of Cherubini, Berton, Boieldieu, Lesueur, and Catel) met in closed session, and the opera was heard and accepted with the greatest signs of approval. My dear friend, how much I regret that you are not a father; this would be the moment to speak of a parent's feelings of happiness, a field in which all sorrows are forgotten. The opera, then, has been accepted and will – in view of the eagerness which the theatre administration here has shown – be given, at the latest, in the early part of October. Curiosity has reached the highest pitch, and envy lurks in expectation; to date the latter has met with no success, and I hope that it will later burn its wings.

Franzi has written two fine concertos, which he wants to have performed in Vienna; did you know that we count on coming to Vienna next March? In November we reckon on going to Holland, the Netherlands, Berlin, and Leipzig, and from there to Vienna; the following autumn we shall then see our beloved Paris once more. I repeat that there is only *one* Paris for art, and we should certainly not visit Vienna if pressing considerations did not call us back there.

Franzi has grown so much that he is almost as tall as I am, much to everyone's astonishment. He knows no other passion than composing, which alone affords him pleasure and enjoyment. A sonata for four hands, a trio, and a quintet ought, I think, to give you pleasure. His concertos are too strenuous, and the difficulties for the performer are prodigious; I always thought Hummel's concertos difficult, but they are easy in comparison. You will be delighted at his left hand. He spends two hours a day practising and an hour reading; all the rest of his time when we are at home is devoted to composition. We go to the theatre regularly, or, rather, we scarcely let a day go by without going there, since we receive free tickets to several theatres including the very best.

Spontini is in Paris and staying with his father-in-law, Herr Erard; we often dine together, and if we had time we could do so daily. Whether Spontini will give a new work here I do not know, but it is assumed that he will. Spontini has offered to help Franzi in every way, and was uncommonly surprised when he heard him improvise without knowing him; in this Franzi has made very great progress, and I look forward eagerly to hearing your opinion when we return to Vienna.

There is nothing I can tell you of any new artists (who are always coming forward in great numbers), since not one has achieved significance to any degree, although the French are very indulgent. [. . .]

Please give our very best wishes to your dear parents, just as we all embrace and kiss you sincerely, holding you, with all reverence and awe, as our fondest of friends.

We also ask to be remembered to Herr Steiner and Herr Haslinger. If you have any news for us, please indicate what it is in your next letter.

Adieu, my dearest and most valued friend, it is 2 o'clock in the morning.

Liszt

Address: 22 Rue neuve St. Eustache.
Hotel de Strassbourg, près la Rue Montmartre.

65 The Paris Opéra. Lithograph by Delpech, ca. 1830.

It was at the Opéra – known at the time as the Académie Royale de Musique – that Rodolphe Kreutzer conducted the first performance of Liszt's opera. Adolphe Nourrit sang the title role.

ACADÉMIE ROYALE DE MUSIQUE.

(PAR EXTRAORDINAIRE)
La Ire représentation de

DON SANCHE
ou
LE CHATEAU D'AMOUR,
Opéra en un acte; suivi de
LA DANSOMANIE,

66 Playbill for the first performance of Liszt's opera *Don Sanche* on 17 October 1825.

67 ''. . . that Franzl has not yet found his match, and Hummel and Moscheles have been knocked into a cocked hat by him . . .'' Adam Liszt's letter to his father in Possendorf, dated 14 August 1825.

The second paragraph contains details of the fourteen-year-old Franz Liszt's opera. (For a translation see p. 335.)

LIFE

January: Accompanied by his father, Liszt embarks on a concert tour of southern France. Among the places visited are Bordeaux, Toulouse, Montpellier, Nîmes, and Marseilles. In Bordeaux he is honoured with a gold medallion inscribed with the words ''La Société Philharmonique de Bordeaux à Fçois Liszt XXV Janvier 1826.''

A lengthy stay in Marseilles ensues. Liszt works on his *Études* and gives six concerts. Later (in August 1877) he told his biographer Lina Ramann in Eisenach that during his stay in Marseilles he had fallen in love with a girl called Lydia Garella: '' 'You can believe me,' he said in a naive and childlike tone of voice, placing his hand on his heart, 'I did not know what a woman was.' ''[8]

May/June: In Lyons, where he gives three successful concerts in the Stock Exchange Hall at the Palais Saint-Pierre.

On his return to Paris, Liszt studies theory and counterpoint with Antonin Reicha (Illus. 53), and works intensively at his keyboard technique.

68 Marseilles. Lithograph by Garneray, based on his own painting, ca. 1825.

At the beginning of 1826 Liszt and his father set off on a concert tour of the French provinces, visiting Lyons, Toulouse, Nîmes, and Bordeaux. The concerts which he gave during a longer stay in Marseilles were especially successful.

69 Title page of the first German edition of Liszt's *Études op. 1*, Leipzig 1835.

These twelve Études, most of which were composed during Liszt's stay in Marseilles, were published by Hofmeister of Leipzig with an accompanying vignette depicting a child lying in a cradle, evidently a reference to the composer's tender years. The first French edition announced 48 Études (the remaining 36 were never written) and was published in 1828 by Boisselet of Marseilles and Dufaut & Dubois of Paris, designated as op. 6. (The opus numbers of Liszt's early works vary according to the country of publication, which has caused problems in identifying when they were written.) These attractive pieces, which can be recommended to young keyboard performers, were rewritten in 1837 (see Illus. 219) and again in 1851 as the well-known *Études d'exécution transcendante*. The dedication of the first French edition to Lydia Garella, a hunchbacked girl, was – according to Liszt's own testimony – intended as an act of homage to what at the time was an unconscious first love.

LISZT

*Lorsqu'oubliant les plaisirs de son age
Et d'heureux chants il s'est abandonné
Le Dieu du genie, couronné
En l'écoutant admire son ouvrage*

WORKS

Études pour le Piano en douze Exercices (12 Piano Studies). Pub. 1828.

Coda to Charles Mayer's Study No. 3 in A flat major. Lost. Auguste Boissier, the mother of one of Liszt's female pupils (see p. 62), mentions in a diary entry of 8 March 1832 that Liszt had composed this Coda at the age of fifteen. Charles Mayer (1799–1862), a pupil of John Field's, had published four Piano Studies in 1823/24. The publisher was Nicolaus Simrock of Bonn.

Préludes et Exercices (for piano) by Muzio Clementi, revised by Liszt. Pub. ca. 1826.[9]

70 Franz Liszt. Lithograph by Boisson, based on a drawing by François Pascal; Marseilles, 1826.

The lithograph was produced to commemorate one of Liszt's concerts in Marseilles in 1826. The lines might be rendered into English as:

When he forgot the pleasures of his youth
And tuned his song to cheerful plaint, in truth
The god who reigns o'er genius did lend
Admiring ear to all that he had penned.

LIFE

January: Liszt sets off on a concert tour which takes him to Dijon, Geneva, Lausanne, Lucerne, and other towns. He probably plays in Berne and Basle, but no reports have survived. The Geneva concerts are mentioned in local press reports of 20 January, 31 January, and 3 February 1827.

Early April to end of July: Liszt in London.

25 May: Concert in the New Argyll Rooms in London, where the audience includes the 75-year-old Muzio Clementi. Charles Salaman describes the sixteen-year-old Liszt as follows: ''He was a charmingly natural and unaffected boy, and I have never forgotten his joyful expression: 'Oh, good! Gooseberry pie!' when his favourite dish was put upon the table.''[10]

9 June: Concert in London (New Argyll Rooms). The famous pianist Ignaz Moscheles is among those present, and he notes in his diary that ''In its power and mastery of every difficulty Liszt's playing surpasses anything previously heard.''[11]

July: Liszt in Paris.

August: To Boulogne-sur-mer to relax. Liszt's father falls dangerously ill.

24 August: The sixteen-year-old Liszt writes to his mother in Austria: ''Best of women, Mother! As I write these lines I am much afraid for my father's health. When he arrived here, he was already a little unwell, but it has grown worse, and today the doctor told me that it may be dangerous . . .''[12]

28 August: Liszt's father dies in Boulogne-sur-mer at the Hibernian Hotel, 36 Rue Neuve-Chaussée. He is 50 years old.

September: Liszt's mother moves to Paris, where she rents rooms at 38 Rue Coquenard. She and her son later move to 7 Rue de Montholon. The young piano virtuoso earns his living by giving piano lessons. Among his first pupils are Comtesse Caroline de Saint-Cricq, Comtesse Montesquieu, and the daughters of the English ambassador, Lord Granville.

25 December: Liszt takes part in a concert with Jacques and Henri Herz at the Théâtre de Madame in Paris.

71 Cover and first page of a hitherto unpublished diary which Liszt kept during part of 1827.

Its contents give details of the sixteen-year-old composer's philosophical and religious ideas, which even at this stage were already clearly thought out.

Liszt explains his sceptical attitude towards diaries. Janka Wohl published these remarks in her memoirs in 1887.[13]

''At a period when the river of life snatched me away with such irresistible force that I was left with no time for self-contemplation, I had the idea of not retiring for the night until I had noted down, fleetingly and in a few terse sentences, the events of the day and the essence of my thoughts. This resolution lasted some eight to ten days, after which some event or other intervened, and I thought no more of my diary. Many years later I was rummaging around in some old papers when a notebook fell into my hands, and, all unsuspecting, I opened it. I was speechless . . . I scarcely believed my eyes! . . . Only my handwriting could convince me that I, and no other, had written these unforgivable lines. The blows rained down upon each other, and the curious thing about the whole affair was that these notes revealed neither my opinion of people and things nor my character. They were simply outbursts of ill temper, anger, irony, or enthusiasm, surly and malicious insights from which not even my friends were spared, like a summary of events whose nullity inflates actuality to larger-than-life dimensions. – Memoirs written from day to day will always present their author, and the time that they aim to reflect, in a more or less false light.

Since discovering this fact to my cost, I have always mistrusted such books . . . they are generally less authentic than one thinks . . . I was passionate and caustic – every passionate individual should be wary of his initial impulses! I did some fine things when I followed mine! – And then, why had I made these notes? In the years 1845–46 mnemotechny was a fashionable science – it sharpened one's memory. – I did not need such science. My terrible ability to remember things has caused me suffering enough. Far rather would I have learned the science of forgetting – unfortunately, this is not a subject that is ever taught!''

WORKS

Piano Concerto in A minor. Liszt played this work in London on 9 June 1827. Ignaz Moscheles noted in his diary that it contained "chaotic beauties." Sixteen pages from the full score of a piano concerto in A minor which were discovered in the Liszt Archive in Weimar almost certainly form part of this work. (See commentary to *Malédiction* under "Works 1834.")

Scherzo in G minor for piano. Pub. 1896 (see p. 50 for facsimile of manuscript).

72 Franz Liszt at the age of sixteen. Coloured chalk drawing by James Anthony Minasi, London 1827.

This almost totally unknown portrait of Liszt was auctioned by Christie's of London on 14 March 1978 and is now owned by the Royal College of Music. In all likelihood it dates from the time of Liszt's visit to London in 1827. Liszt's mother later gave it to Elisabeth Loudon who, together with her younger sister, attended Mademoiselle Alix's Institute at 43 rue de Clichy in Paris. Liszt gave piano lessons here in around 1828, and Elisabeth Loudon was one of his pupils.

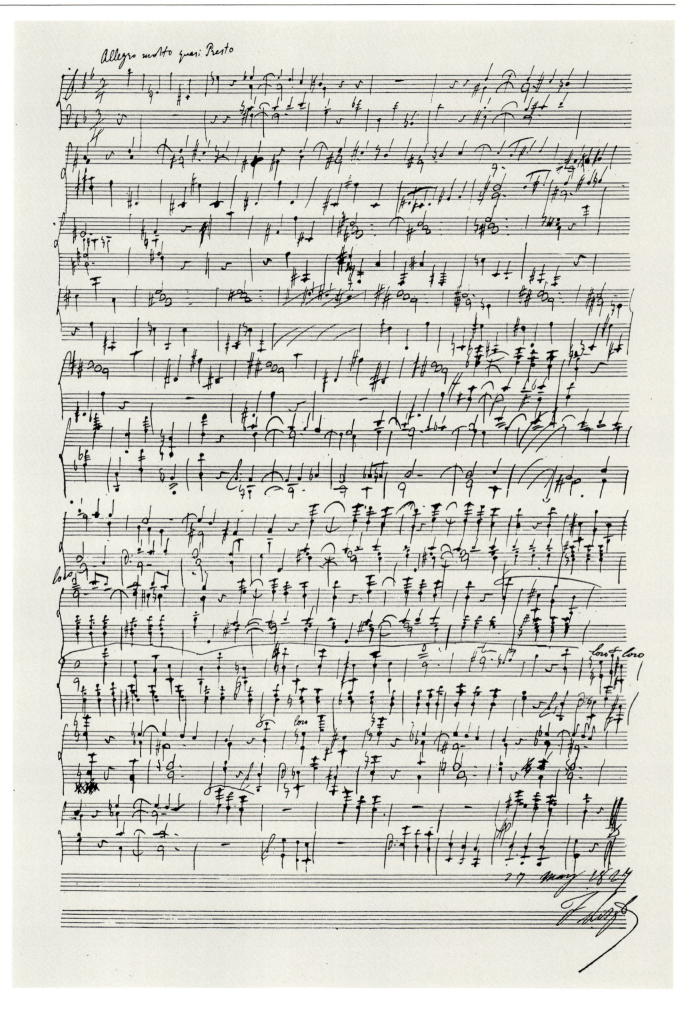

73 Manuscript by the sixteen-year-old Liszt. *Allegro molto quasi Presto* for piano, written in London on 27 May 1827.

The original manuscript was discovered in around 1895 by the Danish pianist Frits Hartvigson, who found it between the pages of an old edition of one of Liszt's piano works. Hartvigson showed it to Otto Leßmann, who published a facsimile of it in 1896.

Hartvigson gave the manuscript to Ferruccio Busoni on 5 April 1909 as a token of his ''supreme admiration'' for the Italian pianist and composer. Busoni published the piece in 1922 in the first issue of *Faust, eine Rundschau*, where a transcription of the original was described as appearing ''for the first time.'' Evidently Busoni was unaware of the facsimile published 26 years earlier.

74 Geneva. Wood engraving by Hallberger, based on a drawing by Kleemann; ca. 1860.

In January/February 1827 Liszt paid an extended visit to Geneva. He felt a particular fondness for the town, to which he returned for a number of visits around 1831 and for a longer stay in 1835/36.

75 Whitechapel High Street, London. Engraving by Cox, based on a drawing by T. H. Shepherd, 1837.

Liszt spent three months in London in 1827, making numerous concert appearances between the beginning of April and the end of June. After Paris, London was the most important port of call in terms of the young virtuoso's pianistic career (see also p. 134 below).

PARIS · GENEVA · YEARS OF PILGRIMAGE

1828–1837

76 Franz Liszt. Watercolour by Nancy Mérienne, 1836.

The first known portrait of Liszt with shoulder-length hair. He usually wore his hair slightly over his ears as was customary at this time, a fashion he followed until his 26th year.

"Desultory studies and creativity
in Paris and, for a time,
in Geneva and Italy,
before my reappearance in
Vienna in 1838,
the success of which launched me
on my career as a virtuoso"

LIFE

27 January: Liszt appears at the Salons Pape in Paris, together with Pixis, Schunke, Rhein, and others.

Once again Liszt feels the desire to become a priest, but the circumstances of his life prevent him from doing so.

"Poverty, this age-old intermediary between mankind and misfortune, tore me from my loneliness, a loneliness which was given over to contemplation, and placed me before a public on which depended not only my own existence but also that of my mother. Young and extravagant, I suffered grievously from all contact with the world around me. It was a source of friction inevitably bound up with my profession as a musician, but it pained me all the more intently in that my heart was wholly filled with the mystical feeling of love and religion," Liszt wrote of this period.[14]

30 March: Appears at the Salons Pape with Osborne, Schunke, and others.

4 April: Liszt plays Hummel's B minor Concerto in Paris. Fétis criticizes the liberties he takes with it.

7 April: Concert at the Salle Chantereine (improvisations, Hummel's Septet, and Herz's Variations).

12 April: Takes part in a concert with Bériot, playing Bériot's Trio and Fantasia.

18 April: Liszt appears at one of Robert's concerts in the Salle Chantereine.

20 April: Liszt performs in the Salons Pape and the Salle Rue de Cléry.

30 April: Takes part in one of Rigal's concerts at the Conservatoire.

Liszt's affair with Caroline de Saint-Cricq ends unhappily; he withdraws from public life.

23 October: *Le Corsaire* carries a report of Liszt's death(!).

Wilhelm von Lenz visits Liszt. He describes him as "a pale and haggard young man with unspeakably attractive features . . . lost in meditation, he lay on a sofa surrounded by three pianos . . . smoking a long Turkish pipe . . . his smile came suddenly, radiantly, and passed as quickly as it had come, like the glint of a dagger in the sunlight . . ."[15]

25 December: Liszt is announced to play Beethoven's E flat major Piano Concerto in Paris, but illness obliges him to cancel his appearance.

Caroline de Saint-Cricq, the beautiful daughter of the French Minister of Commerce, was the great love of Liszt's early years. She was one of his first pupils. Her mother, captivated by the young Liszt's charm, begged her husband not to place any obstacles in the way of a union between the young couple. But the latter drew the artist's attention to the class difference between Liszt and his daughter, and after his wife's death he forbade them to meet. Both were profoundly distressed, and each sought comfort in religion. Caroline wanted to enter a convent; Liszt turned his back on the world and gave himself up to a visionary mysticism.

On a concert tour of southern France in 1844, while passing through Pau on his way to Spain and Portugal, Liszt met his former sweetheart again. Caroline had married Count Bertrand d'Artigaux and was living on his estates near Pau in the Pyrenees. It was not a happy marriage. The profoundly religious woman had evidently not stopped loving Liszt. "I love you still with every ounce of my soul, and I want you to enjoy a happiness which I myself no longer know. I yearn to receive your news but do not dare entreat you. Let me continue to see in you the only guiding star of my life and to pray to Heaven every day for you: reward him, O God, reward him profusely for his unflinching subjection to Thy will," she wrote to Liszt in Weimar in July 1853.

In his will, drawn up in 1860, Liszt remembered Caroline with a "talisman ring," and after her death in May 1872 he wrote to Carolyne von Sayn-Wittgenstein, "She was one of the purest manifestations of God's blessing on this earth. The sufferings which she bore for so long and with such meekness and submission have earned her a place in Heaven. There she will go to her rest to the greater glory of God. The joys of this world never touched her, and immortality alone is worthy of so pure a soul . . ."

77 Caroline de Saint-Cricq. Miniature portrait, ca. 1828.

78 Caroline de Saint-Cricq in old age. Photograph, ca. 1870.
The Comtesse de Saint-Cricq was one of the three most influential women in Liszt's life, the other two being the Comtesse Marie d'Agoult and Princess Carolyne von Sayn-Wittgenstein. The last-named met Caroline de Saint-Cricq in Paris in around 1860 and thereafter corresponded with her until her death, holding the view that Caroline de Saint Cricq would have been the only suitable wife for Liszt.

For a time during 1828 Liszt withdrew totally from public life, thereby sparking off speculation among his followers. The French newspaper *Le Corsaire* even carried a report of his death. It is indicative that in his remarks on his "insignificant career" contained in his letter to Lina Ramann of 30 August 1884 he omitted all reference to the period between 1828 and 1836. He made no important concert appearances and wrote nothing worth mentioning during this time.

DEATH OF THE YOUNG LISZT

Young Liszt has died in Paris. At an age when most children have not even thought of going to school, he had already won the public's heart with his successes. At nine years of age, when other children can scarcely stammer, he improvised on the pianoforte to the astonishment of master musicians, and yet they called him "le petit Litz," seeking to combine his name with that childlike charm which he never left behind. – On that first occasion when he improvised at the Opéra, he had to make the rounds of the boxes and galleries, where all the ladies caressed him; in their naive admiration, suited to the artist's age, they could think of no better way to reward him than to give him kisses and burnt almonds, and to offer him sweets with one hand while with the other they played with his fair silky hair.

This extraordinary boy adds to the list of precocious children who appear on earth only to vanish like hothouse plants, which bear magnificent fruit but die from the effort of bringing them forth. Mozart, too, who like Liszt astonished everyone by his precociousness, died at the age of 31; but the price that he paid for these few extra years was such great sorrow and so much grief that an earlier death might indeed have been a blessing for him as well.

If we consider all the dangers to which talent is exposed, all the monsters which lay siege to genius, persecuting it without cease and accompanying it to its very last step; if we recall that every success awakens envy and goads on intrigue by causing mediocrity to blush, we may perhaps find that it was a far happier fate for the blossom to wither early than to wait for the storms which might overwhelm and crush it later. Young Liszt has had only admirers hitherto. His age was a shield which turned every arrow aside. "He is a child," they said at every success, and envy yielded to patience. But had he grown older, had the divine spark which inspired him been allowed to develop, then they would have looked for failings, would have scorned his merits, and – who knows? – might have poisoned his innermost life. He would have learned the whims of power, the injustice of might; he would have been crushed by the brutal onslaught of worthless and spiteful passions; whereas now, wrapped in his shroud, he begins anew the sleep of childhood and sinks into slumber while yearning, perhaps, to continue the dream of yesterday.

The event is painful, not for his father, who went before him a year ago, but for a family whose name he had begun to make famous. And it is painful for us, for whom no doubt he would have opened up a new spring of musical impulse and joy.

We too mourn his death and join with his family in lamenting their premature loss.

WORKS

Zwei Sätze ungarischen Charakters (Zum Andenken) (for piano). Presumably adaptations of pieces by Bihari and Csermák. At the end of the manuscript are the words, in Liszt's hand, "In memory. Franz Liszt. Paris, 21 May 1828." The present author has been unable to establish when these pieces were first published. A facsimile of the manuscript was reproduced in an anthology, *Rare and Familiar*, published in 1982.

It is not out of the question that these pieces (the first known works by Liszt in the Hungarian style) were written later and that the dedication was merely intended as a reminder of the events of 21 May 1828, but on internal evidence a date before 1830 seems more likely.

Report of Liszt's death in "Le Corsaire," 23 October 1828.

LISZT

Célèbre Pianiste.

Lith. de H. Brunet et Cie à Lyon.

79 Franz Liszt. Lithograph by N. Boucoiran, based on an oil painting by Jean Vignaud of 1828.

The original oil painting is believed to be lost. For a time it was probably in the possession of one of Liszt's friends, the poet Georg Herwegh (1817–1875).

LIFE

Liszt lives a life of seclusion in Paris. His mother complains that, except for his lessons, her son has lost almost all interest in music. He gives no concerts apart from a handful of minor appearances (Salons Pape 22 March, Salon Dietz 7 April, Salon Berlot 11 April, Salon Dietz 15 December). "When death robbed me of my father, and I returned alone to Paris and began to suspect what could become of art and what must become of the artist, I felt as though crushed by the impossibilities that on every side stood blocking the path that I had marked out in my thoughts. And never encountering a sympathetic word on the part of any like-minded soul, I was overcome by a bitter resentment towards the art which I saw before me, an art debased to a more or less remunerative trade and branded as a source of entertainment for polite society. I should have preferred to be anything other than a hired musician in the pay of grandees, patronized and paid by them like a conjuror or like the performing dog Munito . . ."[16] (letter from Liszt to George Sand describing the period 1828/29).

Liszt immerses himself in literature, reading everything that came his way and laying the foundations for his profound erudition. Many of his favourite authors, including Lamennais, Lamartine, Sainte-Beuve, Dumas, Balzac, Hugo, and Heinrich Heine, are to join his circle of friends in the coming years.

It is at this period that *Weltschmerz* is in literary vogue. His favourite reading is Chateaubriand's *René*, a French counterpart to Goethe's *Werther*. The conclusion to which Chateaubriand was drawn – the renunciation of passion, and a willing acceptance of faith and religion – may have brought comfort to the deeply religious Liszt at the end of his unhappy affair with Caroline de Saint-Cricq.

Liszt's constant preoccupation with questions of faith makes it easier for us to accept his entry into the clergy in 1865, a move which even today continues to be treated with scepticism.

80 Franz Liszt. Watercolour by Flora Géraldi, ca. 1829. A rare original portrait of the young Liszt.

81 *Grande Fantaisie* on a theme from Auber's opera *La Fiancée*.
This was almost certainly Liszt's first operatic fantasia. *La Fiancée* was first performed, to great acclaim, in Paris in 1829. Liszt's Fantasia was published the same year by Troupenas of Paris, who numbered it op. 1. (Liszt himself later gave this opus number to the first German edition of his *12 Etüden*; see p. 46.)
Joseph d'Ortigue, the leading music critic in Paris at this time, said that this Fantasia showed "mocking seriousness and Byronic wit," and that it was "flirtatious and brilliant in the manner of Henri Herz."
The title page reproduced here is taken from a shortened version of the piece which Liszt himself prepared and which was published a few years later by Mechetti.

82 Daniel-François-Esprit Auber (1782–1871). Lithograph, ca. 1830.

WORKS

Grande Fantaisie sur la Tyrolienne de l'Opéra ''La Fiancée'' (Auber) (for piano). See Illus. 81. Pub. 1829. The ''Tyrolean Melody'' published in Manchester in 1856 is based on this piece.
Un petit morceau (for cello and piano). Liszt mentions this piece in a letter to M. Curie of ca. 1829. Lost.

83 Saint-Vincent-de-Paul, Paris. Lithograph based on a drawing by T. Mansson; ca. 1860.

Liszt's favourite church – he lived nearby, in the Rue Montholon – had a different façade in 1830.

In the years around 1829 Chrétien Urhan was one of Liszt's closest friends. A violinist in the Paris Opéra orchestra, Urhan was the city's leading viola d'amore player. He was also organist at Saint-Vincent-de-Paul and a well-known figure in Paris's musical life, highly regarded by Berlioz and Meyerbeer (who wrote the viola d'amore part in his opera *Les Huguenots* with Urhan in mind). He was regarded as something of an oddity. Because of his preference for light-blue tail coats, he was known as ''the man in blue.'' Deeply religious, he was a model of moral probity. On being appointed to play in the Paris Opéra orchestra, he made it a condition of his acceptance that he would be allowed to play with his back to the stage during ballet performances, so as not to be exposed to temptation.

According to his mother, Liszt spent most of his time in church during this period and showed scarcely any interest in music, preferring to spend his time with Urhan, whom he saw almost daily.

In January 1837 Liszt wrote to George Sand, ''At about this time I was just recovering from an illness which had lasted two years, and during that period my impetuous need for faith and self-surrender had become immersed in the devotional exercises of Catholicism. My burning brow was bent low over the damp steps of Saint-Vincent-de-Paul! I squeezed the drops of blood from my heart and forced my thoughts to submit. The image of a woman as chaste and as pure as the alabaster of some sacred chalice [Liszt is referring here to his thwarted love for Caroline de Saint-Cricq] was the host which, with tears in my eyes, I offered up to the Christian God. Renunciation of all things temporal was the only lever, the only word in my life . . .''[17]

84 Chrétien Urhan (1790–1845). Organist at Saint-Vincent-de-Paul. Caricature by Dantan, ca. 1830.

85 Paris, Place de la Concorde. Oil painting by Canella, 1829.

Around 1829 Liszt was the favourite piano teacher of the Parisian aristocracy. He often spent the whole day travelling, on foot or by carriage, visiting his pupils in every quarter of the capital. Often when he returned home late in the evening he would sleep in the stairwell in order not to disturb his mother. In later years Anna Liszt liked to tell of this considerate but uncomfortable habit of her son's.

LIFE

22 January: Together with Ferdinand Hiller, Paer, and Pixis, Liszt plays Beethoven's *Fidelio* Overture in a version for eight hands. The concert, given in the Salons Pape, also includes a duet performed by Liszt and Pixis.

2 February: Liszt appears at the Salon Petzold in Paris.

20 and 27 April: Liszt attends two chamber music concerts organized by the violinist Pierre Baillot at the Hôtel du Cardinal Fesch, 59 Rue Saint-Lazare.

28 April: Liszt plays duets with Henri Herz at the Salle Chantereine.

29 April: Liszt takes part in a concert with Karl Schunke in the Salons Erard.

The decisive event of this period is the July Revolution which breaks out in Paris on 27 July 1830. Liszt follows events with all the enthusiasm of youth. He sketches a "Revolutionary Symphony" (see Illus. 92). Probably in imitation of Beethoven's *Battle of Vittoria*, he intends to work three themes into the sketch, a fifteenth-century Hussite song, Luther's *Ein' feste Burg ist unser Gott*, and the national march *La Marseillaise*. The sketch remains unrealized.

Liszt's main interest continues to be directed towards literature, but he also gives piano lessons at Madame Alix's exclusive boarding school in the Rue Clichy, where he is the idol of his aristocratic pupils. He frequents Saint-Simonist circles, sharing their view of the arts as the most suitable means of bringing about a peace-loving and compassionate society. Religion and the arts are an expression of beauty, and dogma and science embody truth, while religious worship and industry serve utilitarian ends.

4 December: Liszt visits Hector Berlioz at his Paris home. It is the first meeting between the two future friends.

5 December: Liszt attends the first performance of Berlioz's *Symphonie fantastique*.

86 Hector Berlioz (1803–1869). Miniature drawing, ca. 1830. Previously unpublished.

Together with Richard Wagner and Frédéric Chopin, Hector Berlioz was another leading nineteenth-century composer with whom Liszt was on friendly terms. Under Berlioz's baton Liszt often performed Weber's *Konzertstück*, Beethoven's E flat major Piano Concerto (see p. 134) and Liszt's own E flat major Piano Concerto (see p. 198). Liszt's piano transcription of Berlioz's *Symphonie fantastique* appeared in 1834, its publishing costs paid for by Liszt himself (see Illus. 108).

Berlioz on the pianist Liszt: ". . . To his preternatural technical command he has added a command of the subtlest shadings and of cantilena, achieving a level of perfection which would have seemed impossible on a piano. As for the prodigious difficulties posed by his compositions, one scarcely notices them, such is the ease with which he is able to overcome them [. . .] . In respect of technique, the only thing that is actually new that I have been able to identify in the endless masses of compositions created by Liszt's hand is restricted to those accents and nuances which it was unanimously agreed could not be produced on a piano and which, until now, were indeed unattainable. Included here are a broad and simple melodic line; sustained notes played with a strict legato; and then at certain points whole bundles of notes thrown in, as it were, with the utmost violence and yet without harshness, without detracting from their harmonic brilliance; in addition, sequences of melody in minor thirds, diatonic runs in the lower and middle registers (where, it is well known, the strings vibrate for a longer period) performed staccato with incredible speed in such a way that each individual note produces only a brief and muted sound which dies away on the instant and is wholly distinct from the notes that precede and follow it . . ."[21] (see p. 86).

87 Franz Liszt. Anonymous oil painting, 1830. Not previously published in colour.

This little-known portrait is owned by the Bory family of Coppet on Lake Geneva. It is believed to be of Liszt.

On 6 December 1830 Berlioz wrote to tell his father that he had made the acquaintance of "Liszt, the famous pianist." The first meeting between the future friends took place on 4 December 1830, on the eve of the premiere of Berlioz's *Symphonie fantastique*.

"We felt an immediate affinity, and since that moment our friendship has grown ever closer and stronger. He came to the concert [i.e. the premiere of the *Symphonie fantastique*] and was conspicuous for the warmth of his applause and his generally enthusiastic behaviour" (*The Memoirs of Hector Berlioz*).

Liszt on Berlioz: ". . . But whatever mood Berlioz's muse might adopt, be it bitter or mild, despairing or smiling, devout or fantastical, his genius presents itself to us, in the church, the theatre, or the concert hall, as one of this century's most powerfully striking phenomena . . ."[18]

". . . The principle embodied in every work by this master is that the artist may pursue the beautiful outside the rules of any school without having to fear that he will thereby fail to find that beauty."[19]

". . . The unforgivable error for which Berlioz's critics reproach him is not his unusual handling of form: no, the reason why they will never forgive him is that form for him is less important than content, and that he is thinker and poet at one and the same time . . ."[20]

WORKS

Revolutionary Symphony. Parts of it were used in later works such as *Héroïde funèbre*. Only sketches exist: see Illus. 92.
Sextet. Written ca. 1830. Mentioned in a letter of 26 July 1835. Lost.
Variations sur une marche du ''Siège de Corinthe'' (Rossini) (for piano). Unpub.

88 Maria Malibran (1808–1836). Oil painting by Decaisne, ca. 1830.

Like her sister Pauline Viardot-García, Maria Malibran was one of the most celebrated singers of her day. Liszt held her in high regard and sometimes accompanied her at the piano. Frédéric Chopin admired her and often mentioned her in his letters: ''Malibran captivates all hearts with her wonderful voice, and she sings like no one else on earth . . .''[22] ''There's no doubt that not Pasta but Malibran is the leading singer of Europe – a miracle!''[23]

When Liszt was in Manchester in December 1840 he found himself staying in the very hotel room in which Maria Malibran had died four years previously, at the age of 28.[24]

Between 1828 and 1832 Liszt not only gave concerts but also taught piano, an activity to which he clearly brought the same intensity that typified everything he undertook.

Auguste Boissier, whose daughter Valérie was a pupil of Liszt's, wrote to her mother in Geneva on 4 January 1832:

"We visited Liszt at his home on 3 January 1832. A wonderful, splendid lesson, which he gave with a zeal which always puts me to shame, with unrivalled talent and the greatest clarity. The study where a man of genius works is an inner sanctum, and I assure you that this small room of Liszt's appears to me like the temple of harmony itself. This young man's intellectual makeup is something quite extraordinary, and not only in music but in everything else that he tackles he bears the stamp of true talent. Unexpected novelty, truth, and profundity are all a part of him; if only I could recall all the judicious remarks, stirring ideas, and original thoughts that fell from his lips. He says things that appear to reveal a whole world of knowledge, and no matter what direction his spirit of observation and his genius were to take he would always be a quite outstanding person. He does not despise the tiniest detail in the course of his teaching, but concerns himself with the most finely nuanced expression marks, with every note, every sound, every bass line, which he insists must be studied in isolation; but it is in executing the melodic line and in the great crescendos that he develops his full authority and that his soul and strength of will appear altogether sublime. While he was giving his lesson and really wearing himself out in order to instruct and encourage his student, his mother kept heaving deep sighs, making signs to me that he was mad, and constantly going over to him with little pills and sweetmeats, which he refused. You cannot imagine two people less like each other, yet they make their way together through life in tender unanimity, and their little household presents a picture of harmony and happiness . . . At a quarter past eight on the evening of the same day, the door of our salon opened and Liszt, who had announced his visit earlier, entered the room. We chatted together for a good hour, and I can tell you that he is a man of very great wit; he speaks with charm and clarity, is altogether natural, and has perfect manners; reflection and experience of the world have matured his mind; on the subject of literature he speaks with passion, refinement, and grace. He has read widely and retained it all, and he expounds his ideas in the most attractive and interesting way, without presumption and without that certain unpleasant tone which artists tend to adopt; you might take him to be thirty years old and brought up in the best society, whereas he was only twenty last October. After tea, he sat down at the piano . . ."[25]

89 Manuscript by Liszt, ca. 1832. Technical exercises for his pupil Valérie Boissier. From a previously unpublished notebook of Valérie Boissier, in the possession of Jean-René Bory.

Even at this early date Liszt was already writing in a virtuoso keyboard style far removed from current practice. The simplicity and conventionality of the present arpeggio exercises are presumably attributable to his pupil's technical limitations.

90 Liszt's pupil Valérie Boissier, later Comtesse Gasparin. Oil painting, ca. 1850.

Opposite page:

91 The July Revolution of 1830. Fighting at the Porte Saint-Denis. Oil painting by Lecomte, 1830.

92 First page of a four-page sketch for a "Revolutionary Symphony."

The dates at the top of the folio (27, 28, 29 July) may refer either to the time at which the piece was conceived, or to its subject matter. In the margin are indications such as *indignation, terreur, liberté, attaque, Bataille*, etc. The work's basic programme was *Attack, Battle*, and *March (Marseillaise)*.

The sketch, which Liszt did not develop further, predates Berlioz's *Symphonie fantastique* and may well be Liszt's earliest essay in programme music.

THE JULY REVOLUTION

"C'est le canon qui l'a guéri!" (It was the cannon that cured him!), Liszt's mother used to say. Indeed, the July Revolution of 1830 appears to have roused the eighteen-year-old Liszt from a lethargy which had lasted almost two years. When the Duc d'Orléans became King Louis-Philippe and attempted to rule the country democratically, Liszt's sympathies were with the revolutionaries. His enthusiasm found expression in his sketch for a *Revolutionary Symphony* (see Illus. 92). If the plan was not realized, it was presumably because Liszt was aware that his knowledge of instrumentation was unequal to such a task. It is worth mentioning that for the three projected themes he chose Slavic, German, and Romance motifs: evidently he regarded the 1830 Revolution as a European event.

Eighteen years later, in 1848, the barricades which brought Wagner to Weimar as a fugitive drew a further series of passionate confessions from Liszt. Above all, the Hungarians' heroic struggle for freedom and their capitulation after initial successes found an echo in his letters and works: ". . . What is happening now is the most astonishing event to have taken place this century," he told Franz von Dingelstedt on 1 March 1848. ". . . My fellow countrymen have taken a step so decisive, so truly Hungarian and unanimous, that it is impossible to deny them our rightful sympathy," he wrote to Carolyne von Sayn-Wittgenstein on 24 March 1848. Musically his sentiments found expression in the cantata *Hungaria*, in the *Arbeiterchor* ("Freedom is a trusty hammer that none shall e'er lay down again"), and in the piano piece *Funérailles*, dedicated to Liszt's fallen friends Prince Lichnowsky, Count Teleky, and Count Batthyány.

LIFE

January: Liszt as guest of Adèle Laprunarède at Castle Marlioz in the Swiss Alps. (See p. 69 below, and n. 35.)

February: Liszt in Geneva (exact dates not known).

March/April: Liszt presumably in Geneva or Marlioz.

May: Visits his pupil Pierre-Étienne Wolff in Geneva.

Liszt spends the summer in Paris. He plays at meetings of the Saint-Simonists at 6 Rue Monsigny and on one occasion accompanies Maria Malibran. General La Fayette is said to have been an occasional visitor.

September: Frédéric Chopin settles in Paris and a short time afterwards meets Liszt for the first time.

October: The earliest sketches for the *Grande Fantaisie de Bravoure sur la Clochette* (see Illus. 93).

93 Page from one of Liszt's sketchbooks with entries for October and December 1831.

At the top of the folio are sketches for the opening bars of the *Clochette* Fantasia, and beneath them an indication of the 20-year-old Liszt's melancholy mood: "Voila que tout cela est passé: mon enfance n'est plus, elle est morte pour ainsi dire quoique je vive encore" (Now all this is over and done with: my childhood is no longer, it is dead, so to speak, for all that I still live). It is possible that the date "1831" was added later, by Liszt or by a third party, and that the correct date should be 1832.

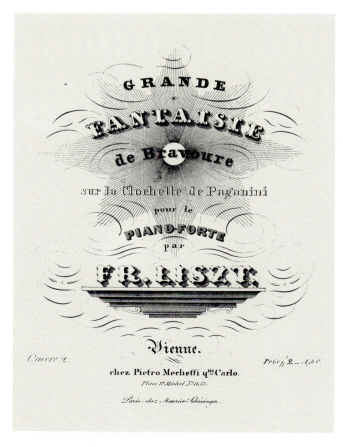

94 Title page of the first edition of Liszt's *Grande Fantaisie de Bravoure sur la Clochette de Paganini*, 1834.

The piece contains several passages marked "tutti," suggesting that Liszt also played or planned the work in a version for piano and orchestra. The sketch reproduced above would seem to suggest that the Fantasia had been drafted as early as 1831, assuming that the corresponding bars were not originally intended for some other work (see p. 67).

In 1831, 1832, and 1833 Niccolò Paganini gave concerts in Paris, and here as elsewhere the style of his playing, his platform manner, and the grotesqueness of his appearance aroused the usual enthusiasm.

Although an entry dated 17 October 1831 in one of Liszt's sketchbooks (see Illus. 93) contains sketches for a Fantasia on Paganini's *Campanella* (the theme, which Liszt was to use later in the third of his *Études d'exécution transcendante d'après Paganini*, derives from the third movement of Paganini's B minor Violin Concerto), there is no evidence that Liszt heard the "devil's fiddler" at his first Paris concerts in March 1831, when Liszt was probably staying in Geneva. But he did hear him the following year, and on 2 May 1832 wrote to Pierre Wolff in Geneva, "What a man, what a violin, what an artist! God, what torments in those four strings! . . . And his expression, his manner of phrasing, and, finally, his soul! . . ."[26] He included in his letter a few musical examples of Paganini's characteristic technical devices, which we shall later encounter in the *Grandes Études de Paganini*. When Paganini died in 1840, Liszt devoted a detailed obituary to him, ending with the words, "May the artist place his goal *inside* and not *outside* himself; may virtuosity be his *means* and never his *end*; and may he never forget that although *noblesse oblige*, it is equally true, if not more so, that *génie oblige!*"[27]

WORKS

Grande Fantaisie de Bravoure sur la Clochette de Paganini (for piano). Earliest sketches (see Illus. 93). The finished piece appeared in 1834.

Liszt told Lina Ramann in December 1876, ''The 'Fantaisie sur le motif de la clochette de Paganini' appeared in Paris in 1834/35 (?), just before I left for Switzerland. It was published at the same time as my 'Partition de Piano' of Berlioz's *Symphonie fantastique* and the fragmentary *Harmonies poétiques* 'avec un profond sentiment d'ennui' (!). My performance of the *Fantaisie* (or, strictly speaking, *Variations*) was not a success when I played it at a number of concerts. Following my first success in Vienna (1838), I took up the Paganini Études again, and Haslinger (Vienna) published the *first* edition of my transcription of the Paganini Études (in 1839) . . . Ten years later, in Weimar, I simplified this first version (which was regarded as unplayable), and persuaded Härtel to bring out a second edition, which has proved fairly popular thanks to Fräulein Mehlig and other pianists whose kind fingers have performed No. 6, *Campanella*, with such brilliant success.''[28]

[*Campanella* is not the sixth of the *Grandes Études de Paganini*, as Liszt states here, but the third.]

95 Niccolò Paganini (1782–1840). Pencil drawing by Ingres, Rome 1819.

The arrival of the famous – or infamous – violinist encouraged Liszt to develop his piano technique and to achieve heights as dizzying as those attained by Paganini. He was often described, not altogether accurately, as the ''Paganini of the piano.''

96 The insurrection in Lyons on 21 and 22 November 1831. Gazette illustration, 1831.

LISZT'S SOCIAL COMMITMENT

Around 1830 Liszt joined the movement of the Saint-Simonians. His religious temperament and capacity for enthusiasm strongly predisposed him to accept the ideas of Claude-Henri de Saint-Simon, who interpreted Christianity in the spirit of early socialism and insisted on the brotherhood of all men.

Liszt's piano piece *Lyon*, with its motto "Vivre en travaillant ou mourir en combattant" (To live working or to die fighting), is the musical product of the silk-weavers' uprisings in Lyons in 1831 and, more especially, in 1834. In 1837 Liszt gave a concert in Lyons in support of the weavers, and he reported to his friend Adolphe Pictet, "I repaired to Lyons, and found myself in the midst of such terrible sufferings and such cruel misery that my whole sense of justice rebelled and my heart was filled with unspeakable sadness. But what torment it is to have to stand by while an entire population struggles in vain to resist a kind of oppression that destroys both body and soul [. . .] . He [the weaver] who does not know where to rest his head works with his hands on costly hangings, weaving the sumptuous fabrics behind which the wealthy weakling sleeps; he who does not own the rags to cover his nakedness weaves the gold brocade which graces princesses, and these children for whom their mother never has a smile stand hunched over the loom, watching with mournful eyes as arabesques and flowers come to life beneath their fingers, decorations intended as toys for the children of the fashionable world . . ."[29]

Liszt's commitment was not confined to rhetorical gestures. Half the income of his virtuoso years was given to charity. Suffice it to mention the donations he made to the Cologne Cathedral building fund in 1841 (1,140 gulden), to the Mozart Foundation in 1841 (900 gulden), to victims of the Hamburg fire of 1842, to the Naumann Memorial in Dresden in 1844 (1,350 thalers), to the Bach Monument in Eisenach, to the Beethoven Monument in Bonn, and to the victims of the flood disaster in Hungary.

From 1848 onwards Liszt performed exclusively for charitable causes, and he taught his pupils in Weimar and Rome for nothing. When he heard that the well-known pianist and piano teacher Theodor Kullak had made no provisions under the terms of his estate for the public good, he wrote an indignant letter to Otto Leßmann, the editor of the *Allgemeine Musikzeitung*. Dated 5 September 1885, it was published that same month: "An estate of several million marks that has been acquired through teaching music cannot be allowed to remain hidden away without consideration for the devotees of art. If the heirs in question are not disposed to establish a Kullak Foundation, I consider it their duty and their obligation to donate 30,000 marks to each of the four existing music foundations – those named for Mozart, Mendelssohn, Meyerbeer, and Beethoven – making a total of 120,000 marks . . ."[30]

97 Four consecutive pages from the rare first edition of Liszt's *Grande Fantaisie de Bravoure sur la Clochette de Paganini*, the earliest sketches of which appear to date from 1831.

LIFE

January: Liszt lives a secluded existence in his garret at 61 Rue de Provence. Auguste Boissier keeps a diary of the piano lessons which her daughter Valérie (later Comtesse Gasparin) receives every three to four days between 3 January and 30 March 1832. We owe to her one of the earliest descriptions of the young Liszt:

''. . . At 1 o'clock yesterday the door of my salon opened, and we saw a slim, fair-haired young man enter, elegant of figure and distinguished of countenance . . . it was Liszt. He paid me a courteous and most obliging visit, and chatted with us for almost an hour. He is an original wit, and avoids merely repeating what others say; his ideas are very acute and entirely his own. He has exquisite manners, nobility, a certain soberness and inner composure, and a modesty which borders on true humility . . .''[31]

28 January: Concert in Rouen.

26 February: Frédéric Chopin gives his first major concert in Paris at the Salon Pleyel. Liszt attends the concert and becomes friendly with Chopin.

15 April: Chopin writes to tell J. Nowakowski that Liszt is in Switzerland.[32] This is our only evidence for a stay in Geneva (?) or Marlioz (?). Madame Boissier's diary ends on 30 March 1832, and it is conceivable that Liszt left Paris immediately after this date.

End of April: Liszt hears Paganini in Paris. Impressed by the latter's demonic virtuosity, he concentrates on his pianistic technique.

2 May: Liszt writes to Pierre Wolff in Geneva:

''. . . For two weeks my mind and my fingers have been working like two damned souls, – Homer, the Bible, Plato, Locke, Byron, Hugo, Lamartine, Chateaubriand, Beethoven, Bach, Hummel, Mozart, and Weber are all around me. I am studying them, observing them, and consuming them with real enthusiasm; and I am also practising four to five hours a day (thirds, sixths, octaves, tremolos, repetitions, cadenzas, etc.) Ah! If I don't go mad first, you'll find me a real artist when we meet again. Yes, an artist of the kind you want to see, and of the kind that is needed today . . .''[33]

28 September: Concert in Bourges.

9 December: Second performance of Berlioz's *Symphonie fantastique* in Paris. Shortly afterwards Liszt begins his piano transcription of the work (see Illus. 108).

98 Franz Liszt. Lithograph by C. Motte, based on a drawing by Achille Devéria, Paris, August 1832.

Marie d'Agoult to Franz Liszt (18 January 1840): ''Devéria's lithograph no longer bears any likeness to you, even if it ever did, but it helped me to rediscover the years of our passion, our sadness and our struggle. Ah, how I love this face!''[34]

99 Franz Liszt. Miniature, oil on ivory. Painted by La Morinière, 1832.

101 Felix Mendelssohn Bartholdy (1809–1847). Anonymous oil painting, ca. 1840. Previously unpublished.

Around the year 1832 Liszt had an affair with Adèle Laprunarède, a young, vivacious, and gifted beauty from the circles which frequented the Faubourg Saint-Germain in Paris. A letter from May 1831 suggests that their affair may already have begun at the end of 1830.

During the winter of 1831 Liszt spent some time in Adèle's company at her castle-like country house at Marlioz in the Swiss Alps, where the lovers were cut off from the world by an unusually heavy snowfall.[35] Liszt then stayed in Geneva before returning to Paris. The letters to Adèle which date from this period onwards he later described as his "first stylistic exercises in the French language."

100 Adèle Laprunarède. Miniature, oil on ivory, signed M.B., ca. 1832. Previously unpublished.

Adèle Laprunarède, later the Duchesse de Fleury, was one of the many women who fell in love with the young Liszt.

WORKS

Grande Fantaisie de Bravoure sur la Clochette de Paganini (for piano). Pub. 1834.
Grand solo caractéristique apropos d'une Chansonette de Panseron (for piano). Ca. 1832. Mentioned in a letter of 12 December 1832. Lost.
Fantasie über eine "Chansonette" (for piano). Unpub. The 36-page manuscript contains thematic material from Liszt's *La Chapelle de Guillaume Tell* of 1835/36 and was auctioned by Sotheby's of London on 27 November 1987. Probably identical with the preceding piece.

In December 1831 the first meeting took place between Liszt and Felix Mendelssohn-Bartholdy. Mendelssohn arrived in Paris from Munich, where he had just given the first performance of his G minor Piano Concerto. He remained in Paris for four months, before continuing his journey to London in April 1832. Together with Ferdinand Hiller, Charles Alkan, and Frédéric Chopin, Mendelssohn was one of Liszt's closest friends and greatest admirers during this period.

In his interesting book on Mendelssohn, Hiller reports how Mendelssohn entered his rooms one day, completely beside himself: "I say, I've just witnessed a miracle, a real miracle. I was with Liszt at Erard's, and I put the manuscript of my concerto in front of him and – though it's scarcely legible – he sight-read it perfectly; he couldn't have played it more beautifully, it was amazing." In 1840 Liszt performed Mendelssohn's D minor Concerto at a public concert, also at sight (see p. 129). For Mendelssohn's assessment of Liszt's piano playing, see p. 255.

102 Frédéric Chopin (1810–1849). Steel engraving published by the music publishers Schuberth & Co., based on Vigneron's 1833 portrait.

Chopin is seen here with the fashionable hair style adopted by elegant male society in Paris around 1830. The portrait matches Liszt's description of Chopin in his biography of the composer (see p. 180): "His blue [!] eyes showed intellect rather than contemplation. His gentle, refined laughter was never bitter. His delicate skin was enchantingly translucent, his blond hair silky; his demeanour bore the hallmark of such nobility that people involuntarily treated him like a lord. [. . .] His whole appearance reminded one of lilies on their swaying and curiously slender stems, with their etherially pale and fragrant calyxes, so fragrant, indeed, that the lightest touch might violate them . . ."

103 Programme for a concert given by Chopin in the Munich Odeon on 28 August 1831.

Chopin played his E minor Piano Concerto and *Fantasia on Polish Airs* (op. 13). A somewhat curious feature of the concert (that would now be unthinkable) was the insertion of an aria between the first and second movements of the concerto. A few days after this concert Chopin set off for Paris.

Opposite page:

104 Paris, Boulevard Poissonnière, at the time when Chopin lived there. Oil painting by Dagnan, 1834.

105 Cité Bergère, Paris. Photograph, 1980.

At the end of 1832 Chopin left the Boulevard Poissonnière and during 1832/33 lived in a second-floor apartment (arrowed on the photograph) at No. 4 Cité Bergère. The house has been substantially altered in the intervening period and is now part of a hotel complex. There is no commemorative plaque to mark Chopin's residence here, and few of the hotel guests who stay in his former rooms are aware of their illustrious predecessor.

106 Chopin's first apartment in Paris, on the fourth floor of 27 Boulevard Poissonnière. Nineteenth-century drawing.

The apartment still exists.

FR. CHOPIN.

MÜNCHEN.

Mit allerhöchster Bewilligung

wird

FRÉDÉRIC CHOPIN

aus Warschau,

Sonntag den 28. August

i m

Saale des philharmonischen Vereins

am Wittelsbacherplatze No. 617.

e i n

Instrumental- und Vocal-Concert

zu geben die Ehre haben.

Erster Satz eines E-moll Concertes für Piano-Forte, componirt und

  vorgetragen vom . . . . Concertgeber.

Cavatine, gesungen von . . . . Herrn Bayer.

Romanze und Rondeau aus obigem Concerte, componirt und vorgetragen vom Concertgeber.

Vierstimmiger Gesang mit Clavierbegleitung, componirt von Herrn Stuntz.

                      Mad. Pellegrini.

  gesungen von . . . . { Herrn Bayer.
                         Herrn Harm,
                         Herrn Lenz.

Phantaisie über polnische National-Lieder für Piano-Forte mit Orchester-

  Begleitung, componirt und vorgetragen vom . . . . Concertgeber.

Billete à 1 fl. sind nur in den Musikhandlungen der Herrn

Falter und Sohn, und Schäffer zu haben.

Anfang Mittags 12 Uhr.

The Polish composer and piano virtuoso Frédéric Chopin had settled in Paris in mid-September 1831. He and Liszt soon became good friends, united in a mutual admiration that may lie behind a paradoxical (indeed, barely intelligible) remark in an open letter of August 1877 from Hiller to Liszt: ". . . And now Chopin appeared – and so, too, did his *Études*, perhaps the only pieces which you have not sight-read by heart [sic: *auswendig vom Blatt gespielt*]." Chopin moved into rooms in the Boulevard Poissonnière. At this time Liszt was living nearby, at 61 Rue de Provence, and was a frequent visitor of Chopin's. The latter wrote to Tytus Woyciechowski on 25 December 1831,

"I am living on the fourth floor, but in the most beautiful part of Paris, on the boulevards, and I have a balcony – a very elegant iron balcony overlooking the street, so that I have a broad view over the boulevards to right and left. On the opposite side of the street, in the so-called Cité Bergère, there is a large courtyard with a public right of way, and it is here that Ramorino lives"[36] [Girolamo Ramorino (1792–1849), a general of Italian and Polish extraction, had been one of Napoleon's officers; he was later shot by the Italians for treason]. A year later, Chopin himself moved to the Cité Bergère (see Illus. 105). His Paris debut took place on 26 February 1832. Liszt attended, as did Mendelssohn, and he applauded enthusiastically.

That Chopin had an exceptionally high opinion of Liszt as a pianist is clear from various letters. The young Liszt may indeed have over-ornamented Chopin's piano works at times; but Chopin's allegedly boundless anger at this – described with monotonous regularity by almost all of Chopin's biographers – is attested by no reliable evidence. Nor are any dismissive remarks by Chopin on the subject of Liszt's compositions authenticated; Liszt's most important works were in any case not written until after Chopin's death. But if one recalls the almost incomprehensible harshness with which Chopin criticized many works by Beethoven, Schubert, and Schumann, it is scarcely likely that he would have felt much enthusiasm for Liszt's B minor Sonata.

In spite of their contrasting temperaments, the relationship between the calm and aristocratic Chopin, who never transgressed the bounds of good taste, and the fiery Liszt, whose character Heine described as "wild, stormy, volcanic, and promethean," remained untroubled for many years. One of the few paintings in Chopin's salon was a portrait of Liszt, and a marble cast of Chopin's hand adorned Liszt's desk as late as 1863 (see p. 228).

A certain estrangement which arose between the two artists in around 1839 is often said to derive from the claim that Liszt used Chopin's rooms for a romantic adventure during the latter's absence, but the only evidence for this is a remark of Liszt's from December 1839 – a remark which may, however, have a perfectly harmless explanation (see p. 106). A more probable cause is suggested by Liszt himself in a breach between George Sand and Marie d'Agoult: "Our ladies had quarreled, and as true cavaliers we each had to side with the relevant party" (Liszt to Friedrich Niecks, ca. 1880).

LIFE

At the beginning of the year Liszt meets the 27-year-old Comtesse Marie d'Agoult at the salon of the Marquise Le Vayer. Their association is to last for almost ten years.

Marie d'Agoult was born on 31 December 1805. Her father, Vicomte Flavigny, was a member of the old French nobility, and her mother was a daughter of the Frankfurt banker Johann Bethmann. She was widely regarded as one of the most cultured and distinguished women in the aristocratic world of Paris. She had married General Charles d'Agoult on 16 May 1827, when one of her witnesses had been Charles X (!). The family owned a house on the Quai Malaquais in Paris and a country house at Croissy, a few kilometres outside the city (see Illus. 119 and 120). Marie d'Agoult left her husband in 1835 and followed Liszt to Switzerland.

19 January: Liszt plays Hummel's Septet and various solo pieces at the Salon Dietz.

February: At Castle Marlioz in the Swiss Alps (?). (See p. 69 above, and n. 35.)

2, 19 and 23 March: Appearances at the Salon Dietz and the Salle du Wauxhall.

2 April: Liszt and Chopin perform together at the Théâtre-Italien in Paris.

3 April: Liszt and Chopin perform together at a concert given by the Herz brothers.

June: Liszt as frequent guest of Heinrich Heine and Frédéric Chopin; the latter's *Études*, op. 10, appear this same year with a dedication ''à son ami F. Liszt.''

July/August: Frequent guest of Marie d'Agoult at Croissy.

3 October: Witness at Berlioz's wedding with Harriet Smithson.

24 November: Liszt takes part in a concert given by Berlioz at the Théâtre Italien.

15 December: Chopin, Hiller, and Liszt play a Triple Concerto by Bach at the Conservatoire; Liszt and Hiller play a duet by Hiller.

22 December: Takes part in a concert given by Berlioz at the Conservatoire.

107 Letter to Liszt from Heinrich Heine, who was a member of Liszt's circle of friends in 1833:
''A thousand apologies for not coming to visit you yesterday evening. But it was too late by the time I had said goodbye to my friend, who was leaving us and in whose company I and a handful of other friends had agreed to spend his last hours here. I embrace you.
19 July 1833. Yours, H. Heine.''

108 Title page of the first edition of Liszt's piano transcription of Berlioz's *Grande Symphonie fantastique*.

109 An invitation from Berlioz to Chopin, informing him that among his expected guests were Hiller, Liszt, and Alfred de Vigny, ca. 1833.

Letter to Ferdinand Hiller written jointly by Liszt and Chopin (with contributions from the cellist Auguste Franchomme) and dated Paris, 20 June 1833.[37] The italicized words are Chopin's. In his open letter to Liszt of August 1877 Hiller remarked, ''I thought I could see your octaves leaping out of your handwriting, while Chopin's *fioriture* leapt out of his.''

Franz Liszt and Frédéric Chopin to Ferdinand Hiller:

''This must be the twentieth time at least that we have met here or at my place with the intention of writing to you, but time and again we have been interrupted by some visitor, or by some other unforeseen circumstance. I do not know whether Chopin will be able to apologize to you: but as far as I am concerned, I believe we have taken incivility and insolence so far that excuses are now neither permissible nor possible. [. . .]

''*I am writing without knowing what my pen is scribbling, because at this moment Liszt is playing my Études and putting honest thoughts out of my head. I should like to steal from him his way of interpreting my Études.* As for those of your friends who have remained in Paris, I have seen the Léo family and their hangers-on on several occasions this winter and spring. [. . .]

Madame Eichthal sends you her very best wishes. The whole Plater family was most upset when you left and has enjoined me to extend their condolences to you. [. . .]

''Do you know Chopin's marvellous *Études? They are admirable pieces! . . . and they will last only until your own appear,* a little modesty from the composer! *A little rudeness on the part of the teacher* – I must explain that it is he who is correcting my spelling mistakes (according to Monsieur Marlet's method).

''*You'll return to us in September,* won't you? *Try* (and let us know the day in good time, because we intend to offer you a serenade or a shivaree). The Society of the City's Most Distinguished Artists – M. Franchomme (present), Madame Petzold, and Abbé Bardin, the leading authorities in the Rue d'Amboise (and my female neighbours); Maurice

Schlesinger, Uncles, Aunts, Nephews, Brothers-in-Law, Sisters-in-Law, (and . . . and . . .) *in the background etc.*

Editorial board
F. Liszt, F. Chopin, Aug. Franchomme''

110 Title page of the first edition of Chopin's *Douze Grandes Études* (op. 10), with a dedication ''à son ami F. Liszt.''

WORKS

Grande Symphonie fantastique (Berlioz) (piano transcription). Pub. 1834. *Un Bal* and *Marche au Supplice* were also published separately.
L'idée fixe (Andante amoroso) from the *Symphonie fantastique* (for piano). Pub. 1833.
Ouverture des ''Francs-Juges'' (Berlioz) (piano transcription). Pub. 1845.
Die Rose (Liszt's first transcription of a Schubert Lied). Pub. 1835, or perhaps as early as 1833.

111, 112 Relievo portraits of Liszt and Chopin in Renaissance frames. Etchings (ca. 1843) by F. Schauer, based on A. Bovy's 1837 medallions.

Liszt's and Chopin's friends confirmed that both portraits were excellent likenesses of their respective subjects.

113 Franz Liszt. Bronze plaquette, probably by David d'Angers, ca. 1833.

114 Marie d'Agoult. Bronze plaquette by David d'Angers, ca. 1833.

Marie d'Agoult entered Liszt's life at the beginning of 1833. Their sensational relationship lasted ten years and produced three children, including Wagner's second wife, Cosima.

115 Marie d'Agoult in old age. Photograph by Nadar, Paris, ca. 1870.

Marie d'Agoult on her first encounter with Franz Liszt:[38]
". . . The Marquise was still speaking when the door opened and a strange apparition met my eyes. I say 'apparition,' for no other word could adequately describe the extraordinary emotion aroused in me by the most unusual person I have ever seen.

Tall and exceedingly thin, a pale visage with large sea-green eyes which would suddenly sparkle with life, like sunlight striking a wave; commanding features which bore the marks of suffering; a hesitant way of moving, appearing to glide rather than walk, seemingly preoccupied yet at the same time restless, like a ghost about to be summoned back to the shades of night. This was my impression of the youthful genius who stood before me and whose mysterious life aroused a curiosity as keen as the envy which his triumphs had earlier inspired in me. Franz asked to be introduced to me, then sat down beside me and with brazen charm began to talk in an intimate tone, as though he had known me for years. Behind the strange exterior which had initially filled me with a sense of amazement, I was attracted by the strength and freedom of an independent mind. And long before our conversation was over I found his character both simple and natural, however unusual it was in my world.

Franz spoke emotionally, breathlessly; he expressed himself with passion and uttered opinions totally strange to ears like mine, accustomed as they were to hearing only banal, conventional views. His flashing eyes, his gestures and smiles – sometimes earnest and infinitely gentle, sometimes satirical – seemed to wish to provoke me into contradicting him or into granting my approval. And I, as I vacillated between these emotions, such was my surprise at the speed of this strange acquaintanceship, answered but little. The lady of the house helped me out of my embarrassment. The piano was opened, and the candles lit on either side. [. . .] When the piece was over, he turned around; a radiance suffused his face, then disappeared again, and for the rest of the evening he made no further attempt to approach me."

Opposite page:

116 Comtesse Marie d'Agoult (1805–1876). Oil painting by Henri Lehmann, 1843.

LIFE

19 January: Liszt and Hiller perform one of Hiller's works for two pianos at the Salon Pleyel.

25 February: Concert at which Liszt, Chopin, and Schunke take part.

7 March: Liszt takes part in a concert with Théodore Haumann.

12 April: Together with Karl Schunke, Liszt plays Schunke's *Duo über Themen Rossinis* at a concert of the composer's.

End of May to 22 June: Liszt at Carentonne, near Bernay, in Normandy.[39]

19 June: Concert for the poor of Bernay.

Liszt's affair with Marie d'Agoult grows more intense. They meet in secret in Liszt's study (his "rat-hole," as he calls it), and he is a frequent visitor at the Château de Croissy. The lovers respond enthusiastically to reading Byron, Senancour (*Obermann*), Lamennais, and Voltaire.

Liszt meets George Sand. He encourages Maurice Schlesinger to found the *Revue et Gazette musicale de Paris* (generally known simply as the *Gazette musicale*), its main contributors being Liszt, Berlioz, Fétis, Janin, and d'Ortigue (see Illus. 199).

September: Lengthy visit to La Chênaie in Brittany as guest of the Abbé Lamennais. Writes his first mature original works (*Lyon, Apparitions, Harmonies poétiques*).

October: Marie d'Agoult's eldest daughter falls ill; she dies two months later. Liszt and the Comtesse do not see each other for several months.

5 November: Liszt appears at a charity concert in the Salon Stoepel; among the works played are his *Clochette* Fantasia (see Illus. 97).

23 November: Berlioz concert at the Conservatoire. Liszt is announced as one of the performers, but he appears to have cancelled. (His name is not mentioned by the critics.)

24 November: Liszt, Urhan and Kreutzer perform together in the church of Saint-Vincent-de-Paul (see Illus. 83).[40]

13 and 27 December: Liszt attends two chamber-music concerts organized by Pierre Baillot at the Salons Duport, 83 Rue Neuve-des-Petits-Champs.

25 December: Liszt and Chopin perform a duet by Moscheles and a piece by Liszt for two pianos (probably on themes by Mendelssohn) at a concert organized by Dr. F. Stoepel. Other participants include Heinrich Wilhelm Ernst, Sabine Heinefetter, and Madame de la Haye (a niece of Jean-Jacques Rousseau).

28 December: Liszt performs his paraphrases of Berlioz's *Un Bal* and *Marche au Supplice* at a concert organized by the latter.

L'ABBÉ DE LA MENNAIS.

Félicité de Lamennais was well known for his writings on the philosophy of religion, the most sensational of which, *Paroles d'un croyant*, was published on 30 April 1834. Liszt was enthralled by the humane ideas and passionate language of the great demagogue, whose demands included total press freedom.

The Abbé Lamennais quickly took the impressionable young man to his heart and in September 1834 invited him to stay at his country house at La Chênaie. Liszt, whose compositions heretofore had almost without exception been transcriptions of other composers' pieces, now worked not only on his *Grande fantaisie symphonique* for piano and orchestra based on themes by Berlioz, but also on his *Apparitions*, his revolutionary piano piece *Lyon*, and the first sketches for his *Harmonies poétiques et religieuses*.[41]

Lamennais helped Liszt and Marie d'Agoult with his advice during the dramatic unfolding of their love affair, and apart from Liszt's mother he was the only person who was told of their plans to move to Switzerland. He later called Liszt "one of the most beautiful souls I have ever met."

Scarcely had Liszt returned from Brittany in October 1834, where he had been staying with the Abbé Lamennais, when the Comtesse's eldest daughter, Louise, fell ill. The six-year-old child died in December 1834; her grief-stricken mother left Liszt's letters unanswered and retired to her country home at Croissy. Only when Liszt wrote in desperation and announced that he was leaving Europe and wished to see her one last time did she agree to a meeting – the encounter which marked the start of their long association.

117 Félicité de Lamennais (1782–1854). Lithograph by Delpech based on a drawing by Belliard; ca. 1835.

Opposite page:

119 Palais Croissy near Lagny. Photograph, ca. 1850. Previously unpublished.

The Palais Croissy, situated a few kilometres outside Paris and built by Colbert in the style of Louis XIV, was acquired by the d'Agoult family in 1832. It underwent numerous structural alterations in the course of the years and no longer exists. During 1833/34 Liszt was a frequent visitor to the house, which served as Marie d'Agoult's summer residence.

120 Hôtel de Mailly, the d'Agoult family residence in Paris, seen here from the Rue de Beaune. Photograph, ca. 1942. Previously unpublished.

The photograph was taken shortly before the building was demolished. Situated on the Quai Malaquais at 1 Rue de Beaune and facing the Louvre, this building was the scene of many meetings between Liszt and Marie d'Agoult during the early days of their love.

121 38 Rue du Général Foy, Paris, Marie d'Agoult's residence 1870–6. Photograph, ca. 1890. Previously unpublished.

Around 1870 the house bore the address Rue Malesherbes.

118 Marie d'Agoult with her daughter Claire-Christine. Crayon drawing by Ingres, 1849.

This portrait was drawn in 1849 in the Comtesse's *salon* at 16 Rue Plumet, shortly before the marriage of her daughter, Claire-Christine (then aged nineteen), to the Marquis Guy de Charnacé.

WORKS

Grande Fantaisie symphonique on themes from Berlioz's *Lélio* (for piano and orchestra). Pub. 1981, together with a version for two pianos.
Malédiction for piano and orchestra. It is not certain when this work was written, but probably ca. 1834. It has come to be known under this title, although Liszt described only the first theme as "Malédiction" ("Curse"). Pub. 1915.

Malédiction is frequently assigned to the year 1827, but this is unlikely if one compares it with other works written at that date. On 26 July 1835 Liszt wrote to his mother from Geneva, asking her to send him his piano concerto; presumably he meant his *Malédiction*. It could be a revised version of the 1827 Piano Concerto, also in A minor. See "Works 1827."
Psaume instrumental (*De profundis*) (for piano and orchestra). Unpublished. The original manuscript (900 bars) is in the Liszt Archive in Weimar. Material from this and *Harmonies poétiques* was used in *Pensée des morts* (see "Works 1847").
Concerto symphonique (for piano and orchestra). Liszt mentions this work in a letter of 26 July 1835. Written winter 1834/35. Very probably identical with the *Psaume instrumental*. Lost or unpublished.
Harmonies poétiques et religieuses (for piano). Originally planned for piano and orchestra. Pub. 1835 (as supplement to Vol. 23 of the *Gazette musicale*). Revised and published in 1853 as *Pensée des morts* (no. 4 of a collection of pieces given the generic title *Harmonies poétiques et religieuses*).[41]
Lyon (for piano), later included in the *Album d'un Voyageur*. Pub. 1840.[42]
Apparitions: No. 1 Senza lentezza, No. 2 Vivamente, No. 3 Fantaisie sur un valse de François Schubert Molto agitato ed appassionato (for piano). Pub. 1835. No. 3 later became no. 4 of the *Soirées de Vienne* (see "Works 1852").
Graßes Konzertstück über Mendelssohns Lieder ohne Worte. Unpublished.
Fünf Variationen über Romanze aus Joseph (Méhul) (for piano). Ca. 1834. Unpub.

WRITINGS:
On the Future of Church Music. A fragment of this article appeared in the *Revue et Gazette musicale de Paris*, No. 35, 30 August 1835.
The essays and travelogues which Liszt published in the *Revue et Gazette musicale de Paris* between 1834 and 1840 were written in collaboration with Marie d'Agoult. All of these essays, with the exception of a piece on Alkan's piano music (1837), were published in German in Vol. II of the collected edition of Liszt's writings, Leipzig 1881.

MARIE D'AGOULT'S HOMES IN PARIS

In November 1839 Liszt embarked upon a series of triumphal concert tours throughout the whole of Europe, while Marie d'Agoult returned to Paris with her children. Between 1839 and her death she lived in the following houses:

1839–1847 10 Rue des Mathurins
1847–1851 16 Rue Plumet (Ingres' drawing [Illus. 118] shows her in the salon of this house)
1851–1859 20 Avenue Marie du Roule. The Comtesse acquired this charming private mansion in 1851. Situated towards the top of the Champs-Élysées, it soon became a meeting-place for the literary élite of Paris. At that date animals still grazed on the undeveloped land around it. The colour of the brickwork and the dense rows of rosebushes surrounding the house led to its being known as the "Maison Rose." The house, situated in an avenue lined with acacia trees, was demolished in 1870.

1860–1861 15 Avenue de l'Impératrice
1862–1869 11 Rue Circulaire (later Rue de Presbourg)
1870–1876 38 Rue du Général Foy

122 Paris photographed from the roof of the Louvre. Daguerreotype by Friedrich von Martens, 1846.

Reproduced in reverse to restore true orientation. Martens used a special camera, which he himself had built: its lens could swivel in front of a curved plate and had an angle of vision of approximately 150°.

In the foreground is the Pont des Arts, leading from the Louvre to the Palais de l'Institut (the domed building in the centre of the picture). To the right of the Institut is the Quai Malaquais, where George Sand and Marie d'Agoult had their town residences. In the background is the Pont Neuf.

123 George Sand and Casimir Dudevant. Oil painting by François Biard, ca. 1834.

The couple were divorced in 1836.

124 George Sand (1804–1876). Photograph by Nadar, ca. 1860.

Franz Liszt first met the 30-year-old George Sand in late summer 1834. On 25 August 1834 he wrote to Marie d'Agoult, "Madame Sand arrived recently. Alfred de Musset told me a great deal about her the day before yesterday. He has said he will introduce me to her when he next goes to visit her . . ."[42]

Alfred de Vigny has left an account of the authoress, who even at that date enjoyed a certain notoriety but whose genius for a modern audience lies rather in her letters than in her novels: "Black curly hair falling down to her shoulders in the style of Raphael's angels. Her eyes are large and dark, shaped like the eyes than you see in portraits of mystics or in the most magnificent Italian heads. Her solemn countenance is motionless. The lower half of her face is unattractive, and her mouth is badly drawn. Charmless in her manner and coarse of speech. Masculine in her habits and her way of speaking, in her vocal timbre and brazenness of speech . . ."

George Sand, who was later to become Chopin's lover, moved into rooms at 19 Quai Malaquais in November 1832, taking over the apartment of the critic and writer Henri de Latouche, and director of *Le Figaro*. The house, situated at the back of the main building, still exists (it was the home of one of Pablo Picasso's daughters until 1984). On the wall overlooking the main street is a plaque which reads, "Ici est la Mansarde Bleue où George Sand vécut de 1832 à 1836. Elle y écrit *Lélia*." – Franz Liszt was soon a welcome visitor here.

125 George Sand. Pencil drawing by Alfred de Musset, ca. 1835.

This drawing dates from the period of the turbulent love affair between Musset and George Sand, which lasted from 1833 to 1835.

From the outset, legend has sought to link together the names of George Sand and Liszt. Was it not inevitable that the handsome, world-famous artist, with his extensive interest in literature, and the intelligent authoress, with her contempt for convention, should feel a mutual sympathy and curiosity?

It must, however, be said that the preconditions for any such affair were highly unfavourable at the time of their earliest meetings. In the autumn of 1834 George Sand was suffering the ups and downs of her desperate love for Alfred de Musset, while Liszt and Marie d'Agoult were currently enjoying the most beautiful and intimate period of their whole ardent relationship. Nonetheless, Musset was jealous. "Can he [Musset] seriously have believed for a moment that I loved Liszt? Does he still think so? . . . If I had been able to love Herr Liszt, I would have loved him to distraction, but I could not . . ." (George Sand and Alfred de Musset: *Correspondance*).

George Sand to Musset: "This evening Liszt said to me that only God deserves to be loved. Perhaps, but once you have loved a man it is difficult to love God; the two are quite different." Liszt to George Sand (March 1835): "Your last letter but one hurt me. How often have I passed your freshly whitewashed house on the Quai Malaquais and felt my heart contract with pain and sadness! . . ." George Sand to Franz Liszt (April 1835): ". . . Come and knock on my door if you like; if not, I shall not be angry with you, but if *yes*, I shall love you all the more for it." Liszt replies by return of post: "Oh, if you knew how happy I am . . . I think it is possible and, indeed, almost necessary for us to be faithful to one another and for our souls to understand each other for a long time to come . . . It is absolutely imperative that I see you again and tell you, prosaically and stupidly, that I love you."

Is this the language of lovers, or are such expressions merely an example of the nineteenth century's effusive way of expressing itself?

126 Alfred de Musset (1810–1857). Photograph by Charles Jacotin, ca. 1850.

127 Franz Liszt. Lithograph by Tavernier, ca. 1834, published as a supplement to the "Galerie de la Presse."

LIFE

14 January: Liszt writes to Lamennais that he is ''leaving tomorrow for two months.''[43] No further details are known.

5 April: Charity concert for Polish refugees at the Théâtre–Italien, Paris. The performers include Liszt, Hiller, Chopin (who plays his E minor Concerto), Ernst, Marie Cornélie Falcon, and Adolphe Nourrit.

9 April: Liszt performs his *Grande Fantaisie symphonique* on themes from *Lélio* at the Hôtel de Ville. During the final *Konzertstück über Mendelssohns Lieder ohne Worte* (with Mlle Vial), Liszt faints and has to be carried from the platform.

23 April: Liszt, Pixis, Alkan, and Liszt's pupil Hermann Cohen (Puzzi) perform at the Salle Chantereine.

3 May: Participates in a concert organized by Berlioz and plays Moscheles's *Variationen über den Alexandermarsch*.

23 May: Appears at Gymnase Musical.

26 May: Marie d'Agoult informs her husband that she is leaving him, after which she sets off for Switzerland.

4 June: Liszt arrives in Basle, where Marie is waiting for him. They remain in the town for a week, before travelling to Geneva via the Furka Pass, Martigny, and Bex. Around 23 June they set off from Hospental for a visit to the St Gotthard Pass. They arrive in Geneva on 19 July and rent rooms at the Hôtel des Balances (No. 47). Soon afterwards they move into rented accommodation in the Rue Tabazan (see Illus. 129). Liszt composes, and attends philosophy lectures at the University. His friends include Pictet, de Candolle, Fazy, Denis, and Sismondi.

1 October: Prince Belgiojoso, an outstanding singer who happens to be in Geneva, organizes a grand charity concert at the Casino. The performers include the violinist Charles Lafont, Bonoldi, Wolff, Cohen, and Liszt, who performs various works including Weber's *Konzertstück* for piano and orchestra.

9 November: The recently opened Conservatoire begins its teaching programme in the rooms of the Casino Saint-Pierre. Liszt gives free piano lessons here.

18 December: Blandine Rachel, the first child of Marie d'Agoult and Franz Liszt, is born in Geneva.

128 Geneva, where Franz Liszt and Marie d'Agoult lived from July 1835 to October 1836. Steel engraving by Weber, ca. 1840.

View of the Quai des Bergues (right of picture), and the Ile Jean-Jacques Rousseau. The Hôtel des Bergues is on the extreme right, at the front of the picture.

129 Liszt's residence in Geneva, on the corner of the Rue Tabazan and Rue des Belles-Filles, now 22 Rue Étienne Dumont. Photograph, ca. 1930.

The marble plaque erected in 1896 was replaced in 1938 by a relief portrait of Liszt in old age!

Liszt left Paris at the beginning of June 1835. On one of his last evenings in the city before his departure, he and Marie d'Agoult visited George Sand in her ''Mansarde Bleue'' on the Quai Malaquais, ascending the winding staircase (almost unchanged to this day) which Balzac, Planche, Sainte-Beuve, Mérimée, Lamennais, Heine, and Musset had all climbed at one time or another.

The scandalous relationship between Liszt and the Comtesse (that ''blonde peri in a sky-blue dress,'' as George Sand described her) was on everyone's lips. The couple decided to move to Switzerland; Marie was already expecting Liszt's child. In the end Liszt left on his own, having arranged to meet her in Basle. The couple stayed there for a week before setting off for Lake Lucerne, where Liszt was inspired to write his piano piece *Le Lac de Wallenstadt*. They travelled via St Gotthard and the Rhône valley, and arrived in Geneva on 19 July. After a brief stay at the Hôtel des Balances, they rented rooms in the Rue Tabazan (see Illus. 129). Liszt immersed himself in work, and in spring 1836 wrote to George Sand: ''For six months I have been doing nothing but writing, scribbling and scrawling music, music of every shape and colour. I'm convinced that if you counted the notes you would find several thousand millions of them . . .''[44]

WORKS

Fantaisie romantique sur deux mélodies suisses (for piano). Pub. 1836.

Grande Fantaisie sur des motifs des Soirées musicales de Rossini. La serenata et L'orgia (for piano). Pub. 1837.

2me Fantaisie sur des motifs des Soirées musicales de Rossini. La pastorella dell'Alpi e Li marinari (for piano). Pub. 1837 (see Illus. 180).

Réminiscences de "La Juive" (Halévy) (for piano). Pub. 1836 (see Illus. 142).

Grande Fantaisie sur la "Niobe" de Pacini (Divertissement sur la Cavatine de Pacini "I tuoi frequenti palpiti") (for piano). Pub. 1837. The early editions also refer to a version for piano and orchestra (lost).

Réminiscences de "Lucia di Lammermoor" (Donizetti) (for piano). Pub. 1840.

Marche et cavatine de "Lucie de Lammermoor" (for piano), intended by Liszt as part of the *Réminiscences de "Lucia di Lammermoor"* but published separately. Pub. 1841.

Marche des Pèlerins (from Berlioz's *Harold en Italie*) (piano transcription). Performed in 1835, but the published version of 1866 almost certainly represents a revision of the original.

Grande Valse di Bravura (also called *Le Bal de Berne*) (for piano). Pub. 1835. Revised version of ca. 1850 published in 1852. A version for piano duet made in 1836 was published in 1842.

Waltz in E major (for piano). Liszt mentions this work in a letter of 26 July 1835. Lost.

Piano Sonata in C minor. Liszt mentions this piece in a letter of March 1836 and writes out the first few notes. Lost.

Piano Tutor for the Geneva Conservatoire. This voluminous manuscript had already been set in Lyons, but the publisher took the plates to the pawnbroker's, where they were destroyed.

WRITINGS:

On the Position of Artists and Their Place in Society, published in six instalments in the *Revue et Gazette musicale de Paris* from May 1835 onwards (Nos. 18, 19, 20, 30, 35, and 41).

Letter from a Bachelor of Music. To George Sand. Pub. in the *Revue et Gazette musicale de Paris*, No. 49, 6 December 1835.

130 Franz Liszt. Oil painting by Jean Gabriel Scheffer.

This romantic portrait, with its dreamily wistful expression and the strikingly beautiful shape of Liszt's right hand, was painted in Geneva at the end of 1835 or the beginning of 1836. Liszt is not yet seen with the shoulder-length hair which he was to wear from 1836 until the end of his life.

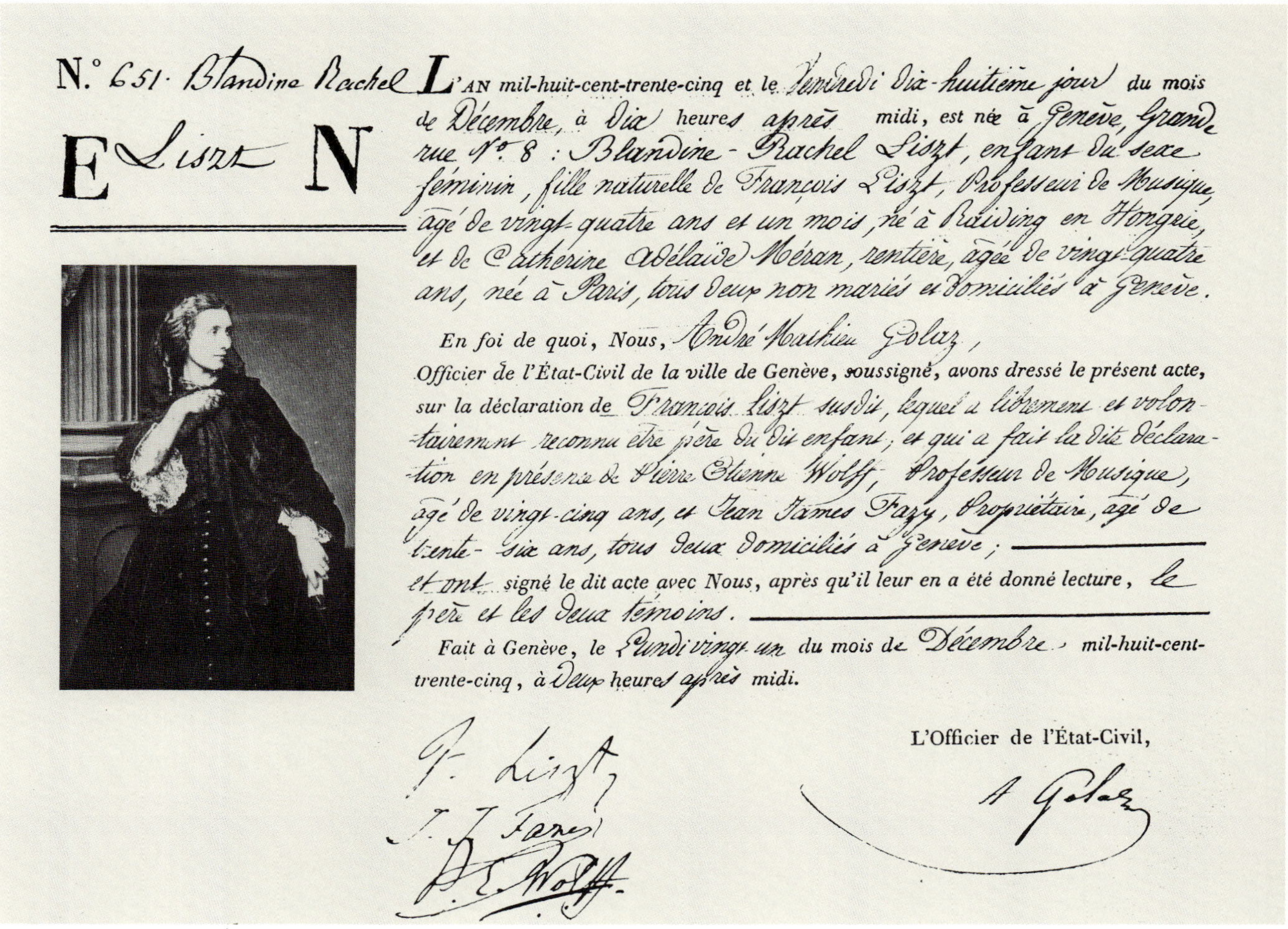

N.° 651 · Blandine Rachel L
E Liszt N

[Handwritten birth certificate in French]

L'AN mil-huit-cent-trente-cinq et le *Vendredi Dix-huitième jour* du mois de Décembre, à *Dix* heures après midi, est née à *Genève, Grande rue N° 8 : Blandine-Rachel Liszt, enfant du sexe féminin, fille naturelle de François Liszt, Professeur de Musique, âgé de vingt-quatre ans et un mois, né à Raiding en Hongrie, et de Catherine Adélaïde Méran, rentière, âgée de vingt-quatre ans, née à Paris,* tous deux non mariés et domiciliés à *Genève.*

En foi de quoi, Nous, *André Mathieu Golay,* Officier de l'État-Civil de la ville de Genève, *soussigné,* avons dressé le présent acte, sur la déclaration de *François Liszt susdit, lequel a librement et volontairement reconnu être père du dit enfant; et qui a fait la dite déclaration en présence de Pierre Étienne Wolff, Professeur de Musique, âgé de vingt-cinq ans, et Jean James Fazy, Propriétaire, âgé de trente-six ans, tous deux domiciliés à Genève;* et ont signé le dit acte avec Nous, après qu'il leur en a été donné lecture, *le père et les deux témoins.*

Fait à Genève, le *Lundi vingt-un* du mois de *Décembre,* mil-huit-cent-trente-cinq, à *Deux* heures *après* midi.

F. Liszt
J.J. Fazy
P.E. Wolff

L'Officier de l'État-Civil,
A. Golay

131, 132 Liszt's daughter Blandine, photograph by A. Solomon, ca. 1855; superimposed upon Blandine's birth certificate, entry of 21 December 1835 in the registry office records of the town of Geneva.

Blandine in 1857 married Émile Ollivier, later to be the French Prime Minister. She died in St Tropez in 1862.

133 Records in Liszt's own hand, giving his opinions on his pupils at the Geneva Conservatoire in 1836.

Blandine's birth certificate in translation:

On Friday, 18 December 1835, at 10.00 p.m. Blandine-Rachel Liszt was born at 8 Grande Rue, Geneva, the natural daughter of François Liszt, professor of music, aged twenty-four years and one month, born at Raiding in Hungary, and of Catherine Adélaïde Méran, lady of property, aged twenty-four years, born in Paris, both parents unmarried and domiciled in Geneva. In witness whereof, we, the undersigned, André Mathieu Golay, acting registrar of the town of Geneva, have drawn up the present certificate on the testimony of the said François Liszt, who has freely and voluntarily acknowledged that he is the father of the said child, and who has made the said declaration in the presence of Pierre Étienne Wolff, professor of music, aged twenty-five years, and Jean James Fazy, householder, aged thirty-six years, both domiciled in Geneva, who have signed the said certificate after having it read back to them.
Witnessed in Geneva, Monday, the 21st day of December 1835, at 2.00 p.m.

F. Liszt   Acting Registrar,
J.J. Fazy   A. Golay
P.E. Wolff

The three witnesses to this document (we note, not without a certain amusement, that they include the future mayor of Geneva) must have been aware that they were adding their names to a certificate which was inaccurate in terms of the name, age, place of birth, and address of the mother!

Liszt's comments on his students (reproduced to the right):
Mlle Marie Demelleyer: Faulty technique (if technique there be). Extreme enthusiasm but little talent. Grimaces and contortions. Glory to God in the highest and peace to men of good will.
Mlle Ida Milliquet: An artist from Geneva. Languid and mediocre. Fairly good fingering. Fairly good posture. Enough "fairly goods," which in all don't amount to much.
Mlle Jenny Gambini: Beautiful eyes!

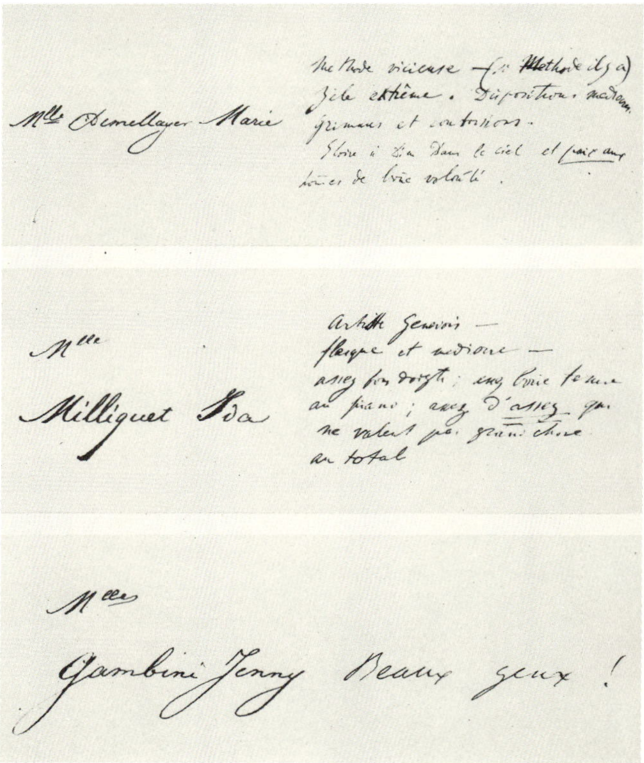

[Handwritten notes]

Mlle Demelleyer Marie — Méthode vicieuse (si Méthode il y a) Zèle extrême. Disposition médiocre. Grimaces et contorsions. Gloire à Dieu dans le ciel et paix aux hommes de bonne volonté.

Mlle Milliquet Ida — Artiste Genevoise flasque et médiocre — assez bon doigté; assez bonne tenue au piano; assez d'assez qui ne valent pas grand chose en total

Mlle Gambini Jenny Beaux yeux!

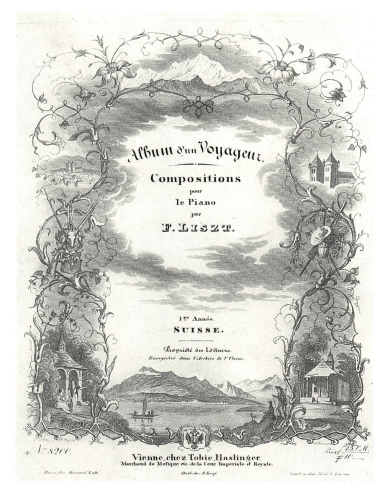

134 ''Au bord d'une source'' from the *Album d'un Voyageur*.

The lithographed title page is taken from the 1855 edition, retitled *Années de Pèlerinage*.

135 Title page of the first edition of ''Orage.''

Liszt reworked his *Album d'un Voyageur* between 1848 and 1854, adding ''Eglogue'' and ''Orage'' and publishing all the pieces under the title *Années de Pèlerinage. Première Année: Suisse*.

136 Title page of the first edition of the complete *Album d'un Voyageur*, published in 1842 by the Viennese firm of Haslinger.

With the exception of ''Lyon,'' which was written in 1834 (see note 41), all these pieces were composed in 1835/36.

137 Lake Geneva around 1836, seen from Pregny. Miniature painting in enamel on a gold snuffbox which Liszt's admirers in Geneva gave him as a present.

The town of Geneva is seen on the right of the picture, with Mont Blanc in the background.

LIFE

January: Compositional work in Geneva.

February: Liszt takes part in a concert in Geneva with his pupil Hermann Cohen.

March: Marie d'Agoult and Liszt undertake various excursions from Geneva, the impressions of which are recorded in the *Album d'un Voyageur*.

6 April: Concert in the Geneva Casino (see Illus. 139).

13 April: Further concert in Geneva.

21 April to 11 May: In Lyons. Concerts on 2, 5, and 7 May in Municipal Theatre and Hôtel du Nord. Nancy Mérienne paints Liszt's portrait (see Illus. 76).

13 May to 3 June: Liszt meets up with old friends in Paris. Chopin refuses to accept that Liszt is remotely comparable to the pianist Sigismond Thalberg, who has conquered Paris in the intervening period.

18 May: Concert at the Salons Erard. Berlioz reviews Liszt's interpretation of Beethoven's *Hammerklavier* Sonata (see p. 86).

5 June: Liszt back in Geneva with Marie d'Agoult. The couple rent rooms in the inn "Zum Genfer Wappen" in Veyrier.

July: They move to a chalet at Monnetier on Mont Salève.

16 July: Concert in Lausanne.

22 and 23 July: Concerts in Dijon.

August: In Geneva and Saint-Gervais.

September: George Sand arrives in Geneva. The friends travel to Chamonix (see p. 87). From there they make an excursion to Fribourg, where Liszt plays on the famous organ in the Church of St Nicholas. "Never did Franz's Florentine profile stand out more palely and clearly than in this dark cloud of mystic terrors and religious mourning . . .", George Sand records. She subsequently lives for several days in the garret of Liszt's house.

26 September: Liszt takes part in a concert given by Hermann Cohen in Geneva.

3 October: Last concert in Geneva (two solo pieces and Beethoven's Piano Trio in B flat major). Shortly afterwards Liszt and Marie relinquish the lease of their house in Geneva.

16 October: Liszt and Marie d'Agoult back in Paris. They live at the Hôtel de France, 23 Rue Laffitte, together with George Sand, who meets Frédéric Chopin here.

13 December: Soirée *chez* Chopin. Liszt and Chopin play Moscheles's Sonata for Four Hands.

18 December: At a concert conducted by Berlioz, Liszt plays his *Lélio* Fantasia, *Un Bal*, and *Marche au Supplice*, and his Fantasia on Themes from Pacini's *Niobe*.

138 Franz Liszt. Pencil drawing by Jean Gabriel Scheffer, Geneva 1836.

Note the raised wrists, a feature of almost all representations showing Liszt at the keyboard (see Illus. 240 and 494). Arm and shoulder action played an important role for Liszt, who rejected bent "crawling fingers." "Do not become stuck to the keys," he would say: "The hands must be more in the air than on the keys!"

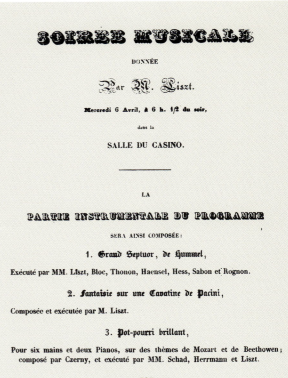

139 Programme for a "Soirée musicale" in Geneva on 6 April 1836.
Hummel's Septet was a work which Liszt held in particularly high regard, and he played it at many of his concerts around 1840. In 1848 he prepared a piano transcription of the piece.

140 Envelope in Liszt's hand, postmarked 28 May 1836 and addressed to "Madame la Comtesse d'Agoult, rue Tabazan, Genève, Suisse" (see Illus. 129).

141 ''Fleurs mélodiques des Alpes'' from the *Album d'un Voyageur*, written 1835/36.

The title page is taken from Haslinger's 1842 edition.

142 Title page of the first edition of Liszt's *Fantaisie Brillante* on Halévy's *La Juive*, composed in 1835 and published in 1836.

Liszt also called his operatic fantasias ''Paraphrases'' or ''Réminiscences.''

143 First page of the manuscript of Liszt's *Grande Fantaisie dramatique* on Meyerbeer's *Les Huguenots*, written in 1836 and published in 1837.

A shorter version appeared in 1842.

144 The opening bars of Liszt's *Huguenots* Fantasia in the composer's hand.

Somewhat remarkably, this Fantasia is the only work which Liszt dedicated to Marie d'Agoult.

WORKS

Album d'un Voyageur (for piano) (see Illus. 136). Written 1835/36.
  I. *Impressions et Poésies*
    1. Lyon [written 1834? cf. note 41]
    2a. *Le Lac de Wallenstadt*
    2b. *Au bord d'une source*
    3. *Les cloches de G.[enève]*
    4. *Vallée d'Obermann*
    5. *La chapelle de Guillaume Tell*
    6. *Psaume*
  published ca. 1840 as *Années de Pèlerinage. Première Année: Suisse.*
  II. *Fleurs mélodiques des Alpes* (see Illus. 141)
    7a. *Allegro*
    7b. *Lento*
    7c. *Allegro pastorale*
    8a. *Andante con sentimento*
    8b. *Andante molto espressivo*
    8c. *Allegro moderato*
    9a. *Allegretto*
    9b. *Allegretto*
    9c. *Andantino con molto sentimento*
  published in 1842 as *Album d'un Voyageur*, II. *Fleurs mélodiques des Alpes.*
  III. *Paraphrases*
    10. *Ranz des vaches*
    11. *Un soir dans les montagnes*
    12. *Ranz des chèvres*
  published in 1836 as *3 Airs suisses*, and reissued in 1877 as *3 Morceaux suisses*; the 1842 edition was entitled *Album d'un Voyageur*, III. *Paraphrases.*

The three parts were published complete in 1842. Seven pieces were taken over from Parts I and II, and to these were added *Orage* (composed after 1848) and *Eglogue* (composed in 1836). *Lento* was renamed *Le mal du pays*. The collection, now entitled *Années de Pèlerinage. Première Année: Suisse*, contained the following pieces:
  1. *Chapelle de Guillaume Tell*
  2. *Au lac de Wallenstadt*
  3. *Pastorale*
  4. *Au bord d'une source*
  5. *Orage*
  6. *Vallée d'Obermann*
  7. *Eglogue*
  8. *Le mal du pays*
  9. *Les cloches de Genève*
  Pub. 1855.

An unpublished version of *Vallée d'Obermann* entitled *Tristia* for piano, violin, and cello was performed in Budapest in 1986.

Rondeau fantastique sur un thème espagnol (El Contrabandista) (for piano). Pub. 1837.

Grande Fantaisie sur des thèmes de l'opéra ''Les Huguenots'' de Meyerbeer (for piano). Pub. 1837 (see Illus. 143 and 144).

Réminiscences des ''Puritains'' de Bellini (for piano). Pub. 1837.

Harold en Italie (symphony by Berlioz) (arranged for piano with solo viola). Pub. ca. 1879.

Eglogue (later taken up into the *Années de Pèlerinage*) (for piano). Pub. 1836.

WRITINGS:

On Popular Editions of Leading Works (essay). Pub. in the *Revue et Gazette musicale de Paris*, No. 1, 3 January 1836.

inspiration (Listz)

pan ? pan ! tzin ? tzin ! patatzin boum boum ! et glaa cl vlaa !!! patatra la la !! (symphonie en ut majeur)

145, 146 Franz Liszt. Two anonymous caricatures, ca. 1836.
Perhaps an allusion to Liszt's interpretation of the *Hammerklavier* Sonata.

In April 1836 Liszt left Geneva for a brief period and returned to Paris, where the name of the piano virtuoso Sigismond Thalberg (see pp. 89 and 90) was on everyone's lips. He was regarded as the equal, if not the superior, of Liszt, who regretted not being able to hear his rival play; but the concert season was over and Thalberg had already left the city.

Liszt gave two concerts. In addition to his own new operatic Fantasias, he also played Beethoven's *Hammerklavier* Sonata. Berlioz devoted a detailed article to him, published in the *Gazette musicale* for 12 June 1836 (presumably through an oversight, it was not included in the German edition of Berlioz's collected writings; there is no English edition). It ends as follows: ''. . . This is the great new school of piano playing! [. . .]

''In support of my view I appeal to the judgement of all who heard him play Beethoven's great sonata (op. 106), this sublime poem which until now has remained the riddle of the Sphinx for almost all piano players. A new Oedipus, Liszt, has solved it, and solved it in such a way that had the composer himself returned from the grave a paroxysm of joy and pride would have swept over him. Not a note was omitted, not a note was added (I followed the performance score in hand), not an inflection was blurred, not a single change was made to the tempo [. . .]

''I know full well that there is nothing more one can say; but it must be said, because it is true. This was an ideal performance of a work regarded as unperformable. By fostering understanding of a hitherto misunderstood work, Liszt has proved that he is the pianist of the future. All honour to him!''

Liszt and Marie d'Agoult gave up their home in Geneva in mid-October 1836. They moved to Paris, renting rooms at the Hôtel de France, 23 Rue Laffitte. The Comtesse's elegant salon soon became a meeting-place for the literary and musical élite of Paris (see p. 92). Ferdinand Hiller describes the atmosphere there in the open letter to Liszt from which we have already quoted:

''They were wonderful times when we met, together with Chopin, at the home of the witty and musical Dr Hermann Franck, or dined with Sainte-Beuve at the Countess d'Agoult's, or attended a dance at the home of one of the Polish émigrées, the charming Countess Plater, where we met Mazurek in the flesh and thought ourselves in Poland. Do you know what an old and supercilious woman from this circle once said to Chopin? (I shall repeat it in the French original, since it would sound far too immoral in German.) 'Si j'étais jeune et jolie, mon petit Chopin,' she said, 'je te prendrais pour mari, Hiller pour ami et Liszt pour amant.' Well, I do not suppose that this remark will surprise you. But perhaps the following one of Chopin's will. One evening you were host to the aristocracy of the French literary world – George Sand must also have been there. As the company was leaving, Chopin turned to me and said, 'What an antipathetic person this Sand woman is! Is she really a woman? I'm half inclined to doubt it.' Louis XIV had similarly found Madame Scarron *insupportable*, but that didn't prevent her from becoming Madame Maintenon. How mysterious are the machinations of fate – completely inscrutable, particularly when it conceals itself in the form of a woman.'' (It was not long afterwards that Chopin fell in love with George Sand.)

147 Liszt on Mont Blanc, September 1836. Caricature by Maurice Sand, 1836.

148 Hôtel de l'Union in Chamonix. Lithograph by Stoehli, ca. 1836.
   Liszt, George Sand, and their companions stayed here in September 1836.

In September 1836 George Sand, together with her children Maurice and Solange and their maid Ursule Josse, accepted Liszt's invitation to Geneva. Liszt, Marie, and "Puzzi" had already set off for Chamonix. In her tenth *Lettre d'un Voyageur*, George Sand later left an amusing account of her arrival in Chamonix and her search for Liszt, with his "very tight smock, long unkempt hair, and necktie rolled up like a length of rope, normally to be found warbling the *Dies Irae* with a cheerful expression on his face." Shortly afterwards, their mutual friend Adolphe Pictet (see Illus. 150) arrived, dressed in a major's uniform. (He, too, later published an equally witty account of the episode in *Une Course à Chamonix* [Paris 1838].) The landlord took him for a policeman and asked whether he had come to arrest "the family of gypsies, with their long hair and smocks, who are making an infernal din upstairs." Pictet read Liszt's entry in the hotel register:

149 Hermann Cohen (1820–1871), Liszt's pupil, also known as "Puzzi." Anonymous plaquette, ca. 1836.

Arriving from:	Doubt
En route for:	Truth
Place of birth:	Parnassus
Profession:	Musician-philosopher

Beneath it was an entry in George Sand's hand:

Names of travellers:	Piffoël family
Domicile:	Nature
Arriving from:	God
En route for:	Heaven
Place of birth:	Europe
Occupation:	Loafers
Date of passport:	Eternity
Issued by:	Public Opinion

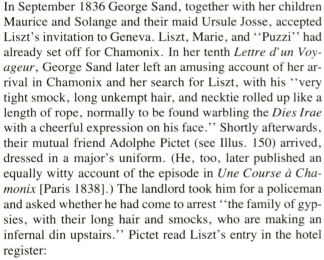

150 Liszt, Marie d'Agoult, and Adolphe Pictet engage in a philosophical discussion in Chamonix. Caricature by George Sand, September 1836.

151 George Sand (left) and Marie d'Agoult in a theatre box on 22 November 1836. Watercolour by Mme Edouard Odier de la Borde, 1836.

LIFE

28 January: First of four chamber music recitals at the Salons Erard with the violinist Chrétien Urhan and the cellist Alexander Batta. The chief works performed are by Beethoven, but Liszt also plays *Études* by Chopin and Moscheles and a number of his own compositions.

2 February: Marie d'Agoult moves to Nohant to spend the next six months with George Sand.

4, 11, and 18 February: Three more chamber music recitals in the Salons Erard.

Liszt publishes various articles written in collaboration with Marie d'Agoult. His chief reading matter is works by his friend Pierre-Simon Ballanche. In February he first hears the pianist Sigismond Thalberg. Paris is divided into supporters of Thalberg and those of Liszt.

March: Liszt spends a few days in Nohant.

9 and 18 March: Minor appearances in Paris.

12 March: Thalberg gives a concert at the Conservatoire.

19 March: Liszt performs at the Grand Opéra before an audience of 3000: ''When the curtain rose and we saw this famous young man, so pale and thin, appear all alone on the stage with only his piano, a kind of fear came over us and our entire sympathy was directed at this noble folly [. . .]; by the fifth bar the battle was already half won . . .'', wrote Ernest Legouvé in the *Gazette musicale*, No. 13, 26 March 1837.

31 March: Liszt and Thalberg appear together in the salons of the Princess Belgiojoso. The occasion gives rise to the *bon mot* ''Thalberg is the first pianist in the world – Liszt is the only one.''

9 April: For the first time Liszt plays unpublished *Études* by Chopin (op. 25) at the Salons Erard (see Illus. 163).

13 and 23 April: Minor appearances at the Salons Pape and Salons du Prytanée.

May to 24 July: Liszt and Marie d'Agoult with George Sand in Nohant. Transcriptions of Beethoven's Symphonies Nos. 5 and 6, together with piano versions of Schubert Lieder.

24 July: Liszt and Marie d'Agoult leave Nohant and travel to Geneva via Lyons (where they stay for some time, including a concert on 2 August for the victims of the Workers' Revolt), Mâcon (where they visit Lamartine), Chambéry (in the company of Louis de Ronchaud), and, by way of a detour, the Grande Chartreuse.

17 August: They arrive on Lake Maggiore.

6 September to end of November: They stay in ''a delicious little inn'' at Bellaggio on Lake Como. Liszt works, in the main, on his *Grandes Études*.

Early December: The couple moves to Como (Hotel dell'Angelo). Liszt pays frequent visits to Milan.

3 December: Concert appearance in Milan.

10 December: Grand concert at La Scala.

24 December: Cosima Liszt born in Como.

WORKS

24 Grandes Études (for piano). Only twelve were published. Revised version of the 1826 *Études* and first version of the *Études d'exécution transcendante* that appeared in 1852. Pub. 1839. See Illus. 219. No. 4 (*Mazeppa*) had been written previously, in 1834. In an edition by Ricordi, Nos. 8–12 are dedicated to Chopin.

Dante Sonata (for piano). First draft. Revised in 1840 and again in 1849. Pub. 1858.

Hexaméron. Variations on a March from Bellini's

Princess Belgiojoso was one of the most remarkable women of the nineteenth century. Visitors to her grotesquely furnished apartments in the Rue d'Anjou (the scene of the ''contest'' between Thalberg and Liszt) included Dumas, Heine, and Musset, who all remarked on her black bed placed, altar-like, on a pedestal and flanked by silver candlesticks, and on her collection of decoratively displayed human skulls.[45]

Restlessly active in political and literary circles, the Princess was taught piano for a time by Bellini and had singing lessons from Giuditta Pasta. On her invitations she was often proud to announce, ''Monsieur Liszt will play.'' Her surviving letters to Liszt (who dedicated his *Réminiscences des ''Puritains''* and his *Hexaméron* [Illus. 161] to her) cover a period of over thirty years and confirm her great admiration for him.

Like her good friends Garibaldi and Mazzini, Christina Belgiojoso was driven into exile in 1849, and it was from Constantinople that she dispatched her famous *Souvenirs dans l'exil* to Paris. Granted an amnesty in 1856, the ardently patriotic Princess founded the journal *Italia*, having already founded both the *Gazetta italiana* and the weekly *Ausonia* in 1843. She wrote for the *Revue des Deux Mondes*, and left a number of other works including *Scènes de la vie turque*, *Asia Mineure et Syrie*, and a four-volume *Essai sur la formation du dogme catholique*.

After being stabbed in the neck by a servant whom she had dismissed from her service, she was condemned to spend the rest of her life carrying her head bent upon her breast, as if in mourning.[46]

THE LISZT-THALBERG PIANO DUEL

During the first half of 1837 the rivalry between Liszt and Thalberg was the main topic of discussion in Paris. In other musical capitals, too, the question as to which of them was the greater pianist refused to go away (see p. 141).

There were lively debates in the press. Liszt had expressed his disappointment at a number of Thalberg's pieces, including the Fantasy on Rossini's *Mosè in Egitto* op. 22 and two *Caprices* opp. 15 and 19, in an article published in the *Gazette musicale* of 8 January 1837. François-Joseph Fétis (1784–1871), the most famous musical scholar of the time, immediately reproached Liszt for having "stood still" in the development of piano playing. His open letter ran to five full pages in the *Gazette musicale* (No. 17, 23 April 1837) and ended with a direct assault on Liszt: "You are the product of a school that has outlived itself and has nothing to look forward to. You are not the creator of a new school. That man is Thalberg; this is the whole difference between you two!"

Rarely in the history of music has there been a more glaring error of judgement. Liszt, whom Berlioz had described less than twelve months earlier as the representative of a "great new school of piano playing" and the "pianist of the future" (see p. 86) rebutted Fétis's attack in a further press article, arguing that "time will tell which of us is wrong and which is right."

Time has indeed provided the answer. Liszt became the leader of a new school and has gone down in musical history as an innovator. Scarcely a note of Thalberg's music is heard any longer.

The Liszt-Thalberg concert took place in Princess Belgiojoso's salons on 31 March 1837, an encounter blown up by the press as a "duel" and a "contest of strength between Carthage and Rome." The oft-quoted final verdict – "Thalberg is the first pianist in the world; Liszt is the only one" – is generally attributed to Princess Belgiojoso, but its author was in fact Marie d'Agoult.

Liszt to Marie d'Agoult (20 March 1840): "They have been quoting your *mot* about Thalberg and me, namely that he is the first and I am the only pianist. Schumann is not pleased with this and asserts that I am both the first and the only one . . ."[47]

*** On annonce une œuvre de charité qui aura lieu à la fois au profit des riches dilettanti et des Italiens indigents. C'est un concert qui sera donné le vendredi 31 mars, dans les salons de la princesse de Belgiojoso. On y entendra les artistes les plus distingués que nous possédions et quelques amateurs dignes du nom glorieux d'artistes. Mais le plus puissant intérêt de cette réunion, la plus attractive de toutes les influences, sera sans contredit le concert simultané de deux talents dont la rivalité agite en ce moment le monde musical, et tient la balance indécise entre Rome et Carthage: MM. Liszt et Thalberg occuperont tour à tour le piano.

152 Announcement (reproduced at original size) in the *Gazette musicale*, No. 13, 26 March 1837, informing its readers of a "contest between Rome and Carthage," i.e. Liszt and Thalberg. (For a translation of the text, see p. 335.)

Opposite page:
153 Princess Christina Belgiojoso (1808–1871). Pencil drawing by Théodore Chassériau, 1847.

154

156

158

159

I Puritani (for piano), by Liszt, Thalberg, Pixis, Herz, Czerny, Chopin. Introduction (theme), second variation, interludes, and finale by Liszt. Pub. 1837. See Illus. 161. A version for piano and orchestra (not orchestrated by Liszt) also exists.

Soirées musicales (piano transcriptions of twelve songs by Rossini): 1. *La Promessa*, 2. *La Regata Veneziana*, 3. *L'Invito*, 4. *La Gita in Gondola*, 5. *Il Rimprovero*, 6. *La Pastorella dell'Alpi*, 7. *La Partenza*, 8. *La Pesca*, 9. *La Danza [Tarantella Napolitana]*, 10. *La Serenata*, 11. *L'Orgia*, 12. *Li Marinari*. Pub. 1838. No. 2 also exists in a version for two pianos, not necessarily by Liszt. Date of publication unknown.

Symphonies Nos. 5, 6, and 7 (Beethoven) (piano transcriptions). Pub. 1840.

Grand Duo concertant sur la Romance de M. Lafont "Le Marin" (for violin and piano). Pub. 1852.

Ouverture du "Roi Lear" (Berlioz) (piano transcription). Pub. Liszt Society, London, 1987.

Esmeralda (opera by Louise Bertin) (vocal score). Pub. 1837. The piano transcription of the *Air de Quasimodo* and three other pieces was published separately, also in 1837. It is unclear whether Liszt himself was responsible for this extensive piece of work or merely supervised its completion, but the vocal score appeared under his name. (The orchestral score appeared under Berlioz's name.)

Marie-Poème. Incomplete. In private collection of J. Pierre, Paris.

WRITINGS:

Articles and travelogues published in the *Revue et Gazette musicale de Paris*:

Thalberg's "Grande Fantaisie" op. 22 and "Caprices" Nos. 1 and 2, op. 15 and op. 19 (2). Pub. in *Gazette musicale*, No. 2, 8 January 1837.

To Professor Fétis. Pub. in *Gazette musicale*, No. 20, 14 May 1837.

On Meyerbeer's "Les Huguenots" (it has not been possible to find this article in any issue of the *Gazette musicale* for 1837).

On C. V. Alkan's Piano Works (Trois morceaux dans le genre pathétique). Pub. in *Gazette musicale*, No. 43, 22 October 1837.

Robert Schumann's Piano Compositions op. 5, op. 11, op. 14. Pub. in *Gazette musicale*, No. 46, 12 November 1837.

Letters from a Bachelor of Music:

To George Sand (January 1837). Pub. in *Gazette musicale*, No. 7, 12 February 1837.

To George Sand (30 April 1837). Pub. in *Gazette musicale*, No. 29, 16 July 1837 (see pp. 94–5).

To Adolphe Pictet (September 1837). Pub. in *Gazette musicale*, No. 6, 11 February 1838.

To Louis de Ronchaud (September 1837). Pub. in *Gazette musicale*, No. 12, 25 March 1838.

To Louis de Ronchaud. On Lake Como (October 1837). Pub. in *Gazette musicale*, No. 29, 22 July 1838.

154 Franz Liszt. Caricature, 1842.
155 Sigismond Thalberg. Caricature, ca. 1840.
156 Franz Liszt. Photograph by Haase, 1860.
157 Sigismond Thalberg. Photograph, ca. 1860.
158 Franz Liszt. Photograph by Petit, 1866.
159 Sigismond Thalberg. Photograph by Nadar, ca. 1866.

160 Sigismond Thalberg (1812–1871). Lithograph by Josef Kriehuber, 1838.

In the years around 1840 Thalberg was accounted the most famous pianist in Europe after Liszt. He wrote the first variation of the *Hexaméron*, and his fame is attested not least by the size of the letters in which his name appears on the title page (see Illus. 161). The incomparably more significant figure of Chopin kept such a low profile as a pianist at this time that when the critic Ernest Legouvé urged him to give concerts in 1838 he wrote, ''And if the question ever resurfaces as to who is the leading pianist in Europe, whether it be Liszt or Thalberg, then the whole world must reply – as all would reply who have heard you play –: 'It is Chopin'.''

HEXAMÉRON.

MORCEAU DE CONCERT.

Grandes

VARIATIONS DE BRAVOURE

pour Piano

sur la

Marche des PURITAINS de Bellini.

Composées

pour le Concert de M.me la Princesse Belgiojoso au Bénéfice des pauvres

par M.M.

LISZT, THALBERG,

PIXIS, HENRI HERZ, CZERNY et CHOPIN.

Propriété des Éditeurs.

N.° 7700.   Enrégistré dans   l'Archive de l'Union.   Prix $\frac{f\,3.-C.M}{fl\,2.-}$

Vienne, chez Tob. Haslinger,

Marchand de Musique etc. de la Cour I. et Roy.
Graben N.° 618.

Paris, chez B.Latte.   Londres, chez M.Mori.

161 *Hexaméron*: Variations on a March from *I Puritani*. Title page of the first edition of 1837.

In 1837 Liszt, Thalberg, Pixis, Henri Herz, Czerny, and Chopin each wrote a variation on the March from Bellini's opera, a piece which was very popular at the time. To Liszt we owe the piano version of the theme, the second variation, the interludes, and the finale. No work appeared more often on his concert programmes during his years as a virtuoso than the *Hexaméron*. He also played it on a number of occasions in a version for piano and orchestra. The piece has now disappeared from the concert hall, and not even the sixth variation by Chopin, the jewel of the entire work, has succeeded in rescuing it from oblivion.

162 Boulevard des Italiens, Paris. Watercolour
by Mozin, ca. 1830.

Following their return from Geneva, Liszt,
and Marie d'Agoult lived at the Hôtel de France
(now demolished) in the Rue Laffitte, one of the
streets running off the Boulevard des Italiens.
They had rooms on the first floor and shared a
salon with George Sand, who had rented a room
on the mezzanine. They were soon receiving
regular visits from Heine, Balzac, Mickiewicz,
Lamennais, Eugène Sue, Berlioz, Rossini, and
other celebrities.

A few steps away, at 5 (later 38) Rue de la
Chaussée-d'Antin, there lived the only pianist
who was Liszt's equal at this time, Frédéric
Chopin. It was in Liszt's and Marie d'Agoult's
salon that George Sand first heard her future
lover.

163 Programme for a concert in the Salons
Erard, Paris, on 9 April 1837.

Liszt played several of the as yet unpublished
Études op. 25 by Chopin.

164 Frédéric Chopin, *Douze Études*, op. 25.
Title page of the first German edition, 1837.

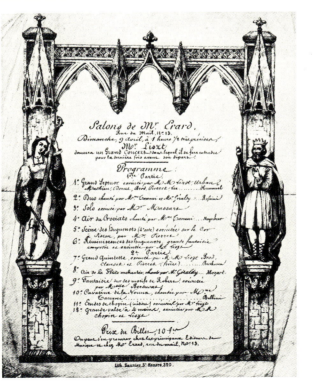

92

165 Frédéric Chopin. Oil painting
by Ary Scheffer, 1847.

166 Franz Liszt. Oil painting
by Ary Scheffer, 1837.

167 Comtesse Marie d'Agoult.
Oil painting by Henri Lehmann,
1839.

Chopin honoured her by
dedicating his *Douze Études*,
op. 25, to her. (Various passages
in letters of the period prove
that Lehmann did not begin work
on this portrait until 1839.
The date ''1838'' on the original
was presumably added in error
at a later stage.)

168 George Sand. Oil painting by
Charpentier, 1837.

169 Heinrich Heine. Oil painting by Moritz D. Oppenheim, 1831.

170 Franz Liszt. Oil painting by F. von Amerling, May 1838.

Heinrich Heine on Liszt, Paris 1837. An extract from Heine's tenth letter "On the French Stage" addressed to August Lewald and published in volume 4 of Heine's collection of critical essays *Der Salon*:

"Liszt has the greatest elective affinity with Berlioz, and he knows best how to execute the latter's music. I do not need to speak of his talent; his fame extends throughout Europe. There is no disputing that as an artist he finds his most unquestioning enthusiasts in Paris, but also his most zealous antagonists. It is significant, surely, that no one speaks of him with indifference. Only the man who has positive merit can arouse the passions of benevolence or hostility in this world, for fire is needed to inflame other people, be it to hatred or to love. The finest evidence in Liszt's defence is the undivided respect with which even his enemies recognize his personal merit. He is a man of eccentric but noble character, selfless and without guile. He is of a highly remarkable turn of mind; he has a profound predisposition towards speculation, and he is interested less in the interests of his art than in the investigations of various schools whose concern it is to solve the great problem encompassing heaven and earth. He was long an ardent supporter of Saint-Simonist views, then his mind was clouded by Ballanche's spiritualistic or, rather, vaporistic ideas, and now he raves about the republican Catholic teachings of a man like Lamennais [. . .]"

Liszt's reply to Heine's attacks (excerpt from a letter written in Venice on 15 April 1838 and published in the *Gazette musicale*, No. 27, 8 July 1838):

"[. . .] If criticism is addressed to me as an artist, I agree with it or reject it, but in neither case will it hurt me; but if it seeks to judge me as a person, each of its words assails my highly irritable sensibility. I am still too young, and my heart still beats too powerfully for me to suffer a hand to be placed on that heart by anyone wanting to measure the rate at which it beats. What I admire, what I hate, and what I hope for – that is so deeply rooted within my soul that it would be hard to lay it bare. Attempts have often been made to do so, attempts undertaken with hostile intent – I answered by saying nothing. You yourself do the same today, acting with the hand of a friend – and it is as a friend that I answer you.

"You say that my character 'sits badly,' . . . and as proof of this you list many matters which, as you claim, I have taken up with great eagerness: the 'riding-stables of philosophy' from which I am said to have chosen one hobby-horse after another. But tell me, in the name of justice and fairness, should not this accusation, which you level at me and at me alone, be laid at the feet of our whole generation? Am I alone in 'sitting badly' in the age in which we live? Notwithstanding our beautiful gothic armchairs and our cushions à la Voltaire, do we not all sit 'very badly' between a past which we refuse to acknowledge and a future which we cannot yet know? [. . .]

"It is true that you have always been far better able than I to dispense with the cross at Golgotha, and yet you emphatically rejected the excuse of being one of those who set it up for him who redeemed the world. – And what do you

say to the Jacobin bonnet? If we look hard enough, shall we really not find it in your wardrobe? Are you sure? – perhaps just a little faded, a little used and, above all, a little ashamed at finding itself in the company of a no longer quite fashionable dressing-gown and a pair of slippers with holes in them?"

Finally even Heine capitulated before Liszt's compelling artistry. In 1841 he wrote about Liszt in *Lutezia*:

"That we are almost drowning in music here, that there is barely a single house where, ark-like, one can escape from this flood of sound, that the noble art of music overwhelms our entire lives – this I regard as a serious sign, and I am often overcome by a sense of ill-humour which degenerates into the most morose injustice towards our great maestros and virtuosos. In the circumstances, it would be wrong to expect me to adopt an excessively cheerful tone in singing the praises of a man whom the *beau monde*, and more especially the hysterical world of women, is currently acclaiming with insane enthusiasm and who is, indeed, one of the most remarkable representatives of the musical movement. I mean Franz Liszt, the brilliant pianist. Yes, the brilliant artist is here again and is giving concerts which exert a magic that borders upon the fantastic. All other pianists pale beside him – all, that is, apart from one, apart from Chopin, the Raphael of the fortepiano. Indeed, all other pianists whom we have heard this year at innumerable concerts are, with this single exception, mere piano players whose brilliance consists in the skill with which they handle the well-strung wood. In Liszt's case, by contrast, one no longer thinks of the difficulty which is being overcome, for the piano disappears and music itself stands revealed [. . .]"

Liszt's letter to George Sand of 30 April 1837 was published in the *Gazette musicale*, No. 29, 16 July 1837. The complete text runs to four times the length of the following abridged extract:

"[. . .] The poet, the painter, or the sculptor accomplishes his work in the quiet of his own studio, and when it is finished he finds libraries to disseminate it and museums to exhibit it; there is no need of any intercession between the work of art and its judges, whereas the composer is obliged by necessity to resort to interpreters who, through their incompetence or indifference, make him suffer the ordeals of a rendition which, however faithful to the letter, reveals only imperfectly the thought behind the work and the genius of its creator. Or – if the composer himself be a performing artist, how rarely is he understood, how much more frequently does it happen that he exposes the turbulent depths of his innermost being to a cold and mocking public, being forced, as it were, to tear his soul from his breast in order to wring some applause from the absent-minded masses! Only by dint of supreme exertions does the white-hot flame of his inspiration cast its pale shadow over these icy brows, only thus can he kindle dull sparks in loveless, unsympathetic hearts.

"I have often been told that I have less right than any other man to give vent to such complaints, inasmuch as, ever since childhood, success has repeatedly outstripped my talent and my wishes. Yet it is precisely this, the thunderous applause, which has convinced me in the saddest way possible that such acclaim has been directed at the inscrutability of fashion, at respect for a great name, and at a certain energetic rendition, rather than at a genuine feeling for truth and beauty. There is more than ample proof of this. – While still a child, I often amused myself by playing mischievous schoolboy pranks, and my audience never failed to fall into the trap. For example, I played the selfsame piece as a work of Beethoven's, Czerny's, and mine. On the day when I presented it as my own, I earned the most encouraging applause: 'It's not at all bad for a boy of his age!' people said; on the day when I played it under Czerny's name, people barely listened; if I played it under Beethoven's authority, I knew I was certain of universal acclaim.

"The name of 'Beethoven' recalls another incident, which occurred at a later date, but which serves all too well to confirm my opinion of our musical audiences' artistic competence. You know that the Conservatoire orchestra has been engaged for some years in public performances of Beethoven's symphonies. His reputation is now universally recognized; the most ignorant of the ignorant entrench themselves behind this mighty name, and impotent envy uses it as a club to beat the contemporary who dares to raise his head. In order to complement the Conservatoire's plan I devoted (albeit most inadequately through lack of time) a number of musical divertissements in the course of last winter almost exclusively to the performance of Beethoven duets and quintets. I was almost certain to inspire boredom, and was just as firmly convinced that no one would dare to admit as much. And indeed, what followed were such dazzling displays of enthusiasm that one could easily have allowed oneself to be deceived into thinking that the audience submits to genius, if this illusion had not been wholly destroyed by a change to the programme on one of the final evenings. Without the audience's being informed, a trio by Pixis was played in place of one by Beethoven. The cries of 'bravo' were more frenzied and numerous than ever; but when Beethoven's trio was performed in the place intended for the one by Pixis, it was found to be cold, mediocre, and boring. Indeed, there were even people who fled the hall, declaring it highly impertinent of Herr Pixis to presume to perform his own work immediately after a masterpiece.

"Far be it from me to assert that the applause which Herr Pixis earned was undeserved by him. But even he could not have responded without a sorrowful smile to applause on the part of an audience which was capable of confusing two works of such totally different styles. It is certain that people who are capable of such a misunderstanding are wholly impervious to the beauties of his work. [. . .]

"I confess that I expected little good of Herr Thalberg's compositions when I heard them praised by people in a way which made it clear that every one of his predecessors, whether Hummel, Moscheles, Kalkbrenner, Bertini, or Chopin, had been hurtled into oblivion through the very fact that he himself had appeared on the scene. I finally grew impatient to get to know these new and profound works for myself – works, moreover, which would allegedly reveal to me a man of genius. I shut myself away for an entire morning in order to study them conscientiously. The outcome of my study was exactly the opposite of what I had expected.

One thing alone astonished me: how such mediocre and insignificant compositions had generally created the effect which they had. From this I concluded that the composer's performing talent must be truly exceptional. I expressed this view in the *Gazette musicale*, without any other aim save that which I have demonstrated on many other occasions: to express my opinion, good or bad, on piano compositions which I had taken the trouble to study. On this occasion it was less than ever my aim to seek to influence or disparage public opinion. I am far from wishing to arrogate to myself so impertinent a right, but I believed that I might be allowed to speak unhindered and say that if this was the new school I was not a part of it; that if Herr Thalberg was taking this new direction I did not feel called upon to go the same way; and, finally, that I could discover no future embryo in his ideas which others should take the pains to develop.

"What I said there I said with regret and, as it were, constrained by a public which had set itself the task of setting the two of us up in competition like two runners competing in an arena for the same prize. I may also have been persuaded to take up my pen and express my opinion in public by a feeling, innate in many persons, which reacts against all acts of injustice and, at even the least provocation, inveighs against error or false belief. Having communicated my views to the general public, I repeated them to the composer himself when we later met. I was pleased to be able to praise his fine performing skill, and to praise it loudly; and he understood more than anyone else what was loyal and liberal about my behaviour. We were now proclaimed as being 'reconciled,' a theme that was soon as stupidly and long-windedly varied as our so-called 'enmity' had been earlier. – In truth there was neither enmity nor reconciliation between us. Are those men enemies if an artist denies to another that quality which the mass immoderately ascribes to him? Are they then reconciled who, above and beyond all questions of art, esteem and respect one another? [. . .]"

171 George Sand. Oil painting by Eugène Delacroix, ca. 1835.

In response to an invitation from George Sand, Liszt and Marie d'Agoult spent the months from May to July 1837 at Nohant.

Liszt worked on his transcriptions of Beethoven's Symphonies Nos. 5 and 6, and completed several transcriptions of Schubert Lieder. George Sand, who generally wrote at night, worked on her novel *Mauprat*.

Her *Journal de Piffoël* contains the following entries for June 1837: "... Arabella's room [i.e. Marie d'Agoult's] is on the ground floor beneath my own. There is space there for Franz's beautiful piano. Beneath my window, with its curtain of green linden branches, notes well out which the whole world would be happy to hear but which here excite only the envy of nightingales. What a magnificent artist, sublime in all that is great and always transcending whatever is trivial – yet oppressed and assailed by some secret pain. Happy man, to be loved by a beautiful, magnanimous, intelligent, and pure woman. What more do you want, you ungrateful man! Oh, if only I were loved like that . . . !''

Marie d'Agoult and her lover left on 24 July 1837. An entry in her *Journal intime* for this same day reveals certain doubts but also a sense of relief: "... I have realized how childish of me it was to believe (and this thought has often filled me with deep sadness) that she alone [George Sand] could have brought true fulfilment to Franz's life, and that I was an unfortunate obstacle in the way of two destinies whose fate it was to merge with each other and complement one another.''

172 Maison Nohant, George Sand's country house. Photograph, 1975.

173 The salon at Nohant, unchanged to this day. Photograph, 1970.

174 Liszt and George Sand. Watercolour by Maurice Sand, ca. 1837.

ÉVENTAIL
GEORGE SAND et ses AMIS en 1838
CHARGÉS par CHARPENTIER et paysage
peint par GEORGE SAND

175 George Sand with her friends. Fan, 1838. The figures were painted by Charpentier, the landscape by George Sand.

In the centre of the picture is Delacroix, with Liszt to the left of him and George Sand to the right. Chopin is portrayed as an exotic bird which she holds tethered to her hand (she had recently made his acquaintance). The artist Calamatta is depicted as a snake, the actor Bocage as a faun, Maurice Sand as Zephyrus, and Solange Sand as a lion. To the right of George Sand is Mallefille, with Grzymala sitting beside the tree on the right, in front of Charpentier. Michel de Bourges is seen holding a pistol, next to Enrico, and the remaining figures on the left of the picture are Didier (wearing a red cloak), Arago (in the water), and Bonnechose (wearing red trousers).

176 George Sand. Photograph by Nadar, ca. 1865.

177 Gioacchino Rossini (1792–1868). Steel engraving, 1849.

In 1837 Liszt transcribed twelve vocal works by Rossini for the piano under the title of *Soirées Musicales*, and in 1838 wrote his paraphrase of the *William Tell* Overture, a showpiece of his virtuoso years.

178 Gioacchino Rossini. Photograph by Nadar, ca. 1855.

179 Milan, view of the town and interior of La Scala. Steel engraving, ca. 1840.

In December 1837 and February 1838 Liszt gave two concerts in the 3000-seat La Scala Theatre, Milan. He later wrote an article about the theatre for the *Revue et Gazette musicale* (see Illus. 199).

180 Title page of the first edition of Liszt's Fantasia *La Pastorella dell'Alpi e li Marinari*, on themes by Rossini.

Liszt spent a considerable part of the winter of 1837/38 in Milan, where he visited various friends, including Rossini, Ferdinand Hiller, and Johann Peter Pixis.

Liszt and the Comtesse d'Agoult spent the months of September and October 1837 on Lake Como. They visited the Villa Melzi at Bellaggio, went on excursions into the mountains, and sailed out on to the lake in the evening.

Liszt wrote prolifically and gave a number of concerts in Milan. In an open letter to Lambert Massart, he reported:

"My first concert I gave in the 'Teatro della Scala,' which, as you know, is one of the largest in the world . . . To tell the truth, I must have cut a curious figure there – I, so thin, so *étriqué*, alone with my trusty Erard . . ."

For an Italian audience, addicted to opera and singing, a concert made up of piano music must have seemed unusual, and when Liszt played one of his new studies, described in the programme as a *studio*, one of the members of the audience shouted to him, "Vengo al teatro per divertirmi e non per studiare!" (I come to the theatre to enjoy myself, not to study).[48]

When, at another concert, Liszt asked for suggestions of themes on which he might improvise, he opened the envelopes which had been submitted to find such motifs as "The Milan Cathedral," "The Railway" (recently invented) and, finally, "Is it better to marry or remain a bachelor?" The final theme he answered orally: "Whatever conclusion one comes to, whether to marry or remain single, one will always repent it."[49]

In a letter of September 1837 Liszt replied to Adolphe Pictet's question whether he would prefer to abandon his career as a virtuoso and devote himself to orchestral composition. His answer attests to his passionate love of the piano: "You have unwittingly touched on a very sensitive point with me; you do not know that to speak to me of giving up my piano would be to announce a day of mourning, robbing me of the light which illuminated all my early life and which has grown to be inseparable from it. For, you see, my piano is to me what his vessel is to the sailor, what his horse is to the Arab – nay more! Until now it has been my very self, my speech, my life! It is the keeper of all that stirred my nature in the passionate days of my youth; to it do I entrust all my wishes and dreams, my joys, and my sorrows. Its strings vibrated to my emotions, and its keys have obeyed my every caprice!

Would you have me abandon it and pursue more brilliant and resounding triumphs on stage or in the orchestra? Oh no! Even were I competent to write music of that kind – which you are undoubtedly premature in assuming to be so – even then it would remain my firm resolve not to abandon the study and development of piano playing until such time as I had done everything possible, everything that it is now possible for me to achieve."[50]

181 Bellaggio on Lake Como. Steel engraving by G. A. Müller, 1834.

182 Villa Melzi in Bellaggio. Photograph, ca. 1930.

183 Cosima Liszt, wife of Hans von Bülow and later of Richard Wagner. Photograph, ca. 1860.
Cosima was born in Como on 24 December 1837; she died in Bayreuth on 1 April 1930.

184 Franz Liszt. Watercolour by
Carl Hartmann, Nuremberg,
11 October 1843.

"Concert tours:
Paris, London, Berlin, Petersburg, etc.:
fantasias, transcriptions,
living like a lord"

LIFE

January: Liszt in Milan. Marie d'Agoult stays behind in Como, but joins Liszt later. He performs frequently in the salons of the Countesses Samoyloff and Jamaglio. He completes his *Twelve Études* and visits Hiller, Pixis, Nourrit, and the soprano Giuditta Pasta, all of whom are staying in Milan. Most of his time, however, is spent with Rossini, whose *Soirées musicales* he transcribes for piano in 1837/38.

18 February: Concert in Milan (see Illus. 186).

15 March: Concert in Milan.

16 March: Liszt and Marie d'Agoult travel to Venice via Brescia and Verona. Two concerts, in the Hall of the Società Apollinex and the Teatro San Benedetto. Because of devastating floods in Hungary, Liszt decides to offer his help with charity concerts.

7 April: Liszt leaves for Vienna. Marie remains in Venice. Liszt writes to her every day.

11 April to 27 May: Eleven concerts in Vienna (for programmes and dates, see p. 104). His success, according to his own testimony, persuades him to embark on a virtuoso career. He is enthusiastically acclaimed by both press and public.

27 May: As Liszt departs for Venice, some of his Viennese admirers form a farewell party in his honour (see Illus. 200).

1 June: Liszt returns to Venice. Marie's pleasure at seeing him again is mixed with jealousy at the infatuation which her lover inspires in other women.

July: In Genoa.

August: Liszt and Marie d'Agoult in Lugano.

September: Liszt in Milan until mid-September; Marie briefly in Como.

End of September to beginning of October: Guest of the Duke of Modena in Cattajo. Performs for the Austrian emperor and empress, who are staying there.

October: Liszt and the Comtesse tour Upper Italy.

November: Liszt and Marie settle in Florence. Friendship with Lorenzo Bartolini, who sculpts marble busts of the couple (see p. 110). Compositional activity and a handful of concerts in the vicinity of Florence.

8 and 17 November: Concerts in Florence.

12 and 16 December: Concerts in Florence.

25 and 29 December: Concerts in Bologna.

185 Venice, the Piazzetta. Steel engraving, ca. 1840.
It was at the Café Florian in the Piazza San Marco that Liszt learned of the devastating Danube floods in Hungary. Without a moment's hesitation he decided to lend his assistance through a series of charity concerts.

186 Programme for a concert given by Liszt at La Scala, Milan, on 18 February 1838.

187 The 1838 floods in Pest. Contemporary illustration.

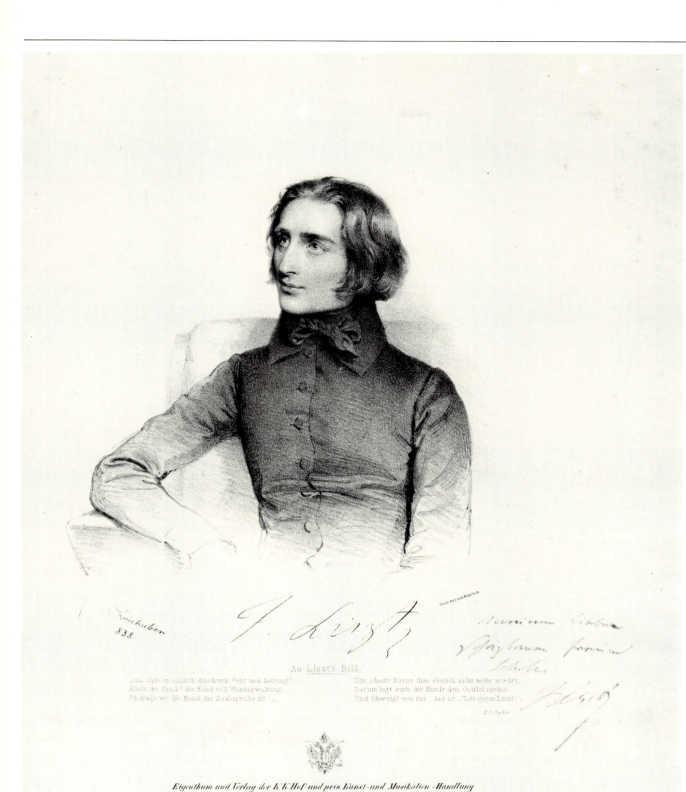

WORKS

Études d'exécution transcendante d'après Paganini (for piano). Pub. 1840/41. First version of the *Grandes Études de Paganini* published in 1851.

Mélodies hongroises (piano transcription for two hands of parts of Schubert's *Divertissement à la hongroise* for four hands). Pub. 1840 (see Illus. 195).

Schwanengesang (14 Schubert Lieder) (piano transcriptions). Written 1838, although some of the transcriptions may date from 1837 or 1839. Pub. 1840 (see Illus. 192).

12 Lieder (Schubert) (piano transcriptions): 1. *Sei mir gegrüßt*, 2. *Auf dem Wasser zu singen*, 3. *Du bist die Ruh*, 4. *Erlkönig*, 5. *Meeresstille*, 6. *Die junge Nonne*, 7. *Frühlingsglaube*, 8. *Gretchen am Spinnrade*, 9. *Ständchen* (''*Horch, horch! Die Lerch*''), 10. *Rastlose Liebe*, 11. *Der Wanderer* (''*Ich komme vom Gebirge her*''), 12. *Ellens Gesang III*. Written 1837/38. Pub. 1838.

Lob der Thränen (Schubert) (piano transcription). Pub. 1838 (see Illus. 193).

Der Gondelfahrer (Schubert) (piano transcription). Pub. 1838.

Soirées italiennes (six piano pieces on motives by Mercadante): 1. *La Primavera*, 2. *Il Galop*, 3. *Il Pastore Svizzero*, 4. *La Serenata del Marinaro*, 5. *Il Brindisi*, 6. *La Zingarella Spagnola*. Pub. 1839.

Grand Galop chromatique (for piano). Pub. 1838 (for two hands and for four hands).

Ouverture de l'opéra ''Guillaume Tell'' (Rossini) (piano transcription). Pub. 1842.

Nuits d'Été à Pausilippe (songs by Donizetti) (piano transcription): 1. *Barcajuolo*, 2. *L'Alito di Bice*, 3. *La Torre di Biasone*. Pub. 1839.

Tre Sonetti di Petrarca (for high voice and piano). Pub. 1847. A second version, for low voice (1865), appeared in 1883. Also from this period (1838/39) dates a version for piano alone (pub. 1846); a second version for piano appeared in 1858. A version of Sonnet 104 for piano duet (''Notturno'') has also been published.

Sposalizio and *Il Penseroso* (for piano). Written 1838/39. Pub. 1858.

WRITINGS:

Letters from a Bachelor of Music:

To Maurice Schlesinger. La Scala (10 March 1838). Pub. in *Gazette musicale*, No. 21, 27 May 1838 (see Illus. 199).

To Heinrich Heine (15 April 1838). Pub. in *Gazette musicale*, No. 27, 8 July 1838 (see p. 94).

To Lambert Massart (April and May 1838). Pub. in *Gazette musicale*, No. 35, 2 September 1838.

To Maurice Schlesinger. On the State of Music in Italy (November 1838). Pub. in *Gazette musicale*, No. 2, 13 January 1839.

To M. d'Ortigue. Raphael's Saint Cecilia (October 1838). Pub. in *Gazette musicale*, No. 15, 14 April 1839.

188 Franz Liszt. Lithograph by Josef Kriehuber, April 1838, with a dedication in Liszt's own hand to ''his dear and valued friend Schober.'' Previously unpublished.

Franz von Schober (1796–1882) had been one of Franz Schubert's closest friends and was also a member of Liszt's circle of acquaintances.

On 28 April 1838 Liszt wrote to Marie d'Agoult about this portrait: ''In twenty-four hours 50 copies of my portrait have been sold, but you will not, I hope, insult me by imagining that this has had the least impression on me? . . .''[51]

We learn from Marie d'Agoult's memoirs of the immediate reason for Liszt's decision to give concerts in Vienna: ''One day Franz stormed into my room with an impetuousness very much out of keeping with his usual custom. He was holding a German newspaper in his hand in which he had read of a terrible flood caused by the Danube bursting its banks. [. . .] 'It's dreadful', he said, 'I wish I could send them everything I own.' Then, with a bitter smile, 'But all I own are my ten fingers and my good name . . .' ''[52]

189, 190 Liszt's Vienna concert programmes of 1838.

Liszt arrived in Vienna around 11 April 1838, intending to stay for ten days. In the event he remained in the Austrian capital for six weeks, his concerts arousing boundless enthusiasm and marking the start of his unique career as a virtuoso pianist.

The programmes for all the concerts at which Liszt appeared in Vienna between 18 April and 25 May 1838. According to some writers, the success of these concerts persuaded him to embark on his career as a virtuoso pianist.

18 April 1838: *Konzertstück* in F minor for Piano and Orchestra by Carl Maria von Weber, and Liszt's own *I Puritani* Fantasia, *Grande Valse di Bravura*, and *Étude* in G minor (''Vision''). He also accompanied Beethoven's *Adelaide*.

23 April 1838: The piano part in Hummel's Septet for Piano, Flute, Oboe, Horn, Viola, Cello, and Double Bass, together with his transcriptions of Schubert's *Ständchen* (''Horch, horch'') and *Lob der Thränen*, and his Fantasia on Pacini's *Niobe*.

29 April 1838: Czerny's Sonata in A flat major (first movement and Scherzo); *Études* by Chopin and Moscheles; *La Serenata e l'Orgia* (Fantasia on themes by Rossini); and piano accompaniments to Schubert's *Liebesbotschaft* and *Erlkönig*.

2 May 1838: Beethoven's Sonata in A flat major (op. 26), Liszt's Fantasia on *Les Huguenots*, A flat major Étude (*Ricordanza*), and *Grand Galop chromatique*, together with the piano parts of Schubert's *Der Hirt auf dem Felsen* and *Ständchen*.

6 May 1838: Weber's *Konzertstück* in F minor for Piano and Orchestra. Liszt was called back to the platform no fewer than seven times, ''an unprecedented occurrence in the annals of Vienna's musical life,'' according to the *Allgemeine Theaterzeitung* of 8 May 1838.

8 May 1838: New *Études* by Chopin and Moscheles, together with Liszt's own Fantasia on Halévy's *La Juive* and the *Hexaméron* (Bravura Variations on the March from *I Puritani*) by Liszt, Chopin, Czerny, Herz, Pixis, and Thalberg.

14 May 1838: Beethoven's Sonata in C sharp minor (op. 27 no. 2); two *Études* by Joseph Christoph Kessler (Andante in A flat major and *Oktavenetüde*); Handel's Fugue in E minor; Scarlatti's ''Cat's Fugue''; and the *Hexaméron* (see programme for 8 May) ''by request.''

15 May 1838: Liszt's transcription of Schubert's *Ständchen*, his own *Grande Valse di Bravura*, and (as an encore) his *Grand Galop chromatique*.

At a further concert on 17 May Liszt also played the Polonaise from *I Puritani*, his transcription of Schubert's *Ständchen*, and the *Grande Valse di Bravura*.

18 May 1838: Liszt's *Fantasia on a Swiss Melody*; his transcriptions of Rossini's *Li Marinari* and *La Tarantella*, and Weber's *Invitation to the Dance*; as encores, his Fantasia on Weber's *Invitation* and his transcription of Schubert's *Erlkönig*.

24 May 1838: Hummel's Septet and Rossini's *Li Marinari*; as encores, selections of his own Fantasias.

25 May 1838: Liszt's paraphrase of Rossini's Overture to *William Tell*; his *Rondo (El Contrabandista)*; his transcriptions of Berlioz's ''Ball Scene'' and ''March to the Scaffold''; his transcriptions of Schubert's *Sei mir gegrüßt*, *Erlkönig*, and *Die Post*; and, additionally, his own *Grande Valse di Bravura*.

191 Franz Liszt. Watercolour by Josef Kriehuber, Vienna 1838.

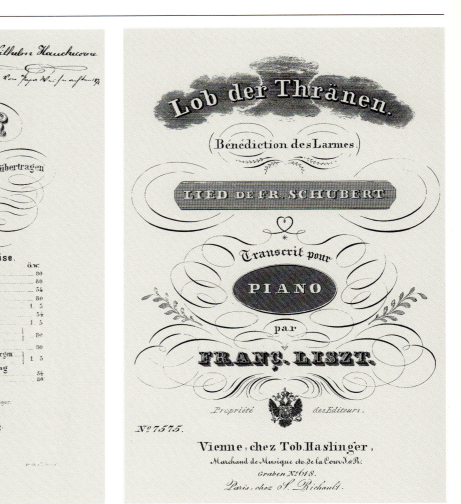

192 Liszt's piano transcriptions of Schubert's *Schwanengesang* and *Winterreise*, written in 1837–39. Title page from an 1840 edition.

193 Title page of the first edition of Liszt's piano transcription of Schubert's *Lob der Thränen*, 1838.

194 *Die Rose*, written in 1833 and published in 1835 (or perhaps as early as 1833); revised in 1838. Title page of an 1840 edition.
  Die Rose is Liszt's first transcription of a Schubert Lied.

195 Title page of Liszt's version for two hands of Schubert's four-handed *Divertissement à la hongroise*, written in 1838 and published in 1840.

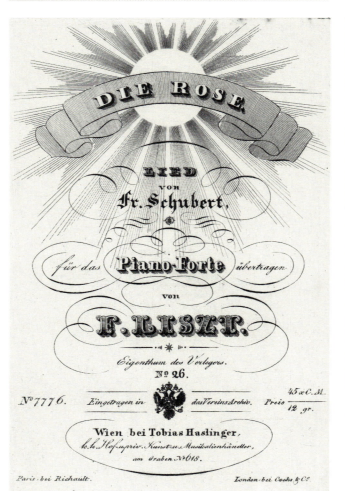

196 Opening bars of the first edition of Liszt's two-handed adaptation of Schubert's third March for four hands, 1847.

197 Franz Schubert. Steel engraving based on a portrait of around 1825.

198 Opening bars of the first edition of Schubert's *Ständchen* ("Leise flehen") in Liszt's piano transcription, written in 1838/39 and published in 1840.

Franz Liszt was the dominant figure in determining nineteenth-century reactions to Schubert's music. Through his piano transcriptions of 56 Schubert Lieder ("In the short space of a single Lied Schubert makes us the spectators of swift and fatal conflicts") he ensured that the composer's name, which around 1835 had barely been heard of outside Vienna, was known throughout the whole of Europe. Even musicians such as Hummel and Hiller were unfamiliar with Schubert's name as late as 1827 when they visited Vienna, the year before the composer's death, and they had certainly not heard a note of his music. Equally hard to believe is the fact that the great song cycles, *Die schöne Müllerin*, *Winterreise*, and even *Schwanengesang*, were scarcely sung by Europe's lyric tenors. Between 1848 and 1861 Liszt prepared orchestral versions of various piano pieces by Schubert, and even his arch-enemy Eduard Hanslick expressed his enthusiasm for them (see p. 257). He first conducted the C major Symphony (D. 944) in 1844, and on 24 June 1854 he gave the first performance of Schubert's opera *Alfonso und Estrella* in Weimar. Nine *Soirées de Vienne*, based on Schubert waltzes, were published in 1853, and in 1870 and 1880 Liszt prepared an edition of Schubert's piano works with Siegmund Lebert, to whom he wrote, "Our pianists scarcely suspect the glorious riches that lie in Schubert's piano compositions."[53] A biography of Schubert, which in 1851 Liszt planned to write in collaboration with Carolyne von Sayn-Wittgenstein, came to nothing. On 19 July 1886, a few days before his death, Liszt played the sixth of the *Soirées de Vienne* in Luxembourg and with it took his leave of the piano, of Schubert, and of his audience.

199 Title page of the *Revue et Gazette musicale* of 27 May 1838, with Liszt's article on La Scala, Milan.

The *Gazette musicale*, founded by Franz Liszt and Maurice Schlesinger in 1834, was the most important music journal in France at this time. It appeared every year until 1880, with the exception of 1870/71 (Franco-Prussian War). Rarely can a journal have had so impressive a roster of illustrious contributors, including Alexandre Dumas, Balzac, Jules Janin, George Sand, François-Joseph Fétis, Joseph d'Ortigue, Ludwig Rellstab, Berlioz, and others. Liszt was one of its most active contributors. The extract reproduced here gives no more than a tenth of the text of Liszt's article.

REVUE
ET
GAZETTE MUSICALE
DE PARIS.

RÉDIGÉE PAR MM. ADAM, G. E. ANDERS, DE BALZAC, F. BENOIST (professeur de composition au Conservatoire), BERTON (membre de l'Institut), BERLIOZ, HENRI BLANCHARD, CASTIL-BLAZE, EDME SAINT-HUGUÉ, ALEX. DUMAS, ELWART, FÉTIS père (maître de chapelle du roi des Belges), F. HALÉVY (membre de l'Institut), JULES JANIN, KASTNER, DE LAFAGE, G. LEPIC, LISZT, MARX, ÉDOUARD MONNAIS, D'ORTIGUE, PANOFKA, RICHARD, L. RELLSTAB (rédacteur de la GAZETTE DE BERLIN), GEORGES SAND, J. G. SEYFRIED (Maître de chapelle à Vienne), STÉPHEN DE LA MADELAINE, J. STRUNZ, etc.

5e ANNÉE. ——— **N° 21.**

PRIX DE L'ABONNEM.

PARIS.	DÉPART.	ÉTRANG
fr.	Fr. c.	Fr. c.
3 m. 8	9 »	10 0
6 m. 15	17 »	19 »
1 an. 30	34 »	38 »

La Revue et Gazette Musicale de Paris
Paraît le DIMANCHE de chaque semaine.

On s'abonne au bureau de la REVUE ET GAZETTE MUSICALE DE PARIS, rue Richelieu, 97; chez MM. les directeurs des Postes, aux bureaux des Messageries, et chez tous les libraires et marchands de musique de France; pour l'Allemagne, à Leipzig, chez KISTNER.
On reçoit les réclamations des personnes qui ont des griefs à exposer, et les avis relatifs à la musique qui peuvent intéresser le public.

PARIS, DIMANCHE 27 MAI 1838.

Nonobstant les suppléments romances, fac-simile, de l'écriture d'auteurs célèbres et la galerie des artistes, MM. les abonnés de la *Gazette musicale* recevront gratuitement, le dernier dimanche de chaque mois, un morceau de musique de piano composé par les auteurs les plus renommés, de 12 à 25 pages d'impression, et du prix marqué de 6 f. à 7 f. 50c.

Les lettres, demandes et envois d'argent doivent être affranchis, et adressés au Directeur, rue Richelieu, 97.

SOMMAIRE. — La Scala, par LISZT. — Séance musicale donnée par les élèves des écoles gratuites, salle Saint-Jean, par Adrien de LA Fage. — Nouvelles.

LA SCALA.

EXTRAIT DES LETTRES D'UN BACHELIER ÈS-MUSIQUE.

Milan, 10 mars.

Le théâtre de la Scala, ouvert en 1778, fut construit d'après les dessins de Piermarini sur l'emplacement de l'ancienne église *Santa-Maria alla Scala;* comme si l'antique serpent, le prince des démons, avait voulu donner un éclatant démenti à la prophétie en posant son pied superbe sur le front brisé de la femme. Je vous ai dit dans ma précédente lettre que la salle est divisée en cinq rangs de loges, non compris la galerie du haut ou *loggione*. Huit cents places distribuées en vingt rangs forment le parterre; le théâtre peut contenir en tout 3,600 personnes. La décoration intérieure va être entièrement renouvelée à l'occasion du couronnement de S. M. l'empereur d'Autriche. C'est une dépense devenue nécessaire : je ne connais rien de plus sale, de plus noir, de plus fétide que les escaliers et les corridors de la Scala, qui est et qui veut être pourtant le premier théâtre du monde.

A Milan on est reconnu pour étranger à cette seule question : Allez-vous ce soir à la Scala? question superflue, oiseuse, inutile, que ne s'adressent jamais les Milanais. Pour eux cela ne fait pas doute; autant vaudrait se demander si l'on vit encore. Hors la Scala point de salut. C'est le lieu de réunion unique, le grand récipient, le véritable centre de gravité de la société milanaise. Quand la Scala se ferme, la société se dissout; on dirait qu'elle a besoin pour exister de l'atmosphère enfumée du théâtre et que le bruit des instruments lui est indispensable pour se dérober à elle-même sa propre nullité. C'est là, dans cet immense vaisseau que se rassemblent chaque soir la société élégante, celle qui l'est moins et celle qui ne l'est pas du tout divisées par rangs de loges, se regardant l'une l'autre à travers l'espace ténébreux qui les sépare. La plupart des loges sont propriété particulière. Cela s'achète comme une maison et le prix varie communément de 20 à 50,000 fr. Quelques-unes sont tendues, meublées et éclairées à l'intérieur comme de petits salons. Chaque femme préside seule dans la sienne et reçoit, durant tout le cours de la représentation, une série de visites auxquelles le mari est obligé de céder de proche en proche la meilleure place; d'où il advient que de visite en visite, de politesse en politesse il se trouve courtoisement mis à la porte. Aussi quelques époux, de ceux qui tiennent à leurs aises, ont-ils

200 Franz Liszt in a travelling coat. Lithograph by Josef Kriehuber (1838), based on a drawing dated 27 May 1838.

When Liszt left Vienna in May 1838, his admirers rode on ahead of him, without his knowledge, to the first mail-coach station at Neudorf, in order to bid him farewell. The artist Josef Kriehuber made a sketch of the composer, entitled "Liszt in a travelling coat," and it was signed by all those present. Kriehuber lithographed the portrait and sent a copy to each of the signatories as a souvenir of the occasion. A comparison with the first known photograph of Liszt (see Illus. 305) reveals this to be one of the most convincing likenesses of the oft-portrayed pianist.

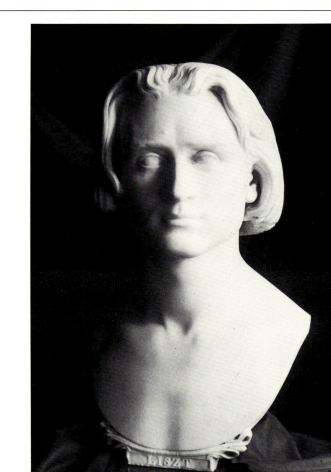

201 Franz Liszt. Marble bust by Lorenzo Bartolini, Florence, begun in 1838 and completed in 1839.

202 Marie d'Agoult. Marble bust by Lorenzo Bartolini, Florence 1839.

203 Lorenzo Bartolini (1777–1850). 1836 steel engraving by Fournier, based on a drawing by Ingres of 1820.

Bartolini became friendly with Liszt in 1838. In the years around 1840 he was Italy's leading sculptor. When Liszt heard how pitifully small the contributions were for the Bonn Beethoven Memorial (France, for example, had contributed a grand total of 424 francs 90 centimes), he informed the relevant committee that he would make available the required sum of 50,000 francs from his own pocket on condition that Bartolini be commissioned to execute the work. The proposal found acceptance, and in 1840 Liszt sent an initial instalment of 10,000 francs. In the event, however, the monument was sculpted by Ernst-Julius Hähnel (1811–1891).

Liszt left Vienna, following his concerts in the city, at the end of May 1838 and travelled to Vienna, where he was reunited with Marie d'Agoult. Various concert commitments continued to keep them apart, albeit for short periods, and during this time they exchanged their feelings in letters.

Marie d'Agoult to Franz Liszt (Genoa, 25 June 1838):
"I love you more than I can say, and I love you for yourself. I believe that you can still love, and therefore that you must still love. Part of your heart remains unsatisfied with me. My love is consuming you. I believe you could love *happily* – but me you have loved *strongly*.

"It has now been five years, and that may be enough. Let me go my own way. When you call, I shall return. As for me, I shall never be able to love anyone again, but why should I deprive you of another love which could be the source of new life for you? At present you are under constraint, and I fear that this stifled need will leave behind worse consequences by causing you to become mentally ill. We must not stand in the way of whatever may help us to develop more perfectly. If I did not love you so reverently and esteem you so highly I should not be able to speak to you in this way, but I have a deep respect for your freedom."[54]

204 Three views of Liszt's life mask, probably made by Bartolini in 1838 as preliminary studies for a bust of the artist. This plaster of Paris mask, taken directly from Liszt's face, offers us the first undistorted, non-idealized impression of Liszt's facial appearance.

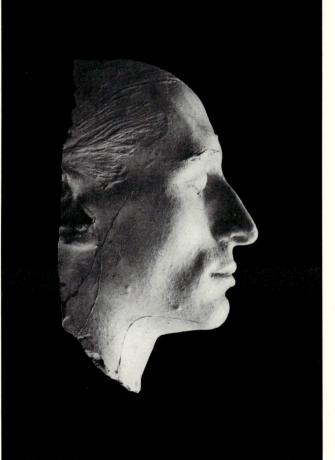

LIFE

1 January: Back in Florence. Bartolini completes the marble busts of Liszt and Marie d'Agoult (Illus. 201 and 202).

February to mid-June: With Marie d'Agoult in Rome. They live close to the Piazza Barberini (80 Via della Purificazione), later in the Via delle Quattro Fontane. Liszt becomes friendly with the painter Ingres, then the director of the Académie de France in the Villa Medici. Liszt busy composing. He discovers the beauties of Bach's Passions. Concerts in aristocratic circles.

March: Notable concert in the Palazzo Poli, the first so-called ''piano recital'' devoted to a single performer. Liszt writes to Princess Belgiojoso on 4 June 1839, ''Just imagine, I took the risk of giving a series of concerts on my own [. . .]. For curiosity's sake I am listing one of the programmes:

''1. Overture to *William Tell*, performed by Monsieur Liszt.

''2. *Réminiscences des 'Puritains.'* Fantasia written and performed by the said Monsieur Liszt.

''3. Studies and fragments by the same.

''4. Improvisations on given themes – again by the same.

''That was everything, no more and no less . . .''[55]

9 May: Liszt's son Daniel born in Rome. Visit to Tivoli and the Villa Adriana in the company of Sainte-Beuve.

Early June: A few days in Albano, then departure from Rome for Lucca.

June to August: Liszt and the Comtesse take up residence in the Villa Massimiliana in Lucca. They become friendly with Henri Lehmann, who paints their portraits (Illus. 207).

September: The couple moves to a log cabin in the forest near San Rossore.

3 October: In Pisa for a few days. In a letter to the Beethoven Committee in Bonn, Liszt offers to make good the sum still needed to erect a Beethoven Monument.[56]

19 October: Liszt leaves Florence for Vienna, while the Comtesse travels to Paris via Livorno and Genoa.

5 and 11 November: Concerts in Trieste.

15 November: Liszt arrives in Vienna. He falls ill the next day with a high temperature.

19 November: First concert in Vienna; then ill in bed until 27 November.

Further concerts in Vienna: 27 November; 2, 5 (midday and afternoon), 8, and 14 December.

Appearances at concerts given by other artists: 29 and 30 November, 15 and 17 December. Effusively praised by both the press and the general public. Haslinger publishes his 12 *Grandes Études* (Illus. 219), the *Hexaméron*, Kriehuber's portrait (Illus. 200), and several transcriptions of Schubert Lieder.

18 to 22 December: In Preßburg. Concerts in the Redoute on 19, 20, and 22 December.

23 December to 16 January 1840: In Pest. Concerts on 27 and 29 December (see ''Life 1840'').

205 Franz Liszt. Drawing by Ingres, Rome, May 1839.

Franz Liszt and the Comtesse d'Agoult left Rome in June 1839. Although their son Daniel had been born shortly before, on 9 May, the Comtesse felt equal to the strains of the journey. Ingres gave her his magical portrait of Liszt on 29 May, presumably as a parting present. He saw the painting again, hanging in Marie's Paris salon, in June 1841: on 13 June she wrote to Liszt, who was then staying in London, ''M. Ingres had a lot to say to me about you. He looked at your portrait with great affection.''[57]

Probably more portraits were made of Liszt than of any other celebrity throughout the nineteenth century, and he may well be described as the most famous man of his day. Even an opponent such as Eduard Hanslick recognized this (see p. 273). Goethe could no doubt have travelled throughout Europe incognito, but Liszt never. At a time when passport photographs did not exist and it was usual to give an exact physical description of the individual concerned, Liszt's passport dispensed with all such details and simply stated, ''Celebritate sua sat notus'' (Sufficiently well known through his celebrity). The beauty of the young man, the middle-aged man's sharply etched and virile good looks, and the ageing Liszt's distinguished appearance provided artists with endless inspiration. ''Rarely does an artist get to work on such a face,'' the well-known sculptor Ernst Rietschel remarked in a letter to Carolyne von Sayn-Wittgenstein of 28 January 1855.

Liszt was rare among musicians in that he was receptive to every aspect of art, and he was on friendly terms or in correspondence with many painters and sculptors of his time, including Lenbach, Kriehuber, Amerling, Delacroix, Zumbusch, and Schwanthaler. In his more intimate circle of friends were Munkácsy, Lehmann, Bartolini, Wilhelm von Kaulbach, and Ary Scheffer.

A particularly close relationship existed between Liszt and the leading French painter Jean Auguste Dominique Ingres (1780–1867), director of the Académie de France in the Villa Medici at the time of Liszt's stay in Rome in 1839. Ingres was an outstanding violinist and was one of the few artists whose intellectual interests transcend their professional boundaries. He had the honour and pleasure of finding in Liszt an accompanist for his violin playing. Liszt dedicated his piano transcriptions of Beethoven's Symphonies Nos. 5 and 6 to Ingres, and wrote a long and appreciative article on him in the form of an open letter to Hector Berlioz, published in the *Gazette musicale* of 24 October 1839. ''Mozart, Beethoven, and Haydn spoke the same language to him as Phidias and Raphael,''[58] Liszt wrote of Ingres. And on 1 March 1839 Liszt told the violinist Lambert Massart that he and Ingres had often made music together and that the latter's violin playing was ''excellent.''

The relationship between Frédéric Chopin and Eugène Delacroix may perhaps be regarded as analogous to this short-lived friendship between Liszt and Ingres. The classical Ingres and the boldly Romantic Delacroix, whose bitter mutual enmity was the talk of Paris, produced perhaps the most important portraits of their two musician friends.

Among Liszt's numerous portraitists there is probably none who gave clearer expression to the musician's sensibility and spirit than Ingres, with his delicate and unwaveringly certain handling of line.

WORKS

Winterreise (12 Schubert Lieder) (piano transcriptions): 1. *Gute Nacht*, 2. *Die Nebensonnen*, 3. *Muth*, 4. *Die Post*, 5. *Erstarrung*, 6. *Wasserfluth*, 7. *Der Lindenbaum*, 8. *Der Leyermann*, 9. *Täuschung*. 10. *Das Wirthshaus*, 11. *Der stürmische Morgen*, 12. *Im Dorfe*. Written 1838/39. Pub. 1840.

Venezia e Napoli (piano pieces): 1. *Lento*, 2. *Allegro*, 3. *Andante placido*, 4. *Tarantelles napolitaines*. Engraved by Haslinger in 1840, but not published. Nos. 3 and 4 were revised in 1859 and published two years later as Nos. 1 and 3 of *Venezia e Napoli*: 1. *Gondoliera*, 2. *Canzone*, 3. *Tarantella*. (*Canzone* is a transcription of a song from Rossini's *Otello* and probably dates from 1859.)

Valse mélancolique (for piano). Pub. 1841. A second version appeared in 1852.

Angiolin dal biondo crin (song for tenor voice and piano). Probably Liszt's first song, presumably written as a lullaby for his daughter Blandine. Pub. 1843. Versions for baritone and tenor appeared in 1856.

Adelaide (Beethoven) (piano transcription). Pub. 1840.

During 1839 Liszt also worked on a number of transcriptions of Beethoven symphonies, in addition to several of the works listed under 1838.

Là ci darem la mano (from Mozart's *Don Giovanni*), mentioned in a letter of 9 November 1839. Probably a preliminary study for the *Réminiscences de ''Don Juan.''* Lost.

Réminiscences des ''Puritains'' de Bellini (version for piano and orchestra), mentioned in a letter of 29 December 1839. Lost or unpublished; or possibly a reference to the accompanying parts for the *Hexaméron* (see ''Works 1837'').

Fantasia on ''Maometto'' (Rossini) (for piano), mentioned in a letter of 24 December 1839. Lost.

La Romanesca (sixteenth-century melody) (for piano). Pub. 1840. A new version appeared in 1852.

Rákóczy March (for piano). First version. Pub. 1846 or 1847.

WRITINGS:

Letter from a Bachelor of Music. To Hector Berlioz (2 October 1839). Pub. in *Gazette musicale*, No. 53, 24 October 1839.

Although Stürler's portrait of Liszt lacks both the fascinating charisma of Ingres's drawing and the Romantic daemonization which Lehmann achieved by the captivating fixity of the subject's gaze and his dramatic chiaroscuro effects, we see here an interesting and, above all, little-known portrait of the composer, whose outstretched hands we must presumably imagine resting on the keyboard of a piano. To be sure, Stürler lacked the gift of going beyond a mere likeness and laying bare the inner essence of the brilliant musician, as Ingres had managed so successfully to do in his drawing of May 1839.

In all probability, it was Liszt's friend the sculptor Lorenzo Bartolini who introduced Stürler to the musician. Stürler occupied a studio in the Via delle Belle Donne in Florence, where he worked for twenty years and where Ingres had had a studio from 1821 to 1824. One of Bartolini's studios was also housed in the same building. Liszt mentions Stürler (who, like Henri Lehmann, was a pupil of Ingres) in his letters, thus allowing us to date the present portrait to September or October 1839. It was with Stürler that Liszt spent his last hours in Florence before setting off for Vienna on 19 October 1839.

Henri Lehmann (1814–1882), one of the leading painters of his day, left two portraits of his friend Liszt and at least five of Marie d'Agoult (see Illus. 116 and 167), remaining the latter's admirer to the end of his days. When Liszt and the Comtesse left Rome in June 1839, Lehmann took charge of their son Daniel who, still too small to cope with his parents' life of restless wandering, was entrusted, in accordance with custom, to a wet-nurse at Palestrina in the Monti Sabini. When Lehmann in turn left Rome on 19 January 1840, his brother Rudolf (to whom we also owe a portrait of Liszt, Illus. 365) assumed responsibility for the child. Liszt, depressed by his inconstant life as a virtuoso, wrote to Henri Lehmann from London on 20 September 1840, ''I would envy you if I did not like you so much, my excellent friend. You live in accord with your thoughts and your heart. What you devise, what you dream, what you believe, you throw at your canvas, depicting it with sincere magnificence, alone and all-powerful in your isolation in the Palazzo Borghese. You avoid all contact with the masses, a contact which is almost always debasing. Genius can dwell peaceably within you; the clangorous discords outside cannot for a moment unsettle it or disturb its slow and dignified revelation with their squalid interruptions [. . .]''[59]

---

206 Franz Liszt. Oil painting by Adolf von Stürler, Florence 1839.

207 Franz Liszt. Oil portrait by Henri Lehmann, 1839.

In the autumn of 1838 and the early months of 1839 Liszt and the Comtesse toured Italy, seeing the sights and visiting the artistic treasures of Pisa, Florence, and Bologna. Liszt also gave occasional concerts ''in order not to forget my trade entirely,'' as he wrote to Hector Berlioz.

On 2 October 1839, Liszt wrote to Berlioz from San Rossore: ''The beauty of this favoured strip of earth revealed itself to me in its purest and most sublime forms. To my astonished eye, art appeared in all its splendour and stood revealed in its universality, its all-embracing unity. Each day confirmed my awareness, through feeling and thinking, of the hidden relationship linking all the works of the creative spirit. Raphael and Michelangelo helped me to understand Mozart and Beethoven; in Giovanni Pisano, Fra Beato, and Francia I found an explanation of Allegri, Marcello, and Palestrina; Titian and Rossini appeared like stars of the same magnitude. The Colosseum and the Campo Santo are not so remote from the *Eroica* Symphony and the Requiem as one thinks . . .''[60]

In mid-October 1839 Liszt went to Vienna, from where his restless career as a piano virtuoso was to take him across the whole of Europe during the eight years that followed. Marie returned to Paris with the three-year-old Blandine and the one-year-old Cosima. The six-month-old Daniel remained with his wet-nurse in the Monti Sabini.

Marie d'Agoult to Liszt in Trieste, letter of 23 October 1839, written from Genoa:
"How could I leave this dear Italian soil without calling after you a last farewell? How could I watch two such beautiful and fulfilling years disappear from my life without grieving for them? Ah my dear Franz! Let me tell you once again from my overflowing heart that you have awoken in me a deep and unalterable feeling which would outlive all others if those others were to change – a feeling of boundless gratitude. A thousand blessings! I have Mistress Cosima with me, whom I had to collect in Genoa, Mistress Cosima (alias Cecchina) who, feature for feature, resembles the enchanting Mouche [Blandine], except that she is much less beautiful and, above all, less distinguished. Their education is the same. The nurse says she must be given everything she wants, without delay, otherwise she will die! I shall endeavour to teach her to live differently. A tedious crossing, dull-witted passengers. I shall be continuing my journey to Marseilles at 12 o'clock. Pesin was civility itself. He settled all my bills with my fellow Comoites, who left delighted with the *regalo* [gift]. Madame Sand dined at Negro's with Chopin. She did not speak, and he did not play. He had a terrible cough . . .

"Fare you well, my love, my beloved, I shall write to you from Lyons. Just as I was boarding the boat in Livorno, the sun was setting in floods of gold, and a melancholy moon rose out of the leaden clouds; by and by it broke free and shone down on our crossing with the most glorious light!

"I accepted this as a symbol of our beautiful evanescent past, but also of our future, a future which has begun so sadly but which will be calm and pure!"[61]

Liszt to Marie d'Agoult, letter written from Venice, Friday, 25 October 1839:
"Here in Venice, Marie, I bid you a final farewell. Henceforth I shall find you only in my heart and my thoughts. But here everything speaks of you, the sea and the sky, San Marco and the gondolas speak of you and repeat your dear name [. . .]"[62]

210 Rome, Forum Romanum. Photograph, ca. 1850.

Liszt and Marie d'Agoult lived in Rome from February to June 1839, staying first in the Via della Purificazione, and then in the Via delle Quattro Fontane. Liszt's son Daniel was born in Rome on 9 May.

Liszt could hardly have foreseen, when he visited the Forum Romanum, that exactly thirty years later he would be wearing the gown of an abbé and living in the cardinal's rooms (marked by an arrow in the photograph) in the monastery of Santa Francesca Romana. (See Illus. 482 and 495.)

211 *Sposalizio*. Painting by Raphael.

Raphael's *Sposalizio* and Michelangelo's *Penseroso* inspired Liszt's piano pieces of the same titles.

Opposite page:

208 Pisa. The Duomo, Baptistery, and Leaning Tower. Photograph, ca. 1880.

209 The Campo Santo in Pisa. Steel engraving, ca. 1845.

The painting *The Triumph of Death* in the Campo Santo (formerly believed to be the work of Andrea Orcagna) was the inspiration behind Liszt's *Totentanz*, a work which consists of variations on the Gregorian melody *Dies irae*. It was sketched in 1838 and completed in 1849, before being revised in 1853 and 1859. It was first performed, with Bülow as soloist, in The Hague on 15 April 1865.

212, 213, 214 Three of Liszt's concert programmes from Vienna in 1839.

The programmes for the remainder of Liszt's concerts in Vienna in 1839 are as follows:

27 November 1839 (originally planned for 24 November): Fantasia on *I Puritani* and Fantasia on *Lucia di Lammermoor* (in place of the advertised *Études*); and Liszt's transcriptions of Schubert's *Die Stadt*, *Das Fischermädchen*, and *Aufenthalt*. On 26 November Liszt appeared at a concert with the violinist Charles-Auguste de Bériot, and on the 29th at a Court concert.

2 December 1839: Beethoven's *Appassionata* Sonata (op. 57) (instead of the advertised B flat major Trio); his Fantasia on Donizetti's *Lucia*; Lickl's *Auf dem Calvarienberg*; his transcriptions of Schubert's *Der Atlas* and *Die Taubenpost*; and, as an encore, the *Grand Galop chromatique*.

5 December 1839: "Fragment nach Dante" (presumably parts of the so-called *Dante Sonata*); Fantasia on Bellini's *La Sonnambula*; and Liszt's *Grande Valse di Bravura*, in addition to some of Chopin's Mazurkas. That same afternoon Liszt played Beethoven's C minor Piano Concerto.

8 December 1839: Beethoven's Sonata in D minor (op. 31 no. 2); Liszt's *Le Lac de Wallenstadt*, *Eroica* Study, and *Tarantelles napolitaines*; also his paraphrases of Rossini's *L'Orgia* and Schubert's *Erlkönig*.

14 December 1839: Beethoven's Grand Trio in B flat major; Liszt's paraphrase on *La Sonnambula* ("by popular request"); and his transcription of Schubert's *Mélodies hongroises* (a two-handed version of the *Divertissement à la hongroise* for four hands).

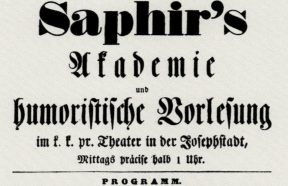

Liszt to Marie d'Agoult, Vienna, 4 December 1839:
". . . since I am no longer under doctor's orders, and have been keeping open house for the last two days, my room has been constantly crowded with people; in addition to which I now find myself suddenly having to learn Beethoven's Concerto in C (which I do not know) and a new Fantasy of my own composition . . ."[63]

The *Allgemeine Theaterzeitung* of 7 December 1839 carried a report on Liszt's performance of Beethoven's Piano Concerto in C minor, which he had had to learn in a matter of hours and which he played with an improvised cadenza:
". . . But everything that we have so far heard about Liszt seems to have been overshadowed by his rendition of Beethoven's Concerto in C minor at the first *Concert spirituel*. The Concerto has been performed here by great artists, but by none has it been performed so brilliantly . . ."

Liszt to Marie d'Agoult, Vienna, 6 December 1839:
". . . Mlle Pleyel arrived here four days ago. She is giving her concert tomorrow. She is now staying at the same hotel as I am. I have heard her a lot. She has a splendid talent, undoubtedly the finest talent as a pianist that there is.
She asked me whether I remembered Chopin's room . . . of course, Madame, how could one forget it, etc. . . . Then Count Dietrichstein came and interrupted our conversation, so I left. [. . .] I was able to be of use to her and even to perform a number of minor services for her [. . .]"[64]

215 Marie Moke-Pleyel (1811–1875), known as Camille Pleyel. Lithograph by Alophe, ca. 1835.

In the years around 1840 Camille Pleyel was widely regarded as the leading woman pianist of her day after Clara Wieck. She was briefly engaged to Hector Berlioz, but later married Camille Pleyel, Chopin's preferred piano maker. She captivated the musical world not only through her pianistic abilities but above all through her beauty. ''Her physical beauty transports the onlooker into the fabulous world of the Lorelei,'' the Viennese art journal *Der Sammler* observed. Berlioz confessed that she ''inflamed him with the fires of Hell,'' and Liszt dedicated to her both his *Tarantelle di bravura d'après la Tarantella de La Muette de Portici* and *Réminiscences de Norma*, while Chopin dedicated his *Nocturnes* op. 9 to her. Schumann called her ''a woman of genius,'' and Clara Schumann confided to her diary that ''Everything I read about her is increasingly clear proof that she must be placed above me, which can only mean total defeat for me . . .''

Camille Pleyel was an ardent admirer of Liszt's. For his part he did her the honour of accompanying her in Herz's *Duo brillant* on themes from *William Tell* (see programme on p. 116). At her first concert in Vienna he led her onto the platform and turned the pages for her (Liszt was the only pianist at this period who played from memory), encouraging Eduard Hanslick to remark that ''If anything more was still needed to dispose the audience in Madame Pleyel's favour, this was it . . .'' (see Illus. 293).

216 Franz Liszt in Hungarian frogged jacket and fur cape. Lithograph by Schier (ca. 1839), based on a watercolour by Kriehuber of 1838 (see Illus. 191).

217 Original review of one of Liszt's concerts from the *Wiener Theaterzeitung* of 30 November 1839 (No. 240, pp. 1175/6). (For a translation of the text, see pp. 335–6.)

Wien.

Zweites Concert des Herrn Franz Liszt.

[The body of the review is printed in German Fraktur type in two columns, signed at the end by Heinrich Adami.]

218 Preßburg. Steel engraving by Bentley based on a drawing by Bartlett; ca. 1840.

View of the palace, formerly the residence of the kings of Hungary. A fire in 1811 reduced the Preßburg Palace to a ruin.

Until the end of the eighteenth century, Preßburg was the most fashionable and beautiful city in Hungary. It was the country's capital, the headquarters of all the imperial authorities and the seat of the imperial primate. Heads of state were crowned here, and the country's parliament met here. Only after 1784 did the city decline in political importance, when Emperor Joseph II chose Ofen as the Hungarian capital.

Liszt's visit to Preßburg between 18 and 22 December 1839[65] was the first time since May 1823 that he had set foot on Hungarian soil, but he was now accepted and acclaimed like a long-lost son by the Hungarian population, who gave him an enthusiastic welcome.

A critic for the Vienna *Allgemeine Theaterzeitung* submitted the following review, dated 23 December 1839:

''I have just come from Liszt's concert. Jubilant shouts of 'Éljen' (Hail!) from the packed hall accompanied every number, and when he finally played a 'Hungarian' piece I thought the applause would never end. Having been overcome by the desire to add somewhat to the effusive remarks which have appeared about Liszt in the papers, I should like to demonstrate, my dear Sir, that we in Preßburg are just as good at praising others as any master critic. But I fear that I shall tax the reader's patience unduly, and so I shall simply report that Liszt caused a furore, as he did in Vienna. He is to give a second concert, probably in the Schauspielhaus.''

Liszt's visits to Preßburg:

1820: 26 November	1874: 18/19 April
1822: 2 January (see note 6)	1881: 3/4 April
1839: 18 to 22 December[65]	1882: 12/13 February
1840: 17 January to 1 February	1883: 17/18 March
1858: 12 April	1884: 24 to 26 February
1872: 19 to 21 January	19 to 21 April
1873: 13 April	30 October
22/23 November	1885: 12 to 14 April

219 Title page of the first edition of the *24 Grandes Études* (first version of the twelve *Études d'exécution transcendante*), written in 1837/38 and published in 1839.

This edition, no longer performed and difficult to obtain nowadays, contained only twelve *Études* and was a revised version of the fifteen-year-old Liszt's twelve *Études en douze exercices* (see Illus. 69). In 1851 Liszt again revised these highly interesting pieces and the following year had them published by Breitkopf & Härtel under the rubric ''seul édition authentique, revue par l'auteur.''

220, 221 Programmes for two of Liszt's concerts in Preßburg in 1839.

222 The Municipal Redoubt in Preßburg. Photograph, ca. 1890.

Liszt performed here on 19, 20, and 22 December 1839, and again on 19 April 1874. The building, a former granary, was demolished in 1911.

223 The Preßburg Theatre, detail of an illustration by Rudolf Alt, 1848.

Liszt performed here on 26 January 1840; it was also here that he conducted his *Legende von der Heiligen Elisabeth* on 18 March 1883. The building was demolished in 1884, and a new theatre was opened on the same site on 2 September 1886.

224 Original review of one of Liszt's Preßburg concerts in December 1839.

The date is misleading. Liszt gave his last concert in Preßburg on 22 December 1839. By 4 o'clock in the afternoon of the 23rd he was already in Pest (see note 65). (For a translation of the text, see p. 336.)

Opposite page:

225 The Redoute in Pest. Steel engraving by Rauschenfels von Steinberg, 1840.

Liszt's concerts in Pest in 1839/40 were held both in the National Theatre and in the Redoutensaal. The Redoute was built by Michael Pollack between 1829 and 1832, but burned down during the Hungarian War of Liberation in 1849. Between 1859 and 1864 Frigyes Feszl's monumental building was erected on the same site, and it was here in 1865 that Liszt's *Legende von der Heiligen Elisabeth* received its first performance (see Illus. 463). The present building, known as the Vigadó, is a reconstruction of this earlier theatre, which suffered severe damage during the Second World War.

222

223

Correspondenz-Nachrichten.

Preßburg, den 23. Dez. 1839.

Liszt gab heute sein zweites und — hoffentlich nur für jetzt — letztes Concert bei uns, nachdem er früher für einen wohlthätigen Zweck im Theater gespielt hatte. Der Enthusiasmus, welchen das erste Erscheinen dieses Kunst-Heros erregte, hat sich als nothwendige Folge seiner außerordentlichen Leistungen erprobt, welche — wie alles wahrhaft Große — durch ihr Wiedererscheinen gewinnen. Man fühlt immer deutlicher, wie Herz und Geist bei Liszt's Spiel eben so thätig sind, als seine Finger, die unter dem auferlegten „Muß" eines eisernen Willens, das Unbegreifliche vollführen; — man ahnt, daß jedes vorgetragene Tonstück — wir möchten sagen „Tongemälde," — ein Spiegelbild seines Innersten — ein Theil seines Lebens ist, und eben diese — wenn gleich dunkle — Wahrnehmung, ergreift den Zuhörer bei den Leistungen Liszt's tiefer, als bei denen jedes Andern. Liszt opfert die eine Hälfte seines Erdenbaseins, um das zu werden, was er ist, und um dieses Erreichte der Welt zu offenbaren, schont er die zweite weniger als er sollte, — denn wer spielt wie Er, dessen Lebenskraft verpufft, während er eine zum Theil rücksichtslose Menge ergötzt. Wir sagen ‚rücksichtslose', denn wären sie dies nicht, so würde wahre Liebe für die Person des Künstlers sie abhalten, nach den erschöpfendsten Anstrengungen, noch Wiederholung zu heischen — oder selbst anzunehmen.

Was die Compositionen dieses musikalischen Byrons anbelangt, so sind sie meist eine Mischung des lyrisch-epischen und romantischen Styles; doch ist letzterer bei Weitem vorherrschender, — oft weich — nie weichlich, bisweilen bizarr, — immer großartig, — nicht ohne Gründlichkeit, doch noch tiefer gefühlt als gedacht, scheinen sie fast mehr Geburten momentaner Seelenstimmung und einer der gewöhnlichen Schranken spottenden Phantasie, als ruhiger Konception, — sie sind bald Licht und Wärme verbreitend — bald wild auflodernde Flammen, — verzehrend für ihren eignen Herd.

Kann übrigens höchste Anerkennung und Auszeichnung jeder Art, Erfolg für das sein, was ein Künstler dem Publikum bietet, so hat Liszt in Preßburg reichlich geerntet, was er gesät, und seine Befriedigung würde sicherlich noch größer sein, wenn bewegte Herzen sich so bemerkbar machen könnten, als bewegte Hände und Lippen.

Der Gefeierte bediente sich bei seinen Produktionen zweier Instrumente unsres ausgezeichneten Klaviermachers Schmidt, und dies auf Anrathen des Herrn Konrad Graf in Wien, dessen Erzeugnisse in diesem Fache bekanntlich einen mehr als europäischen Ruf haben: dieser Umstand ist zu ehrend für beide braven Männer, als daß er mit Stillschweigen übergangen werden dürfte.

J. R.

Liszt arrived in Pest on 23 December 1839, accompanied by Count Kasimir Esterházy, Baron Wenckheim, the two Counts Zichy, and Count Festetics. The enthusiasm which Liszt aroused in the Hungarian capital and, indeed, everywhere he appeared during his virtuoso years has something almost unreal about it today, but it is attested by many eyewitness accounts and contemporary press reports.

Allgemeine Theaterzeitung, 28 December 1839:
"Liszt arrived in Pest at four o'clock in the afternoon of the 23rd of December. The Pest Music Society had made all the necessary preparations at the Hotel Zum Palatin in order to welcome the celebrated virtuoso in a worthy manner; Liszt, however, alighted at the home of Count Leo Festetics, a patron of music, whither the Pest Music Society immediately repaired *in corpore*. A band of musicians welcomed the long-awaited visitor to the hall . . . scarcely had Liszt acknowledged these demonstrations of love and respect with a grateful heart when a military band struck up in the large courtyard, beginning with one of Liszt's *Hungarian* pieces. This was followed by further music from the hall, where Beethoven's Septet was performed, the players including His Excellency Count Brunsvik [Count Franz Brunswick (1776–1849), who had been a friend of Beethoven's and the dedicatee of op. 57, the *Appassionata*]. Refreshments followed. Liszt's first concert takes place on the 27th of December. No one can have any idea of the joyful agitation to which the greater part of the population of Pest and Ofen is already prey . . ."

The question is regularly asked as to when Liszt found time to write any music, given the constant hurly-burly which surrounded him wherever he went. He was exceptionally diligent, however, and used every free minute to work. This alone should be sufficient to dismiss many of his alleged love affairs and consign them to the realm of fiction.

Liszt to Clara Wieck, Pest, 25 December 1839:
". . . I did an enormous amount of work in Italy. Without any exaggeration, I believe I wrote four to five hundred pages of piano music. If you can summon up the patience to listen to even a sixth of it, I should be delighted to play it to you after a fashion.

The Paganini Studies which are dedicated to you will not appear for another two months, but the proofs were corrected some time ago and I shall bring them with me to Leipzig . . ."[66]

Liszt to Marie d'Agoult, Preßburg, 23 January 1840:
". . . I mention the ladies of Pest and Preßburg. You have no doubt convinced yourself that I have made a vast number of conquests and inflamed women's passions. Well, to tell the truth, I have not had a single affair. I was simply what you call 'charming' to two or three of the prettiest and most elegant of them . . ."[67]

Liszt was a man who loved the truth. The descriptions of his concerts and tours contained in his letters to Marie d'Agoult (which he never suspected would later be published) agree in every detail with the eyewitness accounts and press reports which are available to us today.

226 Poem by Franz von Schober on Liszt's arrival in Pest. Reproduced from the 1839 original. The lines were set to music for chorus and string quartet by the conductor of the Pest Opera, Franz Grill. (For a translation of the text, see p. 336.)

227 Title page of the poem (Illus. 226).

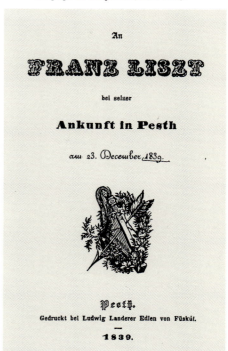

LIFE

The chronicle of Liszt's life for the following years is almost entirely given over to concert dates. Between now and 1847 he spent the greater part of his time on concert tours, and it is remarkable that he found any time at all to compose so many works. He wrote to Marie d'Agoult on 25 December 1839, "I'm really ashamed of my letters, since all I ever talk about is concerts, applause and money . . . But you must remember that that's all my life consists of at present [. . .]"[68]

2, 4, 6, 11, and 12 January: Concerts in Pest.

8 January: Liszt shares a concert platform with J. Táborszky.

9 January: Liszt plays for Count Gabor Keglevich in Buda.

16 January: Concert in Raab (Györ).

17 January to 1 February: Liszt in Preßburg. Concerts on 21, 26, and 27 January. From 28 to 30 January Liszt is the guest of Count Kasimir Esterházy in Gattendorf (Lajtakáta) near Preßburg.

2 to 16 February: Liszt in Vienna. Concerts on 2, 6, 9, 14, and 16 February.

10 and 11 February: Concerts in Brünn (Brno).

17 to 21 February: Liszt in Ödenburg. Concert on 18 February. He is elected an honorary citizen of the town.

19 February: Liszt visits his birthplace in Raiding. He donates 100 ducats towards the cost of a new organ.

20 February: In Eisenstadt (as guest of the Hofer family).

22 February to 1 March: Liszt in Vienna.

3 to 12 March: Liszt in Prague. Concerts on 5, 6, 7, 9, 11, and 12 March.

14 March: Arrives in Dresden. Robert Schumann comes from Leipzig to hear him play.

16 March: Concert in Dresden.

17, 24, and 30 March: Concerts in Leipzig, with a concert in Dresden on the 29th. Liszt becomes friendly with Schumann and Mendelssohn.

April: Liszt in Paris, where he sees Marie d'Agoult and his children. He performs at the home of Princess Belgiojoso and twice, with immense success, at the Salons Erard (before an invited audience).

6 May to end of June: Liszt in London. Solo recitals on 9 and 29 June. Appears at Philharmonic Concerts on 11 May and 8 June, and appears at other artists' concerts on 8 May, and 14 and 22 June. Becomes friendly with Lady Blessington, Count D'Orsay, Moscheles, and Ole Bull (with whom he performs Beethoven's *Kreutzer* Sonata).

7 June: Marie d'Agoult joins Liszt in England. She lives in Richmond.

July: Accompanied by Marie d'Agoult, Liszt travels to the Rhineland via Brussels. Concerts in Baden-Baden, Mainz, Wiesbaden, and Ems (the latter in the presence of the Empress of Russia).

4 to 10 August: Three concerts in Frankfurt.

12 August: Concert in Bonn.

Mid-August to end of September: Liszt on a concert tour of England.

During August his schedule is as follows: 17: Chichester (midday) and Portsmouth (evening); 18: Ryde and Newport (Isle of Wight); 19: Southampton and Winchester; 20: Salisbury and Blandford; 21: Weymouth; 22: Lyme Regis and Sidmouth; 24: Exmouth and Teignmouth; 26: Plymouth; 28/29: two concerts in Exeter; 31: Taunton and Bridgwater.

Concerts during September: 1/2: three concerts in Bath; 3: Clifton (Bristol); 4/5: Northampton; 9:

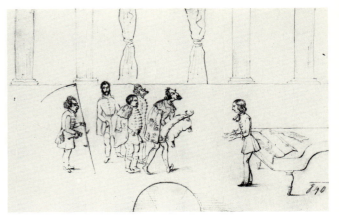

In 1840 Liszt's visit to Pest was accompanied by scenes of unimaginable enthusiasm. His programme at the National Theatre on 4 January including the *Lucia* paraphrase, the *Grand Galop chromatique*, and the *Rákóczy March*. As he stood at the piano at the end of the concert acknowledging the applause, which, according to Franz von Schober, was loud enough "to rouse the dead," he was presented with the famous Sword of Honour by Count Festetics, Count Teleky, Pál Nyáry, Rudolf Eckstein, Baron Antal Augusz, and Baron Bánffy. The blade, curved in the Turkish manner, was of damascened steel inlaid with gold arabesques, while the handle, hilt, and scabbard (which was inscribed with a dedication to Liszt), were set with precious stones, including turquoises, rubies, and emeralds. Liszt bequeathed the sword to the National Museum in Budapest in 1873, and it has formed part of their collection since 1887.

228 Franz Liszt in Hungarian national costume. Plaster of Paris statue by Dosnay, 1840.
229 The presentation of the "Sword of Honour." Caricature signed "Adele," 1840.

230 Memorabilia in Liszt's possession. The 1840 Sword of Honour, with gold and silver wreaths and a walking stick (see Illus. 611).

PROGRAMM.

Sonntag, den 26. Januar 1840,

Mittags um 1½ Uhr,

wird im Preßburger städtischen Theater

ein grosses

Vocal- und Instrumental-Concert,

unter

Leitung und Mitwirkung

des Herrn

FRANZ LISZT,

Ehrenmitglieds des Pressburger Kirchenmusik-Vereins,

zum Besten des Vereins-Fonds

statthaben.

Erste Abtheilung:	Zweite Abtheilung:
1. Ouverture, aus „Wilhelm Tell" von J. Rossini.	4. Ouverture, aus „Oberon" von C. M. Weber.
2. Chor, aus der Oper „Semiramide" mit Doppel-Orchester, von J. Rossini.	5. Chor, aus „Wilhelm Tell" von J. Rossini.
3. Concertstück, für das Pianoforte mit Orchester-Begleitung, von C. M. Weber, vorgetragen von Hrn. Franz Liszt.	6. Hexameron, Bravour-Variationen über ein Thema, aus „Puritani" *), vorgetragen von Hrn. Franz Liszt.

*) 1ste Variation componirt von Thalberg; — 2te von F. Liszt; — 3te von Herz; — 4te von Pixis; — Introduction und Finale von F. Liszt.

HEIMISCHES GEDENKEMEIN.

Gedicht

an Herrn

FRANZ LISZT

bei Gelegenheit des Concerts

am 26. Januar 1840

zu

PRESSBURG.

Buchdruckerei von Anton Edlen v. Schmid.

Ein Sohn Apoll's, gekeimt im Ungarlande,
   Von Gallien grossgezogen in der Kunst,
Erscheinest DU, getreu dem Heimathbande,
   Am Vaterherd', geschmückt mit Göttergunst;
Und reichest Zauberfrüchte zu geniessen,
Wie sie den höhern Welten nur entspriessen.

Bald einen Schacht, gefüllt mit Donnerklängen,
   Enthüllet herrisch DEINE Meisterhand; —
Bald schiffet sie auf wogenden Gesängen
   Die Seelen hin nach einem Feenland,
Wo zauberisch die Finger der Camoene
Entlocken ihrer Lyra holde Töne.

Nimm hin Bewunderung, wie wir sie zollen
   Der Götterlust, die DEINER Hand entspriesst! —
Nicht ziemet uns, — den Meister krönen wollen,
   Den Weltgekrönten; — unser Wunsch nur ist:
In jenen Kranz, den Völker DIR gegeben,
Ein heimisches Gedenkemein zu weben.

J. B. Hollósy.

231 (top left) Programme of a concert given by Liszt in Preßburg in January 1840 on his way back from Pest.

232 (top right) Title page of Hollósy's poem in homage to Liszt (Illus. 234).

233 Gold goblet presented to Liszt by ladies of the Hungarian aristocracy on 27 January 1840, in the presence of the Archduchess Hermine.

On the sides of the goblet, surrounded by garlands, are inscribed the names of its donors, including the Countesses Károlyi, Batthyány, Széchényi, Zichy, and Szapáry. Around the rim is the inscription, ''A'hon' hires müvészének a' hazának ezen hölgyei'' (To our fatherland's famous artist from the ladies of the fatherland). In 1874 Liszt gave the goblet to the National Museum in Budapest.

234 Lines addressed to Liszt. Reproduced from the 1840 edition. (For a translation of the text, see p. 336.)

Market Harborough and Leicester; 10: Derby and Nottingham; 11: Mansfield and Newark; 12: Lincoln; 14: Horncastle and Boston; 15: Grantham; 16: Stamford and Peterborough; 17: Huntingdon; 18: Cambridge; 19: Bury St Edmunds; 21: two concerts in Norwich; 23: Ipswich; 23: Colchester; 24: Chelmsford; 25/26: Brighton.

Liszt undertakes these tours with Louis Henry Lavenu and John Orlando Parry. He subsequently rejoins Marie d'Agoult in Fontainebleau, and then stays for a period in Paris.
26 October to 11 November: Liszt in Hamburg, where he gives six concerts. He donates 3189 thalers to a Musicians' Pension Fund and performs for the poor of Hamburg.
November/December: Concerts in England, Ireland and Scotland. They are a financial failure, and Liszt releases his concert agent, Lavenu, from his obligation to pay him a fee.

Concerts in November: 24: Oxford; 25: Leamington; 26: Birmingham; 27: Wolverhampton; 28: Newcastle under Lyme; 30: Chester.

Concerts in December: 1: Liverpool; 2: Preston; 3: Rochdale; 4: Manchester; 5: Huddersfield; 7: Doncaster; 8: Sheffield; 9: Wakefield; 10: Leeds; 11: Hull; 14: York; 15: Manchester; 18, 21, and 23: Dublin; 28 and 30: Cork.

WORKS

Réminiscences de ''Lucrezia Borgia'' (Donizetti) (for piano). Pub. 1841 or 1842 (Part II only); the whole work appeared in 1848.
Fantaisie sur des motifs favoris de l'opéra ''La Sonnambula'' (Bellini) (for piano) (see Illus. 294). Pub. 1842. Twice revised. A version for four hands appeared in 1876.
Hussitenlied (fifteenth-century melody) (for piano). Pub. 1840, at the same time as a version for four hands.
Morceau de Salon (Étude de perfectionnement) for a piano tutor by Joseph Fétis. Pub. 1841. Revised in 1852 and entitled *Ab Irato*.
Geistliche Lieder (Schubert) (piano transcriptions): 1. *Litaney*, 2. *Himmelsfunken*, 3. *Die Gestirne*, 4. *Hymne*. Pub. 1841.
Geistliche Lieder (Beethoven) (piano transcriptions): 1. *Gottes Macht und Vorsehung*, 2. *Bitten*, 3. *Bußlied*, 4. *Vom Tode*, 5. *Die Liebe des Nächsten*, 6. *Die Ehre Gottes aus der Natur*. Pub. 1840.
Feuille d'Album in A major (for piano) (same theme as *Valse mélancolique*). Pub. 1841.
Grand Septuor (piano transcription of Beethoven's Septet op. 20). Pub. 1841/42. A version for piano duet made ca. 1841 was published ca. 1842.
Marche Héroïque (for piano). May date from this time, although the choral version (*Arbeiterchor*), which has a different middle section, did not go to the publishers until 1848 (see ''Works 1848''). Pub. 1982. Unpub. version for piano duet.
Marche Héroïque dans le genre hongrois (Heroischer Marsch im ungarischen Styl) (for piano). Pub. 1840. (Unrelated to the foregoing work.)
Marche Hongroise (for piano and orchestra). According to the *Gazette musicale* of 14 June 1840, Liszt played a ''Marche Hongroise'' with orchestral accompaniment in London. Presumably it was a version for piano and orchestra (not orchestrated by Liszt) of the above-mentioned *Marche Héroïque dans le genre hongrois*. Unpublished or lost.
Mendelssohn Lieder (piano transcription of opp.

(continued p. 125)

235 Article on Liszt in the *Allgemeine Theater-zeitung* of 18 February 1840. (For a translation of the text, see pp. 336–7.)

236, 237 *How Franz Liszt must join in a banquet in Vienna* and *Invitation to the Dance*. Two watercolours by Johann Peter Lyser, ca. 1840.

These two caricatures illustrate the hurly-burly to which Liszt was perpetually exposed during his years as a virtuoso artist.

238 The programme for Liszt's concert in Vienna on 6 February 1840.

239 Franz Liszt. Lithograph by Lowes Dickinson, based on a drawing by John Hayter; 1840.

"Works 1840" (continued)

19, 34, and 47): 1. *Auf Flügeln des Gesanges*, 2. *Sonntagslied*, 3. *Reiselied*, 4. *Neue Liebe*, 5. *Frühlingslied*, 6. *Winterlied*, 7. *Suleika*. Pub. 1841.

Galop de bal (for piano). Incorporating themes from the *Grande Valse di Bravura* and *Grand Galop chromatique*. May date from this time. Pub. ca. 1840.

Magyar dallok (Ungarische Nationalmelodien) (for piano). Eleven pieces were published under this title in 1843; ten additional numbers were subsequently added; six of them appeared under the title *Magyar rapszódiák (Rhapsodies hongroises)* by 1847. Nos. 18, 19, and 21 were not published until 1973, and No. 20 was first published in 1936 as "Romanian Rhapsody." See "Works 1848."

Fantasia on "Der Freischütz" (Weber) (for piano). Unpublished.

Zwei Stücke im Ungarischen Stil (No. 1 in B flat minor, No. 2 in D minor) (for piano). Written ca. 1840. Pub. 1954. Louis Kentner added a few bars at the end of the first of these pieces, which had been left incomplete by Liszt. The second piece remains unfinished.

Fantasia on English Themes (piano). Written at about this time. Unfinished and unpublished.

An unpublished piece for solo piano based on Italian operatic melodies may date from this time.

WRITINGS:

Paganini. An Obituary. Pub. in *Gazette musicale*, 23 August 1840.

240 Liszt at the piano. Oil painting by Josef Danhauser, 1840.

Originally entitled *Reminiscence of Liszt*, this portrait was commissioned from the Viennese artist Josef Danhauser by the piano maker Conrad Graf. It shows Liszt at the keyboard (an instrument by Graf), with Marie d'Agoult sitting at his feet. George Sand is seen smoking a cigar. Beside her is Alexandre Dumas *père*, and behind her (from left to right) are Victor Hugo, Niccolò Paganini, and Gioacchino Rossini. On the wall is a portrait of Byron, on the mantelpiece a statuette of Joan of Arc, and on the piano a bust of Beethoven by Anton Dietrich.

Danhauser had made Beethoven's death mask in 1827; he later gave the original to Liszt.

241 The piano of Robert and Clara Schumann, made by Graf, 1839. 237 cm long. Made of jacaranda wood.

This instrument was a gift from Conrad Graf to Clara Wieck on the occasion of her marriage to Robert Schumann on 12 September 1840. On Schumann's death in 1856 it passed into the possession of Johannes Brahms, who gave it to the Gesellschaft der Musikfreunde in Vienna in 1873. Liszt also used the instrument.

242 Glazed nameplate over the keyboard of Schumann's piano (Illus. 241).

243 Piano by Conrad Graf of Vienna, 1840. 245 cm long, Viennese action and damper pedals. Probably identical with the instrument seen in Danhauser's painting (Illus. 240). Liszt presumably used this instrument for his Viennese concerts in 1840.

244 Nameplate inlaid in metal on Graf's piano (Illus. 243).

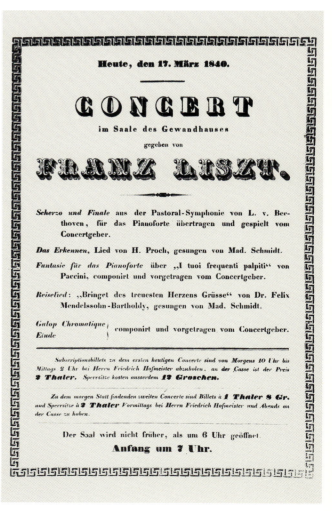

Heute, den 17. März 1840.

CONCERT
im Saale des Gewandhauses
gegeben von

FRANZ LISZT.

Scherzo und Finale aus der Pastoral-Symphonie von L. v. Beethoven, für das Pianoforte übertragen und gespielt vom Concertgeber.

Das Erkennen, Lied von H. Proch, gesungen von Mad. Schmidt.

Fantasie für das Pianoforte über „I tuoi frequenti palpiti" von Paccini, componirt und vorgetragen vom Concertgeber.

Reiselied: „Bringet des treuesten Herzens Grüsse" von Dr. Felix Mendelssohn-Bartholdy, gesungen von Mad. Schmidt.

Galop Chromatique } componirt und vorgetragen vom Concertgeber.
Etude }

Subscriptionsbillets zu dem ersten heutigen Concerte sind von Morgens 10 Uhr bis Mittags 2 Uhr bei Herrn Friedrich Hofmeister abzuholen, an der Casse ist der Preis **2 Thaler.** *Sperrsitze kosten ausserdem* **12 Groschen.**

Zu dem morgen Statt findenden zweiten Concerte sind Billets à **1 Thaler 8 Gr.** *und Sperrsitze à* **2 Thaler** *Vormittags bei Herrn Friedrich Hofmeister und Abends an der Casse zu haben.*

Der Saal wird nicht früher, als um 6 Uhr geöffnet.

Anfang um 7 Uhr.

245 Programme for Liszt's concert in the Leipzig Gewandhaus on 17 March 1840.

246, 247 Robert Schumann (1810–1856) and Clara Schumann, née Wieck (1819–1896). Miniature portraits, ca. 1840.

Liszt and Clara Wieck got to know each other in April 1838. Liszt informed Marie d'Agoult of the meeting in a letter written from Vienna on 13 April 1838: "We are staying at the same hotel, 'Zur Stadt Frankfurt,' and after dining we tinkle away for all we are worth. She is a very simple, very well educated person, not at all c...[*coquette*?], but entirely preoccupied with her art, and preoccupied, moreover, in a distinguished way, without being childish. She was quite amazed when she heard me. Her compositions are very respectable, especially for a woman . . ."[70]

Schumann first met Liszt on 14 or 15 March 1840, having travelled to Dresden to see him. For years the two men had been in correspondence, writing admiring letters and devoting newspaper articles to each other's activities.

ROBERT SCHUMANN ON LISZT'S PIANO PLAYING

Letters to Clara Wieck[69]

18 March 1840:
". . . There isn't space in this letter for everything I have to tell you – Dresden, our first meeting [with Liszt], the concert there, the rail journey here yesterday, the concert yesterday evening, and this morning's rehearsal for the second one. But how extraordinary is his playing, how daring and how frantic, and yet how delicate and fragrant – I have finally heard for myself. But, Clärchen, this world is no longer mine. Art as *you* practise it, and as I often do, too, when composing, this agreeable informality is something that I should not relinquish for all *his* splendour; and there is something tawdry about it . . ."

20 March 1840:
". . . I wish you could have heard Liszt this morning. He really is quite extraordinary. He played from my *Novelletten*, the Fantasy, and the Sonata, in a way that affected me deeply. Much of it was different from what I had expected, but all of it was full of genius, and had a tenderness and sense of daring which is no doubt not an everyday occurrence with him . . ."

22 March 1840:
". . . But to you I say this, that Liszt appears more prodigious every day. This morning he again played at Raimund Härtel's – Études by Chopin, a piece from the Rossini *Soirées* and much else besides, so that we trembled and rejoiced . . ."

25 March 1840:
". . . For the whole of the last few days there has been nothing but dinners and suppers, music and champagne, counts and beautiful women: in a word, he has thrown our entire lives into turmoil. We all love him to distraction, and yesterday, at his concert, he once again played like a god, so that the furore was indescribable. The gossips and backbiters have all been silenced . . ."

Article in the *Neue Zeitschrift für Musik*, April 1840:
". . . It is no longer piano playing of this or that kind, but the expression of a daring character which destiny has allowed him to master and to conquer not through some dangerous instrument, but through the peaceful agency of art. How many leading artists have passed before us in recent years, how many do we ourselves possess who are Liszt's equal in many respects, but who must needs yield before him in energy and daring. [. . .] In a spirit of friendliness, he had chosen for his concert works by three composers living here, Mendelssohn, Hiller, and myself: Mendelssohn's latest Concerto [op. 40 in D minor], Hiller's Studies, and several pieces from one of my older works known as *Carnaval*. To the astonishment of many a more diffident virtuoso, it may be recorded here that Liszt virtually sight-read all these compositions. He had no doubt already had a fleeting acquaintance with the Studies and with *Carnaval*, but he had got to know Mendelssohn's composition only a few days before the concert; ever in demand, he could not possibly have found the time to study it in detail [. . .]"

248 (above) Article by Johann Wilhelm Christern, Hamburg 1840. (For a translation of the text, see p. 337.)

Christern also published a biographical sketch of Liszt in 1841.

249 (left) Advertisement for a concert in Dresden on 29 March 1840, including a declaration by Liszt intended to allay ill feeling which had arisen in the town. (For a translation of the text, see p. 337.)

Liszt left Leipzig on 31 March 1840. Notwithstanding his friendly dealings with Schumann and Mendelssohn, the town was associated in his memory with a series of unpleasant incidents. Clara Wieck's father, Friedrich, who had moved to Dresden from Leipzig that same year, had become his enemy. Either consciously or by mistake, Liszt had failed to send him and the press any free tickets. The local population had already been set against Liszt, even before his arrival in Leipzig, by a report in the *Tagblatt* which had spoken of the ''honour which Liszt's visit is shortly to confer on musical Leipzig.'' Leipzig was to remain hostile to Liszt, his compositions, and even his piano playing until a year before his death, when a German Liszt Society was established in the town.

April 1840 was spent in Paris, where Liszt gave two concerts in the Salons Erard and saw Marie d'Agoult again after an interval of six months. In May and June we find him in London, and then in Frankfurt, Bonn, and other towns along the Rhine. September saw him back in England, followed by visits to Belgium and Hamburg, and then a third concert tour of England. The end of the year found him in Scotland and Ireland.

250 Christern's report on Liszt's first concert in Hamburg, 1840. (For a translation of the text, see pp. 337–8.)

251 Four-octave dummy keyboard.

Liszt occasionally used this keyboard while staying with his uncle, Dr Eduard Liszt, in the Schottenhof district of Vienna. The instrument is now in the Wagner Museum in Bayreuth.

252 Dummy keyboard owned by Liszt.

This instrument, of the type known in Vienna as a "Stummerli," accompanied Liszt on his great European tours. He sometimes used it for finger exercises. He later gave it to Anton Bruckner and it is now in the Liszt Museum at the Academy of Music in Budapest. It has a compass of three octaves.

"Virtuosity exists to enable the artist to reproduce all that is expressed by art. It is indispensable here and cannot be sufficiently cultivated."[71]

"Virtuosity is not an excrescence, but a necessary element in music. [. . .] It is not a passive helpmeet of composition, since the life and death of the work of art entrusted to her care depend upon her breath: it can reproduce that element in the radiance of its beauty, its freshness, and its enthusiasm, but it can also pervert it, making it ugly and distorted. No one will call painting a slavish, material reproduction of nature. As painting is related to nature, so virtuosity is related to creative music making. [. . .] It would be a poor artist indeed (if he deserved that name at all) who simply followed the existing contours with uncomprehending faithfulness, without imbuing them with that life which derives from the artist's perception of passions and feelings. [. . .] Although the virtuoso's rendering of a given theme or subject merely reproduces the ideal which the composer held up to his soul, and although he is, in consequence, merely the interpreter of another's work, he must be as much a poet as the painter and sculptor, who, after all, reproduce nature after their fashion, singing at sight, as it were, from the creator's books of music."[72]

253 A mail coach, the chief form of transport around 1840. Copper engraving, ca. 1830.

For almost ten years Liszt subjected himself to the hardships of a virtuoso's life. He travelled by mail coach from Glasgow to Constantinople, and from Gibraltar to St Petersburg.

254 A steamship on the Danube, with Preßburg in the background. Copper engraving, ca. 1830.

Around 1840 Liszt would cover the distance between Vienna and Pest by mail coach or steamer, but from 1870 onwards he was able to use the railway for his annual visits to Hungary.

Opposite page:

256 Liszt in a travelling coat. Lithograph by Josef Kriehuber, 1840.

Beneath the picture are lines by Lord Byron, written in Liszt's own hand.

255 Page of an autograph letter from Liszt to Count Leo Festetics, 20 June 1842 (reduced in size).

Liszt writes to complain of his life as a virtuoso: "Nothing but concerts! Always dancing attendance on the audience, however reluctantly! What wearisome labour! What a profession!" And he adds a theme from Mozart's *Don Giovanni*, "Notte e giorno faticar" (Night and day I slave away).

Liszt's Piano Practice and Sight-Reading

Anyone who reads Liszt's voluminous correspondence, together with contemporary press reports and eyewitness accounts of his restless progress from concert hall to concert hall, will be forced to the conclusion that the greatest pianist of the nineteenth century never had any time for actual "practising," least of all during the years 1838–47, when he was crossing and recrossing Europe on one concert tour after another. A silent travelling keyboard (see Illus. 252) could of course have served for occasional finger exercises before a concert appearance, but could not have helped him to learn new works.

In drawing a comparison between Liszt, Thalberg, Henselt, and Clara Wieck as pianists, Robert Schumann had noted under the heading *Exercises*: "free: 1. Thalberg, 2. Clara; slavish: Henselt; none: Liszt."

On occasions (and this, too, is confirmed by Schumann) Liszt went straight from the mail coach to the concert hall, even without testing the piano. "Just imagine, he played a Härtel piano [these pianos were well known for their heavy touch], never having seen it before. I like this sort of thing very much, this reliance upon his ten good fingers . . ." (letter to Clara Schumann of 20 March 1840).[74]

Liszt was a phenomenal sight-reader. Saint-Saëns (himself highly regarded in this respect), Ferdinand Hiller, and Wagner frequently expressed their astonishment at Liszt's ability in this regard. In the presence of their respective composers, he sight-read concertos by Mendelssohn and Grieg from the original manuscripts (see pp. 69 and 249). He also mastered works such as Beethoven's C minor Concerto or Mendelssohn's D minor Concerto after reading them through repeatedly in the printed score (see pp. 116 and 129). When Anton Rubinstein handed Liszt a copy of his recently completed Fantasy for two pianos in Vienna, Liszt read through the work, talking as he did so, then sat down at a second piano and played it with the composer. Rubinstein's subsequent comment was "Impossible, impossible, it's unbelievable."

The arduous travelling conditions of the time and the constant hurly-burly which surrounded Liszt robbed him of any opportunity to practise. His few free hours were devoted to his voluminous correspondence (during his five weeks in Berlin in 1842 he wrote over 3000 letters asking for support for himself, and encouraging and recommending others) or to writing out his own compositions. Even here he was rarely left in peace.

Eduard Hanslick on Liszt in 1846:
". . . The whole of Vienna's musical youth was encamped in Liszt's rooms 'Zur Stadt London' during the daytime; he himself sat at the piano, wearing a black silk smock, correcting proofs or, the manuscript paper on his knee, writing down some composition in his sloping, long-stemmed, and not altogether legible handwriting, chatting and smoking the while. Should he also, by a happy chance, sight-read some brand new work, his visitors would have further occasion to marvel at his prodigious musical endowment."[75]

Here's a sigh to those who love me,
And a smile to those who hate;
And, whatever sky 'sabove me,
Here's a heart for every fate

(Byron)

F. Liszt

LIFE

January: Concerts in Ireland, Scotland, and England. 1: Cork; 2: Clonmel; 7: two concerts in Dublin; 9 and 11: Limerick; 12 and 13: Dublin; 15: Belfast; 19, 21, and 23: Edinburgh; 20 and 22: Glasgow; 25: Newcastle upon Tyne; 26: Sunderland and Durham; 27: Richmond and Darlington; 29: Halifax.

3 February: Concert in London.

9 February: Liszt in Brussels. Becomes friendly with François-Joseph Fétis and Prince Felix von Lichnowsky. Gaëtano Belloni enters Liszt's service, continuing as his impresario until 1847.

15 February: Concert in Liège.

16 February: Concert in Brussels.

20 February: Concert in Ghent.

2 and 7 March: Concerts in Antwerp.

27 March: Concerts in Paris (Salons Erard). The programmes include the *Lucia* and *Robert* paraphrases, the *William Tell* Overture, and *Mazeppa*.

April: Liszt performs on a number of occasions at the Salons Erard, each time to overwhelming acclaim. Berlioz observes that no pianist has ever performed or composed like this before (*Robert* paraphrase and *Mazeppa* Study).

25 April: Liszt performs Beethoven's E flat major Piano Concerto, conducted by Berlioz. Wagner is among those present (see right-hand column).

26 April: Liszt attends a concert given by Chopin and writes a review of it (see p. 137).

Beginning of May to 3 July: In London. Liszt works on his operatic paraphrases (*Norma*, *La Sonnambula*, *Der Freischütz*, and *Don Giovanni*). Concert on 12 June, and appearance at a Philharmonic Concert on 14 June.

5 to 11 July: Liszt in Hamburg. Concerts on 7 (Beethoven's *Choral Fantasy*) and 9 July.

13 July: Concert in Kiel.

16 to 25 July: Liszt in Copenhagen. Seven concerts in the presence of King Christian VIII, to whom Liszt dedicates his *Réminiscences de "Don Juan."* He receives the Danebrog Order.

27 July: Liszt in Hamburg. Concert on the 29th. Liszt travels to Nonnenwerth via Rotterdam, Amsterdam, Düsseldorf, and Cologne.

August to October: Liszt and Marie d'Agoult on Nonnenwerth, where a large number of Liszt's songs are written. A constant stream of honours and visits (including one from Felix von Lichnowsky) prevents Liszt from finding any peace and quiet here. From Nonnenwerth he undertakes concert tours to Koblenz, Ems, and Bonn. In Cologne he donates 1140 gulden to the cathedral building fund.

18 September: In Frankfurt Liszt donates 900 gulden to the Mozart Foundation and is enrolled as a Freemason.

12 October: Concert in Aachen.

22 October: Liszt plants a plane tree (which still exists) on the island of Nonnenwerth to mark his thirtieth birthday.

November: Concerts in Germany: Düsseldorf (where he says goodbye to Marie d'Agoult), Elberfeld, Krefeld, Wesel (7 November), Münster (9 and 11 November), Osnabrück (12 November), Bielefeld (13 November), Detmold (15 November), Kassel (19 and 22 November), Göttingen, Gotha, Weimar (26, 28, and 29 November), Jena (30 November), Dresden (4, 9, and 11 December), Leipzig (6, 13, and 16 December), Altenburg (14 December), Halle (18 and 19 December), and Berlin (27 December).

257 The concert hall of the Paris Conservatoire. Wood engraving by P. S. Germain from *L'Illustration* of 15 April 1843.

Liszt gave a benefit performance here in April 1841, the proceeds going towards the Bonn Beethoven Memorial.

258 Richard Wagner (1813–1883). Photograph by Pierre Petit & Trinquart, 1860.

The first known photograph of Wagner. Wagner attended Liszt's concert on 25 April 1841.

On 25 April 1841 Liszt performed Beethoven's E flat major Piano Concerto in the Great Hall of the Paris Conservatoire. In the audience was Richard Wagner, whose review of the concert appeared in the Dresden *Abend-Zeitung* of 5 May 1841:

"What would and could Liszt not be, if he were not a famous man or, rather, if people had not made him famous! He could and would be a free artist, a minor god, instead of which he is now the slave of a most insipid audience which craves to hear only virtuosos. This audience demands at all costs to hear marvels and foolish nonsense; he gives them what they want, is cherished for it, and, at a concert for the Beethoven Monument, performs a Fantasy on *Robert the Devil*! But he did so out of resentment. The programme consisted only of works by Beethoven; yet, notwithstanding this fact, the enchanted audience clamoured to hear Liszt's most exquisite work of art, his *Robert* Fantasy. It redounded to the great man's credit when, with irritable haste, he muttered the words 'Je suis le serviteur du public, cela va sans dire!' and sat down at the piano to play the popular little number with devastating skill . . ."

Only a few days after this concert, Liszt set off back to England. In all he made a total of nine visits to the British Isles, viz. May to August 1824; June/July 1825; April to June 1827; May/June, August/September, and November/December 1840 (between 24 November 1840 and 3 February 1841 Liszt gave concerts almost every day in different towns; see pp. 123 and 134); January and May to July 1841; and April 1886.

Eigenthum und Verlag der K.K. Hof- und priv. Kunst und Musikalien Handlung

des Tobias Haslinger in Wien.

WORKS

Réminiscences de ''Don Juan'' (Mozart) (for piano). Pub. 1843. A version for two pianos appeared in 1877. In 1912 Busoni completed and published a *Fantasia on Themes from ''Figaro''* which Liszt had left in fragmentary form, having played it in Berlin in 1843.

Réminiscences de ''Norma'' (Bellini) (for piano) (see Illus. 293). Pub. 1843. A version for two pianos appeared in 1874.

Réminiscences de ''Robert le Diable'' (Meyerbeer) (for piano). Pub. 1841. A version for four hands appeared in 1843.

Grandes Variations de Concert (abridged version of the *Hexaméron*) (for two pianos). Probably written 1841. Pub. 1870. (This may be the version which Liszt and Clara Schumann performed in Leipzig on 6 and 13 December 1841.)

''I Puritani.'' *Introduction et Polonaise* (Bellini) (for piano). Pub. ca. 1842.

''God Save the Queen.'' *Grande Paraphrase de Concert* (for piano). Pub. 1841 or 1842. In June and July 1842 the Hamburg firm of Schuberth announced a version for piano and orchestra, but this either was not published or is lost. It would not have been orchestrated by Liszt.

Fantasia on Themes from Halévy's ''Guitarero'' (for piano), performed in Kassel on 19 November 1841 and mentioned in the press as ''not yet published.'' Lost or, more probably, never written down.

Fantasia on Themes from Rossini's ''Moïse'' (for piano). Mentioned by Liszt in letters of 14 and 20 May 1841. Lost or, more probably, not completed.

Buch der Lieder (for soprano or tenor and piano): 1. *Loreley*, 2. *Am Rhein*, 3. *Mignons Lied*, 4. *Es war ein König in Thule*, 5. *Der du von dem Himmel bist* (1842), 6. *Angiolin* (already written in 1839, but included in this collection). Written 1841/42. Pub. 1843. A piano transcription, prepared in 1844, was published in 1846. These songs were all revised and published between ca. 1856 and 1860.

Vierstimmige Männergesänge (for unaccompanied men's voices). Pub. 1843: 1. *Rheinweinlied*, 2. *Studentenlied*, 3. and 4. *Reiterlied* in two versions.

Nonnenwerth (for voice and piano). Written ca. 1841. Pub. 1843. A revised version (written ca. 1860) appeared in 1860. A piano transcription was published in 1843, a revised one in 1844, and a final version was written in 1880 and published in 1883. An adaptation (by Liszt?) for piano and violin or cello is unpublished.

Deux Feuilles d'Album (for piano). No. 1 is part of the *Valse mélancolique* (see ''Works 1839'' and ''Works 1840''), while No. 2 is a transcription of the third version of *Nonnenwerth* (see above).

Feuilles d'album (single piano piece) in A flat. Pub. 1884.

Il m'aimait tant (for voice and piano). Written ca. 1841. Pub. (also for piano alone) 1843.

Wo weilt er? (for voice and piano). Written ca. 1841. Pub. 1860.

Das deutsche Vaterland (for men's voices). Pub. 1842 in two versions.

(continued p. 137)

259 Hector Berlioz. Lithograph by Josef Kriehuber, 1845.

 Berlioz conducted Beethoven's E flat major Concerto, with Liszt as soloist, on 25 April 1841.

Left:

260 Johann Peter Pixis (1788–1874).
Liszt's father mentions Pixis in a letter to Czerny (see p. 32).

Right:

261 Henri Bertini (1798–1876).
Bertini's melodic and harmoniously elegant *Études* were highly regarded by Liszt.

FAMOUS PIANO VIRTUOSI IN PARIS
Lithographs, ca. 1840

Left:

262 George Alexander Osborne (1806–1893).
Osborne occasionally appeared on the same platform as Chopin, and has left an account of the latter's concert in Manchester on 28 August 1848.

Right:

263 Friedrich Kalkbrenner (1785–1849).
Kalkbrenner wanted to give lessons to Chopin, who dedicated his E minor Piano Concerto to him. Chopin declined the offer.

''Works 1841'' (continued)

Funeral March (from Beethoven's Symphony No. 3, *Eroica*) (piano transcription). Pub. 1843.
Le Moine (piano transcription of song by Meyerbeer). Written 1841. Pub. 1842.
Carnaval de Venise (Paganini) (piano). Arrangement probably dates from this time. Unfinished and unpublished.
Den Felsengipfel stieg ich einst hinan. Song for low voice and piano. May date from this period. Unfinished and unpublished.

264 Famous pianists around 1840. Lithograph by Nicolas E. Maurin, 1842.
    Back row (from left to right): Rosenhain, Döhler, Chopin, Dreyschock, Thalberg. Front row (left to right): Wolff, Henselt, Liszt. The lithograph was offered to subscribers of the Paris *Gazette musicale* on 1 January 1843.

A whole army of pianists (''I really think there must be more pianists in Paris than anywhere else,'' Chopin wrote to Tytus Woyciechowski[76]) attended Liszt's incredibly successful concerts in Paris in April 1841. When Chopin himself gave a concert on 26 April 1841, Liszt wrote a highly poetical review. Ernest Legouvé, the resident critic of the *Gazette musicale*, describes in his autobiography how Chopin replied to the news that Liszt was planning to review his concert with the words ''He will leave me a little kingdom in his empire.''

Liszt's review of Chopin's concert, *Gazette musicale*, 2 May 1841:

''Last Monday at 8 o'clock, the Salons Pleyel were festively lit. The stairway was decorated with carpets and flowers, and to it came the most elegant ladies and gentlemen, the most celebrated artists, the most prosperous financiers, the most distinguished aristocracy representing the élite of society, all who lay claim to nobility of birth and wealth, talent and beauty.

''A large grand piano stood open on a platform. People flocked around it, eagerly bent on obtaining a seat as close as they could. They all sat down, no other thought in their heads than not to miss a single chord, a single note or nuance, a single thought of him who was now about to take his seat up there. And how fitting it was that these people were all so expectant, attentive, and reverential; for the man whom they were awaiting, whom they wished to see and hear, to admire and overwhelm with acclaim, was not only a brilliant virtuoso, a pianist skilled in the art of the keyboard, not only an artist of great fame and reputation – he was all this and more: he was Chopin.

''[. . .] Chopin has played no part in the exaggerated competitiveness which performing artists all over the world are wont to indulge in at each other's expense. He has al-ways been surrounded by loyal disciples, enthusiastic pupils, and devoted friends, who have protected him from unwanted conflicts and have never tired of spreading abroad their admiration for his name and works. Thus this extraordinary celebrity, truly great and toweringly pre-eminent, has always remained unassailable. All criticism of him is silenced, as though posterity had already spoken. And the glittering audience which flocked to the concert to hear the poet who for far too long had been silent showed no opposition, no reservations: unanimous praise was on everyone's lips.

''[. . .] A wild and volatile element from his native land finds expression in daring dissonances and strange harmonies, while the tenderness and grace of his personality are revealed in the countless nuances and embellishments of his inimitable imagination. [. . .] Since his playing addressed itself to a select gathering rather than to the general public, he was able to reveal himself as he really is, as an elegiac poet, profound, chaste, and visionary. [. . .] Even with his very first chords he established close contact between himself and his listeners. Two Études and a Ballade had to be repeated, and no doubt the audience would have wished to hear every work in the programme repeated again and again if they had not feared tiring the artist, the pallor of whose features signalled his growing fatigue. [. . .]''

265 The island of Nonnenwerth in the Rhine. Steel engraving by A. Fesca, based on a drawing by Eberhard Emminger; ca. 1840.

Liszt and Marie d'Agoult spent the summer months of 1841, 1842, and 1843 here. To the left is Rolandseck, with the Drachenfels behind it.

266 Comtesse Marie d'Agoult. Pencil drawing by Théodore Chassériau, 1841.[77]

267 Liszt's children, portrayed as future celebrities, with Nonnenwerth in the background. Anonymous caricature, ca. 1842.

Blandine is seen on the left, Daniel in the middle, and Cosima on the right. Between them is Liszt, wearing a black top hat and showering young people with money; beside him, holding a sunshade, is Marie d'Agoult.

268 The island of Nonnenwerth. Photograph, 1975.

Liszt first set foot on the island of Nonnenwerth in August 1841. Situated on the Rhine between Koblenz and Bonn, the island was to provide a summer retreat for Liszt and Marie d'Agoult for three consecutive years. He returned with the Comtesse in 1842 and 1843, in the hope of finding the peace and quiet he needed to work. He even planned to purchase Nonnenwerth, but the expense of having to build new supporting pillars, as would have been necessary, discouraged him from doing so.

Nor did Liszt find the peace and quiet he longed for here. His admirers soon tracked him down. As he wrote to Lina Ramann in December 1875, ''These summer months were ruined by incessant visits, and I shall avoid ever again attempting such a *villeggiatura* at a point where railways and steamships intersect.''[78] Nonnenwerth also witnessed the end of his happiness with Marie d'Agoult, who described the island as ''the grave of my dreams and ideals, the mortal remains of my hopes.''

Prince Felix von Lichnowsky (1814–1848), a grandson of the Lichnowsky who had been an intimate of Beethoven's, was a frequent visitor. Liszt had struck up a friendship with the brigadier from Mainz, a man well known for his dazzling appearance and countless duels. The prince accompanied Liszt on a number of concert tours. He was a member of the Frankfurt Parliament before being tortured and murdered by revolutionaries on 18 September 1848.

Bonn, Koblenz, Frankfurt, Cologne, Münster, Bielefeld, and Kassel marked further stages in Liszt's concert career. At the end of November 1841 he paid his first visit to a town which was later to acquire unique significance in his life: Weimar.

269 Programme for Liszt's concert in Weimar on 29 November 1841.

270 Weimar. Steel engraving by Heawood, based on a drawing by Adolf Eltzner; ca. 1845.

Liszt gave a series of concerts in Weimar on 26, 28, and 29 November 1841. Seven years later the town was to become his home. Among the places arrowed on the illustration are the Altenburg (Liszt's home from 1848 to 1861), the Court Theatre (where he held the post of Court Kapellmeister), and the Hofgärtnerei (where he lived from 1869 to 1886).

LIFE

1 January to 3 March: 21 concerts in Berlin. These concerts are undoubtedly the high point of Liszt's career as a virtuoso (programmes and dates at right). Liszt is introduced to Alexander von Humboldt, Bettina von Arnim, Charlotte von Hagn, Varnhagen von Ense, and others.
Liszt receives the Ordre Pour le Mérite, and is elected a member of the Royal Prussian Academy of Arts.
2 January: Concert in Potsdam (Casino).
3 March: Liszt leaves Berlin. Charlotte von Hagn (Illus. 383) is reported to have followed him in secret to spend a few days with him in Müncheberg.
8 March: Concert in Elbing.
10, 11, and 13 March: Concerts in Königsberg.
14 March: Receives honorary doctorate from University of Königsberg.
Following concerts in Tilsit (18 March), Mitau (three concerts), Riga, and Dorpat (8 to 11 April, two concerts) Liszt arrives in St Petersburg on 15 April (new-style dating).
April and May: 20 (8) and 23 (11) April, 10 May (28 April), and 17 (5) May: Concerts in St Petersburg. (The dates in parentheses are in the Russian calendar.) The receipts from one concert are donated to victims of the great Hamburg fire. Liszt becomes friendly with Henselt, Glinka, and Wilhelm von Lenz, and frequents Russian aristocratic circles (Count Wielhorsky, Prince Yusupov, and Princess Pielosulska).
Mid-May: Liszt leaves St Petersburg and returns to Paris via Lübeck (1 June). Various charity concerts in Paris and Neuilly.
30 June: Benefit concert in Paris (Salon Obrist Thorn) for German choristers.
18 July: Liszt in Liège for the unveiling of the Grétry Memorial. He receives the Order of the Lion of Belgium from King Leopold I.
20 July: Concert in the Municipal Theatre in Liège (first movement of Beethoven's E flat major Piano Concerto, *Kreutzer* Sonata with Lambert Massart, *Réminiscences de ''Don Juan,''* and improvisations).
24 July: Concert in Brussels.
August: Liszt, Marie d'Agoult, and his three children on the island of Nonnenwerth.
9 to 13 September: Concert in Cologne for the cathedral building fund.
14 September: Liszt in Koblenz.
September: Concert at Schloß Brühl in the presence of King Friedrich Wilhelm IV. Liszt at Nonnenwerth, then briefly in Paris, Liège, and Aachen.
October: Concerts in Weimar on 23 and 29 October, with concert in Jena in between.
31 October: Liszt accepts the post of Court Kapellmeister in Extraordinary in Weimar with a commitment to conduct the orchestra for three months every year (decree dated 2 November: see Illus. 351).
1 November: Starting in Coburg (1 to 7 November), Liszt embarks on a concert tour with the singer Giovanni Rubini, visiting Gotha (8 November), Frankfurt (11 to 15 November), The Hague (19 to end of November), Rotterdam, Leiden, Utrecht (concert on 9 December), and Amsterdam (12 to 17 December).
End of December: Meeting with Wagner in Berlin.

271 Liszt in a Berlin concert hall. Pastel illustration by Seckert, 1842.

Liszt gave his first concert in Berlin on 27 December 1841. In the audience was Varnhagen von Ense, who noted in his diary, "In the evening concert by Liszt, without orchestra, in the Singakademie; he played all alone, wonderful, matchless, magical, to universal and thunderous applause. Not since Paganini have I heard such a master perform. [. . .] We had seats very near to the front and could observe this intelligent, elegant, handsome man at close quarters. [. . .] The king was in his box, the Count of Nassau, Prince and Princess Karl, Prince August, the Crown Prince of Württemberg. Also Meyerbeer, Felix Mendelssohn, Spontini, Rellstab, Spiker, and a crowd of acquaintances."[79]

Liszt gave 21 concerts in the space of ten weeks (27 December 1841 to 3 March 1842), nine of them for such charitable causes as the Cologne Cathedral building fund, day nurseries, "needy teachers," and poor students.

272 Liszt's programmes for his 21 concerts in Berlin between 27 December 1841 and 3 March 1842.[80] (For a translation of the text, see p. 338.) The relevant dates and venues are as follows:

27 December	Singakademie
1 January	Singakademie
5 January	Singakademie
9 January	Casino (Potsdam)
16 January	Singakademie
21 January	Singakademie
23 January	Singakademie
30 January	Singakademie
3 February	Singakademie
6 February	Singakademie
25 January	Great Hall of the University or Singakademie
4 February	Great Hall of the University
10 February	Schauspielhaus
16 February	Royal Opera House
19 February	Royal Opera House
23 February	Royal Opera House
2 March	Royal Opera House
End of February	Hôtel de Russie
End of February	Hôtel de Russie
End of February	Royal Opera House
3 March	Hôtel de Russie

The music critic Ludwig Rellstab (1799–1860) reviewed Liszt's first concert in Berlin:

"The world has grown weary of drawing witty and sometimes poetic comparisons between Liszt and Thalberg; the latter has been called the 'ange du piano,' the former the 'diable du piano,' and thus they have been coordinated and contrasted. To our own way of thinking, however, these comparisons have not been drawn from the correct point of view; Liszt subsumes the whole of Thalberg. If he does not give the same as the latter, he could none the less do so; he could solve every challenge which Thalberg has been able to solve; whereas the same is not true of Thalberg. Thalberg's art is an harmonically developed, wondrously beautiful corporeality; symmetry, poise, tranquillity, grace, and strength; but he possesses little of that charm which is imparted to the body in exalted states of mind, a quality which Liszt's art possesses in such superabundance that we may well describe that art as endued with the very soul which is missing from Thalberg's art. Nor does he lack tranquillity; Thalberg's tranquillity derives from the fact that no inward ferment or growth disturbs it; it is, rather, a negative quality; Liszt's tranquillity is that of total mastery over all the stirring violence of passion, the positive force of superior might. Thalberg the horseman rides a quiet steed, Liszt, by contrast, a fiery, winged stallion to whose snorting wildness he can give free rein at will or else tame that wildness to the most docile obedience."[81]

From Berlin Liszt travelled to Marienburg, where he made his debut on 8 March 1842. After a series of concerts in Königsberg (modern Kaliningrad), Tilsit (Sovetsk), Mitau (Jelgava), Riga, and Dorpat (Tartu), he arrived in St Petersburg (Leningrad) on 15 April. On the 20th (Old Style, 8th) he gave his first concert in the city, forcing his way through a crowd of more than 3000 spectators in order to gain access to the platform in the great Assembly Hall of the Nobles.

The well-known Russian music critic Vladimir Stasov (1824–1906) reported on the concert:

". . . He tore off his white kid gloves and tossed them on the floor, under the piano. Then, after bowing low in all directions to a tumult of applause such as had probably not been heard in Petersburg since 1703, he seated himself at the piano. Instantly the hall became deadly silent. Without any preliminaries, Liszt began playing the opening cello phrase of the *William Tell* Overture. As soon as he finished, and while the hall was still rocking with applause, he moved swiftly to a second piano facing in the opposite direction. Throughout the concert he used the pianos alternately for each piece, facing first one, then the other half of the hall. [At this time pianos were far less robust than they are today; strings often broke, and for this reason Liszt would sometimes use two pianos.] [. . .] We had never in our lives heard anything like this; we had never been in the presence of such a brilliant, passionate, demonic temperament, at one moment rushing like a whirlwind, at another pouring forth cascades of tender beauty and grace. Liszt's playing was absolutely overwhelming . . ."[82]

Valse à capriccio sur deux motifs de "Lucia" et "Parisina" (Donizetti) (for piano). Pub. ca. 1842. A new version appeared in 1852.
Deux Mélodies russes: 1. *Le rossignol* (Alabyev), 2. *Chanson bohémienne* (for piano). Pub. 1842, No. 1 also in a "Nouvelle édition."
Canzone Napolitana (piano transcription from unknown original). Pub. 1843.
Mazurka (paraphrase of a mazurka "par un amateur de St. Pétersbourg") (for piano). Pub. ca. 1842. Unrelated to the *Mazurka brillante* of 1850.
Élégie sur des motifs du Prince Louis Ferdinand (for piano). Pub. ca. 1842.
Petite Valse favorite (for piano). Written 1842 or 1843. Pub. 1843. Later developed into the *Valse impromptu* of 1850.
Albumblatt in Walzerform (for piano). First published in 1908 in August Göllerich's book *Franz Liszt*.
6 Preludes and Fugues for Organ (J. S. Bach) (piano transcriptions). Begun in 1842 and completed ca. 1850. Pub. 1852.
Songs for men's voices: 1. *Wir sind nicht Mumien*, 2. *Über allen Gipfeln ist Ruh*, 3. *Gottes ist der Orient*, 4. *Das düstre Meer umrauscht.* Pub. 1844. No. 4 with piano accompaniment. Two versions of No. 2 for solo voice and piano were published in 1847 and 1859.
Mignons Lied (for high voice and piano). Pub. 1843; for soprano and orchestra in 1863, and for piano alone in 1844.
L'aube naît et ta porte est close (after Victor Hugo) (for voice and piano). Mentioned in a letter of 7 May 1842. Lost.
Élégie ("En ces lieux tout me parle d'elle," based on a poem by E. Monnier) (for voice and piano). Date of composition unknown. Pub. in Paris before 1855.
Serbisches Lied (song by Prince Konstantin von Hohenzollern-Hechingen). Liszt wrote a piano accompaniment. The present author has been unable to determine when the work was composed or published.
Die Gräberinsel (song by Duke Ernst of Saxe-Coburg-Gotha) (piano transcription). First performed 9 November 1842. Pub. 1983.
Es hat geflammt die ganze Nacht (song by Grand Duchess Maria Pavlovna). A piano accompaniment by Liszt survives in an unpublished manuscript. It is not known when it was written.
Barcarolle vénitienne de Pantaleoni (song by the tenor Pantaleoni). Liszt wrote a piano accompaniment, probably in 1842. Pub. 1842.

273, 274 Programmes of Liszt's first two concerts in St Petersburg (old-style dates).

275, 276, 277 Caricatures published under the title "Das Liszt'ge Berlin" in Volumes 9, 10, and 11 of A. Eyssenhardt's *Berliner Witze*, 1842 [*Last* = burden; *Lust* = delight].

278 (above) *Would you like to play?* Caricatures. Steel engraving published by the Berlin firm of A. Schepeler in 1842.

279 (far right) Title page of *Berlin as it is and . . . drinks*, 1842 (Volume 14), by Adam Brennglas, based on a drawing by Theodor Hosemann.

The hero-worship to which Liszt was forced to submit in Berlin bordered on hysteria. Numerous cartoons and commentaries in the press dealt with this theme.

"He has been fêted and he has been serenaded; a woman knelt down in front of him and begged to be allowed to kiss the tips of his fingers – another embraced him in public in the concert hall – a third poured the remains of his cup of tea into her scent-bottle – hundreds have worn gloves bearing his portrait – many have lost their reason. They all wanted to lose it. An art dealer made glass-paste objects with Liszt's portrait and sold them as ornaments; thousands vied for his favours and begged for his money – and this is only the beginning. Last but not least is Liszt's farewell. Together with the senior students he sat in a carriage drawn by six white horses – never has folly reached such heights!" (*Hell'sche Abendzeitung*, No. 88, 1842)

Newspapers throughout Europe carried reports of the outbreak of Lisztomania in Berlin, provoking disbelief and indignation on all sides. Earlier admirers of Liszt such as Chopin, Schumann, and Mendelssohn felt only anger. Those who were not immediately involved could not understand what all the fuss was about, but even Liszt's enemies succumbed to his spell when exposed to the fascination of the man.

Heinrich Heine (April 1844):
"When I used to hear of the giddiness which broke out in Germany, and more especially in Berlin, whenever Liszt appeared there, I would shrug my shoulders pityingly and think: silent, Sabbath-like Germany does not want to miss

the opportunity to move when permitted to do so, or to shake its sleepy limbs a little . . . Thus did I explain Lisztomania to myself, and I took it to be a characteristic of the state of political immaturity which obtains beyond the Rhine. But I was wrong, and I did not notice my error until last week at the Italian Opera House, where Liszt gave his first concert and gave it, moreover, for a gathering which might well be described as the flower of local society. This was no sentimentally German public, no audience of Berliners falsely adopting the emotions of others – and yet! How powerful, how thrilling was the impression caused by his mere appearance! [. . .]"

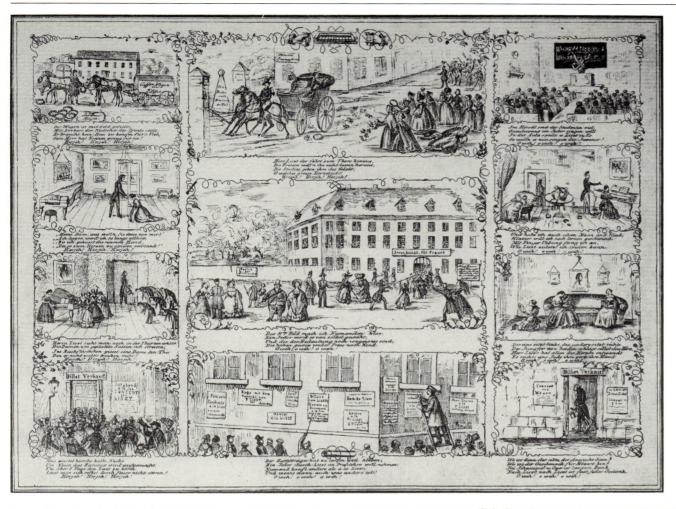

280 Eleven parodistic verses to the tune of *Es ritten drei Reiter*. Lithograph by Schäfer, based on a drawing by Grünspahn; March 1842.

281 Lithograph by Puthalm, based on a drawing by Grünspahn; 1842.

282 ''General Bass'' is taken unawares in his fixed lines, and overpowered by Liszt – and by his homonym List (= cunning). Lithograph, ca. 1842.

The Berlin concerts of 1842 were without doubt the outward climax of Liszt's career as a pianist.

Liszt had everything that it takes to be what is nowadays called a "star": brilliant ability, dazzling good looks, self-confidence on stage, and an energetic constitution. That he gave himself all manner of airs and graces during these years, when, as he himself put it, he "lived like a lord," and that many women literally threw themselves at him, is without question. Unfortunately, many later writers have been influenced by this image, and failed to consider the seriousness and selflessness shown by the Liszt of the Weimar years.

Varnhagen von Ense noted in his diary on 27 January 1842, "Liszt continues to ravish the city; he transfigures the winter here and provides its greatest splendour. His altruism, his unruffled good breeding, his benevolent and charming nature win him acclaim in no less measure than his all-conquering mastery . . ."[84]

Liszt left Berlin on 3 March 1842. He was carried shoulder high to a coach and six, while thirty carriages, driven four in hand, accompanied him out of the city.

This page and opposite:
283–290 Newspaper reports and poems in homage to Liszt, reproduced from journals of the time.[83] (For translations of these texts, see pp. 338–9.)

An Franz Liszt,

nach seinem Concerte für den Bau des kölner Doms.

Der deutschen Ströme Kaiser ist der Rhein;
Der Dom zu Köln ist seines Reiches Krone.
Du fügst zu ihrem Glanze manchen Stein;
Vernimm den Dank von einem Rheinlandsohne.
Dein Name, leuchtend in des Ruhmes Schein,
Gebietend auf dem Dom holdem Throne,
Setzt sich ein Denkmal in dem Zeitenstrome:
Indem du bauen hilfst am Dom der Dome.

Einst, wenn die Wundertöne längst verklungen,
Von denen nun die Seele wiederhallt,
Von ihres Wohllauts Wonne süß durchdrungen,
Erfaßt vom Sturm der mächtigen Gewalt,
Vom Zaubrer Liszt gesagt wird und gesungen,
Der da entflammt die Herzen, die sonst kalt,
Wird man am Dom zu Köln die Inschrift schauen:
„Liszt half an Deutschlands Ruhm und Ehre bauen!"

Berlin, 10. Jan. 1842.   Philipp Kaufmann.

An Franz Liszt.

Kaum flog der Ruf von Hamburg's Schreckensbrande
Durch alle Gauen fort, von Land zu Lande,
Bis an die Newa hin, zu Deinem Ohr:
Da loderte in Deinem edlen Herzen
Das Mitgefühl schon für Hammonia's Schmerzen
Zur lichten Gluth, zur Flamme schnell empor,
Und kaum, daß der Gedanke Raum gefunden,
War er auch mit der That bereits verbunden.

Du großer Meister! Von den Künstlern allen
Warst Du der Erste, der die heil'gen Hallen
Der Kunst zur Hülfe uns geöffnet hat;
Wie Du für uns gewirkt im fernen Lande.
Nah'st Du als Helfer Dich dem deutschen Strande,
Zur Hülfe ward auf's Neu' die erste That;
Ein Ehren-Denkmal wird für ew'ge Zeiten
Dein Werk in der Geschichte Dir bereiten.

Die hohe Kunst, der Du Dich ganz ergeben,
Sie lohnte Niemals schöner noch Dein Streben
Als jetzt, wo Du zum Menschen-Wohl sie übst;
Die wahre Weihe hat sie nun empfangen,
Zu keinem schönern Ziel kann sie gelangen,
Zu keiner Würde, die Du ihr nicht giebst;
Und schöner hat kein Kranz Dein Haupt umschlungen,
Als unser Dank, den Du Dir so errungen!

Den 14. Juni 1842.   M.

Below:
291 Excerpt from the *Leipziger Allgemeine Zeitung* of July 1842, reporting a rumour that Liszt had been expelled from St Petersburg.

Liszt attributed Tsar Nicholas's loss of sympathy to "the irritable and in part inaccurate reports of the then Chief of Police in Warsaw concerning my political sympathies, sympathies which I take pride in not denying. But the report which some newspapers carried of my alleged 'expulsion' from St Petersburg is quite without foundation," Liszt informed Lina Ramann in December 1875.[85] (For a translation of the text, see p. 339.)

Königsberg, 9. Juli. Bei dem gänzlichen Stillschweigen, das russ. Blätter über alle Vorfälle, die nur entfernt die kais. Familie betreffen, beobachten, darf es nicht befremden, daß desto häufiger Gerüchte, die jene Beziehungen berühren, im Publicum Eingang finden. So circulirt schon wieder seit längerer Zeit das Gerücht, die plötzliche Abreise eines berühmten Virtuosen von Petersburg habe in einer Verbannung ihren Grund gehabt. Derselbe habe nämlich, als während eines Concerts in der kais. Loge eine ziemlich laute Conversation Statt gefunden, sich wiederholt nach jener Richtung umgesehen, und da dies unbeachtet geblieben, gleich darauf zu spielen aufgehört. In Folge dessen soll derselbe schon Tags darauf die Weisung erhalten haben, sich sofort aus Petersburg und den Gränzen des russischen Reiches zu entfernen.
(L. Allg. Z.)

Ein überraschender Morgenbesuch bei Franz Liszt.
Unter den vielen Beweisen der Verehrung und des Dankes, welche dem gefeierten Künstler, der nach beinah dreimonatlichem Aufenthalt heut von uns scheidet, hier zu Theil wurden, empfing er gestern eine, seinem mitfühlenden Herzen gewiß vor allen andern Auszeichnungen, besonders wohlthuende. Einhundert Kinder, von denen keines über sechs Jahr alt war, wurden unter Vortritt des Majors von Plehwe von den Vorstehern der verschiedenen Kinderbewahr-Anstalten, zu deren Besten Hr. Liszt ein Concert gegeben, ihm zugeführt, um ihm ihren Dank im Namen der tausend andern Kinder persönlich abzustatten. Eine Anzahl Knaben der Malméneschen Erziehungs-Anstalten hatten sich, von ihren Lehrern begleitet, ebenfalls eingefunden. Der Wirth des Hotel de Russie, Hr. Roth, war so gefällig gewesen, den Kindern seinen großen Saal zu öffnen, in welchem sie sich im Halbkreis aufstellten. Eine Deputation der Vorsteher begab sich hierauf zu Hrn. Liszt, um ihn zu bitten, den Dank der Kleinen anzunehmen. Bei dem Eintritt in den Saal wurde er mit dem Gesange: Lobt froh den Herrn, ihr jugendlichen Chöre, empfangen. Hierauf sprach der Major v. Plehwe einige Worte des Dankes im Namen des Vereins der Kinderbewahr-Anstalten, Herr Borchardt stattete noch besonderen Dank für das, der Anstalt No. 1. zu Theil gewordene, Geschenk ab. Vier von den Kindern traten jetzt vor, sagten ein Verschen, überreichten Kränze und „streuten ihrem Wohlthäter Blumen auf seinen Lebensweg." Alle Anwesende und besonders den Künstler selbst ergriff eine so tiefe Rührung, daß er nicht anders zu antworten wußte, als daß er die Kinder herzlich und liebevoll küßte. Ein Knabe der Malméneschen Anstalt hielt nun ebenfalls eine in Versen abgefaßte, kurze Dankrede, worauf die Kleinen mehrere ihrer Gedächtnißverschen hersagten, wodurch eine heitere Stimmung verbreitet wurde, zumal als die tausend kleinen Fingerchen, mit den Worten: „die sind uns zum Spielen gegeben", in der Luft spielten. Ein scherzhaftes Concert ohne Instrumente und doch mit vollem Orchester von den Malméneschen Knaben ausgeführt, machte den Beschluß. Unter der wiederholten Versicherung, daß ihm dieser überraschende Morgenbesuch eine recht herzliche Freude gemacht habe, nahm der menschenfreundliche Künstler von den Versammelten Abschied, deren Segenswünsche ihn begleiten. —

Danksagungen.
Der Virtuose Herr Liszt
hat seine unermüdliche Wohlthätigkeitsliebe auch der Malméneschen Knaben-Beschäftigungs-Anstalt aus der Einnahme des, zu einem wohlthätigen Zwecke, im Königl. Opernhause gegebenen Concertes, mit einer Gabe von

100 thlr.

zugewendet. Mit der innigsten Freude bringen wir diesem wohlthuenden Virtuosen unsern herzlichsten Dank um so mehr dar, als die guten Knaben der Anstalt, in der neuesten Zeit, ihrem Ernährer so wenig für ihre Erhaltung einzubringen vermögen. Der Segen Gottes ruht auf dieser Gabe! —
Mehrere Freunde der Knaben
der Malméneschen Beschäftigungs-Anstalt.

Königsberg, den 20sten März. (Privatmitth.) Liszt hat uns verlassen, nachdem hier, wie überall, die allgemeinste Bewunderung nicht nur seinen unübertroffenen Leistungen, sondern auch den seltenen Eigenschaften des Geistes und Herzens zu Theil wurde. Wir glauben, den Dank der vielen nahen und fernen Freunde und Verehrer des großen Meisters zu verdienen, wenn wir nachstehendes Schreiben mittheilen, das hier cirkulirt und das er an die philosophische Fakultät hiesiger Hochschule richtete.

„Hochzuverehrende, Hochgelehrte Herren!
Ich würde vergeblich versuchen, Ihnen die tiefe und herzliche Bewegung auszudrücken, in die Sie mich durch Ihre seltene Ehrenbezeugung versetzt haben. Die Doctorwürde aus der Verleihung einer Fakultät, in der sich wie in der Ihrigen, Männer von europäischer Bedeutung versammeln, macht mich glücklich und würde mich stolz machen, wenn ich auch des Sinnes gewiß wäre, in dem sie mir verliehen worden. Ich wiederhole, daß ich mit dem ehrenvollen Namen eines Lehrers der Musik, (und um es hier zu bemerken, kann ich das Wort Musik nur in seiner großen, vollen, antiken Bedeutung gelten lassen) dessen Sie, hochverdiente Herren, mich würdigen, die Verpflichtung unablässigen Lernens und unermüdlicher Arbeit übernommen zu haben mir wohl bewußt bin. In der steten Erfüllung dieser Pflicht: — die Doctorwürde auf eine docte und würdige Weise zu bebauen, den schwachen Theil des Wissens in der Technik, den ich mir anzueignen im Stande bin, als Form und Mittel der Manifestation des Wahren und Göttlichen*) mit Wort und That zu verbreiten: — in der steten Erfüllung dieser Pflicht und bei jedem Erfolge, der mir etwa noch gegönnt ist, wird sich auch die Erinnerung an Ihr Wohlwollen lebendig erhalten und an die rührende Weise, in der ein berühmtes Mitglied**) Ihrer Facultät mich davon unterrichtet hat. Genehmigen Sie, hochgelehrte Herren, den Ausdruck meiner dankbarsten Hochachtung und vollendetsten Verehrung. Königsberg, den 14. März 1842. F. Liszt."

Der neue Pegasus im Joche.

Seht den wunderbaren Reiter,   A a a, als Not', im Wappen,
Der hinauszieht oder ein,   Ein romantisches Gesicht,
Dem die Damen Kränze spenden: Und ein Madschiaren Säbel
Sagt mir nur, wer kann es sein?   Von gewaltigem Gewicht!_
Hinter sich die Notenbündel,   Fast doch will es mich bedünken,
Vor sich gar ein Jnstrument,   Dass man Jemand damit neckt,
Und daneben wieder Etwas,   Dass es irgendwas bedeute,
Das man kennt und doch nicht kennt.   Und dass **LIST** dahinter steckt.

Verlag: Otto'sche Buch- u. Kunsthandlung in Burg.

292 Caricature of Franz Liszt. Steel engraving from around 1842, published by the Otto'sche Buch- u. Kunsthandlung in Burg; a German variant on a lithograph by Lorentz published in the Paris *Miroir drolatique* of 8 July 1842.

Liszt was exposed to caricature as few other artists were: his long hair, his attractiveness to the female sex, and the 1840 Sword of Honour were the constant delight of satirists and caricaturists.

"His name, his figure like some classical cameo, his Neapolitan face, his hair, his appearance, his characteristic manner of speaking: all of this created a type, an individual who aroused curiosity to the highest pitch; he became the lion, the hero of the day. People fought over him, they took his gloves, they cut pieces from his clothing; in the end he no longer dared go out on foot, but when he was seen in a carriage people would unharness the horses and pull the vehicle themselves. Wherever he went, he provoked both frenzy and folly. Yet it was not easy to approach him, particularly for someone like myself who had no title which might recommend me to him whose birth and aristocratic demeanour had opened up the distinguished world of the Faubourg Saint-Germain, the world of princely celebrities such as the Countesses Merlin, the Princess Belgiojoso, and other houses to which he was introduced by letters of recommendation from the leading circles of Hungarian and Austrian society. Forever in the salons of great ladies, he set the barometer to rain or fair, composing for them (as the dedications of many of his glorious works attest), and being worshipped by them. His language, with its wealth of imagery, his refined and witty replies, and the originality of his mind won him the hearts of all his listeners. One can say with certainty that all women were on his side, but one had to see for oneself or, rather, feel what an aristocratic atmosphere he created around himself and what a tremendous sensation he caused whenever he entered a salon, more especially if he was playing there. Though flattered and adored like no one else, he never grew rich. For all that he earned vast sums of money, he gave it away the very next day. I almost died of longing to be introduced to him. I turned to the Belgian ambassador, who finally effected an introduction one evening in Liszt's rooms, when the assembled guests included Jules Janin, Balzac, Alexandre Dumas, George Sand, and Chopin. Moscheles had just published his great Sonata in B flat minor for four hands: a copy was fetched from the publisher Pacini's, and Liszt and Chopin played it at sight as though they had studied it for years. What memories! But

events in Paris were quickly over. Liszt travelled to London, and from there came to Belgium. Fétis had taken him in hand. The best concerts that have ever been held in Brussels were organized by him. Of course I attended. I entreated Liszt to come to Liège, and he finally agreed to perform in the town. The great artist stayed in Brussels, at the Hôtel de Flandre, close to the park. He invited us there to a splendid supper after one of his concerts. We were some 30 to 40 guests: Count Dietrichstein, van Praet, Rogier, Fétis, almost the entire press, Madame Pleyel, and other great musical and literary figures. Everyone has memories of the musical feasts which he gave in our town. Liszt stayed in Liège at the Hôtel de l'Europe, giving dinners and suppers, and spending fabulous sums of money. He had as his secretary a Herr B…, who swindled him out of his concert receipts. I am not afraid of repeating this, since I can prove it. He also had a huge devil of a fellow as his huntsman, merely to shave him and to tie his neckties, which, like his tie-pins, he would change every day. The Grétry Monument was unveiled during his stay in Liège, and he became the hero of the celebrations. King Leopold I sent him the cross of his Order. [. . .]

"Called away to the capitals of Europe, this fabled artist left us. He had undertaken two or three concert tours of Belgium, each of which was a triumphal procession on which he was accompanied by our own celebrities (including women, who dressed up as men in order to follow him . . .), this glorious man, this refulgent meteor, who said 'Au revoir' but not 'Adieu.' "

Liszt's visits to Paris and Belgium in 1842: from the memoirs of the Liège banker Charles Dubois.

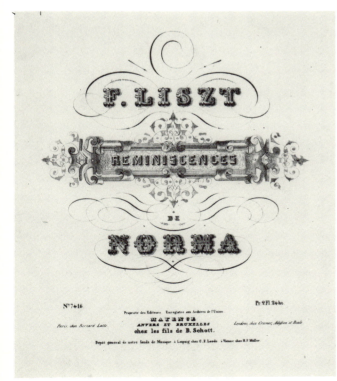

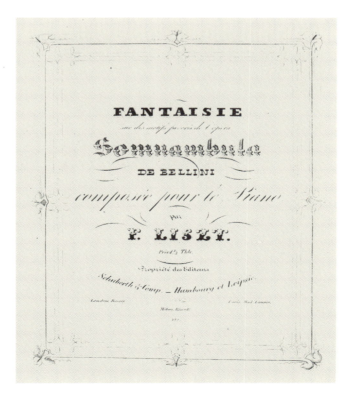

293 Title page of the first edition of Liszt's *Réminiscences de Norma*, 1843.

The first edition included a charming dedication from Liszt to Camille Pleyel (see Illus. 215), reproduced in facsimile. A furious Marie d'Agoult demanded that Liszt withdraw the dedication, but he refused.[86]

294 Title page of the first edition of Liszt's Fantasia on Bellini's opera *La Sonnambula*, 1842.

Most of Liszt's operatic Fantasias were written during his virtuoso years from 1838 to 1847. He often performed these works in the concert hall only hours after noting them down in his hotel room or in the mail coach.

LIFE

January (8, 11, 15, and 18): Concerts in Berlin. Berlin audiences – ashamed of their display of ''Lisztomania'' the previous year, when they had been the laughing stock of Europe – show far greater reserve on this occasion.

21 January to 8 February: Ten concerts in Breslau.

1 February: Liszt conducts Mozart's *The Magic Flute* in Breslau.

2 February: Concert in Breslau (see Illus. 295).

16 February: Liszt in Berlin, where he conducts Beethoven's *Coriolan* Overture, Weber's *Oberon* Overture, and three of his *Vierstimmige Männergesänge*, in addition to playing his *Réminiscences de ''Don Juan''* and Mendelssohn's D minor Piano Concerto.

He also performs in Potsdam, Fürstenwalde, Liegnitz, Brieg, and Neisse, and several times in Breslau.

21, 26, and 27 February: Concerts in Posen.

1 and 3 March: Concerts in Glogau.

7 March: Final concert in Breslau.

10 March: Liszt meets his friend Prince Felix von Lichnowsky and is a guest at the latter's castles in Kryzanowitz and Grätz.

28, 29, and 30 March: Concerts in Cracow.

30 March: Leaves Cracow for Warsaw, where he visits Chopin's father and Józef Elsner, Chopin's composition teacher.

6, 9, 10, and 12 April: Concerts in Warsaw.

Mid-April: Six concerts in St Petersburg; because of his Polish sympathies he loses the Tsar's favour.

25, 27, and 29 April, and 2, 9, and 12 May: Highly successful series of concerts in Moscow. Liszt is fêted by the Moscow aristocracy. After one reception at which Russian gypsies perform, Liszt arrives late at the concert hall and, instead of playing the piece that was announced, he improvises on the gypsy melodies he has just heard.

18 May: Liszt leaves Moscow (with a gift of two bear cubs!) and returns to St Petersburg.

June: Return journey to Germany.

26 June: Concert in Hamburg.

Mid-July to September: Liszt with Marie d'Agoult on the island of Nonnenwerth. Intensive work on Lieder composition, but also excursions to give concerts in Cologne, Solingen, and elsewhere.

24 September: Liszt in Iserlohn, after which he spends a few days in Paris.

3 October: From Frankfurt Liszt sets off on a concert tour of southern Germany: Würzburg (concert on 7 October), Nuremberg (10 to 14 October), Munich (concerts on 18, 21, 25, and 30 October), Augsburg, Stuttgart (4 to 23 November), Hechingen. To Donaueschingen with Prince Konstantin von Hohenzollern, who confers on him the title of Court Councillor. Stays in Karlsruhe, Heidelberg, Heilbronn (15 November), Ulm, Ludwigsburg, Speyer, and Mannheim.

3 and 5 December: Concerts in Mannheim. Visits to Baden-Baden, Darmstadt (6 December), and Frankfurt.

Mid-December: Liszt in Weimar (until 18 February 1844), where he makes his first official appearance as Court Kapellmeister.

Top:
295 Programme for Liszt's concert in Breslau on 2 February 1843.

The ceremonial associated with today's piano recitals goes back to Liszt. He was the first pianist to play his programmes entirely or partially from memory. It was he, moreover, who positioned the piano on the platform in the way that is usual today and who, in addition to performing the customary virtuoso pieces, also played works by older composers such as Handel and Bach. In 1838 he astonished his Viennese audience by playing sonatas by Domenico Scarlatti, a composer unknown in the Austrian capital until then. (Liszt instigated the first complete edition of Scarlatti's sonatas: edited by Carl Czerny, it was published soon afterwards by Haslinger in Vienna.)

Liszt was the first pianist to give an entire concert completely on his own: the very concept of the solo recital is one that we owe to him. Of course, Liszt's recital generally took place at midday or in the late afternoon, in accordance with the spirit of the times. In 1839, while in Rome, he wrote to tell Princess Belgiojoso that he was planning to introduce his ''tedious musical monologues'' to Paris too (see ''Life 1839''). He was also the first virtuoso to appear in halls such as La Scala in Milan, or the Assembly Hall of the Nobles in St. Petersburg, which held more than 3000 spectators.

No virtuoso before Liszt had undertaken concert tours on such a scale. It is difficult for us to imagine nowadays what it must have meant to travel the length and breadth of Europe by mail coach – the main railway lines were not opened until after the end of his virtuoso career. Liszt's concert tours took him from Moscow to Gibraltar, and from Glasgow to Constantinople. He had an iron constitution, and even approaching his sixtieth year could write to Adelheid von Schorn (Rome, 14 May 1869): ''You ask me to send you news of my health as soon as possible; but I have made it my rule for many years now never to concern myself with this subject, either in writing or in conversation, since I find that I am always well enough not to think about it.''[87] Liszt's concert programmes avoided the usual salon music and instead included works by Bach, Beethoven, Weber, Schubert, and Chopin. In his own operatic fantasies and virtuoso pieces he introduced audiences to various innovatory techniques which he himself had developed and which included transferring the melody to the tenor register, glissandos, trilled chords, chromatic and two-handed octave runs, tremolo chord repetitions, and rapid leaps across wide intervals, but above all the interlocking of the hands and interchangeability of the fingers.

Among the works for piano and orchestra which appeared most often in Liszt's programmes are Beethoven's E flat major Piano Concerto and Choral Fantasy, and Weber's *Konzertstück*. Liszt must have taken the performing material for these works with him on his travels.

296 Honoré de Balzac (1799–1850). Daguerreotype, 1842.

WORKS

Tscherkessenmarsch from "Ruslan and Lyudmila" (Glinka) (piano transcription). Pub. 1843.
Russischer Galopp (Bulhakov) (piano transcription). Pub. 1843.
Gaudeamus igitur (piano paraphrase). Pub. 1843. A new edition appeared ca. 1853. Another work on the same theme was composed in 1869.
Autrefois (Ljubila ja) (Wielhorsky) (for piano). Composed and published ca. 1843.
Overture to "Oberon" (Weber) (piano transcription). Pub. 1847.
Ländler in A flat major (for piano). Pub. 1921 (believed to be its first appearance).
6 Lieder (for soprano or tenor and piano): 1. *Du bist wie eine Blume*, 2. *Morgens steh' ich auf*, 3. *Was Liebe sei*, 4. *Die tote Nachtigall*, 5. *Bist du* (1843), 6. *Vergiftet sind meine Lieder*. Written ca. 1843. Pub. 1844.
Oh pourquoi donc (for voice and piano). Pub. 1884. See "Works 1848" for piano version entitled *Romance*.
Seconde marche hongroise (Ungarischer Sturmmarsch) (for piano). Written 1843 and pub. ca. 1844. See "Works 1875."
Piano Piece in F major. Unfinished. Probably written in July 1843.

FRANZ LISZT.

Gez. v. W. Kaulbach. Gest. v. C. Gonzenbach. —

297 Franz Liszt. Steel engraving by Carl Gonzenbach, based on a drawing by Wilhelm von Kaulbach; Munich 1843.

Liszt visited Munich in October 1843 and gave four concerts in the city, two of which were benefit performances ("For the Benefit of the Employment Exchange of the Local Institute for the Blind" and "For the Benefit of the Germans in Greece"). Eminent artists and scholars, including Schwanthaler, Geibel, Thiersch, and Ringeis, sought Liszt's acquaintanceship. His meeting with Wilhelm von Kaulbach, who was later to paint him on many occasions, was the start of a long and friendly relationship. Kaulbach's painting *Die Hunnenschlacht* served as the model for Liszt's Symphonic Poem of the same name.

298–301 Programmes of the four concerts which Liszt gave in Munich in 1843.

Although this was an unfavourable time to give concerts – Munich's burghers were too preoccupied by the insurrection which had broken out in Greece on 15 October, and by their resultant worries for the safety of King Otto – Liszt was none the less the centre of attraction during this period. His first concert was attended by Ludwig I, accompanied by the entire royal household.

Emanuel Geibel, who heard Liszt perform in Munich, wrote that ''He is a poet through and through, and it is his poetic conception, not his technical accomplishment, which involuntarily captivates the masses.''

302 Munich. Max-Joseph-Platz with the National Theatre and Residenz. Oil painting by Heinrich Adam, 1839.

Among the works which Liszt performed in the National Theatre were Beethoven's E flat major Piano Concerto and Weber's *Konzertstück*.

303 Munich. Odeon (to the left of the picture, half obscured), with the Ludwig-Ferdinand-Palais in the background, and the Leuchtenberg-Palais to the right. Watercolour by J. B. Kuhn, ca. 1840.

Liszt gave two concerts in the Odeon in 1843. After the National Theatre it was Munich's most popular concert hall.

LIFE

January to mid-February: Fulfils duties as Court Kapellmeister in Weimar, and also gives concerts in Jena and Rudolstadt.

7 January: Concert in Weimar. Liszt conducts Beethoven's Symphony No. 5 and performs Hummel's B minor Piano Concerto. Hummel had died in Weimar in 1837. His Viennese widow comments on Liszt's performance to Carl Gille, her neighbour at the concert, "So hat's mei Alter halt doch nit g'spielt" (My old man certainly never played it like that).

17 January: Liszt conducts Beethoven's Symphony No. 6 in Gotha.

21 January: Liszt conducts Beethoven's *Eroica* Symphony in Weimar, and performs Weber's *Konzertstück*.

4 February: Beethoven's Symphony No. 7 under Liszt.

18 February: Schubert's C major Symphony and Berlioz's Overture *Le Roi Lear* under Liszt in Weimar.

19 February: Concert in Erfurt.

21 February: Benefit performance in Dresden for a memorial to the composer Johann Gottlieb Naumann. Liszt donates 1350 thalers. Further concerts for the singer Pantaleoni and himself. Meetings with Richard Wagner and Lola Montez.

24 February: Concert in Dessau, then back to Dresden and Bautzen.

5 March: Concert in Bernburg.

7 and 8 March: Concerts in Stettin.

14 and 15 March: Concerts in Magdeburg.

22 and 25 March: Concerts in Braunschweig.

28 and 31 March: Concerts in Hanover. Liszt describes the Hanoverians as "the best audience in North Germany." He then travels to Paris, where his concerts meet with overwhelming acclaim. Final separation from Marie d'Agoult.

16 and 25 April: Liszt gives two solo recitals at the Théâtre-Italien. He is now universally regarded as the world's greatest pianist.

4 May: Under Berlioz's direction, Liszt performs Weber's *Konzertstück* and solo works at the Théâtre-Italien. Further concerts on 11 May (Salle Herz) and 28 May (Hôtel Lambert).

15 June: Concert in Versailles.

23 June: Concert at the Paris Conservatoire.

Concerts in Lyons (2, 5, 9, 12, 14, and 17 July), Marseilles (25 and 29 July, 2 and 6 August), Nîmes (10 August), Montpellier (13 August), and Sète (18 August).

19 August: Two concerts in Sète and farewell concert in Montpellier.

20 August: Concert in Béziers; then guest of the Conte d'Aragon at the Château de Saliès near Albi.

25 August to 5 September: Liszt in Toulouse. Concerts on 27, 30, 31 August, and 1 September.

2 September: Concert in Montauban.

4 September: Farewell concert in Toulouse.

7 September to 6 October: Liszt in Bordeaux. Concerts on 11, 14, and 18 September.

20 September: Concert in Agen.

24 and 27 September: Concerts in Bordeaux.

29 September: Concert in Angoulême.

1 and 2 October: Concerts in Bordeaux.

5 October: Charity concert (for the theatre chorus in Bordeaux) in Libourne.

7 to 21 October: Liszt in Pau (Pyrenees), where he meets his early love Caroline de Saint-Cricq (see p. 54). Concerts on 8, 11, and 17 October. Banquet in his honour on 20 October.

14 and 18 October: Concerts in Bayonne.

22 October to 4 December: Liszt in Madrid,

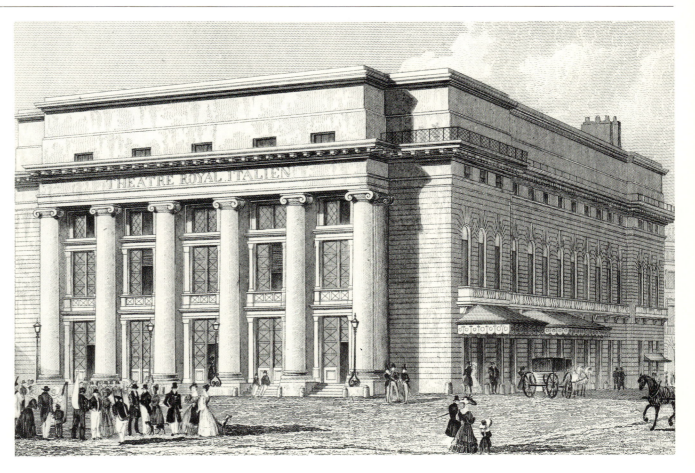

304 The Italian Opera (Théâtre Royal Italien) in Paris. Steel engraving by James Tingle, based on a drawing by Thomas Talbot Bury; ca. 1835. Liszt performed here on 16 and 25 April 1844.

Théophile Gautier on Liszt (*La Presse*, 22 April 1844):
"Much fun has been made of his long hair, of a figure reminiscent of the characters of E.T.A. Hoffmann, of his ecstatic glances, his convulsive gestures, his demonic movements. His tight-fitting black jacket, tailored according to Brandenburg fashion, and his Hungarian sword of honour have been the object of innumerable jokes in more or less bad taste. My own view is that an artist may not, and cannot, look like a chandler; his taste, his way of life, and his thoughts must necessarily give his appearance a certain character, which is simply another way of attracting attention than wearing laced boots, green gloves, and collars of a kind that guillotine the wearer's ears. [. . .]

"What we like about Franz Liszt is that he has always remained the selfsame artist, fiery, wild, and with flowing hair, always the same Mazeppa whom an unbridled piano drags through the steppes of demisemiquavers; if he falls, then it is merely to rise up again as a king! In a word, he is as much a Romantic as ever he was. His hair, scarcely a finger's width shorter, is still long enough to make him look like a Kreisler or a Master Wolfram, an appearance which it would have been wrong for him to abandon. The passing years have not made him any the wiser. He has paid no heed to advice which enlightened critics have given him in their kind insistence that he should put aside all his characteristic qualities: we have rediscovered in him the man whom we have always heard, only perhaps even more astonishing . . ."

The newspaper *Le Corsaire* on Liszt (28 April 1844):
"[. . .] And he comes, sits down at the piano, without noticing anything around him, engrossed in his present task, thoughtful, and trembling with the fever of inspiration. His hand moves absent-mindedly over the keyboard, he tests the instrument, caressing and fondling it, gently at first, in order to ensure that it will not forsake him at the height of the race, that it will not fall apart beneath his fingers; then he warms to his task, lets himself go, and lays into it without pity. He has taken off, let all who can follow him do so! The ecstatic audience, breathing deeply in its rapt enthusiasm, can no longer hold back its shouts of acclaim: they stamp unceasingly with their feet, producing a dull and persistent sound that is punctuated by isolated, involuntary screams, until whispered entreaties restore calm to the hall, a calm which is effortlessly re-established until finally, at the end of the piece, at the climax of the performance, a mighty shout bursts forth, and the entire hall re-echoes with a single roll of thunderous applause.

"Never will an ordinary artist succeed in exercising such an influence on the masses. We may as well admit it: this man has something about him which others lack. He knows how to produce unimaginably wonderful effects on his instrument; he has overcome every material challenge. Ask the most accomplished pianists, they will tell you quite openly: only the devil himself could produce from an indifferently shaped piece of wood what *he* produces from it. He plays overtures with so awesome a force that the orchestra itself is tamed. [. . .]"

305 Franz Liszt. Daguerreotype, 1844. Reproduced actual size. Previously unpublished.

306 Lola Montez (1818–1861). Oil portrait by Joseph Stieler, Munich 1847.

It was at the end of February 1844 that Liszt first met the dancer Lola Montez in Dresden (her real name was Maria Dolores Eliza Rosanna Gilbert; Ludwig I of Bavaria later made her Countess Landsfeld). Rumours of a liaison between them subsequently went all round Europe and are said to have provoked the final breach between Liszt and Marie d'Agoult in 1844. Three years later Liszt was still having to justify himself on the subject of Lola Montez (see his letters to Marie d'Agoult of 3 January 1847 from Bucharest, and May 1847 from Jassy).

Lola's alleged first love letter to Liszt (''I desire you to love me, I desire you to love only me, like all the daughters of my sex I refuse to share you with anyone else . . .'') has as little chance of being authenticated as the claim that to prevent her from pursuing him Liszt locked her in a hotel room with orders not to open it until twelve hours later. And the legend that the dancer accompanied Liszt on his concert tours during the rest of 1844 is refuted by their respective itineraries: Lola went via Paris to Poland and Russia, while Liszt toured southern France, Spain, and Portugal.

There is evidence that Liszt took Lola Montez to a performance of Wagner's opera *Rienzi* in Dresden, and that both were in Paris a month later. But their next recorded meeting was not until August 1845, this time in Bonn.

In her memoirs (which run to several volumes) Lola Montez mentions Liszt only briefly and in passing; indiscreet as she was, she would scarcely have missed an opportunity to add to the list of her lovers by vaunting her conquest of Liszt.[88]

The accompanying daguerreotype of Liszt dates from 1844 and deserves particular attention in that it is the first known surviving photograph of the musician, in addition to being one of the earliest examples of a daguerreotype portrait. Like most daguerreotypes, the original shows its subject the ''wrong'' way round: it is reproduced here in reverse to show Liszt as he was in real life.

The photograph is still in its original red velvet frame. Apart from the 1838 life mask (see p. 111), it is our first objective record of what Liszt looked like. It shows the pianist at the height of his virtuoso career. That he was subsequently photographed on frequent occasions was rarely the result of his own initiative. Photographers pursued him, and his admirers and pupils often dragged him off to the photographer's studio. Among the most noteworthy names who photographed Liszt were Hanfstaengl and Albert in Munich (Illus. 407, 431f, 477ff, 484f, 510), Nadar in Paris (Illus. 649), and above all Louis Held in Weimar (Illus. 582f, 591, 593ff, 596, 602, 605–9, 622).

A variant of this daguerreotype exists, evidently taken on the same occasion. The original is lost, but a copy of it has been reproduced on several occasions in recent years, including *The New Grove*, a record sleeve of Alfred Brendel's, and Alan Walker's *Franz Liszt. The Virtuoso Years*. The daguerreotype reproduced here was previously unknown (it was given to the present author in 1982).

where he gives four solo recitals (31 October, 2, 5, and 9 November) and three charity concerts (13, 14, and 21 November). On 28 October and 22 November he performs at the palace of Prince Villahermosa. In contrast to normal custom, he is received at Court (7 November), where Queen Isabella invests him with the title of Cavalier of the Order of Carlos III and presents him with a valuable diamond tie-pin.

8 December: Arrival in Córdoba. Concert on the 11th.

17 December to end of December: Liszt in Seville.

WORKS

Geharnischte Lieder (for men's voices and piano): 1. *Vor der Schlacht*, 2. *Nicht gezagt!*, 3. *Es rufet Gott*. Pub. 1845; version for piano alone, 1861.

Soldatenlied aus Goethes Faust (for men's voices, with optional trumpets and timpani). Year of publication unknown.

Freudvoll und leidvoll I (for mezzo-soprano and piano). Pub. 1848. A second version appeared in 1860. A different setting of the text was made and published in 1848.

Les Quatre Élémens (for men's voices and piano): 1. *La Terre*, 2. *Les Aquilons*, 3. *Les Flots*, 4. *Les Astres*. Written 1844/45. Unpublished. A number of themes from this work were later reused in the symphonic poem *Les Préludes*.

Die Vätergruft (for bass or baritone and piano). Pub. 1860. The orchestration of this song was the last compositional work of Liszt's life (see Illus. 627).

Marche funèbre de ''Dom Sébastien'' (Donizetti) (for piano). See Illus. 309. Pub. 1845.

Chanson du Béarn and *Faribolo Pastour* (for piano). Pub. 1845.

Overture to ''Le Carnaval romain'' (Berlioz) (piano transcription). Liszt performed this arrangement ca. 1844. Lost, or never printed.

2 Male-Voice Quartets (with piano accompaniment). Written late 1843 or early 1844 and mentioned by Liszt in a letter of 19 January 1844. One of the quartets, *Trinkspruch* (''Gießt Wein in die Gläser, ihr Zecher''), was first published in 1929; the other may be identical with one of the two following entries.

Die lustige Legion (for male-voice quartet and piano). Written ca. 1844. Pub. 1848.

Es war einmal ein König (for bass solo, men's voices and piano). May date from this time. Pub. 1986.

3 Songs (versions for soprano, mezzo-soprano, tenor, baritone): 1. *Ich möchte hingehn wie das Abendrot*, 2. *Laßt mich ruhen*, 3. *In Liebeslust*. Written ca. 1844. Pub. 1859.

6 Songs (for soprano or tenor and piano) to words by Victor Hugo: 1. *Comment disaient-ils* (1842), 2. *Oh! quand je dors* (1842), 3. *S'il est un charmant gazon*, 4. *Enfant, si j'étais roi* (1844), 5. *La tombe et la rose* (ca. 1844), 6. *Gastibelza*. Written 1842–44. Pub. 1844. Piano transcriptions were made ca. 1847. Pub. 1985. See ''Works 1847.''

Marche hongroise in E flat minor (for piano). Pub. 1956, 1972, and 1985.

LIFE

1 January: Concert stop in Cádiz, then on to Gibraltar.

12 January: Liszt leaves Gibraltar on the steamer *Montrose* and sails via Cádiz to Lisbon.

15 January to 25 February: Liszt in Lisbon, where he gives five solo recitals (23, 25, 30, January, 6 and 17 February), and four charity concerts (8, 12, 15, and 22 February). He performs at the Royal Palace on 26 January and on two subsequent occasions. Queen Maria II invests him with the Order of Christ and presents him with a gold snuffbox inlaid with diamonds; the press describes him as ''the God of the piano'' and ''the most wondrous event in Portugal.''[89]

Early March: Liszt in Cádiz and Gibraltar.

8 March: Liszt in Málaga, then Granada and Alicante.

24 March to 4 April: In Valencia. Concerts on 27, 29, and 31 March.

5 to 21 April: In Barcelona. Concerts on 7, 11, 14, 15, 18, and 19 April.

21 April: Leaves Barcelona and sails to Marseilles.

End of April: Several days in Marseilles.

6 May: Liszt in Avignon. Concerts on 8 and 11 May.

14 and 20 May: Concerts in Lyons. On 18 May Liszt stays in Grenoble.

21 May: From Lyons Liszt writes a long letter to George Sand, telling her of his plans to visit Athens, Malta, and Constantinople (of which he will achieve only the last).

24 May and 3 June: Concerts in Dijon, then Besançon, Mühlhausen (three concerts), and Basle, where Raff enters Liszt's service for two months as his secretary, and where Liszt performs on 19 and 23 June, and 11 July.

22 June: Concert in Colmar.

9 and 14 July: Concerts in Zurich.

17 July: Visit to Strasbourg.

End of July: Liszt arrives in Bonn, where he notes the inadequacy of preparations for the Beethoven Festival and persuades the authorities to build a concert hall.

11 to 13 August: Beethoven celebrations in Bonn (see p. 157). Together with Louis Spohr, Liszt is the central figure in terms of both organization and musical direction.

12 August: Unveiling of the Beethoven Monument, financed in part by Liszt's concert activities. ''I think that I have never seen an expression so nobly and serenely radiant on any face,'' wrote Henry Chorley of Liszt.[90] In the evening Liszt performs the E flat major Piano Concerto, and conducts the Symphony No. 5 and the finale from *Fidelio*.

13 August: Performance of Liszt's *Festkantate*. In the evening he performs in Brühl. Afterwards Fétis and Kreutzer find him exhausted and worn out by his restless life in Koblenz and Cologne; according to Liszt's own letter of 25 August to Johann Christian Lobe in Weimar, he is ''blessed with a spectacular bout of jaundice and total exhaustion.''[91]

17 August: Liszt at a meeting for Dutch and German singers in Cleves.

September: Brief stay in Baden-Baden, then further concert tours from September 1845 to January 1846: Colmar, Nancy, Châlons, Rheims, Nantes, and Angers.

8 October: Concert in Darmstadt (see p. 158).

307 A concert grand used by Liszt during his tour of Spain and Portugal in 1845.

The piano makers Boisselot et Fils produced this instrument from their own stock and brought it to Spain for Liszt's concerts. He was accompanied throughout the Iberian peninsula by Louis Boisselot.

At the end of the tour the instrument passed into the possession of the Queen of Portugal, who presented it to the Princess's music teacher; he in turn bequeathed it to the Conservatoire, and it is now in the State Museum in Lisbon.

309 Title page of the first edition of Liszt's transcription of the Funeral March from Donizetti's *Dom Sébastien*.

Liszt transcribed this piece in 1844/45 during his tour of Spain and Portugal.

Marche Funèbre
de
DOM SÉBASTIEN
de C. Donizetti
variée pour le Piano
par
F. LISZT.

VIENNE
chez Pietro Mechetti q.^m Carlo.

Lyons, Marseilles, Toulon, and Bordeaux were the most important ports of call on Liszt's concert tour to the Iberian Peninsula, where he was to remain for half a year from October 1844 to April 1845. His meeting with the sweetheart of his youth, Caroline de Saint-Cricq (see p. 54), may well have coincided with the composition of the song *Ich möchte hingehn*, one manuscript of which bears the words, written in Liszt's hand, ''This song is the testament of my youth – therefore no better, and also no worse.'' It appears to anticipate by some 10 years Wagner's so-called *Tristan* motif (though some scholars suggest that the figure was an allusion added to the song later). Liszt's progress through Spain was blessed by success and rave reviews.

Queen Isabella bestowed on him the title of Cavalier of the Order of Carlos III, gave him a diamond-studded pin, and, contrary to etiquette, received him at Court. On 12 January 1845, Liszt and his Boisselot piano set sail from Gibraltar and headed for Lisbon, where Queen Maria II da Gloria of Portugal created him a Knight of the Order of Christ and presented him with a diamond-encrusted snuffbox. A further series of concerts brought him to Mâcon at the end of May 1845. Here he is said to have proposed marriage to the Comtesse Valentine de Cessiat, the 24-year-old niece of Alphonse de Lamartine. Was it merely a whim, or was Liszt suddenly tired of his life of restless wanderings? She turned him down, as she did all her other suitors, until in 1867, with the permission of Pope Pius IX, she married her uncle, then 31 years older than herself – and found herself a widow seventeen months later.

308 Franz Liszt. Lithograph based on a drawing by Guglielmi; Lisbon 1845.

This little-known portrait of Liszt may have been modelled on the slightly earlier daguerreotype (Illus. 305).

17 October: Liszt in Freiburg.
November: Brief stay in Paris.
19 and 21 November: Concerts in Metz.
24 November: Concert in Luxembourg.
December: Further concerts in France.

WORKS

Festkantate zur Enthüllung des Beethoven-Denkmals in Bonn (for chorus and orchestra). Unpublished. Versions for four hands and for two hands (only 70 bars) were published in 1846.
3 Songs (for tenor or soprano and piano). Written ca. 1849 (Nos. 1 and 2) and ca. 1845 (No. 3): 1. *Hohe Liebe* (pub. 1850), 2. *Gestorben war ich* (pub. 1930), 3. *O lieb, so lang du lieben kannst* (pub. 1847). Piano versions (*Liebesträume*) appeared in 1850. An unpublished version of No. 1 exists for baritone.
3 Songs (for soprano and piano). Written ca. 1845: 1. *Es rauschen die Winde* (pub. 1860), 2. *Wo weilt er?* (pub. 1860), 3. *Wer nie sein Brot mit Tränen aß* (pub. 1848).
Hymne de l'enfant à son réveil (for women's voices, harp and harmonium). Revised 1862 and 1874. Pub. 1875. For piano arrangement see "Works 1847."
3 Songs from Schiller's "Wilhelm Tell" (for tenor and piano): 1. *Der Fischerknabe*, 2. *Der Hirt*, 3. *Der Alpenjäger*. Pub. 1848. A second version appeared in 1859, and an orchestral version (written ca. 1859) was published in 1872.
Le forgeron (for men's voices and piano). Pub. 1962.
Jeanne d'Arc au bûcher (for mezzo-soprano and piano). Pub. 1846. A second version appeared in 1876, and an adaptation for voice and orchestra in 1877.
Ballade No. 1 ("Le Chant du Croisé") (for piano). Begun in 1845 and completed in 1848. Pub. 1849.
Feuille morte (Mariano Soriano) (piano transcription). Pub. 1845.
Große Konzertfantasie über spanische Weisen (for piano). Pub. 1887.
Madrigal (for piano). Early version of the fifth *Consolation*. Unpublished. Manuscript in the possession of Everett Helm.

310 Alphonse de Lamartine (1790–1869). Pencil drawing by Théodore Chassériau, 1844.

At the end of May 1845 Liszt spent three days as guest of his friend Lamartine at the latter's country house, the Château de Saint-Point near Mâcon in Burgundy. With his first melodic and rhapsodic verse collections, *Méditations poétiques* and *Harmonies poétiques et religieuses*, Lamartine, statesman and poet, introduced Romantic ideas to French lyric poetry. Liszt's piano works *Invocations*, *Bénédiction de Dieu dans la solitude*, and *Andante lagrimoso* from his own collection of *Harmonies poétiques et religieuses* took Lamartine's poems as their point of departure. And his symphonic poem *Les Préludes* was prefaced by Lamartine's words, "What is our life but a series of preludes to that unknown hymn whose first and solemn note is sounded by death?"

Langsam – innig –
Du bist wie eine Blume so rein und schön und hold
Ich schau dich an und Wehmuth schleicht mir in's Herz hinein
crescendo
Mir ist als ob ich die Hände aufs Haupt dir legen sollt
Betend
rite – – – nuto
daß dich Gott erhalte so rein und schön und hold

312 Unveiling of the Beethoven Monument in Bonn on 12 August 1845. Anonymous wood engraving from the *Leipziger Allgemeine Zeitung* of 1845.

The Beethoven celebrations in Bonn in August 1845 were the highlight of the musical year. Liszt had given countless concerts to raise funds for the monument and as early as 1840 had sent an initial contribution of 10,000 francs. In Bonn he conducted a number of concerts and declared his readiness to make good the deficit on the Festhalle, which he himself had instigated. Lack of adequate organization and proper invitations, together with inadequate rehearsal facilities, led to several differences of opinion during the festivities.

313 Press report on a concert given as part of the Beethoven Memorial Festival; reproduced from the *Allgemeine Musikalische Zeitung* of 12 September 1845. (For a translation of the text, see p. 339.)

314 Ludwig van Beethoven. Lithograph based on Kloeber's 1818 drawing.

This portrait was hung above a small desk in Liszt's study in Weimar (see Illus. 488). It is still there today.

Das Abendconcert brachte wieder nur Beethoven'sche Werke, als: 1) Die C-moll-Symphonie, von Herrn Liszt burschikos dirigirt, denn die bis nun übliche Art, ein Orchester zu dirigiren, nennt der improvisirte Dirigent „Rococo". Thatsache! Das Orchester, das dieses herrliche Werk bereits auswendig kennt, trug es im Ganzen so gut vor, als wäre ein Rococo-Dirigent am Pulte gestanden. Es ließ sich durchaus nicht durch die ungewohnten Manieren seines Führers stören. 2) Es-dur-Concert für Pianoforte, vorgetragen von Herrn Liszt mit ungewöhnlicher Ruhe und Besonnenheit. Waren auch andere Männer von Fach nicht einverstanden, tadelten sie mit Recht ein auffälliges Coquettiren mit dem Pianissimo und Anderes noch, was schon des großen Raumes wegen hätte unterbleiben müssen, Ref. weiß es seinerseits Herrn Liszt Dank, sich hierbei beherrscht zu haben. 3) Arie des Seraph aus Christus am Oelberg, mehr mit frommem Sinn als theatralischer Bravour von Fräul. Tuczek gesungen. Die Wirkung war eine tiefe. 4) Ouverture zu Coriolan. 5) Canon aus Fidelio, der dahin nicht paßte. Noch weniger passend muß 6) das von dem cölner Quartett gespielte Streichquartett — Es-dur, Nr. 10 — genannt werden. Was wollen vier Saiteninstrumente in einem so großen Raume, die nicht gewohnt sind, in einem kleinen Saal mit ausgiebiger Kraft zu spielen und ein kleines Orchester zu repräsentiren? — Ironie! Endlich 7) zweites Finale aus Fidelio, unter Liszt's Direction. Auch dieses paßte nicht dahin und konnte überdies noch durch mittelmäßige Leistungen einiger Solosänger nur Langweile erzeugen. War dieser Tag schon für die große Zahl verständiger Zuhörer kein freudenvoller, so sollte der folgende und letzte Festtag ein in jedem Betracht leidvoller werden, der das vorausgegangene Gute und Preiswerthe verlöschen und die mitgebrachte Erinnerung in Entrüstung verwandeln mußte.

Opposite page:

311 *Du bist wie eine Blume.*

Liszt composed this song in around 1843. The manuscript has not previously been published.

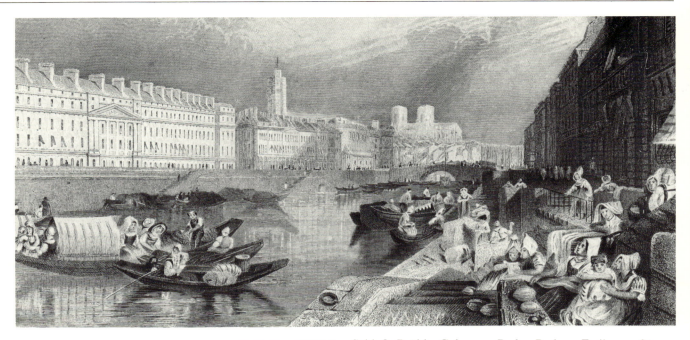

315 Nantes, one of the many towns visited by Liszt in 1845. Steel engraving, ca. 1845.

At right:

316 Article on Liszt published on the occasion of a concert which he was to give in Darmstadt on 8 October 1845. Reproduced from the *Großherzoglich Hessische Zeitung* of 6 October 1845. (For a translation of the text, see pp. 339–40.)

At far right:

317 Review of Liszt's concert in Darmstadt on 8 October 1845. Reproduced from the *Großherzoglich Hessische Zeitung* of 10 October 1845. (For a translation of the text, see p. 340.)

Schloß Brühl, Cologne, Baden-Baden, Freiburg, Strasbourg, Metz, Nancy, Rheims, Paris, and Nantes were among the places which Liszt visited in the autumn of 1845.

A plausible anecdote from the time of his visit to Schloß Brühl tells how Queen Victoria, who was then staying at the castle, asked for the windows to be alternately opened and closed in order to create a current of air. Liszt performed a drastically shortened version of his *Norma* Fantasy and fended off an objection by saying, ''I was afraid of inconveniencing Your Majesty while you were issuing orders.''

** Franz Liszt.

Die Kunstfreunde Darmstadt's haben einen Genuß zu erwarten, der ihnen nur zu lange vorenthalten blieb; sie werden den König aller Virtuosen bewundern Franz Liszt ist angekommen und wird sich hören lassen. Wenn man die Superlative liest, welche heutzutage eine söldnerische Journalistik oft an die Mittelmäßigkeit verschleudert, so geräth man wirklich in Verlegenheit, mit welchen Ausdrücken man das Erscheinen eines europäischen Rennommee's, das Auftreten eines weltbewunderten Genie's anzeigen soll. Ein solches ist Franz Liszt — und der Enthusiasmus, der sich seinen künstlerischen Offenbarungen überall anschloß, hat die außergewöhnlichsten Formen angenommen, um den Hochbegabten würdig zu feiern: Orden, Titel, Stellen, Doctorhüte, Diplome, Ehrensäbel, Triumphzüge bezeichnen seinen Weg von dem heimathlichen Ungarn bis in das gährende Spanien, von dem reichen Petersburg und verzückten Berlin bis in das übersättigte Paris und glänzende London; — wie seine Leistungen, so sind auch seine Erfolge, unerreichte, nie dagewesene. Vor dem Bilde eines solchen Künstlers stempelt sich der Neid zur Dummheit, wie das Beethovenfest in Bonn deutlich bewiesen hat, und ihm gegenüber wird die Caricatur zum Compliment, wie denn der plastische pariser Witzbold Dantan Liszt's Statuette mit zehn Fingern an jeder Hand ausarbeitete. Und Liszt feiert seine Triumphe auf einem Instrumente, das vom Salon bis zur Mansarde verbreitet, von Alt und Jung und Reich und Arm geübt, alle Welt mit Ueberdruß erfüllt und im Concertsaale Schrecken verbreitet; aber Liszt brillirt auch nicht auf dem Pianoforte: unter seinen Händen erwacht ein Orchester; sein Auge weilt nicht auf zweimal fünf Linien: sein Geist durchfliegt Partituren; er spielt nicht, sondern er dichtet und lebt in den Tönen. Dieses Clavier, sonst ein lahmes Werkzeug der Langenweile, wird unter seinen Meisterhänden zum Flügel der Bewunderung; es erfüllt selbst den blasirten Hörer mit Staunen und Entzücken, und die Schauer der Schönheit rieseln ihm durch die Seele, wenn das Genie Liszt's durch ein so unvollkomenes und alltägliches Organ so mächtig und erschütternd und hinreißend zu ihm spricht. Sein Spiel läßt sich nicht beschreiben: das will eben gehört, erfaßt und nachempfunden seyn; es steht um ein Riesenmaß höher als alles was an Instrumental-Virtuosität an uns vorüberzog. Als eilfjähriger Knabe bereits hatte Liszt alle Bethovenschen Compositionen durchdacht und reproducirte sie in der vollendetsten Ausführung; den Jüngling Liszt begeisterten die Leistungen und Erfolge Paganini's, er nahm sich vor, ihm gleich zu werden, und er hat Wort gehalten: denn er steht in technischer Meisterschaft vielleicht noch höher als jener, jedenfalls aber an Compositionstalent und Phantasie überwiegender. Sein Vortrag ist niemals ein mechanisches Vonsichgeben, sondern im eigentlichsten Sinne des Wortes eine Composition, eine ganz für sich bestehende Schöpfung der Kunst, durch Feuer und Leidenschaft von innen heraus wiedergeboren. Jedes Stück, das er spielt, betrachtet er im Allgemeinen als jene, durch welches er phantasirt und fast immer etwas Wundervolles neu erschafft, und wobei sich zugleich die wahrhaft geniale Strebung fundgibt: seine Kunst immer mehr von allen formellen und beängstigenden Fesseln loszumachen, und in wirklicher Begeisterung und unbekümmert um allen äußeren Regelzwang, das sorglos nachzubilden, was unser Auge anerkannt: zu leichterem Verständniß dessen, was er leistet, möchten wir noch hinzufügen: er ist ein „Sohn der Zeit" im schönsten Sinne des Wortes. Ein Genie, das mit den glänzendsten Fähigkeiten ausgestattet und nach allen Richtungen ausgebildet; ein Geist, der sich vermöge erstaunlicher Kraft der Sympathie mit Allem associrt und zusammengelebt hat, was unsere reiche fortschreitende Zeit in Kunst und Leben an Großem, Herrlichem und Neuem aufweist. Daß also von einer gigantischen Schöpfungs- und Reproductionskraft nicht die stillbehagliche Schwärmerei und geglättete Ziererei einer vergangenen Periode, sondern der drängende Sturm der geistigen Bewegung von Jetzt zu erwarten ist, das erräth wohl Jeder, der die Bedeutung unserer Tage und ihre Anspiegelung in einer großen Künstlerseele versteht. Mit seinem Geiste und mit seiner Kunst ist Liszt ein edler Sohn dieser Zeit: seine Biographie und der ihm aller Orten zuschallende Jubel zeugen davon; er ist es aber auch mit seinem fühlenden Herzen, — und was der schlichte Künstler für die Armuth, für anstrebende Kunstjünger, für gemeinnützige Institute und zur Aneiferung mit wahrhaft großmüthigem Sinne thut, das macht, daß neben dem Lorbeer für den Künstler auch die Bürgerkrone für den Menschen von der dankenden Mitwelt hingelegt wurde.   D-M.

** Franz Liszt's Concert.

Liszt hat am 8. sein Concert im Saale der Vereinigten Gesellschaft vor einem glänzenden und sehr zahlreichen Auditorium gegeben. Wir freuen uns vor allem, daß dieses Concert nicht das einzige ist, welches uns den genialen Meister vorführt, sondern daß das Publikum in nächsten Tagen noch das Vergnügen haben soll, ihn im Theater zu bewundern. — Athemlose Aufmerksamkeit folgte den Inspirationen des Virtuosen, der mit seinen Leistungen auf jener Höhe steht, von welcher es kein denkbares „Weiter" gibt, weil der erschöpfte Mechanismus des Instruments die begränzende Schranke bildet. Ein Genie aber wie Liszt kennt in seinem begeisterten Drange nach stetem Vorwärts keine Beschränkung: er ist ein künstlerischer Alchimedes, der sich nur nach dem Raum umsieht, in welcher er seine neuen Schöpfungen versetzen kann. Daher staunen wir gar nicht zu erfahren, daß er soeben mit der Idee umgeht, den Mechanismus seines Instrumentes erfinderisch zu erweitern, um für das, was er in sich fühlt, ein Terrain zur Ausführung zu gewinnen. Wir hörten Liszt in sieben Nummern, darunter nur eine fremde Claviercomposition, die Mazurka von Chopin; denn die Ouverture zu Wilhelm Tell und die reizende Tarantelle sind zwar dem Genius Rossini's entflossen, aber durch diese unvergleichliche und überreiche Transcription für das Pianoforte wirklich ein Miteigenthum Liszt's geworden. Wir haben in unserem Vorartikel auf Eines hingewiesen, das sich gewiß der ganzen Zuhörerschaft als Ueberzeugung eingeprägt hat: unter Liszt's Händen erwacht ein Orchester, ja noch mehr, man hört und fühlt mitten durch die Gewalt der Massen den Gesang durchsilbern. Einen wunderbaren Eindruck brachte die Fantasie über Motive der Norma und der höchst originelle Chromatische Galopp hervor. Das sind Tonstücke, deren Ausführung, wie sie hier dargeboten wurde — Tonfluth, Tempo, Klarheit und Fantasie-Ausstattung erwogen — ons Märchenhafte gränzt. Das Virtuosenthum hat in Liszt seinen Gipfelpunkt erreicht: daß er sich auf diesem behauptet, immer und überall neu und ergreifend wirkt, während Andere nach ein- oder zweijähriger Berühmtheit sich verausgabt haben und schlafen geben, das ist der triftigste Beweis für sein großes musikalisches Genie im Allgemeinen, vermöge dessen er, wie jener griechische Maler, auch ohne Hände ein großer Meister der Kunst geworden wäre. — Ueber ein Concert von Liszt läßt sich kein anderer Bericht schreiben, als: Gehet hin und höret! Wien und Berlin, beide von allen Kunstnotabilitäten überschwemmt, sind nicht satt geworden sich zu seinen je zwölf Concerten hinzudrängen und ihm zu lauschen, wenn seine Finger, bald als zehn Stahlhämmer den schärfsten oder trockensten Ton erzwingen, bald als Streichbogen den sanftesten Klang abschmeicheln und immer die Fülle eines reichen Geistes kundgeben. Sein nächstes Theaterconcert anlangend vernehmen wir, daß durch einen zweckmäßigen Vorbau in's Orchester, das Instrument möglichst in's Auditorium hereingerückt und den Zuhörern keiner seiner Töne entgehen und das Pianoforte unter seinen Händen gewiß raumausfüllend erscheinen wird.   D-M.

The Women in Liszt's Life

Liszt and women: an association of ideas which appears to have left its ineradicable mark on posterity, providing material for many romantic novels and films. And many a life of Liszt seems to fall into this same category. "Franz Liszt, the Don Juan of music" has remained a popular theme.

Adelheid von Schorn, one of his most faithful followers during the last fifteen years of his life, wrote: ". . . That so many women wanted his love and threw themselves at him so passionately does our sex little credit. Men, of course, complained terribly about him, but I am afraid that the reason was mostly envy pure and simple. Liszt respected every honest woman, and once, towards the end of his life, during a moment of seriousness, he told me, 'I never seduced a young girl.' I know that this remark was true. Unfortunately, I saw women importuning him all too often, so that one would have thought their roles were reversed. That Liszt was uniquely attractive to the female sex I often, and much to my horror, had occasion to see. Nor did he cease to be so as he grew older. It was altogether painful to realize that there were still such women who regarded the old man, in need of rest as he was, as desirable prey. But just as Liszt, in spite of everything, saw only the best side of women, so he never allowed himself to be misled when they forced themselves upon him. His chivalry was one of his characteristics which drew the female sex to him, and gave evidence of his noble nature."[92]

318 Franz Liszt. Pastel portrait by Charles Laurent Maréchal ("Maréchal de Metz"), 1845.

Franz Liszt and "La Dame aux Camélias"

It was in November 1845 that Liszt first met Marie Duplessis, who achieved immortality as Alexandre Dumas's "La Dame aux Camélias." Legend claims that Liszt was the last great love of this beautiful and unhappy girl. Among the few possessions found in her room when she died (her apartment, at 15 Boulevard de la Madeleine, still exists but is unmarked by any plaque) was a portrait of Liszt.

What is the actual evidence for such a claim?

In a letter of 12 February 1847 to the Paris doctor David-Ferdinand Koreff, Liszt indicates that he was introduced to Marie Duplessis in November 1845. Koreff (whom André Maurois described as "half charlatan, half genius") was Marie's doctor (in addition to treating Liszt's mother and Marie d'Agoult), and it appears that after her death he suggested that Liszt should settle her unpaid bills.

Liszt to Marie d'Agoult (Lemberg, 1 May 1847): "And this poor Mariette Duplessis who has died . . . the first woman with whom I fell in love, who has now been laid to rest in some unknown cemetery, where the worms will consume her body! Fifteen months ago she said to me, 'Take me, take me with you wherever you want; I shall not be a burden to you, during the day I shall sleep, in the evening you can let me go to the theatre, and at night you can do with me what you want!' I have never told you what a strange attraction I felt for this charming creature at the time of my last stay in Paris. I told her I would take her with me to Constantinople [. . .] but now she is dead . . . I do not know what strange, ancient elegiac note vibrates in my heart at the memory of her!"[93]

319 La Dame aux Camélias (Marie Duplessis, 1824–1847) in her theatre box. Watercolour by Roqueplan, ca. 1845.

LIFE

January: Liszt undertakes a concert tour of northern France (in Rennes on 1 January, then Lille, Douai, Valenciennes), ending up in Brussels.

29 January: Concert in Liège.

Between 25 January and 10 March the *Revue Indépendante* serializes Marie d'Agoult's novel *Nélida*, a satire on her relationship with Liszt (the title is an anagram of her pen name, Daniel [Stern]). Having read only the first instalment, Liszt writes to the authoress on 2 February and expresses his feelings in no uncertain terms.[94]

22 February: Liszt performs Beethoven's E flat major Piano Concerto in Weimar.

1 March to 4 April: Liszt in Vienna. Concerts on 1, 5, 8, 11, 15, 17, 18, 19, 21, 22, 25, 26, 27, 28, 29 (midday and evening), and 31 March, and 4 April.

Liszt receives Beethoven's Broadwood piano as a gift from the publisher Carl Anton Spina. (It is now in the National Museum in Budapest, to whom it passed under the terms of Liszt's will.) See Illus. 437.

12, 14, and 24 March: Concerts in Brünn (Brno).

13, 16, and 19 April: Concerts in Prague.

20 to 25 April: Liszt in Vienna.

26 April: Concert in Olmütz.

29 April: Arrival in Pest. Concerts on 30 April, and 3, 6, 9, and 13 May. Miklós Barabás paints Liszt's portrait (Illus. 331).

17 May: Concert in Vienna; then guest of Prince Felix von Lichnowsky at Schloß Grätz near Troppau.

27 May and 1 June: Concerts in Troppau.

2 June: Concert in Teschen.

13 June: Liszt in Vienna.

14 and 19 June: Concerts in Graz.

16 June: Concert in Marburg.

20 June: Liszt back in Vienna and Brühl.

July: Liszt in Vienna and Rodaun.

2 July: Liszt and Johann Strauß the Elder perform at an open-air concert at the Sperl.

25 July: Concert in Bad Rohitsch-Sauerbrunn (modern Rogaska Slatina).

27 July: Concert in Agram (Zagreb).

3 August: Concert in Ödenburg (Sopron). Liszt is made a magistrate of the County of Ödenburg, after which he visits his hometown of Raiding.

5 August: Back in Vienna, then guest of Count Festetics in Hungary.

26 and 27 September: Liszt in Güns (Köszeg). Concert on the 27th. He had already been given the freedom of the town on the 25th.

6 and 10 October: Stays with Count Festetics in Dáka.

11 October: Charity concert in Pest.

13 to 24 October: Guest of Baron Antal Augusz in Szekszárd. Concert on 18 October.

15 October: Guest of Count Apponyi in Högyész.

24/25 October: Guest of Bishop Scitovszky in Nádasd (Mekseknádasd) (see Illus. 330).

25 and 26 October: Concerts in Fünfkirchen (Pécs).

29/30 October: Guest of Count Guido Karácsonyi in Bánlak.

1 to 7 November: Liszt in Temesvár (Timisoara). Concerts on 2 and 4 November.

7 to 11 November: Liszt in Arad. Concerts on 8 and 10 November.

13 and 17 November: Concerts in Temesvár.

15 November: Concert in Lugos (Lugoj).

19 to 23 November: Liszt in Hermannstadt (Sibiu). Concert on 20 November.

24 November to 7 December: Liszt in Klausen-

320, 321 Franz Liszt. Two lithographs by Josef Kriehuber, 1846.

burg (Cluj). Concerts on 26 and 29 November, and 3 and 6 December.

8 December: Concert in Nagyenyed (Aiud).

9 December: Liszt in Klausenburg.

11 December: Liszt travels to Bucharest via Hermannstadt.

16 to 31 December: Liszt in Bucharest, where he stays with Princess Ghica. Concerts in Bucharest on 21, 23, and 31 December.

WORKS

Five (Six) Choruses (with French words): 1. *Qui m'a donné*, 2. *L'Eternel est son nom*, 3. *Chantons, chantons l'auteur*, 4. *Untexted, in A major*, 5. *Combien j'ai douce souvenance*. Written ca. 1846. In a letter of March 1846 Liszt mentions ''six choruses'', so one of the manuscripts must have gone missing.

''Coriolan'' Overture (Beethoven) (piano transcription). Probably written 1846 or 1847. In a letter dated 14 September 1847, Liszt mentions that it is ''in a portfolio in Germany.'' Lost.

''Egmont'' Overture (Beethoven) (piano transcription). Probably written 1846 or 1847. Mentioned in a catalogue of Princess Wittgenstein. Lost.

Overture to ''The Magic Flute'' (Mozart) (piano transcription). Probably written ca. 1846. Mentioned in the same catalogue. Lost.

Ave Maria I (for chorus and organ). Pub. 1846. Revised and published 1852. See also ''Works 1847.''

Pater noster II (for unaccompanied chorus). Pub. 1846. Revised for men's voices and organ ca. 1848, and published at the same time as a piano version in 1852. See also ''Works 1847.''

Isten veled (Farewell) (for mezzo-soprano or tenor and piano). Pub. 1847.

A patakhoz (To the Brook) (for male-voice quartet). Pub. 1874.

Capriccio alla turca (based on Beethoven's *Ruins of Athens*) (for piano). Pub. 1847.

Jubelouvertüre (Weber) (piano transcription). Pub. 1847.

Overture to ''Der Freischütz'' (Weber) (piano transcription). Pub. 1847.

Leyer und Schwert (piano transcription of Weber's *Schwertlied*). Pub. 1848.

Galop in A minor (for piano). Written ca. 1846. Pub. 1928. Extra variant pub. 1985.

6 Melodien (Schubert) (piano transcriptions): 1. *Lebewohl*, 2. *Des Mädchens Klage*, 3. *Das Zügenglöcklein*, 4. *Trockne Blumen*, 5. *Ungeduld* (1st version), 6. *Die Forelle* (1st version). Pub. 1846.

6 Müllerlieder (Schubert) (piano transcriptions): 1. *Das Wandern*, 2. *Der Müller und der Bach*, 3. *Der Jäger*, 4. *Die böse Farbe*, 5. *Wohin?*, 6. *Ungeduld* (2nd version). Pub. 1847.

Die Forelle (Schubert) (piano transcription) (2nd version). Pub. 1846.

3 Marches for Four Hands (Schubert, D.819 No. 5, D.986b Nos. 1 and 2) (arranged for two hands). Pub. 1847.

Spanisches Ständchen (Festetics) (piano transcription). Unpublished.

Tarantelle di bravura d'après la Tarantella de ''La Muette de Portici'' (Auber) (for piano). Pub. 1847.

3 Pieces, including two on themes from *''La Muette de Portici''*. Year of composition unknown. Unpublished.

(continued p. 162)

"Works 1846" (continued)

Hungarian Rhapsody No. 1 (for piano). Pub. 1851.

Rhapsody (so-called "Romanian Rhapsody") (for piano). Pub. 1936. (*Magyar rapszódiák* No. 20; see "Works 1840".)

Fragment on motifs from Liszt's first Beethoven cantata (see "Works 1845") (piano transcription). Written ca. 1846. Pub. 1846.

Variations on "Tiszántuli Szép Leány" (for piano). Unpub.

Spirito gentile from *La Favorita* (Donizetti) (piano transcription). Unpub.

322 Programme of Liszt's concert in Vienna on 5 March 1846.

Liszt gave more than twenty concerts in March 1846. According to the *Allgemeine Theaterzeitung* of 7 April 1846, he declined a further 172(!) invitations to play.

323 Heinrich Wilhelm Ernst (1814–1865). Lithograph by P. Münzer, ca. 1845.

Ernst and Liszt had already performed together in Paris in 1834 and 1835. They appeared on the same platform again in Vienna on 15, 21, and 25 March 1846 (see Illus. 324 and 461).

Zweites CONCERT von Franz Liszt

Donnerstag den 5. März 1846,
Mittags um halb 1 Uhr,
im Saale der Gesellschaft der Musikfreunde.

Programm.

1. **Ouverture** aus Wilhelm Tell, arrangirt von Liszt
2. a) **Le Lac de Wallenstadt.**) Aus dem Album d'un
   b) **Au bord d'une source.**) voyageur.
3. **Fantasie in C**, von Fr. Schubert,
4. **Zwei Etuden** von Chopin,
5. **Fantasie aus Norma**, von Liszt

gespielt von LISZT.

Heinrich Adami: "Herr Franz Liszt's First Concert" from the *Allgemeine Theaterzeitung* of 3 March 1846:

"If we had to say who, in the case of any other instrument, was its first and greatest master, we should be at a loss for an answer; only with the piano have we no need for even a moment's reflection, for there is but a single name to name: that of Franz Liszt. As for the other great celebrities who play the piano, we are astonished at their exceptional achievements, their supreme technical accomplishment, we admire their clever accounts, their noble and worthy artistic endeavours; but Liszt alone can enchant his listener, Liszt who, himself inspired, inspires others; and though they were to imitate all his technical tricks, and even seek to surpass that skill, they have failed to learn this one special secret, no matter how intently they may have listened. The magic spell may very well lie in the blue ring which Liszt wears on his finger! Six whole years have gone by since Liszt was last in Vienna. During that time we have digested an unbelievably vast amount of keyboard music, our audiences have grown aweary of concerts, and our better critics have severely attacked all pitiful virtuosity. Many a famous name has sought in vain to rouse old sympathies; it was a hard and difficult time for all virtuosos who had learned nothing new and who had cause to complain at their public's 'shocking indifference' and their critics' coldly hostile tone. But then Franz Liszt arrived on the scene and, like some latter-day Caesar, threw into the scales the ever-victorious weapon of his great and wondrous talent, in order to rescue a virtuosity which was sorely oppressed and wellnigh an object of mockery. But why do I speak of talent? That is most certainly not the right term. All the famous representatives of piano playing have talent, great and distinguished talent; Liszt's talent, by contrast, is something original, a facet of genius, a quality unique to him alone, and it is this that places him so far above all others and thus prevents his being compared with anyone else.

"It was indeed, a remarkable occasion, this first concert, the day before yesterday, the 1st of March, at midday, in the Musikverein. In the entire hall there was only just sufficient room for the two magnificent Streicher pianos; everywhere else, including the pit and the chorus gallery (with its two rows of seats at 3 gulden apiece), the stalls and all the galleries, were full to overflowing, but what an elegant and select audience it was, the élite of local society. Downstairs by the main entrance, the servants who crowded the stairs were more numerous than the audience has been at many of our concerts. This bevy of fair ladies in the most tasteful of dresses offered a glorious spectacle. And finally Liszt appeared, welcomed with shouts of acclaim which we thought would never end, unchanged in his appearance and – to judge by his playing in the very first piece – unchanged in his artistry, too."

324 A matinée at Liszt's. Lithograph by Josef Kriehuber (1846), clearly influenced by Danhauser's oil painting (Illus. 240).

The artists seen here are Liszt at the piano, Czerny (wearing glasses) with Berlioz beside him, Ernst (with a violin) on the right, and Kriehuber (who made the lithograph) on the left.

Liszt is playing on an instrument by Conrad Graf. On the music stand are his own *Ungarische Nationalmelodien* and Beethoven's Sonata in A flat major, op. 26.

325, 326 Franz Liszt. Bronze medallion by Conrad Lange, 1846. Presented to Liszt by the ladies of Vienna.

The Latin inscription on the reverse of the medal (''Perituris sonis non peritura gloria'') might be translated, ''Though sound may perish, glory will not.''

327 Hotel "Römischer Kaiser," Hermannstadt (modern Sibiu, Romania). Photograph, ca. 1885.

Liszt stayed here during his visit to Hermannstadt in November 1846. The building (at the centre of the photograph) is no longer standing.

328 Hermannstadt, with the Munţii Făgăraşului in the background. Photograph, ca. 1940.

Apart from Leipzig, Hermannstadt was the only town where Liszt was booed, largely on account of his open sympathy with the cause of Hungary.

329 Liszt's programme in Pécs, Hungary, on 25 October 1846.

The University of Pécs owns the only known copy of this programme, a work of art in its own right, embellished with a steel engraving of Liszt by Josef Tyroler.

330 Palace of Nádasd (modern Mecseknádasd, Hungary), summer residence of the Bishop of Fünfkirchen (Pécs). Photograph, ca. 1950.

Liszt stayed here in 1846 as a guest of Bishop Johann (János) von Scitovszky (later the Primate of Hungary). A marble tablet commemorating Liszt's visits on 24 October 1846 and 21 September 1870 was erected on 21 October 1956. The building is now used as a school.

In the autumn of 1846 Liszt undertook a concert tour of the Banat, a region between Transylvania and Romania: Temesvár, Arad, Klausenburg, Hermannstadt, Bucharest, and Jassy were his main ports of call.

He travelled in the company of Hungarian aristocrats including Count Teleky and Count Bethlen. In Hermannstadt, where the inhabitants were almost all from Swabia, he incurred the displeasure of the Transylvanian aristocracy. The local population was locked in conflict with the Hungarians, and engaged in the most violent political struggle for its very existence. As an encore Liszt ignored requests for *Erlkönig* and played the *Rákóczy March*. The Hermannstadt audience saw this as a provocation, and press reactions were muted.

A report in the *Siebenbürger Wochenblatt*, No 95 (Kronstadt, 26 November 1846), p. 385, was headed "From Hermannstadt: 21 November 1846": "In the middle of the hall, on a raised section, stood two pianos on which Liszt performed by turns. [. . .] A number of magnates, counts, and barons surrounded the virtuoso, and we may assert without exaggeration that the highest of state officials never had a more splendid escort. Liszt plays. He leaves behind in the listener a feeling rather of astonishment and admiration than contentment and satisfaction. There is no time to comprehend it all, since scarcely has he begun to play when a violent thunderclap suddenly rings out, so that all the notes become blurred, and everything appears confused . . ."

Der Siebenbürger Volksfreund, No. 48, p. 375 (Hermannstadt, 27 November 1846): "Impossible though it must seem, the world-famous piano virtuoso came, a man who, the son of German parents, chanced to see the light of day in Hungary. All who could afford 1, 2, or 3 gulden were certainly not going to stay home. The hall was packed to the rafters. The clock had already struck a quarter to seven; no one dared breathe. [. . .] If London and Paris have experienced their moments of happiness, as I do not doubt for a moment, it does not by any means follow that Hermannstadt must also have known such happiness, for such moments cannot be obtained by coercion . . ."

331 Franz Liszt. Oil portrait by Miklós Barabás, 1846.

LIFE

13 (1) January: Arrival in Jassy (Romania). Concerts in Jassy on 17 (5), 20 (8), and 23 (11) January (old-style dates in brackets). Liszt stays with the Minister of Finance, Alecu Bals. He gets to know Vasile Barbu's popular melodies, and is introduced to the poet Vasile Alexandri. From Jassy he sets off for the Ukraine.

14 (2) and 19 (7) February: Concerts in Kiev. Meets Princess Carolyne von Sayn-Wittgenstein.

February/March: As guest of Carolyne at Woronince. A few concerts in neighbouring towns.

13 April to early May: Liszt in Lemberg. Four concerts.

16 May: Liszt passes through Stanislav.

19 to 26 May: Liszt in Czernovtsy. Concerts on 24 and 25 May.

27 May: Liszt in Jassy.

4 June: Liszt in Galatz (in quarantine).

8 June to 13 July: Liszt in Constantinople. He performs twice at the royal palace in Tchiraghan and on several occasions at the Russian Embassy. Abdul-Medjid Khan decorates him with the Order of Nichan-Iftikhar and presents him with a gold casket.

17 July: Two days in Galatz (in quarantine).

July/August: Liszt in Odessa, where he gives ten concerts. During this period many Russian dignitaries are in the town in connection with massive troop manoeuvres.

14 September: Liszt in Elisabetgrad. He gives his last concert here (a benefit performance for himself).

In Elisabetgrad Liszt ends his virtuoso career for ever. His years as a pianist become a legend.

22 October: Liszt celebrates his birthday at Woronince, where he remains until the end of January 1848. He gives a number of concerts in the surrounding towns of Podolia.

Letter of 25 January 1847 from Herr Eisenbach, the Austrian consul in Jassy, to Prince Metternich:

". . . On the 13th instant the famous pianist Franz Liszt arrived in the city from Bucharest; the three concerts which he gave here having met with the most brilliant acclaim, he left today for Kiev and Odessa, from where he plans to set off next spring for Constantinople. The first visit which he and his travelling companion, the Hungarian nobleman Guido de Karácsonyi, paid on anyone here was on the imperial representative, whom they saw the very day after their arrival; the restrained, respectable, and tactful behaviour which these two gentlemen showed throughout their stay here might serve as an example to many travellers abroad . . ."

332 Odessa. Steel engraving, ca. 1845.

Liszt was in Odessa from the end of July to the beginning of September 1847. In the nearby city of Elisabetgrad, where he was to end his career as a virtuoso in the middle of September, he saw Tsar Nicholas I review eighty thousand of his troops. Liszt's audiences here consisted chiefly of Russian officers in their splendid uniforms. He gave ten concerts in Odessa, of which six took place in the Theatre, three in the Hall of the Stock Exchange, and one in the Hôtel Richelieu.

333 The Château of Woronince in the Ukraine. Photograph, ca. 1940. Previously unpublished.

It was here that the *grand amour* between Liszt and the châtelaine, Carolyne von Sayn-Wittgenstein, began.

WORKS

Harmonies poétiques et religieuses (for piano): 1. *Invocations*, 2. *Ave Maria*, 3. *Bénédiction de Dieu dans la solitude*, 4. *Pensée des morts*, 5. *Pater noster*, 6. *Hymne de l'enfant à son réveil*, 7. *Funérailles*, 8. *Miserere*, 9. *Andante lagrimoso*, 10. *Cantique d'amour*. Written 1847–52 (No. 3 in 1845). Pub. 1853. *Hymne du matin*, *Hymne de la nuit*, and *Invocations* (1st version) were discarded from this collection and were not published until 1981. *Litanie de Marie*, also originally intended for this collection, remains incomplete.

Hungarian Rhapsody No. 2 (for piano). Pub. 1851.

"Cujus animam" from *Stabat mater* and *La Charité* (Rossini) (for piano). Pub. 1848. Liszt added cadenzas and elaborations in the 1880s; first complete publication 1972.

Songs (to texts by Victor Hugo) (piano transcriptions) (see "Works 1844"). Transcribed ca. 1847. Pub. 1985. The transcription of *Enfant, si j'étais roi* was first published in 1975.

Le célèbre Zigeunerpolka (Conradi) (piano transcription). Pub. 1849.

Le juif errant (poem by Béranger) (for baritone and piano). Unpublished.

Schwanengesang and March from "Hunyadi László" (Erkel) (piano transcription). Unpublished.

Concert Paraphrase on themes from "Ernani" (Verdi) (for piano). Unpublished. Not the same as *"Ernani": paraphrase de concert* of 1849 (see "Works 1849").

Grande paraphrase de la marche de Giuseppe Donizetti [sic: not Gaetano Donizetti] (for piano). Pub. 1848.

Titan (for baritone solo, male voice chorus and piano). Unpublished.

Drei Lieder von Dessauer (piano transcriptions). Pub. 1847.

Glanes de Woronince (for piano): 1. *Ballade d'Ukraine, dumka*, 2. *Mélodies polonaises* (the first melody was also used in the Duo for violin and piano [see "Works 1851"], while the second melody is identical with Chopin's *Mädchenswunsch*), 3. *Complaintes, dumka*. Pub. 1849.

Mazeppa (for piano). Revised version of No. 4 of the *24 Grandes Études* (see "Works 1837"). Written ca. 1847. Pub. 1847.

3 Songs (for chorus, No. 1 with solo quartet, No. 3 with solo tenor): 1. *Die alten Sagen kunden*, 2. *Saatengrün*, 3. *Der Gang um Mitternacht*. Year of publication unknown.

334 Princess Carolyne von Sayn-Wittgenstein at the time of her first meeting with Liszt. Daguerreotype, Odessa 1847.[95]

335 Carolyne von Sayn-Wittgenstein. Daguerreotype, St Petersburg 1847. Previously unpublished.

Princess Jeanne Elisabeth Carolyne von Sayn-Wittgenstein was born on 8 February 1819, the daughter of the Polish aristocrat and landowner Peter von Ivanovsky and his equally well-born wife Pauline. She lived at Woronince, a country house built in the early eighteenth century and situated between Kiev and Odessa. All descriptions of her agree that, except for her dark and expressive eyes, she was not a beautiful woman. She was, however, notable for her intelligence and education, her lively temperament, and her deeply fanatical and unshakable Catholicism. She had travelled throughout the whole of fashionable Europe. In 1836, when she was seventeen, she had been married, at her father's behest, to Prince Nicholas von Sayn-Wittgenstein, adjutant to the governor of Kiev and the youngest son of the victorious Russian field marshal Prince Wittgenstein.

The Princess's fateful meeting with Liszt persuaded her to leave Russia in April 1848, taking her eleven-year-old daughter Marie with her. For twelve years she lived with Liszt in Weimar, quickly surrounding herself with artists and scholars (see p. 177). Tireless in her campaign to obtain a divorce, she moved to Rome in 1860 and after two papal audiences was finally granted permission to marry Liszt. The wedding was planned to take place in Rome on Liszt's fiftieth birthday, but on the very eve of the ceremony the plan was frustrated (see p. 221). After that she rarely left her rooms in the Via Babuino, but devoted herself to theological studies, smoking vast numbers of extremely strong cigars. She died on 8 March 1887, shortly after completing her 24-volume *Inner Causes of the External Weakness of the Church*. She is buried in the Vatican cemetery (see Illus. 646).

336 Princess Carolyne von Sayn-Wittgenstein with her young daughter, Princess Marie Wittgenstein. Lithograph by Carl Fischer based on a portrait by Casanova; 1844.

337 Franz Liszt. Pencil drawing by Julius Kossak, Lemberg 1847. A little-known portrait of Liszt.

338 Carolyne von Sayn-Wittgenstein. Undated pencil drawing by Vilna. Previously unpublished.

On the occasion of Liszt's concerts in Constantinople, a Muslim with a remarkable knowledge of the subject was heard to observe that, although many virtuosos had performed in the seraglio, none had moved his fingers as quickly as Liszt.

". . . Liszt is currently in Constantinople, where he is inspiring the Muslims. The unanimous cry, 'never before have we heard anyone play so quickly,' shows us clearly enough how profoundly and for what reasons the apogee of art is known, felt, and honoured in Istanbul, too,'' the *Siebenbürger Volksfreund* wrote in its issue of 15 July 1847.

In a letter which Erard received in Paris on 5 August 1847, Liszt described the magnificent view of the Bosporus and the Sea of Marmara (''Europe and Asia at one and the same time''),[96] which he could see from the Russian Embassy, where he gave a series of concerts.

The magnificent Erard piano which had been brought from Paris to Constantinople for Liszt's concerts was subsequently sold for 16,000 piastres to a certain M. Baldagi, who gave it as a wedding present to his fiancée.

An amusing incident in passing: on his arrival in the city, Liszt was brought before the Sultan with a warrant for his arrest. A fellow pianist had used the similarity of their names to advertise himself as the famous Liszt, so that the real Liszt was taken to be an impostor. The error was soon cleared up. ''A pianist, Listmann by name, begged my forgiveness in Constantinople for having removed the second syllable of his name from his concert programme. His reward was a lavish gift from the then Sultan,'' Liszt later told Henriette von Liszt in a letter of 8 February 1884.[97]

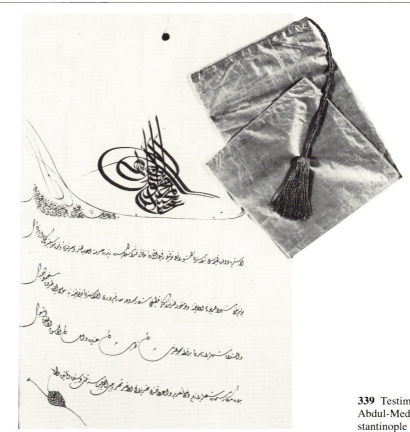

339 Testimonial presented to Liszt by Sultan Abdul-Medjid Khan during Liszt's visit to Constantinople from 8 June to 13 July 1847.

Liszt ended his virtuoso career in September 1847, stepping down from the platform at the pinnacle of his fame. For years he had been obliged to earn money to support not only himself and his mother, but also his children's education and maintenance. Similar constraints forced him to write and play operatic fantasies, a genre which to modern ears sounds distinctly dated.

It has often been claimed that Liszt's encounter with the Princess was his reason for giving up his concert career, but he had already long been toying with the idea of doing so. His letters contain frequent passages such as the following: ''What a loathsome necessity it is for a professional virtuoso to have to keep on chewing over the same old things! How often have I not had to mount the *Erlkönig* mare!'' (Liszt's piano transcription of Schubert's *Erlkönig* was always in great demand with audiences.) In October 1846 he wrote to Grand Duke Carl Alexander of Weimar, ''. . . The moment will come when I break out of the chrysalis state of a virtuoso's existence . . .'' Much earlier than this his dissatisfaction with his fate had already found expression in a letter to Lamennais of 18 December 1837: ''. . . Will my life always be ruled by this sense of otiose futility which so oppresses me? Will the hour of surrender and man's work never come? Am I then mercilessly condemned to ply the trade of a clown whose task it is to amuse people in their salons? . . .'' (see Illus. 255). Liszt felt he had been wasting his time. It may also be that the hope of finding, with Carolyne von Sayn-Wittgenstein, a home where he could finally realize his plans and compose in peace contributed to his decision to bid farewell to the concert platform.

340 Programme for Liszt's concert in Kiev on 2 February 1847.
It was probably at this concert that Carolyne von Sayn-Wittgenstein first saw and heard Liszt.

341 Liszt's handwriting in
1847 (facsimile, two-thirds of
original size). The last four
pages of Liszt's letter to Baron
von Gutmansthal, written in
Woronince on 25 October
1847. The autograph letter,
which is owned by the present
author, runs to eight pages.

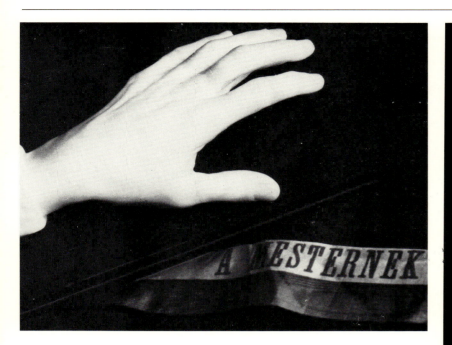

FRANZ LISZT'S HANDS

Liszt's hands are mentioned admiringly in many contemporary accounts. Even today we can still gain a lively impression of their beauty through plaster casts, paintings, and photographs (see also Illus. 130, 431, 461, 468, 487, 570).

Liszt had large but very narrow hands, with long slender fingers and thumbs which he could stretch further than most other people. According to the pianist Karl Klindworth, "He did such amazing things with the thumb of his left hand that you would think it was twice the length of an ordinary thumb." It is known that Liszt could play runs in tenths perfectly cleanly, often adding thirds and even chords.

In some of his earlier works such as his transcription of the *Oberon* Overture or Schubert's *Mélodies hongroises*, and the first version of his sixth Paganini Study (Variation VI), Liszt demanded runs of tenths to be played at speed. From around 1850 onwards he avoided excessive difficulties when writing for the keyboard: ". . . My 40 years of pottering around with the piano have now made me much more concerned not to torment the player unnecessarily, but to leave it to his discretion to produce the greatest possible effects of tone and strength through moderate effort," Liszt wrote to Julius Schuberth from Rome on 5 September 1863.[98]

342 Liszt's left hand. Anonymous sculpture in Carrara marble.

343 Plaster cast of Liszt's right hand, holding Carolyne von Sayn-Wittgenstein's left hand, as a symbol of their attachment.

344 Plaster cast of Liszt's right hand.

345 Plaster cast of Liszt's right hand in old age, photographed by Louis Held in Weimar.

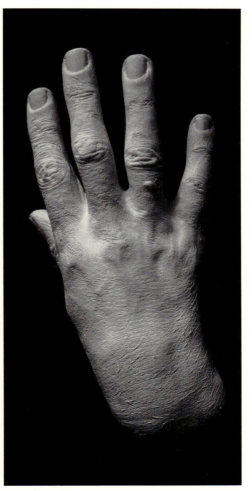

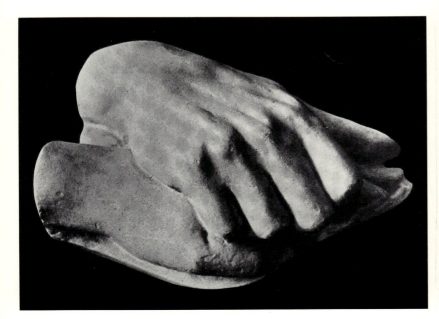

346 Franz Liszt. Photograph by Ghemar, Brussels 1854. Previously unpublished.

"Self-composure and work in Weimar"

1848–1860

LIFE

January: Liszt at Woronince, then (without giving concerts) in Lemberg (22 January), Cracow (25 January), Ratibor (26 January, where he meets Prince Felix von Lichnowsky at Kryzanowitz), and in Löbau (29 January).

February: At the beginning of the month Liszt takes up his duties as Court Kapellmeister in Weimar.

16 February: Liszt conducts Flotow's *Martha* in Weimar. He performs Henselt's Piano Concerto at two Court concerts.

28 February: Liszt conducts Gustav Schmidt's *Prinz Eugen* in Weimar.

Liszt expresses his enthusiastic support for the early successes of the Hungarian uprising; a year later he will dedicate his *Funérailles* to the fallen heroes.

26 March: Travels via Dresden (27 March) and Cosel (28 March) to Ratibor, where he meets Prince Lichnowsky.

28 March to mid-April: Guest of Prince Lichnowsky at Kryzanowitz. (The Prince will be murdered in Frankfurt only a few months later: see p. 139.)

18 April: Liszt meets Carolyne von Sayn-Wittgenstein at Grätz, on Lichnowsky's estates near Troppau. They remain until May, then travel to Vienna, Eisenstadt (where they visit Pater Albach), and Raiding.[99]

June: The couple travels via Prague to Weimar, where the Princess moves into the Altenburg, while Liszt rents rooms at the Hotel Erbprinz.

July: With the support of the Grand Duchess of Weimar, Maria Pavlovna, a sister of Tsar Nicholas I, Carolyne von Sayn-Wittgenstein writes to the Tsar asking for a divorce.

August: Wagner visits Liszt in Weimar.

September/October: Carolyne suffers a setback in her efforts to obtain a divorce: she refuses to obey the Tsar's instructions to return to Russia, and her husband transfers to Nicholas I his parental rights to their surviving daughter. When finally banished from Russia, the Princess may no longer be received at the Weimar Court.

12 November: Liszt conducts Wagner's *Tannhäuser* Overture in Weimar.

December: Liszt works at the Altenburg; officially his residence remains the Hotel Erbprinz.

WORKS

Ce qu'on entend sur la montagne ("Bergsymphonie") (symphonic poem, first draft). Four versions in all. The definitive version appeared in 1857.

Les Préludes (symphonic poem, first draft). Revised in 1850. Pub. 1856. A version for two pianos prepared ca. 1854–6 was published in 1856, and a version for piano duet made ca. 1858 appeared in 1859.

348 The titles of Liszt's twelve symphonic poems. Title page of the 1856 first edition of *Mazeppa* in the composer's arrangement for two pianos.

This innovatory musical genre, often described as "programme music," met with little approval in the years around 1850.

347 The Court Theatre in Weimar. Anonymous lithograph, ca. 1840. From 1848 onwards this was the focal point of Liszt's activities as Court Kapellmeister. Many works by famous and unknown composers received their first performances here under his baton.

It is worth bearing in mind what it meant for the greatest pianist in the world to retire from the concert platform and take up an appointment as Court Kapellmeister in a small town in central Germany (Weimar numbered some 13,000 inhabitants in the years around 1848). Financial considerations did not play a part in Liszt's decision; as a piano virtuoso he could have earned more by giving a single concert than his appointment as Kapellmeister brought him in a whole month.

Liszt felt the need to perform here works which he must have known in advance would bring him no great acclaim from the general public. By and large, he avoided the traditional repertory and devoted his energies instead to works such as Schumann's *Genoveva*, Berlioz's *Benvenuto Cellini*, Schubert's *Alfonso und Estrella*, and Wagner's *Tannhäuser*, *Lohengrin*, and *The Flying Dutchman*.

It is also worth recalling the circumstances in which these performances took place. Following the deaths of Schiller and Goethe Weimar had again become a sleepy provincial capital, dreaming of its great past. Liszt's orchestra comprised some 35 (!) musicians in around 1850, and the chorus numbered ten men and thirteen women. Although the lustre of Liszt's name was able to attract a handful of leading artists to the town, including Joseph Joachim as Konzertmeister, his orchestra never rose above 40 players.

Opposite page:

350 Programme of a concert conducted by Liszt in Weimar on 12 November 1848.

Although typical of the period around 1850, this kind of programme is scarcely conceivable today. The first half consisted of three vocal numbers, Wagner's *Tannhäuser* Overture, and a movement from Henselt's Piano Concerto, in addition to Liszt's own *Tarantelle di bravura* from Auber's *La Muette de Portici*; the second half of the evening was a staged performance of Act IV of Meyerbeer's *Les Huguenots*.

Hungaria (cantata for baritone solo, chorus and piano). Pub. 1961.

Weimars Toten (for baritone or bass and piano). Pub. 1849.

Die Macht der Musik (for tenor or soprano and piano). Pub. 1849.

Klinge leise, mein Lied (for tenor and piano). Pub. 1918. A second version appeared in 1860.

Schwebe, schwebe, blaues Auge (for tenor and piano). Pub. 1918. A second version appeared in 1860.

Arbeiterchor (for solo baritone, solo quartet, men's voices and piano). Although the piece was engraved, its publication was prevented by the outbreak of the Revolution. It was not published until 1953; but Anton von Webern arranged the work for bass solo, chorus, and orchestra in 1924, and his edition of the vocal score was published the same year.

Le vieux vagabond (for bass and piano). Pub. 1918.

Trois Études de concert (for piano): 1. *Il Lamento*, 2. *La Leggierezza*, 3. *Un Sospiro* (the titles are probably not by Liszt). Pub. 1849. Elaborations to No. 3 were composed in the 1880s and published in 1911.

Ballade No. 1 (for piano) (the first draft dates from 1845). Pub. 1849.

Romance (for piano). Pub. 1908. For the version for voice and piano also written at this time and entitled *Oh pourquoi donc*, see ''Works 1843.'' (See also ''Works 1880.'')

Overture to ''Tannhäuser'' (Wagner) (piano transcription). Pub. 1849.

Widmung (Robert Schumann) (piano transcription). Pub. 1848.

Er ist gekommen (Robert Franz) (piano transcription). Pub. 1849.

Einsam bin ich (Weber) (piano transcription). Pub. 1848; new edition 1876.

Schlummerlied (Weber) (piano transcription). Pub. 1848.

Salve Maria from *I Lombardi* (Verdi) (piano transcription). Pub. 1848.

Wasserfahrt (Mendelssohn) (piano transcription). Pub. 1849.

Der Jäger Abschied (Mendelssohn) (piano transcription). Pub. 1849.

Septet (Hummel, op. 74) (piano transcription). Pub. 1849.

Mass (Szekszárd Mass) (for men's voices and organ). Pub. 1853. A second version was written and published in 1869.

Années de Pèlerinage. Première Année: Suisse (for piano). The 1836 version was revised (with the addition of a number of new titles) between 1848 and 1854. Pub. 1855. See ''Works 1836.''

12 Lieder von Robert Franz (from opp. 2, 3, and 8) (piano transcriptions). Written ca. 1848. Pub. 1849.

Hungarian Rhapsodies Nos. 3–15 (for piano). In most of these pieces Liszt reused melodies and whole passages from his *Ungarische Nationalmelodien* of 1840–47. These new pieces, written between 1848 and 1853, were published in 1853; Nos. 9 and 15 also appeared separately, in 1848 and 1851 respectively.

Freudvoll und leidvoll (for mezzo-soprano and piano) (second setting). Written ca. 1848. Pub. 1848.

349 The Residenz in Weimar. Steel engraving by Knopfmacher after a drawing by Pozzi; ca. 1850.

351 Decree appointing Liszt Grand Ducal Director of Music Extraordinary at Weimar, issued on 2 November 1842.

Not until 1848, when Weimar became his permanent home, did Liszt perform all the functions of his office.

352 ''Hotel Erbprinz'' in Weimar. Undated drawing by Lorenz Wiest, nineteenth century.
Liszt lived here from June 1848 until he moved to the Altenburg to be with Princess Carolyne von Sayn-Wittgenstein. The Weimar Court took no official notice of his move, and for the following twelve years continued to send written communications to the ''Erbprinz.'' The building still exists, as do the rooms in which Liszt stayed. Johann Sebastian Bach and Richard Wagner also stayed at the ''Erbprinz'' in their time.

353 The Altenburg in Weimar. Anonymous nineteenth-century woodcut based on a drawing by Jordan.
Liszt – ''half Franciscan, half gypsy,'' as he called himself – found his first and only refuge here. The building in which he wrote his B minor Sonata, both his piano concertos, and all his symphonic poems has survived almost unchanged on the outside, but the splendid interior is scarcely recognizable any longer.

Opposite page:

354 The Altenburg in Weimar. Photograph by Louis Held of Weimar, ca. 1900.

355 The Altenburg in Weimar. Watercolour by Carl Hoffmann, December 1859.

356 The Altenburg library. Wood engraving from the *Illustrirte Zeitung* of 26 May 1855.
On the right is Beethoven's Broadwood piano, on the left an Erard grand.

357 The Altenburg music room. Wood engraving from the *Illustrirte Zeitung* of 2 June 1855.
Beside the huge pedal pianoforte (see Illus. 391) is an instrument once owned by Mozart.

The Altenburg

The Altenburg in Weimar was Liszt's home from 1848 to 1861. As such it became one of the nineteenth century's most resplendent centres of art. Musicians, writers, and scholars met here, as did painters, sculptors, and theatre artistes. Among those who enjoyed the generous, not to say lavish, hospitality of Liszt and the Princess were Richard Wagner, Hector Berlioz, Johannes Brahms, Clara Schumann, Anton Rubinstein, Alexander von Humboldt, Varnhagen von Ense, Hoffmann von Fallersleben, Bettina von Arnim, Gustav Freytag, Emanuel Geibel, Paul Heyse, Wilhelm von Kaulbach, Moritz von Schwind, Adolph von Menzel, Ary Scheffer, Friedrich Preller, Ernst Rietschel, and Gottfried Semper. Friedrich Hebbel spent some time at the Altenburg in 1861, and Hans von Bülow, Carl Tausig, Joachim Raff, and Peter Cornelius could always board there free of charge. Many pianists were lured to the Altenburg by the chance to hear their idol play, or even to be taught by him. Dionys Pruckner, Hans von Bronsart, and Karl Klindworth were among the lucky few to whom Liszt passed on his knowledge – without asking for anything in return.

The Altenburg was, and is, a lordly edifice situated on a pine-forested elevation in the Jenaer-Straße. It had been built in 1811 by Friedrich von Seebach, a colonel in the Hussars, on the very spot where Henry the Fowler and his son, the Emperor Otto the Great, had held their Imperial Diets. In 1851 it came into the possession of the Grand Duchess Maria Pavlovna, who had placed it at the disposal of Carolyne von Sayn-Wittgenstein three years earlier.

The ground-floor salon was used for chamber music; above its door was a humorous drawing by Bettina von Arnim (see Illus. 384), and on the wall was Beethoven's original death mask, together with medallions of Wagner, Berlioz, and Schumann. Next to this room was a study decorated with weapons and smoking paraphernalia which had been given to Liszt as presents. Upstairs on the first floor was the library (Illus. 356), the dining room, the "Green Study," and the Princess's Oriental corner salon. The second floor comprised Liszt's living quarters, including the music room (Illus. 357 and 391), and a series of guest-rooms. At the back of the house was Liszt's "Blue Study" with its three windows overlooking the garden (see Illus. 355), the Boisselot grand piano (see Illus. 648), and doors leading to Liszt's bedchamber and to a room which contained only a crucifix and two prie-dieux for Liszt and the Princess.

358 Manuscript of the first page of Liszt's *Hungarian Rhapsody* No. 19 with the composer's dedication to Lina Schmalhausen (see Illus. 603).

359 Gypsy family in Puszta Telecska. Oil painting by Julius Muhr, ca. 1857.

Liszt's "Hungarian Rhapsodies" and His Book on the Gypsies

The term "Hungarian Rhapsody" involuntarily conjures up the figure of Franz Liszt, whether it be in recalling Zsolt von Harsanyi's biographical novel of the same title, or the no less popular piano pieces by Liszt.

It was in 1848 – the year of the great Revolution which sent a wave of sympathy for the brave freedom fighters of Hungary right across Europe – that Liszt began to revise his *Ungarische Nationalmelodien* or *Magyar dallok* of 1840–47 and turn them into the *Hungarian Rhapsodies*. The rhetorical *melos* of the Gypsy violin, the recitative-like qualities of the *lassu*, the infectious élan of the *friss* or of the *csárdás* with its clatter of spurs were forms of expression which suited Liszt's style of composing and playing as well as reflecting his rhapsodical life-style. He may also have been attracted by the tonal colour of Gypsy music, standing as it does outside the usual major and minor systems.

The first two Rhapsodies were published in 1851, Nos. 3–15 following in 1853. (Early versions of No. 9, *Pester Karneval*, and No. 15, *Rákóczy March*, had already appeared in 1847 and 1851 respectively.) The last three differ from the earlier ones inasmuch as they are not based on borrowed themes. No. 16 was published in 1882, No. 17 in 1886, No. 18 in 1885, and No. 19 in 1886. (The numbering does not correspond to the order in which they were written: No. 17 was composed in 1884, No. 18 in 1885, and No. 19 in 1884.) The so-called "Romanian Rhapsody" (the title is not Liszt's), which includes themes from Transylvania and Walachia, was probably conceived in 1846 during Liszt's concert tour of this region. It was not published until 1936. A Rhapsody allegedly newly discovered and published in 1969 as No. 20 is in fact No. 9 of the *Magyar dallok*.

In 1936 Béla Bartók wrote, "In the name of truth, I must stress that the Rhapsodies, especially the Hungarian ones, are consummate creations of a unique kind. The material which Liszt used here could not have been handled with greater beauty or genius. The value of the material itself, however, is quite a different matter, which is evidently the reason why the general value of these works is so slight and their popularity so great [. . .]".

Liszt's book *Des Bohémiens et de leur Musique en Hongrie* (*On the Gypsies and Their Music in Hungary*) appeared in French in 1859 and in a German translation (by Peter Cornelius) in 1861. Liszt was not the man to engage in pedantic, time-consuming source studies, as his book on Chopin had already made clear. He wrote in an impetuous, poetical style, and unfortunately he left Carolyne von Sayn-Wittgenstein to fill in far too many of the details in her inimitably effusive manner. Hungarian folk music had not been properly investigated at this time (not until ca. 1920 were Bartók and Kodály to do so), and Liszt made the mistake of confusing the music of Hungary with that of the Gypsies. It was an error which the Hungarians were slow to forgive.

LIFE

January: Liszt works on various compositions in Weimar, including his Piano Concertos and his *Totentanz*.

16 February: Liszt conducts Wagner's *Tannhäuser* in Weimar, only the second production of the work since its Dresden premiere on 19 October 1845.

27 February: Liszt conducts Gustav Schmidt's *Prinz Eugen* in Weimar.

14 April: Liszt conducts *Tony oder Die Verstellung* by Duke Ernst von Saxe-Coburg-Gotha.

13 May: Wagner arrives in Weimar, a revolutionary fleeing from the Dresden Uprising. He stays first at the Altenburg, then (from the 20th) in Magdala. Liszt finances his flight to Zurich and also his return from Paris in July.

June/July: Compositional activity.

1 August: First version of *Tasso*.

28 and 29 August: To mark the centenary of Goethe's birth, Liszt conducts Beethoven's Symphony No. 9, part of Schumann's *Faust*, the first performance of his own *Tasso* (in the form of an overture), and his *Festmarsch zur Goethejubiläumsfeier*.

September: With the Princess and her daughter Marie in Helgoland.

October: On the return journey, Marie falls ill with typhus; the party remains in Bad Eilsen, near Bückeburg.

17 October: Frédéric Chopin dies in Paris. Shortly afterwards Liszt and the Princess begin their biography of Chopin.

November: Liszt in Bad Eilsen. Joachim Raff, who has entered Liszt's service, helping him orchestrate his works and to write out the fair copies of his full scores, follows him to Bad Eilsen, where the two men work together every day.

8 December: Full score of the E flat major Piano Concerto completed. The A major Piano Concerto (originally entitled *Concert Symphonique*) is also finished.

WORKS

Piano Concerto No. 1 in E flat major. First sketches 1830 (!). Completed in 1849 and revised in 1853. Further alterations in 1856. Pub. 1857. A version for two pianos appeared at the same time.

Piano Concerto No. 2 in A major. Written 1839 (!). Orchestrated in 1849; revised in 1853, and altered in 1857 and 1861. Pub. 1863. A version for two pianos appeared in 1862.

Totentanz (for piano and orchestra). First sketches 1838. Completed 1849, revised in 1853

360 Place Vendôme, Paris. Anonymous oil painting, ca. 1849.

Frédéric Chopin died on 17 October 1849 in the house to which he had moved only weeks previously, behind No. 12 Place Vendôme (not, as generally assumed, in the building at the front which bears a commemorative plaque). He was laid out in the first-floor room at the front building, behind the windows next to the plaque.

361 12 Place Vendôme. Interior of the Louis XIV salon in which Chopin's friends paid him their last respects. (Decorated with genuine gold leaf, this room is now the main showroom of the jewelry firm of Chaumet & Cie.)

The portrait on the wall, that of the Empress Marie-Louise, seen wearing diamonds from the firm of Chaumet & Cie, was not in the room in 1849. The Place Vendôme can be seen through the windows.

362 Title page of Liszt's biography of Chopin, 1852 edition.

F. CHOPIN

PAR

F. LISZT

LEIPZIG

BREITKOPF ET HAERTEL
IMPRIMEURS-ÉDITEURS

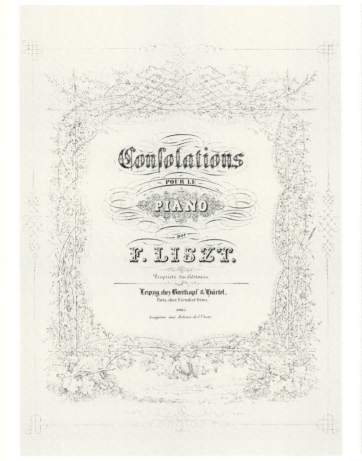

363 *Consolations*, composed in 1849 and published by Breitkopf & Härtel in 1850.

These six piano pieces (the most famous of which, No. 3, bears a strong resemblance to the melody of Wagner's "Nie sollst du mich befragen" from *Lohengrin*) are among the easiest of Liszt's works from a technical point of view, and for many young students of the piano they are their first encounter with the composer's sound-world.

In September 1849 Liszt and the Princess spent a number of weeks on Helgoland, where they met the brother of Henri Lehmann (see Illus. 207), Rudolf, himself an artist, who on 25 September sketched the portrait of Liszt reproduced here. It is to Rudolf Lehmann that we owe the following description of Liszt:

"[. . .] In his youth he had been of slim and delicate appearance, and even now was both elegant and prepossessing; his mobile features were full of character and life, his forehead not very high, while his temples – where phrenologists place the feeling for music – were notable for their uncommonly sharp edges. Shortsighted by nature, his grey eyes were shaded by heavy eyebrows but filled with life and an expression of benevolence. His nose was elongated, somewhat Roman, while his nostrils twitched in constant, nervous movement. The corners of his mouth were strongly accented and this, together with his slightly projecting lower lip, gave character to his finely chiselled mouth, while a well-developed chin completed his clean-shaven face. His auburn hair, combed upwards and backwards to either side of his forehead, fell low over his neck in a straight soft mane" (Rudolf Lehmann, *Erinnerungen eines Künstlers*, Berlin 1896).

364 Playbill for Liszt's performance of *Tannhäuser*, 1849.

Wagner on Liszt: "What I felt when I created this music, he too felt when he performed it; what I wanted to say when I wrote it down, he too said when he gave it expression. Wondrous! Through this rarest of all friends' love I found a true home for my art, a home which I had long desired and looked for everywhere, but always in the wrong place, but which I finally found at the very moment when I myself became homeless . . ."[100]

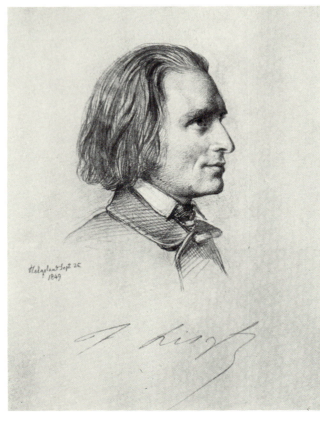

365 Franz Liszt. Drawing by Rudolf Lehmann, Helgoland 1849.

and again in 1857. Pub. 1857. Versions for two hands and for four hands appeared at the same time.

Ce qu'on entend sur la montagne ("Bergsymphonie"). Revised version. The definitive version appeared in 1857.

Tasso. Lamento e Trionfo (Symphonic Poem). The definitive version of 1854 appeared in 1856. A version for two pianos prepared ca. 1854–6 was published in 1856, and a version for piano duet made ca. 1858 appeared in 1859.

Festmarsch zur Goethejubiläumsfeier (for orchestra). First version. Revised in 1857 and published in 1859. A piano version appeared in 1849.

Chor der Engel (from Goethe's *Faust*) (for mixed voices and harp or piano). Pub. 1849.

"Ernani": paraphrase de concert (Verdi) (for piano). Written ca. 1849. Pub. 1860.

Großes Konzertsolo (for piano). Pub. 1851. Revised for two pianos as *Concerto pathétique* in 1856 and published in 1866. A version for piano and orchestra ("Grand Solo de Concert") dating from ca. 1850 is unpublished.

Funérailles (for piano). Pub. 1853.

6 Lieder von Goethe (Beethoven, from opp. 75, 83, and 84) (piano transcriptions). Written ca. 1849. Pub. 1849.

Dante Sonata (for piano). Revised version of the 1837 draft. Pub. 1858.

Canzonetta del Salvator Rosa (for piano). Pub. 1858.

Wedding March and *Dance of the Elves* (Mendelssohn) (piano transcription). Pub. 1851.

Quatre Illustrations du "Prophète" (Meyerbeer) (three pieces for piano and one for organ): 1. *Prière, Hymne triomphal, Marche du sacre*, 2. *Les Patineurs, Scherzo*, 3. *Choeur pastoral, Appel aux armes*, 4. *Ad nos, ad salutarem undam* (see "Works 1850"). Pub. 1849/50.

Cavatine (*Robert le Diable*) (Meyerbeer) (piano transcription). May date from this time. Unpub.

Licht, mehr Licht (for men's voices and brass). Pub. 1849.

An die ferne Geliebte (Beethoven) (piano transcription). Pub. 1850.

O du mein holder Abendstern (Wagner) (piano transcription). Pub. 1849.

Halloh! Jagdchor und Steyrer from *Tony* (Duke Ernst II of Saxe-Coburg-Gotha) (piano transcription). Pub. 1849.

Über allen Gipfeln ist Ruh (for men's voices and two horns). Second version. Pub. 1849.

Consolations (for piano). Pub. 1850.

Grand Duo concertant sur la Romance de M. Lafont "Le Marin" (for violin and piano). Revision of 1837 version. Pub. 1852.

Quand tu chantes bercée (for voice and piano). Pub. 1973.

WRITINGS:

Chopin (biography). Published in
1851 *La France musicale* (in French)
1852 Breitkopf & Härtel (in French)
1877 W. Reeves, London (in English)
1880 Breitkopf & Härtel (in German)
1910 Breitkopf & Härtel (new edition).

Liszt's essay *Tannhäuser and the Song Contest on the Wartburg* was published in 1851.

The essays published between 1849 and 1859 were written in collaboration with Princess Carolyne von Sayn-Wittgenstein. They were published, in a German translation by Lina Ramann, in *Franz Liszt, Gesammelte Schriften*, Vols. I, III, IV, V, and VI (Leipzig 1880–83).

LIFE

2 January: Liszt and the Princess in Braunschweig. On 3 January in Leipzig.

5 January: Back in Weimar.

Mid-January to mid-March: Liszt's mother and his former secretary Gaëtano Belloni pay an extended visit to the Altenburg. Joachim Raff also moves in.

11 February: Liszt conducts Beethoven's Symphony No. 8, Scribe's *Une Femme qui se jette par la fenêtre*, and Fischer's *Das Hausgesinde*.

19 February: Liszt conducts the second performance of his *Tasso* in Weimar. It is followed, at the end of February, by the premiere of the first version of *Ce qu'on entend sur la montagne*.

March: Trips to Dresden and Leipzig.

1 April: Liszt conducts Rossini's *Le Comte Ory* in Weimar.

7 April: Liszt conducts the local premiere of Hoven's *Ein Abenteuer Carls des Zweiten*.

12 June: Liszt conducts local premiere of Saloman's *Das Korps der Rache*.

July: Liszt works on various compositions and on his Chopin biography at the Altenburg.

24 August: First performance of Liszt's *Prometheus*, given in the form of an overture to his *Chöre zu Herders "Entfesseltem Prometheus,"* which also receives its world premiere under the composer's baton.

25 August: Premiere of Liszt's *Festchor* to mark the unveiling of the Herder Monument in Weimar.

28 August: Liszt conducts the premiere of Wagner's *Lohengrin* in Weimar.

28 September: Liszt conducts Donizetti's *La Favorita* in Weimar.

13 October: Joseph Joachim takes up the post of Konzertmeister in Liszt's orchestra; he will remain in Weimar for two years.

23 October: The Princess goes to take the waters in Bad Eilsen, near Bückeburg, in the hope of curing her rheumatism.

November/December: Liszt in Bad Eilsen (until 20 January 1851).

366 Playbill for the first performance of *Lohengrin*, 1850.

367 Richard Wagner. Photograph by Joseph Albert, 1864.

At right, and opposite page:

368 Opening section of Liszt's essay on *Lohengrin* as first published in the *Illustrirte Zeitung* of 12 April 1851. (For a translation of the text, see pp. 340–1.)

Liszt conducted the premiere of Wagner's *Lohengrin* in Weimar on 28 August 1850. It was a work which set new artistic and technical standards, and Liszt was untiring in his efforts to do it justice. Although the production met with considerable critical success, the reports which reached Wagner (now living in exile in Zurich) were instrumental in persuading him to break with the contemporary theatre and to set up a festival of his own for the exclusive presentation of *The Ring*.[101]

More than a year later, on 14 January 1852, Liszt wrote to the Grand Duchess Maria Pavlovna, ''In order, for example, to make the performance of *Lohengrin* acceptable, we would have needed a dozen extra choristers, both men and women, without whom the splendid choruses contained in this work lose much of their effectiveness, [. . .] more supernumeraries, to avoid the absurd situation whereby, in Act II, a march was played without a solemn procession passing over the stage, [. . .] furnishings that were somewhat less patriarchal than Elsa's seat in Act III, which consisted simply of four bare boards, [. . .] and, finally, more orchestral players.'' Liszt also complained of the inadequate sets and costumes.[102]

WORKS

Ce qu'on entend sur la montagne (''Bergsymphonie''). Second version. (The definitive version appeared in 1857.)

Chöre zu Herders ''Entfesseltem Prometheus'' (for six soloists, chorus, and orchestra). Revised and pub. 1855.

Prometheus (in the form of an overture to the above). First version of the symphonic poem of 1855.

Festchor zur Enthüllung des Herder-Denkmals in Weimar (for men's voices and piano). Pub. 1850.

Héroïde funèbre (symphonic poem). Pub. 1857. A version for two pianos appeared in 1856.

Pater noster IV (for four-part chorus and organ). Unpublished.

Fantasie und Fuge über den Choral ''Ad nos, ad salutarem undam'' (based on a theme from Meyerbeer's *Le Prophète*) (for organ or pedal pianoforte). Pub. 1852. A piano version for four hands appeared at the same time.

6 Preludes and Fugues for Organ (Bach) (piano transcription). Pub. 1852.

Mazurka brillante (for piano). Pub. 1850.

Valse impromptu (for piano). Pub. 1850.

Liebesträume (3 Notturnos) (for piano): 1. *Hohe Liebe*, 2. *Seliger Tod*, 3. *O lieb, so lang du lieben kannst*. Transcribed ca. 1850. Pub. 1850. See ''Works 1845.''

La cloche sonne (piano transcription of a French song). Written ca. 1850. Pub. 1958.

Bunte Reihe (piano transcriptions of 24 pieces for violin and piano by Ferdinand David). Pub. 1851.

Polonaise brillante (Weber) (for piano and orchestra). Orchestrated 1850/51. Pub. ca. 1852. A version for piano solo was made ca. 1851 and published ca 1851–3.

Sardanapale (opera). As early as 1845 Liszt had considered writing an opera on this Byronic subject. He worked at it for a time in 1850, but gave up the plan in 1851; 111 pages of sketches have survived in short score.

WRITINGS:

On the Goethe Foundation at Weimar (ca. 100 pages). Pub. 1851.

Richard Wagner's ''Lohengrin''. Pub. 1851. See this page and facing page.)

---

dem man nicht bloße Gewissenhaftigkeit in seiner Liebe zum Schönen nachrühmen kann, — denn er ist verzehrt von der edlen, innerlich brennenden Wunde des Kunst-Fanatismus. Wagner, dessen Geist durch seine natürlichen Fähigkeiten wie durch seine hohe Bildung gleich empfänglich für die Reize aller Künste war, und diese Küste einen Theil von der so vollkommen compacten Einheit loszutrennen, die diese Opern durch die Wirkung ihres durchgehends in noch nie erforschten Regionen gehaltenen, fast ebenso vom einfachen Recitativ als von den cadenzengeschmückten Phrasen unserer großen Arien entfernten Stols auszumachen.

Heinrich der Finkler.

Elsa.

Lohengrin.

Liszt's liaison with Marie d'Agoult produced three children. Following their birth, they were left behind with wet nurses (the eldest, Blandine, was left in Geneva, Cosima in Genoa, and Daniel in Palestrina near Rome) before joining Liszt's mother in Paris. Between 1844 and the autumn of 1848, Blandine and Cosima attended the exclusive boarding school in Paris run by Laure Bernard, who later became governess to the children of the Duc de Nemours. They were then placed in the keeping of Madame Patersi de Fossombroni, at 6 Rue Casimir Périer, Paris. In the autumn of 1855 they were taken to Berlin to spend two years with Hans von Bülow's mother. Daniel, Liszt's highly gifted son, spent the first few months of his life with a wet nurse in the Monti Sabini, where he was also looked after by the brothers Henri and Rudolf Lehmann. He enrolled at the Lycée Bonaparte in Paris in 1850.

369 The children of Franz Liszt and Marie d'Agoult. Pastel drawing by Amélie de Lacépède, Paris 1843. Left to right: Blandine, Daniel, Cosima.

371 Blandine (left) and Cosima Liszt. Pastel drawing by L. Demazey, ca. 1843.

370 Cosima (left) and Blandine Liszt. Pencil drawing by Henri Lehmann, 1842.

372 Cosima, Blandine, and Daniel Liszt. Pencil drawing by Friedrich Preller, Weimar 1855.

FRANZ LISZT'S CHILDREN
Photographs ca. 1850

Blandine-Rachel, born in Geneva on 18 December 1835, married the French statesman Émile Ollivier on 22 October 1857. Ollivier became Prime Minister of France on 2 January 1870, but was driven from office on 9 August 1870 in the wake of France's involvement in the Franco-Prussian War. Blandine died in St Tropez on 11 September 1862, two months after the birth of her first child, a boy. She was 26 years old. (See Illus. 445.)

Cosima Francesca Gaëtana was born in Como on 24 December 1837. She married Hans von Bülow on 18 August 1857, but their marriage was annulled on 20 July 1869, and on 25 August 1870 she became the second wife of Richard Wagner. She died in Bayreuth, at the age of 92, on 1 April 1930. (See Illus. 183 and 497.)

Daniel Heinrich, born in Rome on 9 May 1839, was awarded the Grand Prix d'Honneur at the Lycée Bonaparte in 1856, and the following year began to study law at the University of Vienna. He succumbed to a chest infection on 13 December 1859. (See Illus. 429.)

373 Liszt's children. Daniel (left), Cosima (standing), Blandine (sitting at the front), Liszt's mother (on the left, wearing a white bonnet), and the children's governess (on the right). Photograph, ca. 1852.

374 Blandine Liszt. Daguerreotype, ca. 1852.

375 Cosima Liszt. A little-known photograph, ca. 1855.

376 Cosima Liszt. Daguerreotype, ca. 1852. Previously unpublished.
The indistinctness of the image is due to the poor quality of the original.

LIFE

January: Liszt in Bad Eilsen.

21 January: Liszt back in Weimar.

16 February: Concert in the Court Theatre at which Liszt performs *Les Patineurs* (the second of his *Illustrations du Prophète*).

17 February: Liszt leaves for Bad Eilsen.

March: With Carolyne von Sayn-Wittgenstein in Bad Eilsen.

3 April: Liszt leaves Bad Eilsen and, after a brief stay in Halle, returns to Weimar.

7 April: Liszt submits his essay on the Goethe Foundation to the Grand Duchess of Weimar.

13 April: Liszt conducts Berlioz's *Harold en Italie* in Weimar. At the same concert Jadassohn performs Liszt's adaptation of Weber's *Polonaise brillante* for piano and orchestra.

April: Liszt conducts Mozart's *Don Giovanni*, Beethoven's *Fidelio*, Donizetti's *La Favorita*, and Meyerbeer's *Robert le Diable* in Weimar.

26 April: The Weimar Hofkapelle is placed under Liszt's sole direction.

May: Liszt reads the final proofs of his *Études* and *Hungarian Rhapsody* No. 1. Towards the end of May he leaves for Bad Eilsen.

June: Hans von Bülow moves to the Altenburg as Liszt's pupil.

14 July: Liszt back in Weimar. Trial performances of the revised versions of *Ce qu'on entend sur la montagne* and *Tasso*.

August: Liszt fetches the Princess from Bad Eilsen, after which the couple set off on a journey along the Rhine Valley before returning to Weimar.

September/October: Compositional activity in Weimar.

11 November: Liszt conducts Schumann's Overture *Die Braut von Messina* in Weimar, on the occasion of a performance of Schiller's drama.

13 December: Liszt conducts the premiere of Bülow's Overture *Julius Cäsar* (the first performance of any piece by Bülow) at a performance of Shakespeare's play in Weimar.

14 December: Liszt's adaptation for piano and orchestra of Schubert's *Wandererfantasie* receives its first public performance in Vienna; the soloist is Julius Egghard and the conductor Joseph Hellmesberger.

377 Franz Liszt conducting. Caricature by Gottlob Theuerkauf, ca. 1851.

During his period as Court Kapellmeister in Weimar, Liszt conducted a total of 43 operas, half of which were contemporary works.

Opinions were divided as to Liszt's abilities as a conductor. Wagner, for example, admired them, but they frequently met with disapproval, which arose in part from the fact that many of the works he performed were modern pieces (by Berlioz and Wagner among others), requiring a novel style of conducting.

Hans von Bülow, who was himself one of the greatest conductors of the nineteenth century, said of Liszt:

"[. . .] Yesterday I attended a rehearsal of *Fidelio* with Liszt; I was completely captivated by his conducting; wholly admirable and quite astonishing!"[103]

Arthur Nikisch, another leading conductor who had played under Liszt many times in Vienna, admitted that he had learned a great deal from watching Liszt conduct.

378 "*Forte*" and "*Piano.*" Two anonymous caricatures of Liszt, ca. 1851.

". . . at a *piano* entry his whole body seems to sink down, while it grows, conversely, to gigantic proportions whenever a *crescendo* is due to appear; Liszt then often stands on his toes, as high as he can, stretching his arms above his head . . ."[104]

HANS VON BÜLOW

It was in June 1851 that Bülow came to the Altenburg in Weimar to study with Liszt. One of the most talented and intelligent musicians of his day, Bülow won the admiration of Brahms, Wagner, and Liszt both as pianist and as conductor. He married Liszt's daughter Cosima in 1857.

Bülow idolized Liszt. "This devotion is the result not simply of my gratitude, but of a wholly involuntary fondness for him, since the mere sight of his noble and expressive features gladdens me and causes my soul to dilate with joy [. . .],"[105] Bülow once wrote. Liszt for his part wrote to Bülow's mother, "I regard myself as his father, and shall feel exactly the same ten years from now."[106] Liszt remained true to his word. When Bülow turned increasingly away from Liszt in the years around 1880 and lent his support instead to Brahms, Liszt retained his former love and respect for him.

379 Hans von Bülow (1830–1894). Oil portrait by Wilhelm Streckfuß, 1855.

WORKS

Mazeppa (symphonic poem). Pub. 1856. A version for two pianos, prepared in February 1855, also appeared at this time; a version for four hands, made in 1874, was published in 1875.
Grandes Études de Paganini (for piano). Revised version of the *Études d'exécution transcendante d'après Paganini* (see "Works 1838"). Pub. 1851.
Études d'exécution transcendante (definitive version) (for piano). Revision of the 1839 version. Pub. 1852.
Wandererfantasie (Schubert) (for piano and orchestra). Pub. 1857/58; repub. 1874. A version for two pianos appeared in 1862.
Fantasie über Motive aus Beethovens "Ruinen von Athen" (for piano and orchestra). Written between 1848 and 1852. Pub. 1865, together with piano versions for two hands and for four hands.
Two Polonaises (in C minor ["Polonaise pathétique"] and E major) (for piano). Pub. 1852.
Duo (Sonata) (for violin and piano), based on Chopin's *Mazurka*, op. 6 no. 2. Pub. 1964. The earlier dating of 1835 proposed by Humphrey Searle and others is called into question by the degree of thematic transformation contained in the work.
Scherzo und Marsch (for piano). Pub. 1854.
Beethoven's Symphony No. 9 (transcription for two pianos). Pub. ca. 1851.

380 Liszt's set of playing cards (later owned by Rosa von Milde).

Throughout his life Liszt liked to relax after a meal with a few games of cards. His preferred game was whist. His partners were his pupils, who would cheat in his favour in order to keep him in a good mood.

LIFE

January/February: Compositional activity in Weimar, including *Hungarian Rhapsodies*, *Soirées de Vienne*, and *Fantasie über ungarische Volksmelodien*.

5 March: Peter Cornelius pays his first visit to Weimar in order to make Liszt's acquaintance. "After Mendelssohn, Liszt was almost the only person whose physiognomy was not in conflict with the image which I had formed in my innermost thoughts," he writes in his diary after their first meeting.

20 March: Liszt conducts Berlioz's *Benvenuto Cellini* in Weimar, the first revival of the work since its premiere in 1838.

12 and 13 April: Liszt conducts the premiere of Hoven's *Der lustige Rat* in Weimar.

11 May: Liszt conducts Wagner's *Faust* Overture (first version) in Weimar.

13 June: Liszt conducts a stage performance of Schumann's *Manfred* in Weimar. This and two later revivals by Liszt will be the only performances for decades to come.

Liszt's mother, after visiting her son in Weimar, breaks her leg in Erfurt on the way back to Paris. She returns to the Altenburg for a lengthy convalescence.

18 June: Liszt arrives in Ballenstedt, where he directs the music festival on 22/23 June. The programme includes Beethoven's Symphony No. 9 and Berlioz's *Harold en Italie*. He is violently attacked in the press for his novel programming and style of conducting.

3 July: At the Braunschweig Music Festival. In Ettersburg on the 14th.

15 August: First performance of Liszt's Mass (*Szekszárd Mass*) under the composer's baton in the Catholic church in Weimar.

Autumn: Peter Cornelius at the Altenburg. He writes to tell his mother, "Liszt shall have the best that I am capable of, since he is so great a friend, far above all petty censure, one of those spirits which the centuries produce so rarely."[107]

14 November: Hector Berlioz arrives in Weimar. Liszt organizes a Berlioz Week.

20 November: Berlioz conducts his *Roméo et Juliette* and *La Damnation de Faust* in Weimar.

December: Liszt works intensively at his B minor Sonata.

Joseph Joachim resigns his post as Konzertmeister in Liszt's orchestra.

381 Autograph letter from Liszt to the Frankfurt Kapellmeister Gustav Schmidt, written from Weimar on 18 May 1852.

Liszt expresses deep respect for Louis Spohr as "a promoter of the cause of music" and recommends him, in preference to himself, as chairman of a meeting of conductors which Schmidt had suggested convening. Liszt also mentions performances which he is planning to give of Wagner's *Tannhäuser* and *The Flying Dutchman*, Schumann's *Manfred*, and Spohr's *Faust*.

WORKS

Sonata in B minor (for piano). Completed on 2 February 1853. Pub. 1854.

Soirées de Vienne (paraphrases of Schubert's Waltzes, opp. 9, 33, and 77) (for piano). Pub. 1852/53. Republished in 1873, 1874, 1883, and 1885.

Fantasie über ungarische Volksmelodien (for piano and orchestra). Based on the *Hungarian Rhapsody* No. 14. Pub. 1864.

Entry of the Guests on the Wartburg (*Tannhäuser*) and *Elsa's Bridal Procession* (*Lohengrin*) (piano transcriptions). Pub. 1853.

Ab irato (*Étude de perfectionnement*) (for piano). Pub. 1852.

Bénédiction et serment, deux motifs de "Benvenuto Cellini" (Berlioz) (piano transcriptions). Pub. 1854, together with a version for four hands.

Kirchliche Festouvertüre über den Choral "Ein' feste Burg ist unser Gott" (Nicolai) (for organ). Pub. 1852.

O du mein holder Abendstern (*Tannhäuser*) (for cello and piano). Unpublished. A fragment of the autograph was reproduced in Julius Kapp, *Franz Liszt*, Berlin 1911.

382 Bettina von Arnim (1785–1859). Pastel drawing by Achim von Arnim-Bärwalde, based on a miniature of ca. 1820.

Bettina von Arnim was a witty and charmingly eloquent woman who had been on intimate terms with both Beethoven and Goethe. She entered Liszt's circle of friends in 1842, and was one of the few women with whom he used the "Du" form of address. She visited him at the Altenburg on several occasions, and stayed in Weimar from October 1852 to January 1853. An extensive correspondence between them has survived. In 1842 Bettina wrote to Liszt, "Whatever it may be that moves me about you, it inspires me to make something better of myself. [. . .] I cannot help dreaming whenever I think of you. You are a spokesman for the age. [. . .] I am fond of you, I love you. The days have bedewed me as though with a fructifying rain. [. . .] I owe this to having listened to your music . . ."[108]

384 A drawing by Bettina von Arnim dedicated to Liszt; it hung in Liszt's chamber music room at the Altenburg.

383 Charlotte von Hagn (1809–1891). Lithograph by August Selb, based on a painting by Joseph Stieler; ca. 1830.

The Munich Court actress Charlotte von Hagn was one of the most celebrated and popular beauties of her time. Her admirers included King Ludwig I. "She combined the most outstanding talent that has perhaps ever been witnessed on the stage with perfect physical beauty and charm [. . .], diversity of character, passion and deep emotion, perspicuity, wit, elegance and sophistication . . ."[109]

Liszt and Charlotte von Hagn first met in Berlin in 1842. There were rumours of a passionate affair, and it is said that Charlotte secretly followed the pianist when he left the city. The two remained in correspondence for years. Charlotte to Liszt (letter of 24 May 1849): "Years have passed since I found and lost you, but I must confess that because of you I am out of sorts with the rest of mankind; for not *one*, not one can sustain the merest comparison. You are *unique*, and always will be . . ."[110]

LIFE

January: Agnes Street arrives in Weimar to study with Liszt. An intimate relationship develops between him and the quiet, reserved woman. Following her departure from Weimar in April 1855, Liszt will write to her almost every week (from 1869 to 1878 no letters have survived, and from 1878 to 1886 their correspondence is only sporadic); Agnes's letters to Liszt express a sense of abandonment and longing.

13 January: Ferdinand Laub takes over Joachim's position as Konzertmeister.

2 February: The B minor Sonata is completed.

16 and 19 February: Liszt conducts Wagner's *Flying Dutchman* in Weimar.

27 February: Performance of *Tannhäuser* in Weimar.

2 March: Liszt conducts *The Flying Dutchman*. His last appearance on the conductor's podium in Weimar until October.

5 March: *Lohengrin* performed in Weimar.

19 March and 17 April: Raff's opera *König Alfred* performed at Liszt's instigation.

1 June: First performances in Pest of Liszt's *Fantasie über ungarische Volksmelodien* and *Fantasie über Motive aus Beethovens "Ruinen von Athen"*, with Bülow as soloist and Erkel as conductor.

15 to 24 June: Johannes Brahms at the Altenburg in Weimar.

End of June: Liszt calls in at Karlsruhe to make preparations for the music festival before continuing his journey to Zurich.

2 to 10 July: Liszt stays with Wagner in Zurich.

6 July: Liszt, Wagner and Herwegh visit Brunnen on Lake Lucerne.

7 July: Wagner, Liszt, and the poet Georg Herwegh swear eternal friendship while drinking from the three springs on the Rütli. Liszt returns to Weimar via Badenweiler (11 July), Frankfurt (12/13 July, where he meets Gustav Schmidt and Henri Vieuxtemps), and Wiesbaden (15 July).

30 July to 15 August: In Carlsbad with Carolyne von Sayn-Wittgenstein, Bülow, Edmund Singer, and Ferdinand Laub. Emanuel Geibel, who is also present, expresses his enthusiasm at meeting Liszt.

16 August to early September: Liszt and the Princess in Teplitz. They discuss the final steps needed to marry. Liszt is a frequent guest of the pianist Alexander Dreyschock.

Carl Alexander becomes Grand Duke in Weimar.

12 September: Liszt in Dresden, where Bülow performs Liszt's paraphrase of Weber's *Polonaise* for piano and orchestra, with Rietz conducting.

18 September to 5 October: In Karlsruhe, with excursions to Darmstadt, Mannheim, and Baden-Baden.

3 to 5 October: Liszt conducts the Karlsruhe Music Festival. The orchestra, made up of musicians from Karlsruhe, Darmstadt, and Mannheim, plays Beethoven's Symphony No. 9, Joachim's Violin Concerto, and works by Wagner, Berlioz, Mendelssohn, Liszt, and others. Violent attacks in the press.

6 October: Accompanied by the Princess, Cornelius, Joachim, Bülow, Reményi, Pohl, and Dionys Pruckner, Liszt travels to Basle where he meets Wagner.

9 October: Wagner, Liszt, and the Princess arrive in Paris. The next day Wagner is introduced for the first time to the fifteen-year-old Cosima Liszt.

Jn verschiedenen mir zu Gesicht gekommenen Berichten über das Karlsruher Musikfest fand ich einen Punkt, über welchen genügende Übereinstimmung zu herrschen scheint: über die Unzulänglichkeit meiner Befähigung als Musikdirigent.

Ohne hier den Grad des absichtlichen zu dieser Meinung beitragenden Vorurtheils weiter zu berühren, ja ohne untersuchen zu wollen, inwieweit zu dieser Ansicht die einfache Thatsache mitgewirkt hat, daß die Wahl zum Dirigenten mit Übergehung der Kapellmeister von Karlsruhe, Darmstadt und Mannheim auf mich gefallen sei, würde es mir nicht zukommen Ansprüche zu erheben, die mit jener Versicherung, welche man festzustellen eifrig bestrebt ist, im Widerstreit stünden, wäre dieselbe auf eine Thatsache oder eine Berechtigung gegründet. Aber gerade dieses muß ich mit aller Entschiedenheit zurückweisen.

Was zunächst die Thatsache betrifft, so scheint niemand bestreiten zu können, daß das gesammte Programm sich einer vorzüglichen Ausführung erfreute, daß das Verhältnis und die Klangwirkung der Instrumente, mit Berücksichtigung auf die gewählte Lokalität zusammengestellt, befriedigend und selbst vortrefflich genannt werden mußte. Alles das giebt man naiverweise sogar mit dem Beisatz zu: es habe wahrhaft überrascht, daß das Ganze so vortrefflich ausgefallen sei — "trotz" der Unzulänglichkeit meiner Leitung.

Ich bin weit davon entfernt, mich mit den Pfauenfedern der Orchester von Karlsruhe, Mannheim und Darmstadt schmücken zu wollen — und gewiß: mehr als irgend jemand bin ich geneigt, den ausgezeichneten Talenten ihrer einzelnen Mitglieder volle Gerechtigkeit widerfahren zu lassen; — dennoch muß ich es durch das Zeugniß meiner Gegner selbst als erwiesen betrachten, daß die Aufführung sich zuweilen überraschend und im Ganzen weit besser erwies, als man angesichts meiner Direktion zu erwarten sich berechtigt glaubte.

Ist diese Thatsache einmal zugegeben, so bliebe nur noch übrig zu untersuchen, ob ich denn wirklich derselben so völlig fremd sei, wie man mit besonderem Vorliebe zu behaupten sucht, und aus welchen Gründen man einen Orchesterdirigenten dergestalt auf die öffentliche Anklagebank setzt, trotzdem die Ausführung seines Orchesters zufriedenstellend war, zumal wenn man gerechterweise die Neuheit der gebotenen Musikstücke für beinahe das ganze Personal in Betracht zieht. Denn, wie es in Karlsruhe hinreichend bekannt ist, war — mit Ausnahme des Satzes von Berlioz, den nur ein Theil der Karlsruher Kapelle unter des Komponisten eigener Leitung (in Baden) mitgespielt hatte — die neunte Symphonie, ebenso wie die Werke von Wagner, Berlioz, Schumann ꝛc. gründlich nur mir allein bekannt, was daraus erklärlich ist, daß sie früher an diesen Orten noch zu keiner Aufführung gelangt waren.

Indem ich mich nun zur Berechtigung des oben angeführten Urtheils wende, frage ich: ob man mir gegenüber den Thatsachen mit gutem Gewissen und vollkommener Sachkenntniß den Vorwurf machen kann, ein unzulänglicher, unerfahrener, unsicherer ꝛc. Dirigent zu sein?

Ohne mich vertheidigen zu wollen — was ich bei denen, die auf mein Verständniß eingehen, nicht nöthig zu haben glaube — möge mir dennoch gestattet sein eine Bemerkung zu machen, welche auf den Grund der Sache selbst zurückgeht. Die Werke nämlich, für welche ich öffentlich meine Bewunderung und Vorliebe bekenne, gehören der Mehrzahl nach zu denjenigen, welche die mehr oder minder namhaften, insbesondere die sogenannten "tüchtigen" Kapellmeister gar nicht oder so wenig ihrer persönlichen Sympathie werth finden, daß eine von ihnen veranstaltete Aufführung zu den Seltenheiten gehört.

Diese Werke zählen zu denen, welche man jetzt gewöhnlich als dem Stile der letzten Periode Beethoven's angehörig bezeichnet

und deren Ursprung man vor noch nicht langer Zeit mit großem Mangel an Ehrfurcht durch die „Taubheit" und „Geistesverwirrung" Beethoven's erklärte(!). Sie erfordern meinem Urtheile nach von Seiten der ausführenden Orchester einen Fortschritt, dem wir uns jetzt zu nähern scheinen, der aber noch weit entfernt ist aller Orten seine Verwirklichung entgegenzusehen; einen Fortschritt in der Betonung, in der Rhythmisirung, in der Art gewisse Stellen im Detail zu phrasiren, zu deklamiren und Schatten und Licht im Ganzen zu zu vertheilen — mit einem Wort: einen Fortschritt im Stil der Ausführung selbst. Dieser knüpft zwischen dem dirigirten und dem dirigirenden Musiker ein Band, welches durch einen unverwüstlichen Taktschläger geknotet wird. Denn an vielen Stellen arbeitet die grobe Aufrechthaltung des Taktes und jedes einzelnen Takttheiles | 1, 2, 3, 4 | 1, 2, 3, 4 | einem sinnig- und verständnißvollen Ausdruck geradezu entgegen. Hier wie allerwärts, tödtet der Buchstabe den Geist — ein Todesurtheil, das ich nie unterzeichnen werde, wie gehässig auch in ihrer erheuchelten Unparteilichkeit die Angriffe ausfallen, welchen ich ausgesetzt sein mag.

Für die Werke von Beethoven, Berlioz wie ihnen verwandten Meistern sehe ich noch weniger als für andere die Vortheile ein — die ich auch anderwärts mit Überzeugung bestreiten möchte —, welche daraus entstehen könnten, wenn ein Dirigent die Funktion einer Windmühle zu der seinigen macht und im Schweiße seines Angesichts seinem Personal die Wärme der Begeisterung mitzutheilen sucht.

Da namentlich, wo es sich um Verständniß und Gefühl, um ein geistiges Durchbringen zu einem Entflammen der Herzen zu geistiger Gemeinschaft im Genusse des Schönen, Großen und Wahren in der Kunst und Poesie handelt: da dürfte die Selbstgenügsamkeit und handwerksmäßige Fertigkeit der gewöhnlichen Kapellmeister nicht mehr genügen, sondern dürfte sogar mit der Würde und erhabenen Freiheit der Kunst in Widerspruch stehen! Auch werde ich — mit Erlaubniß meiner gefälligen Kritiker — bei jeder weiteren Gelegenheit es bei meiner ungenügenden Fähigkeit oder "Unzulänglichkeit" bewenden lassen, und zwar principiell und einer inneren Überzeugung folgend, welche mich niemals zu der Rolle eines Takt-Profoßen herabsinken lassen wird — einer Rolle, zu der mich fünfundzwanzig Jahre Erfahrung, Studium und aufrichtige Begeisterung für die Kunst in keiner Weise geeignet machten.

Bei aller Hochachtung, welche ich vielen meiner Kollegen zolle, und bei aller Bereitwilligkeit, die guten Dienste, die sie der Kunst geleistet haben und noch leisten werden, mit Vergnügen anzuerkennen, glaube ich mich denn doch nicht verpflichtet in jedem Punkt ihr Beispiel nachahmen zu müssen — und zwar eben so wenig, was die Wahl der aufzuführenden Werke, als was die Art ihrer Auffassung und Direktion betrifft.

Ich glaube es schon einmal ausgesprochen zu haben, daß nach meiner Meinung die wirkliche Aufgabe eines Kapellmeisters darin besteht, sich augenscheinlich überflüssig zu machen — und mit seiner Funktion möglichst zu verschwinden. Wir sind Steuermänner und keine Ruderknechte.

Und selbst wenn dieser Ausspruch auf noch größere Opposition Einzelner stoßen sollte, bin ich außer Stande eine Meinung, die ich für die richtige halten muß, zu ändern. Für die Weimarer Kapelle hat die Anwendung dieses Princips vorzügliche Resultate herbeigeführt — Resultate, welche selbst einige meiner jetzigen Tadler seinerzeit lobend anerkannt haben. Darum werde ich fortfahren, ohne Entmuthigung, ohne falsche Bescheidenheit, der Kunst meine Dienste so zu weihen, wie ich es für das Beste halte — und wie es wohl auch am besten sein wird. —

Nehmen wir also den Fehdehandschuh, welcher uns in Gestalt von Schlafmützen hingeworfen wurde, ohne Unruhe und Sorge auf und beharren wir im Bewußtsein unseres guten Rechtes — und unserer Zukunft. —

Weimar, den 5. November 1853.   F. Liszt.

---

21 October: Liszt back in Weimar. At the end of the month he conducts Wagner's *Flying Dutchman*.

4 November: Peter Cornelius moves into the Altenburg as guest of Princess Wittgenstein.

18 and 26 December: *Tannhäuser* under Liszt.

WORKS

Festklänge (symphonic poem). Pub. 1856. A version for two pianos also appeared in 1856, while a version for four hands was published in 1861.

An die Künstler (for men's voices and orchestra). Two versions. Pub. 1854.

Huldigungsmarsch (for orchestra). Pub. 1859. A piano version for two hands had appeared in 1858.

Vom Fels zum Meer (march for orchestra). Written between 1853 and 1856. It is not known when it was published. A piano version appeared in 1865. A piano duet version is unpublished.

Domine salvum fac regem (for solo tenor, men's voices, and organ). Pub. 1936.

Piano Concerto No. 1 in E flat major. Revised version; also version for two pianos, the latter published in 1857.

Andante finale and *March* from Raff's *König Alfred* (piano transcription). Pub. 1853, together with a version for four hands.

Te Deum II (for men's voices, organ, brass, and timpani). Pub. 1936.

Ballade No. 2 (in B minor) (for piano). Pub. 1854.

Gebet (for organ). Arranged from *Ave Maria I*. Date of publication unknown, but reprinted 1971.

WRITINGS:

A Letter on Conducting. Pub. 1853 (see Illus. 386).

Sobolewski's "Vinvela." Pub. 1855.

Opposite page:

385 Liszt conducting. Lithograph based on a drawing by Carl Hoffmann; ca. 1853.

Liszt's towering authority often led to his being invited to conduct so-called "music festivals." He generally found himself facing a motley assortment of amateur musicians, and inferior performances were often unavoidable. Following the 1853 Festival in Karlsruhe, he had to contend with the following criticism from the *Niederrheinische Musikzeitung*:

"Our concern is not Liszt the pianist of genius, the man of deep erudition, the noble and fiery individual, but Liszt the apostle of the music of the future, Liszt the conductor and composer of works that belong to this selfsame genre. Yes, Liszt the conductor. Following the Karlsruhe Music Festival there is but *one* opinion in the matter, namely that he is not the right person to wield a baton, least of all to conduct sizeable masses. Not only does he not beat time (in the simplest sense of the word and in the traditional way that even the greatest masters have learned in the past to adopt), but his eccentric and animated movements mean that the orchestra is perpetually and often precariously adrift . . ."[111]

---

386 "We are steersmen, not oarsmen." Liszt's open letter on conducting, reproduced from Volume V of *Franz Liszts Gesammelte Schriften* (Leipzig 1882).

Liszt never adopted a defensive stance towards the attacks that were made on his progressive style of composing and conducting. None the less, he published the present essay by way of a reply to a criticism which seemed to him to be wide of the mark (see caption to

Illus. 385). Ten years later, he inserted in the full score of his *Heilige Elisabeth* a remark to the effect that he regarded conventional conducting as nonsensical and brutal, and that he would prefer to have it banned in the case of his own works. "Music is a sequence of notes which demand to enfold one another, not something to be bound together by dint of violent beating." (For a translation of the text, see p. 341.)

387 Autograph letter written from Weimar on 25 October 1853. Previously unpublished.

The recipient is not indicated, but it was probably Siegfried Wilhelm Dehn, Peter Cornelius's teacher and a friend of Liszt's. The letter gives details of Liszt's plans for the winter of 1853/54, and also mentions the exact date of his return from a journey to Paris with Wagner in October 1853.

389 Hans von Bülow. Photograph, ca. 1853.

Bülow's studies with Liszt began in 1851 and ended in 1853, whereupon he embarked on a successful career as a pianist. He felt the warmest affection for Liszt, and was the latter's leading interpreter from 1850 to 1860. Liszt entrusted him with the first performance of the B minor Sonata on 22 January 1857, the same year in which Bülow married Cosima Liszt.

390 Joseph Joachim (1831–1907). Photograph, ca. 1853.

From October 1850 to December 1852 Joachim, a famous violinist and a close friend of Liszt's, was Konzertmeister of the Weimar Court Orchestra. In spite of their difference in age, he was one of the few friends whom Liszt addressed as ''Du'' and in the years around 1850 was Liszt's preferred chamber music partner.

388 Johannes Brahms (1833–1897) and (seated) Ede Reményi (1828–1898). Daguerreotype, January 1853.

This is believed to be the earliest surviving photograph of Brahms. In the past it has generally been reproduced the wrong way round but is correctly shown here. The original is lost; a copy from Brahms's estate is owned by Kurt Hofmann in Hamburg.

Together with the violinist Ede Reményi, the twenty-year-old Brahms arrived in Weimar on 15 June 1853 and for the next ten days enjoyed Liszt's hospitality at the Altenburg. Associated with this visit is the (apparently indestructible) legend that Brahms fell asleep during a performance (by the composer) of Liszt's B minor Sonata, and was

thereupon shown the door. The story must be dismissed as a fabrication, not least because on his departure Brahms was presented with a cigar case by his well-disposed host. We do know, however, that Brahms was invited to perform his E flat minor Scherzo but that his courage failed him. Liszt immediately played the piece at sight, using a scarcely legible copy, much to the astonishment of the composer.

It must none the less soon have become clear to Brahms that the course adopted by the so-called ''New German School'' was not his own. Like Joachim, he turned away from Liszt as a composer but continued to value the man and admire the pianist until the end of his life (see ''Brahms on Liszt's piano playing,'' p. 267.)

391

392

393

Only rarely in the course of his life did Liszt have to buy his own instruments. Great piano manufacturers such as Erard, Graf, Streicher, Boisselot, Steinway, Bechstein, Bösendorfer, Blüthner, and Chickering reckoned it an honour – and a source of free publicity – to give him their pianos or to place them at his disposal for concerts. It must often have been difficult for Liszt not to offend these various manufacturers, many of whom were friendly with him, in choosing which piano to use.

39

391 Liszt's giant pedal pianoforte, a combination of piano and organ, built over a period of years by the Paris piano makers Alexandre and Erard in accordance with Liszt's instructions.

This instrument was the only one of its kind. It had three manuals, sixteen stops, and organ-like pedals. From 1853 onwards it graced the Altenburg, where it was admired by Berlioz and Rubinstein. In 1887 it passed into the possession of the Gesellschaft der Musikfreunde in Vienna as part of Liszt's estate, and is now exhibited in the Kunsthistorisches Museum. The bench containing the pipes, which originally went with the instrument, no longer exists (see Illus. 357).

392 Composing desk, a combination of desk and three-octave playable keyboard, built by Bösendorfer for Liszt.

Liszt wrote to Ludwig Bösendorfer on 15 November 1875, "How can I thank you for your great kindness and consideration? I am awaiting the 'piano' and mysterious 'composing desk' . . . with sincere gratitude, and with sincere good wishes to Frau Bösendorfer, your most devoted servant Franz Liszt." This original instrument is now in the Liszt Museum at the Academy of Music in Budapest.

393 Bösendorfer grand. 187 cm long.

Liszt used this instrument during the last years of his life. It is now in the Liszt Museum at the Academy of Music in Budapest.

394 Liszt's Bechstein in the Hofgärtnerei in Weimar.

Trembling to a greater or lesser extent, all the great virtuosos of the years around 1885 played on this instrument in the presence of Liszt. It still stands in the position it occupied during his lifetime.

395 Piano-harmonium, built by Alexandre and Erard in 1864/65 and used by Liszt in Rome and Budapest.

This instrument is now in the Liszt Museum of the Budapest Academy of Music.

396 A piano by Chickering, exhibited at the 1867 Paris World Exhibition, where Chickering won a gold medal.

Liszt was given this huge instrument as a present at Christmas 1867. On the inside of the lid are the words "à F. Liszt. Chickering & Son." The piano stood in Liszt's study in the monastery of Santa Francesca Romana in Rome. When Liszt had to give up this room, following the secularization of the monastery, Princess Carolyne von Sayn-Wittgenstein negotiated the instrument's transfer to Baron Augusz of Szekszárd. On Liszt's death it passed to the Academy of Music in Budapest, where it is now in the Director's reception room. The legendary pianist Josef Lhévinne played on another Chickering piano formerly owned by Liszt at a concert in Carnegie Hall on 31 October 1927.

397 Liszt's Steinway grand.

The firm of Steinway had presented Liszt with one of their grand pianos as early as 1873. A second Steinway (depicted here) came to Weimar in 1883, but since there was already a grand piano at the Hofgärtnerei this particular instrument was housed in the Weimar home of the Baroness Meyendorff. Liszt wrote to the firm in November 1883 to thank them for the "imposing masterpiece with its strength and melodiousness, its singing qualities and perfect harmonic effects . . ." This instrument was later owned by Liszt's granddaughter Daniela at the Vittoriale in Gardone on Lake Garda. (The house was previously known as the Villa Cargnacco and was owned by Henry Thode, Daniela's husband, before being acquired by Gabriele D'Annunzio in 1921.) Under the terms of Daniela's will, the instrument has been on exhibition in the Museo Teatrale della Scala since 1940.

398 The Ibach piano on which Liszt liked to accompany his pupils at piano recitals, seen here in the Hofgärtnerei in Weimar. Beside it is the Bechstein grand shown in Illus. 394.

396

397

395

398

7 January: Liszt hears *Lohengrin* in Leipzig. The following day he writes Wagner a detailed account of the performance's deficiencies.

22 January: Premiere of Heinrich Dorn's opera *Die Nibelungen* under Liszt in Weimar.

27 January: Liszt conducts Berlioz's *La Fuite en Égypte* from *L'Enfance du Christ*.

He conceives his book on the Gypsies.

16 February: Liszt conducts the premiere of his symphonic poem *Orpheus* in Weimar.

19 February to 30 April: During this period Liszt conducts performances of the works discussed in the first ten essays listed on the facing page under "Writings."

23 February: Liszt conducts the premiere of *Les Préludes* in Weimar. He subjoins to this best-known of his symphonic poems the words of Alphonse de Lamartine: "What is our life but a series of preludes to that unknown hymn whose first and solemn note is sounded by death?"

March: Liszt conducts a performance of Duke Ernst's *Santa Chiara* in Gotha.

16 April: Liszt conducts the premiere of his symphonic poem *Mazeppa* in Weimar.

19 April: First performance of the definitive version of *Tasso* under Liszt in Weimar.

16 May: Liszt visits Joachim in Leipzig, then travels to Hanover and Braunschweig, where he sees Henry Litolff.

7 June: Performance of Donizetti's *La Favorita* under Liszt in Weimar.

24 June: Liszt conducts the first performance of Schubert's opera *Alfonso und Estrella*.

8 and 9 July: Visit to Frankfurt.

10 to 16 July: Accompanied by Anton Rubinstein, Liszt travels to Rotterdam as guest of honour at the local music festival. The two men are joined by Ferdinand Hiller for a visit to Ary Scheffer in Scheveningen. On the 20th Liszt meets his daughters in Brussels, before returning to Weimar via Cologne and Bonn, where he calls on Hiller.

August: Works on his *Faust Symphony*.

September: Anton Rubinstein stays at the Altenburg.

Wagner writes to Liszt: "For who was there who understood me?? – You – and no one else! [. . .] there is not a single fibre of my being nor even the slightest quivering of my heart-strings which you yourself have not also felt."[112]

27 October: Clara Schumann plays Schumann's A minor Piano Concerto in Weimar, with Liszt conducting. Liszt's appreciation of Clara Schumann appears in the *Neue Zeitschrift für Musik* a few months later.

9 November: Premiere of Liszt's symphonic poem *Festklänge* in Weimar.

10 November: Liszt conducts his *Orpheus* in the Stadthaus in Weimar.

11 November: Liszt conducts the premiere of Rubinstein's opera *Die sibirischen Jäger* in Weimar. He becomes friendly with the poet Hoffmann von Fallersleben, who has settled in the town. The two men will later found the New Weimar Society.

10 December: Liszt conducts *Tannhäuser* in Weimar.

31 December: The New Weimar Society is established.

Liszt's most significant piano piece, his B minor Sonata, appeared at the beginning of 1854 with a dedication to Robert Schumann, who in turn had dedicated his C major *Phantasie* to Liszt. With the exception of Wagner, neither the general public nor Liszt's musical colleagues found much to admire, still less to understand, in the piece. Clara Schumann, not exactly overjoyed by either of the two dedications, hated it: "I received a friendly letter from Liszt today, enclosing a sonata dedicated to Robert and a number of other things. But what dreadful things they are! Brahms played them to me, and I felt quite ill [. . .]. It's much ado about nothing – not a single sound idea, but altogether confused, and not a clear harmonic progression to be found anywhere!" (25 May 1854)

The work opens up a wide field of vision, and could scarcely gain a fair hearing in the Biedermeier music salons of the 1850s. Eduard Hanslick was arrogant enough to exclaim that "The B minor Sonata is a brilliant steam-driven mill which almost always runs idle. Never have I experienced a more oversophisticated, more brazen juxtaposition of the most disparate elements – such dissolute raging, and so bloody a battle against all that is musical."

Liszt refused to be misled. When, around 1880, Carolyne von Sayn-Wittgenstein demanded that he defend himself against the ironical and even spiteful attacks of the influential Viennese critic, he merely reacted by saying, "*He has to play his self-important role, not I.*"[113]

The B minor Sonata is now a part of the repertory of every leading pianist and may even be the most frequently performed piano piece in the concert hall. Liszt's remark "I can wait" has come true. Composers such as Debussy, Ravel, Scriabin, and Bartók have admired the work. "If Liszt had written nothing more than his B minor Sonata, this gigantic work sprung from a single cell, it would have been sufficient to show the sort of man he was," Richard Strauss said in Montreux in 1948, and, according to Wilhelm Kempff, he once got so worked up in the course of a conversation on how much Liszt had been misjudged that the people around him became seriously concerned about the state of his health. Strauss described Liszt as "tragically misunderstood in Germany."

Wilhelm Backhaus wrote, "[. . .] as a pianist I regard it as my bounden duty to show my gratitude and respect for the memory of the glorious master who gave us his B minor Sonata. It remains unsurpassed to this day as the most magnificent piano sonata of the post-Beethoven period. Had he written nothing else, he would still be immortal" (*Musik und Musiker*, 31 July 1936).

One of the ways of approaching Liszt (albeit a way reserved almost exclusively for musicians) is through the B minor Sonata. The work not only reveals the composer's great and proud spirit; it also demonstrates the "technique" of his compositional method, namely the art of motivic variation of which he was the unchallenged master. It is an art which consists in varying the themes according to changes of mood (in the widest sense of the term), thus creating ever new structures which, however intimately interrelated, are nevertheless contrastive in effect. To the extent that this transformation was applied to the rhythmic structure of the theme Liszt's technique was even taken over by the young Brahms, who, it may be added, was one of the

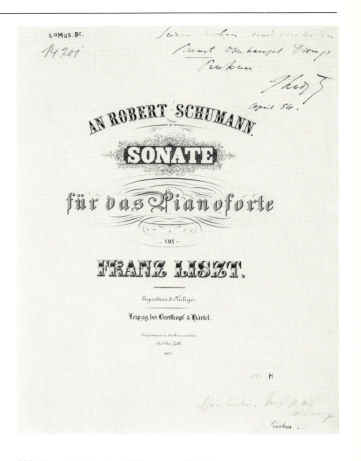

399 Sonata in B minor. Title page of the first edition of 1854, with a dedication by Liszt to his Munich pupil Dionys Pruckner.

first to hear this work performed, when Liszt himself played it in June 1853.

The B minor Sonata shows the immense achievements of which Liszt would have been capable if he had had the peace of mind necessary to devote himself solely to his creative work. But his admirers and pupils, his fame as a pianist, his social commitments and epistolary obligations, not to mention his constant travelling and his involvement in the destinies and problems of others, all robbed him of this peace of mind. Certainly, his dealings with others were often more important to him than concentrating on his work.

Liszt's whole being is reflected in the B minor Sonata. No one has expressed this more beautifully than Wagner, who wrote to Liszt in 1855, after Karl Klindworth had played the work to him, "My dearest Franz! you too were in the room with me! The Sonata is beautiful beyond belief; great, lovable, deep, and noble – as sublime as yourself."[114]

The Sonata was first performed in public in Berlin on 22 January 1857, when Hans von Bülow played it to inaugurate the first Bechstein grand.

400 Franz Liszt. Medallion by Ernst Rietschel, 1854.

This marble relief is one of the most valuable representations of Liszt from an artistic point of view.

WORKS

Eine Faust-Symphonie in drei Charakterbildern (for orchestra and tenor solo; the final chorus was not added until 1857). Written between August and 19 October 1854. Pub. 1861. A version for two pianos appeared in 1863, at the same time as the *Gretchen* movement for piano solo.
Orpheus (symphonic poem). Composed within the space of fifteen days at the beginning of 1854. Pub. 1856. A version for two pianos was also published in 1856, and a version for four hands followed in 1859.
Tasso (symphonic poem). Definitive version. Pub. 1856.
Ce qu'on entend sur la montagne ("Bergsymphonie") (symphonic poem). Revised version.
Andante religioso (organ). Based on *Ce qu'on entend sur la montagne*. May date from around this time. Date of publication unknown.
Hungaria (symphonic poem). Pub. 1857. A version for two pianos was published in 1861, and a version for four hands in around 1874.
Berceuse (for piano). Pub. 1854. A second version (1862) appeared in 1865.
Années de Pèlerinage. Première Année: Suisse (for piano). Further (and final) improvements to the second version (pub. 1855).
Petrarch Sonnet No. 104 (for mezzo-soprano or baritone and piano). First version. Unpublished.
2 Pieces from "Lohengrin": 1. Festival and Bridal Song, 2. Elsa's Dream and Lohengrin's Rebuke (piano transcriptions). Pub. ca. 1854.

WRITINGS:
1. *Gluck's "Orpheus,"* 2. *Beethoven's "Fidelio,"* 3. *Weber's "Euryanthe,"* 4. *On Beethoven's Music to "Egmont,"* 5. *On Mendelssohn's Music to "A Midsummer Night's Dream,"* 6. *Scribe and Meyerbeer's "Robert le Diable,"* 7. *Schubert's "Alfonso und Estrella,"* 8. *Auber's "La Muette de Portici,"* 9. *Bellini's "I Capuleti e i Montecchi,"* 10. *Boieldieu's "La Dame blanche,"* 11. *Donizetti's "La Favorita,"* 12. *The Flying Dutchman*[115] (by Richard Wagner), 13. *The Rhinegold* (by Richard Wagner). On 1 January 1855, 14. *Clara Schumann*. Pub. 1854/55.

Liszt visited Rotterdam in July 1859. In his open letter to Liszt of August 1877, Ferdinand Hiller recalled the occasion:

"We spent a series of busy, interesting days in Holland. [. . .] You were the only celebrity present, although your companion Anton Rubinstein was later to become one. At that time we none of us knew much about him, and the unavoidable sense of unease that must have come over him at finding himself among so many people who had no inkling of his true merit persuaded him to shun the many occasions when everyone else came together, and to prefer the pleasant domesticity which had come his way. But what you said then in praise of him has been confirmed in every respect. [. . .] On your return via Antwerp you gave us the pleasure of your visit to Bonn, where I and my family were in *villeggiatura*. It was a fiendishly hot day, and in a vain attempt to freshen himself up poor Rubinstein used all the eau de cologne he could lay his hands on. But you had a siesta by playing the recently published second series of my Rhythmic Studies (the first series was dedicated to you), playing them, moreover, in such a way that I stared at the title page for a while attempting to convince myself that it was I who had in fact written them. Your dear mother was no doubt right when she said to me, in her linguistically somewhat vague manner, 'Mon fils, he has nerves – qui sont de fer.' "

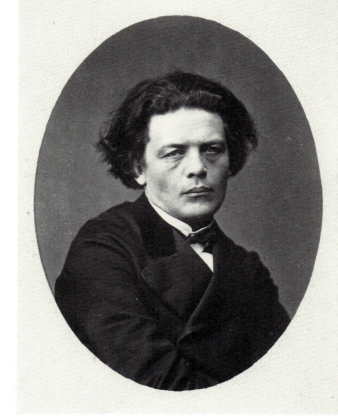

401 Anton Rubinstein (1829–1894). Photograph by Fritz Luckhardt of Vienna, ca. 1865.

The eminent pianist and composer Anton Rubinstein accompanied Liszt to Rotterdam in 1854.

LIFE

January: Liszt works on several essays (see "Works 1855").

Mid-February: Berlioz Week in Weimar. Berlioz stays at the Altenburg.

17 February: First performance of Liszt's E flat major Piano Concerto in the Weimar Castle. Berlioz conducts, with Liszt as soloist.

21 February: Stage performance of Berlioz's *Lélio* (with Liszt as soloist) and *Symphonie fantastique*, both conducted by the composer.

March: Compositional activity in Weimar.

9 April: Liszt conducts the first performance of Schumann's opera *Genoveva*. The audience includes Giacomo Meyerbeer. Liszt travels to Leipzig for a performance of his *Ave Maria* for four-part chorus, composed in 1846 and published in 1852. He works on the Mass which Primate Johann von Scitovszky has commissioned for the consecration of the cathedral in Gran (Esztergom): "I prayed over it more than I composed it," Liszt writes to Wagner on 2 May 1855.[116]

1 May: Liszt completes the "Gran" Mass.

26 to 30 May: Liszt at the Lower Rhenish Music Festival in Düsseldorf. He visits the Schumanns and plays Bach's *Chromatic Fantasia* and (with Clara Schumann) an arrangement for four hands of Schumann's *Genoveva* Overture.

1 June: Liszt back in Weimar. At the end of the month he travels to Jena for a performance of his *Szekszárd Mass*.

21 July: The thirteen-year-old Carl Tausig arrives at the Altenburg to study with Liszt.

15 August: Liszt conducts a new Mass by Peter Cornelius in Weimar's Catholic church.

Liszt's children visit him at the Altenburg. In September Blandine and Cosima move to Berlin (to stay with Bülow's mother), while Daniel remains with his father until early October.

25 October: Liszt travels to Merseburg for the first performance of his *Fantasie und Fuge über den Choral "Ad nos, ad salutarem undam"* performed by his pupil Alexander Winterberger to mark the inauguration of the cathedral organ.

14 October: Liszt in Braunschweig, where, on the 18th, he conducts a performance of his symphonic poem *Orpheus* and the world premiere of the symphonic poem *Prometheus*.

6 December: Concert at the Berlin Singakademie, including works by Liszt. He is attacked by the press, which finds his newer works strange and inaccessible. The works performed in Berlin include *Tasso*, *Les Préludes*, the E flat major Piano Concerto (with Bülow as soloist), *Psalm xiii* (first performance), and *Ave Maria I* (for choir and organ).

12 December: On his return from Berlin, Liszt is welcomed back by the Weimar Court, "wreathed in laurel." "And in thistles," Liszt is reported to have added.

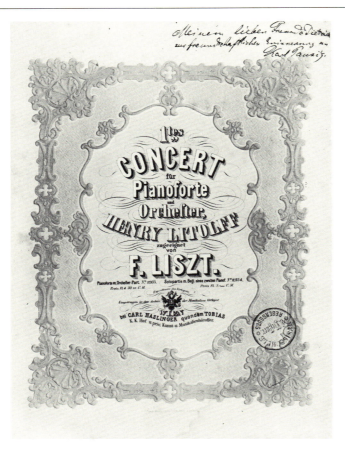

The first performance of Liszt's E flat major Piano Concerto was a notable occasion: Liszt himself played the piano solo, while Berlioz conducted. The work, whose most interesting movement is an effectively sparkling Scherzo, was dismissed in its day as a "triangle concerto." Liszt himself analysed part of it in a letter of 26 March 1857, reproduced here from the first edition of his letters.[117] (An English translation appears on pp. 341–2.)

er ist nur eine gedrängte Recapitulation des früher Gebrachten mit erfrischten, belebteren Rhythmen und enthält *kein neues Motiv*, wie es Dir bei Durchsicht der Partitur gleich deutlich werden wird. Diese Art von *Zusammen*fassen und Abrunden eines ganzen Stückes bei seinem Abschluss ist mir ziemlich eigen; sie lässt sich aber von dem Standpunkt der musikalischen Form gänzlich behaupten und rechtfertigen.

Die Posaunen und Bässe

nehmen den 2. Theil des Motivs von dem Adagio (H-dur) auf:

Celli

Die darauf folgende Clavierfigur

ist nichts anders als die Wiederbringung des Motivs, welches im Adagio durch die Flöte und Clarinett angegeben war,

Flöte

(Clavier-Triller auf G.)

so wie die Schluss-Passage eine Variante und Steigerung in Dur des Motivs des Scherzo,

bis endlich das erste Motiv

auf dem Pedal der Dominante *B* mit Trillerfiguration-Begleitung

eintritt und das Ganze abschliesst. —

Das Scherzo Es-moll vom Anbeginn des Triangels gebrauchte ich als vermittelnden Contrast.

Was den Triangel anbelangt, verhehle ich nicht, dass er Anstoss geben kann, besonders wenn er zu stark und nicht präcis geschlagen wird. Gegen den Gebrauch der Schlag-Instrumente herrscht überhaupt eine vorgefasste Abneigung und Perhorrescirung, die durch den häufigen Missbrauch derselben nicht ungerechtfertigt ist. Wenig Dirigenten sind auch umsichtig genug, um sie in den Compositionen, wo sie mit Bedacht verwendet sind, nach der Absicht des Componisten — ihr rhythmisches Element ohne die rohe Zuthat des plumpen Gelärms — zur Geltung zu bringen. Die dynamische und rhythmische Würze und Steigerung, welche die Schlag-Instrumente bewirken können, wäre in den meisten Fällen durch sorgfältiges Probiren und Proportioniren derartiger Ein- und Zusätze weit effectvoller herzustellen. Die ernst und gediegen scheinenwollenden Musiker aber ziehen es vor, die Schlag-Instrumente *en canaille* zu behandeln, die sich in der anständigen Gesellschaft der *Symphonie* nicht einfinden darf. Auch beklagen sie tief innerlich, dass Beethoven sich verführen liess, im Finale der 9ten Symphonie die grosse Trommel und den Triangel zu gebrauchen. Von Berlioz, Wagner und meiner Wenigkeit darf es nicht wundern, »gleich und gleich gesellt sich gern«, und da wir als impotente *Canaille* unter den Musikern behandelt werden, ist es ganz natürlich, dass wir uns mit der *Canaille* unter den Instrumenten gut vertragen. Allerdings ist es hier wie in allem das Richtige, das harmonische Mass zu treffen und festzuhalten. Dem hochweisen Bannspruch der doctrinären Kritik gegenüber werde ich aber eine Zeitlang noch die Schlag-Instrumente verwenden müssen und gedenke, ihnen noch einige wenig bekannte Effecte abzugewinnen.

WORKS

Eine Symphonie zu Dantes "Divina commedia" (*Dante Symphony*) (for orchestra and women's or boy's voices). 1. *Inferno*, 2. *Purgatorio-Magnificat*. Begun in summer 1855, completed 8 July 1856. Pub. 1859, together with a version for two pianos.

Missa solemnis zur Einweihung der Basilika in Gran (Esztergom) ("*Gran*" *Mass*) (for chorus, soloists and orchestra). Pub. 1859.

Prometheus (symphonic poem). Revision of the 1850 version. Pub. 1856, together with a version for two pianos. A version for four hands was published in 1862.

Die Seligkeiten (for baritone solo, chorus and organ). Begun in 1855 and completed in 1859. Pub. 1861. Later incorporated in the oratorio *Christus*.

Psalm xiii ("How long wilt thou forget me, O Lord?") (for chorus, soloists and orchestra). Revised in 1859. Pub. 1864.

Präludium und Fuge über das Motiv BACH (for organ). Pub. 1855. A piano arrangement of this version remained unpublished until 1983. A second version entitled *Fantasie und Fuge über das Thema BACH* appeared in 1870, and a piano transcription of this version, prepared ca. 1870, was published in 1871. A new edition, described as "the only correct version," appeared in 1872.

Was Liebe sei (for soprano or tenor and piano). Second setting, ca. 1855. Pub. 1879.

Ein Fichtenbaum steht einsam (for baritone or mezzo-soprano and piano). First setting, composed ca. 1855. Pub. 1860.

Ihr Auge ("*Nimm einen Strahl der Sonne*") (for baritone or mezzo-soprano and piano). Composed ca. 1855. Pub. 1860.

Mazeppa (version for two pianos). Pub. 1856.

WRITINGS:

Berlioz and His "Harold" Symphony (ca. 100 pages).

Robert Schumann (ca. 80 pages).

Robert Franz (conceived chiefly by Robert Franz and Friedrich Hinrichs).

No Entr'acte Music!

Marx and His Book "The Music of the Nineteenth Century" [Adolph Bernhard Marx, 1795–1866]. Pub. ca. 1855.

404 Franz Liszt. Photograph by Ghemar, Brussels 1854.

405 Hector Berlioz, conductor of the first performance of Liszt's E flat major Piano Concerto. A little-known photograph, ca. 1855.

406 The Ducal Palace in Weimar. Miniature painting on a gold watch which Princess Augusta of Prussia, later to become Empress of Germany, had given to Liszt on his birthday in 1842, taking the opportunity to point out that she had been born in the same year as the composer.

It was in the Ducal Palace that the E flat major Piano Concerto had its premiere on 17 February 1855.

Opposite page:

402 Title page of the 1857 first edition of Liszt's E flat major Piano Concerto, with a handwritten note by the pianist Carl Tausig.

403 Liszt's published letter of 26 March 1857 (see note 117), with analytical comments on his E flat major Piano Concerto. (For a translation of the text, see pp. 341–2.)

LIFE

7 January: Liszt attends the Berlin premiere of Wagner's *Tannhäuser*.

15 January: Liszt sets off for Vienna, where he has been invited to conduct the festival concerts held to mark the centenary of Mozart's birth.

27 and 28 January: Liszt conducts various works by Mozart in Vienna, including the Overture to *The Magic Flute*, the G minor Symphony, and the C minor Piano Concerto.

4 February: Liszt hears an act of Mozart's *Don Giovanni* in Prague.

8 February: Berlioz arrives in Weimar.

16 February: Liszt conducts Berlioz's *Benvenuto Cellini* in Weimar.

17 February and 1 March: Berlioz conducts his Overture *Le Corsaire* and *La Damnation de Faust* in Weimar. (Both works had been rehearsed by Liszt.) Liszt's attempt to interest Berlioz in Wagner's works, especially *Lohengrin*, comes to nothing.

10 March: Liszt in Jena, where his secular cantata *An die Künstler* is performed. He later works on the full scores of some of his symphonic poems.

20 April: Hans von Bülow asks for Cosima's hand in marriage.

2 May: Liszt in Merseburg, where Winterberger gives the first performance of his *Präludium und Fuge über das Motiv BACH* on the cathedral organ.

11 May: Bülow visits Liszt to discuss his marriage with Cosima.

Mid-May: The first movement of the *Dante Symphony* is completed.

12/13 June: Liszt attends the music festival in Magdeburg. In May and June he works on the definitive version of *Ce qu'on entend sur la montagne*.

8 July: Completion of the *Dante Symphony*. Voluminous correspondence dealing with the intrigues surrounding the forthcoming performance of the ''Gran'' Mass, which was being opposed by Count Leo Festetics.

7 August: Departure for Hungary.

8 August: Liszt spends half a day in Prague in the company of Dreyschock, Kittl, Ambros, and Count Nostitz.

10 August to 14 September: Liszt in Hungary.

20 August (in Gran), and 26 and 27 August (in the Banqueting Hall of the Pest National Museum): Liszt rehearses his ''Gran'' Mass.

31 August: First performance of the ''Gran'' Mass to mark the consecration of the basilica in Esztergom.

3 September: Liszt as guest of Count Károlyi in Fót.

4 September: The ''Gran'' Mass is performed in Pest's parish church in the Eskü-Ter in the inner town.

8 September: Liszt conducts his *Szekszárd Mass* in Pest and, on the same day at the National Theatre, his *Les Préludes* and the first performance of *Hungaria*, a performance which is greeted with immense acclaim.

14 to 19 September: Liszt in Vienna.

20 to 29 September: Liszt in Prague.
Friendship with Smetana and Dreyschock.

22 and 27 September: Rehearsals for the ''Gran'' Mass.

28 September: Liszt conducts his ''Gran'' Mass in Prague's St Vitus's Cathedral.

29 September: On his way back to Weimar, Liszt calls on Burgrave Karel Chotek at his castle in Großpriesen.

8 to 10 October: Liszt stays in Stuttgart.

407 Franz Liszt. Photograph by Franz Hanfstaengl, Munich, November 1856; the earliest known photograph of Liszt by this leading photographer.

Unlike Hanfstaengl's later portraits of Liszt (Illus. 431, 432, 479, 484, and 485), this photograph is virtually unknown.

Robert Schumann died on 8 June 1856. Liszt had always revered him deeply. The Schumanns for their part had been great admirers of Liszt around 1840 (see pp. 129 and 267) but with the passage of time had moved increasingly away from him both as man and as artist, finding his innovative works alien to their nature. Liszt had grown up against the background of French Romanticism and lacked the Schumanns' beloved ''German soul.'' Nonetheless, they rarely missed an opportunity to beg favours of Liszt, who was untiring in his support of Robert Schumann's works. ''Could you, and would you, be kind enough to forward some letters for us to Petersburg? Perhaps also to Moscow? Please, please do so, it would be of great help to us [. . .].'' ''Dear Herr Liszt, could you not speak to the Grand Duchess about it, [. . .] a word from you would no doubt do the trick [. . .].''[118]

Liszt's favourite works by Schumann were the F sharp minor Sonata, the *Symphonische Etüden*, *Carnaval*, the C major *Phantasie*, *Novelletten*, the *Phantasiestücke*, and the *Manfred* Overture. Tradition has it that he was able to negotiate the notorious leaps in the C major *Phantasie* without looking at the keys and while continuing to hold a conversation. He never allowed his students to play the ''Chopin'' episode from *Carnaval*, but always performed it himself – twice: the first time refined, graceful, and poetic, the second time mysteriously, as though form and sound were slowly floating away.

The well-known writer Fanny Lewald has left an impressive description of Liszt during this period: ''[. . .] Liszt was still as slim and as graceful in all his movements as he had been when I saw him in Königsberg. I was as surprised on this occasion as I had been then [. . .]: the cheerful brightness of his eyes and the way he would open them wide, together with the peculiar majesty which suffused the whole of his countenance. Neither his shoulder-length auburn hair, beginning with a high sweep in the middle of his forehead, nor his complexion and facial features were in any way Germanic, but nor could they be described as Slav or Sarmatian, since at least until he grew heavier in old age, in profile they recalled Dante. Whenever he looked around him, he seemed like someone who owned the world and for whom that ownership was so innate as to appear entirely natural. So noble was his head that during the years from 1830 to 1840, when he was living mainly in Paris, he had as much influence upon visual artists as did the classical beauty of the Comtesse d'Agoult [. . .]. In the period around 1848 Liszt spoke mostly French; but he handled it in a way that struck me as something unusual, something utterly charming, just as I was struck by the way he would offer people his hand, shaking it cordially. This is not something I could explain or describe, yet it was something people felt to be both liberal and beautiful, something which momentarily brought him closer to the stranger in question, something, finally, which showed trust and inspired confidence.''[119]

408 Clara and Robert Schumann. Copper engraving based on a daguerreotype produced in Hamburg in March 1850.

13 October to 27 November: Liszt visits Wagner in Zurich, where he arrives on the 13th. They are joined a few days later by Carolyne and her daughter Marie. Liszt, who is confined to his bed by a leg injury throughout part of his visit, acquaints Wagner with his *Faust Symphony* and *Dante Symphony*.

22 October: To mark Liszt's 45th birthday, Wagner improvises a performance of Act I of *The Valkyrie* at the Hotel Baur au lac. Liszt plays the piano, and the audience includes Gottfried Keller, Georg Herwegh, Jakob Sulzer, and Gottfried Semper.

23 November: At a gala concert in St Gall Liszt conducts his *Orpheus* and *Les Préludes*, and Wagner conducts Beethoven's *Eroica* Symphony.

27 November: Liszt and the Princess set off for Munich, where they remain until 12 December. At the National Theatre Liszt hears performances of *La Clemenza di Tito*, *Jessonda*, *Le Prophète*, and *Tannhäuser*. He spends time with Lachner, Liebig, and Förster, and forms a "close friendship" with Kaulbach.

16 December: Wagner describes Liszt's friendship as the most important and significant event in his life.[120]

WORKS

Dante Symphony. Definitive version. Pub. 1859. See "Works 1855."

Faust Symphony. Version for two pianos. Revised in 1860 and published in 1863. See "Works 1854."

Preludio pomposo (Festvorspiel-Prélude) (for piano). Pub. 1857, together with a version for orchestra.

Concerto pathétique (for two pianos). Based on the *Großes Konzertsolo*. Pub. 1866. A revised version, with an interpolation by Hans von Bülow made with Liszt's approval in 1884, was published in 1886.

Anfangs wollt ich fast verzagen (for mezzo-soprano or baritone and piano). Pub. 1860.

Vereinslied (for men's voices). Pub. 1861.

Ständchen (Rückert's "Hüttelein, still und klein") (for men's voices with tenor solo). Pub. 1861.

Ce qu'on entend sur la montagne ("Bergsymphonie"). Definitive version. Pub. 1857. A version for two pianos prepared ca. 1854–7 was published in 1857.

Hungaria (symphonic poem). Corrections to 1854 version.

Cantique d'amour (adapted for harp). Unpublished. The manuscript is known to have been in the possession of Richard Pohl ca. 1895.

Wie singt die Lerche schön (for tenor or soprano and piano). Written ca. 1856. Pub. 1856. (See p. 204.)

WRITINGS:

"Dornröschen." Genast's Poem and Raff's Music of the Same Title. Pub. 1856. Consists of (a) "Sleeping Beauty" (fairy-tale retold by Liszt) and (b) essay *Genast's poem and Raff's music*.

Mozart: On the Occasion of his Centenary Festival in Vienna. Pub. 1856.

409 Franz Liszt. Oil portrait by Richard Lauchert, 1856.

In a letter to Carolyne von Sayn-Wittgenstein of 5 August 1857, Liszt described this portrait as a "fiasco."

23. November 1856

410 Souvenir of the concert in St Gall on 23 November 1856, reproduced from the *St. Galler Tagblatt*, No. 544, 1856.

The themes from *Orpheus* and *Les Préludes* are in Liszt's handwriting, while the *Eroica* motive plus accompanying sentence (''Thus Beethoven thought on heroic matters'') are in Wagner's hand.

411 Page from the guest book of the St Gall Foundation with entries by Liszt, Wagner, Herwegh, and Semper, dated 24 November 1856.

412 Franz Liszt. Lithograph by Josef Kriehuber, 1856.

During a six-week stay in Zurich with Richard Wagner in October/November 1856, Liszt was invited to appear at a concert in St Gall on 23 November. He conducted his symphonic poems *Orpheus* and *Les Préludes*, and Wagner conducted Beethoven's *Eroica* Symphony. After the concert, Wagner wrote to Otto Wesendonck, ''Liszt's *Orpheus* has left a deep impression upon me; it is one of the most beautiful, most perfect, indeed, most matchless of tone poems. Great was my enjoyment in this work. It made Liszt very happy to hear my undisguised appreciation of his works.''

The *St. Galler Tagblatt* carried an enthusiastic report on the concert: ''That such heroes of music should conduct concerts in St Gall is a phenomenon the like of which will scarce be repeated for centuries to come. [. . .] Here we see two men, united in aim and lacking all sense of envy, but rejoicing only in each other's greatness: one of them an outlaw, garnering a rich and ample garland of honour on foreign soil – the other, formerly rushing from triumph to triumph, now suddenly withdrawing into himself with a free and firm resolve in order to pour his great, unbroken strength into pure and noble works of art'' (*St. Galler Tagblatt*, Sunday edition No. 544, p. 31).

Opposite page:

413 Manuscript in Liszt's hand, dated Zurich, 16 November 1856, with motives from Scene 4 of *The Rhinegold* and Wagner's signature. Previously unpublished.

Diese Stelle tritt ein nach dem Donner
gesagt hat =
Schwüles Gedünst
schwebt in der Luft
lästig ist mir
der trübe Druck:
Das bleiche Gewölk
samml' ich zu blitzendem Wetter
Das fegt den Himmel mir hell!
Er schwingt den Hammer –
Zürich 16 November 56.
pour copie conforme
Richard Wagner

414 *Wie singt die Lerche schön*, written ca. 1856.
Manuscript previously unpublished.

Opposite page:

415 Franz Liszt. Oil portrait by Wilhelm von Kaulbach
(see also Illus. 424), 1856.

LIFE

5 January: Liszt begins his symphonic poem *Hunnenschlacht*.

7 January: In the Weimar Court Theatre Liszt conducts the first performances of his A major Piano Concerto, with Hans von Bronsart as soloist, and the final version of *Ce qu'on entend sur la montagne*.

22 January: First performance of Liszt's B minor Sonata given in Berlin by Hans von Bülow, to inaugurate the first grand piano made by Carl Bechstein; the work meets with unexpected acclaim. A critical review in the *Spenersche Zeitung* leads Bülow to engage in a long and bitter correspondence with the critic Gustav Eduard Engel in the columns of that paper.

10 February: Liszt completes his symphonic poem *Hunnenschlacht*.

15 February: Wagner writes an appreciative letter on Liszt's symphonic poems.

22 February: Liszt travels to Leipzig for a week.

26 February: Liszt conducts *Les Préludes*, *Mazeppa*, and his E flat major Piano Concerto (with Bülow as soloist) in the Gewandhaus. Violent attacks in the press.

15 March: Liszt's *Psalm xiii* performed in Jena.
A leg injury confines Liszt to his bed until mid-April.

20 May: Liszt travels to Aachen to conduct the 35th Lower Rhenish Music Festival.

31 May: Liszt conducts Beethoven's *Zur Weihe des Hauses* and Handel's *Messiah* in Aachen.

1 June: Concert in Aachen, including Schubert's C major Symphony and Liszt's *Festklänge*.

2 June: Third concert in Aachen, including Liszt's E flat major Piano Concerto (with Bülow as soloist), Beethoven's Violin Concerto (with Edmund Singer as soloist), and Wagner's *Tannhäuser* Overture. Considerable opposition from Liszt's former friend Ferdinand Hiller.

End of July to mid-August: Back in Aachen, seeking treatment for his leg injury. Works on symphonic poem *Die Ideale*.
Sits for a medallion by Christian Mohr in Cologne.

18 August: Attends the wedding in Berlin of his daughter Cosima and Hans von Bülow.

3 September: Rietschel's Goethe and Schiller Memorial is unveiled in Weimar, the foundation stone of the Carl August Memorial is laid, and Liszt's *Weimars Volkslied* receives its first performance.

4 September: The Wieland Memorial is unveiled in Weimar. Liszt conducts his *Festvorspiel*.

5 September: Liszt conducts the first performance of his *Faust Symphony* and *Die Ideale* in Weimar. Smetana visits Liszt in Weimar.

12 September: Trial performance of Liszt's symphonic poem *Hunnenschlacht* in Weimar.

22 October (Liszt's birthday): Liszt's daughter Blandine marries Émile Ollivier.

1 to 8 November: Liszt in Dresden. On the 7th he conducts his *Prometheus* and *Dante Symphony*.

10 November: Moritz Schön conducts the first performance of *Héroïde funèbre* in Breslau.
Revisions to the *Faust Symphony* and *Dante Symphony*.

29 December: Liszt conducts the first performance of his *Hunnenschlacht* in Weimar.

416 Title page of the 1876 first edition of the second movement (''Gretchen'') of Liszt's *Faust Symphony* in a piano arrangement by the composer.

417 Liszt's *Faust Symphony*. Title page of the first edition of the full score, 1861.

The *Faust Symphony* is counted among Liszt's most significant works. It was begun in August 1854 and completed on 19 October 1854, although the final chorus was not added until 1857.

Dante's *Divine Comedy* and Goethe's *Faust* accompanied Liszt throughout his life, and he took copies of both texts with him on almost every journey he made. Certainly, there is something Faustian about Liszt's character with his magus-like magnetism, his love of experimentation, and his constant search for a (musical) secret. As a mere curiosity it may be mentioned that a number of portraits of Liszt recall both Dante (see facing page) and Faust (see Illus. 478 and 479).

Liszt's *Faust Symphony* was dedicated to Hector Berlioz and first performed, under the composer's baton, on 5 September 1857 as part of the celebrations held to mark the unveiling of the Goethe and Schiller Memorial and the Wieland Memorial, and the laying of the foundation stone of the Carl August Memorial in Weimar. It was performed in various towns during the years that followed, but without achieving any real success. Mention should, however, be made of performances under Ferruccio Busoni (1920), Leonard Bernstein (1976), and Daniel Barenboim (Bayreuth 1986).

418 The Goethe and Schiller Memorial in Weimar. Steel engraving by Alfred Krause, ca. 1860.

The Goethe and Schiller Memorial in front of the Weimar Court Theatre was unveiled on 3 September 1857. It was the work of Ernst Rietschel, to whom we owe an excellent relief portrait of Liszt (Illus. 400). The ceremony was accompanied by the first performance of Liszt's *Weimars Volkslied*.

WORKS

Die Ideale (symphonic poem). Pub. 1858, together with a version for two pianos.
Hunnenschlacht (symphonic poem). Written between 5 January and 10 February 1857. Pub. 1861, together with a version for two pianos.
Festvorspiel (Preludio pomposo) (for orchestra). Pub. 1857. See "Works 1856."
Künstlerfestzug (for orchestra). Pub. 1860, together with piano versions for two hands and for four hands.
Festmarsch zur Goethejubiläumsfeier (for orchestra). Reorchestration of the older version. Pub. 1859, together with piano versions for two hands and for four hands.
Weimars Volkslied (for chorus). Six versions. Pub. 1857, together with versions for solo voice and piano, piano solo (two versions), and piano duet. A version for organ appeared in 1873.
Die Legende von der heiligen Elisabeth (generally called "Saint Elisabeth" by Liszt) (oratorio). Begun ca. 1857, completed in August 1862. Vocal score pub. 1867 (see Illus. 448), full score 1869. Individual sections appeared in 1867/68 in arrangements for two hands and for four hands.
Final chorus of the *Faust Symphony*. Pub. 1861. See "Works 1854."
Es muß ein Wunderbares sein (for soprano or baritone and piano). Pub. 1859.
Muttergottes Sträußlein zum Mai-Monate (for soprano and piano): 1. *Das Veilchen*, 2. *Die Schlüsselblumen*. Pub. 1859. A third song, *Das Glöckchen*, mentioned in a catalogue of Princess Wittgenstein, is lost.
Pilgrims' Chorus from "Tannhäuser" (Wagner) (piano transcription). Pub. 1865. A second version appeared in 1885.
Ich liebe dich (for tenor or soprano and piano). Pub. 1860. A version for piano alone was published in 1980.
Revision of Beethoven's works. All the piano works, chamber music, and the Masses in C major and D major. (Some of these works were revised in 1861.)

WRITINGS:
Weimar's September Festival in Honour of the Centenary of Carl August's Birth. Pub. 1857.
Criticism of Criticism: Ulibishev and Serov. Pub. 1858.

At the end of May 1857 Liszt travelled to Aachen to conduct the 35th Lower Rhenish Music Festival. Once again he was faced with the thankless task of turning a group of amateurs into a festival orchestra and mastering an extensive programme. And once again he had to put up with the criticism, this time on the lips of his former friend Ferdinand Hiller, of "not knowing how to conduct" (*Kölnische Zeitung*, No. 155, 6 June 1857):

"Now that I have heard him rehearsing and performing the most disparate works at five great rehearsals and at three great concerts, I have come to the conclusion that Liszt is no conductor – at least not in proportion to the task which he has set himself and the demands which we are entitled to make of such a man [. . .]."

Liszt and Hiller embody two totally different types of musician. In 1855 Liszt told Carolyne von Sayn-Wittgenstein what he thought of Hiller as a conductor: "Hiller's direction, like his entire personality, is adaptable, well-rounded, thoroughly respectable, and even distinguished, but without any kind of energetic vigour and therefore without authority and without the power to captivate an audience. He could be reproached for making too few mistakes, and for giving insufficient grounds for criticism."[121]

Rosa von Milde has left an account of how Liszt worked with an orchestra when there was sufficient time at his disposal: "Everything had to work right down to the minutest detail before he would allow the rehearsal to continue, and it might happen that if the woodwind, for example, had not played a passage to his satisfaction he would rehearse that passage with them for between half an hour and three quarters of an hour [. . .]."[122]

419 Liszt conducting in the Aachen Stadttheater on 1 June 1857. Wood engraving, 1857.

420 Franz Liszt. Medallion by Ludwig von Schwanthaler, 1857.

421 Liszt and the soprano Rosa von Milde. Medallion cast in 1857 to mark the 35th Lower Rhenish Music Festival.

CARL TAUSIG (1841–1871)

422 From left to right: Hans von Bülow, Carl Tausig, Karl Klindworth. Photograph by Joseph Albert, Munich 1865.
These three great pianists, who were all on terms of the closest friendship with each other, were among Liszt's most distinguished pupils in the years around 1855. Few other pianists were as justly entitled as these three to describe themselves as their revered master's "favourite pupils," and few were as lavishly housed and entertained at the Altenburg as they.

favour with the Princess Liszt packed him off to Wagner in Zurich: "Dearest Richard, I am sending you an amazing fellow. Give him a friendly welcome, and tell him to give your Erard a good working over and to play all manner of things for you."[124] Wagner's reaction was one of delight and horror: "My childless marriage has suddenly been blessed with a real catastrophe, and I am enjoying, in rapid succession, the quintessence of a father's cares and troubles. [. . .] Musically, however, he is enormously talented, and his furious piano playing makes me shudder. It inevitably reminds me of you and of the remarkable influence which you exercise over so many, often highly gifted, young men."[125] "I recently wrote to you in uninhibited terms concerning this young Tausig. Two things make me overlook all his shortcomings, and bind me to him to such a degree that I am almost inclined to trust him: they are his boundless love of you and the way he stops being naughty the moment that conversation turns to you, when he shows the most tender and profound reverence towards you [. . .]."[126]

Tausig seemed uniquely suited to a virtuoso career, yet it was not one which gave him any lasting satisfaction. He studied philosophy, mathematics, and natural science. In 1862 he went to Vienna and conducted concerts made up entirely of Wagner's works. In 1865 he founded a "School of Advanced Piano Playing" in Berlin. On 2 July 1871 he travelled to Leipzig with Liszt, and the next day contracted typhus. He died on the 17th, and hands which Liszt had described as "des mains de bronze et de diamants" were laid to rest for ever.

Liszt wrote to Carolyne von Sayn-Wittgenstein on 23 July 1871, "Tausig's loss affects me deeply. He possessed the nerve, the intelligence, the uniqueness, the consistency, the talent, and the perseverance of a great artist! He was, moreover, a highly cultured person of great practical skill, well suited to fill a leading position in the world of music. He was familiar with the ideas of Kant, Schopenhauer, and Darwin. At the same time he showed admirable care in revising and perfecting several musical works – piano studies, a concerto, unedited transcriptions of several Beethoven quartets, Bach chorales [. . .]."[127]

Karl Klindworth was one of Liszt's first pupils in Weimar. From 1854 to 1868 he lived in London, where he played the piano and conducted concerts, before taking up a position as Professor of Piano in Moscow from 1868 to 1882. He then moved to Berlin, where he was active as a piano virtuoso, teacher, and conductor. He published an edition of Chopin's works of which Liszt thought very highly, and he also edited Beethoven's sonatas. Wagner entrusted him with the task of preparing vocal scores of some of his operas. He was the adoptive father of Siegfried Wagner's later wife, Winifred.

Wagner wrote to Liszt from London on 5 April 1855: "Klindworth has just played me your great Sonata! [. . .] He has amazed me with his playing: no lesser man than he could have dared perform your work for me for the first time. He is worthy of you: indeed he is! – It was wonderful! [. . .]"[128]

Tausig must have been a phenomenal pianist. Everyone who heard him spoke of his uniquely brilliant technique, which was even said to equal Liszt's. (He could play the *prestissimo* passage in broken octaves at the end of the third movement of Chopin's E minor Concerto at breathtaking speed.) Even his greatest rivals were full of praise for his playing. Anton Rubinstein called him "infallible," Bülow "unsurpassable, superb." Liszt described him as his finest pupil.

"This morning I received a pupil by the name of Tausig, aged thirteen and a half. He is one in a thousand, and I firmly believe that in two to three years from now he will have an extraordinary career. He already plays every work in the most astonishing way and composes the most piquant things," Liszt reported on 21 July 1855.[123]

Apart from a few interruptions, Tausig remained Liszt's pupil from 1855 to 1859. Some of the tricks he played were not always entirely harmless (on one occasion, lack of money forced him to sell Liszt's as yet unpublished manuscript of the *Faust Symphony* for 5 thalers, without his teacher's knowledge), so that when he temporarily fell into dis-

425 Document, dated 23 June 1857, attesting to Liszt's admission into the Order of St Francis.

423 Agnes Street-Klindworth (1825–1906) in later life. Photograph, ca. 1870.

Agnes Street was Liszt's pupil from 1853 to 1855. She became his intimate friend, and rumours even began to circulate in Weimar that Liszt intended to marry her. Agnes Street is the (unnamed) recipient of *Franz Liszts Briefe an eine Freundin*, published in 1894 and still awaiting translation into English, a collection of 133 letters covering the years from 1855 to 1886 which is of immense value not least because Liszt, untypically, discusses his own works here.

424 Franz Liszt. Oil portrait by Wilhelm von Kaulbach, 1857.

Kaulbach was a member of Liszt's circle of friends in Munich. In the letters (all in French) between Liszt and Carolyne von Sayn-Wittgenstein, Kaulbach is generally referred to as Liszt's "excellent friend," without any mention of his name. He produced two oil portraits of the composer (Illus. 415 and 424), one pencil drawing (Illus. 297), and one caricature (Illus. 486).

LIFE

1 January: Eduard Lassen takes up his appointment as music director in Weimar.

14 January: Tausig performs Liszt's A major Piano Concerto under Bülow in Berlin. Both the concerto and the symphonic poem *Festklänge* meet with a lively response.

27 January: Liszt conducts an evening of Mozart's works in the Weimar Court Theatre.

February: Liszt works on *Hamlet*.

11 March: The Sophiensaal in Prague is full to overflowing for performances of Liszt's *Die Ideale*, *Dante Symphony*, and A major Piano Concerto, all under the composer's baton. The soloist is Carl Tausig, who also plays one of Liszt's Rhapsodies.

14 March: Liszt conducts his E flat major Piano Concerto (with Pflughaupt as soloist) and *Tasso* in the same hall. The composer and his works inspire a sympathetic response in Prague audiences. The same day Liszt leaves for Vienna.

15 to 31 March: Liszt in Vienna.

22 and 23 March: Liszt conducts his "Gran" Mass in the Redoutensaal.

1 to 12 April: Liszt in Pest.

10 April: Liszt conducts his "Gran" Mass in the Banqueting Hall of the National Museum.

11 April: Liszt conducts his "Gran" Mass in the Pest parish church and afterwards receives holy orders as a member of the Order of St Francis in Pest's Franciscan Church.

12 April: Breaks journey in Preßburg.

20 and 21 April: Breaks journey in Prague.

23 to 27 April: Liszt in Löwenberg. On the 25th he conducts performances of *Les Préludes*, *Tasso*, and *Festklänge*.

27 May: First performance of the *Festgesang* (dedicated to German primary-school teachers) at a teachers' assembly held in Weimar.

25 June: Trial performance of *Hamlet* in Weimar. Friedrich Hebbel visits Liszt.

Towards the end of July: Liszt in Wilhelmsthal for a few days, then back in Weimar from the 27th.

August: Wilhelm von Kaulbach stays with Liszt in Weimar.

15 August: Liszt conducts a concert to mark the tercentenary of the founding of Jena University.

26 August: Liszt leaves Weimar for Bavaria.

September: Liszt, the Princess, and her daughter in Innsbruck, after which they convalesce in the Ötztal Alps.

October: Liszt in Munich, where he sits for the photographer Franz Hanfstaengl (see Illus. 431 and 432).

8 and 9 October: In Salzburg.

30 October: Liszt conducts the first performance of Sobolewski's *Comala* in Weimar.

15 December: Liszt conducts the first performance of Cornelius's *Der Barbier von Bagdad* in Weimar. The work (which is dedicated to Liszt) is dismissed as a "modern fabrication," and both it and Liszt are booed. The result is one of the greatest theatre scandals of the nineteenth century. Following the premiere Liszt asks to be relieved of his post.

17 December: Beethoven Festival in Weimar. Liszt conducts the Overture *Zur Weihe des Hauses* and the Symphony No. 7. He receives a rare ovation, but his decision to leave Weimar is unshakeable, and not even a private audience at Court (along with Cornelius) can persuade him to change his mind.

On 15 December 1858 Peter Cornelius's comic opera *The Barber of Baghdad* received its first performance under Liszt's baton in the Weimar Court Theatre. The work became the victim of a demonstration directed against the whole of the New German camp. Cornelius has left us his own account of the evening:

"A degree of opposition unprecedented in the annals of the Weimar theatre, and involving persistent hissing, sought to counteract the applause from the very beginning. At the end, fighting broke out and went on for ten minutes. The Grand Duke had applauded throughout, but this did not stop the others from hissing. Finally Liszt and the whole orchestra applauded, and Frau von Milde dragged me out on to the stage. The artists all took my part with real enthusiasm. Liszt's treatment of me was exemplary. I pray that everyone who takes an interest in me may risk life and limb for this man who is the standard-bearer of a new age."[129]

Following the premiere Liszt resigned his position as Court Kapellmeister in Weimar. "My decision to break with the public was not made yesterday. It was left to chance to decide whether I broke with it on the occasion of a success or of a failure. Chance *has* decided."[130]

426 Eduard Lassen (1830–1904). Photograph by Friedrich Hertel, ca. 1880.

Lassen was appointed Music Director in Weimar on 1 January 1858, when he succeeded Liszt as Court Kapellmeister.

427 The Weimar Court Theatre. Photograph by Louis Held, ca. 1890.

Many important works were performed in this theatre during Liszt's tenure as Court Kapellmeister.

428 Opening page of Daniel Liszt's study book.

Liszt's son Daniel spent the years 1857 to 1859 studying law in Vienna. He stayed in the Schottenhof with Liszt's uncle, the lawyer Dr Eduard Liszt.

429 Liszt's son Daniel (1839–1859). Medallion by Adolf Donndorf, 1856.

Liszt described the death of his only son as the greatest and most painful loss of his entire life.

WORKS

Hamlet (symphonic poem). Pub. 1861, together with a version for two pianos. A version for four hands appeared in 1875.

Festgesang (for chorus). Written for the opening of the 10th General Assembly of German School-teachers. Pub. 1859.

Hungarian Rhapsodies Nos. 2, 5, 6, 9, 12, and 14 (arranged for orchestra by Liszt and Franz Doppler). Written 1858–60. Pub. 1874/75. No. 9 (''Pester Karneval'') also exists in a version for piano, violin, and cello; it was published in 1892.

3 Songs: 1. *Air de Chateaubriand*, 2. *Strophes de Herlossohn*, 3. *Kränze pour chant*. These three songs, mentioned in a catalogue by Carolyne von Sayn-Wittgenstein, are believed lost.

Jeanne d'Arc au bûcher (contralto solo and orchestra). Reworking of a version of 1845; unpublished. Revised in 1874 and published in 1877.

6 Chants polonais (from Chopin's op. 74) (piano transcriptions). Written ca. 1858: 1. *Mädchenswunsch*, 2. *Frühling*, 3. *Das Ringlein*, 4. *Bacchanal*, 5. *Meine Freuden*, 6. *Heimkehr*. Pub. 1860.

Années de Pèlerinage. Deuxième Année: Italie (for piano). New edition of the earlier versions, most of which had been revised ca. 1849: 1. *Spozalizio*, 2. *Il Penseroso*, 3. *Canzonetta del Salvator Rosa*, 4. *Sonetto 47 del Petrarca*, 5. *Sonetto 104 del Petrarca*, 6. *Sonetto 123 del Petrarca*, 7. *Après une lecture de Dante, Fantasia quasi Sonata*. Pub. 1858.

Lenore (melodrama with piano). Pub. 1860.

Variations on Pásztor Lakodalmas (Festetics) (piano). Pub. 1859.

430 Two pages of a letter dated 5 October 1854 from Liszt to the singer Salvatore Cavaliere de Castrone, the husband of the well-known singing teacher Mathilde Marchesi (see Illus. 502). Previously unpublished (reduced in size). The complete letter runs to four pages.

431, 432 Franz Liszt. Photographs by Franz Hanfstaengl, Munich 1858.

LIFE

14 January: Bülow conducts Liszt's *Die Ideale* in Berlin; when a handful of demonstrators begin to hiss, he shouts at them angrily, ''I would ask the gentlemen who are hissing to leave the room; it is not usual to hiss in this hall!'' The audience falls silent, but Bülow and Liszt's work are attacked all the more vociferously in the press.

February: The Grand Duke asks Liszt to explain what must be done so that the Weimar Theatre may keep his services. Liszt makes detailed suggestions, although he has long since felt an inner aversion to Weimar.

25 February to beginning of March: With Bülow in Berlin. On the 27th he conducts *Die Ideale*.

12 March: Bülow conducts *Mazeppa* and *Festklänge* in Prague. The concert also includes the first performance of Wagner's Prelude to *Tristan and Isolde*.

9 April: Liszt conducts the first performance of his *Huldigungsmarsch* in Weimar.

10 April: Liszt is invested with the Austrian Order of the Iron Crown.

End of April to 7 May: Liszt as guest of Prince Hohenzollern in Löwenberg, Silesia.

8 to 11 May: Liszt in Breslau.

20 May: Liszt conducts Handel's *Judas Maccabaeus* to mark the centenary of the composer's death.

28 May: Leaves for Leipzig, where he is the first to sign the foundation charter of the Allgemeiner Deutscher Musikverein.

1 to 5 June: To celebrate the 25th anniversary of the founding of the *Neue Zeitschrift für Musik*, the editor, Franz Brendel, organizes a gathering of musicians in Leipzig. Liszt conducts his ''Gran'' Mass.

23 June: Grand Duchess Maria Pavlovna, a great admirer of Liszt's, dies in Weimar.

July/August: Liszt works on the revision of *Psalm xiii*, and the composition of *Psalms xxiii* and *cxxxvii*.

29 August: At the invitation of Berlioz and the singer Pauline Viardot, Liszt takes part in a music festival at Baden-Baden.

2 October: First performance of Liszt's *Die Seligkeiten* in the Weimar parish church. Feodor Milde sings the baritone solo.

15 October: Princess Marie Wittgenstein, Carolyne's daughter, marries Prince Konstantin von Hohenlohe-Schillingsfürst and moves to Vienna.

30 October: Liszt is raised to the Austrian nobility by the Emperor Franz Joseph I.

9 November: First performance of Liszt's melodrama *Vor hundert Jahren* in Weimar.

15 to 18 November: Liszt in Zwickau.

11 December: Liszt travels to Berlin, where his son Daniel is gravely ill.

13 December: The twenty-year-old Daniel Liszt dies in his father's arms at the home of Hans and Cosima von Bülow.

18 December: Liszt returns to Weimar.

At right, and top of opposite page:

434 *Festlied zu Schillers Jubelfeier*, first published in the *Illustrirte Zeitung* of 12 November 1859.

330   Illustrirte Zeitung.   [№ 854. 12. November 1859.]

433 Patent of nobility conferring a knighthood on Liszt.

The hereditary title of Knight of the Austrian Empire was conferred on Liszt on 30 October 1857. He never made use of the title, and in 1867 transferred it to his uncle Dr Eduard Liszt.

435 Certificate conferring the freedom of the city of Weimar on Liszt, dated 26 October 1860.

WORKS

Venezia e Napoli. Supplément aux Années de Pèlerinage. Deuxième Année: Italie. Revision of the two 1839 pieces, together with a new second piece based on a song from Rossini's *Otello:* 1. *Gondoliera,* 2. *Canzone,* 3. *Tarantella.* Pub. 1861.

Paraphrases of Verdi's operas (for piano): 1. *Rigoletto,* 2. *Il Trovatore* (''Miserere''), 3. *Ernani.* Pub. 1860. The *Ernani* paraphrase had been conceived ca. 1846 but was radically revised in 1859. The *Don Carlos* and *Aida* paraphrases were written later.

Phantasiestück on themes from ''Rienzi'' (Wagner) (for piano). Pub. 1861.

''Weinen, Klagen, Sorgen, Zagen,'' Präludium (for piano). Pub. 1863. Not to be confused with the later *Variationen über das Motiv von Bach* (from BWV 12, *Weinen, Klagen, Sorgen, Zagen*) (see ''Works 1862'').

First Mephisto Waltz (Der Tanz in der Dorfschenke) (for piano). Pub. 1862. The 1860 orchestral version was published in 1865.

Final chorus from ''Der Barbier von Bagdad'' (Cornelius) (piano transcription). Announced in a letter to Cornelius of 23 August 1859. Not written, or lost.

Künstlerfestzug zur Schillerfeier (piano transcriptions for two hands and for four hands of the 1857 orchestral version). Pub. 1860.

Te Deum I (for mixed voices, organ, brass and drums). Pub. 1936.

Psalm xxiii (''The Lord is my shepherd'') (for voice, harp, and organ; also version for optional men's voices made in 1862) and *Psalm cxxxvii* (''By the rivers of Babylon'') (for soprano solo, women's voices, violin, harp, and organ). Pub. 1864.

Psalm xiii (reworking of 1855 version). Pub. 1864.

Festlied zu Schillers Jubelfeier (for solo baritone and men's voices). Pub. 1859. See Ilus. 434.

Festmarsch nach Motiven von E.H. zu S.-C.-G. (on themes from Duke Ernst of Saxe-Coburg-Gotha's *Diana von Solange*) (for orchestra). Pub. 1860, together with versions for piano solo and duet.

4 Marches by Franz Schubert (orchestral versions of Schubert's piano duets D.818 No. 2, D.819 No. 5, and D.968b Nos. 1 and 2). Pub. 1871 and 1880. A transcription for piano duet was prepared in 1879. Year of publication unknown.

Mit klingendem Spiel (for children's voices). Pub. 1860.

Morgenlied (for female or children's voices). Pub. 1861.

Die Seligkeiten (for baritone solo, chorus and organ). (See ''Works 1855.'') Pub. 1861.

Vor hundert Jahren (melodrama with orchestra). Unpublished.

Nocturnes (John Field). Revised by Liszt. Pub. 1859. According to August Göllerich, twelve of these *Nocturnes* also appeared in a piano duet transcription.

WRITINGS:

John Field and His Nocturnes. Pub. 1859.
Pauline Viardot-Garcia. Pub. 1859.
On the Gypsies and Their Music in Hungary. (Most of the chapters were written by Princess Carolyne von Sayn-Wittgenstein.) Published in French in 1859 and in a German translation (by Peter Cornelius) in 1861.

LIFE

January: Liszt in Weimar, where he works on various orchestral pieces and songs.

17 January: Invited to Berlin for a performance of Count Redern's opera *Christine*.

26 February: The first performance of Liszt's *Chöre zu Herders "Entfesseltem Prometheus"* in Vienna ends in loud demonstrations of disapproval.

Early March: The *Berliner Echo* carries a "Declaration" directed against "the music of the future" and its leaders (Liszt and Wagner). The declaration, written by Joseph Joachim and Bernhard Scholz and signed by Brahms and Julius Otto Grimm, is as ill-conceived as it is silly. Joachim's defection in 1857 may well have hurt Liszt personally; but he reacts to it with his customary nobility of mind:

"Several of my closer friends, including Joachim and, at an earlier date, Schumann and others, have adopted a remote, timid, and ill-disposed attitude towards my musical creations, but I certainly do not hold this against them and cannot make them pay for it, since I continue to share a deep and sincere interest in their own works," Liszt wrote to Wagner on 19 April 1857.[131]

April: Liszt in Weimar, where he works on the instrumentation of various works.

17 May: Carolyne von Sayn-Wittgenstein travels to Rome to ask the Pope to acknowledge her divorce decree, which has finally arrived from Russia. Her husband, Prince Nicholas, has remarried in 1856, and it is now in his own interest too to obtain a divorce. Liszt's and the Princess's hope that they may finally be married after years of struggle seems about to be realized.

June: Trips to Zwickau and Magdeburg for performances of the *Festmarsch zur Goethejubiläumsfeier* and *Les Préludes*.

July: Compositional work in Weimar. Excursions to Leipzig and Ettersburg.

August: Elected Officer of the French Legion of Honour.

22 to 28 August: With Cosima in Berlin.

14 September: Liszt writes his will.

12 October: Birth of Liszt's first grandchild, Daniela, daughter of Cosima and Hans von Bülow.

26 October: On his return from a journey to Vienna, Liszt is given the freedom of the city of Weimar.

8 November: First performance of Liszt's *Künstlerfestzug* in the Weimar Court Theatre.

22 to 28 November: In Berlin for the baptism of his grandchild Daniela on the 24th.

December: Liszt in Weimar, where he revises various older works.

Liszt drew up his last will and testament in September 1860, naming his children and the Princess as his heirs and bequeathing various keepsakes to his more intimate friends. Later, in 1873, 1874, and 1879, he made provision for the majority of his more valuable possessions – mostly gifts acquired during his virtuoso years and including Beethoven's Broadwood piano (Illus. 437), gold and silver wreaths, his ceremonial sword (Illus. 230), and cups and medallions – to be bequeathed to the Hungarian National Museum following the death of the Princess. They duly passed into the Hungarian collection in 1887.

Liszt's will gives an instructive insight into his frame of mind, and it is therefore worth quoting extracts from it here.

My Testament

Weimar, 14 September 1860.
I am writing this on 14 September, the day on which the Church celebrates the Feast of the Exaltation of the Holy Cross. The very name of this feast evokes that ardent and mysterious feeling which, like some sacred stigma, transfixes my entire being. [. . .]

The good that I have thought and done during the last twelve years I owe to Jeanne Elisabeth Carolyne Princess Wittgenstein, née Ivanovska, on whom I so desperately yearn to bestow the sweet name of wife. Alas, human spitefulness and the most despicable intrigues have hitherto doggedly frustrated that wish. [. . .] I beg her to forgive the sad inadequacy of my artistic works, and the yet sadder frailty of my good intentions, which is mingled with so many shortcomings and so many inconsistencies. She

knows the smarting pain of my life; she knows that I feel unworthy of her and that I cannot rightly ascend to those pure and sacred regions where her spirit and virtue dwell. If I may yet live for some time on this earth, I vow to strive increasingly to improve, to reduce and correct my mistakes, to gain a greater sense of moral balance, and to miss no opportunity to leave behind the reputation of setting a good example. – Lord, have mercy upon me! Be Thou merciful unto me, and may Thy grace and blessing be with me now and always!

Thus do I owe Carolyne the little good which is in me. But I also owe her the few material possessions which I own: in short, the little that I am and have. She has taken care that my inheritance has been preserved, increased, and properly invested. It amounts to some 220,000 francs (two hundred and twenty thousand francs) deposited with Rothschild in Paris, together with a small sum which my father left with Prince Esterházy and which is now with my cousin Dr Eduard Liszt, District Court Councillor in Vienna.

I ask Carolyne to ensure that this inheritance which I shall leave behind is divided equally and as fairly as possible between my two daughters, Blandine and Cosima Liszt. The former is married to Monsieur Émile Ollivier, Deputy of the City of Paris with the Corps Législatif and a lawyer; the second – Cosima – is married to Baron Hans Guido von Bülow in Berlin.

It goes without saying that my mother, Madame Anna Liszt in Paris, will continue to receive intact the modest pension which has accrued to her over several years from the interest on my capital. In the event of her death, this sum too will be divided in equal shares between my two daughters, who are legitimate heirs.

The perfectly harmonious concord, the honest and childlike frame of mind, which has always obtained between my mother and my children is a source of great comfort to me. May God grant that they remain just as unshakeably friendly after my death. With tender reverence I thank my mother for the constant demonstrations of her kindness and love. In my youth I am said to have been a well-behaved child. She alone must take credit for that; for who could not be a well-behaved child with a mother who sacrificed her very self in so exemplary a way? – If I die before her, her blessing will accompany me to my grave.

I bless my two daughters, Blandine and Cosima, and thank them with all my heart for the ardent, overflowing joy and satisfaction which they have brought me through their noble hearts and honest minds. May they follow the ways of God and remain perpetually true to the Cross of Christ, without expecting the world, with its vanity and passion, to give them what it cannot. [. . .]

In contemporary music there is already a name which is growing increasingly famous: Richard Wagner. His genius was a signal to me! I followed it! My friendship with Wagner had all the character of a noble passion. [. . .] I therefore ask Carolyne to continue her friendly relations with Wagner after my death. Who better than she could understand so strong an impulse as that which Wagner has so boldly given to art through his heavenly feelings of love and poetry.

[Liszt here catalogues the various *objets d'art* which are to remain in the Princess's possession until her death, bequeathing individual keepsakes to his friends and pupils, making provision for the publication of a number of his works, and ending his testament with the following wish:]

I simply wish to be buried, if possible, at night, and without any ceremony.
May the light everlasting shine upon me!
My dying breath will be a blessing upon Carolyne.

F. Liszt.

Opposite page:

436 Franz Liszt. Steel engraving by A. Weger, based on a photograph taken by Hanfstaengl in 1858; ca. 1860.

437 Beethoven's Broadwood piano, owned by Liszt and bequeathed by him to the Hungarian National Museum (see Illus. 356).

The frame bears a handwritten inscription, "Hoc Instrumentum est Thomae Broadwood (Londini) donum propter ingenium illustrissimi Beethoven." To the right of it are the signatures of the committee of experts who helped to choose the instrument, "Ferd. Ries, J. B. Cramer, Ferrari, Knyvett."

In addition to Beethoven's grand piano (a gift to Liszt from the Viennese publisher Carl Anton Spina), Liszt, a great admirer of Beethoven, also owned the composer's original death mask, a present from the painter Josef Danhauser.

438 Platinum inkwell presented to Liszt as a gift and later bequeathed to the Hungarian National Museum.

Like the Beethoven grand, this precious inkwell is mentioned in Liszt's will. On the front, beneath the arching leaf-like decoration, is Liszt's coat of arms; on the left-hand side is an eagle staring into the sun, its wings outstretched; and on the back is a bird charmed by a snake. The top is decorated with a turquoise and gold inlay work, together with an inscription in Turkish. The bottom of the inkwell is undecorated save for the maker's signature, "G. Fabergé à St. Petersburg."

WORKS

Les Morts (for orchestra). Written in memory of Liszt's son Daniel, who had died in 1859. A chorus for men's voices was added in 1866. Pub. 1916. Liszt also wrote piano versions for two hands (pub. 1908) and for four hands (unpub.) and a version for organ (pub. 1890).
Psalm xviii ("The heavens declare the glory of God") (for men's voices and orchestra or wind band). Both versions pub. 1871.
Lieder (for tenor or mezzo-soprano and piano): 1. *Ich scheide*, 2. *Die stille Wasserrose*, 3. *Jugendglück*, 4. *Wieder möcht ich dir begegnen*, 5. *Blume und Duft*, 6. *Nonnenwerth* (second version), 7. *Wer nie sein Brot mit Tränen aß* (second version). Pub. 1860. A new setting of No. 7 for alto or baritone and piano was also made around this time and published in 1862.
Die drei Zigeuner (Lenau) (for tenor or mezzo-soprano and piano). Pub. 1860. A version for voice and orchestra, written in 1860, appeared in 1872; and a version for violin and piano, arranged in 1864, was published in 1896.
Marche au Supplice (fourth movement of Berlioz's *Symphonie fantastique*) (for piano). Reworking of the 1833 version with an introduction arranged from the *Idée fixe* (see "Works 1833".) Pub. 1866.
Der traurige Mönch (melodrama with piano). Pub. 1872.
Mignons Lied (third version) (for mezzo-soprano and piano). Pub. 1863.
An den heiligen Franziskus von Paula (for men's voices, organ, brass, and timpani). Pub. 1875.
Responses and antiphons (for four-part chorus and organ). Pub. 1936.
Pater noster I (for chorus and organ). Pub. 1864. Later taken up into *Christus*.
Two episodes from Lenau's Faust (for orchestra): 1. *Der nächtliche Zug*, 2. *Der Tanz in der Dorfschenke (First Mephisto Waltz)*. Pub. 1865. A version for piano duet appeared in 1862.
Introduction and Fugue from "Ich hatte viel Bekümmernis" BWV 21, and *Andante from "Aus tiefer Not"* BWV 38 (Bach) (organ transcriptions). Pub. 1862.
Pilgrims' Chorus from "Tannhäuser" (Wagner) (organ transcription). Pub. between 1860 and 1862. Revised 1862 and pub. 1864.
Spinning Chorus from "The Flying Dutchman" (Wagner) (piano transcription). Pub. ca. 1861.
Helges Treue (Draeseke) (arranged as a melodrama with piano accompaniment). Pub. 1874.
Danse des Sylphes de "La Damnation de Faust" (Berlioz) (piano transcription). Pub. 1866.
Festmarsch zu Schillers 100jähriger Geburtsfeier (Meyerbeer) (piano transcription). Pub. 1866.
Polonaise martiale and *Une petite mélodie*. Both of these pieces are mentioned by Liszt in a letter of 13 November 1860. Unpublished or lost.
Loreley (for voice and orchestra). Pub. 1863.
Ein Fichtenbaum steht einsam (for baritone or mezzo-soprano and piano). Second setting. Written ca. 1860. Pub. 1860.
Erlkönig, Gretchen, Die junge Nonne, Mignon, Der Doppelgänger, and *Abschied* (Schubert) (orchestrations). The first four orchestrations appeared in 1863; that of *Der Doppelgänger* is unpublished, and that of *Abschied* is lost.

ROME, WEIMAR, BUDAPEST

DEATH IN BAYREUTH · 1861–1886

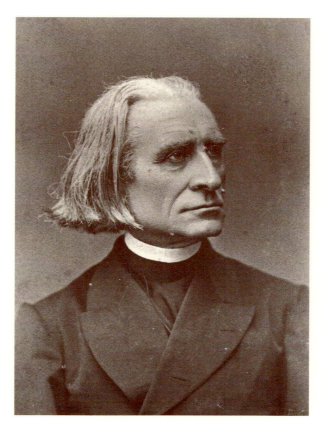

439 Franz Liszt. Photograph by Fritz Luckhardt, 1871.

''. . . logical continuation
and conclusion, in Rome,
Pest, and Weimar . . .''

LIFE

8 to 21 January: Cosima visits her father at the Altenburg in Weimar.

15 to 17 February: In Löwenberg. Performances of *Mazeppa* and *Die Ideale*.

17 to 20 February: In Leipzig. Performance of *Prometheus*.

8 March: First performance of *Der Tanz in der Dorfschenke* (First Mephisto Waltz, for orchestra) at the Weimar Court Theatre.

End of April: Liszt leaves Weimar and travels to Paris via Frankfurt (1 May), Mainz, and Brussels.

May: Extended visit to Paris. Napoleon III creates Liszt an Officer of the French Legion of Honour.

26 May: Wagner arrives in Paris, accompanied by Carl Tausig, and sees Liszt again for the first time since 1856.

3 June: Liszt and Tausig travel to Brussels, where Liszt sees Agnes Street-Klindworth again; then back to Weimar.

25 June: First performance of *Psalm xviii* in Weimar.

July: Carolyne von Sayn-Wittgenstein continues her efforts to obtain a divorce in Rome. A meeting of cardinals decides in her favour. The wedding is planned to take place in Rome in October.

2 August: Wagner arrives in Weimar and stays at the Altenburg.

7 August: The Allgemeiner Deutscher Musikverein is founded at a *Tonkünstlerversammlung* in Weimar. Among those present are Wagner, Bülow, and Cornelius. Liszt conducts his A major Piano Concerto with Tausig as soloist.

12 August: Liszt leaves the Altenburg and moves into the Hotel Erbprinz: ''I left the house, in glorious sunshine, at 2 o'clock in the afternoon, this house in which for twelve years you did good deeds with such ardent enthusiasm, and in which you sought after beauty. [. . .] When I passed through the rooms this morning, I could not restrain my tears. But after a final pause by your prie-dieu – where you always knelt with me before I set off on a journey – I had a feeling of liberation which restored my former strength,'' Liszt wrote to Princess Carolyne on 12 August 1861.[132]

17 August: Liszt leaves Weimar and sets off for Silesia, calling at Wilhelmsthal, where he takes his leave of the Grand Duke and is appointed Gentleman of the Ducal Bedchamber.

22 August to 19 September: Guest of Prince Hohenzollern in Löwenberg.

19 September to 6 October: Liszt in Berlin, after which he travels to Marseilles for several days' visit, then on to Rome.

20 October: Arrival in Rome.

22 October: The wedding is due to take place on Liszt's 50th birthday. A papal legate arrives on the eve of the ceremony with orders to delay until the legal documents can be examined.

November/December: After years of effort to legitimize their union, Liszt and the Princess are definitively thwarted in their plans. They resign their hopes. The Princess refuses to allow the records to be examined. She scarcely sets foot outside her apartment at 89 Via Babuino any longer. Liszt moves into rooms at 113 Via Felice (now Via Sistina) and devotes himself exclusively to his compositional activities.

440 Place de la Concorde, Paris. Photograph, ca. 1865.

In the background (encased in scaffolding) is the Madeleine. Immediately next to it, in the Rue Malesherbes, was Marie d'Agoult's final home in Paris.

441 Programme for a concert on 7 August 1861.

One of the last concerts in the Weimar Court Theatre prior to Liszt's departure for Paris and Rome. The *Faust Symphony* was conducted by Hans von Bülow.

In May 1861 Marie d'Agoult and Liszt met again in Paris after many years of separation. In the interim Marie's novel *Nélida*, an account of her affair with Liszt, had won a wide readership. In it she had cast Liszt in the part of the artist Guermann who, following a brilliantly successful career, is commissioned by a German Grand Duke to paint murals (an allusion to Liszt's virtuoso years and his subsequent appointment in Weimar). He fails utterly, and the walls remain unpainted.

Liszt now stood in Marie's presence, and told her straight out: ''The walls *are* painted, and others, too, will be painted, without our worrying in the least about the stupid things which are said and printed about us [. . .]. You did not believe in me, but you can see now that I have really made it!''

''Marie's face was covered in tears. I kissed her forehead, for the first time in many years, and said to her, 'Now, Marie, let me say to you in the language of the peasants, God bless you! Do not wish me harm!' ''[133]

It was Liszt's long-cherished wish to legalize his irregular relationship with Carolyne von Sayn-Wittgenstein: ''You know that in my union with the Princess lies my honour and all the happiness which I strive and hope for in this world,'' he wrote to Grand Duke Carl Alexander of Weimar on 19 August 1860.[134] The Grand Duke interceded on the Princess's behalf with Cardinal Antonelli, Pope Pius IX's secretary of state: ''As proof of Herr Liszt's entitlement to a sympathetic hearing from His Holiness one could cite the following: the numerous donations which Herr Liszt has made to Catholic churches and religious foundations in every country; the concerts which he has given in Berlin and Cologne in support of the [Cologne] Cathedral building fund; the concert he gave in Pest for the Church of St Leopold; and the concert in Brussels for restoration work on the church [. . .].''[135]

After two audiences with Pius IX, the ceremony was fixed for 22 October 1861. A cousin of the Princess who happened to be in Rome chanced to visit the Church of San Carlo al Corso, which was already decorated for the forthcoming ceremony; on the very eve of the wedding he persuaded the authorities to order an investigation into the records of the Princess's divorce. She refused to release them; the wedding did not take place.

442 Princess Carolyne von Sayn-Wittgenstein. Photograph by Fratelli d'Alessandri, Rome 1860.
On the back of this photograph is an inscription, written by the Princess, to the effect that these were the clothes she wore for her audience with the Pope in the Sistine Chapel in 1860, when she petitioned His Holiness for a divorce.

443 San Carlo al Corso, Rome. Photograph, ca. 1920.
The church in which Liszt's planned marriage to Carolyne was to have taken place.

444 Piazza di Spagna, Rome. Photograph, ca. 1860.
Princess Carolyne lived at 93 Piazza di Spagna before moving to 89 Via Babuino, where she had second-floor rooms during the winter and third-floor rooms in summer. The Via Babuino begins between the two rows of houses on the right of the picture.

WORKS

Die Legende von der Heiligen Elisabeth (oratorio). Work on various movements. The entire work appeared in 1867.
Valse de l'opéra ''Faust'' (Gounod) (piano paraphrase). Written ca. 1861. Pub. 1862.
Der nächtliche Zug (from Lenau's *Faust*) (for piano duet). Pub. 1862.
Pastorale (''Schnitterchor'' from *Chöre zu Herders ''Entfesseltem Prometheus''*) (piano transcriptions for two hands and for four hands). Pub. 1861.
Löse Himmel meine Seele (Lassen) (piano transcription). Pub. 1866.
Lieder by Robert Schumann: 1. *An den Sonnenschein*, 2. *Dem roten Röslein* (piano transcriptions). Written ca. 1861. Pub. 1861.
Revision of Beethoven's works (see ''Works 1857'').

LIFE

January/February: Liszt in Rome, where he works on compositions of a predominantly religious nature. An élite of artists and scholars, aristocrats, and clerics gathers around Liszt, and, as at every period of his life, he is idolized by women. The historian Ferdinand Gregorovius notes in his *Roman Diaries* how an American lady framed the cover of a chair on which Liszt had sat, and hung it on her wall. ''If, like Liszt, a man manages to avoid despising the whole of the human race at such moments, then he deserves high praise.''[136]

11 March: Liszt's *Faust Symphony* is performed in Leipzig under the direction of Hans von Bronsart.

April/May/June: Liszt works on *Die Legende von der Heiligen Elisabeth* in Rome.[137]

3 July: Blandine's son, Daniel Émile, is born.

12 July: Liszt writes to Franz Brendel in Leipzig to tell him that he has completed 140 pages of the full score of his oratorio.

10 August: *Saint Elisabeth* finally completed. Various excursions from Rome, including Albano and Frascati. Giovanni Sgambati becomes a pupil of Liszt's.

11 September: Liszt's daughter Blandine dies at the age of 26 in St Tropez.

October: Liszt suffers much from the loss of his daughter; he is ''so to speak not responsible for his actions, as far as all external affairs are concerned,'' he tells Franz Brendel.[138]

November: Completes his *Variations* on *Weinen, Klagen, Sorgen, Zagen.*

December: Decides to write a *Christus* oratorio.

Liszt's arrangement of the Waltz from Gounod's *Faust* is one of those virtuoso pieces which generally arose at a publisher's request but which he often also transcribed purely out of pleasure in dazzling virtuosity.

His famous pupil Eugen d'Albert, who was a composer and pianist in his own right, once said, ''I should like to compare the virtuoso with the courtesan, the creative artist with the mother. As far as Liszt is concerned, it is doubly amazing that a man who was so much celebrated and so greatly loved should remain personally unaffected by all the glitter and attention with which his triumphant career was accompanied. He was the very embodiment of kindness, modesty, and selflessness, and it was these qualities, combined with brilliant intellectual gifts, which gave his character its transfigured fascination.''[139]

445 Liszt's eldest daughter, Blandine. Photograph by Adam Salomon, Paris, ca. 1860. Born in Geneva on 18 December 1835, Blandine died in St Tropez on 11 September 1862.

Following the death of his twenty-year-old son Daniel in 1859 (see pp. 185 and 211), Liszt was to mourn the passing of his 26-year-old daughter Blandine in 1862. She died two months after the birth of her first son.

446 Title page of an early edition of Liszt's brilliant paraphrase of the Waltz from Gounod's *Faust*, which had first been performed in 1859.

447 Autograph folio sketching out the contents of Liszt's large-scale oratorio *Christus*, begun in 1862 and completed in 1866.

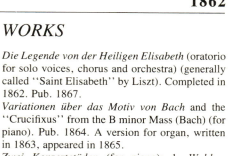

Die Legende von der Heiligen Elisabeth (oratorio for solo voices, chorus and orchestra) (generally called "Saint Elisabeth" by Liszt). Completed in 1862. Pub. 1867.

Variationen über das Motiv von Bach and the "Crucifixus" from the B minor Mass (Bach) (for piano). Pub. 1864. A version for organ, written in 1863, appeared in 1865.

Zwei Konzertetüden (for piano): 1. *Waldesrauschen*, 2. *Gnomenreigen*. Written 1862 or 1863. Pub. 1863.

Berceuse (for piano). Second version. Pub. 1865.

Cantico del Sol di San Francesco d'Assisi (for baritone solo, men's voices, and orchestra). Pub. 1884. A version for piano, written in 1881, was published in 1983. See also "Works 1880."

Alleluja (motives from the *Cantico del Sol*) (for piano). Pub. 1865.

Ave Maria (Arcadelt, arranged by Dietsch) (piano transcription). Pub. 1865. An organ transcription, prepared in 1865, was published at the same time.

Ave Maria (for a piano tutor by Lebert and Stark). Pub. 1863.

A la Chapelle Sixtine, a one-movement work for piano combining variations on the *Miserere* of Gregorio Allegri with Mozart's *Ave verum corpus*. Pub. 1865, together with an organ transcription. A piano duet version appeared in 1866; an orchestral version is unpublished. The *Ave verum corpus* was also issued separately as a piano solo.

Hosannah (from the *Cantico del Sol*) (for organ and trombone). Pub. 1867.

Cujus animam (from Rossini's *Stabat mater*) (for organ and trombone). Written ca. 1862. Pub. 1870. A piano transcription of 1847 had appeared in 1848; a version for high voice and organ was published in 1874.

---

448 *Die Legende von der Heiligen Elisabeth*, title page of the 1867 vocal score.

After many years' work, Liszt completed this oratorio on 10 August 1862. It was dedicated to King Ludwig II of Bavaria and was first performed in Pest on 15 August 1865.

From 1862 onwards the main emphasis of Liszt's creative work shifted to church music. Unlike his other works, his Masses and oratorios are much less frequently performed nowadays than they were in their composer's lifetime, and their occasional appearances in modern concert programmes must be seen as owing mainly to Liszt's great name.

LIFE

January/February: Initial and intensive work on the large-scale oratorio *Christus*.

11 March: Cosima's second child is born. She is christened Blandine after Liszt's eldest daughter, who has died six months earlier.

April/May: Because of disruptive social commitments, work on *Christus* proceeds only slowly. Liszt begins on his piano transcriptions of Beethoven's Symphonies Nos. 1, 2, 3, 4, and 8. He writes in a remarkable vein to Breitkopf & Härtel: ''None the less, a piano arrangement of these works must be content with producing a very feeble and remote approximation. How can one breathe life and soul, sound and strength, fullness and solemnity, colour and accent into the piano's flimsy hammers? – Yet I shall try to get round the worst of its disadvantages, at least, and provide the piano-playing world with the most faithful possible outline of Beethoven's genius. [. . .] The more familiar one becomes with Beethoven, the more one gets attached to certain details and finds that even insignificant things are not wholly worthless . . .''[140]

3 June: First performance of *Slavimo slavno slaveni!* (for men's voices and organ) in Rome.

20 June: Liszt moves from the Via Felice to the Oratorio della Madonna del Rosario on the Monte Mario at the edge of the city (see Illus. 450 and 451).

11 July: Liszt receives a visit from Pope Pius IX in his monastic cell.

16 July: Liszt has a private audience with Pius IX, who gives him a cameo.

August: Liszt works on the piano scores of Beethoven's symphonies.

10 September: Liszt expresses to Carl Gille his thoughts on the meaning behind his stay in Rome (see right-hand column, this page).

October: Liszt immersed in his work on the Monte Mario.

11 November: ''In spite of being withdrawn and cut off, I continue to be much disrupted by visits, social obligations, musical foster children, lengthy – and generally useless – correspondence, and various duties,'' Liszt writes to Franz Brendel.[141]

December: The two *Légendes* for piano are completed. Work on *Christus*.

Liszt settled in Rome in October 1861. From 1869 onwards the Abbé Liszt generally spent the months of January to March/April in Pest (renamed Budapest in 1872), the summer months in Weimar, and the autumn and winter in Rome and Tivoli.

The presence of the Princess, his chosen ecclesiastical status, and the mild winter climate in Rome continued to exercise their sway over him until the end of his life. In the idyllic Villa d'Este he found that sense of seclusion for which he often yearned but which he was scarcely ever allowed to enjoy.

On 10 September 1863 he wrote to Carl Gille from Rome: ''My sojourn in Rome marks the third and probably the last period of my life, which has always been troubled but always industrious and striving upwards. Thus I need a good deal of time to bring various long works – and my life itself – to a satisfactory conclusion. This need I find fulfilled in my present retirement here, which will yet become more extreme. My present monastic abode affords me not only a glorious view over the whole of Rome, the Campagna, and the mountains but also what I had longed for: seclusion and peace [. . .].''[142]

A. Marchetti inc. il paesaggio

1. Monte Mario	13. Chiesa di S. Andrea della Valle
2. Ponte Molle	14. Monte Cavallo
3. Chiesa di S. Giovanni de' Fiorentini	15. Chiesa del Gesù
4. Piazza del Popolo	16. Chiesa di S. Carlo a Catinari
5. Porto di Ripetta	17. Palazzo Farnese
6. Chiesa Nuova	18. Chiesa della Trinità de Pellegrini
7. Chiesa di S. Carlo al Corso	19. Tivoli
8. Chiesa di S. Agnese a Piazza Navona	20. Chiesa di S. Maria Maggiore
9. Scalinata e Ch. della Trinità de Monti	21. Foro Trajano
10. Piazza Colonna	22. Campidoglio
11. Università Romana della Sapienza	23. Tempio della Pace
12. Pantheon	24. Colosseo

VEDUT.
PRESA DAL
Alla Guardia Civica

Liszt's residences in Rome:

1839 (February–June): Via della Purificazione and Via delle Quattro Fontane

1861 (October) – 1863 (June): Via Felice 113

1863 (June) – 1865 (April): Monastery of the Madonna del Rosario on the Monte Mario

1865 (May) – 1866 (June): Vatican, opposite Raphael's *Loggie*

1866 (June–November): Madonna del Rosario[143]

1866 (November) – 1871 (October): Monastery of Santa Francesca Romana; in May and July 1867 he returned briefly to the monastery of the Madonna del Rosario

1868 (October) – 1885: Villa d'Este, Tivoli

1873 (October) – 1880: Via (or Vicolo) dei Greci 43

1880 (December) – 1886 (January): Hotel Alibert, Via Alibert, not far from the Via Barberina and Piazza del Popolo

WORKS

Christus (oratorio) (for chorus, solo voices, and orchestra). Begun in 1863 and completed in 1866. Pub. 1872. A transcription for organ of the chorus *Tu es Petrus* was prepared in 1867. The date of publication is not known. Piano transcriptions of the movements *Hirtengesang* and *Die heiligen drei Könige* appeared in 1873.

Symphonies Nos. 1, 2, 3, 4, and 8 (Beethoven) (piano transcriptions). Nos. 5, 6, and 7, which had appeared at an earlier date, were revised at this time. All the symphonies, including No. 9 (transcribed in 1864), were published in 1865.

Légendes (for piano): 1. *St François d'Assise: la prédication aux oiseaux*, 2. *St François de Paule marchant sur les flots*. Pub. 1866. An orchestral version dating from 1863 was published in 1983. A simplified piano version of No. 2 appeared in 1976.

Salve Polonia (for orchestra). Pub. 1884. Piano versions for two hands and for four hands appeared in 1884.

Slavimo slavno slaveni! (for men's voices and organ). Pub. 1930. Versions for piano, piano duet, and organ ("Andante maestoso") were published ca. 1910.

Rhapsodie espagnole (for piano). Written ca. 1863. Pub. 1867.

Christus ist geboren I and II (words by Theophil Landmesser) (versions of I and II for mixed voices and organ; version of I for men's voices and organ; and versions of II for men's voices with organ postlude, for women's voices, and for piano). Pub. 1865.

Stabat mater speciosa (from *Christus*). Completed in September 1863. Pub. 1872.

Les Sabéennes (*Berceuse* from Gounod's opera *La Reine de Saba*) (piano transcription). Written ca. 1863. Pub. 1865.

2 Preludes from op. 28 (nos. 4 and 9) (Chopin) (organ paraphrase). Written ca. 1863. Pub. 1869.

Pio IX ("*Der Papsthymnus*") (for organ). Written ca. 1863. Pub. 1865, together with versions for piano solo and piano duet. There is also an unpublished transcription for orchestra.

L. Nisi-Cavalieri inc. il Panorama.

ROMA

GIANICOLO

della Città di Bologna

25. Palestrina
26. Chiesa di S. Giovanni Laterano
27. Palazzo de Cesari
28. Tempio di Vesta
29. Acquedotti
30. Frascati
31. Monte Aventino
32. Mura di Roma
33. Sepolcro di Cecilia Metella
34. Piramide di Cajo Cestio
35. Chiesa di S. Paolo
36. Chiesa di S. Pietro

37. Giardino e Palazzo Pontificio
38. Porta Angelica
39. Castel S. Angelo
40. Chiesa di S. Spirito
41. Quercia di Tasso
42. Palazzo e Giardino Corsini
43. Ponte Sisto
44. Isola Tiberina
45. Chiesa di S. Maria in Trastevere
46. Chiesa di S. Pietro in Montorio
47. Fontana dell'Acqua Paola
48. Bosco Parrasio

449 Rome around the time Liszt settled there. Lithograph based on a drawing by A. Marchetti and L. Nisi-Cavalieri; ca. 1860.

Towards the top left-hand corner is the Monte Mario (numbered 1), with the Oratorio della Madonna del Rosario (arrowed), where Liszt lived from 1863 (see Illus. 450 and 451). In front of it is the Vatican whither he moved in 1865 after receiving the four minor orders of the Catholic Church. In front of the Colosseum (24) is the Forum Romanum, where he lived from 1867 (see Illus. 482 and 495), and in the background (19) is Tivoli, which served as Liszt's autumn and winter retreat from 1869. Here in the Villa d'Este Cardinal Gustav von Hohenlohe placed several rooms at Liszt's disposal (see Illus. 530 and 543).

450 The Ponte S. Angelo with the Castel S. Angelo, Rome. Photograph, ca. 1865.

In the background is the Monte Mario, with the Oratorio della Madonna del Rosario (arrowed) in the top left-hand corner.

451 Oratorio della Madonna del Rosario. Photograph, ca. 1970.

Liszt occupied a number of rooms on the first floor (farthest left in the picture, behind the window beneath which a white plaque can be seen). The Oratorio still exists, scarcely altered, its official address being 177 Via Trionfale.

Opposite page:

452 Autograph alterations in a new version of Liszt's four-part Mass for male voices. Previously unpublished.

These two pages of sketches (in the possession of Frau Eleonore Recher) were only partially used in the definitive version of 1869.

On 20 June 1863 Liszt moved into a small apartment in the sixteenth-century monastery of the Madonna del Rosario on the Monte Mario outside Rome. He lived there for two years, before moving to the Vatican on 25 April 1865. In June 1866 he returned to the Monte Mario.

On 25 July 1863 Liszt wrote to his mother from Rome: "[. . .] My new apartment has awakened in me the greatest desire to work. You know the extraordinary honour which the Holy Father has shown me [Pius IX had visited him on 11 July], and you will understand that such a visit, to which no worldly honour can compare, has merely confirmed me in a resolve which I had already taken to settle permanently in Rome. Apart from me, the only other people in the building are the priest, a brother who supervises the kitchen in most excellent fashion, and my manservant [. . .]."[144]

Liszt's pupil August Stradal visited his mentor's former apartment in 1885: "There was a magnificent view from the monastery. Far below lay the Eternal City, behind it the Campagna Romana, and beyond that the Monti Sabini and Monti Albani. [. . .] I visited the room: a stone floor without carpets or rugs, a bed, a crucifix, a prie-dieu, a simple table! A deep sense of sadness came over me. After a life filled with the greatest successes which a virtuoso has ever known – such poverty, privation, and immersion in unworldly isolation! I saw two worlds: Liszt traversing the whole of Europe showered with honours and marks of distinction from the highest potentates, and then – Santa Maria del Rosario!"[145]

LIFE

January: Liszt lives in seclusion in the Oratorio della Madonna del Rosario, although even here he is perpetually interrupted by visits from friends and admirers.

22 January: Liszt rejects all attempts to lure him back to Germany: ''Leave me in peace, leave me to dream, not, it is true, beneath the 'blossoming almond trees' that Hoffmann sings of, but comforted and secure in the protection offered by the 'Madonna del Rosario,' who has granted me this cell. My German friends would be far wiser to visit me here than to entice me back to their German provinces,'' Liszt writes to Franz Brendel.[146]

March: Liszt appears at a concert in Rome for the benefit of Peter's Pence. At the request of Breitkopf & Härtel he has been preparing piano scores of all the Beethoven symphonies. He now completes this work, adding the fourth movement of the Ninth Symphony at a later date.

May: Ede Reményi, a violinist friend of Liszt's, is in Rome for two months, and the two men meet almost daily.

4 May: King Ludwig II of Bavaria enters Wagner's life as a generous benefactor. ''What a royal miracle, this letter of Ludwig of Bavaria's to Wagner! It really ought to be carved in letters of gold in Valhalla. I only wish a few other princes would adopt such a style,'' Liszt writes to Franz Brendel from Rome on 28 May 1864.[147]

July: Liszt spends a few days in the Villa d'Este as guest of Cardinal Hohenlohe. Towards the end of the month he plays for the Pope at Castel Gandolfo.

9 August: Liszt sets off for Karlsruhe, his first visit to Germany since 1862.

21 to 26 August: Tonkünstlerversammlung in Karlsruhe, where Liszt meets many of his old German friends; then to Munich to see Cosima. He visits Bülow, who is confined to bed, seriously ill, at the Hotel Bayerischer Hof.

30/31 August: Guest of Wagner at Haus Pellet on Lake Starnberg, where Liszt gets to know those parts of The Mastersingers which have so far been completed. Visits Kaulbach and then spends a few days in Stuttgart.

5 September: Revisits Weimar, including the ''Blue Room'' at the Altenburg.

13 to 17 September: As guest of Prince von Hohenzollern in Löwenberg, then a few days in Berlin.

24 September: In Weimar; then, on the 27th, back in Berlin with Hans and Cosima von Bülow.

28 September to 2 October: As guest of the Grand Duke's family in Wilhelmsthal.

4 to 12 October: Accompanies Cosima to Paris. Reunion with his mother and the Comtesse d'Agoult.

12 October: Liszt travels via Toulon to St Tropez to visit the grave of his daughter Blandine, two years after her death. After a brief stay in Marseilles, he returns to Rome.

15 November: Liszt writes a generous letter to Marie d'Agoult, commenting on his controversial works: ''Should it come about that my Divine Comedy Symphony or the symphony that I was inspired to write by Goethe's Faust are ever performed in Paris, I would ask you only to be kind enough to give them a patient hearing . . .''[148]

14 December: Liszt is invited by Baron Prónay to conduct the first performance of his Saint Elisabeth in Paris.

Liszt had chosen his new residence in the hope of being able to devote himself to his work, cut off from the world in his monastic cell on the Monte Mario. But his admirers soon ran him to ground, and scarcely a day went by when he was not visited by friends and pupils or by others whom mere curiosity had brought to the monastery gates.

The violinist Ede Reményi (whom no less a person than Johannes Brahms had accompanied on the piano around 1850; see Illus. 388) gave six concerts in Rome's Teatro Argentina in 1864. He visited Liszt almost every day and finally talked him into agreeing to a photographic souvenir of the occasion (Illus. 453). Reményi died during a concert in San Francisco in 1898. It was for Reményi's wedding to Gizella Fay in 1872 that Liszt wrote his Epithalam.

Also seen in the photograph is the Hungarian pianist Ferdinand Plotényi (1844–1933), whom Reményi adopted as his son and whom he trained as his regular accompanist. Plotényi returned to his native Hungary in 1890 and built a castle which soon became the centre of musical life in Upper Hungary. He continued to play the piano until his death at the age of 89, but he performed in public only for charity.

453 Left to right: Ede Reményi, Ferdinand Plotényi, and Franz Liszt. Photograph by ''Photo Americaine,'' Rome 1864 (see Illus. 477).

''Photo Americaine'' was the name of a studio opened by Achille Sanglau in the Palazzo Lovati in the Piazza del Popolo on 1 January 1863.

The diplomat and historian Kurd von Schlözer (1822–1894), in a letter of 1 June 1864:

''The day before yesterday I visited Liszt at his monastery of Santa Maria del Rosario on the Monte Mario, with its magnificent view of Rome and the mountains. It used to be densely populated, for the number of cells is by no means insignificant. Now the only people who live there are a single Dominican, the monastery servant, and Liszt. Every morning the Dominican says mass in the small church that faces the country road. Liszt is always there; he sits, prince-like, in an enclosed balcony with a window, situated only a few paces from his cell – just like Carlos V in the monastery of San Just, where, if necessary, he could hear mass from his bed. [. . .] Liszt owes this apartment to his friend Father Theiner, a man known for his ultramontane views, whom he had told of his desire for a calm and quiet cell.

''In the middle of a fairly large room is a long desk, with a small private library arranged along the walls; here and in the window alcoves I also counted some twelve pictures of saints, of varying sizes. On a corner table is Chopin's hand carved in marble; beside it is an etui containing a ring which Pius IX gave Liszt when he visited him last year. Next to the desk is a fairly ancient piano which also suffers from being badly tuned, and – funniest of all – the D in the bass does not work. It is at such an instrument that Franz Liszt now works, the same man before whom the most massive grand pianos of Europe once trembled and who for half a generation has ruled the entire artistic world like some Jupiter tonans. He scarcely ever plays any longer; in his apartment he uses the piano only for composing. He is at present occupied in transcribing Beethoven's Ninth Symphony. [. . .]

''I was just on the point of leaving him two days ago when his fellow countryman Reményi arrived, a brilliant violinist, who brought with him not only his violin but the English vice-consul in Naples, a Mr Douglas, together with the latter's wife and daughter. And since Liszt had recently composed Lenau's Gypsy song [Die drei Zigeuner] Reményi, who has arranged it for the violin, played it for us. Liszt accompanied him on the piano, without its D. But it is a highly original composition, and while he was playing it Reményi's Hungarian blood was so stirred that he all but danced around, just like his fellow Magyars on the puszta.

''When they had finished, there followed a typically British scene. Mr Douglas suddenly rushed up to Liszt and said: 'May I beg a favour of you?' 'By all means.' 'May I play just one chord on your instrument?' 'Play as many as you like,' Liszt answered. Whereupon Mr Douglas strode majestically over to the piano, struck a chord, and then took out his notebook and entered in it that on Monday, 30 May 1864, at four o'clock in the afternoon in the monastery of Santa Maria del Rosario, where Liszt was staying, he, Douglas, had played a chord on the great man's piano.''[149]

454 Cosima von Bülow. Photograph by Joseph Albert, ca. 1864. In 1864 Liszt visited Karlsruhe, Munich, and Paris in the company of his daughter Cosima, who was later to become Wagner's wife.

On 27 January 1864 Liszt wrote to Carl Gille: "[. . .] What satisfaction could it give me to gad about so idly and so fruitlessly? Have not many years of superficial activity taught me the advantages of isolation?

" 'Aemulomini antem charismata meliora!' My higher calling is to be free to feel and create, not to play and beg for success. For that reason, all I need is calm and secluded independence, an independence which I have finally gained here and which no kingdom on earth can ever replace. [. . .] To return to Germany I should first have to step over a grave – beyond which a further grave awaits me. This, my dear friend, is no figurative way of speaking, for you know what I have lost with Blandine and Daniel! [. . .]"[150] (Shortly before this Liszt had lost his nineteen-year-old son Daniel and his 26-year-old daughter Blandine.) His longing to find peace was to remain unfulfilled. He spent the last twenty years of his life travelling back and forth every year among his three homes in Rome, Budapest, and Weimar. Between mid-August and October 1864 alone we find him in Rome, Karlsruhe, Munich, Stuttgart, Weimar, Löwenberg, Berlin, Wilhelmsthal, Paris, Toulon, St Tropez, Marseilles, and back again in Rome.

J. ALBERT
Königl. bayer. u. kaiserlich russischer
HOF-PHOTOGRAPH
MÜNCHEN.

WORKS

Symphony No. 9 (Beethoven) (piano transcription). Pub. 1865 (together with the other eight Beethoven symphonies).
La Notte (for orchestra). Pub. 1916. A piano version of ca. 1864 appeared as late as 1980; and a version for piano duet, prepared in 1866, is unpublished. The version for violin and piano dating from ca. 1865 was published in America ca. 1978. (See also "Works 1866.")
Ora pro nobis. Litany (for organ). Pub. 1865.
Urbi et orbi. Bénédiction papale (for piano). Pub. 1878.
Vexilla regis prodeunt (for piano). Pub. ca. 1982. A version for orchestra is unpublished.
Stabat mater (for piano), using a theme also found in the twelfth movement of *Christus*, possibly dates from this time. Published in 1978. See "Works 1866."
Soldiers' Chorus from *Faust* (Gounod) (piano transcription). Mentioned by Liszt in a letter to Bülow of 20 December 1866, where it is said to have been "prepared two years ago." Lost.
Confutatis and *Lacrymosa* (from Mozart's *Requiem*) (piano transcriptions). Pub. 1865.
Der, welcher wandelt diese Straße ("Adagio") from *The Magic Flute* (Mozart) (piano duet transcription). Year of composition unknown. Unpublished. Manuscript in Library of Congress.

Shortly before receiving the four minor orders, Liszt busied himself with the task of preparing piano transcriptions of Beethoven's Symphonies Nos. 1, 2, 3, 4, 8, and 9, and of revising his transcriptions of Symphonies Nos. 5, 6, and 7, which had already been published. For Liszt these works were the most glorious music ever written, and his aim in preparing these arrangements was to make them known to a wider audience. The piano offered this possibility, not least because good orchestral performances were still a rarity at this time. On 14 September 1864 he wrote to Breitkopf & Härtel, "I hope you will not take it amiss if I regard my revision of Beethoven's Symphonies as fully complete with the third movement of the Ninth, since it is not in my line to prepare a simple piano reduction of this momentous fourth movement for the use of choral conductors. [. . .] Schott's edition of the Ninth Symphony for two pianos made it possible to reduce the essential elements of the orchestral polyphony to ten fingers and hand over the chorus to the other performer. But to reduce both parts, instrumental and vocal, to two hands is possible neither *à peu près* nor even *à beaucoup près*!"[151] (In response to Härtel's insistent demands, Liszt later agreed after all to arrange the Ninth Symphony for piano solo.)

455 Franz Liszt. This little-known photograph, taken around 1864, is also one of the last photographs to show Liszt not wearing his abbé's cassock.

LIFE

January: Liszt in Rome, where he works on his *Missa choralis*, which is dedicated to the Pope. He expresses his delight at Mosonyi's "magisterial and exemplary" piano score of the *"Gran" Mass.*[152]

24 February: Liszt takes part in a concert in Rome organized by the banker's wife Isabel Cholmeley, who sings a number of Liszt's songs.

23 March: At a concert in the Great Hall of the Capitol Liszt performs his *Cantique d'amour* and piano transcription of Rossini's *La Charité*.

15 April: First performance of *Totentanz* in The Hague, with Bülow as soloist.

20 April: At the Palazzo Barberini Liszt performs Weber's *Invitation to the Dance* and his transcription of *Erlkönig*. It is his concert farewell to the glamour of secular music. The very next day he repairs to the Lazarite monastery in Rome to begin his spiritual exercises.

25 April: Liszt enters the clergy and receives minor orders. The ceremony of tonsure is performed by the Lord Almoner, Prince Hohenlohe.

May: Liszt moves into rooms opposite Raphael's *Loggie* in the Vatican, having left his apartment on the Monte Mario immediately after receiving minor orders.

25 May: First performance of Liszt's *Pater noster* from *Christus* in Dessau, on the occasion of the *Tonkünstlerversammlung* organized by the Allgemeiner Deutscher Musikverein.

July: Liszt spends a few days as guest of Gustav von Hohenlohe at the Villa d'Este.

30 July: Liszt receives three further ecclesiastical orders.

8 August to 12 September: In Hungary.

14 August: Public dress rehearsal of Liszt's *Saint Elisabeth* in the Redoute in Pest.

15 August: Liszt conducts the first performance of *Saint Elisabeth* in the Redoute in Pest.

17 August: Liszt conducts his orchestral version of the *Rákóczy March* and the first part of his *Dante Symphony* in Pest.

23 August: Further performance of *Saint Elisabeth* in the Redoute in Pest.

25 August: As guest of Count Károlyi in Fót.

27/28 August: Liszt, Cosima, Bülow, Reményi, and Plotényi as guests of Primate Scitovszky in Gran (Esztergom).

29 August: Liszt gives the first performance of the two piano *Légendes* in the Redoute in Pest; Bülow and Reményi also appear at the same concert.

2 to 8 September: Liszt, Cosima and Hans von Bülow, Reményi, and Plotényi are guests of Baron Antal Augusz in Szekszárd.

18 September: Back in Rome, where Liszt works on his choral arrangement of *Pio IX* ("Tu es Petrus").

29 September: Remembering the poor response to his *Prometheus-Chöre* in Vienna in 1860, Liszt declines Herbeck's offer to perform *Saint Elisabeth* in the city.[153]

October: King Ludwig II commands a performance of *Saint Elisabeth* in Munich. (It takes place on 24 February 1866.)

November: Liszt works on *Christus* in the Vatican.

December: After an interruption lasting several weeks, Liszt resumes work on his *Christus*.

456 Decree concerning Liszt's taking minor orders.

457, 458 Franz Liszt. Photographs by Canzi és Heller, August 1865. The first photographs to show Liszt dressed as an abbé.

On 25 April 1865 Liszt received the tonsure from the Grand Almoner (later Cardinal) Gustav von Hohenlohe, the brother of the German Chancellor Prince Konstantin von Hohenlohe-Schillingsfürst. He received three more orders on 30 July 1865, making a total of four out of the seven degrees of priesthood. As such he was a cleric but not a priest. He could still have married or resumed his secular status, but he was obliged to hear mass once a day and to wear clerical vestments. Until the end of his life Liszt read his Breviary every day, although only those ordained as deacons are strictly obliged to do so.

"He received the tonsure and the first of the minor orders from Monsignor Hohenlohe in St Peter's," Ferdinand Gregorovius wrote in his *Römische Tagebücher* in May 1865. "He now wears the abbé's cassock, lives in the Vatican, and is said to look well and to be satisfied. This is the end of the brilliant virtuoso, and of a truly sovereign personality. I am glad I heard Liszt play; he and the instrument seemed to have grown together as a single being, a sort of piano centaur [. . .]."

The whole world was mystified by Liszt's surprising step, or else they ridiculed it. It was said that he wanted to attract attention (although at no time in his life did Liszt need to stage-manage his own affairs). Liszt himself made his reasons clear on several occasions: "Convinced, as I was, that this act would fortify me on the path of righteousness, I performed it without compulsion, in all simplicity and honesty of intention. It is consistent, moreover, with the early intentions of my youth [. . .].[154] I really have accepted clerical status – but certainly not out of any contempt for the world, still less from aversion to art [. . .].[155] My predisposition towards Catholicism dates back to my childhood, and has become a constant and dominating feeling [. . .]."

WORKS

Missa choralis (for mixed voices and organ). Pub. 1869.

Crux! (sailors' hymn) (versions for male voices and for female/children's voices and piano). Pub. 1865.

Christus (oratorio) (*Introduction, Pastorale, Annunciation, Entry into Jerusalem*). The complete oratorio was published in 1872.

Ave maris stella (for mixed voices and organ). Pub. 1870. A version for voice and piano appeared in 1868, a piano transcription in 1871, and an organ transcription in 1880.

Weimars Volkslied (organ transcription). Pub. 1873. (See "Works 1857".)

Regina coeli laetare (Lassus) (organ transcription). Pub. 1869.

Rákóczy March (orchestral version). Pub. 1871, together with a piano version for four hands, and two versions for piano solo. (There is also a version for two pianos, and another, at least supervised by Liszt, for two pianos eight hands.)

Mazurka-fantasie (Bülow) (orchestral transcription). Pub. ca. 1890.

Illustration de "l'Africaine" (Meyerbeer) (for piano): 1. *Prière des matelots*, 2. *Marche indienne*. Pub. 1866.

Adagio and *Moderato* (two short piano pieces eventually grouped together with three other pieces, all in the collection of Baroness von Meyendorff). Pub. 1928.

Tre Sonetti di Petrarca (second version, for baritone or mezzo-soprano and piano). Written ca. 1865. Pub. 1883.

459 A moving letter written by Liszt's mother to her famous son on 4 May 1865, following the news that he had taken holy orders.

". . . So live happily, my dear child, and if the blessing of a feeble old mother can achieve aught with the Almighty, then I bless you a thousand times . . ." (For a translation of the complete text, see p. 342.)

460 Abbé Liszt. Silhouette by Fritz Schulz, ca. 1868.

463 Liszt conducting the first performance of his *Legende von der Heiligen Elisabeth* in the Redoutensaal in Pest on 15 August 1865. Wood engraving from the *Illustrirte Zeitung* of 16 September 1865, based on a drawing by Jean Hubert Reve.

The world premiere of Liszt's three-hour oratorio *Die Legende von der Heiligen Elisabeth* in the new Redoute in Pest (opened on 15 January) was widely regarded as a major musical event. Many leading musicians came from far and near, including Bedřich Smetana from Prague. The auditorium, which held almost three thousand people, was sold out days in advance. The chorus and orchestra, under the composer's baton, comprised around five hundred performers.

№ 1159. 16. September 1865.]   Illustrirte Zeitung.   193

Franz Liszt als Dirigent beim ersten Musik- und Sängerfest in Pest am 15. August. Nach einer Zeichnung von J. Reve.

461 From left to right: Cosima von Bülow, Heinrich Wilhelm Ernst (?), Franz Liszt, and Hans von Bülow. Photograph, Pest 1865.

Bülow and his wife (who by this time was already Wagner's mistress) attended the premiere of Liszt's *Die Legende von der Heiligen Elisabeth* in Pest in August 1865, after which they were invited to Gran, with Liszt, as guests of Primate Johann von Scitovszky. The three of them then travelled to Szekszárd to spend a few days with Baron Antal Augusz.

462 (right) A review of the Pest premiere of Liszt's *Die Legende von der Heiligen Elisabeth*, reproduced from the *Illustrirte Zeitung* of 16 September 1865. (For a translation of the text, see p. 342.)

Franz Liszt als Dirigent beim ersten Musik- und Sängerfeste in Pest.

R. — Am 15. Aug. wurde der 25jährige Bestand des pest-ofener Conservatoriums durch ein Musikfest im größten Stile begangen. Franz Liszt, der Liebling der Nation und die erste musikalische Größe des Landes, war die Seele dieses Festes, welches von einem Comité unter dem Vorsitze des Frhrn. Béla v. Orczy ins Werk gesetzt wurde. Wie auf Liszt stets die Aufmerksamkeit und die Bewunderung des Landes von dem Augenblicke an hafteten, wo der neunjährige Knabe sein erstes öffentliches Concertstück spielt, bis zu dem Momente, wo die von Träumen des Ehrgeizes bewegte Brust des Künstlers sich unter das Kleid der Entsagung geflüchtet, so war der Jubel außerordentlich, als Liszt am 15. Aug. an das Dirigentenpult trat, um sein Oratorium: „Die heilige Elisabeth von Ungarn", in dem festlichen Redoutensaale zum ersten mal in lebendigen Tönen erklingen zu lassen. Der Autor, den man bisher gewohnt war, in seinen symphonischen Dichtungen unaufhaltsam vorwärts stürmen zu sehen, führt in diesem Oratorium mit fester Hand die Zügel der Töne. Es ist von einer großartigen Conception und fesselt durch eine farbenvolle Instrumentirung. In dem Festconcerte vom 17. Aug. wurde der erste Theil von Liszt's „Dante-Symphonie" aufgeführt. Außerdem hatten Robert Volkmann, Generalmusikdirector Franz Erkel und Mosonyi neue Compositionen für das erste ungarische Musikfest geliefert, die Beifall errangen. Sonntag am 20., als am Tage des heiligen Stephan's, Schutzpatrons von Ungarn, wurde ein Ausflug der versammelten 50 Sängervereine nach dem Stadtwäldchen unternommen; Musikkapellen spielten an allen Orten, mit dem Gesang der tausendstimmigen Chöre abwechselnd. Freudenfeuer erleuchteten die Wälder und erst spät abends gingen die unendlichen Menschenmassen jubelnd nach Hause.

LIFE

4 January: First performance of the *Stabat mater speciosa* from *Christus* in the Franciscan church of S. Maria in Aracoeli in Rome.

Liszt works on *Christus* in the Vatican.

6 February: Liszt's mother dies in Paris.

24 February: First performance in Germany of Liszt's *Die Legende von der Heiligen Elisabeth* (in Munich).

26 February: Sgambati conducts Liszt's *Dante Symphony* in Rome to inaugurate the Sala Dante. At the same time an exhibition is held at which the main scenes from Dante's *Divine Comedy* are shown on 27 large canvases by contemporary Italian painters.

1 March: Repeat performance of *Die Legende von der Heiligen Elisabeth* under Bülow in Munich.

3 March: Liszt arrives in Paris, where he stays with his son-in-law Émile Ollivier.

5 March: Repeat performance of the *Dante Symphony* under Sgambati in Rome.

8 March: Liszt plays his two St Francis *Légendes* for Princess Metternich in Paris; he also plays duets with Camille Saint-Saëns.

15 March: Performance of the "*Gran*" *Mass* in St-Eustache in Paris. Inadequate rehearsals mean only a limited success. A few days later Liszt breaks definitively with Marie d'Agoult.

April: Liszt is decorated with the Order of St Michael by King Ludwig II of Bavaria. In Paris he invites Berlioz, Kreutzer, d'Ortigue, Damcke, and other critics who have reproached him for "unresolved dissonances" in the "*Gran*" *Mass* to his apartment, where he demonstrates their resolution.

21 April: Liszt visits the Emperor Napoleon III.

24 April: In Amsterdam.

25 April: Liszt concert in Amsterdam, including *Psalm xiii*, various piano pieces played by Bülow, and Liszt's transcription for piano and orchestra of Schubert's *Wandererfantasie*.

27 April: Second concert in Amsterdam. Bülow plays Liszt's *Rhapsodie espagnole* and Beethoven's G major Piano Concerto. The programme also includes *Les Préludes*.

29 April: "*Gran*" *Mass* in Amsterdam. Liszt returns to Paris via The Hague (30 April) and Brussels (1 May).

Early May: Liszt performs at one of Rossini's matinees, playing his arrangements for two pianos (with Francis Planté) of *Les Préludes* and *Tasso*; he plays the same pieces on 9 May at the home of Chopin's pupil Princess Czartoryska; and on 11 May he and Saint-Saëns play the *Dante Symphony* for two pianos at the home of the famous illustrator Gustave Doré.

15 May: Liszt leaves Paris for Rome.

Early June: Liszt's friend Gustav von Hohenlohe becomes cardinal and gives up his rooms in the Vatican, where Liszt has been living. Liszt returns to the Oratorio della Madonna del Rosario.

July/August/September: Liszt works on *Christus* in Rome.

1 October: Completes *Christus*.

23 October: Liszt to Carl Gille on his oratorio: "When and where I have it performed does not worry me in the slightest. It is an artistic necessity for me to write my things; it is enough for me to have written them, without laying claim to other favours . . ."[156]

December: Liszt works on his *Hungarian Coronation Mass*.

464 The Palace of Count István Károlyi in Fót. Photograph, ca. 1970.

Towards the end of August 1865 Liszt came to Fót on his second visit to Count Károlyi (the first had been on 3 September 1856). Liszt frequently stayed with Hungarian friends at their country houses, including visits to Dáka (Count Festetics), Högyész (Count Apponyi), and Bánlak (Count Karácsonyi) in 1846, Szekszárd (Baron Antal Augusz) in 1865, 1870, and 1877, Horpács (Count Széchényi) in 1872 and 1874, Hosszúpályi (Count Ernö Zichy) in 1879, Ödenburg (Prince Esterházy) in 1881, and Tetétlen (Count Géza Zichy) in 1884.

465 Salon in Rome, with Liszt and Anton Rubinstein in the background. Wood engraving "taken from life" by H. Bürck, ca. 1875.

Kurd von Schlözer: "How many times is he invited to play for society gatherings when he has no desire to do so! He then becomes effusively polite towards his hosts, speaks wittily about music, goes over to the piano, strikes some chord or other, takes in the whole room with his flashing and demonically sarcastic gaze, and then, murmuring the words 'You blockheads!' to himself, takes his hat and slips away."[157]

466 Abbé Liszt with Pope Pius IX and (to Liszt's right) Cardinal Antonelli, in the cloisters of the Church of St John Lateran in Rome. Wood engraving based on a drawing by Paul Thumann, ca. 1866.

Pope Pius IX held Liszt in high regard. Accompanied by Monsignor Merode and Lord Almoner Gustav von Hohenlohe, Pius IX visited Liszt at the Oratorio della Madonna del Rosario on 11 July 1863, and heard Liszt perform his recently completed *Légende* for piano, *St François d'Assise: la prédication aux oiseaux*. At the end of July 1864 Liszt was the Pope's guest at Castel Gandolfo.

467 View of the Vatican from the Monte Pincio. Photograph, ca. 1868.

Liszt received minor orders on 25 April 1865 and moved to the Vatican, where he occupied an apartment facing the *Stanze* decorated with Raphael's frescoes. He was a frequent guest in clerical circles. On 21 July 1868, to mark the twentieth anniversary of Pius IX's coronation, Liszt played a number of his own piano works in the Vatican Library for an audience including the Pope himself (see Illus. 481).

WORKS

Christus (*Stabat mater dolorosa*, *Resurrexit*, and *Tristis est anima*). The work is now complete, save for the movements *O filii et filiae* and *Die Gründung der Kirche*, added in 1867. Complete work published in 1872.

Hungarian Coronation Mass (for the coronation of the Emperor Franz Joseph I and Empress Elisabeth as King and Queen of Hungary on 8 June 1867). Written 1866/67. Pub. 1869. The *Benedictus* and *Offertorium* appeared in 1871 in a piano version for two hands dating from 1867, in a piano version for four hands from 1869, and versions for violin and organ (ca. 1870) and violin and piano (1869). The *Benedictus* was arranged for violin and orchestra in 1875 and published in 1877. The *Offertorium* was arranged for organ/harmonium/pedal pianoforte at some date after 1867.

Dall"alma Roma (for two-part chorus and organ). Based on *Die Gründung der Kirche* from *Christus*. Unpub.

Trois Odes Funèbres (for orchestra):
1. *Les Morts* (with chorus added in 1866). Pub. 1916. See ''Works 1860.''
2. *La Notte*. See ''Works 1864.'' In 1866 Liszt asked that this work be played at his funeral. It was not.
3. *Le Triomphe funèbre du Tasse*. Pub. 1877. A piano version for two hands, prepared in 1866, appeared in 1878; versions for piano duet and for two pianos, written in 1866 and 1869, are unpublished.

Hymne an die Heilige Cäcilie (for piano). Lost. Possibly contains material used in the choral work of 1874. May be identical with an unpublished piano transcription of Gounod's *Hymne à Sainte Cécile* made in 1866.

Piano piece in A flat. Published by the Liszt Society, London, 1988, and previously printed in *The Piano Student* in 1935. Not to be confused with the piano piece in A flat No. 2, containing the theme of the first *Ballade*, which was probably written down between 1845 and 1848 and published in 1966.

471 The interior of Saint-Eustache, Paris. Lithograph by Philippe Benoist, based on a drawing by Chapuy; ca. 1865.

Liszt's *"Gran" Mass* was performed here on 15 March 1866. The proceeds (which according to the *Gazette musicale* and by Liszt's own reckoning amounted to 50,000 francs) were donated to Paris's schools.

The definitive breach between Franz Liszt and Marie d'A-goult took place in March 1866. Her disparagement of Liszt in her 1846 novel *Nélida* can perhaps be regarded as a thoughtless act of revenge; but her publishing a new edition of the novel in 1866, twenty years after its first appearance, almost certainly contributed to the tone of hostility on which their final encounter ended.

On 13 April 1866 Liszt wrote to Carolyne von Sayn-Wittgenstein from Paris, "Here is a brief report on the evening I spent with Nélida [Marie d'Agoult], who will not of course be inviting me again. I have hesitated to tell you about it until now, although I saw her twice on her own. [. . .] Né-lida told me that she was intending to publish her memoirs. I replied that I considered it impossible for her to write any such memoirs, since anything so entitled would be nothing but dissimulation and lies. – This was the first time I have ever really sorted things out with her on the question of truth and falsehood. These are harsh words, but it was my duty to speak them. [. . .] I may add that the role of Guermann [Liszt's code name in *Nélida*] is a foolish conceit. It is time to put an end once and for all to this kind of didactic senti-mentalism. Madame d'Agoult does not *need* to show le-niency towards me. With my hand on my heart I believe I may say that I have the truth on my side, and I have nothing else to reproach myself for except the occasional violence in my manner. Unfortunately, however, there is no way of say-ing such things in a form which would be agreeable to those who are hurt by them. Hitting people with a fan is not the way to conduct a surgical operation."[158]

468 Franz Liszt. Photograph by Pierre Petit, Paris 1866.

469, 470 Comtesse Marie d'Agoult. Two pho-tographs taken in Paris around 1866, the year of her last encounter with Liszt.

In October 1866 she opened her old diary from 1839 and added a resigned postscript to the earlier entries: "Reread these lines in Saint-Lu-picin, 15 October 1866. – 28 years later! What has *he* done with these 28 years? And what have *I* done? He is the Abbé Liszt, and I am Daniel Stern [her *nom de plume*]! And so much despair, so many deaths, so much weeping, sobbing, and grief between us!"[159]

LIFE

January to March: Liszt works on his *Hungarian Coronation Mass* in Rome.

March: Liszt tranfers his hereditary knighthood to his uncle, Dr Eduard Liszt. Liszt himself has never used the title.

14 April: Liszt completes his *Hungarian Coronation Mass*.

May: King Ludwig II of Bavaria expresses his enthusiasm for Liszt's *Die Legende von der Heiligen Elisabeth*, which is dedicated to him. A vocal score of the work is published by Kahnt in 1867 (see Illus. 448).

4 to 16 June: Liszt in Pest.

6 June: Audience with the Emperor Franz Joseph I, to whom Liszt presents a holy relic as a gift from the Pope. On 7 June he is invested with the Commander's Cross of the Order of Franz Joseph.

8 June: Performance of the *Coronation Mass* in St Michael's Church in Buda on the occasion of the coronation of the Emperor Franz Joseph I and Empress Elisabeth as King and Queen of Hungary.

6 July: Sgambati conducts the first performance of the *Christmas Oratorio* from *Christus* in the Sala Dante in Rome.

25 July: Liszt travels to Weimar at the invitation of the Grand Duke Carl Alexander.

29 July: Liszt arrives in Weimar, where he stays in his "Blue Room" at the Altenburg (see Illus. 355).

23 to 25 August: At the *Tonkünstlerversammlung* in Meiningen.

28 August: Successful performance of *Die Legende von der Heiligen Elisabeth* under Liszt's baton in the Hall of Song on the Wartburg to mark the 800th anniversary of the Wartburg.

31 August to 18 September: As guest of Grand Duke Carl Alexander in Wilhelmsthal. Liszt travels to Munich via Meiningen (19 September).

21 September to 28 October: In Munich (Hotel Marienbad), including an excursion to Lucerne to see Wagner.

3 October: Arrives in Stuttgart for three days' stay.

9 October: Hoping to avert a public (and personally distressing) scandal arising from the affair between Wagner and his daughter Cosima, Liszt travels to Lucerne to discuss the matter with Wagner, but in vain.

20 October: Liszt writes to his uncle, Eduard von Liszt: "If Bülow remains active here for a few years, Munich will become the musical centre of Germany. Apart from musical matters, my stay here has offered me a great deal of interest and pleasure through my meetings with Kaulbach, Liebig, Heyse, Geibel, Redwitz, etc. . . ."[160]

November: Liszt works at the Monastery of Santa Francesca Romana in Rome (see Illus. 482).

3 December: To Liszt's regret, the Neu-Weimar-Verein (founded is 1854) is disbanded.

475 Franz Liszt wearing the cowl of a Franciscan monk. Anonymous bronze plaquette, ca. 1865.

476 An example of Liszt's calligraphy around 1870 (reduced in size). Original manuscript of a heretofore unknown cadenza by Liszt for Beethoven's Third Piano Concerto in C minor, op. 37.[161]

WORKS

Hungarian Coronation Mass (completed in April). Pub. 1869. (See "Works 1866".)
Christus. Added movements *Die Gründung der Kirche* and *O filii et filiae*. Complete oratorio published in 1872.
Marche funèbre (on the death of the Emperor Maximilian of Mexico), No. 6 of the *Années de Pèlerinage. Troisième Année* (for piano). Pub. 1883.
Benedictus and *Offertorium* from the *Hungarian Coronation Mass* (piano transcriptions). Pub. 1871.
Isoldens Liebestod from *Tristan and Isolde* (Wagner) (piano transcription). Pub. 1871.
Fantaisie sur l'opéra hongrois Szép Ilonka (Mosonyi) (piano paraphrase). Pub. 1868.

473 Grand Duke Carl Alexander of Saxe-Weimar. Photograph by Louis Held, Weimar 1888.

472 Grand Duchess Sophie, daughter of King William II of the Netherlands and, from 1842, wife of Grand Duke Carl Alexander of Saxe-Weimar. Photograph by Louis Held, Weimar 1889, taken three years before the couple's golden wedding.

When Carl Alexander became Grand Duke of Weimar in 1853, Liszt found himself serving an honest individual who was to become, as far as their difference in status would allow, an intimate friend. Notwithstanding the Princess's epistolary remarks that "the Grand Duke does not deserve Liszt and cannot give him what he does deserve" and that "they have a Liszt, a man of such farsighted vision, and they employ him beating time for *La Favorita* and *Martha*," the two men remained devoted to each other until Liszt's death.

Liszt gave up his appointment as Court Kapellmeister in Weimar in 1859 and left the town two years later, but Carl Alexander succeeded in persuading him to return there in 1869. The Grand Duke placed rooms in the Hofgärtnerei at his disposal, and Liszt spent several months there every year, devoting himself to composing and teaching. An extensive correspondence between the two men has survived and was published in Leipzig in 1909.

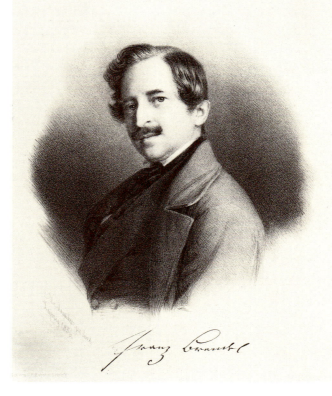

474 Franz Brendel (1811–1868). Lithograph by Otto Merseburger, Leipzig 1856.

In 1844 Brendel became editor of the *Neue Zeitschrift für Musik*, which Robert Schumann had founded ten years earlier, but far from continuing in the spirit of its founder he guided the journal in the direction of the "New German School." Together with Liszt he established the Allgemeiner Deutscher Musikverein in 1859, becoming its president two years later.

Brendel was one of Liszt's most loyal friends. Between 1861 and 1865 he kept him informed of all the important musical events in Germany, which Liszt could follow only at a distance because of his absence in Rome. Around 1862 Brendel was Liszt's most favoured correspondent.

That Liszt's name was used as a musico-political tag for the so-called "New German School" (a term for which it is nowadays difficult to imagine any precise meaning) has always stood in the way of an objective assessment of his works. The words "music of the future" were on everybody's lips and were sneered at by every satirical journalist and cartoonist in Europe, and, although they tended to refer to the music of a Wagner or a Berlioz, they so inflamed the passions of musicians and literati generally that two factions sprang up and became involved in the most bitter disputes. Manifestos were printed which had been written and signed by such leading musicians as Brahms, Joachim, Julius Otto Grimm, and Bernhard Scholz.

If Liszt was proclaimed leader of this school, it was because he was a well-known personality with numerous titles and appointments and because he was ready to help everyone who asked him for his support, not least his friend Wagner. It was Wagner, indeed, who symbolized the real "musician of the future," but the Saxon composer was little suited to this role since he was solely concerned with promoting his own life's work. Accordingly, it was Liszt to whom others turned, regarding him as the embodiment of New Weimar, just as Goethe had embodied Old Weimar. Since the description "New Weimar School" seemed too restricted, the concept of the "New German School" was chosen instead.[163]

477 Franz Liszt, the violinist Ede Reményi, and Ferdinand Plotényi (Reményi's usual accompanist at this time). Photograph by Joseph Albert, Munich 1867.

478 Franz Liszt. Photograph by Joseph Albert, Munich 1867.

Around the middle of the nineteenth century Joseph Albert and Franz Hanfstaengl were Bavaria's leading photographers. Wilhelm von Kaulbach described the present photograph as "unsurpassable."[162] The magazine *Münchner Punsch* adopted a less complimentary tone in its issue of 20 October 1867: "One of Rome's more remarkable ruins is available from Joseph Albert; one feels almost uncomfortable observing this mass of lines and furrows, produced by the ravages of time and now reproduced with all too conscientious accuracy by means of modern photography. We refer to the Abbé Liszt."

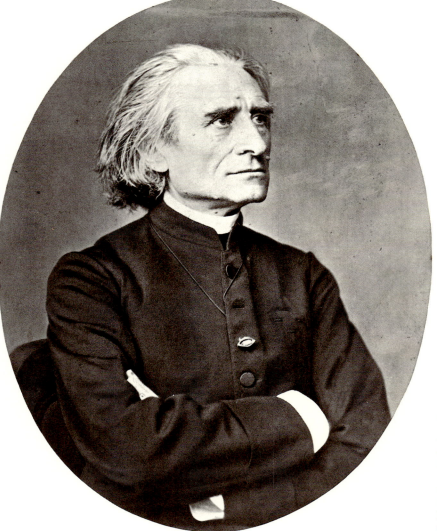

Opposite page:

479 Franz Liszt. Photograph by Franz Hanfstaengl, Munich 1867. Previously unpublished.

The inscription (dated 3 December 1920) to the well-known pianist Josef Pembaur (1875–1950) was added by Liszt's granddaughter Blandine von Gravina. Pembaur's widow gave the portrait to the present writer in 1982.

GALLERIE DER ZEITGENOSSEN.

FRANZ LISZT.

LIFE

January to 2 July: Liszt in Rome.

24 January: Liszt takes part in a concert in the Deutscher Verein in Rome to raise funds for the needy of East Prussia. His favourite pupil in Rome, Giovanni Sgambati, also appears at the concert, performing in Schumann's Quintet and playing Schubert's *Wandererfantasie*.

February/March/April: Liszt works in Rome on various choral pieces. He spends most of his time with Giovanni Sgambati.

31 March: Liszt writes to Franz Brendel: "Sgambati is certainly no 'spa artist,' although his virtuosity is exceptional and of undoubted impact. He plays Bach, Beethoven, Chopin, Schumann, and my most difficult compositions with complete mastery and independence. His artistic propensities and sympathies are entirely 'New German' . . ."[164]

10 May: Bülow conducts Liszt's *Legende von der Heiligen Elisabeth* in Munich.

21 June: To celebrate the twentieth anniversary of Pope Pius IX's accession to the See of Rome, Liszt performs at a concert held in the great Banqueting Hall of the Vatican Library in the presence of the Pope and other Church dignitaries.

2 July: Accompanied by the professor of theology Abbé Solfanelli, Liszt sets off on a pilgrimage to Spoleto, Cascia, Portiuncula, Assisi, Fabriano, and Loreto.

11 July to 29 August: Liszt in Grotta Mare near Ancona as guest of Count Fenili, an uncle of Solfanelli's. Liszt completes twenty pages of his *Technische Studien* and studies the texts of the Office and Breviary with Solfanelli. He writes to Carl Gille, "My apartment is close to the edge of the sea, surrounded by lemon and orange groves. The chief advantage of this *villeggiatura* is the total absence of pianos. Of course, they kindly offered to provide me with an instrument and place it in my sitting-room, but I raised the most decided protest . . ."[165]

1 September: Liszt arrives back in Rome. He revises Weber's piano works.

19 October: Liszt completes his revision of Weber's piano works, and turns his attention to an edition of Schubert's piano pieces.

17 November: Liszt moves to the Villa d'Este near Tivoli for a month's stay.

25 November: Franz Brendel dies in Leipzig. He is 57.

2 December: Liszt completes his revision of Schubert's piano works at the Villa d'Este. He returns to Rome in mid-December.

31 December: The poet Henry Wadsworth Longfellow and the painter George Healy visit Liszt in Rome (see p. 243).

480 Gold pocket watch with an engraving of Pope Pius IX. On the reverse is a representation of St Peter. A present to Liszt from Carolyne von Sayn-Wittgenstein.

Liszt enjoyed the especial favour of Pope Pius IX (see Illus. 466). He played for him on repeated occasions, was his guest at Castel Gandolfo, and on 11 July 1863 received His Holiness in his cell at the monastery of the Madonna del Rosario. It was often assumed that Liszt had chosen the abbé's cassock in order to commend himself to the Pope as a church musician. Liszt himself expressed his view of this suggestion in a letter to Carolyne von Sayn-Wittgenstein:

"I have never demanded any position or any title in Rome. If the Holy Father had appointed me to the Sistine Chapel, I would have accepted out of respect for his kindness and out of obedience to him – in the perhaps erroneous belief that I might be of service to religious art, but under no illusion as to the difficulties or the vexations which such a task would have brought me. That he has not done so is not a cause of sorrow to me – quite the opposite, it alleviates the sorrow I already feel [. . .]."[166]

481 Liszt performing in the Vatican Library on 21 June 1868 for Pope Pius IX. Wood engraving based on a drawing by Otto Günther; 1868.

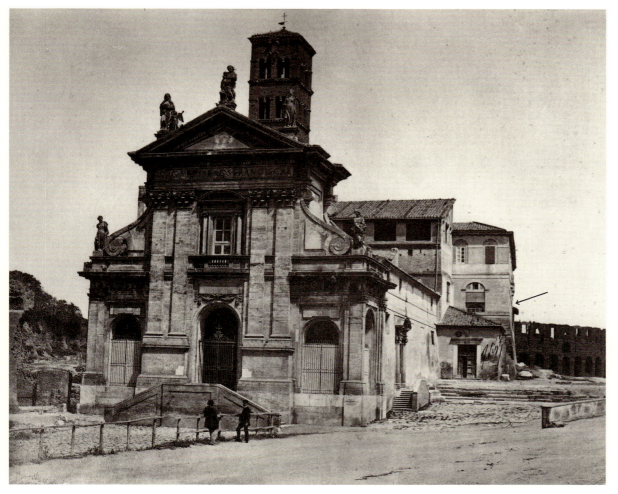

482 The Monastery of Santa Francesca Romana in Rome, Liszt's home from 1866 to 1871. Photograph by Pompeo Molins, ca. 1870.

This photograph was owned by Liszt himself. To the right of the entrance leading to his rooms is his autograph signature. The Colosseum can be seen in the distance. Liszt's fame meant that many travellers to Rome regarded it as *de rigueur* to call on him when visiting the Forum Romanum; one result was that the composer was rarely able to work in peace here in Santa Francesca Romana, which, together with the Villa d'Este, was without doubt the most idyllic of all his residences.

From November 1866 Liszt lived in first-floor rooms in the right-hand wing of the monastery of Santa Francesca Romana, which stands in the middle of the Forum Romanum. The poet Henry Wadsworth Longfellow visited Liszt here on New Year's Eve 1868 in the company of the painter George Healy. Healy reported on the visit as follows:

"We drove to the old monastery and rang at Liszt's private entrance. It was already fairly dark in the vestibule, the door of which was opened by a piece of string attached to the inside. There was not a servant in sight. But the abbé himself came down to greet us, a Roman candlestick held aloft to light the way. His characteristic head, with its long iron-grey hair, sharply etched features, and penetrating black eyes, and his tall, slim figure shrouded in priestly vestments produced so impressive a picture that Longfellow let out an involuntary whisper, 'Mr Healy, you must paint this for me [. . .].' "

WORKS

Technische Studien (for piano). Begun in 1868 and continued over the next twelve years. Pub. 1886, shortly after Liszt's death.

Die Heilige Cäcilie (for piano). Composed in 1868 or 1869, and mentioned by Carolyne von Sayn-Wittgenstein in a letter of 2 July 1876. Lost, unless it is identical with the *Hymne an die Heilige Cäcilie* (see "Works 1866").

Introduction to Study in C "sur des notes fausses" (Rubinstein) (piano). May date from around this time. Unpublished.

Mihi autem adhaerere (for men's voices and organ). Pub. 1871.

Requiem (for chorus, soloists, organ, and brass). Pub. 1869.

Don Carlos: Coro di festa e marcia funebre (Verdi) (piano paraphrase). Written ca. 1868. Pub. 1868.

Les Adieux, Rêverie from Gounod's *Roméo et Juliette* (for piano). Written ca. 1868. Pub. 1868.

Revision of Carl Maria von Weber's piano works. Prepared in 1868 and 1870 (Sonatas opp. 24, 39, 49, 70; *Konzertstück* op. 79; *Momento capriccioso* op. 12; *Grande polonaise* op. 21; *Rondo brillante* op. 62; *Invitation to the Dance* op. 65; *Polacca brillante* op. 72). Vol. I pub. 1875, Vol. II 1883.

Revision of Schubert's piano works. Revised in 1868 and 1880 (Sonatas opp. 42 and 53; Fantasias opp. 15 and 78; *Impromptus* opp. 90 and 142; *Moments musicaux* op. 94; Waltzes and Ländler opp. 9, 18, 33; *Valses sentimentales* op. 50). Pub. 1875 and 1880. The pieces for four hands were revised in 1878.

483 Liszt at the door of the Monastery of Santa Francesca Romana on 31 December 1869. Oil portrait by George P. A. Healy, January/February 1869.

LIFE

12 January: After calling in at Florence and Munich, Liszt arrives in Weimar. He moves into the former studio of the artist Friedrich Preller in the Hofgärtnerei, which until the end of his life remains his home in Weimar. One of his first visitors is Anton Rubinstein.

20 January: Liszt performs at a Weimar Court concert.

February: Liszt works on sacred choral pieces in Weimar.

21 March: Liszt stays with the Duke of Coburg in Gotha, after which he spends two days in Meiningen.

26 March to 16 April: Liszt in Vienna. He stays with Dr Eduard von Liszt in the Schottenhof district. The building still exists.

4 and 11 April: Successful performances of *Die Legende von der Heiligen Elisabeth* under Herbeck in Vienna.

17 to 19 April: Liszt in Regensburg. He becomes friendly with the publisher Friedrich Pustet, and also with Franz Witt, founder of the Cäcilienverein and of the periodicals *Fliegende Blätter für katholische Kirchenmusik* and *Musica viva*.

21 April to 4 May: In Pest.

26 April: Liszt Concert in the Redoute, including the *Dante Symphony* and *Hungaria* (under Erkel), the *Geharnischte Lieder* (under Antal Knahl), and the *Coronation Mass* (under Liszt).

29 April: First meeting with Sophie Menter, one of his leading pupils (see Illus. 516).

30 April: Second Liszt Concert in the Redoute: *Hungaria* and *Psalm cxxxvii* (under Erkel) and the *Coronation Mass* (under Liszt).

Liszt returns to Rome via Sagrado (5/6 May, as guest of Princess Hohenlohe) and Florence (7 May).

15 May: Witt conducts the first performance of Liszt's *Ave maris stella* as a solo quartet in Regensburg.

June/July: Liszt revises his *Coronation Mass* and *Szekszárd Mass* in Rome.

24 to 31 August: In Munich to attend the first performance of Wagner's *The Rhinegold*, staged at the Court Theatre on Ludwig II's orders.

27 August: Final dress rehearsal of *The Rhinegold* in Liszt's presence. Because of technical deficiencies, the performance is postponed. Liszt returns to Rome.

September/October: Preparatory work on the oratorios *St Stanislaus* and *St Stephan* (both will remain unfinished).

22 September: Liszt attends the premiere of *The Rhinegold* in Munich, a performance which takes place against Wagner's wishes.

17 October: Performance of Liszt's *Requiem* in Lemberg.

Mid-October to end of March 1870: At the Villa d'Este as guest of Cardinal Hohenlohe-Schillingsfürst; in between times in Rome for a number of brief visits.

17 November: Liszt to Carl Gille: "In order to escape the intolerable interruptions that I suffer during the winter season in Rome, I have emigrated here – to the Villa d'Este – and shall remain a Tiburtine hermit until the beginning of April. I felt the urge to stop dissipating the days of my old age as I had wasted my youth . . ."[167]

December: Liszt works on his second Beethoven cantata.

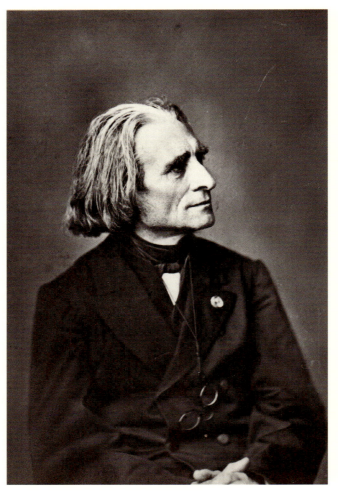
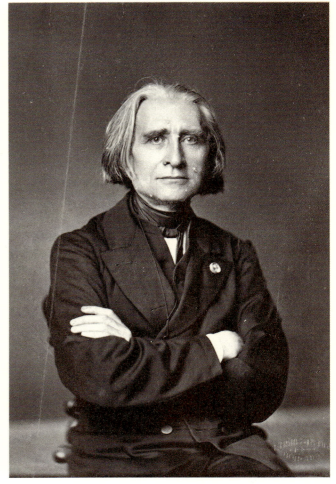

484, 485 Photographs by Franz Hanfstaengl, Munich 1869.

486 Franz Liszt. Caricature by Wilhelm von Kaulbach, Munich 1869.

In August/September 1869 Liszt spent several weeks in Munich, a visit which culminated in his attending the first performance of Wagner's *The Rhinegold* on 22 September. (The performance took place against Wagner's wishes.)

In her 1911 memoirs Josepha Dürck-Kaulbach recalled the caricature which her father drew of Liszt at this time: "[. . .] The Master (as he was universally known) had been visiting my parents for years, each time he passed through Munich. He was always accompanied by a swarm of admirers, both male and female, all of whom worshipped him and dogged his footsteps wherever he went. I can still recall many of the scenes in which Liszt played a leading role.

"I can see him, for example, sitting in our salon with my mother and a number of friends. Liszt spoke animatedly and interestingly in his typically restless manner, often using only gestures to indicate what he meant. The sense generally had to be imagined or guessed, since he did not trouble to complete words or sentences; he merely sketched out his thoughts, so to speak. A characteristic movement of his long fingers, a few mumbled words, a friendly nod of his head – and that was all; you could then imagine the rest. Or perhaps not. On that particular evening – Liszt was engaged in a lively discussion – my father was sitting in the adjacent room which was divided from the salon only by portières. He kept on peering through the gap in the curtains, laughing contentedly to himself. He then asked me for a pencil and a piece of paper and sketched a portrait [Illus. 486] of the famous artist. When Liszt got up to take his leave, my father cried out with a smile, 'Oh bother, it's turned into a caricature!' "

WORKS

Ave Maria II (for mixed voices and organ). Pub. 1870. Two very different piano versions in D and D flat appeared in 1871 and 1873, and a version for voice and organ in 1936.

Pater noster III (for mixed voices and organ). Pub. 1870. A version for men's voices and organ appeared in 1936.

Tantum ergo (for women's voices and organ). Pub. 1871, together with a version for men's voices and organ.

O salutaris hostia I (for women's voices and organ). Pub. 1871, together with a version for mixed voices and organ.

Szekszárd Mass. Second version. Pub. 1869. See ''Works 1848.''

Inno a Maria Vergine (for mixed voices, organ, and harp). Pub. 1936, together with a version for mixed voices, harmonium, piano duet, and harp.

Zur Säkularfeier Beethovens (second Beethoven cantata) (for mixed voices, soloists and orchestra). Written 1869/70. Pub. 1870. The introductory section (*Andante*), which is an orchestration of the slow movement from Beethoven's ''Archduke'' Trio, op. 97, also appeared separately.

Gaudeamus igitur (for mixed voices, soloists, and orchestra). Pub. 1871, together with a piano version. A piano duet version followed in 1872. (This is a different work from the 1843 piece of the same title.)

Benedictus and *Offertorium* (from the *Hungarian Coronation Mass*) (for violin and piano). Pub. 1871. (See ''Works 1866''.)

Tanzmomente (Herbeck) (piano transcription). Pub. 1870.

La Marquise de Blocqueville. Portrait en musique: a continuation to two musical sketches by Henri Herz and Francis Planté (for piano). Pub. 1889.

Adagio from Violin Sonata BWV 1014 (Bach). Transcription for organ. May date from this period. Date of publication unknown.

487 Franz Liszt. Oil portrait by George P. A. Healy, 1868/69.

According to the artist's own testimony, Healy had the rare pleasure of being able to listen to Liszt playing for hours on end on the piano which had been moved into his studio specially for the occasion.

In December 1868 the poet Longfellow saw both this portrait and a cast of Liszt's hands which Healy had made, whereupon he expressed a desire to make Liszt's acquaintance (see p. 243).

488 Liszt's study at the Hofgärtnerei in Weimar. Photograph by Louis Held of Weimar, ca. 1890 (see Illus. 596).

This room was the scene of Liszt's famous matinées, at which his most important pupils performed.

489 The dining room at the Hofgärtnerei. Photograph, ca. 1950.

After dining Liszt used to enjoy a few games of whist. Guests were present almost every day.

490 Liszt's bedroom at the Hofgärtnerei. Photograph, ca. 1950.

As he grew older Liszt showed a surprisingly unassuming nature (see p. 292). Whenever his friend Carl Gille came to spend the night, for example, he made a point of offering him his bed, himself spending the night on a *chaise-longue* in the salon. When staying at hotels he would occasionally ask for "modest rooms for myself and something more comfortable for Signor Spiridione [Liszt's manservant from 1875 to 1881]."[168]

On 12 January 1869 Liszt moved into a small apartment in the Grand Ducal Hofgärtnerei in Weimar's Belvedere-Allee. It was here that he composed and gave lessons during his annual visits to Weimar henceforth and to the end of his life. By this time in his life Liszt was above such externals and found the apartment somewhat too luxurious, as he told

Princess Carolyne: "I am informed that the Grand Duchess and the Princesses have been laboriously involved in choosing carpets, curtains etc. And indeed, the apartment is of a 'Wagnerian' luxury, of a kind that the good people of Weimar are not at all used to."

491 The Hofgärtnerei in Weimar, seen here from the park. Photograph by Louis Held, ca. 1890.

Liszt's housekeeper Pauline Apel is seen standing at the garden gate. Every year from 1869 to 1886 Liszt spent several months in Weimar, where he occupied the whole of the first floor of the Hofgärtnerei. The rooms now house a Liszt Museum.

492 The Weimar Hofgärtnerei seen from the street. Photograph by Louis Held, 1886.

The photographer Louis Held, to whom we owe many valuable photographs of Liszt, settled in Weimar at 16 Schillerstraße in 1882. In 1886 he moved his studio to 1 Marienstraße (on the right, at the end of the street shown here).

LIFE

January to late March: Apart from brief visits to Rome, Liszt remains at the Villa d'Este.[169]
He completes his second Beethoven cantata (written for the centenary celebrations in Weimar), and also a piano score of it. Ferdinand Gregorovius helps with the interpolated lines of verse.

2 April: Liszt leaves Rome for Weimar, arriving at the Hofgärtnerei on 6 April. The soprano Pauline Viardot visits him. Preparations for the Beethoven celebrations.

29 May: Beethoven celebrations organized by the Allgemeiner Deutscher Musikverein in Weimar. Liszt conducts the first performance of his Beethoven cantata and the Symphony No. 9, and Tausig plays the E flat major Piano Concerto. Saint-Saëns is among those present.

3/4 July: In Leipzig for a performance of the *Kyrie*, *Gloria*, and *Credo* from his *Missa choralis*.

5 July: A performance of the complete *Missa choralis* takes place in Jena in Liszt's presence.

9 to 12 July: In Liebenstein.

13 to 26 July: In Munich, where he attends performances of *The Rhinegold* and *The Valkyrie* on 13, 17, 20, and 22 July. Reunion with Kaulbach. Sittings for Lenbach.

23 July: Attends the Passion plays at Oberammergau.

26 July: Liszt leaves Munich and sets off for Regensburg, from where he travels by boat to Vienna, arriving in the Austrian capital on 27 July. On 30 July he leaves for Szekszárd.

31 July to 16 November: In Szekszárd as guest of Baron Antal Augusz.

21/22 August: Liszt attends concerts given by the Pest Vocal Society.

25 August: Cosima and Richard Wagner are married in Lucerne.

17 to 19 September: Liszt in Kalocsa as guest of Cardinal Haynald. On the 18th he and Reményi give a concert in the Archbishop's Residence. The audience includes Sophie Menter, Olga Janina, and Baron Antal Augusz.

21 September: Liszt in Nádasd as guest of the Bishop of Pécs.

25 September: Concert in Szekszárd in support of the local Women's Association. The performers include Sophie Menter, Olga Janina, Ödön von Mihalovich, François Servais, and Liszt.

October: While in Szekszárd, Liszt works on the orchestrations of four Schubert Marches and revises his orchestral versions of six *Hungarian Rhapsodies*.

18 October: Olga Janina gives a banquet in Liszt's honour in Szekszárd.

16 November to 22 April 1871: Liszt in Pest, where he attends concerts almost every day.

16 December: To mark the centenary of Beethoven's birth, Liszt conducts a concert in the Redoute, including Beethoven's Symphony No. 9, his Violin Concerto (with Reményi as soloist), and Liszt's own Beethoven cantata.

18 December: Liszt in Rákospalota as guest of Ede Reményi.

Wilhelm von Csapó (1840–1933), who in 1911 published 177 letters from Liszt to Baron Augusz, recorded in his memoirs the events that took place in Szekszárd on 27 September 1870:

"Szekszárd yesterday offered its visitors a rare delight. Sophie Menter, who is at present staying with Liszt's entourage at Baron Augusz's, gave a charity concert; the audience was attracted not so much by the distinguished artiste as by the news that the Master himself might perhaps also perform something outside the official programme – and so indeed it proved. When the concert organizer announced that Reményi was unwell, a great cry of 'Liszt' went up on all sides. For quite some time he refused to comply with the general request. But when he saw that it was all in vain, he made a gesture as if entreating patience. Each of his movements is so singular and expressive; he stands before his fellow humans like some mythical phenomenon incarnate. Everyone waited with tense curiosity as he finally sat down at the piano. He chose one of his *Hungarian Rhapsodies*, but I noticed only his manner of playing it: his facial expression changed from a fiery glance to a delicate smile; his fingers glided over the keys with magical tenderness or descended on them like lightning! He seemed to delight in the unbounded enthusiasm. In the background Augusz winked and smiled like a happy impresario."

493 Baron Antal Augusz (1807–1878). Lithograph by Strixner, ca. 1855.

494 Liszt as guest of Baron Antal Augusz in Szekszárd. Wood engraving by Rusz, based on a drawing by Kollarz; 1870. From left to right: Liszt, Mosonyi, Abrányi, Augusz, and Reményi.

WORKS

Ungarischer Geschwindmarsch – Magyar Gyors induló (for piano). Pub. 1871.
Rákóczy March (piano duet version). Pub. 1871.
Mosonyi gyázmenete – Mosonyis Grabgeleit (on the death of Mihály Mosonyi) (for piano). Pub. 1871.
Szózat und Hymnus (Egressy/Erkel) (piano transcription). Written ca. 1870. Pub. 1873. A version for orchestra appeared in 1878. There is also a version for piano duet, pub. 1873.
Fantasie und Fuge über das Thema BACH (for organ). Second version. Pub. 1870. (See ''Works 1855''.)
Siegesmarsch – Marche triomphale (for piano). Written ca. 1870. Pub. 1982.
Ungarischer Marsch zur Krönungsfeier in Ofen-Pest am 8. Juni 1867 (for orchestra). Written in 1870 (not 1867, as the title might suggest). Pub. 1871, together with piano versions for two hands and for four hands.
Der Schwur am Rütli (Draeseke) (vocal score of Part I only). Unpublished.

495 The Monastery of Santa Francesca Romana in Rome. Photograph, 1984 (see Illus. 482).
It was here that the 27-year-old Edvard Grieg visited Liszt in 1870.

Edvard Grieg describes his second meeting with Liszt in a letter to his parents of 9 April 1870:
''I had the good fortune to have just received back from Leipzig the manuscript of my piano concerto [in A minor, op. 16, first performed in the Leipzig Gewandhaus on 22 February 1872 with Erika Lie as soloist], so I took it with me. As well as myself there were present Winding, Sgambati, and a German Lisztian unknown to me. [. . .] Winding and I eagerly waited to see whether he really would sight-read my concerto. For my part I considered it impossible, but Liszt took a different view. 'Would you like to play it?' he asked me. 'No, I can't,' I replied at once: 'I haven't yet had a chance to practise it.' Picking up the manuscript, he went to the piano and said to the assembled guests with his characteristic smile: 'Very well, now I'll show you that I can't either.' With that he began to play. I must confess that he took the first movement too fast, so that the beginning sounded confused. But later, when I had found an opportunity to indicate the correct tempo to him, he played it as only he could. It is significant that he played the cadenza – in other words, the most difficult section – best of all. [. . .] At the end he handed back the manuscript and said, with unusual warmth: 'You must go on in the same vein – you're cut out for it. And don't allow yourself to be discouraged!' This last injunction meant a very great deal to me. There was something about the way he spoke that made his words sound like a kind of blessing. I intend to recall his words whenever I am overcome by disappointment and bitterness, and the memory of that hour will have a wonderful power to sustain me when times are bad.''

496 Edvard Grieg (1843–1907). Photograph, ca. 1880.
Grieg was a great admirer of Liszt's and visited him frequently in Rome. In 1870, much to the younger man's astonishment, Liszt sight-read Grieg's A minor Piano Concerto from the composer's own manuscript.

497 Franz Liszt with his daughter Cosima. Photograph by Franz Hanfstaengl, Munich 1867.

498 Richard Wagner with his wife Cosima. Photograph by Fritz Luckhardt, Vienna, 9 May 1872.

Opposite page:

499 Franz Liszt. Oil portrait by Franz von Lenbach, ca. 1870. Previously unpublished.

WAGNER ON LISZT

"Do you know a musician who is more musical than Liszt? who holds within his breast the powers of music in richer, deeper store than he? who has felt more sensitively and more tenderly, who knows more and who can do more, who is more gifted by Nature and who, by educating himself, has developed his potential more forcefully than he? – If you cannot name a second one like him, oh, you may confidently trust in this unique individual!"[170]

At a banquet held on 18 August 1876 during the first Bayreuth Festival, Wagner pointed to Liszt: "Here is the man who first had faith in me at a time when no one knew of my existence, and without whom you would perhaps not have heard a single note of my music, my dear friend – Franz Liszt!"

From Wagner's letters to Franz Liszt[171]

9 May 1853: "[. . .] Has ever an artist or a friend done for another what you have done for me!! In truth, though I might despair of the whole world, a single glance in your direction holds me aloft, high aloft, filling me with faith and hope [. . .]."

8 April 1853: "[. . .] Your greatness is also your misery – both are inextricably bound up with each other and must needs torment and torture you [. . .]."

19 July 1849: "You dear, kind Liszt! See what you can and might do! Help me, help me, dear Liszt! Fare you well, and – help me!"

14 October 1849: "[. . .] We are about to run out of our last gulden – and a wide and glorious world lies before me in which I have nothing to eat and nothing to provide me with warmth! – See what you can do for me, prince among men! [. . .]"

COSIMA ON HER FATHER

"How could I give you a proper picture of my father? From childhood, when he would pay us brief visits, to the end of his life, the impression he made on me was that of some fantastically legendary figure. In his features I could imagine Nornagest, and I was once told by a painter that his head and his whole physiognomy had influenced French painting. My mother told me of her first meeting with him when he was about twenty, saying that she thought that one of Hoffmann's characters had come to life before her very eyes. To say he was good or witty or to say he was a great composer or a great virtuoso or a pious believer is wrong. All opposites came together within his heart, and I could equally well imagine this utterly worldly existence transformed into an ascetic one. *Greatness*, wholly unbounded, in his perception of all things, and *fire*: these are the two qualities which I should most like to ascribe to him. From them sprang the originality of his thinking. But I should not like to risk characterizing him any further, for I should then have to fall back on antitheses, which would confuse everything. It's best if I tell you anecdotes about him when we meet" (Cosima Wagner to Houston Stewart Chamberlain, letter of 17 April 1889).[172]

Two of the anecdotes which Cosima told about her father: "When a young author brought him a fairly worthless composition, Liszt said, 'My friend, when one invites guests to dine, one does not offer them cigarette ash and wood shavings.' – When the Duke of Saxe-Coburg begged Liszt to ask Wagner for some tips on instrumentation, Liszt replied, 'You know, Your Highness, when Wagner sets about orchestrating a work, it is because he has already been struck by a good idea.' "[173]

LIFE

1 January to 22 April: Liszt in Pest.

2 January: The musicologist Ludwig Nohl delivers a lecture on Beethoven in the Salon placed at Liszt's disposal by Mihály Schwendtner. Liszt and Reményi perform the *Kreutzer* Sonata. During the following weeks Liszt attends concerts almost every day.

February/March: Liszt works on the proofs of several new editions of his works, including the "*Gran*" Mass, the piano version of the *Fantasie und Fuge über das Thema BACH*, various versions of the *Rákóczy March*, the *Hungarian Coronation Mass*, and *A lelkesedés dala*.

18/19 April: Liszt gives charity concerts in the Karácsonyi Palace.

22 April: Liszt leaves Pest and travels to Vienna, where he stays till the end of the month.

2/3 May: Liszt in Prague, where he frequents the company of Ambros, Hostinsky, Smetana, and Smetana's pupil Jiránek.

3 May: Arrives in Weimar around evening.

11 June: Performance of *Die Legende von der Heiligen Elisabeth* in the parish church in Weimar.

13 June: Liszt is appointed Hungarian Royal Councillor.

29 June: Liszt stays in Jena for a performance of his *Requiem*.

2 July: Together with the great pianist Carl Tausig, Liszt travels to Leipzig, where a number of his works are performed.

17 July: Tausig dies in Leipzig (see p. 208).

22 July (to the end of the month): Liszt at Schloß Wilhelmsthal as guest of the Grand Duke.

22 to 28 August: Back at Schloß Wilhelmsthal as guest of the Grand Duke.

3 to 7 September: In Eichstätt for the Annual General Meeting of the Cäcilienverein.

Mid-September: Back in Rome.

22 October: Liszt celebrates his 60th birthday in Rome in the company of Hans von Bülow.

16 November to 26 December: Liszt in Pest, where he moves into his first permanent apartment in the city, at 20 (now 23) Nádorgasse.

25 to 27 November: Scandal surrounding Olga Janina, who has fallen madly in love with Liszt. When he rejects her, she threatens to kill herself and Liszt (she finally relinquishes a revolver intended for him). Ödön von Mihalovich persuades her to leave Pest. She avenges herself by writing defamatory novels (*Les souvenirs d'une cosaque* and *Mémoires d'une pianiste*).

26 December: Count Széchényi, Mihalovich, Reményi, and Liszt travel to Vienna for a performance of part of *Christus*.

31 December: Anton Rubinstein conducts the *Christmas Oratorio* from *Christus* in Vienna in the presence of the composer. Anton Bruckner accompanies on the organ.

Berthold Kellermann, a pupil of Liszt's from 1873 to 1879, has left an instructive picture of his mentor's habits:

"Liszt got up at 4 o'clock every morning, even if he had drunk a lot of wine the previous evening and had not gone to bed until very late. Soon after rising, and without having breakfasted, he would go to church. At about 5 o'clock he drank coffee with me and also ate a couple of dry rolls. After that he began the day's work, writing or glancing over letters, correcting music proofs, and various other things. The post arrived at around 8 o'clock, invariably bringing with it a whole host of things. He now glanced through the correspondence, reading and replying to private letters, and correcting sheet music. I was the only person allowed to play to him during this time. At around 9 I generally returned to my own rooms. The Master then wished to work undisturbed. He rarely received visitors during the morning. [. . .]

"Liszt worked unusually easily and quickly. He wrote full scores with fluent speed, from the bottom of the page to the top, just as you or I would write a letter. Only thus can one understand how a man who, socially, was always in such incredible demand could produce such a multitude of compositions, which a practised copyist would have taken an entire lifetime merely to copy out. When, towards the end of his life, Liszt was passing through Munich, I and my young wife visited him at the Hotel Marienbad where he was staying. The Master was just working on a new piece and greeted us warmly. But then he sat down again immediately at his desk, excusing his behaviour by explaining that the work was urgent. He refused, however, to let us go but, kindness itself, continued to talk to us for quite some time, while simultaneously writing away uninterruptedly at his score [. . .]."[174]

500 Wilhelmsthal near Eisenach, house and park. Steel engraving, ca. 1850.

Liszt spent several days in Wilhelmsthal in July and August 1871. He was a welcome guest of the Grand Duke's family and was a visitor here in 1858, 1861, 1864, 1867, 1875, 1876, 1877, and 1883.

501 A letter from Liszt to an unnamed recipient, dated Wilhelmsthal, 25 August 1871. Previously unpublished.

WORKS

Ave verum corpus (for mixed voices and organ). Pub. 1871.

Benedictus and *Offertorium* from the *Coronation Mass* (for violin and organ). Written ca. 1871. Pub. 1875.

Libera me (for men's voices and organ). Pub. 1871. The piece was also used in Liszt's *Requiem*.

Fantasie und Fuge über das Thema BACH (piano transcription of the organ version of 1870). Written 1870 or 1871. Pub. 1871. (See ''Works 1855''.)

Die Allmacht (Schubert) (adaptation for tenor or soprano solo, chorus, and orchestra). Pub. 1872.

Am stillen Herd (from Wagner's *The Mastersingers of Nuremberg*) (piano transcription). Pub. 1871.

Die Fischerstochter (based on a poem by Count Carl Coronini) (for baritone or mezzo-soprano and piano). Pub. 1879.

A lelkesedés dala – Das Lied der Begeisterung (for men's voices). Pub. 1871.

502 Franz Liszt. Photograph by Fritz Luckhardt, Vienna 1871, with a handwritten dedication from Liszt to the soprano Mathilde Marchesi, dated March 1886.

Mathilde Marchesi (1821–1913) was widely regarded as one of the nineteenth century's leading singing teachers. She studied with Nicolai in Vienna and García in Paris, and she in her turn taught many famous singers including Nellie Melba.

LIFE

1 to 8 January: Liszt in Vienna. He attends concerts given by Bülow and Rubinstein.

9 January to 1 April: Liszt in Budapest. He attends Bülow's Beethoven concerts on 9 and 11 January.

19/20 January: Liszt in Preßburg, where he attends a concert given by Bülow.

4 February: Performance of Liszt's *Missa choralis* in the parish church in Budapest.

9 February: First performance of *Epithalam* at a soirée given by Count Széchényi.

18 March: Liszt performs in the presence of the Court at the Redoute in Budapest, the proceeds being donated to charity (see Illus. 505).

19 March: Liszt conducts a Mass by Hans Leo Hassler in St Michael's Church in Budapest.

25 March: Repeat performance of the *Missa choralis*.

1 April: Liszt travels to Vienna, where he stays as usual with his uncle Eduard von Liszt in the Schottenhof district.

6 April: Liszt returns to Weimar via Prague and Dresden. His chief social contacts, apart from the Grand Duke's family, are with Baroness Olga von Meyendorff.

2 May: Performance of *Die Legende von der Heiligen Elisabeth* in Erfurt, attended by the composer.

8 May: Accompanied by Adelheid von Schorn, Liszt attends a performance of Berlioz's *Requiem* in Leipzig.

18 May: After a long silence, Richard Wagner approaches Liszt with an invitation to the foundation-stone ceremony in Bayreuth (see Illus. 503 and 504).

26 to 30 June: Liszt in Kassel for the annual meeting of the Allgemeiner Deutscher Musikverein. It includes a performance of *Die Legende von der Heiligen Elisabeth*.

July: Musicians arrive in Weimar from every quarter of Europe to study with Liszt.

11 August: Liszt in Sondershausen for a music festival, including a performance of the *Faust Symphony*.

3 to 5 September: Richard and Cosima Wagner visit Liszt in Weimar, the first meeting between the two men since October 1867.

12 to 14 September: In Magdeburg for a performance of *Saint Elisabeth*.

5 October: Liszt leaves Weimar and travels to Eisenach for a two-day visit.

8 to 14 October: Liszt in Schillingsfürst, near Ansbach, as guest of Cardinal Hohenlohe.

15 to 21 October: Liszt's first visit to Bayreuth as guest as Richard and Cosima Wagner. (A detailed account of this visit is provided by Cosima's Diaries.)

22 October: En route to Hungary, Liszt celebrates his 61st birthday alone in Regensburg, at the Hotel "Zum Goldenen Kranz."

23 to 26 October: In Vienna.

26 October to 10 November: Guest of Count Imre Széchényi at Horpács, near Ödenburg.

4 November: In the company of Count Széchényi and Mihalovich, Liszt visits his home town of Raiding.

11 November to 1 April 1873: Liszt in Budapest.

21 November: The "Gran" Mass in Preßburg.

23 and 25 November: Liszt attends Bülow's chamber music concerts in Budapest.

24 December: Liszt spends Christmas Eve with Baron Antal Augusz in Budapest.

503 Liszt's own copy of Wagner's letter to him of 18 May 1872. Wagner's marriage to Cosima and Hans von Bülow's consequent fate had led to a cooling of the friendship between Liszt and Wagner, and for several years they had not even written to each other. This letter of Wagner's, inviting Liszt to Bayreuth, was the first successful step in the direction of a reconciliation.

504 Draft of Liszt's reply to Wagner's letter of 18 May 1872. (For a translation of both these letters, see p. 342.)

Liszt paid his first visit to the Wagners in Bayreuth from 15 to 21 October 1872.

Cosima's diary entry for 17 October 1872: "Long talk with my father; Princess Wittgenstein is tormenting him on our account – he should flee from Wagner's influence, artistic as well as moral, should not see me again, his self-respect demands this, we murdered Hans [von Bülow] from a moral point of view, etc. I am very upset that my father should be tormented like this – he is so tired and is always being so torn about! Particularly this wretched woman in Rome has never done anything but goad him – but he does not intend to give me and us up. This conversation keeps me long at my father's side, and unfortunately R[ichard] is offended by my leaving him alone so long."[175]

Opposite page:

505 Concert in the Redoutensaal in Budapest, 18 March 1872. Oil painting by Schams and Lafitte, 1872.

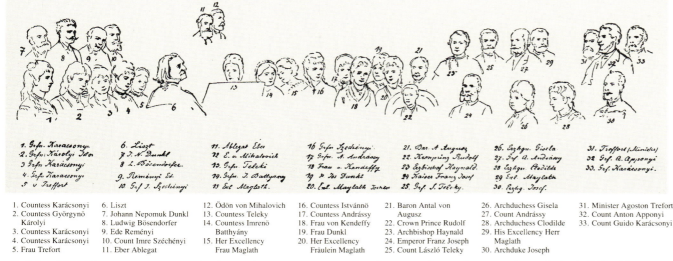

1. Countess Karácsonyi	6. Liszt	12. Ödön von Mihalovich	16. Countess Istvánnö	21. Baron Antal von	26. Archduchess Gisela	31. Minister Agoston Trefort
2. Countess Györgynö Károlyi	7. Johann Nepomuk Dunkl	13. Countess Teleky	17. Countess Andrássy	Augusz	27. Count Andrássy	32. Count Anton Apponyi
3. Countess Karácsonyi	8. Ludwig Bösendorfer	14. Countess Imrenö Batthyány	18. Frau von Kendeffy	22. Crown Prince Rudolf	28. Archduchess Clodilde	33. Count Guido Karácsonyi
4. Countess Karácsonyi	9. Ede Reményi	15. Her Excellency Frau Maglath	19. Frau Dunkl	23. Archbishop Haynald	29. His Excellency Herr Maglath	
5. Frau Trefort	10. Count Imre Széchényi		20. Her Excellency Fräulein Maglath	24. Emperor Franz Joseph	30. Archduke Joseph	
	11. Eber Ablegat			25. Count László Teleky		

In May 1872 Liszt gave a concert in the Budapest Redoute for the benefit of a local orphanage, and a monastery which had burned down. The Emperor Franz Joseph and his Court attended, and the programme included Beethoven's "Moonlight" Sonata and Chopin's B flat minor Nocturne, F sharp major Prelude, and A major Polonaise.

Although opinions varied widely as to Liszt's compositions, his status as an outstanding pianist was never in question.

Felix Mendelssohn to Ignaz Moscheles, letter of 21 March 1840: "[. . .] Liszt has been here for six days, and his truly masterly playing and the inward musical character which he exudes from his fingertips have given me great pleasure. His speed and agility, but above all his sight-reading, his memory, and the way he is completely imbued with music are utterly unique in character, and I have never seen them surpassed [. . .]."

Camille Saint-Saëns, *Portraits et Souvenirs*, 1899: "[. . .] Surmounting a difficulty in art becomes an act of beauty. But beauty arises only once the technical difficulties have been overcome, so that the listener is not aware of them. Here one enters the realm of perfect playing, where Liszt with his godlike ease was absolute ruler. Power and delicacy, rhythmic accent and charm – his playing possessed all this, together with unparalleled warmth and impeccable precision."

Carl Tausig to Wilhelm von Lenz, 1860: "I said to myself that in the Don Juan Fantasia I was not *above* the difficulty, but *in* it; only he was above it, only he! [. . .]" On another occasion Tausig remarked, "No mortal man can measure himself with Liszt. He dwells upon a solitary height" (Amy Fay, *Music-Study in Germany*, Chicago 1881).

Anton Rubinstein in Preßburg on 13 April 1885, when he and Liszt were celebrated at a banquet as the two greatest living pianists: "I cannot accept that. I and others like me are but common soldiers next to our field marshal Franz Liszt."

WORKS

Sunt lacrymae rerum (No. 5 of the *Années de Pèlerinage. Troisième Année*) (for piano). Pub. 1883.

Epithalam (on Reményi's marriage) (for violin and piano). Written ca. 1872, and published, together with piano versions for two hands and for four hands, in 1872.

J'ai perdu ma force et ma vie (for contralto or baritone and piano). Pub. 1879.

La Perla ("Ich bin des Meeres zartweiße Tochter") (for female voice and piano). Pub. ca. 1873.

Wartburglieder (from Scheffel's *Der Braut Willkomm auf der Wartburg*): 1. *Die Erde ist erschlossen* (for chorus), 2. *Als wir mit deutschen Klingen* (for baritone), 3. *Hab ich geträumt* (for tenor), 4. *Beim Scheiden der Sonne* (for tenor), 5. *Ich schrieb allzeit nur wenig* (for baritone or bass), 6. *Thüringens Wälder senden* (for 2 baritones), 7. *Wo liebende Herzen sich innig vermählt* (for tenor). All with piano accompaniment. Pub. 1873. The original orchestrated version is unpublished.

La Marseillaise (for piano). Written ca. 1872. Pub. 1872.

Bevezetés és magyar induló – Einleitung und Ungarischer Marsch (Széchényi) (piano transcription). Pub. 1873.

Fantasia and Fugue in G minor for organ (Bach) (piano transcription). Pub. 1872.

Ich weil in tiefer Einsamkeit (Lassen) (piano transcription). Written ca. 1872. Pub. 1872.

Lieder by Robert Schumann (piano transcriptions): 1. *Weihnachtslied*, 2. *Die wandelnde Glocke*, 3. *Frühlings Ankunft*, 4. *Des Sennen Abschied*, 5. *Er ist's*, 6. *Nur wer die Sehnsucht kennt*, 7. *An die Türen will ich schleichen*, 8. *Frühlingsnacht* (*Überm Garten durch die Lüfte*). Written ca. 1872. Pub. 1872.

Lieder by Clara Schumann (piano transcriptions): 1. *Warum willst du andere fragen?*, 2. *Ich hab' in deinem Auge*, 3. *Geheimes Flüstern*. Written ca. 1872. Pub. 1872.

Impromptu (for piano). Pub. 1877. An earlier variant version entitled *Nocturne* is unpublished.

Ballad from "The Flying Dutchman" (Wagner) (for piano). Pub. 1873.

LIFE

1 January to 1 April: Liszt in Budapest.

12 January: During a soirée at the Hungaria Hotel, Liszt plays his transcription of Széchényi's *Bevezetés és magyar induló* and (together with Mihalovich and Dunkl) one of Bach's triple concertos.

31 January: Liszt hears his *Gaudeamus igitur* (for chorus and orchestra) for the first time at a performance in Budapest.

8 February: To Liszt's gratification, the Hungarian Parliament agrees to provide the funds to establish an Academy of Music in Budapest.

2 March: Concert in honour and benefit of the Lieder composer Robert Franz at the Hungaria Hotel. Among the works which Liszt plays are Beethoven's Sonata op. 26 and his own *Soirées de Vienne* Nos. 4 and 6.

19 March: At an orchestral concert under Hans Richter in the Redoutensaal Liszt conducts his paraphrase of *Szózat und Hymnus*.

21 and 31 March: Charity concerts in the Redoute, at which Liszt plays (inter alia) Beethoven's Sonata op. 27 no. 1, and Nocturnes, Preludes, and Mazurkas by Chopin.

2 to 12 April: In Vienna (in the Schottenhof).

12 April: Liszt leaves Vienna for Preßburg.

13 April: Performance of the ''Gran'' Mass in Liszt's presence in Preßburg Cathedral.

15 April: In Vienna for a Court concert, then on to Leipzig.

16/17 April: Liszt in Leipzig, where he meets the President of the Allgemeiner Deutscher Musikverein, Carl Riedel.

17 April to 26 July: Compositional and teaching activities.

29 May: First complete performance of *Christus* under Liszt in Weimar. Among those present are Cosima and Richard Wagner, Countess Schleinitz, Marie von Muchanoff-Kalergis, Mihalovich, and Raff.

23 to 26 June: In Dornburg, then on to Berlin, where he visits Countess Schleinitz, then Leipzig (for a performance of the *Missa choralis*), and finally back to Weimar.

26 July to 5 August: Liszt in Bayreuth for the topping-out ceremony on the Festival Theatre. (Cosima's Diaries describe the course of this visit.)

6 to 13 August: Liszt in Schillingsfürst as guest of Cardinal Hohenlohe, then in Langenburg as guest of Hermann von Hohenlohe.

7 September: To mark the marriage of the Grand Duke's heirs, Liszt plays his adaptation of Weber's *Polonaise brillante* and his *Fantasie über ungarische Volksmelodien*, both with orchestra.

8 September: Liszt conducts Beethoven's Symphony No. 9 in Weimar.

23 September: Liszt attends a performance of his *Wartburglieder* on the Wartburg.

28 September: Performance of *Two Episodes from Lenau's ''Faust''* in Sondershausen, in Liszt's presence.

4 to 23 October: In Rome. Audience with the Pope on the 22nd (Liszt's birthday), followed by a few days in Vienna.

30 October to 17 May 1874: Liszt in Budapest, where he moves into rooms at 4 Hal tér.

8 to 11 November: Budapest celebrates the 50th anniversary of Liszt's first major concert appearance in Vienna in 1823 (see Illus. 512 and 513).

9 November: Performance of *Christus* under Hans Richter in the Budapest Redoute.

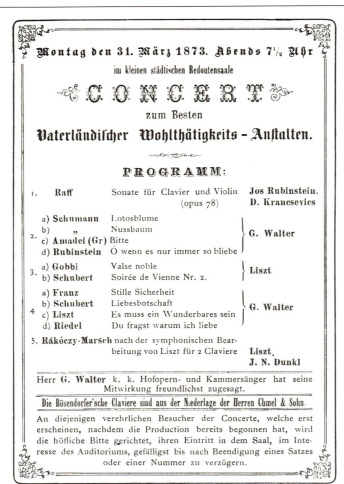

506 Caricatures of Liszt by János Jankó, published in *Borsszem Jankó*, 6 April 1873.
The captions were originally in Hungarian:
[1] Liszt appears, his cassock tempering the arrogance of his smile. – Thunderous applause
[2] Opening chords. He turns his head to be certain of his audience. . .
[3] closes his eyes and seems to play for himself alone
[4] Pianissimo: Saint Francis of Assisi speaking to the birds
[5] Hamlet-like broodings, Faustian despair, sighs. . .
[6] Reminiscences: Chopin, George Sand, youth, moonlight, love. . .
[7] Dante: Inferno, the groans of the damned, crashing thunderclaps. . .
[8] He played just for us – bravo! hurray!

507 Programme for a charity concert on 31 March 1873.
Liszt also played Chopin's Nocturne in A flat major as an encore, and accompanied the soprano Irma Semsey in a number of Lieder.

508 Caricature of Liszt by Karl Klič, published in the *Humoristische Blätter*, Vienna 1873.
The figure on the left is Ludwig Bösendorfer. The quatrain beneath the caricature might be translated as follows:
The ladies' man of yesteryear
Assists the poor and underfed;
Enchanted music feasts our ear
And serves us as our daily bread.

509 Franz Liszt wearing his decorations. Photograph by Ferencz Kózmata, Budapest 1873.
  The photograph was taken on the occasion of the fiftieth anniversary of Liszt's first concert appearance in Pest.

A review by Eduard Hanslick from 1873. Even from his position of declared hostility Hanslick could not conceal his admiration for Liszt's art of instrumentation:

''Another novelty was Liszt's orchestral adaptation of Schubert's Funeral March in E flat minor [No. 5 of the six *Grandes Marches* D.819]. As a piano piece the work is typically Schubertian, tuneful and naturally flowing, but in no way significant; with its harmonic and rhythmic simplicity and threadbare quaver accompaniment the Trio in E flat major, which in any case sounds far too cheerful for a Funeral March, becomes all too tiresome when repeated so often. But what has Liszt been able to make of this small-scale drawing! He has turned it into an impressive and colourful picture which one never tires of admiring and which constantly reveals new coloristic miracles. There is true poetry in the instrumentation, unlike that heartless technical skill which one is bound to praise in so many modern orchestral pieces. The way in which the theme first emerges from the darkness of the violas and low-register clarinets, growing brighter with the addition of violins and flutes, until finally the horns, the trumpets, and the three trombones and tuba gradually begin in the second part to suffuse the whole with their solemn splendour, like some refulgent sunset is impossible to describe.

''And this E flat major Trio: how Liszt has enriched and enhanced it by his varied and finely shaded instrumentation! The cellos begin by intoning the melody in a song-like tenor register, it is then taken up by the violins, on the G string, and finally by French horn, clarinet, and flute over a gently flowing triplet accompaniment played by the violins. In the second part of the Trio, the first horn takes the melody, supported by the three lower horns (muted), while two flutes flutter gently above it in legato arpeggios; finally all the violins and cellos take up the theme in octave unison, building up to the greatest climax until, at the very end, a further new development takes us by surprise: the melody returns in the oboes. Liszt appears here in the full splendour of his art – as he always does when Schubert provides him with his ideas. In its sheer genius this adaptation of Liszt's is very much a re-creation, yet not a single bar of the original has been altered, not a single note of Schubert's March has been gainsaid. And if Schubert could hear his March in Liszt's orchestration I believe he would utter the selfsame cry of admiration that Voltaire is said to have done on seeing one of his tragic roles performed by Clairon as no other actress before her had rendered it: 'Was it I who wrote that?' ''[176]

Franz Liszt's Titles and Orders

Franz Ritter von Liszt (hereditary Austrian knighthood).
Honorary doctorate from Königsberg University.
Court Councillor of Hohenzollern-Hechingen.

Court Kapellmeister in Extraordinary Service.
Royal Hungarian Councillor.
President of the Hungarian Academy of Music, Budapest.
Chamberlain of the Grand Duchy of Saxony and Weimar.
Honorary President of the Allgemeiner Deutscher Musikverein.
Honorary Canon of S. Albano, Rome.
Officer of the French Legion of Honour.
Grand Officer of the Order of Guadeloupe.
Holder of the Prussian Order *Pour le mérite*.
Member of the Académie des Beaux-Arts, Paris.
Member of the Prussian Academy of Arts.
Order of Merit of St Michael.
Maximilian Order for Art and Science.
Holder of the Commander's Cross of the Order of Franz Joseph.
Member of the Freies Deutsches Hochstift of Frankfurt.
Member of the Frankfurt Lodge ''Zur Einigkeit.''
Member of the Zurich Lodge ''Modestia cum libertate.''
Member of the Weimar Order of the Falcon, the Order of St Gregory, the Order of the Oak Crown, the Order of Vigilance, the Spanish Order of the Cross of Carlos III, the Portuguese Order of Christ, and the Belgian Order of Leopold.
Freeman of Ödenburg, Weimar, Jena, etc.

Franz Liszt:
''I was never affected by the prevailing feverish desire for orders – I regard them as a sign of the good will of princes and as something granted to talent and merit, but not as attributes of talent or merit. I cannot treat them as articles of my wardrobe, but nor can I ascribe to them an inner worth which they in no way possess [. . .].''[177]

  When someone spoke contemptuously of orders, Liszt replied, ''Orders are an embarrassment only to those who do not have them.''[178]

16/17 November: Liszt in Gran (Esztergom) as guest of Primate János Simor.
22/23 November: In Preßburg for the third performance of the ''Gran'' Mass on the 23rd.
December: Liszt attends musical events in Budapest almost every day. He works on his *St Stanislaus*.

WORKS

12 große Etüden (part of a *Great Technical Piano Tutor*). Believed to have been in the possession of Olga Janina, who is said to have lost it. In fact identical with part of the *Technische Studien* in twelve volumes published in 1886.
Walther von der Vogelweide (presumably No. 4 of the *Wartburglieder*, ''Beim Scheiden der Sonne'': see ''Works 1872'') (version for tenor, violin, and piano). The autograph score turned up in 1925 at a Berlin auction. Its present whereabouts are unknown.
Fünf ungarische Volkslieder (piano transcriptions). Written ca. 1873. Pub. 1873.
Klavierstück in F sharp major. Written ca. 1873. Pub. 1928.
Ave Maria II (second piano transcription). Written ca. 1873. Pub. 1873. See ''Works 1869.''
Klavierstück (Adagio) (one of five pieces for Baroness Olga von Meyendorff). Pub. 1928.

AMY FAY: LETTERS FROM WEIMAR
May to June 1873

The American Amy Fay studied with Liszt for a period in 1873. In the letters she wrote to her family in America she reveals herself as an acute observer. Of Liszt's piano playing she once said that he "showers pearls and diamonds over the keyboard." Her collection of letters appeared in America in 1881 and in a German translation the following year. In addition to a chapter on Liszt, from which the accompanying extracts are taken, the volume also contains an account of her piano lessons with Tausig, Kullak, and Deppe.

1 May 1873

"Last night I arrived in Weimar, and this evening I have been to the theatre, which is very cheap here, and the first person I saw, sitting in a box opposite, was Liszt, from whom, as you know, I am bent on getting lessons, though it will be a difficult thing, I fear, as I am told that Weimar is overcrowded with people who are on the same errand. I recognised Liszt from his portrait, and it entertained and interested me very much to observe him. He was making himself agreeable to three ladies, one of whom was very pretty. He sat with his back to the stage, not paying the least attention, apparently, to the play, for he kept talking all the while himself, and yet no point of it escaped him, as I could tell by his expressions and gestures.

"Liszt is the most interesting and striking looking man imaginable. Tall and slight, with deep-set eyes, shaggy eye brows, and long iron-gray hair, which he wears parted in the middle. His mouth turns up at the corners, which gives him a most crafty and Mephistophelean expression when he smiles, and his whole appearance and manner have a sort of Jesuitical elegance and ease. His hands are very narrow, with long and slender fingers that look as if they had twice as many joints as other people's. They are so flexible and supple that it makes you nervous to look at them. Anything like the polish of his manners I never saw. When he got up to leave the box, for instance, after his adieux to the ladies, he laid his hand to his heart and made his final bow, – not with affectation, or in mere gallantry, but with a quiet courtliness which made you feel that no other way of bowing to a lady was right or proper. It was most characteristic.

"But the most extraordinary thing about Liszt is his wonderful variety of expression and play of feature. One moment his face will look dreamy, shadowy, tragic. The next he will be insinuating, amiable, ironical, sardonic; but always the same captivating grace of manner. He is a perfect study. I cannot imagine how he must look when he is playing. He is all spirit, but half the time, at least, a mocking spirit, I should say. I have heard the most remarkable stories about him already. All Weimar adores him, and people say that women still go perfectly crazy over him. [. . .]"

7 May 1873

"[. . .] Liszt looks as if he had been through everything, and has a face *seamed* with experience. He is rather tall and narrow, and wears a long abbé's coat reaching nearly down to his feet. He made me think of an old-time magician more than anything, and I felt that with a touch of his wand he could transform us all. [. . .]"

21 May 1873

Liszt plays the last three movements of Chopin's B minor Sonata: "[. . .] It was the first time I had heard him, and I don't know which was the most extraordinary, – the Scherzo, with its wonderful lightness and swiftness, the Adagio with its depth and pathos, or the last movement, where the whole keyboard seemed to *donnern und blitzen* (thunder and lighten). There is such a vividness about everything he plays that it does not seem as if it were mere music you were listening to, but it is as if he had called up a real living *form*, and you saw it breathing before your face and eyes. It gives *me* almost a ghostly feeling to hear him, and it seems as if the air were peopled with spirits! [. . .]"

29 May 1873

"[. . .] Yesterday I had prepared for him his *Au Bord d'une Source*. I was nervous and played badly. He was not to be put out, however, but acted as if he thought I had played charmingly, and then he sat down and played the whole piece himself, oh, *so* exquisitely! It made me feel like a wood-chopper. The notes just seemed to ripple off his fingers' ends with scarce any perceptible motion. [. . .] Do you wonder that people go distracted over him? [. . .]"

6 June 1873

"[. . .] His touch and his peculiar use of the pedal are two secrets of his playing, and then he seems to dive down in the most hidden thoughts of the composer, and fetch them up to the surface, so that they gleam out at you one by one, like stars! [. . .] I often think of what Tausig said once: 'Oh, compared with Liszt, we other artists are all blockheads.' [. . .]"

19 June 1873

"[. . .] When Liszt plays anything pathetic, it sounds as if he had been through everything, and opens all one's wounds afresh. All that one has ever suffered comes before one again. Who was it that I heard say once, that years ago he saw Clara Schumann sitting in tears near the platform, during one of Liszt's performances? Liszt knows well the influence he has on people, for he always fixes his eyes on some one of us when he plays, and I believe he tries to wring our hearts. [. . .] But I doubt if he feels any particular emotion himself when he is piercing you through with his rendering. He is simply hearing every tone, knowing exactly what effect he wishes to produce, and how

to do it. [. . .] Liszt hasn't the nervous irritability common to artists, but, on the contrary, his disposition is the most exquisite and tranquil in the world. We have been there incessantly, and I've never seen him ruffled except two or three times, and then he was tired and not himself, and it was a most transient thing. [. . .]"

24 July 1873

"[. . .] Liszt is going away to-day. He was to have left several days ago, but the Emperor of Austria or Russia (I don't know which) came to visit the Grand Duke, and of course Liszt was obliged to be on hand and to spend a day with them. He is such a grandee himself that kings and emperors are quite matters of course to him. Never was a man so courted and spoiled as he! The Grand Duchess herself frequently visits him. But he never allows any one to ask him to play, and even she doesn't venture it. That is the only point in which one sees Liszt's sense of his own greatness; otherwise his manner is remarkably unassuming. [. . .]"

510 Franz Liszt. Photograph by Franz Hanf-staengl, Munich 1869.

Amy Fay: ''Liszt knows well the influence he has on people, for he always fixes his eyes on some one of us when he plays, and I believe he tries to wring our hearts . . .'' (see facing page). A variant of this photograph was widely circulated at the time, but the present study is little known.

511 Liszt revisits his birthplace in Raiding.
Wood engraving, 1873.

512 Lithograph produced by the publishing
house of Stephan Halász in Budapest to mark the
fiftieth anniversary of Liszt's concert career in
1873.
  Top left is Beethoven's symbolic ''Weihekuß'' (see Illus. 35), and top right the concert
given before Emperor Franz Joseph I (see Illus.
505); bottom left is a wholly distorted impression of Liszt's birthplace, and bottom right an
imaginary Memorial to Liszt.

On several occasions during his lifetime Liszt revisited his birthplace at Raiding, the village he had left, apparently for good, at the age of ten:

On 19 February 1840 in the company of Franz von Schober; Liszt gave 200 forints for the church organ and for the poor people of the village (see Illus. 11).

On 3 August 1846 on the occasion of his concert in Ödenburg.

In May 1848 with Princess Carolyne.

On 4 November 1872 with Count Széchényi and Count Mihalovich (Illus. 511).

On 7 April 1881 in the company of Ludwig Bösendorfer, Count Zichy, and Adalbert von Goldschmidt.

Count Albert Apponyi (see Illus. 513) described Liszt as "a noble and kind-hearted man, one of the finest men I have ever met. Envy and resentment were unknown to him; how many musicians became famous thanks to him and owed the recognition they found to the publicity which he gave them! The discovery of some new talent was always a source of immense delight to him, and all who were serious about the advancement of art could always count on his active support. I emphasize this characteristic lack of envy because I have never encountered it to such a degree in any person who has rivals in his or her particular field of activity.''[179]

513 The Festival Committee on the occasion of the fiftieth anniversary of Liszt's first concert appearance in Budapest. Photograph, Budapest 1873.

From left to right: Archbishop Lajos Haynald (chairman of the committee), Imre von Huszár, Franz Liszt, Count Imre Széchényi, Ödön von Mihalovich, Baron Antal Augusz, Count Albert Apponyi, Hans Richter, Count Guido Karácsonyi, and Johann N. Dunkl.

LIFE

1 to 6 January: Liszt in Budapest.

7 January: Departure for Vienna.

11 January: Concert in the Vienna Musikvereins-saal for the benefit of the Emperor Franz Joseph Foundation (see Illus. 517). Liszt plays his adaptation of Schubert's *Wandererfantasie* and one of his own *Hungarian Rhapsodies*, both for piano and orchestra. At a banquet afterwards, also attended by Johannes Brahms, who had conducted at the concert, Liszt receives the Order of Franz Joseph.

14 January: Soirée at Bösendorfer's. Liszt plays works by Chopin and some of his own pieces.

15 January to 16 February: Liszt in Horpács as guest of Count Imre Széchényi. He writes the melodrama *A holt költö szerelme* here.

12 February: Charity concert in Ödenburg. Liszt plays a Nocturne and Mazurka by Chopin, together with his *Soirées de Vienne*.

18 February to 17 May: In Budapest, with excursions to Vienna, Kalocsa and Preßburg.

4 and 23 March: Liszt appears at charity concerts in Budapest.

25 March: Liszt conducts his *Coronation Mass* in the parish church in Budapest.

1 to 7 April: In Vienna.

15 to 17 April: Liszt in Kalocsa as guest of Cardinal Haynald.

18/19 April: Liszt in Preßburg. On the 19th a charity concert in the Redoute at which Sophie Menter appears. The performance also includes *Die Seligkeiten* from Liszt's *Christus*.

10 May: Performance of *Saint Elisabeth* in Düsseldorf under Theodor Ratzenberger.

17 May: Liszt leaves Budapest and returns to Rome via Florence, where he visits Bülow.

7 June to end of September: At the Villa d'Este outside Rome. Liszt expresses his pleasure at the life of seclusion which he leads here. He works on his sacred choral pieces *St Stanislaus* and *St Cecilia*, *Die Glocken des Straßburger Münsters*, and the *Hymne de l'enfant à son réveil*, and on piano transcriptions of several of his Symphonic Poems.

October: In Rome at 43 Vicolo dei Greci, then back to the Villa d'Este from the end of the month.

November/December: Liszt at the Villa d'Este, with excursions to Rome in between times.

21 November: First performance in Preßburg of Liszt's *Hungarian Coronation March*.

''Jubilantly greeted, Liszt appeared in the long robe of an abbé, seated himself at the piano and began Schubert's *Wandererfantasie*, op. 15. His playing is perfect, as of old, with more spiritual repose and greater moderation. It is not so stunning or so gripping as it used to be, but it is more unified, more solid. He was more brilliantly effective in his second number, the *Hungarian Rhapsody* for piano and orchestra. This original work – which begins in real Gypsy style, with a free and melancholy improvisation, and then leaps up, with a rattling of spurs, in a vigorous, czárdás-like orgy, whirling and swirling with ever more frenzy – seemed to awaken his youthful spirits. The Allegro offered many astounding effects exclusively associated with Liszt, such as the hammering with both hands on a single key and the characteristic imitation of the cimbalom. The way he reproduces the whirring, hammering sound effects of this quintessential and best-loved Hungarian instrument is quite inimitable.

''His playing was free, poetic, replete with imaginative shadings, and at the same time characterized by noble, artistic repose. And his technique, his virtuosity? I hesitate to speak of it. It suffices to observe that he has not lost it but has rather added to it in clarity and moderation. What a remarkable man! After a life incomparably rich and active, full of excitement, passion, and pleasure, he returns at the age of 62 and plays the most difficult music with the ease and strength and freshness of a youth. Not only does one listen with breathless attention to his playing; one also observes its reflection in the fine lines of his face. His head, thrown back, in its expression of powerful gravity still suggests something of Jupiter. Sometimes the eyes flash beneath the prominent brows; sometimes the characteristically upturned corners of the mouth are raised a little higher in a gentle smile. Head, eyes, and sometimes even a helping hand maintain constant communication with orchestra and audience. Sometimes he plays from notes, at other times from memory, putting on and taking off his spectacles accordingly. Sometimes his head is bent forward attentively, sometimes thrown back boldly. All this has the utmost fascination for his listeners – particularly feminine listeners. It has always been one of Liszt's unique qualities to create an effect in his great art by means of all kind of lesser arts, as indeed we know: 'God moves in a mysterious way.'

''Liszt brought the Rhapsody to a conclusion in a storm of octaves. The audience applauded, shouted, cheered, rose to its feet, recalled the master again and again, indefatigably. The latter in his turn, with the quiet, friendly, gracious bearing of the habitual conqueror, let it be known that he too was not yet tired. For the Liszt of today it was a great accomplishment; and yet he went about it as if it were nothing, and he himself still the Liszt of 1840. A darling of the gods, indeed!''[180]

514 Caricature of Liszt by F. Grätz, 1874.

The satirical figure of ''Kikeriki'' asks the Austrian Minister of Education Karl von Stremayr (seen here leaning over the piano), ''Why does Your Excellency not look at the fingers of other members of the clergy?''

515 The Bayreuth Musical Steam Engine. Caricature by Karl Klič from the Vienna *Humoristische Blätter* of 20 August 1876.

Wagner's spirit rises up out of the musical sounds, while the piano maker Ludwig Bösendorfer stokes the fires of Liszt's instrument.

Opposite page:

516 Sophie Menter (1846–1918). Photograph by J. Löwy, Vienna 1873.

Liszt described her as ''the greatest pianist of her day'' and called her his ''only legitimate daughter as a pianist.''

Born in Munich, Sophie Menter studied with Tausig and (from 1869) with Liszt. From 1883 to 1887 she was professor of music in St Petersburg, where she became friendly with Tchaikovsky. She later divided her life between Schloß Itter in the Tyrol and Stockdorf near Munich (where she surrounded herself with an army of cats).

517 Programme of a concert on 11 January 1874.

Liszt played his arrangement of Schubert's *Wandererfantasie* and one of his own Hungarian Rhapsodies (presumably his *Fantasie über ungarische Volksmelodien*) for piano and orchestra.

WORKS

Die Glocken des Straßburger Münsters (after a poem by Longfellow) (for chorus, soloists, and orchestra): 1. *Prelude: Excelsior!*, 2. *Die Glocken*. Pub. 1875. Versions of *Excelsior!* for piano four hands and for organ appeared in 1876; a version for voice and organ is unpublished.

Symphonic poems (*Ce qu'on entend sur la montagne*, *Mazeppa*, *Hamlet*, and *Hungaria*) (transcriptions for piano duet). Pub. 1875.

Hungarian Rhapsodies Nos. 2, 5, 6, 9, 12, and 14 (transcriptions for piano duet of the 1858 orchestral versions). Pub. 1875.

Ihr Glocken von Marling (for mezzo-soprano and piano). Pub. 1879.

Und sprich (''Sieh auf dem Meer'') (for mezzo-soprano and piano). Pub. 1879.

A holt költő szerelme (*Des toten Dichters Liebe*) (melodrama with piano). Pub. 1874.

Anima Christi sanctifica me (for men's voices and organ). Two versions, both pub. 1882.

Hymne de l'enfant à son réveil (for women's voices, piano, and harp) (definitive version). Pub. 1875.

Die Heilige Cäcilie (for mixed voices, soprano solo, and orchestra or piano, harp, and organ). Pub. 1876.

Die Legende von dem Heiligen Stanislaus (oratorio). Unfinished. Begun ca. 1874 and worked on intermittently over the following years.

Weihnachtsbaum – Arbre de Noël. Twelve piano pieces: 1. *Psallite*, 2. *O heilige Nacht!*, 3. *Die Hirten an der Krippe*, 4. *Adeste fideles*, 5. *Scherzoso*, 6. *Carillon*, 7. *Schlummerlied*, 8. *Altes provençalisches Weihnachtslied*, 9. *Abendglocken*, 10. *Ehemals! – Jadis*, 11. *Ungarisch*, 12. *Polnisch*. Written 1874–76. Pub. 1882, together with transcriptions for piano duet. No. 2 (*O heilige Nacht!*) was arranged for tenor solo, women's voices, and organ after 1876 and published in 1882.

[Erste] Elegie (for cello, piano, harp and harmonium). Pub. 1875, together with versions for piano solo, piano duet, cello and piano, and violin and piano.

Jeanne d'Arc au bûcher (for mezzo-soprano and piano). Second version. Pub. 1876. A version for contralto solo and orchestra prepared at this time was published in 1877.

Tanto gentile e tanto onesta (Hans von Bülow) (piano transcription). Pub. 1875.

LIFE

1 January to 8 February: Liszt at the Villa d'Este and in Rome. On 9 February he leaves for Budapest.

11 February to 1 April: Liszt in Budapest.

3 March: Performance of the *Chöre zu Herders "Entfesseltem Prometheus"* in Budapest. Liszt and Antal Siposs perform the piano accompaniment for four hands.

10 March: Joint concert featuring Liszt and Wagner, held in the Redoute in aid of the Bayreuth Festival fund. Liszt plays Beethoven's E flat major Piano Concerto, conducted by Hans Richter.

15 March: Liszt performs at a charity concert in the Redoute. The following day he resolves ''not to open the piano again for a very long time,'' i.e. not to perform in public.[181]

22 March: Liszt advises the Hungarian Minister of Culture, Agoston Trefort, to appoint Franz Witt of Regensburg and Hans von Bülow to professorial chairs at the Academy of Music.

30 March: Trefort personally brings Liszt the news of his election as President of the Budapest Academy of Music.

2 to 8 April: In Vienna (Schottenhof).

9 to 13 April: In Munich.

12 April: Successful performance of *Saint Elisabeth* in Munich. King Ludwig II immediately commands two further performances in the Court Theatre.

13 April to 15 September: Apart from a few interruptions, Liszt is in Weimar throughout this period.

28 April: Liszt performs his Variations on *"Weinen, Klagen, Sorgen, Zagen"* at a concert in Hanover in support of the Bach Memorial in Erfurt.

2 to 12 May: Liszt at Het Loo, near Arnhem, as guest of King William III of the Netherlands; then back to Weimar.

17 June: Memorial concert in Weimar's Tempelherrenhaus for Marie von Muchanoff-Kalergis, who had died in 1874. The programme consists of works by Liszt, including the *Elegie* written in her memory.

19 to 28 July: In Wilhelmsthal as guest of the Grand Duke and his family.

29 July to 17 August: Liszt in Bayreuth (see Cosima Wagner's Diaries), then a few days in Liebenstein, before returning to Weimar.

13 September: In Leipzig.[182]

16/17 September: Liszt stays with his biographer Lina Ramann in Nuremberg, before returning to Rome.

19 September to 2 October: In Rome.

3 October to 5 February 1876: Liszt at the Villa d'Este, with occasional visits to Rome in between times. He busies himself with various choral works and the piano versions of the *Ungarischer Sturmmarsch* for two and four hands.

14 November: Official opening of the Budapest Academy of Music. Liszt had been appointed its President in March 1875.

4 December: The Leipzig publisher Julius Schuberth invites Liszt to edit Chopin's works, but Liszt refuses, arguing that ''Chopin, following the supreme example of Beethoven, left detailed instructions on how to phrase his works, even adding the pedals with the utmost care in almost every instance, so that scarcely anything of a superficial and technical kind was left to others apart from ensuring correct notation and fingering: to elucidate Chopin's soul with the aid of pedantry is wholly impossible.''[183]

Count Albert Apponyi describes Liszt's piano playing before and during his concert on 10 March 1875:

''I believe I am not wrong in thinking that the performance of Beethoven's E flat major Concerto which Liszt gave within the framework of the open rehearsal marked the high point of his career as a performing artist; indeed, it may even have been the peak of all that has ever been achieved in the realm of artistic rendition. Hans Richter and the orchestra followed the great master's intentions spellbound, and nothing in their accompaniment could have destroyed the perfection of the impression or, rather, the impression of perfection which emanated from Liszt. It is now 57 years since I first experienced Liszt interpreting Beethoven for Wagner, but I can still hear the sound of it in my ears and in my mind as though it were yesterday. At each significant development in this wondrous work one could sense how both these living artists, the performer and the listener, were communing spiritually the one with the other, and how happy they felt in the harmonious understanding which they shared with the long-dead genius. Invisible threads of suggestive empathy passed from this hearth of the deepest emotion to us profane listeners and imbued our unresisting souls with a feeling of true happiness. No words can describe what we experienced then: it was just music, resonant feeling raised above concepts and words. [. . .]

''The concert took place the following evening, and during the morning I went with Mihalovich to visit Liszt in his apartments where we discussed a number of details relating to Wagner's stay in the city. To our dismay we found him with a bandage on the third finger of his right hand. 'Yes,' he said to us with a smile, 'you can see I've cut myself slightly.'

''We thought that this was the end of the concert and asked the Master what his thoughts were on the matter. 'Why do you ask?' he replied, 'of course I'll play this evening.' 'But your injured finger?' 'Well, I'll just have to do without it,' was his reply.

''And, indeed, he really did play the E flat major Concerto that evening without using his third finger and without anyone noticing: this was Liszt the pianist!''[184]

518 Programme for the concert on 10 March 1875 which both Cosima (opposite page) and Count Apponyi (above) described.

519 Programme for a concert on 15 March 1875.

WORKS

Ungarischer Sturmmarsch. Second version (for piano). Pub. 1876, together with a piano version for four hands and an orchestral adaptation.

Der blinde Sänger (melodrama based on a ballad by Tolstoi). Pub. 1878. A piano version was prepared in 1878 and published in 1881.

Der Herr bewahret die Seelen seiner Heiligen (for mixed voices, organ, and wind instruments). Pub. 1887.

Carl August weilt mit uns, festival chorus written for the unveiling of the Carl August Memorial in Weimar on 3 September 1875 (for men's voices, brass, and drums). Pub. 1887.

2 Polonaises from Stanislaus (for piano). Published 1983.

Vive Henri IV (French folk song) (piano transcription). Written ca. 1875. Pub. 1950.

520 Franz Liszt. Photograph by György Klösz, Budapest 1875.

This photograph was taken on the occasion of a concert at which Liszt conducted his *Die Glocken des Straßburger Münsters* and played Beethoven's E flat major Concerto (see Illus. 518). Cosima Wagner attended the dress rehearsal and noted in her diary on 9 March 1875, "My father absolutely overwhelms us with the way he plays the Beethoven concerto – a tremendous impression! Magic without parallel – this is not playing, it is pure sound. R[ichard] says it annihilates everything else . . ." Of the performance itself she wrote, "Tired and visibly bowed with age, Liszt approached the piano and seemed scarcely to have touched the keys when, as though by magic, such fullness of sound rang out and the plasticity of Beethoven's themes emerge so forcefully – in his playing of powerful and delicate passages alike – that we wondered whether even in his youth he had been able to play in so incomparable a manner . . ."

LIFE

1 January to 5 February: Liszt works at the Villa d'Este. After brief stays in Florence (10 February) and Venice (12/13 February), he arrives in Budapest.

15 February to 30 March: Liszt in Budapest.

27 February: First performance in Budapest of Liszt's *Hunnenschlacht*.

5 March: Marie d'Agoult dies in Paris.

20 March: Charity concert for the victims of the Danube floods.

26 March: Liszt's Budapest pupils give their first concert in the new Academy of Music at 4 Hal tér (Liszt has an apartment on the first floor of the building).

2 to 5 April: During a visit to Vienna, Liszt sees Bösendorfer, but spends most of his time with Saint-Saëns, whose *Danse macabre* he arranges for piano.

7 April to mid-September: Liszt in Weimar; several excursions interrupt him in his work.

30 April: Liszt travels to Düsseldorf for three days for performances of his *Chöre zu Herders ''Entfesseltem Prometheus''* and *''Gran'' Mass*. He meets Ferdinand Hiller and Clara Schumann (see p. 267).

4 to 14 May: Liszt in Hanover for a performance of his *Faust Symphony*.

15 to 25 May: Liszt as guest of King William III of the Netherlands at Het Loo, for a meeting of artists. On the 26th he is in Weimar, and on the 27th in Altenburg for the annual *Tonkünstlerversammlung*.

June: In Weimar, composing and teaching.

26 June: Performance of *Die Heilige Cäcilie* in Jena.

2 July: Liszt hears his symphonic poem *Hamlet* for the first time at a concert in Sondershausen, conducted by Max Erdmannsdörfer.

29 July to 1 August: Liszt in Wilhelmsthal as guest of the Grand Duke and his family.

1 August to 2 September: In Bayreuth for the first complete performance of Wagner's *Ring* in the presence of King Ludwig II.

18 August: At a banquet held in Bayreuth, Wagner stresses that without Liszt his music would never have found acceptance (see p. 250).

1 September: During a soirée at Wahnfried, Liszt plays the first and third movements of Beethoven's *Hammerklavier* Sonata.

2 September: Liszt returns to Weimar, then travels to Godesberg to visit Bülow, who is seriously ill.

24 September to 5 October: Liszt in Hanover. Hans von Bronsart looks after Bülow in Hanover.

6 to 9 October: Liszt stays with his biographer Lina Ramann in Nuremberg.[185] He then travels to Budapest via Regensburg and Vienna.

15 October to 11 March 1877: Liszt in Budapest, where he teaches at the Academy of Music.

21 to 31 October: Liszt in Szekszárd as guest of Baron Antal Augusz.

1 and 2 November: In Kalocsa as guest of Cardinal Haynald.

27 December: Liszt writes to Leopold Damrosch to announce that he has sent him the score of his *Triomphe funèbre du Tasse*. Damrosch conducts the first performance of the work in New York in 1877.

521 The tomb of Marie d'Agoult at Père Lachaise, Paris. Photograph, ca. 1960.

LISZT ON SAINT-SAËNS

To Carolyne von Sayn-Wittgenstein, 8 April 1876:
''[. . .] For many years I have thought very highly of his talent, which is certainly remarkable. If I were to describe it in a word, I would say he was the French Rubinstein – in other words, both an outstanding virtuoso and a highly creative composer, so universally gifted that he can shine in every field: symphony, oratorio, chamber music, salon music, and opera. In addition, he plays the organ wonderfully well. On a personal level, I am even closer to him than I am to Rubinstein [. . .].''[186]

To Carl Gille, 17 December 1877:
''[. . .] Saint-Saëns deserves far more success than he has been accorded so far, although everywhere – in France, Russia and Germany – he is already regarded as a distinguished composer who is striving with solemn resolve and mastery to achieve the highest that art that attain [. . .].''[187]

To Ludwig Bösendorfer, 19 February 1879:
''[. . .] Perhaps you and Hellmesberger would care to attend the soirée which we are holding here on 7 March, when we shall be honoured by a visit from that superb composer and splendid virtuoso, my admirable friend Saint-Saëns [. . .].''[188]

Saint-Saëns on Liszt (see pp. 255 and 332):
''The memory of having heard him play consoles one for no longer being young.''

THE DEATH OF MARIE D'AGOULT

Marie d'Agoult, the mother of Liszt's three children, died on 5 March 1876. Liszt had last seen her exactly ten years previously, in March 1866 (see p. 237). He described his total estrangement from his erstwhile lover in a letter to Princess Carolyne of 14 March 1876:

''[. . .] The newspapers report that Daniel Stern [Marie d'Agoult's pen name] has died. Casting hypocrisy aside, I could not bring myself to weep any more now, after her passing, than during her lifetime. La Rochefoucauld has well said that hypocrisy is homage paid to virtue, but one is still entitled to prefer true homage to false. Well, Madame d'Agoult had a great liking, nay, a real passion, for falsity – except at certain moments of ecstasy, which she subsequently could not bear to remember.

''Moreover, at my age condolences are as embarrassing as congratulations. *Il mondo va da sè* – one lives one's life, occupies oneself, grieves, suffers, deceives oneself, changes one's views, and dies as best one can. The sacrament to be most desired seems to me to be that of extreme unction.''[189]

522 Camille Saint-Saëns (1835–1921). Photograph by Paul Nadar, ca. 1895.

Liszt and Saint-Saëns felt the highest admiration for each other both as composers and as pianists.

WORKS

Danse macabre (Saint-Saëns) (piano transcription). Pub. 1876.
Andantino (short piano piece) (No. 4 of the five short piano pieces dedicated to Baroness Olga von Meyendorff). Pub. 1928.
Walhall (from Wagner's *Ring*) (piano transcription). Written ca. 1876. Pub. ca. 1880.
Festpolonaise (for four hands). Pub. in 1908 in August Göllerich's book on Liszt, and again in 1971. Also arranged for piano solo and published in 1981.
Via Crucis. Les 14 stations de la croix (for mixed chorus, solo voices, and organ). First sketches.

CLARA SCHUMANN ON LISZT'S PIANO PLAYING

To Johannes Brahms, May 1876:
"Just imagine: on my way back I heard Liszt again, for the first time in many years, and was utterly captivated by a number of pieces by Schubert which he played wonderfully well – but not, of course, by his own things, including a duo for two pianos on BACH, which was dreadful and became diverting only when his passagework encompassed the whole keyboard. But he has a unique mastery of it – a pity that one is permitted so little calm enjoyment but is always driven forward by a demonic force. I observed him closely, his sophisticated coquetry, his aristocratic amiability, etc. [. . .]"[190]

Diary entry of 9 April 1838 (Vienna):
"We have heard Liszt. There is no other player with whom he can be compared – he stands quite alone. He arouses terror and amazement, and is a most amiable artist. His appearance at the piano is indescribable – he is an original figure – he is absorbed by the piano [. . .]."

To Robert Schumann, Berlin, 20 March 1840:
"[. . .] But how lucky is Liszt to be able to play everything at sight, when the rest of us toil away and still achieve nothing [. . .]."[191]

To Robert Schumann, Berlin, 22 March 1840:
"The first time I heard Liszt in Vienna I could not bear it (we were at Graf's) but sobbed aloud, so deeply moved was I [. . .]."[192]

JOHANNES BRAHMS ON LISZT'S PIANO PLAYING

"He who has not heard Liszt play really cannot speak on the subject. He leads the way, and then, a long way behind, there is no one else. His piano playing was something unique, incomparable and inimitable."[193]

To the North German poet Klaus Groth (1819–1899):
"We, too, can play the piano" – and he named himself and other contemporary pianists – "but between the lot of us we've only a few of the fingers from both *his* hands."

Even Liszt's operatic fantasies, whose place in musical history is nowadays generally not considered worth defending, found a supporter in Brahms: "Anyone who really wants to know what Liszt has done for the piano should study his early operatic fantasies. They represent the rudiments of piano technique."[194]

LISZT ON BRAHMS'S B FLAT MAJOR PIANO CONCERTO

In 1882 Brahms sent Liszt his recently published Second Piano Concerto, asking him for his opinion. Although Liszt knew how much his own works had met with merciless disapproval on Brahms's part, his reply was typically generous: "To be frank, I found at an initial reading that it left a somewhat grey impression; but I have gradually seen the light. It has the succinct character of an outstanding work of art in which thoughts and feelings move in noble symmetry."[195]

523 Clara Schumann. Photograph by Fritz Luckhardt, ca. 1876.
In 1876 Clara Schumann heard Liszt play again for the first time in many years. She wrote to Brahms to tell him about it (left-hand column).

524 Johannes Brahms. Photograph, ca. 1895 (see p. 193).

Since the breakdown of their marriage plans in October 1861 (see p. 221), Liszt's relations with Carolyne von Sayn-Wittgenstein had entered a noticeably resigned phase, albeit still as inwardly intimate as ever. The Princess was now living in Rome, where she remained, with rare exceptions, until her death in 1887. Liszt divided each year about equally among Weimar, Budapest, and Rome. From 1876 onwards Carolyne worked with Lina Ramann on Liszt's biography. As Lina Ramann commented, ''The Princess is the only person on earth who knows everything about the Master; she is familiar with all the invisible threads, and she possesses the key to many incomprehensible facets of his life [. . .].''

During the periods when he was in Rome, Liszt would dine with the Princess: from 1880 onwards he lived in the Hotel Alibert, only a stone's throw from her apartment. When absent from Rome he would inform her by letter of his daily activities.

After the death of Prince Nicholas Wittgenstein in March 1864 there was no longer any obstacle in the way of their marriage. But either because Liszt and the Princess had long since grown reconciled to their fates, or because the Princess could not – or would not – bind Liszt to her for the rest of his life, there was no longer any talk of marriage.

What still bound these two people to each other was the memory of the thirteen years they had spent together and an ardent commitment to the Christian faith. There is no doubt that the Princess influenced Liszt's decision to receive minor orders.

525 Franz Liszt. Photograph by Friedrich Hertel, Weimar 1876.

Malwida von Meysenbug on Carolyne von Sayn-Wittgenstein:

''[. . .] She was not beautiful and never had been, and she once told me with a laugh that her mother, a beautiful and elegant woman fond of the pleasures of the world, had been saddened by how ugly she was, and that to console her mother she had told her to wait patiently for the resurrection, when she would be a miracle of loveliness. She also had one of those faces that have no real youth and which therefore tend to improve with age; and if one spoke with her and the object of the conversation aroused her interest or enthusiasm her features would become so animated and so expressive, and her eyes would glint with such ardour, that one would forget to notice whether she was beautiful or not, for one felt under the sway of an extraordinary personality, an unusual intellect which had no need of superficial charms to hold one's attention. [. . .] She once said to me, since I wore black a lot, that she too had worn black in the past, but that it had then become clear to her that it was not the dear Lord's wish that she should do so, since he had decorated the earth so beautifully with flowers of every colour; since that time she had worn clothes of all the colours of spring and summer, particularly in the fluttering ribbons of the bonnets which she wore – bonnets which, I may add, were hideousness itself [. . .].''[196]

From Weimar Liszt wrote to his mother in 1849: ''I do not know on what occasion Princess G. told you that Princess Wittgenstein was not beautiful. I flatter myself that I know something about beauty, and I maintain that Princess W. is beautiful – indeed, that she is very beautiful – for her soul transfigures her countenance and makes it supremely beautiful [. . .].''[197]

526 Princess Carolyne von Sayn-Wittgenstein. Photograph, Rome 1876.

527 Franz Liszt. Oil portrait by Mór Than, 1878.

LIFE

1 January to 11 March: Liszt in Budapest. He teaches four times a week, from 3 till 6 in the afternoon, at the Academy of Music.

15 February: The Artists' Society gives a Liszt Concert in the Hungaria Hotel. Liszt plays several piano pieces.

5 March: Liszt conducts his *Saint Elisabeth* in the Redoute.

10 March: Sophie Menter plays at a Liszt Concert in aid of charity.

11 March: Arrival in Vienna (Schottenhof).

16 March: Concert in aid of the Beethoven Monument in Vienna. Liszt plays Beethoven's E flat major Concerto and *Choral Fantasy*.[198]

18 March: Joseph Böhm conducts Liszt's *Missa choralis* and *Pater noster* at a concert held in the composer's presence in Vienna.

24 March to 3 April: Liszt in Bayreuth.

2 April: Liszt plays his B minor Sonata at Wahnfried. Wagner gives him a signed copy of his autobiography. Cosima notes in her diary, ''A lovely, cherished day, on which I thank Heaven for the comforting feeling that nothing – no deeply tragic parting of the ways, no malice on the part of others, no differences in character – could ever separate us three. – Oh, if only it were possible to add a fourth to our numbers here [Hans von Bülow]! But that an inexorable Fate forbids, and for me every joy and every exaltation ends with an anxious cry to my inner being! . . .''[199]

April: Compositional activity in Weimar.

15 May to the end of the month: Liszt attends the annual *Tonkünstlerversammlung* in Hanover. He plays (with Ingeborg von Bronsart) Saint-Saëns's *Variations on a Theme of Beethoven* and his own *Concerto pathétique*, together with his *Cantique d'amour* and *Mélodies hongroises*. He also takes over as conductor of his *Saint Elisabeth* when the scheduled conductor proves too drunk to appear.

12 June: Performances of the ''Gran'' Mass and *Psalm xiii* conducted by Karl Müller-Hartung in the Weimar parish church.

17 June: Performance of part of *Christus* in Liszt's presence in Leipzig.

1 July: Alexander Borodin visits Liszt in Weimar. He remains in Liszt's circle for three weeks.

23 to 28 July: Wagner and Cosima visit Liszt in Weimar. Cosima remains until the 30th.

9 to 12 August: Liszt in Wilhelmsthal, after which he travels to Rome via Bayreuth (12 to 15 August), Schillingsfürst (15/16 August), and Munich (16/17 August).

19 to 27 August: Liszt in Rome.

27 August to 27 October: Liszt at the Villa d'Este, where he writes piano pieces on the villa's cypresses and fountains.

23 September: Liszt writes to Carolyne von Sayn-Wittgenstein, ''I spent the whole of these last three days beneath the cypresses! I was as though possessed, and it was impossible to think of anything else – even in church – their ancient boles would not leave me in peace, and I heard their branches singing and weeping, weighed down by their everlasting leaves. Now, at last, they have come to rest on the pages of my music manuscript paper . . .''[201]

27 October to 17 November: Liszt in Rome.

21 November to 31 March 1878: Liszt in Budapest, where he teaches at the Academy of Music.

WORKS

Années de Pèlerinage. Troisième Année (for piano): 1. *Angelus!*, 2. *Aux Cyprès de la Villa d'Este (Andante)*, 3. *Aux Cyprès de la Villa d'Este (Andante non troppo lento)*, 4. *Les Jeux d'Eau à la Villa d'Este*, 5. *Sunt lacrymae rerum*, 6. *Marche funèbre*, 7. *Sursum corda*. Nos. 1–4 written in 1877; No. 5 in 1872; No. 6 in 1867; No. 7 ca. 1877. Pub. 1883.
Zweite Elegie (for piano). Pub. 1878, together with a version for piano and violin or cello (also written in 1878).
Sancta Dorothea (short piano piece). Pub. 1927.
Valse d'Adèle (piano transcription of a piece by Géza Zichy for left hand alone). Written ca. 1877. Pub. 1877.
Die Rose (romance by Louis Spohr) (piano transcription). Written ca. 1877. Pub. 1877.
Sei still ("Ach, was ist das Leben") (for mezzo-soprano or baritone and piano). Pub. 1879.
Resignazione (for organ or piano). Published in 1908 in August Göllerich's book on Liszt.
Petofi szellemének – Dem Andenken Petöfis (for piano). Pub. 1877, together with a version for four hands.
Agnus Dei (from Verdi's *Requiem*) (transcription for organ, harmonium, or piano). Pub. 1879.
Ave maris stella (for harp). Mentioned by Liszt in a letter of 12 October 1877 to the publisher Kahnt. Lost. See "Works 1865."
Orchestration of the second Overture to Cornelius's "Der Barbier von Bagdad". This Overture was only sketched by Cornelius and was orchestrated by Liszt. The year of publication is not known.
Salve Regina (for organ or harmonium). Pub. 1880.

Hanslick's review of the concert on 16 March 1877.

"Interest in the concert during the past week has revolved exclusively around Liszt, the king of pianists, and around his splendid support for the Beethoven Monument concert. We can but admire the strength and stamina of a man in his 66th year who has in fact given three concerts in a row, since the two public rehearsals for the gala concert were packed out and brought in a tidy sum for the charity organizers. And if a fourth preliminary rehearsal, however brief, had been arranged at which Liszt had not played but had merely been placed on public display – even then the tickets would no doubt all have been snapped up. What supreme good fortune to be able to exercise such power of attraction and fascination over one's fellows, and to be able to do so, moreover, uninterruptedly, irresistibly, from childhood to old age! At the Beethoven Concert Liszt played the E flat major Concerto and the Choral Fantasy (op. 80), both with his characteristic nobility and intellectual refinement, performing the tender song-like passages best of all. He delighted his audience and lent generous support to the splendid aim of erecting a monument to Beethoven in Vienna. For this we owe him our gratitude, and our gratitude alone. But do we not also owe our readers something? Do we not owe them the whole unvarnished truth? Can we really call Liszt an eternally youthful virtuoso and describe him now with the selfsame words and the same unqualified praise that we used after Liszt's last appearance in January 1874? It is of course inevitable that old age should make its presence felt, knocking gently and discreetly at the artist's door – it would be a miracle if it were otherwise, and not even an abbé believes in miracles nowadays. It was his closest friends most of all who were the first to deny his old strength of attack, the stamina and bold self-certainty which Liszt had formerly shown in playing bravura passages. For my own part, I will say only that three years ago Liszt played his *Hungarian Rhapsody* and Schubert's *Wandererfantasie* much more pas-

sionately and much more brilliantly than he played the two Beethoven pieces on this occasion. But the younger generation should not rejoice too loudly: they will still not catch up with the old man."[200]

Grosser Musikvereins-Saal.

Freitag den 16. März 1877:

CONCERT

zu Gunsten des

Beethoven-Denkmals

IN WIEN.

Mitwirkende: *Die Damen und Herren* Caroline Gomperz-Bettelheim, *k. k. Kammersängerin,* Marie Wilt, *k. k. Kammer- und Hofopernsängerin,* Franz Liszt, Josef Hellmesberger, *k. k. Hofkapellmeister und Director des Conservatoriums,* Reinhold Hummer, *Mitglied des k. k. Hofopernorchesters,* der Singverein, das Gesellschafts-Orchester.
Leiter des Concertes: *Director Johann Herbeck.*

PROGRAMM:

1. Marsch und Chor aus den „Ruinen von Athen". — Singverein.
2. Arie „Abscheulicher" aus „Fidelio". — Wilt.
3. Clavier-Concert Es-dur. — Liszt.
4. Schottische Lieder. — Gomperz-Bettelheim, Liszt, Hellmesberger, Hummer.
5. Clavier-Fantasie mit Chor. — Liszt, Singverein.
   Soli: *Die Damen Wilt und Gomperz-Bettelheim;* die Vereinsmitglieder: *Frau Gugler, Herr Wanicek, Herr Dunkl, Herr Graf.*

Sämmtliche Tonwerke von Beethoven.

Clavier: Bösendorfer. — Streichinstrumente: Lemböck.

Dieses Programm unentgeltlich. *Texte auf der Rückseite.*

531 The Musikverein building in Vienna. Wood engraving based on a drawing by E. Petrovics; ca. 1870.
Major performances of Liszt's works were given in this building in the years around 1875.

532 Programme for a concert in Vienna on 16 March 1877.

Opposite page:

528 Title page of an early edition of Liszt's piano piece *Aux Cyprès de la Villa d'Este*.

529 Title page of the first edition of Liszt's *Années de Pèlerinage. Troisième Année*, 1883.
The first four pieces were written in 1877 in the Villa d'Este. A number of works in this cycle, especially *Les jeux d'eau à la Villa d'Este*, anticipate the tonal visions of Debussy and Ravel.

530 Garden of the Villa d'Este. Photograph taken ca. 1880, with a dedication in Liszt's own hand dated January 1886 and addressed to his pupil August Stradal.

LIFE

1 January to 31 March: Liszt in Budapest, where he teaches at the Academy of Music.

20 January: Matinée at the Academy of Music in honour of Cardinal Haynald. The programme includes Liszt's *Die Heilige Cäcilie*, dedicated to the Cardinal, and the performers include Count Zichy.

7 February: Death of Pope Pius IX in Rome. Liszt had held him in high esteem and been received by him on several occasions.

21 March: Liszt gives a concert at the Institute for Young English Ladies in Budapest.

27 March: Performance of part of Liszt's *Dante Symphony* under Sándor Erkel.

1 to 7 April: Liszt spends a week in Vienna, as he does almost every year.

8 to 17 April: Liszt in Bayreuth. (Cosima's Diaries include an account of the harmonious course of this visit.) Liszt admires Act I of *Parsifal*, the second complete draft of which has recently been completed.

17 April to 17 August: Apart from a few excursions, Liszt is in Weimar throughout this period. His pupils include Adele aus der Ohe, Eduard Reuß, Moriz Rosenthal, and the fourteen-year-old Alfred Reisenauer.

25 May to the end of the month: Liszt in Hanover, visiting Hans von Bülow and Hans von Bronsart. He hears a performance of Wagner's *Rienzi* under Bülow. He returns to Weimar, then sets off on 8 June for Paris.

9 to 18 June: Liszt attends the World Exhibition in Paris as President of the Jury in the section devoted to musical instruments. He stays with the Erards at 13 Rue du Mail (see pp. 273 and 40).

21 to 26 June: At the annual *Tonkünstlerversammlung* in Erfurt, Liszt conducts his *Hungaria* and a piano concerto by Bronsart, in which the soloist is Hans von Bülow.

July: Back in Weimar, Liszt revises Schubert's piano works.

20 to 31 August: Liszt in Bayreuth. According to Cosima's Diaries, Wagner "enlarges on my father's unique, aristocratic personality, everything about him refined, princely, grand, yet at the same time full of artistic genius."[202] Liszt admires Act II of *Parsifal*, on which Wagner is currently working. Liszt travels to Rome via Munich (1 September). Franz von Lenbach accompanies him to the station in Munich.

3 to 12 September: Liszt in Rome, where he sees Carolyne von Sayn-Wittgenstein again.

9 September: Death of Liszt's loyal friend Baron Antal Augusz.

12 September to the end of the year: Liszt at the Villa d'Este, with visits to Rome in between.

October: Intensive work on *Via Crucis* and the *Septem Sacramenta*.

21 November: Completion of *Via Crucis*.

December: Piano transcription of Eduard Lassen's incidental music to Hebbel's *Die Nibelungen* (see Illus. 426).

533 Linus and Hercules. Liszt caricatures, 1878.

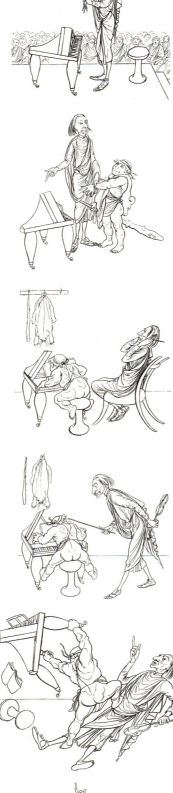

Liszt caricatures from 1878, with verses by F. van Hoffs.

When Hercules was still a child,
The greatest living pianist
On whom fair destiny had smiled
Was Linus, alias Franz Liszt.

Throughout the season he would go
On tour and play his cembalo.
He lived – or so it is related –
In ancient Thebes the Hundred-Gated.

His fame and his desire to please
Drew acolytes from near and far.
And so young Master Hercules
Enrolled at his Conservatoire.

When Linus saw the massive mitt
That spanned a twelfth (I'll swear to it),
He cried, "Andante lagrimoso!
He'll be a famous virtuoso."

But hands alone are not enough
To make a cembalist; in truth
A pianist's made of stronger stuff
Than this tone-deaf and idle youth.

Although he tried to persevere
And studied with him for a year,
He found the easiest étude
Exposed his gross ineptitude.

And finally there came the day
When Hercules proved doubly deaf
To all his preceptor might say
And struck F sharp instead of F.

Thinking "This will do the trick,"
Linus seized his fiddlestick,
And when he heard the next wrong note
His pupil vengefully he smote.

In this he showed a lack of tact,
For Hercules was not the sort
Of man you'd say was slow to act.
He gave the piece no further thought

But grabbed the clavicembalo
And dealt it an almighty blow,
Then swung it round and brought it down
With all his might on Linus' crown.

The cembalo now lay in bits
(Believe me, not a word is false)
But, worse than that, "le petit Litz"
Would never play another waltz.

Every story has a moral:
Music teachers should not quarrel
With their students. If they do,
Their lives and instruments they'll rue.

WORKS

Via Crucis. Les 14 stations de la croix (for mixed chorus, solo voices, and organ or piano). Written 1878/79. Pub. 1936. A version for piano duet, also prepared at this time, remains unpublished, but the piano solo version was published in 1980. A version for organ also prepared at this time is believed to be unpublished.

Septem Sacramenta (Responsories) (for solo voices, chorus, and organ). Pub. 1936. On No. 7 (*Matrimonium*) Liszt noted, ''Not published to date, December 84.'' In other words, No. 7 may have appeared at the end of 1884.

Zwölf alte deutsche geistliche Weisen (transcriptions for piano or organ): 1. *Was Gott tut, das ist wohlgetan*, 2. *O Traurigkeit*, 3. *Nun ruhen alle Wälder*, 4. *Meine Seel' erhebet den Herrn*, 5. *O Haupt voll Blut und Wunden*, 6. *O Lamm Gottes*, 7. *Wer nur den lieben Gott läßt walten*, 8. *Es segne uns Gott*, 9. *Vexilla regis*, 10. *Crux benedicta*, 11. *Jesu Christe*, 12. *Nun danket alle Gott*. (The numbering varies from edition to edition.) Some of the pieces were conceived for choir or for a single accompanied voice. No. 4, in spite of its title, has the words, ''Gott sei uns gnädig und barmherzig.'' Written 1878/79. Nos. 1 and 3–8 were published in 1921, Nos. 1–7 and 9–12 in 1980.

Songs (for mezzo-soprano or tenor/baritone and piano): 1. *Der Glückliche*, 2. *Einst*, 3. *An Edlitam* (''Zur Silberhochzeit''), 4. *In Stunden der Entmutigung (Gebet)*. Written ca. 1878. Pub. 1879.

Die tote Nachtigall (for soprano or mezzo-soprano and piano). Second version. Pub. 1879.

Excerpts from Incidental Music to Hebbel's ''Die Nibelungen'' and Goethe's ''Faust'' (Lassen) (piano transcriptions): I. *Nibelungen*: 1. *Hagen und Krimhild*, 2. *Bechlarn*. II. *Faust*: 1. *Osterhymne*, 2. *Hoffest: Marsch und Polonaise*. Written and published in 1878/79.

Der blinde Sänger (Tolstoi) (piano transcription). Pub. 1881. See ''Works 1875.''

Revision of Schubert's piano works for four hands. Pub. 1880.

Erbgroßherzog Karl August. Franz Lißt.
Kapellmeister Laffen. Gräfin Mouchanoff.
Eine Soiree bei Franz Lißt in Weimar.
Großherzog Karl Alexander Opernregiffeur Schmidt
Kammerfänger Ferenczy. Prof. Müller-Hartung. Dr. Hermann Uhde. Dr. Julius Groffe.
Hoftheaterintendant Freih. v. Loën.
Kammermufikus Kömpel. Kammerfänger v. Milde.

534 Soirée at the Hofgärtnerei in Weimar. Wood engraving from *Das Neue Blatt*, ca. 1878.

Liszt travelled to Paris for the 1878 World Exhibition, staying in the city from 9 to 18 June as honorary president and member of the jury of the section devoted to musical instruments. Hanslick's delightful description shows once again the sensation that Liszt caused wherever he appeared:

''Liszt appeared at our first jury meeting and was enthusiastically greeted on every side. I seized the opportunity to suggest that our jury might acclaim Liszt as its honorary president. Which they did, much, it seemed, to the great man's delight [. . .]. That Hungary, with its few musical instruments, had sent its own juror to Paris and that it had, moreover, given the office to no less a person than Liszt seemed somewhat curious, but it turned out for the best. No one else could outshine him. It was as though our Emperor had been elected to serve in Parliament (as indeed happens in certain rural communities). Liszt maintained a diplomatic reserve in his judgement. When faced with the various piano makers he found himself very much in the delicate situation of a real live monarch.

''And so he walked everywhere with us, giving an encouraging word here, a friendly smile there, but without studying any of the instruments himself [. . .]. More and more people attached themselves to our party, and time and again I had to reply to the polite questioning of some total stranger, 'De grâce Monsieur, n'est-ce pas Litz?' [. . .] In his day Liszt was indubitably the most widely known personality in the whole of Europe. Even if only from pictures of him, everyone knew the slim figure in his abbé's coat and broad-brimmed hat, not to mention the sharply outlined Jupiter-like head so characteristically framed by a mane of white hair.

''Towards midday he stopped in his tracks, somewhat weary, and confessed that he was now ready to award first prize to a knife and fork. We were all happy to accept his invitation to breakfast in the Hungarian 'Czarda' in the exhibition park. The sun-tanned landlord laughed with delight under his upturned moustache, the cook did his best, the Gypsy musicians likewise, and thus we were soon enjoying the most delightful home comforts. Rarely have I seen Liszt so good-humoured and so communicative – I might even say so amiable, if I had ever known him to be other than amiable [. . .]'' (*Aus meinem Leben*, Berlin 1911, vol. II, pp. 184–6).

LIFE

2 to 12 January: In Rome, then via Florence (for a few days' stay with Jessie Laussot) to Budapest.

18 January to 2 April: Liszt in Budapest, where he teaches at the Academy of Music.

8 February: Court Councillor Eduard von Liszt, Liszt's uncle and a man very dear to him, dies in Vienna.

7 March: Saint-Saëns gives a concert in the Redoute in Budapest. In addition to his piano quartets, he performs Liszt's *Venezia e Napoli*. For years the two composers have been on the friendliest terms.

10 to 15 March: With Count Géza Zichy in Klausenburg.

12 March: Performance of part of *Saint Elisabeth* in the Redoutensaal in Klausenburg.

14 March: Liszt and Zichy give a concert in aid of the victims of the Danube floods in Szeged.

16 March: Liszt in Hosszúpályi (near Debrezen) as guest of Count Ernö Zichy.

26 March: Liszt takes part in a concert in the Budapest Redoute in aid of victims of the flood disaster in Szeged.

2 to 9 April: Liszt in Vienna. Celebrations to mark the silver wedding anniversary of the Austrian imperial couple.

3 April: Liszt attends a concert given by the Hellmesberger Quartet and is tumultuously received (see p. 274).

4 April: Liszt soirée at the Bösendorfersaal.

5 April: A concert in Liszt's honour is held at Bösendorfer's. Among the performers are Toni Raab.

6 April: Concert by the Vienna Philharmonic including Liszt's *Loreley* and *Mignon* for orchestra.

7 April: Liszt gives a charity concert in the salon of Count Gyula Andrássy.

8 April: In the morning Hellmesberger conducts two of the *Septem Sacramenta* (*Eucharistia* and *Matrimonium*) in the Burgkapelle; in the evening Liszt conducts his *"Gran" Mass* in the Musikvereinssaal.

9 April: Liszt attends a concert, then sets off for Hanover.

13 April: Bülow conducts Liszt's *Prometheus* in Hanover. After a performance of Beethoven's Symphony No. 9, Liszt describes Bülow as "the most eminent of all conductors" after Wagner.[203]

18 April: Liszt leaves Hanover for Frankfurt. On the 21st Kniese conducts a performance of *Christus* in Frankfurt.

May: Liszt in Weimar, composing and teaching.

3 to 9 June: Liszt attends the annual *Tonkünstlerversammlung* in Wiesbaden. Bülow conducts a performance of the *Faust Symphony* in the composer's presence.

6 and 7 July: Liszt in Sondershausen for a performance of *Ce qu'on entend sur la montagne*.

10 July: Complete performance of the *Septem Sacramenta* in the Weimar Parish Church.

26 July: Adolf von Henselt visits Liszt in Weimar.

21 to 31 August: Liszt in Bayreuth. To mark Goethe's birthday (28 August) he plays his *Faust Symphony* on the piano in Wahnfried. He sets off for Rome, calling on Lenbach in Munich (1/2 September) on the way.

3 to 7 September: Liszt in Rome.

8 September to 6 January 1880: Liszt at the Villa d'Este, where he works on various compositions including his transcriptions of Beethoven's 3rd, 4th, and 5th Piano Concertos for two pianos, and a piano paraphrase of the *Polonaise* from Tchai-

Liszts „Graner Messe" und „Loreley".

Es geschah in Hellmesbergers letzter Quartett-Soirée, daß während des Schubertschen Es-dur-Trios unbemerkt Liszt in den Saal trat. Bescheidentlich hielt er sich bis zum Schlusse des Stückes im Hintergrunde, um dann, die Reihen der Zuhörer entlang, seinen Sitz im „Cercle" aufzusuchen. Die allgemeine Aufmerksamkeit, die schon während des Schubertschen Finales stark ins Schwanken gerathen war, warf sich nun ausschließlich und in so gehobener Stimmung auf den berühmten Ankömmling, daß die ganze Versammlung wie auf ein Zeichen zu applaudiren begann und so lange damit fortfuhr, bis Liszt vortrat und sich dankend verbeugte. Es war ein reizender, unvergeßlicher Moment. Wir kennen keinen zweiten Fall, daß ein Künstler, der weder als Componist noch als Mitwirkender, sondern als einfacher Zuhörer einen Concertsaal betritt, vom ganzen Publikum laut und einhellig begrüßt worden wäre. Wenn heute Bismarck und Gambetta, Richard Wagner und Verdi, die jüngste, schönste Primadonna und der älteste Virtuose im Concert oder Theater erscheinen würden, sie dürften sich keiner solchen Scene rühmen. Niemand in ganz Europa, als gerade Liszt. Das in der Mehrzahl der Zuhörer instinctiv aufblitzende Gefühl, Liszt zu begrüßen, setzte sich wie an einer electrischen Kette fort, bis es fast gleichzeitig im ganzen Saale zum dröhnenden Ausbruche kam. Ein gemüthvoller, liebenswürdiger Zug, der wahrlich unser Publikum ziert, wie er den Gefeierten ehrt. Diese allgemeine, nicht blos dem Künstler, sondern ebensosehr dem Menschen geltende Sympathie kommt auch überall sonst zum Vorscheine, wo Liszt intervenirt. Welcher Zauber umgiebt noch immer den bejahrten Mann! Dirigirt er selbst eine seiner Compositionen, so schweigen nicht blos die bekannten Mißlaute der Opposition — wie sich das ja bei einem wohlerzogenen Publikum versteht — nein, das Opponiren selbst, das innere Widerstreben so mancher Zuhörer gegen Liszts Schöpfungen schweigt besänftigt, wenn das von Geist und Wohlwollen leuchtende Antlitz des alten Feuerkopfes sie anblickt und Liszts Musik gleichsam durch seinen eigenen Mund zu uns spricht. Die gestrige Aufführung der Graner Festmesse im großen Musikvereinssaale lieferte den jüngsten Beleg für jene auffallende Erscheinung. Die Festmesse, jedenfalls Liszts größte Arbeit, wurde in Wien bekanntlich im März 1858 zuerst gegeben. Daß seit einundzwanzig Jahren keine unserer weltlichen oder geistlichen Musik-Autoritäten an eine Wiederholung dieses Werkes gedacht hat, zeigt, wie gering in Wien das Bedürfniß danach war. Auch heute mochte hinreichende Betheiligung des Publikums zweifelhaft sein ohne das anlockende persönliche Erscheinen Liszts. Die Gesellschaft der Musikfreunde hatte sich dieses Talismans weislich versichert, der auch diesmal nicht versagte. Mir persönlich fällt das Bekenntniß schwer, daß ich von diesem Werke keinen anderen Eindruck empfing, als vor 20 Jahren, so redlich ich mich jetzt bemühte, Gefallen daran zu finden. Einige Dornen hat diese Composition wohl seither verloren, aber es sind ihr keine Rosen nachgewachsen. Wir haben in diesen 20 Jahren musikalisch viel erlebt und viel erlitten — manches ungewöhnlich Formlose, Gewaltsame, Mißtönende übt heute nicht mehr die frühere aufreizende, ärgerlich provocirende Macht über uns. Die „Graner Messe" hat uns

nach 20 Jahren sanfter gefunden, aber nicht glücklicher gemacht. Von welcher ihrer zwei Seiten wir diese Kirchenmusik betrachten, von der kirchlichen oder musikalischen, sie bietet uns wohl Anregungen, aber Befriedigungen nimmermehr. An der individuellen Frömmigkeit und Religiosität des Componisten zweifeln wir keinen Augenblick, vermögen aber für unser Theil nichts von dem verklärten Frieden und der Heilkraft des Gebets in einer Musik zu finden, die das ganze Wirrsal der menschlichen Leidenschaften aufstört, ein Drama irdischer Unrast und Zerrissenheit. Interessant durch zahlreiche geistvolle Züge, durch eindringende musikalische Exegese, imponirend durch Ernst und Größe ihrer Intentionen, merkwürdig endlich als die Schöpfung eines phänomenal organisirten, genialen Mannes, bleibt uns die „Graner Messe" doch schließlich ein durchaus unerquickliches, ungesundes und raffinirtes Werk, in welchem das Ringen nach religiösem Ausdruck und der unüberwindliche Hang nach theatralischer Effecthascherei fortwährend um die Herrschaft kämpfen. Wie Mahomeds Sarg, so schwebt Liszts Festmesse heimathlos zwischen Himmel und Erde. Die Aufführung der „Graner Messe" bot einen merkwürdigen Anblick — das Sehen war ja dem Publikum in erster Linie wichtig. Auf einer erhöhten Dirigenten-Tribüne steht Liszt, in langem schwarzen Abbékleid, aus dessen oberen Knopflöchern ein langes schweres Büschel von Miniaturorden herabhängt, eine wahre Malaga-Traube von Ordenskreuzchen. Zahlreiche um das Pult gehängte und gelegte Blumen-Guirlanden und Lorbeerkränze bilden eine Art kleineren Bosquets, von dessen dunklem Grün sich das imposante weiße Haupt Liszts effectvoll abhebt. Liszt dirigirt, wenn man einige leicht andeutende Handbewegungen so nennen kann. „Der Dirigent soll Steuermann sein und nicht Ruderknecht," lautet ein bekannter Ausspruch Liszts. Wenn man glücklicherweise zwei treffliche „Ruderknechte" arbeitend zur Seite hat, dann verschlägt es freilich wenig, daß der Steuermann zeitweilig die Hände in die Taschen steckt. Herr Kremser, der die ganze Aufführung sorgfältigst vorbereitet hatte, dirigirte mit dem Taktstock, Herr Hellmesberger desgleichen mit dem Violinbogen; über beiden schwebte, so ganz im allgemeinen, als heiliger Geist Franz Liszt. Wenn er manchmal die Hand weit ausstreckte über Sänger und Musiker, da sah es mehr wie ein Segnen aus, als wie ein Dirigiren. Alles aber, er mag thun was immer, kleidet ihn vornehm und bedeutsam und übt den bekannten, halbhundertjährigen Zauber auf jung und alt. Auch auf die Solosänger blieb dieser Zauber nicht ohne Einfluß: sie sangen ihre schwierigen Partien mit wahrhaft apostolischer Hingebung.

Auch im letzten Philharmonischen Concert gehörte Liszt das lebhafteste Interesse: sang doch Frau Pauline Lucca — offenbar dem anwesenden Componisten zu Ehren — zwei Lieder von Liszt: „Mignon" und „Loreley". Von allen Compositionen Liszts sind seine Lieder — es giebt deren ein halbes Hundert — am wenigsten gekannt und gesungen. Das verbreitetste und beliebteste ist jedenfalls: „Es muß ein Wunderbares sein", eines der wenigen Lieder von Liszt, dessen zarte einheitliche Stimmung nirgends gewaltsam zerrissen wird und das rein genossen werden kann. Bemerkenswerth sind sie alle, diese Lieder, als höchst individuelle Äußerungen einer interessanten Persönlichkeit, die sich allerdings den meisten Gedichten gegenüber sehr souverän benimmt.

535 Eduard Hanslick's review of the *"Gran" Mass* and a number of Liszt's Lieder, reproduced from *Concerte, Componisten und Virtuosen der letzten fünfzehn Jahre 1870–1885*, Berlin 1886. The article (from which the final 32 lines have been cut here) first appeared in the morning edition of the *Neue Freie Presse* of 10 April 1879. (For a translation of the text, see p. 342.)

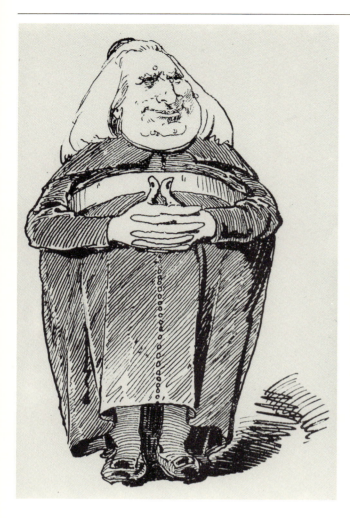

Abbé Liszt und Frau Gomperz-Bettelheim.

(Gez. von **Kliē.**)

Franz Liszt in Wien.

LISZT CARICATURES FROM 1879

Famous and instantly recognizable, Liszt was one of the most widely caricatured of nineteenth-century personalities. In the years around 1875 numerous caricatures (some more witty than others) appeared in *Humoristische Blätter*, *Der Floh* and above all *Borsszem Jankó*.

Liszt's dislike of caricatures was well known; nor did he have any time for so-called humorous magazines.

"I have never taken any great pleasure in cartoons and caricatures. They pander to universal vulgarity, and that is not a sentiment Franz Liszt can subscribe to [. . .]" (from an unpublished letter, 1882).

"It is not to my liking to sup with wits and satirists; jokes are like pepper – they should be used in moderation [. . .]" (letter to Carolyne von Sayn-Wittgenstein, 9 October 1872).[204]

Top of page:

536 Caricature from *Borsszem Jankó* of 27 July 1879.

537 Caricature from *Der Floh* of April 1879.
The soprano Caroline von Gomperz-Bettelheim took part in Liszt's concerts in Vienna on 7 April (a charity performance in aid of flood victims of Szeged, when the piano accompanist was Felix Mottl) and 8 April 1879 (as soloist in Liszt's "Gran" Mass).

kovsky's *Eugene Onegin*. Liszt is appointed Honorary Canon of San Albano.
30 December: Grand charity concert at the Villa d'Este in aid of the poor of the Sabine Hills. The performers include Liszt, Nadine Helbig, and the fifteen-year-old Alfred Reisenauer.

WORKS

Polonaise from Tchaikovsky's *Eugene Onegin* (piano transcription). Pub. 1880. Normally dated 1880; but it is clear from Liszt's letter to Olga von Meyendorff of 25 October 1879 that the piece was written in 1879.
Tarantelle (Dargomïzhsky) (piano transcription). Pub. 1880. Originally for three hands: Liszt perpetuates Dargomïzhsky's original joke of having one hand sustain a pedal point on two A's throughout the piece.
Sarabande and Chaconne from Handel's "Almira" (for piano). Pub. 1880.
Was Liebe sei (for mezzo-soprano and piano). Third setting. Written ca. 1879. Pub. 1879.
Go not, happy day (to words by Tennyson) (for mezzo-soprano or tenor and piano). Pub. ca. 1880.
Rosario (for mixed voices and organ or harmonium): 1. *Mysteria gaudiosa*, 2. *Mysteria dolorosa*, 3. *Mysteria gloriosa*, 4. *Pater noster* (for baritone or unison men's voices). Pub. 1936. Nos. 1–3 also for organ, pub. 1971.
Ossa arida (for men's voices and organ four hands). Pub. 1936.
Revive Szegedin, Hungarian March (Szabady) (piano transcription of Massenet's orchestration). Pub. 1892.
Missa pro organo lectarum celebrationi missarum adjumento inserviens (for organ). Pub. 1880.
Cantantibus organis (for contralto solo, mixed voices, and orchestra). Pub. 1880.
Danza Sacra e Duetto Finale (from Verdi's *Aida*) (piano transcription). Pub. 1879.
Gebet (for organ). Pub. 1970. Adapted from the *Graduale* of the *Missa pro organo* of 1879. (No connection with the *Gebet* of 1853 for organ or with the song *In Stunden der Entmutigung* of 1878.)
O Roma nobilis (for mixed voices or solo voice and organ). Written ca. 1879. Pub. 1936. Piano version pub. 1983.
Toccata (for piano). May have been written at this time. Pub. 1970.
Carousel de Mme Pelet-Narbonne (for piano). May have been written at this time. Pub. 1970.
Una Stella Amica. Walzer (Pezzini) (piano transcription). May have been written at this time. Pub. by Ricordi, date unknown.
Sospiri! (for piano) (No. 5 of the Olga von Meyendorff pieces). Pub. 1958.
Beethoven's Piano Concertos in C minor, G major, and E flat major (arranged for two pianos for study purposes and for the concert hall). The *tutti* passages are scored for both pianos. Pub. 1882. Liszt wrote cadenzas for the Third and Fourth Concertos for this publication.

538 Liszt and Bösendorfer. Caricature from *Humoristische Blätter*, 1879.

LIFE

1 to 6 January: Liszt at the Villa d'Este, then in Rome until the 10th. He leaves for Budapest on the 11th.

12 to 14 January: Liszt in Venice, where he visits Jessie Laussot-Hillebrand, Princess Therese Hohenlohe, Talleyrand, and Count Harry von Arnim.

15 January to 20 March: Liszt in Budapest.

30 January: Liszt writes to the mother of Alfred Reisenauer, ''Mendelssohn's admirable concertos always prove safe, especially since Berlioz claimed in his witty essay (published almost 30 years ago) that these concertos play themselves, without any additional effort on the pianists' part . . .''[205]

February: Teaching commitments at the Budapest Academy of Music, where Liszt holds a master class for fifteen pianists.

14 March: Liszt's pupils give their first concert in the new Music Academy building at 67 Sugár út.

21 March: Liszt arrives in Vienna.

23 March: Liszt conducts *Die Ideale*, *Die Glocken des Straßburger Münsters*, and his *Szekszárd Mass* in the Musikvereinssaal. The concert is followed by a banquet attended by, among others, Leschetizky, Scharwenka, Essipoff, Zichy, Hellmesberger, and Raab.

25 March: *Missa choralis* under Joseph Böhm.

28 March: *Les Préludes* under Hans Richter.

1 April: Liszt leaves Vienna and travels to Weimar via Dresden (2/3 April).

3 April to 19 August: Liszt in Weimar.

27 April: Empress Augusta in Weimar. Performances of *Les Préludes* and the *Grand Galop chromatique* (in Doppler's orchestration).

17 to 24 May: Annual meeting of the Allgemeiner Deutscher Musikverein in Baden-Baden. Performance of *Jeanne d'Arc* and parts of *Christus*. Saint-Saëns is among those present. Liszt returns to Weimar via Frankfurt (where he visits Raff on the 24th) and Gießen (25 May).

13 to 27 June: Hans von Bülow in Weimar; he sifts through the crowd of pianists which has continued to grow around Liszt.

27 June: Müller-Hartung conducts Cherubini's Requiem in C minor and Liszt's *Coronation Mass* in the Weimar parish church.

7 July: Performance of Rossini's *Petite Messe solennelle* in Jena.

August: The Freies Deutsches Hochstift appoints Liszt an honorary member and master.

19 August: Liszt leaves Weimar and travels via Liebenstein and Munich (where he sits for Lenbach on the 25th) to Rome, arriving there on 29 August.

4 September to 11 January 1881: Liszt at the Villa d'Este, with excursions to Siena and Rome.

16 to 25 September: Liszt visits Richard and Cosima Wagner in Siena (Villa Torre Fiorentina). On the 21st he plays Beethoven's Sonatas op. 27 no. 2 and op. 28 for Wagner; and on the 24th Wagner sings through Act III of *Parsifal*, accompanied on the piano by Liszt.

October/November: Liszt at the Villa d'Este, composing and dealing with a huge correspondence. Asked by Olga von Meyendorff why he had not entered a seminary in 1830, he confirms that only his mother's wishes had prevented him from doing so.

29 December: Liszt attends a concert given by Sophie Menter in Rome (see Illus. 516). Afterwards, he says that ''there is no one to compare with her among women pianists.''[206]

540 Autograph letter from Smetana to Franz Liszt, dated 19 March 1880.

In old age Liszt led a very unpretentious life. A single manservant was ''the only luxury'' he permitted himself, as he once told Carolyne von Sayn-Wittgenstein. After the Princess had gone to Rome in 1860, the following servants were employed by Liszt:

1860–1861: ''Otto'' (last name untraceable).

1862–1870: Fortunato Salvagni, from Rome.

1871–1875: Miska Sipka, whom Liszt brought with him from Szekszárd (Hungary). He died in Rome in February 1875.

1875–1881: Spiridion Knezevits from Montenegro, an imposing figure with an imperial beard and an enormous moustache. He was extremely demanding and was regarded by Liszt's pupils as a figure of fearsome authority. In his letters Liszt occasionally calls him ''the famous Spiridion.''

1882–1884: Achille Colonello, an Italian with a good knowledge of languages. He died on 1 February 1884. (See Illus. 591.)

1884–1886: Michael Kreiner, known as Mihály or Mischka.

Karl Lehmann served Liszt briefly in March 1884.

539 Franz Liszt. Photograph by Vianelli, Venice 1880.

541 Bedřich Smetana (1824–1884). Photograph, ca. 1880.
Smetana was a loyal and genuine admirer of Liszt's; for his part, the older man helped the Czech composer in every conceivable way.

542 Pauline Apel. Photograph by Louis Held, ca. 1890.
Helped by a single servant, Pauline Apel looked after Liszt's household in Weimar. After his death she ran the Liszt Museum in the Hofgärtnerei, regaling the numerous visitors with many an anecdote about her master which only she knew.

WORKS

La Mandragore (Delibes). Incomplete piano arrangement of ballad from Delibes' *Jean de Nivelle*. Dates from 1880 or later. Unpublished.

Second Mephisto Waltz (for orchestra). Written 1880/81. Pub. 1881, together with piano transcriptions for two hands and for four hands.

Romance oubliée (for viola and piano). Pub. 1881, together with versions for violin and piano, cello and piano, and piano alone. The piece derives from the *Romance* of 1848 (see ''Works 1848'').

In festo transfigurationis Domini nostri Jesu Christi (for piano). Pub. 1927.

Pro Papa (Pope Leo XIII): 1. *Dominus conservet eum* (for mixed voices and organ), 2. *Tu es Petrus* (for unison men's voices and organ). Written 1880 or 1881. Pub. 1881. (Unconnected with the *Tu es Petrus* from *Christus*.)

Angelus (for string quartet) (transcription of the *Angelus* from the *Années de Pèlerinage. Troisième Année* : see ''Works 1877''). Pub. 1883. Also a version for string orchestra, identical to quartet version with added double-bass part by Liszt.

Des Tages laute Stimmen schweigen (for contralto or baritone and piano). Pub. 1923.

Verlassen (''Mir ist die Welt so freudenleer'') (for mezzo-soprano and piano). Pub. 1880.

San Francesco (Prelude to *Cantico del Sol di San Francesco*) (for organ). Pub. 1936. Version for piano pub. 1983.

Variants for a piano transcription (by Count Géza Zichy) of Bach's Chaconne for unaccompanied violin. Mentioned in a letter to Zichy of 30 August 1880. Lost.

Die vier Jahreszeiten (draft of a string quartet). Ca. 1880. Left uncompleted.

Seconda Mazurka Variata (P. A. Tirindelli) (piano transcription). Pub. Turin, date unknown.

O, wenn es doch immer so bliebe (Anton Rubinstein) (piano transcription). Pub. 1881. Identical to *Gelb rollt*, listed in some catalogues as missing.

Variation on a theme on which Borodin, Cui, Lyadov, and Rimsky-Korsakov had already published variations (for piano duet). Liszt wrote a variation (''Andante'') as a prelude to the new edition of this piece entitled *Paraphrasen über ein enfaches Thema*. Liszt's prelude is for piano solo, not duet as stated in all catalogues.

543 Villa d'Este at Tivoli outside Rome, Liszt's home during the winter months between 1869 and 1885. Photograph, ca. 1880, mounted with pressed leaves and twigs from the gardens of the Villa d'Este, and with a handwritten dedication from Liszt to his pupil August Göllerich. Previously unpublished.

Opposite page:

544, 545, 546, 547 Franz Liszt during a studio sitting in Rome. Water-colours by Nadine Helbig, Rome 1880.

On this occasion Liszt was sitting to several artists at once and also using the time to carry on a conversation with his pupil Giovanni Sgambati. On the left is the sculptor Richard Greenough, working on his medallion (Illus. 547); in the centre is the easel belonging to Nadine Helbig, who has yet to begin her portrait (Illus. 544), preferring first to sketch the entire scene (Illus. 545) while signing her empty canvas with the initials "N.H." At the right is the painter Moritz Treuenfels, whose sketch already hints at his finished portrait (Illus. 546).

544

geg. von Nadine Helbig,
geb. Prinzessin Schahawskoy

545

546

547

LIFE

1 to 11 January: Liszt at the Villa d'Este.

12 January: Sgambati conducts the first performance in Rome of *Tasso: lamento e trionfo* in the composer's presence.

15/16 January: Liszt in Florence, where he visits Jessie Laussot-Hillebrand, Laura Minghetti, Countess Dönhoff, Sophie Menter, and Princess Rospigliosi. He then travels to Budapest via Venice, where he meets Ugo Bassani and Rodolphe Lichtenstein on 17/18 January.

20 January to 3 April: Liszt in Budapest, where he teaches at the Academy of Music and occupies rooms in the Academy building.

14 February: Bülow gives a recital of Liszt's piano works in Budapest, followed by a concert with Beethoven's last five sonatas.

15 February: Liszt writes to the editor of the *Gazette de Hongrie*: "25 years ago Bülow was my pupil in music, just as I was a pupil of my revered and cherished Czerny 25 years before that. But Bülow has the ability to fight more effectively and more tenaciously than I. His wholly admirable edition of Beethoven is dedicated to me as the 'fruits of my teaching.' But here the teacher had everything to learn from the pupil . . ."[207]

9 March: Sándor Erkel conducts the first performance of the *Second Mephisto Waltz* for orchestra in Budapest.

3/4 April: Liszt in Preßburg. On the 3rd a concert is given in aid of the Hummel Memorial (see Illus. 557).

5/6 April: Accompanied by Bösendorfer, Zichy and Goldschmidt, Liszt spends the night in Ödenburg. Concert in the Casino on the 6th.

7 April: Liszt attends the unveiling of a memorial plaque on the house where he had been born in Raiding (see Illus. 26 and 558).

8 to 13 April: Liszt in Vienna. Concerts on the 9th (Liszt plays the piano part in Beethoven's Trio op. 70 no. 1) and on the 11th (performance of the *Dante Symphony*).

14 to 16 April: Liszt in Nuremberg with his biographer Lina Ramann.

16 April to 21 September: Liszt in Weimar, apart from a few journeys elsewhere.

23 to 28 April: Liszt in Berlin. Liszt concert under Bilse on the 23rd; on the 24th performances of *Les Préludes* (under Mannstädt), *Festklänge* (under Leßmann), and *Jeanne d'Arc* (with Marianne Brandt); on the 25th a performance of *Christus*.

29 April to 3 May: At the music festival in Freiburg. Performance of *Christus* on 1 May. At a matinée on 3 May in the Great Hall of the Museum, Liszt plays three piano pieces. He travels to Karlsruhe on the 4th and arrives in Baden-Baden on the 5th, where Felix Mottl conducts performances of *Mazeppa*, *Hunnenschlacht*, the *Second Mephisto Waltz*, and parts of *Christus*. Liszt then returns to Weimar.

23 to 30 May: Liszt attends the music festivals in Antwerp and Brussels (see p. 283). *"Gran" Mass* and *Totentanz* in Antwerp, *Faust Symphony*, *Tasso*, and *Concerto pathétique* in Brussels.

31 May: Liszt receives the Order of Leopold from the King of Belgium.

9 to 12 June: *Tonkünstlerversammlung* in Magdeburg. Performance of *Ce qu'on entend sur la montagne*.

2 July: Liszt slips on the steps of the Hofgärtnerei in Weimar, and the injury that he sustains plagues him for the rest of the summer.

548 The former Academy of Music in Budapest. Photograph, 1982.

Liszt taught here for several months (generally from mid-January to early April) each year between 1881 and 1886. (The building was number 67 in a street then known as Sugár út or Radialstraße, in 1885 renamed Andrássy út, and now called Népköztársaság útja.) From 20 January 1881 a number of rooms on the first floor were placed at Liszt's disposal as living quarters, the salon of which led directly into the great organ and concert room where his Chickering grand piano stood (see Illus. 396).

549 Liszt's piano room at 4 Fisch-Platz (Hal tér), Budapest. Wood engraving from the *Illustrirte Zeitung* of 15 August 1886, based on a drawing by J. J. Kirchner.

Liszt lived at 4 Fisch-Platz in Budapest from 1873 to 1880. Between 1875 and 1880 the Academy of Music was also housed under the same roof.

The two grand pianos at the left in the picture are by Bösendorfer and Beregszászy. The instrument on the right, Liszt's piano-harmonium (see Illus. 395), is surmounted by a miniature copy of the Beethoven Monument in Vienna, for the erection of which Liszt had contributed some 25,000 gulden in 1877.

550 Liszt courted by his admirers. Caricature, ca. 1881.

551 Liszt, Hans von Bülow (on the left), and Richard Wagner. Caricature from *Der Floh* of 27 November 1881.

552 Liszt and Bösendorfer. Caricature from the *Humoristische Blätter*, 1881.

553 Entry into Budapest. Caricature from *Borsszem Jankó*, ca. 1881.
At the head of the procession is Kornél Abrányi, followed by Count Géza Zichy, Liszt, and Irinyi (with clarinet). The drummer is Count Albert Apponyi.

554 Liszt leaves the Budapest Academy of Music. Caricature from *Borsszem Jankó* of 23 January 1881.
Inquisitive onlookers have waited to catch a glimpse of Liszt. Abrányi (as a poodle) carries his master's watching stick.

555 Liszt has to pose as a model. Caricature from *Borsszem Jankó*, 1879.

CARICATURES OF LISZT FROM CA. 1881

A note on Illus. 555: A journalist went to invite Liszt personally to an organ recital by Saint-Saëns, who was then staying in Budapest, but he was not admitted as Liszt was having his portrait painted. After a long and violent exchange of words, the journalist finally pushed the doorkeeper aside and forced his way into the vast hall, where Liszt was sitting on a platform, surrounded by various pianos, while between six and eight ladies were busily immortalizing his features on canvas. In the deep and intently filled silence the Master had nodded off. Roused by the sound of approaching footsteps, he turned to his visitor with a smile: "You see me like Saint Sebastian: the arrows are these brushes."[208]

9 July: Having spent two weeks in Weimar with his daughter, Hans von Bülow sets off for Nuremberg for his first meeting with Cosima since their divorce.

22 September to 10 October: Liszt in Bayreuth. At Wahnfried, he performs Beethoven's Sonatas opp. 101, 109, 110, and 111. He returns to Rome with his granddaughter Daniela, travelling via Nuremberg (where he visits Lina Ramann on 10 October) and Venice (14/15 October).

16 October to 20 January 1882: Liszt in Rome at the Hotel Alibert.

22 October: Gala concert at the German Embassy in Rome to mark Liszt's 70th birthday.

25 December: Liszt's Christmas song, *O heilige Nacht*, receives its first performance in Rome.

WORKS

Von der Wiege bis zum Grabe (symphonic poem). Written 1881/82. Pub. 1883, together with piano versions for two hands and for four hands which had been prepared before the full score.

A magyarok Istene – Ungarns Gott (for baritone, men's voices, and piano). Pub. 1881, together with a piano version for two hands and a version (prepared for Géza Zichy) for left hand only. A transcription for organ or harmonium appeared in 1882.

Psalm cxxix (De profundis) (for baritone solo, men's voices and organ). Pub. 1881. A shorter version for bass and piano or organ appeared in 1883.

Cantico del Sol di San Francesco (piano transcription). Pub. 1983. A transcription for organ (mentioned by Liszt in a letter to Carolyne von Sayn-Wittgenstein of 6 September 1881) appeared in 1971.

Csárdás macabre (for piano). The (unfinished) first draft is dated "February 1881, Budapest," while a copy which Liszt prepared bears the date "April 1882." Pub. 1950. János Végh prepared a version for four hands which Liszt himself completed, together with a transcription for eight hands on two pianos.

Wiegenlied – Chant du berceau (for piano). Adapted from *Von der Wiege* (above). Pub. 1958.

Dances galiciennes (Zarembski) (orchestrated by Liszt). Pub. ca. 1882.

O Meer im Abendstrahl (duet for soprano and contralto with piano or harmonium accompaniment). Written ca. 1881. Pub. 1883.

Liebesszene und Fortunas Kugel from Goldschmidt's *Die sieben Todsünden* (piano transcription). Written ca. 1881. Pub. 1881.

Valse oubliée No. 1 (for piano). Pub. 1881.

Nuages gris (for piano). Pub. 1927.

Ave Maria IV (for voice with organ or harmonium). Pub. 1890. A piano transcription prepared at this time appeared in 1958.

Elaboration on Abrányi's *Virag Dál* (for piano). Unpublished.

556 Franz Liszt and Count Géza Zichy (see p. 296). Photograph by Ede Kozics, Preßburg, 4 April 1881.

Zichy lost his right arm in a hunting accident but still continued to appear all over Europe as a piano virtuoso.

557 Programme of a concert on 3 April 1881, at which Liszt and Zichy appeared together.

558 Liszt surrounded by the Raiding villagers at the unveiling of a commemorative plaque on the house where he was born. Photograph by M. Rupprecht of Ödenburg, 7 April 1881.

To the right of Liszt is Count Géza Zichy; the figure on the podium is the senior notary of the region, József Hannibal.

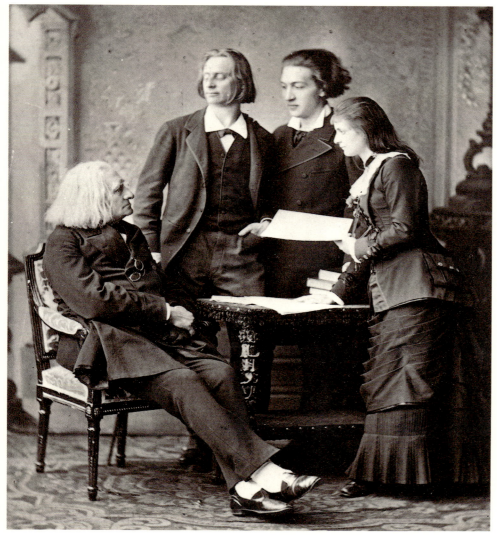

In May 1881 Liszt honoured the music festivals of Antwerp and Brussels with his presence. Soon after his arrival in Antwerp on 23 May he attended a performance of his *''Gran'' Mass*. This was also the first time that he had heard a performance of his *Totentanz* with orchestra. The soloist was his Polish pupil Jules de Zarembski (1854–1885), whose real name was Juliusz Zarebski (Illus. 559). Two days later we find Liszt in Brussels, where his pupil François Servais conducted performances of the *Faust Symphony* and *Tasso*, in addition to which Zarembski and his wife, Johanna Wenzel, another of Liszt's pupils, performed the *Concerto pathétique* for two pianos.

François Servais (born in St Petersburg in 1846, died in Asnières in 1901: Illus. 559), a composer and conductor who had won the Belgian Prix de Rome in 1873, founded the Concerts d'Hiver in Brussels in 1887. Because of his physical likeness to Liszt he was often thought to be the latter's son. Even the serious and reliable *Riemann-Musiklexikon* (Mainz 1961, II, 675) claims he was ''the illegitimate son of Franz Liszt and Princess Wittgenstein.'' But Servais was born in 1846, whereas we know that Liszt did not meet the Princess until February 1847. Suggestions that the Princess bore Liszt other illegitimate children stand up no better under examination.

559 Liszt, François Servais, Jules de Zarembski, and Johanna Wenzel-Zarembski. Photograph by J. Ganz, May 1881.

560 Medallion by Edouard Louis Geerts, Brussels 1881.

A gold copy of this medal was presented to Liszt. On the reverse, framed by palm leaves, are the words ''To Franz Liszt to commemorate 29 May 1881. From the musicians of Brussels.''

561 Franz Liszt. Bust by Ernst G. Herter, 1881.

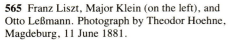

THEODOR HOEHNE   MAGDEBURG.

11. 6. 87.

565 Franz Liszt, Major Klein (on the left), and Otto Leßmann. Photograph by Theodor Hoehne, Magdeburg, 11 June 1881.
  This photograph was taken while Liszt was attending the *Tonkünstlerversammlung* in Magdeburg between 9 and 12 June 1881.

566 Page from a letter written by Carolyne von Sayn-Wittgenstein on the occasion of Liszt's seventieth birthday, on 22 October 1881.

567 Franz Liszt's address book. A gift from the Vienna Akademischer Wagner-Verein to mark his seventieth birthday.

568 Book cover presented to Liszt by the city of Budapest on his seventieth birthday. Gilt bronze decorations and coloured enamelwork on velvet, with Liszt's initials in the centre.

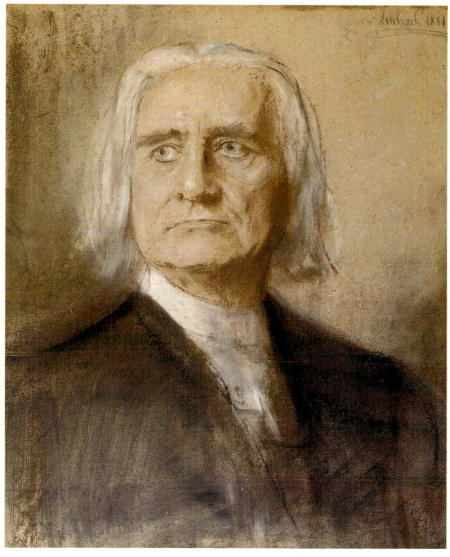

562 (above left) Franz Liszt. Pastel portrait by Franz von Lenbach, Munich, 1 September 1884, with a dedication from Lenbach to Liszt's granddaughter Countess Blandine von Gravina.

Lenbach belonged to Liszt's circle of friends. When Liszt visited Munich Lenbach would often accompany him to the station; and during his winter visits to Rome the painter generally called on Liszt or arranged to meet him at the Café Greco. Lenbach is known to have completed seven portraits of Liszt (see Illus. 499).

563 (above right) Franz Liszt. Oil and charcoal portrait by Franz von Lenbach, 1881.

564 (below right) Franz Liszt. Pastel portrait by Franz von Lenbach, ca. 1884.

LIFE

January: Liszt in Rome. Three days with Cardinal Hohenlohe at the Bishop's Palace in Albano.

28 January: Liszt leaves Rome and travels to Florence, where he is guest of Count Resse at the Palazzo Guadagni on 28/29 January; there he meets the writer Angelo de Gubernatis. On 30 January he meets Count Alberti in Venice, and between 1 and 3 February is in Vienna.

2 February: Liszt attends a Brahms recital given by Bülow in Vienna.

4 February to 14 April: Liszt in Budapest, where he teaches at the Academy of Music.

12 February: Liszt attends a concert given by Bülow in Preßburg to raise funds for the Hummel Memorial.

25 February: At a reception held in Budapest to honour the painter Mihály Munkácsy, Liszt plays his 16th *Hungarian Rhapsody*, which is dedicated to the artist.

25 March: Performance of the *Hymne de l'enfant à son réveil* at a matinée concert held by the Institute of Young English Ladies in Budapest.

5 to 11 April: Liszt in Kalocsa as guest of Cardinal Haynald. Concert in the Archbishop's Palace on 9 April.

Brahms sends Liszt his B flat major Piano Concerto for his comments (see p. 267).

18 April to mid-November: Liszt in Weimar, apart from occasional journeys elsewhere. His *Angelus* (for string quartet) receives its first performance at a Court concert in April.

1 to 8 May: Visit to Brussels and Antwerp (5/6 May). First performance of *Saint Elisabeth* in French in Brussels. The audience includes Saint-Saëns, Massenet, and Francis Planté.

22 June: Karl Müller-Hartung conducts *Christus* in the Weimar parish church.

1 to 6 July: Liszt in Freiburg for performances of the *"Gran" Mass* and *Die Glocken des Straßburger Münsters*. The audience includes Saint-Saëns and Sophie Menter.

5 July: Liszt in Baden-Baden for a Liszt concert organized by Richard Pohl.

8 to 14 July: Liszt in Zurich for a music festival. Performances include *Saint Elisabeth*, the A major Piano Concerto (played by Robert Freund), and the *Illustrations du "Prophète"* (played by Saint-Saëns).

15 July to 5 August: Liszt in Bayreuth, where he attends performances of *Parsifal*.

25 July: At a gathering of artists in the Bayreuth theatre restaurant Wagner stresses Liszt's contribution to all that he had achieved.

Liszt's granddaughter Blandine von Bülow marries Count Biagio Gravina.

Profoundly impressed by Wagner's *Parsifal*, Liszt writes his piano transcription of the *Feierlicher Marsch zum heiligen Gral*. He revises the third volume of his *Années de Pèlerinage*.

23 September: The artist Paul von Joukovsky is Liszt's guest in Weimar, where he remains for some time, completing Liszt's portrait (see Illus. 570).

24 September: Together with Gottschalg, Liszt travels to Arnstadt for an organ concert given by Ernst Schilling.

8 October: Liszt completes his symphonic poem *Von der Wiege bis zum Grabe*.

22 October: Müller-Hartung conducts a concert in the Weimar Court Theatre to mark Liszt's birthday. The programme includes the Prelude to *Parsifal*, *Ce qu'on entend sur la montagne*, the E flat major Piano Concerto (played by Eugen d'Al-

LISZT ON HIS OWN WORKS

"Vast experience has taught me that my things tend to make enemies for me rather than friends" (to Eduard Liszt, 22 May 1863).[209]

"[. . .] Herr Hanslick will soon be taking the trouble to pass on his good advice to me – and I, as befits me, shall be told of my total incompetence in matters of musical composition [. . .]" (to Carolyne von Sayn-Wittgenstein, 27 December 1871).[210]

"[. . .] I admit that I once suffered occasional attacks of vainglory – but they have now completely stopped; neither success nor diversion nor honours of any kind have any appeal for me any longer! As for what little I create in my music, it would be better if I were to create it after my own fashion in some remote place and not importune others with it [. . .]" (to Carolyne von Sayn-Wittgenstein, 23 July 1868).[211]

"[. . .] No one feels more deeply than I do the imbalance between noble intentions and what I in fact achieve in my compositions [. . .]" (to Camille Saint-Saëns, 6 December 1881).[212]

569 Franz Liszt. Photograph by H. von Langsdorff, Freiburg 1881. With a dedication in Liszt's hand on the rolled-up sheet of music, "Poor composer, F. Liszt."

570 Franz Liszt. Oil portrait by Paul von Joukovsky, 1882.

LISZT'S AMERICAN ADMIRERS

It is remarkable that Liszt was the most famous musical personality of nineteenth-century America, although he never visited the country. In the present day, too, America is a centre of the Liszt renaissance.

In the summer of 1885 Liszt received a visit from an American concert agent, who offered him two million marks to come to America the following season. Liszt would share the concert platform with other performers and play only a single item at each concert. The offer amused Liszt, who wrote to the agent: "What, at the age of 74, am I supposed to do with two million marks? Do you expect me to play the *Erlkönig* three hundred times in America? You can't teach an old dog new tricks!"[213] When a beautiful and amiable American lady told him on one occasion that he could make a "vast fortune" if he came to America, his gallant response was, "Madame, if it were *you* who required this fortune, I should most certainly come!"[214]

The portrait of Liszt (Illus. 570) by Paul von Joukovsky (who also designed the famous sets for Wagner's *Parsifal*) was commissioned by the piano maker Risch of Toronto, Canada. On receiving the portrait Risch wrote to Liszt: "[. . .] For weeks our salon has been besieged by thousands upon thousands of people, including the élite of Toronto society. Their heads bared, solemnly and composedly, as though in church, the onlookers observe these revered features, features they know and admire. [. . .] Canada feels richer and happier for possessing you [. . .]."[215]

bert), *Pester Karneval*, *Rákóczy March*, *Du bist wie eine Blume*, and *Jeanne d'Arc au bûcher*.

14/15 November: Liszt visits Lina Ramann in Nuremberg, then travels via Zurich (16 November) to Venice.

19 November to 13 January 1883: With Cosima and Richard Wagner in the Palazzo Vendramin in Venice, the first winter for many years which Liszt has not spent in Rome or the Villa d'Este. The two versions of *La lugubre gondola* date from this time. Wagner frequently asks Liszt to play works by Beethoven, Weber, and Schubert, and he discusses with Liszt his plans to write one-movement symphonies. They play whist together almost every day: the favourite card game of both men helps to relax the occasional tensions which develop between them. Wagner is to die four weeks after this final meeting with Liszt.

571 Liszt surrounded by his admirers, on the occasion of the music festivals held in Brussels and Antwerp in 1882. Photograph by F. van Boghout, May 1882.

Front row, from left to right: Peter Benoit, Vrouw Lynen, Liszt, Vrouw von Haroen, Victor Lynen. Back row, from left to right: F. von Knyck, F. Lamoriniere, Gustave Léon Huberti, J. Pecher.

WORKS

Réminiscences de Simone Boccanegra (Verdi) (for piano). Pub. 1883.

Valse oubliée No. 2 (for piano). Pub. 1884.

Hungarian Rhapsody No. 16 (for piano). Pub. 1882, together with a version for four hands.

La lugubre gondola I (for piano). In 6/8. Pub. 1916.

La lugubre gondola II (for piano and violin or cello). In 4/4. Pub. 1974. A version for piano solo was published in 1886. The version for piano and violin (or cello) may be the original setting, but Liszt added 17 bars to the ending of it after he had made the piano version.

Feierlicher Marsch zum heiligen Gral from Wagner's *Parsifal* (piano transcription). Pub. 1883.

3 Songs from J. Wolff's "Tannhäuser" (Leßmann). Written and published in 1882.

Symphonisches Zwischenspiel zu Calderons Schauspiel "Über allen Zauber Liebe" (Lassen) (piano transcription). Written ca. 1882. Pub. 1883.

Provenzalisches Lied (Robert Schumann) (piano transcription). Written ca. 1882. Pub. 1882.

A magyarok Istene (orchestration). See "Works 1881." Mentioned in a letter to Kornél von Abrányi of 23 July 1882. Lost.

Die Wiege (for four violins), evidently an adaptation of the identically titled first part of the symphonic poem *Von der Wiege bis zum Grabe*. The manuscript, formerly in the possession of Nadine Helbig, is now lost.

Prelude (for violin). Mentioned by Nadine Helbig in 1906 as being "dedicated to her daughter." Written ca. 1882. Lost.

572 Pupils and friends of Liszt around 1880. Photograph, 1911.

Back row, from left to right: 1. Unknown, 2. Liszt's pupil István Thomán, 3. Martin Krause, 4. Liszt's pupil August Stradal (?), 5. Unknown, 6. Liszt's pupil August Göllerich, 7. Liszt's pupil Bernhard Stavenhagen, 8. Unknown, 9. Liszt's pupil Lina Großkurth (?),

10. Liszt's pupil Berthold Kellermann. Front row, from left to right: 1. Frau Göllerich, 2. Liszt's pupil Sophie Menter, 3. Liszt's pupil Count Géza Zichy, 4. Liszt's pupil Vera Timanoff, 5. Count Apponyi.

573 Richard and Cosima Wagner outside the Palazzo Vendramin (landward side), where Liszt stayed from 19 November 1882 to 13 January 1883. Anonymous oil painting, winter 1882/83.

574 *La lugubre gondola*. Title page (showing Wagner's grave) of the first edition for piano, 1886. Written in Venice in December 1882 and originally scored for violin or cello and piano.

575 Soirée at Wahnfried, Bayreuth. Oil painting by Georg Papperitz, 1882.
  Seated, from left to right: Franz von Lenbach, Siegfried and Cosima Wagner, Amalie Materna, Wagner, Fritz Brandt, Hermann Levi, Liszt, Franz Betz, Countess Marie Schleinitz, Paul von Joukovsky. Standing, from left to right: Emil Scaria, Franz Fischer, Hans Richter (behind Liszt), Albert Niemann, Countess Hildegard Usedom.

576 Liszt as Wagner's guest at Wahnfried, Bayreuth. Oil painting by Wilhelm Beckmann, 1882.

From left to right: Cosima Wagner, Richard Wagner, Franz Liszt, Hans von Wolzogen. In the background is Lenbach's portrait of Cosima, with a portrait of Schopenhauer on the wall. A bust of King Ludwig II can be seen through the window.

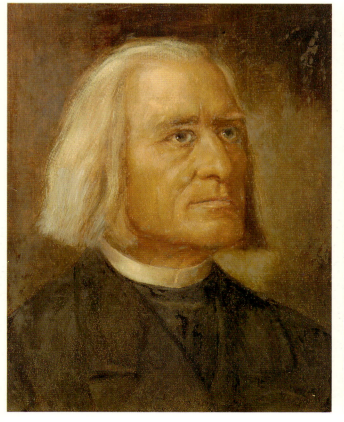

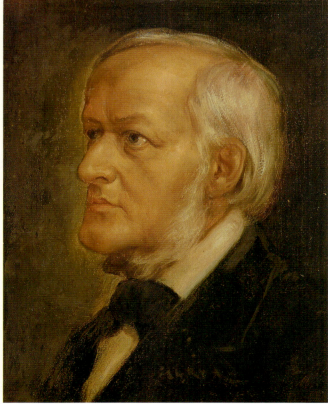

577, 578 Franz Liszt and Richard Wagner. Anonymous portraits, ca. 1882.

Liszt stayed with the Wagners in Venice during the winter of 1882/83. On one occasion Wagner is reputed to have approached Liszt on his knees, saying: ''Franz, you one can approach only on all fours!''[216]

LIFE

13 January: Liszt ends his two-month visit to Wagner in Venice.

14 January to 3 April: Liszt in Budapest, where he teaches at the Academy of Music.

13 February: Richard Wagner dies in Venice.

16 February: Ceremonial inauguration of the organ in the Concert Hall of the Budapest Academy of Music immediately next to Liszt's apartment.

17 to 19 February: Liszt stays with his niece, Baroness von Saar, at Stuhlweißenburg (Székesfehérvár).

11 March: Liszt performs at the Institute for Young English Ladies in Budapest.

17 to 19 March: Liszt in Preßburg. On the 18th he conducts the local premiere of *Saint Elisabeth* in the Estates Theatre.

4 to 7 April: Liszt in Vienna, where he frequents the circle of friends surrounding Marie von Hohenlohe-Schillingsfürst, the daughter of Carolyne von Sayn-Wittgenstein.

7 April to 31 January 1884: Liszt in Weimar. His usual winter visit to Rome does not take place.

1 May: Performance of *Saint Elisabeth* in Marburg in Liszt's presence.

2 to 7 May: In Leipzig for the *Tonkünstlerversammlung* (3 to 6 May).

10 May: Liszt hears Bach's B minor Mass in Erfurt conducted by Peter Ludwig Hertel.

22 May: At a memorial concert held in Weimar to mark Wagner's birthday, Liszt conducts the Prelude and Good Friday Music from *Parsifal*, and Müller-Hartung conducts the Preludes to *Lohengrin* and *Tristan and Isolde*, Isolde's *Liebestod*, *The Ride of the Valkyries*, the *Siegfried Idyll*, and the Funeral March from *Götterdämmerung*.

18 June: Liszt attends a concert given by Bilse in Erfurt. On the 20th, he hears Beethoven's *Missa solemnis* here.

30 June: *Szekszárd Mass* and *Nun danket alle Gott* in Liszt's presence in Jena.

27 to 31 July: Liszt in Wilhelmsthal.

3 August: Together with Olga von Meyendorff, Liszt hears Berlioz's *Benvenuto Cellini* in Leipzig.

Musical matinées or soirées are held almost every week in the Hofgärtnerei in Weimar.

6 September: Liszt's granddaughter Daniela visits him in Weimar. At the end of the month he returns to Leipzig for a further performance of *Benvenuto Cellini*, a work very close to his heart.

22 October: Stage performance of *Saint Elisabeth* to mark Liszt's birthday. Géza Zichy, who is present at the performance, will later recall with what kindness and civility Liszt deals with the crowd of supplicants who surround him, demanding his patronage, his autograph, and his money.[217]

19 November: Surprisingly successful Liszt Concert in Leipzig. One of the soloists is Liszt's new pupil Alexander Siloti.

24 November: Cardinal Hohenlohe-Schillingsfürst visits Liszt in Weimar.

1 December: Liszt travels to Meiningen, where Bülow conducts a Beethoven concert on the 2nd. The two men travel together to Weimar, where Bülow conducts a Raff concert.

16 December: Liszt returns to Meiningen for an orchestral concert conducted by Bülow. In his admiration for the conductor he writes a *Bülow-Marsch*.

WORKS

Magyar király-dal – Ungarisches Königslied (for baritone). Pub. 1884. A piano version prepared at this time appeared in 1884/85. Six versions for various choral combinations and a piano version for four hands appeared in 1883/84.

Nun danket alle Gott (for organ, men's or mixed voices, brass, and drums). Pub. 1884.

Unstern (for piano). Written ca. 1883. Pub. 1927.

R.W.-Venezia (for piano). Probably written on the occasion of Wagner's death (R.W. = Richard Wagner). Pub. 1927.

Am Grabe Richard Wagners (for piano). Pub. 1956, together with a version for harp and string quartet; a version for organ was published in 1973.

Third Mephisto Waltz (for piano). Pub. 1883.

Valse oubliée No. 3 (for piano). Pub. 1884.

Bülow-Marsch (for piano). Pub. 1884, together with a version for four hands. An unpublished version for eight hands prepared in 1884 may not be by Liszt.

Zur Trauung (based on the 1838 piano piece *Sposalizio*) (for organ, with optional chorus and contralto solo). Pub. 1890.

Schlaflos, Frage und Antwort (Nocturne) (for piano). Pub. 1927.

Kavallerie-Geschwindmarsch (piano transcription). Pub. 1883. Liszt did not want this piece to be published. He could not remember the name of the composer.

2 Songs by Francis Korbay (orchestration). Unpublished. An unpublished arrangement of Korbay's *Gebet* for voice and organ may also date from this time.

Cadenzas to Nos. 6 and 9 of *Soirées de Vienne* (for piano). Pub. 1883 in a new edition of the *Soirées de Vienne*.

Requiem für die Orgel (for organ). Pub. 1885.

Mephisto Polka (for piano). Pub. 1883.

Recueillement (for piano). Written and published ca. 1883.

Liszt's son-in-law Richard Wagner died in Venice on 13 February 1883. When Liszt heard the news of his death, he said simply, ''Today him, tomorrow me.'' Wagner had described his friendship with Liszt as ''the most beautiful thing that has ever happened in my life,'' and Liszt had nurtured his genius almost to the point of self-sacrifice. As early as 1849 he had commented, ''Here is a man of astonishing genius – indeed, such skull-splitting genius – as is uniquely suited to this country, a new and brilliant manifestation in art [. . .].''[218]

Franz Liszt on Richard Wagner

''His true glory consists in never having wavered from his great calling – a calling which he has followed in spite of the most multifarious setbacks. The immortality of leaving a great name on earth is assured to him.''[219]

''When one has written the *Nibelungs* and *Parsifal* one has no need to say charming but superficial things to one's friends and acquaintances.''[220]

''[. . .] What he demands most of all from his listeners is refinement of feeling, a profound insight into the heart's sufferings and the ability to grasp its inner actions. Anyone who goes to hear Wagner in order to see a grand opera and to take home the crumbs of simple melodies as a good petty bourgeois would take home sweets from a gala dinner, anyone who likes to weep without good cause, can only be bored by Wagner's operas.''[221]

579 Wagner's grave in the garden at Wahnfried, Bayreuth. Photograph, ca. 1890.

580 The last portrait of Wagner. Pencil drawing by Paul von Joukovsky, in a notebook of Cosima's; beneath it the words, in Cosima's hand, ''R[ichard] reading – 12 Febr. 1883.''

Opposite page:

581 Richard Wagner. Photograph by Franz Hanfstaengl, Munich 1871.

religion of his forebears. But Liszt, too, is a strict believer, and the epiphany of our Saviour is his guiding star as, trusting in God like St Francis of Paola, he battles against life's tempests. Nor does he fear death, or complain about spiteful attacks or the non-appreciation of his works. Yet it would be an error to believe that Liszt might abandon his free-thinking ways because of clerical influence, for to him everything in art is progress: he knows of no 'being' but only 'becoming'; his motto is 'ever onward towards the light of truth.' Liberal and conservative feelings combine within him to produce the noble, kind, and high-minded man that he is.

"Liszt remains extremely calm in every situation, nothing can disconcert him, and he does not know the meaning of nervous irritation. In Rome, for example, in the tiny room where the Master taught and where there were often as many as twenty listeners with whom he conversed in French between the musical numbers, we pupils would sometimes become very irritable, especially since the occasion generally went on for over three hours yet the Master did not show the least signs of tiredness. His nervous system was in splendid condition, and his physical constitution excellent. If only Liszt had taken some daily exercise he might not have been affected by dropsy and could certainly have reached a much greater age. But Liszt never went for walks, and even for short distances he would take a carriage. In Pest he even had a permanent carriage, which would wait for him outside the Academy of Music."[222]

AUGUST STRADAL ON FRANZ LISZT

582, 583 Franz Liszt. Photographs by Louis Held, Weimar 1883.

Opposite page:

584 *Magyar király-dal (Ungarisches Königslied).* Title page of the first edition of 1884.
Liszt composed this work in 1883 for the opening of the Royal Hungarian Opera House in Budapest. Shortly before the opening ceremony, in September 1884, the piece was rejected on the grounds that it incorporated a revolutionary hymn from the time of Rácóczy. Liszt, replying to the charge of disloyalty, remarked that "Music should remain music, without pernicious and unnecessary interpretations," and quoted historical examples of the ways in which melodies change. But the authorities refused to relent, and the work was not performed.

August Stradal (1860–1930), a Bohemian pianist and composer, and a pupil of Door, Leschetizky, and Anton Bruckner, studied with Liszt from 1884 to 1886. He prepared numerous piano transcriptions of Liszt's orchestral works. Liszt was very fond of Stradal (whom he called "Stradalus") and took him with him to Rome, Budapest, and Weimar; Stradal's memoirs of Liszt, published in 1929, must therefore be regarded as a reliable account of the last years in Liszt's life.

"Particularly striking is the extreme modesty of his personal needs. He is content with everything: his various domiciles are quite unassuming, in no way luxuriously appointed; one sees in his room only the bare essentials. He always travels by second class, never orders a cab for himself, and chooses very simple hotel rooms. How primitive, for example, were his two day-rooms in the Hotel d'Alibert in Rome! He does not even own a fur coat for travelling in winter, and even when the weather is very cold he goes around in his ordinary coat. His diet is almost spartan. In Weimar and Pest (in Rome he always dined with the Princess Wittgenstein) he was content to eat canned meat; he drinks only a light Château Paluggyai wine, and never smokes any other cigar than a cheap Virginia. If anyone presents him with a box of fine cigars he gives them away to his guests and pupils. He owns no jewellery, or if he has any he never wears it.

"His religious outlook is all-encompassing, embracing many philosophical systems and having nothing in common with the piety of a man like Bruckner, who clings to the

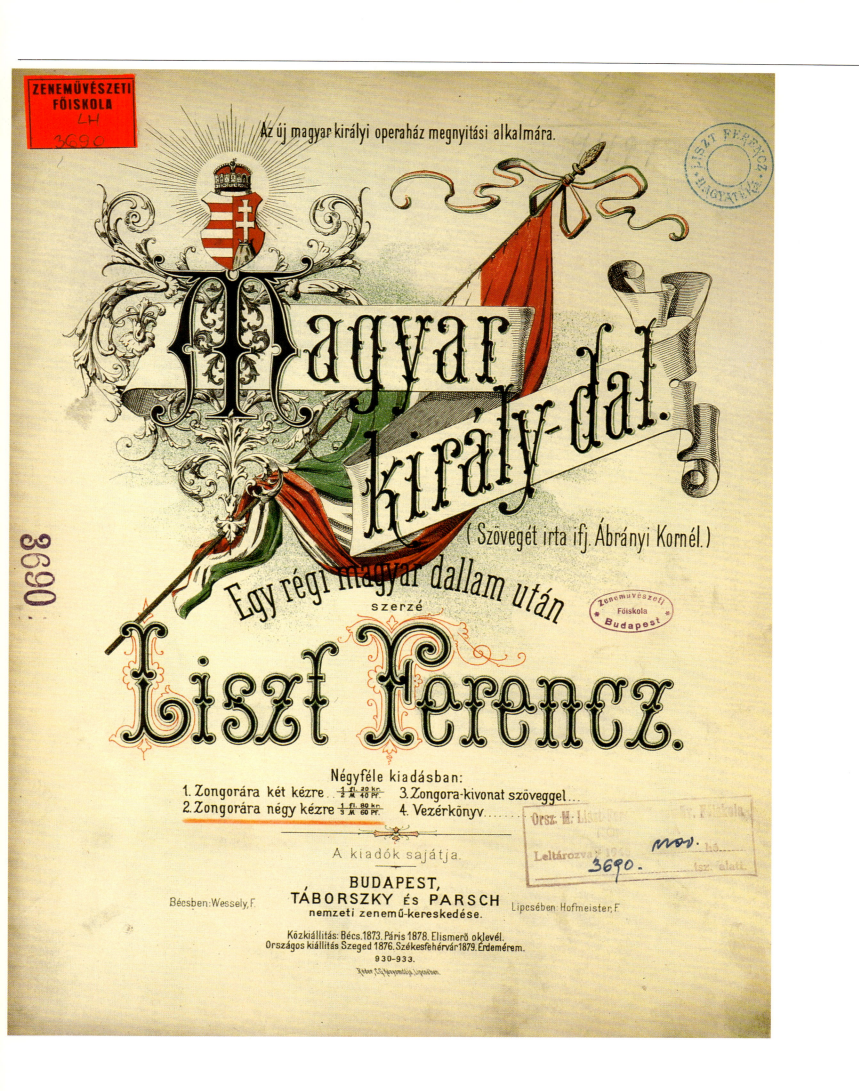

Az új magyar királyi operaház megnyitási alkalmára.

Magyar király-dal.

(Szövegét irta ifj. Ábrányi Kornél.)

Egy régi magyar dallam után szerzé

Liszt Ferencz.

Négyféle kiadásban:

1. Zongorára két kézre   1 fl. 20 kr. / 2 M 40 Pf.   3. Zongora-kivonat szöveggel…
2. Zongorára négy kézre   1 fl. 80 kr. / 3 M 60 Pf.   4. Vezérkönyv……

A kiadók sajátja.

Bécsben: Wessely, F.

BUDAPEST,
TÁBORSZKY és PARSCH
nemzeti zenemű-kereskedése.

Lipcsében: Hofmeister, F.

Közkiállitás: Bécs. 1873. Páris 1878. Elismerő oklevél.
Országos kiállitás Szeged 1876. Székesfehérvár 1879. Érdemérem.
930–933.

585–590 Some of Liszt's pupils. Concert studies by Hans Schließmann, ca. 1890.
585. Eugen d'Albert (1864–1932), 586. Emil von Sauer (1862–1942: see Illus. 602), 587. Frederic Lamond (1868–1948), 588. Moriz Rosenthal (1862–1946: see Illus. 602), 589. Sophie Menter (1846–1918), 590. Bernhard Stavenhagen (1862–1914: see Illus. 600).

Frederic Lamond (Illus. 587) on his teacher Liszt, on the occasion of the 50th anniversary of the latter's death (*Musik und Musiker*, 31 July 1936):

"I shall never forget the moment when I first stood in Liszt's presence. It was a dream of my childhood and youth to be allowed to study one day with the greatest master of the keyboard. It was on the recommendation of one of Liszt's former pupils that I came to visit the Master in Weimar in the summer of 1885. Liszt was then living in the Hofgärtnerei, which had been placed at his disposal by the Duke of Weimar, a small house idyllically situated at the end of the romantic park where Goethe and Schiller had often walked in animated conversation. One of the Master's pupils met me at my hotel and escorted me to the Hofgärtnerei, where I was led up a narrow flight of stairs until I found myself in a not over-large room furnished in modest comfort. It was here that the Master used to give the lessons which became world-famous. Before me stood a distinguished old man wearing the clothes of a secular priest. His long white hair hung down in strands over his strikingly noble brow. Two intelligent eyes looked at me earnestly, but kindly. My heart was beating wildly: this, then, was Franz Liszt, that legendary personality who had once been friendly with Chopin, who had fought for Richard Wagner with the most disinterested self-sacrifice and had contributed to the great Bayreuth enterprise! I shuddered with awe as I recalled how, as a boy, Liszt had received the kiss of consecration from Beethoven. Now I saw the Master standing before me in the flesh. [. . .]

"Liszt's teaching was a revelation. Of course the Master expected the highest technical proficiency of his pupils. It was a self-evident precondition that the pupil must be able to master every technical difficulty, so technical problems were never once mentioned. Only the spirit of the music and its innermost essence were elucidated by Liszt with lightning flashes of insight. For that reason less gifted students gained next to nothing from such instruction. The Master barely listened to them, although he normally allowed them to finish what they were playing, or else he would dismiss their playing with a jocular remark which was none the less devastating as an assessment. Towards his gifted students, however, the Master showed an inexorable strictness, particularly where tempo and interpretation were concerned.

"Sometimes Liszt himself sat down at the piano, and then a magic spell was cast by his fascinating personality, a spell which it is beyond our human language to describe. I recall, for example, the penultimate variation in G sharp minor from Robert Schumann's *Symphonic Studies*. Never have I heard this wonderful variation played like this by a pianist. Some of the passages in his own works Liszt called 'fripperies.' These included the cadenza-like parts of his works. But even here he proved himself to be not merely a virtuoso, but an incomparable artist.

"Liszt did not charge for his teaching. But these were no ordinary lessons. Could their immeasurably great value ever be reckoned in terms of money? No living soul could have managed such a calculation, not even the finest mathematician. The Master's watchword was 'Noblesse oblige.' No one was as noble in his calling as was Liszt. He was indeed a true Christian in the very best sense of the word. I thank my creator that it was granted to me to know this glorious and unique human being, the artist Franz Liszt, and to be permitted to follow his teachings throughout the whole of my life."

It seems impossible to calculate the number of pupils who flocked to Weimar to be taught by Liszt. Carl von Lachmund alone (Illus. 597) names more than three hundred. So good-natured was Liszt that he allowed even unworthy individuals to visit and pester him with their playing, so that they might henceforth describe themselves as "Liszt's pupils." His most important pupils were Hans von Bülow, Eugen d'Albert, Sophie Menter, Emil von Sauer, Alexander Siloti, Moriz Rosenthal, Arthur Friedheim, Alfred Reisenauer, José Vianna da Motta, Giovanni Sgambati, Karl Klindworth, Dionys Pruckner, Vera Timanoff, Conrad Ansorge, Frederic Lamond, Hans von Bronsart, Bernhard Stavenhagen, August Stradal, and, above all, Carl Tausig, whom Liszt described as his finest pupil.

August Stradal recalls, "I was out walking with Liszt. Suddenly we heard the sounds of his second Ballade coming towards us from a house. The Master listened and said it was dreadful how the piece was being played. He went to the house with me and knocked on the door. The culprit, a very attractive young lady, opened it and almost fainted on seeing the Master. Liszt was most amiable and showed the young lady a number of passages. A week later Gille came to see the Master in Weimar and reported that the girl had had a notice placed outside her house which read, 'H.J., pupil of Franz Liszt.' – The affair amused the Master greatly."[223]

A short time after this photograph (Illus. 591) was taken Liszt's servant fell ill, and he died on 1 February 1884. A letter which Liszt wrote the following day to Carl Gille is indicative of his charitable cast of mind:

"Physical death was bound to overtake Achille sooner rather than later. May his soul rest in eternal peace! He was an estimable man, a devout Catholic, and the best, the quietest, and the most accomplished of my manservants. His failings always seemed much less serious than my own; and his qualities were most praiseworthy. There was never an ambiguous word between us. –

"Uncertain as to whether you are still in Weimar, I have just telegraphed Adelheid, asking her to ensure that the Catholic clergyman prays over Achille's coffin. I should also like a stone cross to be placed upon his grave with the inscription, 'Achille Colonello, manservant to Franz Liszt, Honorary Canon.' I trust in your kindness to arrange this. The money to reimburse you for the burial, the cemetery, the hospital, and the cross will be sent to you immediately from Budapest, where I shall be arriving on Tuesday and where I shall await your letter.

Your truly grateful
F. Liszt.

2 February 84 – Nuremberg"[224]

591 A gathering of Liszt's pupils outside the Hofgärtnerei, with Liszt at the window. Photograph by Louis Held, Weimar 1883.

Walter Bache (seventh from left, with bald head), Alexander Siloti (eleventh from left, resting his arm on his neighbour's shoulder), Alfred Reisenauer (centre of picture, with his hands in his pockets, wearing a light-coloured suit), Henri van Zeyl (standing in the doorway, wearing glasses), Carl von Lachmund (right foot on steps, flower in buttonhole), Frau Lachmund to his left (between the two women dressed in white – see Illus. 597), William Dayas (third from right), and Wilhelm Posse (second from right). In the left-hand window is Liszt's servant Achille Colonello.

LIFE

6 January: Accompanied by Felix von Weingartner, Liszt attends a concert given by Bülow in Eisenach.

1 February: Death of Achille Colonello, Liszt's highly valued servant (see p. 295). Liszt sets off for Budapest, calling at Nuremberg (where he visits Lina Ramann on 2/3 February) and Gran.

4 February to 19 April: Liszt in Budapest, where he teaches at the Academy of Music.

24 to 26 February: Liszt in Preßburg.

On 25 February Liszt conducts his *Hungarian Coronation Mass* in Preßburg Cathedral. The performers include the Hellmesbergers (Ferdinand, Joseph senior, and Joseph junior) and Hans Richter.

3 March: Guest of Primate Simor in Gran.

12 March: Liszt writes to Olga von Meyendorff, "My eyes are growing so weak that it is almost impossible for me to make demands on them for more than two hours a day. The extensive period of time that I have devoted to music manuscript paper has badly affected my eyesight [. . .] At Christmas I intend to make myself a most unwelcome present and stop writing any more music . . ."[225] (This helps to explain the decrease in Liszt's productivity in old age.)

2, 4 and 5 April: Liszt attends matinées given by Kalman Vörös, Emma Földváry, and the Institute of Young English Ladies, occasionally responding to invitations to play.

9 to 15 April: Liszt in Kalocsa as guest of Cardinal Haynald.

19 to 20 April: Liszt in Preßburg as guest of Bishop Heiller, then in Vienna until the 24th.

20 April: First performance in Vienna of *Tasso*.

25 April to 25 October: Apart from a few excursions, Liszt remains in Weimar throughout this period.

8 May: In Leipzig for a performance of Goldschmidt's *Helianthus*.

18 May: Liszt hears his *Christus* conducted by Carl Riedel in Leipzig.

23 to 28 May: Annual *Tonkünstlerversammlung* in Weimar (see p. 298); among those present are Pauline Viardot, Saint-Saëns, and Eugen d'Albert. Stage performance of *Saint Elisabeth* on the 23rd. On the 25th Liszt conducts Bülow's *Nirwana* and the first performance of his own *Salve Polonia*. A performance of the "Gran" Mass is given on the 26th, and on the 28th there are performances of Liszt's *Die Ideale* and Weingartner's *Sakuntala*.

26 June: Performance of the "Gran" Mass in Jena.

12 July to 9 August: Liszt in Bayreuth, where he stays at the house in which he is to die two years later (see Illus. 632). He attends performances of *Parsifal* on 21 and 23 July.

26 August to 2 September: Liszt in Munich. Together with Géza Zichy, Berthold Kellermann, Blandine von Gravina, and Isolde and Siegfried Wagner, he attends a performance of the *Ring*. Excursion to Schloß Itter to see Sophie Menter. He visits Lenbach's studio on 1 September for a portrait session.

5 to 7 September: In Eisenach.

28 September: Liszt returns to Eisenach for a series of concerts conducted by Joachim and held to inaugurate the town's Bach Monument, towards which Liszt has given 3000 thalers.

1 October: Liszt in Leipzig, where Siloti and Friedheim perform his *Faust Symphony* and *Dante Symphony* for two pianos in the Gewandhaus.

COUNT GÉZA ZICHY ON FRANZ LISZT

"If true nobleness of heart forms the substance and core of saintliness, Franz Liszt was a saint. A worldly, amiable saint. Capable of making any sacrifice, always willing to help, wholly lacking in vindictiveness, oblivious to the wrongs he suffered, one of the most noble and humane of human beings ever to set foot on earth. Strict and tolerant, and not one of those Catholics who can sometimes be so unchristian. His magnanimity and kindness of heart were even greater than his genius. He was incapable of turning down a request. He recommended everyone, which meant that his letters of recommendation lost much of their weight. Through living in the sultry atmosphere of the Eternal Feminine, his kindness of heart and incomparable courtesy brought him the reputation of a Don Juan, something he most certainly was not. He said to me, 'If women appear ingratiating and men remain steadfast, they are bound to be brutal or ridiculous. Both are difficult!' He liked splendour and magnificence, yet his own way of life was as simple and modest as possible. I dined with him for several months, and the menu always consisted of ragout, boiled vegetables, fruit, and cheese. He drank very little during the meal; his favourite drink was a light Hungarian wine and – unfortunately – cognac. He took sips of it throughout the day, but I swear that I never saw him in a condition unworthy of his person. He never drank strong wines. When I presented him with some bottles of Bakator wine from 1827 and 1834, he said to me, 'My dear Géza, this is stronger than wine and weaker than cognac; I should have to drink very little to replace my table wine, and a very great deal to be able to manage without my cognac!'

592 Count Géza Zichy (1849–1924) and Franz Liszt. Photograph by Ede Kozics, Preßburg, 4 April 1881.

Liszt was bound to Zichy by the strongest ties of friendship. On 12 November 1884 he played for the Hungarian villagers on Zichy's estates at Tetétlen. A simple farmer told him, "The Count has told us what your name is, you yourself have shown us what you can do, but we ourselves have found out who you really are, and that is why we pray to the great God of Hungary to bless you."[226]

"He was an early riser; he would be in church by six, or by seven at the latest. Even in the depths of winter he wore only a light overcoat with a tartan travelling rug which trailed behind him over the ground. He smoked a good deal, generally black Italian cigars and mostly smoked only halfway; the other half he would chew at for hours. At night he slept very little; he would pace up and down in his room, occasionally sitting down at the piano or writing. He made up for his lack of sleep at night by resting in the afternoon for one and a half or two hours. Liszt was of a cheerful disposition and usually in good spirits, although he suffered sometimes from deep melancholia. The wretchedness suffered by those around him and human misery in general saddened him greatly. He must have been very fond of me to have repeatedly vented his grief in my presence. He could never speak of his son Daniel's premature death without tears in his eyes. 'That was the greatest affliction of my life,' he told me. His mind was often elsewhere; if a thought passed through his head he would look up at the ceiling and begin to beat time with one of his long fingers.

"On one occasion I found him composing at his desk. Outside the window an organ grinder was playing. 'For heaven's sake, why don't you drive the man away?' I asked the Master impatiently. Liszt said with a smile, 'He has been playing for two hours, but I don't want to offend him.' At which he rose to his feet, opened the window, threw out a silver florin and said, 'My dear colleague, I like your music very much, you have a real sense of rhythm, and you turn the handle with feeling; but I'm just composing a tune which can't be combined with yours – would you mind not playing until I've finished? Next time you're here I'll play you the piece, and if you like it I'll let you make a new cylinder from it.'

"One day we were sitting drinking black coffee when a visitor was announced who had behaved badly towards Liszt in the past and even caused him material harm. 'Surely you don't intend to receive him, Master?' I said. 'Of course, I forgave him long ago.' The man came in, Liszt embraced him and said with a smile, 'Here is the biggest rogue in the whole of Europe, but a charming fellow none the less.' "[227]

Opposite page:

593 Franz Liszt. Photograph by Louis Held, Weimar 1884.

The portraits of Liszt in old age show the superior but simple dignity of regal modesty, an irresistible unity of noble bearing and submission to fate.

25 to 27 October: Liszt visits Lina Ramann in Nuremberg, then spends two days in Vienna. On the 30th he visits János Batka in Preßburg, and on the evening of the 30th arrives in Budapest.

1 to 17 November: Liszt in Tetétlen as guest of Count Géza Zichy. He gives a concert at the castle for the Hungarian peasants.

22 and 24 November: Liszt attends Bülow's concerts in Budapest.

8 December: Liszt leaves Budapest and sets off for Rome, travelling via Florence, where he meets Arnold Böcklin and the Scottish composer Alexander Mackenzie.

12 December to 25 January 1885: Liszt in Rome.

WORKS

Der Zaubersee (ballad for tenor solo and piano by Géza Zichy). Liszt orchestrated the ballad ca. 1884. The score was destroyed during World War II.

In domum Domini ibimus (for mixed voices, organ, and brass). Written ca. 1884. Pub. 1920. The Prelude to this work exists in a piano transcription (published in 1983) and in a version for organ (published in 1908 in August Göllerich's book on Liszt).

Mariengarten (Quasi cedrus) (for soprano, contralto, tenor, and organ). Written ca. 1884. Pub. 1936.

Sancta Caecilia (for contralto and organ or harmonium). Written ca. 1884. Pub. 1936.

Sankt Christoph (Legend for baritone solo, women's voices, piano, harmonium, and harp). May have been written in the 1880s. Unpublished. First performed in 1967 and recorded in 1968.

Introitus (for organ). Pub. 1887. The work was republished in 1890 together with *Les Morts*.

Le Crucifix (for contralto and piano/harmonium). Published (in three versions) in 1884.

Qui seminant in lacrimis (for mixed voices and organ). Pub. 1936.

Concert Waltz (based on *2ème Suite en forme de valse* for four hands by János Végh) (piano transcription). Pub. 1889.

O sacrum convivium (for contralto solo, women's voices, and organ or harmonium). Written ca. 1884. Pub. 1936.

Und wir dachten der Toten (for contralto or baritone and piano). Written ca. 1884. Pub. 1923.

Puszta-Wehmut – A Puszta keserve (piano transcription of a Hungarian song by Zámoyská). Written ca. 1884. Pub. ca. 1885. An unpublished version for violin and piano is in the private collection of H. Cardello in New York.

Der Asra (song by Anton Rubinstein) (piano transcription). Written ca. 1884. Pub. 1884.

Sanctus (probably for piano or organ). Mentioned in Gottschalg's diary of 7 October 1884 and described as a ''chordal-style prelude.'' Probably part of another work.

Two Csárdás: 1. *Allegro*, 2. *Csárdás obstiné* (for piano). Pub. 1886.[228] A version of No. 2 for piano duet may also date from this time.

Valse oubliée No. 4 (for piano). Written ca. 1884. Pub. 1954.

Hungarian Rhapsodies Nos. 17 and 19 (for piano). Pub. 1886. No. 19 also exists in an unpublished version for piano duet.

594 Liszt with members of the Allgemeiner Deutscher Musikverein outside the headquarters of the Crossbow Society in Weimar, on the occasion of the 1884 *Tonkünstlerversammlung* between 23 and 28 May 1884. Photograph by Louis Held, May 1884.

Liszt (Honorary President of the Allgemeiner Deutscher Musikverein) in the centre of the picture; to his left Carl Gille (holding his hat), and to his right the publisher C. F. Kahnt; to Kahnt's right the bearded figure of Otto Leßmann, editor of the *Allgemeine deutsche Musikzeitung*. In front of Liszt are his pupils Arthur Friedheim (with his right hand on his left knee) and (to Friedheim's right) Richard Burmeister. On the right, in the third row from the front, are Liszt's pupils Alexander Lambert (third from right) and Alfred Reisenauer (to Lambert's right). In front of the second column from the right is August Göllerich (bearded), with Anna and Helene Stahr on his left and right (wearing similar hats). The figure on the extreme left of the first row is the harpist Wilhelm Posse, and the young man between the fifth and sixth figures from the right in this row is Felix Weingartner, whose opera *Sakuntala* was performed in Weimar, at Liszt's instigation, on 28 May 1884.

595 Report on the *Tonkünstlerversammlung* in Weimar, reproduced from *Schorers Familienblatt*, 1884. (For a translation of the text, see p. 343.)

Die Musik hat bekanntlich ihre Parteien fast ebenso, wie die Politik. Wer hat nicht einmal von dem Kampfe der Glucklisten und Piccinisten gehört? So stehen sich auch in unsern Tagen die Freunde des Alten und die Anhänger des Neuen, die Verehrer Liszts, Wagners, Berlioz' entgegen. Das Neue freilich wird mit der Zeit gleichfalls alt, und was anfangs heftig bekämpft wurde, läßt man sich schließlich gefallen. Der „Allgemeine deutsche Musikverein" ward 1859 auf einer nach Leipzig berufenen Tonkünstlerversammlung gestiftet. Zweck dieser Versammlung war, das fünfundzwanzigjährige Bestehen der einst von Robert Schumann gestifteten „Neuen Zeitschrift für Musik" zu feiern, die damals der verdiente Musikhistoriker Franz Brendel redigierte. Wie diese Zeitschrift stets für alles Neue eingetreten war, so hatten sich auf dem Feste auch fast nur die gleichgesinnten Geister eingefunden. Den Mittelpunkt bildete Franz Liszt, der seit einer Reihe von Jahren am Hoftheater zu Weimar als Hofkapellmeister wirkte. „Lohengrin" hatte in jenem Jahre in Berlin seine erste Aufführung erlebt. Wenn selbst dieses Werk auf so lebhaften Widerstand stieß, kann man sich denken, wie es mit der in Leipzig zum erstenmale gespielten Einleitung zu „Tristan und Isolde" oder mit Franz Liszts „Graner Festmesse" ging. Aber im Kampfe thun sich Freunde zusammen, und so ward der „Allgemeine deutsche Musikverein" gegründet. Sein Protektorat übernahm der kunstsinnige Großherzog Karl Alexander von Sachsen-Weimar, in dessen Residenz in nächsten Jahre das erste Musikfest des neuen Vereines stattfand. Zwanzig Musikfeste hat derselbe seitdem abgehalten und überall nach Kräften dafür gearbeitet, daß auch der Gegenwart ihr Recht wird und der heranstrebende junge Künstler zu Gehör kommt. Zur Erinnerung an Beethovens hundertjährigen Geburtstag ist eine „Beethovenstiftung" ins Leben gerufen worden, die bestimmt ist, sich der Musiker in ähnlicher Weise anzunehmen, wie die Schillerstiftung der Schriftsteller. Der „Allgemeine deutsche Musikverein" kann mit Genugthuung auf seine fünfundzwanzigjährige Geschichte zurückblicken. Noch immer ist seine Mitgliederzahl im Wachsen begriffen; nicht nur Musiker gehören demselben an. Wer irgend Musik liebt, kann hier mit dem geringen Jahresbeitrag von sechs Mark etwas für die Zwecke dieser Kunst thun und sich zugleich den Eintritt zu den alljährlich, bald hier, bald dort stattfindenden Musikfesten und damit eine Fülle musikalischen Genusses erkaufen.

Das fünfundzwanzigjährige Jubelfest des Vereins fand in den Tagen des 23. bis 28. Mai zu Weimar statt, seiner eigentlichen Heimstätte, der Stadt, wo heute noch Liszt alljährlich die Sommermonate im Kreise seiner Schüler und Schülerinnen verlebt. Gar manches hat sich in den verflossenen fünfundzwanzig Jahren geändert, gar mancher, der damals noch frisch ins Leben hineinsah, ist jetzt zur letzten Ruhe eingegangen. Auch der Geschmack des Publikums ist ein anderer geworden. Was 1859 verdammt wurde, findet Bewunderung. Der „Graner Festmesse" lauschte ein begeistertes Publikum und die „heilige Elisabeth" — gleichfalls eine oratorische Komposition Liszts — von der man sonst nicht einmal im Konzertsaale etwas wissen wollte, findet ein solches jetzt sogar bei einer scenischen Darstellung im Theater. Nur der Verein ist seinen Principien treu geblieben: das Jubelfest zeichnete sich durch die Vorführung einer ganzen Reihe neuer oder selten gehörter Kompositionen aus. Auch Liszt ist noch derselbe. Zwar wallt ihm, wie unser Bild zeigt, das Haar jetzt schneeweiß um die Stirn. Aber es sind noch dieselben unvergeßlichen, charakteristischen Züge. Noch durchglüht den greisen Meister dieselbe Begeisterung für alles Große und Schöne, dieselbe hingebende Bereitwilligkeit, dafür einzutreten, noch wirkt er in unverminderter Schaffenskraft, und wenn er in dem zur Ehre des Festes aufgeführten Festspiele von Adolf Stern mit dem greisen Goethe verglichen wurde, so drängt sich dieser Vergleich fast von selber auf. Liszt ist Ehrenpräsident des Vereins, eigentlicher Vorsitzender Professor Karl Riedel in Leipzig, gleich rühmlich bekannt als Komponist, wie als Musikforscher und Leiter eines trefflichen Gesangvereins, dessen Leistungen diesen Winter auch in Berlin allgemeine Bewunderung erregt haben. Liszt wie Riedel sind die Charakterköpfe dieser Tonkünstlerversammlungen. Aber auch sonst fehlt es nicht an bekannten Namen, freut man sich der heranwachsenden Generation, der heranstrebenden Talente und hat die Gewähr, daß die Kunst in unserm Vaterlande nicht brachliegen, sondern immer wieder Pflege und Förderung finden wird. Der Dresdner Felix Draeseke freilich, dessen Bild wir gleichfalls bringen, gehört gleichsam dem mittleren Geschlechte an, da wir seinen Namen schon auf den ersten Festen des Vereins finden. Seitdem hat er unablässig an sich selber gearbeitet: eine Symphonie Draesekes, welche in Weimar gespielt wurde, ist von so klarer Schönheit, daß sie in jedem musikalischen Lager Anerkennung gefunden hat. Die Gegensätze gleichen sich eben allmählich aus. Auch August Klughardt, jetzt Hofkapellmeister in Dessau, von dem ein Quartett vorgeführt wurde, vertritt einen solchen ausgleichenden Standpunkt. Klughardts Instrumentalkompositionen sind von großem melodischen Reize und Formvollendung; weniger Glück hat er auf dem Gebiete der Oper gehabt, für welche ihm der große dramatische Zug zu fehlen scheint. Jedenfalls darf er zu den bedeutendsten unter den jüngeren Komponisten gerechnet werden. Der jüngeren, nicht der jüngsten. Der jüngste dürfte vielmehr Felix Weingartner sein, der, 1863 zu Zara in Dalmatien geboren, erst einundzwanzig Jahre zählt, und der trotzdem schon eine große Oper im Wagnerschen Stile, „Sakuntala," geschrieben hat, Text und Musik. Es versteht sich von selbst, daß ein solches Werk vielfach die Spuren jugendlicher Unreife trägt, und es wäre schlimm, wenn es nicht so wäre, denn wie sollte sich der Künstler sonst entwickeln? Daß Weingartner dies aber wird, darf man schon um deswillen hoffen, weil er durch und durch Musiker ist: das beweist nicht nur das wunderbare Geschick, welches er als Komponist entfaltet, man spürte es auch an der vortrefflichen Art, wie er zur Nachfeier des Festes seine eigene Oper dirigierte. Jedenfalls ist Weingartner ein Beleg des Goetheschen Wortes, daß immer wieder ein frisches junges Blut cirkuliert. Und so wollen wir dem Vereine wünschen, daß dies auch mit ihm der Fall sei, vor allem aber, daß ihm noch lange sein Ehrenpräsident, Franz Liszt, als leuchtender Führer diene!

A note on Illus. 596: The burden of correspondence became more and more unbearable for Liszt (according to his own testimony he had more than 3000 letters to answer every year), and he called it his ''earthly purgatory.'' His protests in 1882 against the indiscriminate sending of letters proved ineffectual. It is astonishing that in spite of everything he replied to all the requests that were put to him and scarcely ever left a letter unanswered. At the beginning of 1886 the first issue of the magazine *Zenelap* carried the following piece:

''Not a day goes by during each of the Master's two-month stays here but one or more future Richard Wagners or Goldmarks turn up first thing in the morning and, with the most unobtrusive insistence, knock at his door, armed with enormous bundles of music and laying claim to his precious time. Only a very small proportion of them comes with the intention of learning anything. Most of them think they are already proficient and wish only to receive a written testimonial or at least find a publisher who pays well. On almost every occasion the Master sits down at the piano and plays through their compositions with encouraging civility, praising or criticizing in places, according to the merit of the pieces in question, adding extra bits and altering empty or monotonous chords etc. Compositions are sent in from every part of the country, and Liszt looks through them with the greatest care, always returning them with a few lines of his own. It is worth adding that the Master pays the postage.''

596 Liszt at his desk in the Hofgärtnerei in Weimar. Photograph by Louis Held, June 1884.

597 Liszt with his pupil Carl Lachmund and Lachmund's wife, Caroline. Photograph by Louis Held, Weimar 1884.

''. . . Shortly afterwards a door opened, and Liszt stood there in its frame; motionless, like a picture, with his long white hair falling almost to his slightly stooping shoulders, a compelling grandeur in his features – and yet his face seemed serene and friendly as his keen grey eyes observed the stranger standing before him. I felt as though an electric current flowed outwards from him. During the silence, which lasted no more than a few seconds, I thought a celestial being stood before me . . . My restless imagination had earlier depicted him as the youthful Liszt, the perfect lissome cavalier and conqueror. The man who stood before me now was another Liszt, crowned by his seventy years, gently stooping, and with a sacred calm unclouded by arrogance . . .'' (Carl von Lachmund, *Mein Leben mit Franz Liszt*, on his first meeting with Liszt in April 1882.)

598 Liszt and his pupil Alexander Siloti, who later taught Sergei Rachmaninov. Photograph by Louis Held, Weimar 1884. (The lower left-hand corner of the original negative of this photograph is missing.)

". . . In the autumn of 1884 I informed Liszt that I should like to be photographed in order to send my photograph to Russia. He said that he would have himself photographed with me, and that this group photograph would always be a splendid souvenir for me. It is remark-able how Liszt found a special meaning in everything. For the photo-graph I wanted Liszt to sit on a chair with myself on the ground at his feet; but he refused to accept this, explaining that he was old, that he had said all there was to say, and that he could sit, but that I was still young and had my whole life ahead of me, which was why I had to stand in order to be ready to advance . . ." (Alexander Siloti, "Meine Erinnerungen an Liszt": see note 229).

Liszt's pupil Alexander Siloti:

"It is impossible to recount how Liszt played. In spite of the fact that I myself am a pianist, I can neither demonstrate nor describe his way of playing. He did not produce a large volume of sound, but when he played the piano sound simply did not exist. He played on the same unequal instrument on which we pupils had played. But as soon as he sat down at this worn-out instrument he played in such a way that anyone who never heard him could not imagine what it sounded like. I am a great admirer of the playing of Anton Rubinstein, and I find that we living pianists are pitiful pygmies next to him. I know that Anton Rubinstein used to say that as a pianist he was insignificant compared to Liszt."

Siloti wrote of Liszt's interpretation of the first movement of Beethoven's "Moonlight" Sonata, "Scarcely had he played the opening triplets when I felt I no longer existed in the same room; but when the G sharp entered in the right hand four bars later, I lost all sense of reason. He did not accent this G sharp, but it was a sound never heard before, a sound which even now, 27 years later, I can still hear clearly. He played the whole of the first movement and then the second, but only the beginning of the third, saying that he was too old and did not have sufficient physical strength [. . .]."[229]

Liszt's pupil Moriz Rosenthal:

"How did he play? Like no one before him, and probably like no one after him. When I was still a boy and went to see him in Rome for the first time, he used to play for me in the evening for hours on end – nocturnes by Chopin, his own études – everything he played had a gentle dreamlike quality, and I was astonished at the fabulous delicacy and perfection of his touch. The ornaments were as delicate as a spider's web or the veins in precious lace. After what I had heard in Vienna I thought no fingerwork could surprise me any longer, since I had, after all, studied with Joseffy, the greatest master of this art. But Liszt was more marvellous than anyone else I have heard, and there were other surprises too which he had up his sleeve . . .

"I spent ten years with him and flatter myself that I really got to know him. I may say that I have never met so noble and kind-hearted a man. The whole world knows of his willingness to help struggling and aspiring artists, and of his inclination to work for charitable ends. And when has there ever been a friend like him? [. . .] For Liszt the composer my love is just as great. Even in his less significant works the stamp of genius is evident [. . .]."[230]

Liszt's pupil August Stradal:

"Many people will ask me how he played in his old age. One can imagine how this titan of the piano must have played at the height of his brilliance. But it is difficult to describe how the Master performed at the piano in his later years. First and foremost, it was a miracle of technique! Liszt, who had ended his virtuoso career in Elisabetgrad (Russia) in 1847, at the age of 36, and thereafter played only occasionally in public for charity, even at the time when I got to know him [1885] still commanded that same prodigious technique which was innate and not learned. [. . .]

"Since the Master never did any technical exercises, devoting himself only to his compositions and touching the piano only to play something for his pupils and admirers, it remains an absolute miracle that even in old age Liszt was still the same unsurpassable virtuoso. I heard many great artists play when they were well advanced in years – Joachim, Ole Bull, Sarasate, etc. – all of whom were by then capable of only mediocre achievements technically. Joachim, in particular, played a lot of wrong notes in his later years.

"Nor did Liszt's playing lose any of its demonic passion, since he could still attack the keys in the truest sense of the word."[231]

602 Franz Liszt surrounded by his pupils. Photograph by Louis Held, October 1884.

Front row, from left to right: Saul Liebling, Alexander Siloti, Arthur Friedheim, Emil von Sauer, Alfred Reisenauer, Alexander W. Gottschalg.

Back row, from left to right: Moriz Rosenthal, Viktoria Drewing, Mele Paramanoff, Franz Liszt, Friedheim's mother, Hugo Mansfeld.

As a pedagogue, too, Liszt was the central figure of the nineteenth century. In turn, his pupils were active all over the world: Rosenthal, Sauer, Göllerich, and Stradal in Vienna, Friedheim in Munich and Canada, Siloti in Moscow (Rachmaninov was a pupil of Siloti's) and New York, Lamond in The Hague and Glasgow, Sgambati in Rome, Tausig in Berlin, Dayas in Helsinki (where he succeeded Busoni), Zarembski in Brussels, Stavenhagen in Munich and Geneva, Vianna da Motta in Lisbon, Sophie Menter in St Petersburg, Berthold Kellermann in Berlin and Munich, and István Thomán (Bartók's teacher) in Budapest. Since Liszt had himself been taught by Czerny and since Czerny in his turn had had lessons with Beethoven, many of Liszt's pupils made the proud claim that they were, indirectly, "Beethoven's pupils."

LISZT'S REMARKS WHILE TEACHING

Liszt would accompany the pieces which his pupils performed with a running commentary, mostly witty, sometimes sarcastic.

On Brahms's B flat major Piano Concerto: "This is one of Brahms's very finest works. He himself plays it somewhat carelessly – Bülow plays it particularly well." At a one point he would say, "Now he's putting on his great boots."

When a female pupil played his *Jeux d'eau à la Villa d'Este* very badly, he said to her: "My dear young lady, that was not the fountains in the park at the Villa d'Este but the plumbing in the smallest room in the Villa d'Este; I have no wish to hear that noise and must ask you to do your dirty washing at home!" ("Washing one's dirty linen in public" was Liszt's criticism for poor playing.)

To a composer who brought him his latest work: "Your music contains many new and beautiful things, but the beautiful ones are not new, and the new ones are not beautiful."

To a female pupil who excused her poor performance of a Bach fugue by saying that she had been too busy travelling: "Well, then, you must have left some of the music behind you on your journey, since I didn't hear all the notes. You'd better telegraph for them at once!"

"To play Beethoven requires more technique than ideally belongs to it."

"Schumann must be well phrased in every detail. He must be played firmly and resolutely and be rhythmically well articulated. With him the ritenutos should be just as effective as the accelerandos and animatos are with Mendelssohn. Mendelssohn flows along clearly and quickly, Schumann breathes, but Chopin has more appreciable stature."

When a pupil played clattering scales, Liszt imitated the appropriate sound, saying, "Don't wash your mouth out," and when Amy Fay made too much movement with one of her hands, he told her, "Don't make omelette!"

Opposite page:

599 Liszt's pupil Alexander Siloti (1863–1945). Photograph by Louis Held, ca. 1884.

600 Liszt's pupil Bernhard Stavenhagen (1862–1914). Photograph by Louis Held, ca. 1884.

601 Liszt's pupil Arthur Friedheim (1859–1932). Photograph by Louis Held, ca. 1884.

LIFE

1 to 25 January: Liszt in Rome.

26 to 28 January: Liszt in Florence, where he sees Count Gubernatis (director of the *Revue internationale*), Jessie Laussot-Hillebrand, Alexander Mackenzie, and Princess Rospigliosi.

30 January to 13 April: Liszt in Budapest.

February: Liszt works on his 18th and 19th *Hungarian Rhapsodies* and his *Trauervorspiel* and *Trauermarsch* in Budapest.

8 March: Liszt in Rákospalota as guest of Ferenc Vargas.

23/24 March: In Gran as guest of Primate Simor.

2 to 5 April: In Kalocsa as guest of Cardinal Haynald.

13/14 April: In Preßburg. On the 13th Liszt attends a concert given by Anton Rubinstein in support of the Hummel Memorial.

14 to 18 April: Liszt in Vienna. On the afternoon of the 18th he attends the dress rehearsal of Anton Rubinstein's opera *Nero* in the Court Theatre.

19 April to the end of September: Liszt in Weimar, apart from occasional visits elsewhere.

25 May: Liszt travels to Mannheim and that same evening hears a performance of Wagner's *Götterdämmerung*, after which he travels to Karlsruhe with his two granddaughters Isolde and Eva Wagner for the annual *Tonkünstlerversammlung* (27 May to 1 June) at which Felix Mottl conducts his *Dante Symphony*.

3 and 4 June: Liszt in Strasbourg for a performance of *Die Glocken des Straßburger Münsters*.

5 to 10 June: Liszt in Antwerp. Liszt Concert under Servais on the 7th, and the *Szekszárd Mass* in St Joseph's Church on the 8th. On the 9th Liszt is honoured by the King and Queen of Belgium at the Brussels World Fair.

13 to 15 June: Liszt in Aachen. Liszt concert under Kniese on the 14th.

July/August: Liszt in Weimar, composing and teaching. Among the works written at this time are *Historische ungarische Bildnisse*.

3 September: Liszt attends a concert in the Leipzig Gewandhaus consisting exclusively of his works.

5 September: Liszt addresses an indignant letter to Otto Leßmann on the subject of the million marks left by Theodor Kullak on his death in 1882. ''As an artist you don't rake in a million marks without performing some sacrifice on the altar of art,'' he told Lina Ramann, who was visiting him in Weimar.[232]

15 October: Liszt leaves Weimar and travels to Rome, accompanied by Friedheim, Stavenhagen and Thomán.

16 October: Liszt in Munich, where he hears Cornelius's *Der Barbier von Bagdad*. The opera has now gained acceptance in a version revised by Mottl and Levi, and with Liszt's orchestration of the second Overture.

18 October: Liszt spends a few days with Sophie Menter at Schloß Itter in the Tyrol.

22 October: Liszt is honoured by the Innsbruck Male Voice Choir on the occasion of his birthday. A Liszt Society is founded in Leipzig.

25 October to 21 January 1886: Liszt in Rome at the Hotel Alibert. He teaches and works on his oratorio *St Stanislaus*. In mid-November he spends a few days at the Villa d'Este.

A mon bon Ami
Baille
Gustave Durand

Litz . Rome
écoutant une Messe
de Palestrina
1885

WORKS

Historische ungarische Bildnisse – Magyar történelmi arcképek (for piano): 1. *Stephan Széchényi*, 2. *Josef Eötvös*, 3. *Michael Vörösmarty*, 4. *Ladislaus Teleky*, 5. *Franz Deák*, 6. *Alexander Petöfi*, 7. *Michael Mosonyi*. Pub. 1956. The pieces devoted to the memory of Petöfi and Mosonyi had already been written in 1877 and 1870 respectively, but Liszt expanded them slightly for this collection.

Concerto in the Hungarian Style (for piano and orchestra). September/October 1885. It was orchestrated by Tchaikovsky and published ca. 1895, when it was attributed to Sophie Menter, for whom Liszt had corrected and prepared the short score. It was republished by Schirmer in 1909 and by Kalmus ca. 1976. There is no evidence that Liszt actually composed this work. The style has nothing in common with the Liszt of this period, and not until 1981 was there any suggestion that it might be by Liszt.

Hungarian Rhapsody No. 18 (for piano). Pub. 1885. A version for piano duet was also published at this time.

Trauervorspiel and *Trauermarsch* (for piano). Pub. 1887. The Funeral March is almost identical with the fourth of the *Historische ungarische Bildnisse* but is 27 bars longer.

Abschied (Russian folk song) (for piano). Pub. 1885.

Tarantelle (Cui) (piano transcription). Pub. 1886.

Fourth Mephisto Waltz (for piano). Unfinished version pub. 1954. Completed from Liszt's sketches by Leslie Howard and published 1988.

Pax vobiscum! (for men's voices or male voice quartet and organ). Pub. 1886.

Qui Mariam absolvisti (for baritone, mixed voices, and organ). Pub. 1886.

(continued p. 307)

Opposite page:

603 Liszt and his pupil Lina Schmalhausen. Photograph by Koller, Budapest 1885, with a dedication to Lina Schmalhausen in Liszt's hand, ''Different again, but of the same mind'' – an allusion to Lina Schmalhausen's collection of photographs of Liszt.

Fashionable salons and the Eternal Feminine on the one hand and mystic contemplation on the other were the two poles between which Liszt's final years were acted out. Lina Schmalhausen, Olga Janina (albeit briefly), and above all Baroness Olga von Meyendorff were the women with whom the ageing Liszt was on closest terms.

604 Liszt listening to a Mass by Palestrina in Rome. Pencil drawing by Gustave Durand, 1885.

''Liszt was devout through and through, devout to the point of ecstasy. I was often granted the privilege of seeing him pray, either in the old, venerable, and silent church of San Cosimo e Damiano or in the Chiesa dell'Anima, either in the perfect stillness of a deserted sanctuary or during wonderful performances of Palestrina's Masses. He was no longer aware of earthly matters, but seemed transfigured!'' (Nadine Helbig, *Deutsche Revue*, 1907). ''From his seat Liszt would recite the words of the Latin liturgy in such a loud voice that it seemed to be *he* who was celebrating mass'' (reminiscences of the poet Karl Linzen, who had been an altar boy in Weimar).

605 Liszt, Albert Morris Bagby (right of picture), and Brodkorb. Photograph by Louis Held, Weimar 1885.

606 Liszt and the violinist Arma Senkrah. Photograph by Louis Held, Weimar, 31 July 1885.

LISZT ON THE CRITIC'S ROLE

''If the critic is not also an artist, if he is unable to practise what he professes to preach, one mistrusts his expert judgement (and one is probably right to do so), and one denies that he is competent to understand and criticize results. If as a critic he is solemn and severe, people will laugh at him for failing to understand the inner processes at work and will regard his severity as rage and impotence. Artists will spurn him, and whatever he may do he will suffer not only the hatred but also the contempt of those on whom he lavishes the most extravagant praise.

''The position of the artist-critic is ten times worse. If he dares to pass conscientious judgement on what he finds unsatisfactory in the works of great masters, his temerity is intolerable; if he criticizes his colleagues and contemporaries, he is said to be driven by 'pure envy.' Those composers with whom he is on terms of personal friendship accuse him of 'ingratitude,' while those who have never met him wonder what they have done to deserve such treatment. Although he believes he has raised only questions of art, it transpires that he has raised personal questions affecting hundreds, and that he has attracted as many enemies as the people he criticized have spouses, brothers, cousins, patrons, and sometimes even fellow countrymen!''[233]

LISZT ON CRITICISM

''Without imagination there is neither art nor science, and therefore no criticism either'' (1854).[234]

''[. . .] An excellent prescription against unjustified criticism is to criticize oneself properly both beforehand and afterwards – and also to remain quite calm and continue on one's way [. . .]'' (letter to Jules de Zarembski, 13 December 1877).[235]

''A critique which sought only to emphasize the *weak* points in a work of art would be too critical. It should also seek out the *beauties* of the work'' (1854).[236]

''[. . .] Would not the best result of criticism be for it to inspire the artist to renewed creativity? [. . .]'' (letter to Carl Reinecke, 25 March 1849).[237]

''Literature can *feel* art, but only artists can *assess* it in detail. [. . .] The non-artist can speak only of his individual unauthenticated impressions, since he does not possess the necessary foundation on which to build those impressions'' (1855).[238]

''Criticism appears useful, effective, and difficult (and for that reason deserving of respect) as soon as it fulfils the requirements of conscientiousness, fairness, knowledge, and decency; but because of the way in which it is normally practised it sinks to the level of a degrading job, or else the persecutions which it brings down upon itself on the part of all who would remain conscientious and independent reduce it to an act of chivalrous submissiveness'' (1838).[239]

"Works 1885" (continued)

Salve Regina (for four-part *a cappella* chorus). Pub. 1936.

Gruß (15 bars to the words "Glück auf") (for men's voices). Pub. 1885.

Bagatelle ohne Tonart – Bagatelle sans tonalité (for piano). Pub. 1956.

Klavierstück ("Ruhig"). Published in 1982 in an edition by Joseph Banowetz, who did not notice that it was Liszt's introduction and coda to Tausig's piano transcription of Johann Strauß's *Waldstimmen*.

En Rêve. Nocturne (for piano). Pub. 1888.

Concerto pathétique (for piano and orchestra). Arranged by Eduard Reuß from the earlier piece for two pianos (see "Works 1856"). The beginning and ending were altered and many corrections and changes made by Liszt himself, who approved the final publication. Pub. 1886.

607 Liszt and the violinist Arma Senkrah performing Beethoven's F major Sonata in Louis Held's Weimar studio. Photograph by Louis Held, Weimar, 31 July 1885.

In his *Erinnerungen an Franz Liszt* August Stradal writes, "In July there appeared a violin virtuoso who performed for the Master on a handful of occasions, and I had to accompany her. The young lady flattered Liszt a great deal and dragged him to the photographer's studio, where an enormous photograph was taken. It showed Liszt accompanying her at the piano, and underneath it the Master wrote, 'To the distinguished violin virtuoso – her most devoted accompanist F. Liszt.' Fräulein Senkrah sent the photograph to all the towns she was due to visit on her concert tours and, thanks to this publicity, always played to full houses."[240]

608 Franz Liszt. Photograph by Louis Held, Weimar 1885. (The original negative is damaged in the top right-hand corner.)

In the years around 1840 Liszt had been one of the most ele- gant figures in European circles, but in old age he scarcely troubled any longer about his physical appearance. Carolyne von Sayn-Wittgenstein wrote to Baron Antal Augusz (in her fractured German), ''I may mention in passing that his cloth- ing has become terribly inelegant. He no longer looks like *un homme de la société*, but like an old organist. And what shoes! – You could float from Civita-Vecchia to Naples in them . . .''[241]

609 Franz Liszt. Photograph by Louis Held, Weimar 1885.

In his final years Liszt suffered from dropsy, and by the end of his life he was almost blind: both ailments he ignored. He never liked to be asked about his health, and generally responded with an ironic remark. When his pupil Carl Pohlig began to go into details about the smallpox from which he was suffering, Liszt cut him off with the words "A most wholesome illness!"[242]

LIFE

1 January: On the first day of the year (the year of his death) Liszt greets his pupils in Rome with the words, ''A bad year! It begins on a Friday, and my birthday too falls on a Friday . . .'' (Liszt regarded Friday as his unlucky day and avoided taking important decisions on Fridays.)

15 January: Farewell concert at the Palazzo Barca. The performers include Göllerich, Stradal, Stavenhagen, Ansorge, and Liszt (13th Rhapsody).

21 January: Accompanied by his pupil Stavenhagen, who reads to him from Tolstoi's *Religion*, Liszt leaves Rome for Budapest. On the way he visits Jessie Laussot-Hillebrand in Florence and Princess Hatzfeld at the Palazzo Malipiero in Venice.

30 January to 11 March: Liszt in Budapest.

February: Teaching commitments at the Academy of Music. Apart from his Hungarian students, Liszt also gives lessons here to Stradal, Göllerich, Stavenhagen, and Ansorge.

10 March: Farewell concert in Budapest. The performers include Stradal (*Funérailles* and 19th *Hungarian Rhapsody*), Mlle Krivácsy (*Don Carlos* paraphrase), and Lina Schmalhausen (11th *Hungarian Rhapsody*). Kornél Abrányi delivers a speech.

11 March: Liszt leaves Budapest in the evening.

12 to 15 March: Liszt in Vienna, where he spends time with Bösendorfer and Marie von Hohenlohe-Schillingsfürst.

15 (evening) to 18 March: Liszt in Liège, where he stays with Countess Mercy-Argenteau. A Liszt Concert on the 17th includes the ''Gran'' Mass, the A major Piano Concerto, a *Hungarian Rhapsody*, and two Lieder.

19 March: Liszt stays with Victor Lynen in Antwerp.

20 March to the morning of 3 April: Liszt in Paris. *Les Préludes* under Edouard Colonne (20 March); matinée at Mihály Munkácsy's (23 March); highly successful performance of the ''Gran'' Mass under Colonne in Saint-Eustache (25 March); *Les Préludes*, *Orpheus*, and a *Hungarian Rhapsody* (28 March); a repeat performance of the ''Gran'' Mass in Saint-Eustache (2 April). The proceeds from the Paris concerts, some 42,000 francs, are donated at Liszt's request to various charities. Meeting with Claude Debussy.

3 to 18 April: Liszt in London (Westwood House, Sydenham). Successful performance of *Saint Elisabeth* under Mackenzie in St James's Hall on 6 April: the Prince of Wales (later King Edward VII) escorts Liszt from the Green Room to the auditorium. The next day he is invited by Queen Victoria to perform at Windsor Castle; among the pieces he plays are a Nocturne by Chopin. The Queen presents him with a marble bust of her by Joseph E. Boehm. On the 8th is a soirée at the Grosvenor Gallery organized by Walter Bache; among those present are Joachim, Lamond, and Vladimir von Pachmann. Liszt plays from his 13th *Hungarian Rhapsody* and *Mélodies hongroises*. On the 9th Emil Bach gives a Liszt Concert (see Illus. 624), and on the 10th there is a Liszt Concert at the Crystal Palace. A repeat performance of *Saint Elisabeth* takes place on 17 April. Between these engagements are dinners in Liszt's honour, invitations, and visits to concerts and the theatre.

20 to 26 April: Liszt in Antwerp (with Victor Lynen).

610 Letter of 25 February 1886 from Liszt's servant Mihály Kreiner to the photographer Louis Held, asking for photographs for his master's last journey. Previously unpublished.

613 Liszt's travelling bag with his coat of arms: a rampant silver unicorn in two of the fields, a bar set with a golden star in the other two.

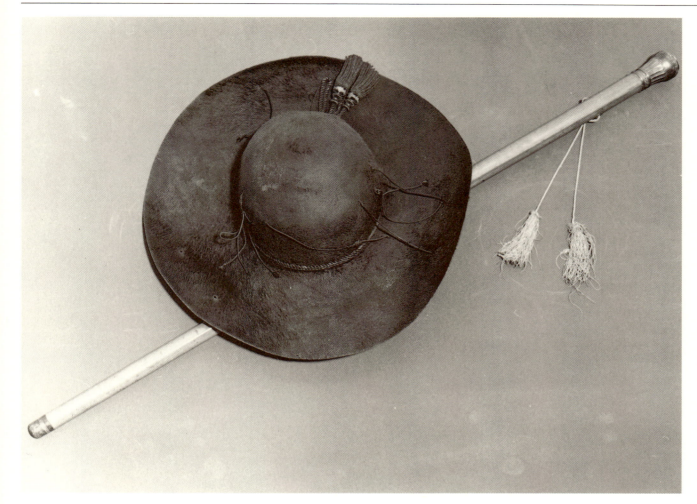

611 Liszt's walking stick and his abbé's hat. The walking stick, of brown cane with a silver handle, was a present from Pope Pius IX.

It is remarkable that a man who in the *Années de Pèlerinage* had given such movingly atmospheric expression to nature had clearly so little time for rural beauty. His travelling companions report that he "never looked out of the cab window" but remained preoccupied with reading and writing; and it was often remarked that he never went for walks and even for short journeys used a carriage, which was kept at the ready outside his door in Budapest.

In September 1875 he told Lina Ramann: "Thanks to your careful preparations, I had splendid travelling companions for my two days' journey from Nuremberg to Rome. Your monograph on Bach and Handel was more entertaining than the famous scenery of the Brenner Pass [. . .]."[243]

On 11 March 1886 Liszt set out from Budapest on his last great journey. When his friends said goodbye "until we meet again," his reply was "In the next world." Towns which had once prostrated themselves before the virtuoso once again prepared to honour him, and his compositions were given an unexpectedly warm reception. The world of music sensed that it would never again see this impressive figure with his snow-white mane of hair. Vienna, Liège, Paris, London, Antwerp, Brussels, Paris again, Weimar, and Luxembourg were only some of the places he stayed on this journey, which ended in Bayreuth on 31 July.

612 Liszt's portable writing desk (25 x 32 cm), which he took with him on his travels.

27 April: Liszt in Brussels (with Monsignor Ferrata).

28 April to 15 May: Liszt in Paris, where he stays with his friend the painter Mihály Munkácsy. Concerts of Liszt's music meet with astonishing acclaim. A performance of *Saint Elisabeth* is given in the 7000-seat hall of the Trocadéro (8 May).

17 May: Liszt arrives back in Weimar suffering from a cold. He receives a visit from Cosima, who has avoided him since her husband's death. Liszt accepts her invitation to attend performances of *Tristan* and *Parsifal* in Bayreuth.

1 June: Liszt travels to Halle for a medical examination. He is diagnosed as suffering from dropsy and cataracts. A course of treatment in Kissingen during August and an eye operation in Halle during September are prescribed and accepted.

3 to 6 June: Annual *Tonkünstlerversammlung* in Sondershausen, which Liszt attends. Performances of *Christus*, *Hamlet*, *Totentanz* (with Siloti), *Ce qu'on entend sur la montagne*, *Die Ideale*, *Hunnenschlacht*, and Friedheim's orchestration of the *Historische ungarische Bildnisse*. On his return to Weimar, Liszt undertakes excursions to Dornburg (23/24 June), and to Jena (25 June) for a performance of Mendelssohn's *Paulus*.

1 to 4 July: Liszt in Bayreuth for the wedding of his granddaughter Daniela and the art historian Henry Thode.

5 to 19 July: Liszt at the Château of Colpach in Luxembourg as guest of Mihály Munkácsy.

19 July: At the request of Munkácsy's wife, Liszt makes his last public appearance in the packed hall of the Luxembourg Casino. He plays the first of his *Liebesträume*, the *Mélodies polonaises* from *Glanes de Woronince*, and the sixth of the *Soirées de Vienne*. In all probability this is the last time he ever played the piano.

20 July: Liszt leaves Luxembourg and travels via Frankfurt (where he spends the night) to Bayreuth.

21 July: Liszt arrives in Bayreuth. He attends performances of *Parsifal* (on the 23rd) and *Tristan* (on the 25th). On the course of these final days and hours of Liszt's life, see pp. 324–25.

31 July: Franz Liszt dies in Bayreuth.

WORKS

Ne brani menya, moy drug (Do not reproach me, my friend). Song for solo voice and piano to words by Tolstoi. Published Moscow 1958.

Die Vätergruft. The orchestration of the accompaniment to this song (to a poem by Ludwig Uhland) was Liszt's final compositional task (see Illus. 627).

Because of his progressive blindness Liszt was virtually unable to write music during his final months.

614 Caricatures of Liszt from *La Vie Parisienne* of 3 April 1886.

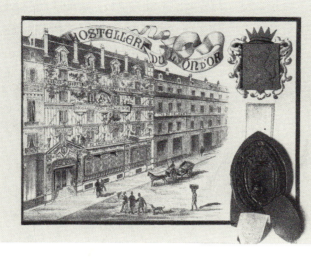

615 The Hotel ''Lion d'Or'' in Paris.

616 Menu for the dinner held in Liszt's honour on 31 March 1886.

617 Soirée at the home of Mihály von Munkácsy in Paris on 23 March 1886. Wood engraving, 1886.

Front row of audience (from left to right): Alphonse Daudet (with the painter Munkácsy behind him), Diémer, Count Hoyos, Count Pourtalès, Countess Hervey, Count Ferrière, Saint-Saëns, Countess Pourtalès, Liszt, Monsignor Czaski, Charles Gounod, Frau von Munkácsy.

618 Programme for the soirée on 23 March 1886.

Saint-Saëns and Diémer (Alfred Cortot's teacher) played duets by Liszt, who ended the evening with an epilogue. Liszt enjoyed the rare pleasure of being recognized as a composer during his final visits to Paris in March and April 1886.

619 Liszt is honoured in the studio of the sculptor Cyprien Godebski, March 1886. Wood engraving from *Le Monde illustré* of 3 April 1886, based on a drawing by Reichan.

620 Franz Liszt in London in April 1886.
Wood engraving from *The Graphic* of 10
April 1886, based on a drawing by
Charles Renouard.

MR. OTTO GOLDSCHMIDT   MR. AUGUST MANNS

MR. J. E. BOEHM, R.A.   SIR ARTHUR SULLIVAN   REV. HENRY WHITE   THE ABBE LISZT   MR. W. SHAKSPE.

621 Liszt greeting Joseph Joachim at a reception held in London's Grosvenor Gallery. Wood engraving from *The Graphic* of 17 April 1886.

MR. WALTER BACHE   SIR F. LEIGHTON, P.R.A.   MR. CHARLES HALLE   MADAME ALBANI

RR JOACHIM   MR. ARTHUR CHAPPELL   MADAME ANTOINETTE STERLING   SIR GEORGE MACFARREN

622 Liszt's pupils, among them Arthur Friedheim (leaning forward with arms outstretched), Alexander Siloti (semi-recumbent), and Bernhard Stavenhagen (top of picture, with his left arm round Siloti's neck). Photograph by Louis Held, Sondershausen, 5 June 1886.

The men are clearly enjoying themselves. The photograph was taken immediately before or after the group photograph (Illus. 625) shown opposite, in which all the men in this scene also figure.

623 (at right) Liszt and his pupil Bernhard Stavenhagen. Photograph by W. & D. Downey, London, April 1886.

Stavenhagen accompanied Liszt on his last journeys to London and Luxembourg. The composer was almost blind by now and in June and July 1886 dictated most of his letters to Stavenhagen. The composer of two piano concertos, Stavenhagen was appointed Court Kapellmeister in Weimar in 1895, and from 1901 to 1904 was director of the Akademie der Tonkunst in Munich.

624 (far right) Liszt and his pupil Emil Bach. Photograph by W. & D. Downey, London, April 1886.

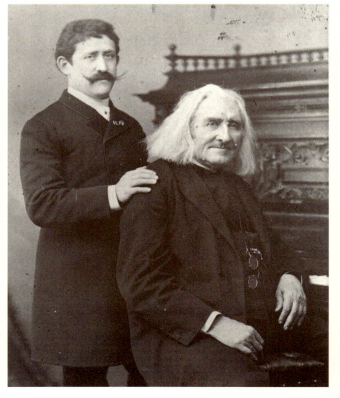

625 Liszt surrounded by his admirers at the 1886 *Tonkünstlerver-sammlung* in Sondershausen. Photograph by Louis Held, Sonders-hausen, 5 June 1886.

626 The persons who can be identified in Illus. 625: 1. Paul Knüpfer, 2. Alexander Glazunov, 3. Arthur Seidl, 4. Max Grünberg, 5. Julius Klengel, 6. Frau Klengel, 7. Gunther Mahlendorf, 8. Carl Goepfart, 9. August Bieler, 10. Salomon Jadassohn, 11. C. F. Kahnt, 12. August Göllerich, 13. Carl Gille, 14. Otto Leßmann, 15. Adolf Schultze, 16. Willy Rehberg, 17. Alexander Ritter, 18. Lina Ramann, 19. Liszt, 20. Karl Hill, 21. Marianne Brandt, 22. Carl Schröder, 23. Carl Halir, 24. Martin Krause, 25. Alexander Siloti, 26. William Dayas, 27. Bernhard Stavenhagen, 28. Arthur Fried-heim, 29. August Stradal.

Liszt's final works – studies in sound, or monologues with occasional outbursts – are notably sparing of melody. The composer laid aside, so to speak, the coat of many colours with which he had typically clothed so many other works; instead he sought ways of extending tonality, developing a style of writing which was increasingly ascetic and often consciously monochrome. Liszt knew that he had "thrown his spear too far into the future," and, indeed, a whole century was to pass before the general public was made aware of these later pieces, not least through the pioneering work of the pianist Alfred Brendel.

In describing Liszt's late piano works, Peter Raabe wrote perhaps the finest tribute ever penned to the composer: "[. . .] Just as at the end of his life he renounced all sense of magnificence, so here he renounces what the world understands as expression. What he says here is devoid of hope, and the man who feels no hope no longer speaks in choicely elegant forms. He no longer speaks to others, rarely even to himself. In *Nuages Gris* melody-less schemes float past, and in *Unstern* the dissonances hammer away one after the other, like a prisoner beating at the wall with his fists although he knows that no one is listening. He then attempts to pray, but his voice is reduced to a stammer – he stares into space awaiting an answer which never comes.

"This was Liszt, the lifelong exile, the solitary figure. The Liszt whom the world knew was of course a different man. What he gave to the world was accepted as he wished only if no real demands were thereby made on that world – which then took pleasure in him and called him amiable, without suspecting what they really meant: that the man was worthy of being loved."[244]

627 Probably the last music that Liszt wrote. A page from the full score of Liszt's orchestration of Uhland's ballad *Die Vätergruft* ("Es schritt wohl über die Haide").

The orchestration of this Lied was the last compositional task undertaken by Liszt. He had set the poem for bass or baritone voice while staying in Port Marly in 1844.

628 Liszt's letter to Lina Schmalhausen, 21 June 1886.

Almost blind, Liszt had to dictate his extensive correspondence and have letters read out to him during the final weeks of his life. The lines reproduced here are among the last that he wrote with his own hand.

629 The last photograph of Franz Liszt, seen here on the arm of Frau von Munkácsky leaving the Château at Colpach, the Luxembourg home of the painter Mihály von Munkácsy. The photograph must have been taken around 15 July 1886, and in all likelihood on the 19th, the date on which Liszt left Colpach.

This photograph – virtually unknown – is almost certainly the last ever taken of Liszt. It is also the only known candid "snapshot" of the composer, in addition to being the only one that shows him wearing a top hat.

Liszt travelled to Bayreuth on 1 July 1886 in order to attend his granddaughter Daniela's wedding to the art historian Henry Thode on the 3rd. Two days later we find him at the Château of Colpach in Luxembourg, as guest of his friend the painter Mihály Munkácsy. Although he normally turned down the idea of performing in public, he sat down at the piano here once again. ("It seems they are intending to put me in front of a piano in London. This is something I can no longer tolerate in public, since my fingers are now 74 years old and are no longer equal to such exertions. And Bülow, Saint-Saëns, Rubinstein, and you, my dear Bache, play my works much better than my own insignificant and decrepit self. Perhaps it would be acceptable to indicate to the public that Liszt can appear only as a grateful visitor, and that neither London nor anywhere else can count on the active participation of his fingers.")[245]

On 19 July, at a concert in the Luxembourg Casino, Liszt played his first *Liebestraum*, the *Mélodies polonaises* from *Glanes de Woronince*, and his sixth *Soirée de Vienne*. It was his farewell to the concert hall.

On 21 July Liszt arrived back in Bayreuth suffering from a chill. Utterly exhausted, he attended performances of *Parsifal* and *Tristan* on the 23rd and 25th. Six days later he departed this life. For an account of his final days see pp. 324-5.

630 Bayreuth, the stage and auditorium of the Festspielhaus. Photograph, ca. 1890.

Huddled in his box, and wracked by coughing, Liszt attended performances of *Parsifal* and *Tristan und Isolde* during the days that preceded his death. During the intervals he dragged himself to the front of his box to applaud.

631 The Bayreuth Festspielhaus. Photograph, ca. 1890.

632 The house in which Liszt died in Bayreuth, at 9 Wahnfriedstraße (then known as Siegfried-straße). Photograph, ca. 1950.

During his last visits to Bayreuth, Liszt occupied the small room on the ground floor of this building (the two middle windows). To the right (with the commemorative plaque) is the room in which he died on 31 July 1886.

633 The house in which Liszt died, seen from the garden. Photograph, ca. 1900.

Liszt's loyal pupils kept a vigil on the steps outside his room during the night of his death.

634 Franz Liszt on his deathbed. Photograph by Hans Brand, Bayreuth, 1 August 1886, together with a lock of Liszt's hair. Previously unpublished.

From the estate of Lina Schmalhausen (see Illus. 603), this photograph bears the inscription, ''These forget-me-nots and red roses were placed in his hands by me before the coffin was closed. No one but me garlanded the 'body' with flowers. This photograph was taken at my request. The lock of hair was cut from his left temple and handed to me by Frau Cosima Wagner at his deathbed at 6 o'clock in the morning, 1.8.1886.''

Opposite page:

635 Franz Liszt on his deathbed. Photograph by Hans Brand, Bayreuth, 1 August 1886. Previously unpublished.

The photograph is framed by flowers and leaves from the funeral wreaths presented by Sophie Menter, Arma Senkrah (see Illus. 516 and 607), Adalbert von Goldschmidt, the sculptor Moses Jakob Ezéchiel, and Grand Duke Carl Alexander of Weimar (see Illus. 473), and from the Conservatoires in Moscow, Prague, and elsewhere. Beneath the photograph is a lock of Liszt's hair.

636 Liszt's death mask, taken at 1 o'clock in the afternoon of 1 August 1886.

The death mask was prepared in the room in which Liszt had died by Weißbrod, Schnappauf, and Kästner in the presence of the painter Paul von Joukovsky, before being taken the short distance to Wahnfried. The photographs reproduced here, taken by Louis Held around 1890, show the original mask, which is now in Weimar.

637 Liszt's death mask, seen from the side.

On the right of the cast the original stamp ''Weißbrod & Schnappauf'' is clearly identifiable.

Opposite page:

638, 639 Local press reports of Liszt's death. (For translations of these texts, see pp. 343–4.)

LISZT'S DEATH IN BAYREUTH

''Since the years of my youth I have regarded dying as much easier than living. Although death is often preceded by terrible and protracted suffering, it none the less releases us from the involuntary yoke of our existence. Religion eases this yoke, but our hearts continue to bleed beneath it [. . .]'' (Liszt to Lina Ramann, 22 February 1883).[246]

Franz Liszt was not fated to die a simple death. The groans and cries brought on by spasms of the heart and difficulty in breathing during his final night could be heard in the entire neighbourhood of the house in which he died, in Bayreuth's Siegfriedstraße (now Wahnfriedstraße 9).

As with the death of Frédéric Chopin, a circle of legends has been woven around Liszt's final days and hours, whose most confusing aspect is the claim that his daughter Cosima, who was living only a few steps away in Wahnfried, ignored her dying father during this period. If we compare all the statements left by Liszt's relatives and by those of his friends and pupils who were with the dying man during these final days – Cosima and Siegfried Wagner, Daniela von Bülow-Thode, Paul von Joukovsky, Lina Schmalhausen, August Stradal, Liszt's manservant Mihály, and, above all, August Göllerich – the following picture emerges:

Wednesday 21 July: Liszt arrives in Bayreuth from Luxembourg at half past three in the afternoon. He is suffering from a cold, is feverish, and coughs a lot. He goes straight to bed, but in the evening is woken by his grandchildren Eva and Siegfried Wagner and taken to Wahnfried for a musical soirée.

Thursday 22 July: While August Göllerich (Illus. 626, no. 12) is reading to the now almost totally blind Liszt from a Breviary, Lina Schmalhausen (Illus. 603) arrives in Bayreuth. It is around 7 o'clock in the morning. These two pupils of Liszt's remain with him from now on, seeing to his needs and reading aloud to him. Liszt keeps nodding off, but notices each time they stop reading. Violent coughing fits rack his body in between times.

Friday 23 July: Liszt's condition remains poor. At 4 o'clock in the afternoon he attends the opening ceremony of the Festival. During the evening's performance of *Parsifal* he sits in the Wagners' box, leaning against a pillar, utterly exhausted, struggling to stifle his violent coughing with a handkerchief pressed to his mouth in order not to disturb the performance.

Saturday 24 July: No improvement in his health. Cosima now comes to see him every day between 6 and 7 in the morning in order to breakfast with her father. For his midday and evening meals Liszt is invited to Wahnfried. Many of Liszt's pupils, having heard of the worrying state of his health, travel to Bayreuth. During a game of whist with Eduard Lassen (Illus. 426), Otto Leßmann (Illus. 565, no. 14), Alexander Siloti (Illus. 598) and Sophie Menter (Illus. 516), Liszt is scarcely able to hold the cards or put them in order.

Sunday 25 July: Liszt's condition is becoming more and more critical, but he refuses to be dissuaded from attending the performance of *Tristan*. ''Cosima wishes me to attend, I have promised her I would, and I am going,'' he replies to his pupils' protestations. (Liszt was honorary president of the Wagner Society.) At the beginning of the performance and during the intervals Liszt appears at the front of his box.

Monday 26 July: Liszt's health continues to deteriorate. His remark to Lina Schmalhausen, ''I do not believe I shall get up from here,'' is to prove correct. The local doctor Karl Landgraf tells him to stop drinking alcohol, which for Liszt, accustomed to his daily intake of cognac, is bound to lead to a further loss of strength. Since Göllerich himself falls ill for two days, Liszt's only attendants are Lina Schmalhausen and the manservant Mihály.

Tuesday 27 July: After a sleepless night, Lina asks Liszt how he is, to which he replies with a solemn, prescient look, ''No better.''

Wednesday 28 July: Dr Fleischer arrives from Erlangen and diagnoses that Liszt has been suffering from pneumonia for a week. Cosima gives orders for no one else to be admitted; Lina Schmalhausen has to leave the house, and Stavenhagen is stationed in the entrance hall to keep all visitors out.

Thursday 29 July: From now on Cosima sleeps in the room next to her father, who is delirious most of the time.

Friday 30 July: Liszt is barely concious any longer. At 2 o'clock in the morning he leaps out of bed, repeatedly clutching his heart and crying out for air in a booming voice. By the time Dr Landgraf arrives, he is lying motionless and apparently dead. He revives after lengthy massage but remains unconscious.

Saturday 31 July: Cosima spends the whole day at her father's bedside. Dr Fleischer is summoned back and prescribes strong wine and champagne. Liszt continues to groan loudly until half past ten, when his breathing becomes silent and irregular. After two injections in the region of the heart, the body convulses violently three times, then falls back, lifeless. At half past eleven his heart stops beating.

1886. XXXI. Jahrgang.

№ 212.

Montag den 2. August

Erscheint täglich. Alle kgl. Post=anstalten u. Landpostboten liefern das Tagblatt vierteljährlich für 1 M. 60 Pfg. Preis für den 2. u. 3. Monat des Quartals 55 Pfg. per Monat.

Bayreuther Tagblatt.

Oberfränkische Volkszeitung.

(Die Verantwortlichkeit für Inserate trägt deren Einsender.)

Bei Anfragen von Auswärts ist Franco = Marke für die Rückantwort beizulegen.

Abonnements für Bayreuth 1 M. 40 Pfg. vierteljährlich, bei freier Zustellung in's Haus 1 Mark 60 Pfg. Preis für den 2. u. 3. Monat des Quartals 1 Mark, frei in's Haus 55 Pfg. per Monat.

* Liszt. †

Mitten in die Freude und die Begeisterung, welche der glückliche, ja glänzende Fortgang der Festspiele hervorgerufen, fiel gestern Nachts die Trauernachricht, daß Franz Liszt, der große Tonmeister, dessen Ruhm die ganze civilisirte Welt erfüllt, Liszt, der vertraute Freund und Förderer Wagners, Liszt, der Vater der Frau Wagner, Samstag Nachts ½ 12 Uhr das Zeitliche gesegnet hat.

War man auch durch die vor einigen Tagen erfolgte Erkrankung des verehrten Mannes, die bei dem hohen Alter desselben von Anfang an die schlimmsten Befürchtungen erwecken mußte, auf die Katastrophe vorbereitet, so glaubte man noch bis zu den zwei letzten Tagen das Ende nicht so nahe, und um so schmerzlicher traf deshalb die Todesbotschaft die hier versammelten Gäste und die Einwohnerschaft der ganzen Stadt.

Das tiefste Mitgefühl Aller wendet sich zunächst der Wagner'schen Familie, insbesondere der schwergeprüften Frau Wagner zu, die inmitten der Festspiele, inmitten der schweren Aufgabe, die sie mit der Leitung der Aufführungen übernommen, von diesem schweren Schicksalsschlage heimgesucht wurde, der das Herz der zärtlichen Tochter auf das Tiefste treffen mußte. Wer des großen Tonmeisters treue Liebe zu seinen Angehörigen kannte, der fühlt mit der hochverehrten Familie. Wagner die ganze Größe des Verlustes, und die innigste Theilnahme Aller, das kann versichert werden sich in vollem Maße den Trauernden gezollt.

Heute, in den ersten Augenblicke der höchsten Trauer, vermögen wir nicht ein erschöpfendes Lebensbild des großen Todten zu geben, dessen Verdienste von berufeneren Federn gewürdigt werden müssen; wir beschränken uns deshalb auf einige allgemeine Daten:

Franz Liszt ist geboren am 22. October 1811 in dem ungarischen Orte Raiding, als der Sohn eines fürstlich Esterhazy'schen Rechnungsofficianten. Schon frühzeitig zeigte er ein eminentes Talent für die Musik. Im neunten Jahre spielte Liszt zum ersten Male öffentlich auf dem Claviere und erregte allgemeines Staunen. Mit Unterstützung der Grafen Amade und Szapary brachte der Vater Liszt's seinen talentvollen Sohn nach Wien, wo er den Unterricht Czerny's und Salieri's genoß. Nach 18 monatlichem Unterricht trat Liszt mit glänzendem Erfolge in Wien auf. Bald darauf wandte sich Liszt nach Paris, wo sich sein eminentes Talent trotz mannigfacher Anfeindungen, deren Seele Cherubini war, alsbald unwiderstehlich zu den höchsten Triumphen Bahn brach. Liszt wurde rasch der Liebling der Pariser Welt. Er wandte sich dann nach England, wo er ähnliche Triumphe erzielte. 1827 folgte ein Ausflug in die Schweiz, von wo aus Liszt nach England zurückkehrte; bald zwang ihn aber seine angegriffene Gesundheit, sich in die Bäder von Boulogne zu begeben. Hier starb Liszt's Vater, und Ersterer kehrte nach Paris zurück. 1831 hörte er Paganini, was seine ganze spätere Richtung beeinflußte. Von 1833—1835 lebte Liszt in Genf in ziemlicher Zurückgezogenheit, kehrte dann nach Paris zurück, wo er mit Thalberg in Rivalität trat; 1837 begab er sich nach Italien und verweilte daselbst bis Ende 1839.

Im Jahre 1848 verließ Liszt die Laufbahn des reisenden Virtuosen und wandte sich nach Weimar. Hier wirkte er fortan als Hofcapellmeister in außerordentlichen Diensten als Mittelpunkt eines Kreises von Anhängern und Schülern, der für die Ideen und Erzeugnisse Richard Wagner's und Berlioz', sowie für die daraus hergeleiteten Bestrebungen eifrigste Propaganda machte. 1859 wurde Liszt zum großherzogl. weimar'schen Kammerherrn ernannt und wandte sich dann nach Rom, wo er im selben Jahre in den geistlichen Stand trat und fortan als Abbé lebte. In neuester Zeit hielt er sich zeitweilig in Pest auf, wo er an der neugegründeten königlichen ungarischen Musikakademie als Präsident wirkte. Bei den Bayreuther Festspielen war Liszt ein steter Gast; er wohnte sämmtlichen Aufführungen bei und trug durch die Theilnahme seiner illustren Person nicht wenig zu dem Erfolge des großen Unternehmens bei.

Was Liszt als Virtuos und Tonheros geleistet, mögen die Federn der Männer vom Fach schildern; wir beschränken uns darauf, die hauptsächlichsten seiner Compositionen hier aufzuführen:

An symphonischen Dichtungen hat Liszt componirt: „Tasso", die „Hunnenschlacht", „Faust", „die Ideale", „Orpheus", „Prometheus", dann

an kirchlichen Werken: eine große Messe, dann die Oratorien: „Die heilige Elisabeth", „Christus" u. a. Auch als geistvoller Schriftsteller wirkte Liszt in hervorragenden Journalen und durch Monographien.

Ueber die Krankheitsgeschichte Liszt's gehen uns von eingeweihter Seite folgende Mittheilungen zu:

Liszt hatte mit ungestörtem Wohlbefinden seiner Enkelin am 4. Juni beigewohnt und dann Tags darauf eine Reise nach Luxemburg angetreten. Hier zog er sich wiederholt Erkältungen zu und in Folge derselben Bronchialcatarrh, mit welchem behaftet er am 21. Juni zu den Festspielaufführungen hier ankam, der damit verbundene quälende Husten besserte sich indeß, und Liszt konnte noch den beiden ersten Vorstellungen beiwohnen; es war ihm vergönnt, die Premiere des „Tristan" und den großartigen Erfolg dieses musicalischen Schmerzenskindes der Wagner'schen Muse noch anzusehen, zu erleben. In der Nacht vom 25. auf 26. Juli trat große Unruhe ein und der behandelnde Arzt Dr. Landgraf u. constatirte bei seinem Morgenbesuch das Vorhandensein von Fieber und den drohenden Ausbruch einer Entzündung der rechten Lunge. Der Patient durfte das Bett nicht mehr verlassen und wurde in strengster Ruhe gehalten, auch Universitäts-Professor Dr. Fleischer von Erlangen, ein den nächsten Bekannten der Familie Wagner befreundeter Arzt, wurde zu einem Consilium herbeigerufen. Die Krankheitserscheinungen waren anfänglich nicht bedrohlich, steigerten sich aber allmälig, und Sonnabend, den 31. Juli zeigte sich die ganze rechte Lunge im Zustande der Entzündung. Die Kräfte und die Herzthätigkeit, auf deren Erhaltung von Anfang an die ärztliche Behandlung bedacht war, erhielten sich bis dahin in befriedigender Weise, und das Bewußtsein war nicht erloschen, wenn auch der Kranke viel delirirte. Daß eine Krisis bevorstehe, war ersichtlich, und auch Hoffnung vorhanden, daß dieselbe günstig verliefe, als Abends gegen 8 Uhr die ersten Zeichen eines bevorstehenden Collapses eintraten, und die Herzthätigkeit merkbar erlahmte. Es wurde von beiden Aerzten Alles aufgeboten, dieselbe durch die kräftigsten Reizmittel zu verstärken, allein ohne Erfolg. Nachts gegen ½12 Uhr hörte die Respirations- und Herzthätigkeit auf und trat in ganz sanfter Weise der Tod ein, wie auch während der ganzen Krankheit der Sterbende keine besonderen Schmerzen erkennen ließ.

Liszt wird — nach seinem eigenen ausdrücklichem Wunsch — auf hiesigem Friedhofe, Dienstag, Vormittag 10 Uhr zur letzten Ruhe gebettet werden. (Siehe Neuestes.)

Bayreuth, 1. August 1886.

Extra-Blatt
der Oberfränkischen Zeitung.

* Bayreuth, 1. August. Kaum ist eine Säule der ersten Bühnenfestspiele gebrochen, kaum Scaria geschieden, so rafft der Tod den bewährtesten Freund und Förderer Wagners und seines Werkes in den schlimmsten Tagen hinweg. **Dr. phil.** und **Abbé Franz Liszt**, geb. am 22. October 1811 zu Reiding bei Oedenburg (in Ungarn) als Sohn eines Rechnungs-Beamten, ist 75 Jahre alt gestern um 11½ Uhr Nachts gestorben.

Der erste Klavierspieler der Welt, ein bedeutender Tondichter, ein für seine Ideale begeistert wirkender Mann, ein verläßiger Freund und großer Wohlthäter von unvergleichlicher Güte ist mit Liszt geschieden.

Liszt lebte fast in allen großen Kunstsitzen Europas längere Zeit, so in Wien, London, Rom, in Pest und neuerlich in Weimar, wo er zuerst außerhalb Dresdens, Richard Wagners, der später sein Schwiegersohn wurde, bahnbrechendes Tonwerk „Tannhäuser" am 16. Februar 1849 aufführen ließ, dem am 28. August 1850 die allererste Aufführung des „Lohengrin" folgte. Die Universität Königsberg, bezw. deren philosophische Fakultät verlieh Liszt 1842 das Diplom eines Doctors der Musik, Papst Pius IX. 1865 den Titel eines Abbate.

Für specielle Ausbildung Liszt's in Wien bei Czerny und Salieri, nach im Konservatorium zu Paris hatten reiche ungarische Grafen, wie Amadé und Szapary die Mittel gewährt. Den Titel eines Hofkapellmeisters in Weimar erhielt Liszt schon 1844, die Funktion desselben führte er von 1848—1859 in jenem Jahre ward er zum herzoglichen Kammerherrn ernannt. In den geistlichen Stand trat er 1865, und wurde später, in den siebziger Jahren, zum Hostkanonikus von San Albano ernannt.

640 Liszt's funeral procession on its way to the Bayreuth cemetery. Wood engraving from *Le Monde illustré* of 21 August 1886, based on a drawing by Gérardin (after the photograph Illus. 642).

641 Press report on Liszt's funeral from the *Oberfränkische Zeitung* of 4 August 1886. (For a translation of the text, see p. 344.)

642 Franz Liszt's funeral procession in Bayreuth. Photograph by Hans Brand, 3 August 1886.

* Bayreuth, 3. Aug. (Begräbniß von Franz Liszt. Schluß.) Im Zuge befanden sich alle hier weilenden Musik- und Kunstgrößen, insbesondere auch fast sämmtliche bei den Bühnenweihfestspielen Mitwirkenden, die Vertreter der Stadt, der k. Regierung und des Militärs, und zahlreiche Fremde und Einheimische der verschiedensten Stände. In den Straßen wehten von vielen Häusern Trauerflaggen.

Den Trauerwagen mit seinem düstern Schmuck hatte Herr Eyser (Dammallee) geziert. Um halb 11 Uhr erreichte der Trauerzug den Friedhof, und nun trugen, gefolgt vom Trauerzuge, eine Reihe Herren vom Liederkranz Bayreuth den schwarzen, mit goldenen Kanten und seinen Spitzen gezierten Metallsarg vom Leichenhause bis zum gemauerten Grabe, das etwa 100 Fuß nordwestlich vom Eck der Kirche sich befindet.

Hier hielt nun Hr. Geistlicher Rath Korzendorfer den kirchlichen Theil der Leichenfeierlichkeit ab, und tiefste Rührung bemächtigte sich — beim Vernehmen der ergreifenden Bittgebete für den Abbé Franz Liszt und der kirchlichen Segenswünsche — der großen Trauerversammlung. Wohl kein Friedhof mochte jemals eine Versammlung gesehen haben, in welcher mehr hervorragende Künstlergrößen vereint waren.

Neben dem Sarge waren bereits kostbare Kränze aus Nah und Fern niedergelegt, auf einem Sammtkissen befanden sich die zahlreichen Orden des Verstorbenen.

Nun trat Herr Bürgermeister Muncker an das Grab, und sprach mit tiefbewegter sonorer Stimme folgende ergreifende Worte:

„Werthe Trauerversammlung!

Was der große Meister, den wir nun zur Erde bestattet haben, das letzte Mal, da er mit den Seinen in dem Kunsttempel drüben auf der Höhe unserer Stadt verweilte, als unheilvolle Verkündigung an den Helden Tristan vernahm: „Todtgeweihtes Haupt, todtgeweihtes Herz" das rufen wir nun tieferschüttert als bittere Klage an seinem Grabe aus.

Ja ein Haupt hat sich geneigt, vor dessen erhabener Größe wir bewundernd stehen. Und ein Herz ist nun dem Tode geweiht, dessen innige Hingebung wir am Besten und Schönsten im Kreise der Familie seiner Tochter kennen und verstehen lernten.

Wohl ihm! — und das sagen wir zum Troste auch für uns — wohl dem Vielgewanderten, daß es ihm beschieden war, hier umgeben von seinen Enkeln in den Armen der liebenden Tochter die Seele auszuhauchen.

Nun ist es Nacht im Hause, aber die Leuchte seines Ruhmes löscht nicht aus. Liszt, der geniale Virtuose, der Meister der Töne, wird ewig leben.

Auch ihn betten wir, wie unsern vor Jahren heimgegangenen Meister, in Bayreuther Erde, möge sie ihm leicht sein!

Die Stätte, wo er schläft, wird von uns heilig gehalten werden. Dem innigsten Freunde und großen Förderer unseres seligen Meisters Wagner und seiner Werke schulden wir und bewahren wir den wärmsten und ehrfurchtvollsten Dank.

(Nach Niederlegung eines von der Stadt Bayreuth gewidmeten Kranzes auf das Grab):

Nimm selig Entschlafener unsere letzte Liebesgabe! ruhe bei uns sanft! mögen die Engelschöre, unter denen in Deinem letzten großen Tongebilde die erlöste Seele sich zum Paradiese aufschwingt, mögen sie auch Dich ins Jenseits emporgeleiten!"

Auch im Namen und Auftrag der dem Seligen stets treuen Stadt Wien legte Hr. Bürgermeister Muncker einen herrlichen Kranz am Grabe nieder. Nach ihm widmete Herr Kapellmeister Reuß von Karlsruhe im Namen der Schüler Liszts, mit Worten des tiefsten Dankes gegen den väterlichen Freund, der wie kein Anderer voll Herzensgüte gewesen, einen Kranz. Diesem folgte Herr Krause im Namen des Leipziger Liszt-Vereines mit dem gleichen Weihgeschenk. Noch rief der vieljährige Freund des Verewigten Hofrath Dr. Gille in Jena volltönende Abschiedsworte ins Grab nach, dann warfen die Herrn und Damen der illustren Trauerversammlung — unter ihnen Frau Cosima Wagner und ihre Kinder, welche im tiefsten Schmerze aufgelöst waren — voran Hr. Bürgermeister Muncker und sämmtliche Mitglieder des Festspielkomites, geweihte Erde in das Grab des theuren großen Dahingeschiedenen. Damit ging Liszts Bestattung zu Ende, die Meisten schieden nassen Auges von der Trauerstätte. Ave anima pia!

Beim Grabe waren indeß immer neue Kränze niedergelegt worden, darunter ein bewundernswerther vom deutschen Kronprinzen gespendet, fünf von der großherzoglichen Familie in Weimar, andere von der Fürstin Hatzfeld, vom Fürsten Hohenlohe, zwei von Graf und Gräfin Wolkenstein, ein wundervoller Edelweißkranz von Sofie Menter, zwei Riesenkränze vom Orchester- und Theaterpersonal der Bühnenfestspiele u. s. w. Wer nennt sie alle, die da kamen?

Erst spät um Mittag schieden die Letzten von der ernsten Stätte, die nun einen der größten Künstler und besten Menschen deckt. Friede seiner Asche!

FUNÉRAILLES

The room where Liszt had died was draped in black and the body laid out at 10 o'clock on the morning of 1 August. A peaceful expression on his face, Liszt lay between a bust of Richard Wagner at his head and a large crucifix at his feet, with palms, flowers, and burning candles in between. Siloti, Göllerich, Stradal, Friedheim, Stavenhagen, Thomán, Krause, Joukovsky, and the manservant Mihály mounted a guard of honour in the adjoining room.

The coffin was closed on 2 August and taken to Wahnfried, where it was once again laid out in state. The body was blessed the following morning, after which the funeral procession set off to the Bayreuth Cemetery at 10 o'clock. They were preceded by two heralds and the Bayreuth fire brigade, followed by a carriage drawn by black-draped horses and bearing flowers and wreaths from many countries; then came the black-curtained funeral carriage with its canopy-like mounting, carrying the coffin covered with a large laurel wreath from the Crown Prince of Germany. Cosima had refused to allow Liszt's pupils to carry the coffin, so they walked alongside with burning candles. The four corners of the pall were held by Felix Mottl, Hans von Wolzogen, Baron von Loën, and Ödön von Mihalovich.

Behind the funeral carriage came Liszt's servant, Pauline, and Mihály, who carried his master's decorations on a velvet cushion. They were followed by the clergy, and by Siegfried Wagner, Henry Thode, Adolf Groß, and Ernst von Wedel. Next came a carriage with the Wagner family, Baroness Meyendorff, and Princess Hatzfeld, then friends, artists, and the townspeople of Bayreuth. Somewhere in the crowd was Anton Bruckner.

LISZT'S DAUGHTER ON HER FATHER

"He was poor and wanted to be so. Here we touch on a point which, above and beyond the irresistible charm of his being, lent his present life [i.e., the final third of his life] its peculiar character, providing the key to his conduct towards others: love of his neighbour. This expression of Christianity animated his entire being and did so, moreover, to such a boundless extent that many who thought Christian love should be kept within certain bounds were unable to understand either him or his behaviour. That his help and advice were available to all, both worthy and unworthy; that he never asked on what ground his seed had fallen or whether his goodness had kindled even the tiniest spark of love: this was of course beyond the grasp of conventional souls. But anyone who saw him involuntarily removing his hat when giving alms to the beggar could say that he was in the presence of a Christian. At the same time, he once let slip the remark, 'I have no illusions about charity' ('je n'ai pas d'illusions sur la charité'), a remark which, on the lips of a man who gave away everything, certainly means a great deal [. . .]."[247]

643 Liszt's grave covered in wreaths. Photograph, 4 August 1886.

644 The chapel in which Liszt is buried, with the inscription "I know that my Redeemer liveth." Photograph, ca. 1900.
  The chapel was destroyed in 1945 but was restored to its original state in 1978/79 by the town of Bayreuth, which thus paid worthy tribute to the great man in death.

645 Liszt's grave before the chapel was restored. Photograph, 1974.

For a time uncertainty surrounded the selection of Liszt's final resting place. Disappointingly, the Grand Duke of Weimar had merely demanded to know, "Where and when will Liszt be buried?" Baron von Loën waited and waited for new information, but it never arrived, since Liszt's friend the Grand Duchess Sophie was taking the waters in Bad Gastein. Later the Court in Weimar intended to erect a mausoleum to Liszt at the Altenburg, but the idea was turned down by Frau Wagner, as was a private request to transfer Liszt's body to Hungary. It is clear from two of Frau Wagner's letters published at this time that she was prepared to hand over Liszt's body only on two conditions: "First, if a demand be made by His Royal Highness the Grand Duke of Weimar to preserve my father's mortal remains in the royal vault, and, secondly, if a resolve be taken by the representatives of both houses of the Hungarian Parliament to honour my father's memory by solemnly transferring his body from Bayreuth to Pest." But neither suggestion was made. The Grand Duke was opposed to the idea of burying Liszt in the royal vault, and the Hungarian nation refused on a governmental level to reclaim the body because of the allegedly "anti-nationalistic" sentiments in Liszt's essay *The Gypsies and Their Music in Hungary*. When Parliament met on 27 February 1887, a request by the Pest Society of Writers and Artists was rejected, more especially because of opposition from the then Prime Minister Kálmán Tisza, who called Liszt a "common actor." And later plans by Abrányi and Haynald to bring the body back to Hungary by private means came to nothing because of Frau Wagner's counter-

demand. In the meantime claims had been made on Liszt's remains from another quarter. The Franciscans, to whose order Liszt had of course belonged, demanded the body under the terms of their statutes. Princess Wittgenstein, who under Liszt's last will and testament of 1860 was regarded as his heiress and executrix, lent her support to this appeal in a lengthy document compiled from biographical notes. The matter was closed by the death of the Princess, who followed her great friend into the next world on 7 March 1887, only a few days after completing her *magnissimum opus*, the 24-volume *Des causes intérieures de la faiblesse extérieure de l'église*. She was laid to rest in the German Cemetery at St Peter's in Rome. Liszt's Requiem accompanied her to her grave.

Immediately after Liszt's death, the Grand Duke of Weimar had suggested the idea of a "Liszt Foundation under the aegis of the Allgemeiner Deutscher Musikverein to encourage the new direction in German music." Carolyne's daughter (and hence her heiress), Princess Hohenlohe, donated the impressive sum of 70,000 marks for this purpose, decreeing that unless Liszt himself had made other arrangements to dispose of them, the treasures and memorabilia contained in Liszt's and her mother's estates should be entrusted to a Liszt Museum. The rooms which Liszt had inhabited in the Hofgärtnerei were made available as a museum "for all time" by the Grand Duke, who requested that they be kept in their unaltered state.

Bayreuth, accordingly, remained Liszt's last resting place. In the Municipal Cemetery the town erected a small mausoleum designed by his grandson Siegfried Wagner. The fact that he is buried in Bayreuth may be a source of

646 The grave of Carolyne von Sayn-Wittgenstein in the German Cemetery at the Vatican. Photograph, ca. 1890.

Princess Wittgenstein sought by every means available to her to have Liszt's body handed over to the Franciscans, of whose order he had been a member since 1857; these efforts ended only with her death on 7 March 1887.

647 Princess Marie von Hohenlohe-Schillingsfürst, daughter of Carolyne von Sayn-Wittgenstein. Photograph, ca. 1870.

She gave 70,000 marks to help establish a Liszt Foundation, while to the Liszt Museum in Weimar she generously bequeathed all the Lisztian memorabilia which she had inherited from her mother.

648 A glimpse of the Liszt Museum in Weimar. Photograph by Louis Held, ca. 1900.

Following Liszt's death, Grand Duke Carl Alexander made available Liszt's rooms in the Hofgärtnerei for use as a museum. (The illustration shows the main room ca. 1900, the exhibits having since been rearranged.) Together with the Goethe and Schiller Memorials, the Liszt Museum in Weimar is now one of the main tourist attractions in a town already rich in tradition. In the foreground is Liszt's Boisselot grand, to which a glass top has been added. In the centre are weapons and gifts of honour presented to Liszt, framed by lithographs and the medallions by Rietschel and Schwanthaler (see Illus. 400 and 420). Above them is Lauchert's portrait of Liszt (see Illus. 409), and to the left a portrait of Berlioz by the same artist. On the right, in a wide gold frame, is Carl Rahl's 1858 portrait of Liszt.

sadness to many, in view of the events surrounding his final illness and death. On the other hand, it is a happy chance that Liszt now rests in the very place where the artistic ideal which he fought and yearned for throughout his life has taken on solid shape, and that this selfsame place offers him the home which he longed for and which he helped to create. His willing self-sacrifice in pursuit of an ideal forms the worthy keystone of his whole existence. Just as he always lived and fought for others, encouraging and supporting them without thought for himself, so he died in the service of a great cause. In Liszt were contained the elements of a Christian soul: capable of every self-sacrifice, he felt neither envy or anger towards his enemies, but was a man of the greatest sincerity and an extraordinary, almost criminal, goodness.

Clara Schumann (Diary entry of 1 August 1886).
Liszt died in Bayreuth yesterday, 31 July – another man borne to his grave, and a rare one at that! But how it pains one not to be able to mourn him whole-heartedly. All that tawdriness around him obscures one's picture of him as man and artist. He was an eminent keyboard virtuoso, but as such a dangerous example for young people to follow. Almost every up-and-coming player imitated him, but they lacked his spirit, genius, and charm, and so there emerged only a handful of great and pure technicians and a great many caricatures [. . .]. And then Liszt was a poor composer – here, too, a pernicious example to many, albeit not so lastingly harmful since his compositions lack those very qualities which he possessed as a virtuoso; they are trivial and tedious and will certainly soon disappear from the world in the wake of his passing. He always impressed people by his amiableness and virtuosity, and that was why they performed his works. As a young man he was deeply fascinating, but later on there was so much coquettishness about him, for all his intelligence and charm, that it often offended me.

Peter Cornelius (Yearbook of the Allgemeiner Deutscher Musikverein, 1868).
It required courage to include Beethoven's great sonatas in a concert programme at a time when these works were still considered insane and hare-brained by the vast majority of real connoisseurs, to say nothing of the windbags of the time. It required courage to play the Ball Scene by Berlioz when an authority such as Rossini had said the young man in question could do everything except write music. It required courage to perform Weber's *Konzertstück* before a classically minded Parisian audience which knew not the first thing about a Monsieur Weber. We do not need to go on: it required courage for *Tannhäuser* and *Lohengrin*, courage for *Benvenuto Cellini*, courage and enthusiasm for all the rich and bold artistic deeds which Liszt performed in the face of unprecedented scorn and misunderstanding. It required, finally, the most decisive inner courage to descend from the throne of a universally admired virtuoso and, striving for lofty spiritual goals, to experiment right in front of an audience which hated having its comfortable outlook disturbed, which had admired and then dismissed Liszt as a virtuoso, and which was now expected to start afresh by studying Liszt as a tone-poet.

Ernest Newman (*The Man Liszt*, 1934).
Liszt was no simple saint, but an exceedingly complex human being who was torn in twain, his whole life through, between his religious instincts and the imperious demands of the flesh, a man with undoubtedly a strong strain of chivalry in him, but also a man to whom play-acting was second nature [. . .].

Alfred Einstein (*Music in the Romantic Era*, 1947).
He was a born revolutionary; and one might say – if it were compatible with a regard for his magnificent personality – he was a born libertine, a born Bohemian [. . .]. His strange artistic career and spiritual development caused him to be the most independent and unrestrained of Romantic musicians [. . .].

Ludwig Kusche (*Porträt eines Übermenschen*, 1961).
Liszt's life should not be a novel which we read only to return to the bookshelf with the remark, ''Most interesting!'' Liszt's life, one of the most real that have ever been lived, should set us an example in the sense of Rilke's *Archaischer Torso Apollos*: ''You must change your life.'' This demand applies to artists as it does to non-artists. Only he who takes great men as his model and who strives to emulate their intellectual agility of mind, their urge to work, and their lofty humanitarianism can lay claim to being considered a human being, now or in the future. Even if the day should come when not a note of Liszt's compositions is ever again to be heard, his life and achievements would remain a *memento vivere* for all who still exist and who wish, if possible, to counteract the law of inertia which typifies human nature. This urge to advance – this instinctual drive towards openness, towards the attainable and even the unattainable – is the reason why Liszt should always remain worthy of our admiration. He had an immensely high opinion of art and of all that is needed to make art possible. His artistic fanaticism might have enabled him to utter that same confession which we owe to one of the greatest and most steadfast figures of the visual arts with which Liszt had so deep and inward a relationship, the French painter Edgar Degas: ''You must have a high opinion of the work of art, not the work of art you are currently engaged on, but the one you will one day achieve. Without this there is no point in working.''

Karl Schumann (*Das Kleine Lisztbuch*, 1974).
At an early date Liszt's radiant personality became the object of male sexual jealousy, that most sly of all resentments. It did not even allow the dead man to rest in peace. Following Liszt's death, and encouraged by the Wagnerians' disparagement of him, this jealousy assumed the mask of scientific objectivity and subjected him to strict quality control: Liszt's compositional achievements were belittled or, like his late piano pieces, were simply ignored; his music was dismissed as ''sophisticated light music,'' relegated to popular concerts and played as encores; his erstwhile canonization in writings emanating from the Sayn-Wittgenstein Chancellery made him additionally suspect. His reputation as a virtuoso was already enough to cast him in a suspicious light; a true genius should have been misjudged in his lifetime, should have been impoverished, unprepossessing, and dependent upon the good will of posterity. Serious investigations were rarely undertaken, least of all in Germany. The mere mention of Liszt's name in a seminar on music met, as I can testify, with scornful laughter and indigna-tion. Peter Raabe's pioneering biography and admiring statements from such composers as Schoenberg, Debussy, Ravel, and Bartók remained isolated phenomena which were not taken seriously. Except outside Germany, Liszt was not a subject for serious enquiry; popular novels and films could claim him as their own, at which they were so successful that they conditioned the current view of Liszt in much the same way that our understanding of Schubert was once determined by *Lilac Time*. This trivialization of Liszt culminated in an assault on his ethically based emotional outlook: during the campaign on the Eastern Front, special broadcasts on ''Greater German Radio'' were introduced by the theme from *Les Préludes* as a ''Fanfare for Russia.'' Liszt as a harbinger of Nazism was the final fatuous consequence of a process of degradation which had been going on for decades.

What angered people about Liszt as a person also angered them about his works: his anti-bourgeois outlook, the absence of all pettiness, the renunciation of bulls'-eye window panes, lavender, and the other accessories associated with sentimentality, his tendency towards grandiloquence, and the emotiveness of ambitious demands. Liszt's works are garrulous and repetitive, mannerist and sentimentally gushing, but they are never grimacingly, whiningly middle-class; they are not botched-up affairs that limp along using formal support, with wry-faced profundity and impotence hidden behind decent craftsmanship and intellectual pretentiousness. Liszt's passionate nature would sometimes dissolve into rhetoric, but it was a passion that refused to be tamed. To be merely lukewarm seemed to Liszt the worst of all evils. He always performed from a pedestal and not from behind a homely hearth, never relying on his secure but confining status as ''Master.'' And his subdued late piano pieces with their whole-tone scales, ''sans tonalité,'' verge upon the outrageous, heralding future storms. He maintained the *élan* with which he entered his century, for all the appointments and honours, the hero-worship and disappointment to which he was subjected. Liszt never gave in. The world is loath to forgive him for that.

649 Franz Liszt. Photograph by Paul Nadar, March 1886.

Johannes Brahms to Richard Heuberger, 1888.
"It really is rather tiresome to have lady pianists forever playing the same works by Liszt! I have nothing but praise for Frau Jaëll! An intelligent, ingenious person who writes her own things for the piano, which are just as bad as Liszt's!" (Marie Jaëll, 1846–1925, was a well-known pianist who was also a composer.)

Camille Saint-Saëns, 1890.
"[. . .] He has been accused of stupid things – he is said, for example, to have read philosophical systems into music. But this is wholly false. Liszt only ever translated poetic ideas, and if one wishes to condemn everything that diverges from "pure" music it is not only *his* music that must be rejected, but the "Pastoral," Mendelssohn's symphonies and characteristic overtures, the whole of Berlioz, and the whole of Wagner."

Claude Debussy, concert review (*Gil Blas*, 16 February 1903).
"This Symphonic Poem [*Mazeppa*] is full of serious faults; it is sometimes even cheap. Yet the tempestuous passion which it maintains to the end holds the listener enthralled with such force that one finds it magnificent without asking why. At the end of the concert you can feign disgust because it turns out so well. It is sheer hypocrisy, believe me [. . .]!"

Maurice Ravel, concert review, 1912.
"[. . .] Are the failings in all Liszt's works really so important to us? Are there not sufficient strong points in the tumultuous, seething, vast, and glorious chaos of musical material on which several generations of famous composers have drawn? Let us be honest: it is very much to these shortcomings that Wagner owes much of his declamatory vehemence, that Strauss owes his overenthusiasm, Franck his prolix sublimity, the Russian School its occasional harsh and pittoresque style, and the French School the uncommon coquettishness of its harmonic charm. For all their dissimilarity, do not these writers owe the best of their qualities to the overflowing musical generosity of their great predecessor?"

Ferruccio Busoni, *Zürcher Programme*, 1916.
"[. . .] Liszt was an artist and a prince among men, and a legend even during his lifetime. Among his princely qualities were his cast of mind, his appearance, and his conduct, while a happy combination of talent, intelligence, steadfastness, and idealism marked him out as an artist. As such he possessed all the characteristics of the great: the universality of his art, three creative periods, and an eternally questing outlook; the mystifying aspect of his abilities, the element of prestidigitation that typified his performing style, and the magnetic effects of his skill were the "legendary" side of Liszt.

"His goals were advancement, ennoblement, and liberation. Only a sublime individual strives for advancement, only one innately noble seeks ennoblement, only a freeman can grant freedoms. He became the symbol of the piano, which he raised to princely status so that it might be worthy of him."

From a letter to Alfred Kastner, 1920: "It was with dismay that I gathered from your essay that you dismiss Liszt with a mere wave of the hand [. . .]. I know Liszt's weaknesses, but I do not misjudge his strength. Basically we are all descended from him – Wagner not excepted – and we owe him the little of which we are capable. César Franck, Richard Strauss, Debussy, all the older Russian composers are branches of the same tree. That is why it is wrong to praise Respighi and dismiss Liszt in one and the same sentence. A *Faust Symphony*, a *Saint Elisabeth*, a *Christus* – no later composer has succeeded in writing such works. Even today *Les Jeux d'Eau* remains the model for all the musical fountains which have flowed since then [. . .]. At all events, if you have good reasons for rejecting Liszt, you should enumerate those reasons and not assume in advance that every reader knows what they are and that every musician agrees with you. I personally do not see how Liszt has ruined Schubert's *Wandererfantasie*. Quite the opposite: I have long since been forced to recognize how well Liszt helps the listener across certain stretches of the original. No piano player, therefore, can lose face by sharing Liszt's views, unless, of course, he is demonstrably superior to Liszt as a musician and as a pianist. But I have yet to encounter such a piano player; I myself am respectfully conscious of the distance which separates me from this great man [. . .]."

Béla Bartók, from his public lecture *Problems of Liszt*, 1934.
"If we compare Liszt as a composer with his predecessors and contemporaries, we find features in his works which we search for in vain elsewhere. We discover that among all the greater composers of his own day and of the previous age there was not a single one on whom so many disparate influences were at work [. . .]. Liszt never set out from a single point, nor did he combine several interrelated things in his works; he abandoned himself to the influence of the most varied, most contradictory, one might almost say most irreconcilable elements [. . .]. We must seek the essence of his works in those new ideas to which Liszt was the first to give expression, and in his brave and pioneering penetration of the future. These qualities raise Liszt as a composer to the ranks of the great, and it is because of them that we love his works as they are, regardless of their weaknesses."

Richard Wagner (*On Franz Liszt's Symphonic Poems*, 1857).
[. . .] Since I have never felt the blissful, freshly instructive effect of this love more clearly than in my love for Liszt, I should like to call upon those who mistrust him: place your trust in him, for you will be amazed what you achieve through that trust. If you hesitate because you fear betrayal, examine him more closely and see who it is that you are to trust. Do you know a musician who is more musical than Liszt? who holds within his breast the powers of music in richer, deeper store than he? who has felt more sensitively and more tenderly, who knows more and who can do more, who is more gifted by Nature and who, by educating himself, has developed his potential more forcefully than he? – If you cannot name a second one like him, oh, you may confidently trust in this unique individual, a man who, moreover, is far too noble a human being ever to think of deceiving you. And you may be sure that you will be most enriched by this trust precisely where you most fear, in your mistrust, to be harmed by him!

Arnold Schoenberg, *Franz Liszts Werk und Wesen*, 1911.
"Liszt created an art form which our own age must regard as an aberration, whereas a later age may perhaps see only the brilliant insight on which it was based. Both views are justified, but perhaps because we are developing that insight along a different path we tend to notice the other one more [. . .]. Although his works thus appear not to come up to certain expectations, we should not forget how modern they are in purely musical terms, how much their ideas are inspired by real intuition. He was, after all, one of those who led the struggle against tonality, both in his use of themes which do not necessarily point to such a centre and in the many harmonic details which his successors would pursue to exhaustion – but most of all in the many ideas which he bequeathed to those who came after him. His influence here is perhaps even greater than that of Wagner, whose creative work was far too perfect for later composers to be able to add anything to it. But it is certainly not necessary to see him only in this way. One need only recall his *Christus* to see a work whose impact is still to be felt. Perhaps the coming age will latch on to its sound and its intentions. For our own age is once more searching for its god; and that is more characteristic of it than the most outstanding technical accomplishments."

650 Franz Liszt. Photograph by Paul Nadar, March 1886.

APPENDIX

17 Carl Czerny's autobiographical report

In 1819, a short time after Mlle Belleville had left us [in 1816 Czerny had assumed responsibility for the musical education of the then eight-year-old Ninetta Belleville, "one of the rarest of musical talents," who had lodged with Czerny's parents], I received a visit one morning from a man accompanied by a boy some eight years of age, who bade me invite the lad to play something on the fortepiano. He was a pale, sickly-looking child who, while playing, swayed to and fro on the stool as if drunk, so that I kept thinking he would fall to the floor. His playing, moreover, was quite unrhythmical, untidy, and confused, and he had so little idea of fingering that he threw his fingers over the keys in a wholly arbitrary fashion. Yet notwithstanding this I was astonished at the talent which Nature had bestowed upon him. Certain of the pieces which I placed before him he played *a vista* [at sight] like a pure "natural"; but by that very token one saw that Nature herself had formed a pianist. It was just the same when, at his father's request, I gave him a theme on which to improvise. Without the slightest knowledge of harmony, he brought a sense of inspiration to the manner in which he played it.

His father told me his name was Liszt, that he was a subordinate official on Prince Esterházy's estates, and that until now he had taught his son himself, but he asked me whether I might not be prepared to take on his little Franzi if he should come to Vienna the following year.

Naturally I agreed, and at the same time gave him instructions as to the manner in which he should meanwhile continue the boy's education, showing him scale exercises etc. About a year later Liszt and his son came back to Vienna, and moved into rooms in the same street where we ourselves were living (in the Krugerstraße), and I devoted almost every evening to the boy, having little time to do so during the day.

Never had I had so eager and industrious a pupil, nor one of such genius. Since I knew from many a past experience that, in those cases where mental gifts outstrip physical powers, such geniuses are wont to neglect all basic technique, it seemed to me necessary above all else to spend the early months controlling and consolidating his mechanical proficiency, so that in later years he would no longer go astray.

Within a short space of time he was playing scales in every key with all the masterly fluency that was made possible by fingers supremely well designed for playing the piano; and through a serious study of Clementi's sonatas (which will always remain the best form of training for the keyboard performer *providing they be studied in the spirit of the composer*) I accustomed him to playing in time, a skill he had totally lacked so far, and to achieving an attractive touch and tone, the most correct fingering, and correct musical declamation, although these compositions initially struck the boy, lively and forever high-spirited as he was, as somewhat dry in nature.

So successful was this method that when, a few months later, we went through the works of Hummel, Ries, Moscheles, and then Beethoven and Sebastian Bach, it was no longer necessary to pay undue heed to the mechanical rules, for I could now allow him to grasp the spirit and character of these various composers. Since he had to rehearse each piece of music extremely quickly, he finally became so adept at performing the music at sight that he was capable of playing, unrehearsed, even long and difficult works *in public* as though he had been studying them for some considerable time. I was equally at pains to teach him how to extemporize, by frequently setting him themes on which to improvise.

Little Liszt's unshakable liveliness and great good humour, together with this extraordinary unfolding of his talent, ensured that my parents came to love him as a son, and I as a brother;

and as well as teaching him without any thought of remuneration I also gave him all the necessary sheet music, by which I mean all the good and useful pieces that existed at that time. Within a year I was already able to allow him to play in public, and he aroused a degree of enthusiasm in Vienna such as few artists have succeeded in awakening. The very next year, his father gave public benefit concerts with him, at which the lad performed Hummel's Concertos in A minor and B minor (both completely new at that time), Moscheles's Variations, Hummel's Septet, the concertos by Ries, and many of my own compositions, in addition to improvising on each occasion upon themes proposed by the audience; and the world was indeed not wrong at that time to see in him a second Mozart.

Unfortunately, his father wished to derive great pecuniary benefit from him, and just when the lad was doing so well with his studies and I was on the point of introducing him to composition, he set off on tour, first to Hungary and finally to Paris and London etc., where, as all the journals of the time attested, he caused the greatest sensation. In Paris, where he settled with his parents, he admittedly earned a great deal of money but lost a great many years in time, since his life, like his art, had taken the wrong turning. When I came to Paris sixteen years later (1837), I found his playing in every respect quite dissolute and confused for all its tremendous bravura. I believed I could give him no better advice than to travel the length and breadth of Europe, and when he came to Vienna a year later his genius gained renewed momentum. Amidst the boundless acclaim of our keenly appreciative public, his playing soon assumed that brilliant yet clear sense of direction for which he is now so well known in the world. None the less, I remain convinced that, had he continued his youthful studies in Vienna for a few more years, he would in composition too now justify all the high hopes which we were right to place in him then.

24 Report in the *Preßburger Zeitung* describing Liszt's concert on 26 November 1820

Hungary.

Preßburg. Last Sunday, the 26th, at midday, the nine-year-old virtuoso Franz Liszt had the honour of performing on the pianoforte before a numerous company made up of the local nobility and a number of patrons of the arts in the residence of His Excellency Count Michael Esterházy. This artist's extraordinary dexterity, together with the speed and skill which he brought to bear when performing at sight everything, however difficult, which was placed before him, gave rise to universal admiration and justifies the highest hopes.

45 Review of Liszt's Strasbourg concerts on 3 and 6 December 1823

On the 3rd of December in the Saal zum Geist, and on the 6th in the Theatre, the eleven-year-old Liszt surprised us with his accomplished and expressive piano playing; his free improvisations in particular earned the most extraordinary applause. Among the works which he played was a Piano Concerto in B minor by Hummel (not Himmel, as was advertised), together with Variations on Moscheles's *Alexander March*, both of which he executed with admirable dexterity and feeling. He has now left with his father for Paris.

67 Adam Liszt's letter to his father of 14 August 1825

Paris 14 Aug [1]825.

Dear Father,

It is our most ardent wish that you and our mother and children are in good health and keeping well, as we ourselves are, having – God be praised – nothing to complain about. As each day passes, France convinces us more and more that there is only

one France. This year we were in England again and were well content when we returned to Paris, having previously enjoyed fifteen days' bathing at Boulogne on Sea.

My lad has written an opera which will be given in the leading Royal Theatre in Paris at the beginning of October or end of September. The title of the opera is /: *Don Sanche ou Le Château d'amour* (in German, *The Castle of Love*):/. We shall wait until after the first few performances have taken place, when we plan to travel to Holland, the Netherlands, Prussia, and Germany, before arriving in Vienna by March of next year.

> Man proposes,
> God disposes.
> Everything hinges on chance.
> But at all events we shall not remain in the Austrian States
> for more than two months, after which we shall either
> go to Italy and Switzerland or else return directly to
> Paris.
> Dear Father, if there is anything you want, please write at
> once and I shall regard it as my most solemn duty to
> meet your wish at once.
> Write out the address as follows
> Monsieur
> Monsieur Liszt.
> Rue neuve St. Eustache N° 22.
> Hôtel de Straßbourg près la
> Rue Montmartre.
> Herr Hofer in Eisenstadt will be able to tell you more
> about us.
> We embrace you all many times with all our hearts.
> Franzel is almost as tall as I am.
>
> Your
> honest son
> Adam

I shall spare myself from weeping by writing to tell you of the tremendous progress the boy has made in everything, nor shall you yourself have cause to weep when you read what I have to say. You will be pleased, I am sure, when I tell you that Franzl has not yet found his match, and that Hummel and Moscheles have been knocked into a cocked hat by him. His compositions are beyond the laws of reason. He is so well-behaved in his conduct, and so kind-hearted; he speaks of you often and is very much looking forward to being able to bring something for you from Paris and London.

152 Announcement in the *Gazette musicale* of 26 March 1837

A charity event is announced that will benefit both the well-to-do dilettanti and the indigent Italians. It is a concert which will take place on Friday 31 March in the salons of the Princess Belgiojoso. The most distinguished artists that we possess will be heard there, together with a number of amateurs worthy of the glorious name of artist. But the greatest interest at this gathering, and the most compelling of all attractions, will be without question the simultaneous appearance of two talents whose rivalry excites the musical world at present, maintaining as it does an indecisive balance between Rome and Carthage. Messrs. Listz [*sic*] and Thalberg will take turns at the piano.

217 Review of Liszt's concert in Vienna on 27 November 1839, from the *Wiener Theaterzeitung* of 30 November 1839

Vienna.

Second Concert of Herr Franz Liszt.

It is impossible to describe the enthusiasm which this great virtuoso has once again aroused in Vienna. – His mighty art has imperiously forced all other present-day musical interests into the background, and scarcely is one of his concerts over when everyone is already asking, longingly, when the next one will be. Not since Paganini has another artist made so apparently magical an impression as Liszt upon the Viennese public, which has been overpowered at every level from the strict connoisseur and scholar down to the ordinary concert enthusiast, and years will pass before a third name is discovered worthy of being placed alongside these two great masters. We are, however, convinced that, if we are not to await him in vain, this unknown third person will surpass the triumphs of these other two neither on the violin nor on the piano, for regarding those two instruments the competition may be regarded as settled. Only those who have never heard Liszt perform may perhaps be inclined to suspect exaggeration when they read the reports in our newspapers, and they will not understand how the piano, with its predetermined sound structure, could be capable of such extraordinary effects, – but anyone who has ever witnessed a Lisztian performance has in truth no need of any further explanation, for he will have heard for himself how at the hands of *this* master the instrument is raised to a hitherto unsuspected pitch of the highest perfection and rendered capable of standing comparison even with that king of instruments, the violin.

Years of unremitting study are necessary if, in a branch of art in which so many great and famous masters have already expended such a wealth of talent, wit, and ingenuity, the performing artist is to acquire the skill he needs simply to render existing compositions or to play works that require elaboration according to patterns already laid down; but Liszt, once having finished all these studies, set off in a new direction in which his genius bore him aloft on the wings of an eagle. He gave new form and a new direction to his manner of playing. In matters of technique he became master of his instrument as none had been before him, so that it was easy for him to devise wholly characteristic ways of playing which before him would scarcely have been deemed possible, and which even now of course he alone commands. His artistic understanding, however, has at the same time prevented him from allowing the mechanical aspect of his playing to become the central issue, and even when he has plunged into a sea of difficulties a nobler and loftier aim has continued to predominate. But the great and apparently unfathomable power of his playing rests in the fact that, even before the listener has recovered from his astonishment at the performance of some immense bravura passage, Liszt is able to lure from the strings of his instrument moving sounds so full of soul that they stir the listener's heart. It would be an erroneous view, and one which must most emphatically be rejected, to believe that this contrast is merely artificially induced and that the entire effect is contrived, as is no doubt the case with many another concert performer. But the joy which seizes possession of Liszt, inspiring him to ever greater enthusiasm, reveals that this way of playing, far from straining for empty effect, is but the expression of his innermost being and of the sentiment that dominates him. The applause on the part of a large and educated public may certainly produce a mood of inspiration in the virtuoso, and not even Liszt will remain indifferent to the enthusiasm of the Viennese; but I am convinced that at the moment he sits down at the piano he has forgotten the audience packed closely around him and is so preoccupied with his performance that he no longer has eyes or ears for anything else besides. It is this that marks out the genuine artist, and those who maintain that at his concerts Liszt performs for his public alone, and not for himself as well, have never understood or apprehended him!

Liszt gave his second concert three days ago, the 27th of November, at midday, at the Musikverein. In consequence of an indisposition, which happily had no more serious consequences, he had been obliged to postpone it from the 24th. Scarcely recovered, and still somewhat ailing, he sat down at the piano, welcomed by the thunderous applause of the crowded hall, and began with a Fantasy of his own composition on themes from *I Puritani*, a highly demanding piece full of the most surprising effects, which he performed with a power and stamina that would have been a source of astonishment in any other player, but not in Liszt who, when carried away by his own inspiration, appears to forget all physical suffering and not to notice any weariness until the final chord has died away beneath his hands. Experience has long since shown that artists never play better than in an agitated, ailing condition, and thus it seemed to me and many others that never had we heard Liszt play better than he did on this occasion! The Fantasy on *I Puritani*, which was greeted with endless applause and which, more especially in those themes taken from the part of Elvira, was a masterpiece of elegance, grace, and delicacy of execution, was followed not by the two *Grandes Études* which had been announced but by another work of his own composition, a Fantasy

on themes from *Lucia di Lammermoor*, with which he threw the audience into such a state of agitation that it seemed as though the applause and calls to return to the platform would never end. In place of the Studies which, at the performer's request, had been omitted from the programme as too exhausting, the audience requested a repeat of the Fantasy, a request which the artist, flushed by his playing and its brilliant reception, was only too pleased to meet. As compositions these two Fantasies may be held out as models to all who believe it sufficient to throw together a few well-known themes, to vary them, and then to describe the whole concoction without further ado as a Fantasy. Finally, Herr Liszt played three Schubert songs, "Die Stadt," "Das Fischermädchen" and "Aufenthalt" from *Schwanengesang*, which – if the audience had had its way – would no doubt all have had to be repeated; in the event they had to make do with a repeat of the final one. The intervals between the piano pieces were filled by Mlle Tuczek, who performed the song *Il Platano*, only recently heard here, and a new Italian song by *Curci*, *Il Concedo*, after which Messrs Steiger, Anger, Rabeneck, and Reichmann of the Court Opera chorus performed a vocal quartet by Cherubini. Mlle Tuczek was applauded, and it is certainly much to her credit that she was able to draw attention to her charming talent before an audience as numerous and distinguished as is to be found at any concert given by Liszt. – The piano upon which Herr Liszt performed on this occasion was not the same as at his first concert, although it too was a Graf instrument of most solid and elegant construction, superb tone, and excellent volume and strength. The instruments produced by this firm certainly enjoy the best reputation at home and abroad – but Liszt's concerts are bound to make them even more famous.

Heinrich Adami.

224 Review of Liszt's concert in Preßburg on 22 December 1839

Reports from Our Correspondents.

Preßburg, 23 December 1839.

Liszt gave his second and – we hope only for now – his last concert with us, having earlier performed in a charitable cause at the Theatre. The enthusiasm aroused by the first appearance of this hero of art proved to be the inevitable consequence of his extraordinary achievements, achievements which – like all that is truly great – gain through being repeated. The listener is made increasingly aware that, when Liszt plays, his heart and mind are just as active as his fingers which, following the imperative dictates of a will of iron, perform feats that defy comprehension; one suspects that every piece of music performed – one might almost say every *"tone painting"* – is a reflection of his innermost being, a part of his very existence, and that this perception, however vague, grips the listener more deeply in the case of Lißt's achievements than with any other performer. *Liszt* sacrifices the *one* half of his earthly existence in order to become what he is, but to reveal this to the world he spares the *second* half less than he should – for who else plays like him, whose vital spark evaporates as he entertains an in part unheeding mass. We say "unheeding" for, were this not so, *true love* of the artist's person would discourage them from demanding, or even expecting, that after the most exhausting exertions he might play an encore.

As for the compositions of this musical Byron, they are mostly a mixture of the lyrico-epic and romantic styles; but the latter is definitely what predominates – often tender, never mawkish, sometimes bizarre, always grandiose – not without solid foundations, but always more deeply felt than thought, seeming almost to be products of momentary moods and of an imagination that scoffs at common limitations, rather than the result of calm conception, spreading light and warmth or flaring up in fiercely raging flames which consume their own hearth.

If, moreover, the highest acclaim and distinctions of every kind can reward an artist for what he offers his public, then Liszt has richly reaped what he sowed in Preßburg, and his contentment would surely be even greater if the hearts he has moved could attract as much attention as the hands and lips which moved on his behalf.

For his performances the celebrated artist used two instruments by our excellent piano maker Schmidt, having been advised to do so by Herr Konrad Graf of Vienna, whose products in this department enjoy of course a more than European reputation: this circumstance does too much credit to both these worthy men to be passed over in silence here.

J.N.

226 Franz von Schober's poem welcoming Liszt to Pest

While yet a child of tender years,
Thou feltst chill destiny's firm hand
As fate decreed an exile's life
And spake: "Thou hast no fatherland!"

On pinions of transfiguring art
To art's enchanted realm thou'rt flown
Wherein the spirits of the great
Do dwell and claim thee as their own.

Luxurious and caressing life
Now lures thee back to earth again
And, dowering thee with all his gifts,
Commands thee tarry here and reign.

Thou'rt borne aloft by fame herself,
Embracing all within thy gaze:
"The world itself is now thine home!
All nations of the earth thee praise."

Whatever fate has granted thee,
Whate'er of art and fame and joy,
With loyal heart thou yet recallst
The land that knew thee as a boy.

Thou com'st to us in time of need,
Where art is in its infancy.
Though poor, our hearts yet overflow
With love and thus we welcome thee!

We welcome thee with laurel crown
Which thou has earned so gloriously,
Thou matchless artist, noble, true,
Franz Liszt! Thy land is proud of thee!

234 Verses in homage to Liszt by J. B. Hollósy

Apollo's son, whom Hungary has bred
And whom the men of Gaul have reared in art,
Returnest thou, to Nature's bonds still wed,
To joy thy father's hearth with filial heart.
Enchanted fruit thou offerest us as fare
From higher worlds whose higher joys we share.

A chasm echoing with thunderous roar
Now stands revealed by thy commanding hand;
Or else our souls, on surging billows borne,
Are ferried to a distant faery land
Where Camenean hands enchantingly
Entice sweet sounds from lyre and psaltery.

Accept the admiration that we owe
The godlike joy that at thy hands we learn!
Our wish is not to crown thee whom we know
Already crowned our master; no, we yearn
To weave forget-me-not from local haunts
Into the garland that thy brow now vaunts.

235 Review of Liszt's concerts in Vienna, from the *Allgemeine Theaterzeitung* of 18 February 1840

Liszt's Soirée and Farewell Concert.

With his two last concerts Liszt took his leave of Vienna in a manner entirely worthy of his position as man and artist. Last Friday, the 14th of February, after the theatre, he gave a soirée in the Musikvereinssaal for the benefit of the Vienna Hospital Fund, to which a most handsome contribution was made in consequence; and the day before yesterday, the 16th of February, at midday, he gave his farewell concert in the Great Redoutensaal. The receipts from this latter concert may well have amounted to some few thousand florins, for, although the price of the tickets had been raised, the hall and gallery were packed, and by eleven o'clock no more tickets for the stalls were being handed out by the box office. Liszt had already given eight concerts, two of which were for charity, in addition to which he had performed at the academies of Saphir, Bériot, and Pleyel and at the Concerts spirituels, in other words fourteen times in all; and after all this, in the midst of the heady diversions of the Carnival, he now gave this brilliant farewell concert, truly a success of a kind never before witnessed in Vienna with any other artist, and certainly one which will not be equalled, at least for some time to come.

Now that those sounds which so often enthralled and enchanted us have died away, perhaps for some time to come, it is almost a sad reminder to sift through what we heard and recall that at his soirée Liszt performed Hummel's Septet in truly magnificent fashion, and that he created the most extraordinary effect with his rendition of a Fantasy on Pacini's "I tuoi frequenti palpiti'' and with the two Hungarian pieces performed at his seventh concert; that at his farewell concert he played the *Concertstück* by Karl Maria von Weber which he himself has made so famous, an improvisation on given themes, Beethoven's Fantasy for Pianoforte, Orchestra, and Chorus, and, by request, a further Hungarian piece and his Chromatic Galop. There is such a mass of impressions here that only with difficulty can they be sorted out in the listener's memory and characterized according to their artistic content. At these two final concerts Liszt played works by three great masters, and it must remain a matter of uncertainty which of these three beautiful tone poems was most enhanced by him. The way in which the young artist succeeded in finding the magic formula needed to breathe form and life into the slumbering spirits of these notes is a question I leave for him to answer who can give an exhaustive account of the meaning of the word ''genius.'' It often remained a matter of wonderment to me when I heard Liszt performing great classical works, for I could not fathom how a man on whom life makes no fewer demands than does his art could find the time for such comprehensive studies, in addition to working so unremittingly to developing modern piano playing to a hitherto unknown pitch of perfection. But Liszt is a virtuoso from head to toe, a virtuoso in the noblest sense of the word. He practises his art not as a form of speculation, but out of an inner need, and I would maintain that in such a state of mental agitation he himself is perhaps the most inspired of his listeners, and certainly the severest of his critics. But it is true virtuosity to pour into the lap of poverty a generous share of that which good fortune has given him. True virtuosity is also piety towards the great masters of the past, a piety which has found such fine expression in the letter which Liszt published in this journal wherein he mentions the monument for Beethoven.

248 Johann Wilhelm Christern's article on Liszt published in the *Blätter für Musik und Literatur* of October 1840
Franz Liszt the Romantic Artist.
The so-called Young German movement, a community sprung from the most recent period of literature, has consigned itself as a quincunx. By the same token people have spoken, or would like to have spoken, of a phalanx of music, a musical Young Germany; and is it now by chance or is it, rather, by design on the part of some higher world spirit that here too a fateful pentagram, a rune with magic Romantic sounds, has been formed as though of its own volition? Chopin, Liszt, Thalberg, Henselt, Schumann – behold the new Olympus with its young heroic gods, a thyrsus-wielding host drunk with youthful fire, passing through the world from dawn to dusk as the followers of a smiling Dionysus once did, young and old, men and women joining the surging mass and swelling its numbers in their yearning desire! –

I am thinking now of *Liszt* alone. I am thinking of his character, his personality, and everything bound up with the strength of his art and with the fire of his inspiration – but not of the date and year of his birth, nor of his name or anything else that is merely vain and empty noise. Who will prevent me from contemplating this single rune from the aforesaid pentagram simply as though it had issued from the melting-pot of the present, as something modelled on so much else that is great in time and history, as something that passes through life to equal effect?

Has Liszt a character? Can his nature be briefly epitomized? I should have thought that it could by surveying his works, by logical argument, by considering their inner music and outer poetry, and, one might almost say, by visionary insight in moments of sanctified silence. Ah, how the soul dilates with joy, casting off the bonds that fetter petty narrow hearts, when it breathes Polhymnia's fragrancy. I have drunk from thy beaker, young eagle, I have tasted of thy wine, it was sweet and strong, and its golden spray imbued my soul with its dulcet sounds! –

Let me begin by speaking of history, the best instructress, as all would acknowledge. When Moscheles' star was in the ascendant, the worthy Clasing, respected then as now in Hamburg and throughout the world, had no idea of the other man's style or music. He expressed his amazement, clearly and openly, that anyone could play such things! – When, in Vienna, Mozart stood before Austria's Emperor, the latter said to him, no less sagaciously by his own lights: ''Very pretty, dear Mozart, but what a lot of notes!'' And what did the twelve-year-old child reply? ''No more than are necessary, Your Majesty.''

''But what a lot of notes'' – this is something that clever people occasionally say, no doubt, about the Romantic Liszt. And what is his answer? ''No more than are necessary, you stupid rabble.'' All with eyes to see such things will no doubt see how fragile a thing is prejudice; that it is really not a question of the

number or multitude of notes which *you*, poor artist, can only play; you who without fault, as you stand and move, as you speak and behave, would have condemned Mozart in that tribunal before the Emperor. Thus do I dismiss you, begrudger of notes; remain outside in the cold, you Judas, you who betrayed the eternal advance of beauty and infinite art!

It is said that *simple* beauty typifies the past. Very well, I concede that to be so. But I would also say that *sublime* beauty typifies the present, and that first and foremost it typifies our Liszt. Chopin, Thalberg, and Henselt are all individually somewhat different, not generally so, but specifically. If we follow the glorious Liszt's compositions from the first to the last, we shall find that they all express the idea of sublimity, a taste for grandiose intentions and the wondrous hieroglyphs of the spirit of our age. This is no more than a summary view, for it lies outside our scope on this occasion to furnish proof from each work in turn. But if I am to indicate anything definitive (with the request that it be not misinterpreted), I should say that Chopin loves all that is pithy, affective, and terse; Henselt loves elf-like gambolling; Thalberg a solemnity now brilliant, now melancholic; Schumann humorous profundity; Liszt, the great Liszt, a serious, sublime style of writing; and all of these composers both plenitude and fullness. I stood before Liszt's magnificent *Erard* piano. I compared its mechanism with spiritualism. I observed its broad, dare I say vigorous, black keys, its formal proportions far removed from those of Viennese instruments, the waves of sound produced by its bell-like bass – and I asked myself whether or not there was any relationship between the magnificence and tuning of this instrument and the way of playing associated with it; and my answer was yes! And all the players of genius who have touched its keys and strings awoke of a sudden and echoed that cry of ''Yes'' in a thousand-strong chorus of hallelujahs!

As I write these lines, I live in the hope of yet hearing Liszt the Romantic playing his own poems and works. By the time this appears in print, this may already have happened, may already be realized, and an even more vivid comparison and systemization will then be possible. For what is freshly experienced expresses itself in a different way from the silently deciphered hieroglyph. Music remains a sacred mystery. Wise men refuse to admit as much, and yet it is true none the less. Living sentient induction reveals it all to us.

Christern.

249 Advance notification of Liszt's concert in Dresden on 29 March 1840
For the Benefit of the Local Armies
Today, Sunday the 29th of March
Franz Liszt's Final Concert
By reason of the performer's departure
12.30 midday.
The Royal Court music dealer, C. F. Meser, will oversee the sale of tickets for numbered seats @ 2 thalers, and for the remaining seats @ 1 thaler, between 8 and 12 o'clock on the ground floor of the Hôtel de Saxe.
Doors open 11.30.

Declaration.
It is with as much surprise as sadness that I heard of an article sent in and published by a journal in Leipzig in which a number of accusations have been made against me.

Accustomed to having only my artistic achievements criticized, I could scarcely have expected that I would be reproached for having failed
(1) to announce my concerts,
(2) to issue complimentary tickets.
As far as announcements were concerned, the majority of these had already been placed in local newspapers before my arrival, but none of them had been edited by me nor furnished with my signature.

Never have I refused to hand out complimentary tickets, but since my concert took place only a few hours after my arrival, it is no doubt possible that during this brief space of time those people who might normally expect to be sent complimentary tickets were overlooked, an omission which I most sincerely regret.

Although Herr Hofmeister assumed responsibility for the entire arrangements with a willingness matched only by his industry and obligingness, the unfortunate misunderstandings which have arisen are a consequence of the aforesaid announcements and arrangements, and although I was certainly the last to be apprised of them their effect upon me was no less disagreeable for that.

All the more gratifying was it to discover among the educated classes of Dresden and Leipzig unsolicited supporters of my cause; such flattering appreciation amply compensated me in both these cities; I recall the mark of distinction kindly shown me by Dr Mendelssohn, whom I revere and admire greatly, and by the distinguished Leipzig Orchestra and Chorus, and it is with genuine delight that I seize this opportunity to express the fact that I take my leave of these two cities with a feeling of deep-seated gratitude and reverence.
Dresden, 27 March 1840. F. Liszt.

250 Johann Wilhelm Christern's review of Liszt's concert in Hamburg in late October 1840
Franz Liszt's First Concert.
When it is generally agreed that a certain person stands out as the leading figure of his day in one particular art or science or trend in human thinking, and that he not only stands out but dictates the future course and development of thousands of others, it will always seem hard to observe the golden mean between sufficient circumspection on the one hand and active enthusiasm on the other, and, instead of a one-sided panegyric, to express an impartial view that attests to the writer's refinement of taste in passing critical judgement. In general, the hot-blooded southerner may perhaps have an easier task, for the sympathy born of enthusiasm is granted greater due, the more subordinate a role is played by cold and sober reason. Yet let us not be ashamed of the unfolding of the spirit, nor of the resurrection of the mind on the occasion of a jubilant Eastertide, when a glorious, wondrous genius unfolds his wings above us; for otherwise the simple child of nature, abandoning himself to the charm of the senses and the whim of the moment, would have the advantage over us, the advantage of greater enjoyment and of the most blissful sense of contentment!

The genius obeys the voice of genius. With this axiom in mind, Franz Liszt adapted Beethoven's Symphonies for the piano, and performed a part of the ''Pastoral'' Symphony to open his evening's concert. In the spirit of pure and noble art, there could indeed be no bolder undertaking than to strive for the palm of new artistic merit through independently mastering this ethereally rural painting! Whoever had any notion of the free effusion of Beethoven's orchestra, or of his instrumental writing in general, must admit that to reproduce this – nay, even to indicate or hint at it – on the piano involves a gigantic task tantamount to piling Ossa on Pelion in order to reach the heavens themselves. But listen! The sounds of music and song, of babbling brooks and rolling thunder, the whole of nature's springtime stirrings are audible here: as in that admirable painting by David whose basic idea is itself essentially imperial, the new hero tames his rearing stallion on the highest cloud-covered rocky promontory, gazing down calmly and self-assuredly upon the joyful world! Yes, you are the master of us all, Liszt! How splendidly, and with what soul and life, you have reproduced the fullness of the orchestration of a kindred spirit whose light is a beacon that guides your steps. It is Beethoven to the life, although Beethoven could not become so. How impoverished is our dear German tongue, how lacking in words to express the impression behind such forces; what use are such words as *good*, *beautiful*, and *admirable* which have been used and abused a thousand times over for less worthy objects! Only the language of a Tacitus, a Demosthenes, a Johannes von Müller would be worth coveting here. *And yet* the profoundest depths of poetry and art have revealed their effects upon the hearts and souls in the echoing hall. A peal of thunder was this cry of ''Ah!''

The *second*, *greatest* force, a bright point of light of wondrous perfection, was reserved for Liszt's rendition of two ''Songs without Words'' adapted from Schubert. Felix Mendelssohn captured this province with his singing keys, and how our Liszt now graces it with the garlands of celebration and sadness associated with the deep-souled Schubert! Do you know the double appoggiatura to the delicate echo of *this* ''Serenade''? We may impudently claim that through *his* originality Liszt has invested *this* kind of playing, too, with a *wholly new* and *loftier* spirit. The piano is no longer so weak, no longer so stupid. It reproduces in all their nuances the emotions felt by its greatest master and its greatest conqueror. – The finesse of the ensemble, the magnificence of logical conjecture and virtuoso boldness were especially developed in the Fantasy movement for two pianos as played by the strong yet graceful hands of Liszt and by the young and talented Herr [Gottfried] He[r]rmann, who has made such valiant progress. This is perhaps the best moment to say a word about Liszt's characteristic calm and the tense expression of his soul's very essence. If a man's eyes and countenance be the image of his innermost being, his purest self, then this is certainly true of Liszt. Who can observe these nervous features, which *no* portrait has yet reproduced like *this*, and not read into them the whole poetry of Romanticism, the wondrous history of a titanic world spirit? Ever struggling, ever contending with an immensely vast vision, eternally great and sublime through this contest which knows no victory and never ends! –

In appending the entire programme for the benefit of our foreign readers, we take the liberty of adding a number of factual comments.

Part I.

(1) "Pastoral" Symphony by Beethoven, arranged for piano solo by the performer.

(2) Vocal number.

(3) Part of a concerto for violoncello, performed by the Konzertmeister, Herr Knoop.

(4) Fantasy from *Lucia di Lammermoor*, arranged for piano solo by the performer.

Part II.

(5) Two songs by Franz Schubert, *Ständchen* and *Ave Maria*, arranged for piano solo by the performer.

(6) Duet for two pianos, performed by Messrs Herrmann and Liszt.

(7) Vocal number.

(8) Chromatic Galop, composed and performed by Herr Liszt.

On the very morning of the concert a rumour passed through the town like wildfire: "The directors of the Municipal Theatre have sent a circular to their singers, forbidding them to appear at Liszt's concert, notwithstanding the fact that the latter has personally paid his respects to both colleagues." – When the "Pastoral" Symphony was finished, Liszt said something along the following lines in regard to this matter: "I am very sorry to have to inform this distinguished audience that, in spite of the fact that two or even, I believe, three vocal pieces were advertised, all of these numbers will have to be omitted from this evening's programme, since the directors of the Municipal Theatre have forbidden their singers to sing at my concert. (Several cries of dismay.) I must therefore beg your forgiveness if in consequence a significant degree of monotony should arise, although, in order to satisfy this distinguished audience I should gladly agree to performing six or more additional pieces!" (Loud cries of Bravo!)

The following morning the weekly news included an advertisement by the directors of the Municipal Theatre in which it was explained that the performer had merely been guilty of a *faux pas* inasmuch as there is a law forbidding all theatre singers to appear at concerts without the special consent of their superiors. – We hope that in the light of this the two sides will be brought together and reconciled.

In a forthcoming issue we shall be publishing a further biography of Franz Liszt.

272 The programmes, where known, of Liszt's 21 concerts in Berlin between 27 December 1841 and 3 March 1842, as recorded by Lina Ramann (see note 80):

First programme [27 December]: *Ouverture de l'opéra "Guillaume Tell"* (Rossini/Liszt), *Réminiscences de "Lucia di Lammermoor"* (Donizetti/Liszt), *Réminiscences de "Robert le Diable"* (Meyerbeer/Liszt), *Adelaide* (Beethoven/Liszt), *Chromatic Fantasy and Fugue* in D minor (Bach), *Erlkönig* (Schubert/Liszt), *Grand Galop chromatique* (Liszt).

Second programme [1 January]: Sonata in C sharp minor ("Moonlight") (Beethoven), *Grande Fantaisie sur des thèmes de l'opéra "Les Huguenots"* (Meyerbeer/Liszt), *Invitation to the Dance* (Weber), Fugue in E minor, and Theme and Variations (from D minor Suite) (Handel), *La Danza [Tarantella Napolitana]* from *Soirées musicales* (Rossini/Liszt), Mazurkas (Chopin), Polonaise from *I Puritani* (Bellini/Liszt), *Marche Héroïque dans le genre hongrois* (Liszt).

Third programme [5 January]: *Septet* (Hummel), Aria by Pacini sung by Luigi Pantaleoni, *Ständchen* and *Ave Maria* (Schubert/Liszt), *Rheinweinlied* from *Vierstimmige Männergesänge* (Liszt), Prelude and Fugue in A minor (Bach), *Grande Valse di Bravura* (Liszt).

Fourth programme [9 January]: *Élégie sur des motifs du Prince Louis Ferdinand de Prusse* (Liszt), *Réminiscences de "Don Juan"* (Mozart/Liszt), *Momento capriccioso* (Weber), Studies by Moscheles and Chopin, Prelude and Fugue in E minor (Bach), *Hexaméron* Variations.

Fifth programme [16 January]: Scherzo, Storm and Finale from Beethoven's "Pastoral" Symphony; *Fantaisie sur des motifs favoris de l'opéra "La sonnambula"* (Bellini/Liszt), *Ma-*

zeppa (Liszt), Sonata and "Cat's Fugue" (Scarlatti), *Valse à capriccio* (Liszt).

Sixth programme [21 January]: *Konzertstück* (Weber), *Marche et cavatine de "Lucie de Lammermoor"* (Donizetti/Liszt), Sonata in D minor (Beethoven), *Lob der Thränen* (Schubert/Liszt), Scherzo a capriccio in F sharp minor (Mendelssohn), *"Heil Dir im Siegerkranz"* ("God Save the Queen") (Liszt).

Seventh programme [23 January]: *Réminiscences de "Don Juan"* (Mozart/Liszt), *Ständchen*, *Ave Maria* and *Erlkönig* (Schubert/Liszt), *Invitation to the Dance* (Weber), Free improvisation on Russian National Anthem and Caspar's Drinking Song (*Der Freischütz*), *Réminiscences de "Robert le Diable"* (Meyerbeer/Liszt).

Eighth programme [30 January]: *Réminiscences des "Puritains"* (Bellini/Liszt), *Magyar dallok* (Liszt), Sonata in F minor ("Appassionata") (Beethoven), *La campanella* and arrangement of *Carnaval de Venise* (Paganini/Liszt), Prelude and Fugue in C sharp minor (from *The Well-Tempered Clavier*), *La Serenata e L'Orgia* (Rossini/Liszt).

Ninth programme [3 February]: *Divertissement sur la cavatine "I tuoi frequenti palpiti"* (from *Niobe*) (Pacini/Liszt), Funeral March from the "Eroica" Symphony (Beethoven/Liszt), Sonata in A flat major (Weber), *Réminiscences de "Norma"* (Bellini/Liszt), *Au Lac de Wallenstadt* (Liszt), *Au Bord d'une source* (Liszt), Improvisation on three themes.

Tenth programme [6 February]: Sonata in A flat major ("Funeral March") (Beethoven), *Réminiscences de "Lucrezia Borgia"* (Donizetti/Liszt), *La campanella* (Paganini/Liszt), Scherzo and Fugue from the Sonata in B flat major (*Hammerklavier*) (Beethoven).

Eleventh programme [25 January]: *Ouverture de l'opéra "Guillaume Tell"* (Rossini/Liszt), *Erlkönig* (Schubert/Liszt), *Invitation to the Dance* (Weber), Agathe's Aria arranged for piano (Kullak), *Grand Galop chromatique* (Liszt). Two of Liszt's songs for four-part chorus, *Rheinweinlied* and *Studentenlied* ("Es war eine Ratt' im Kellerloch"), were also performed at this concert.

Twelfth programme [4 February]: The performers included Pantaleoni and Zschiesche. Apart from a paraphrase of *Gaudeamus igitur*, the remainder of the programme is unknown. After the concert Liszt was driven back to his hotel by local students.

Thirteenth programme [10 February]: At this concert Liszt performed three pieces, including *"Heil Dir im Siegerkranz."* His remaining programme is unknown. Two of his quartets were sung, viz.: *Rheinweinlied* and *Das deutsche Vaterland*.

Fourteenth programme [16 February]: Piano Concerto in E flat major (Weber), *Hexaméron* Variations, *Réminiscences de "Don Juan"* (Mozart/Liszt), *Réminiscences de "Lucia di Lammermoor"* (Donizetti/Liszt), *Grand Galop chromatique* (Liszt). The orchestra performed the *Oberon* and *Leonore* Overtures; two vocal numbers from Bellini's *I Puritani* completed the programme.

Fifteenth programme [19 February]: Overture to Gluck's *Iphigénie en Aulide*, Piano Concerto in E flat major ("Emperor") (Beethoven), Overture to Rossini's *William Tell*, *Invitation to the Dance* (Weber), improvised encores, Choral Fantasy (Beethoven).

Sixteenth programme [23 February]: *Fantaisie sur des motifs favoris de l'opéra "La sonnambula"* (Bellini/Liszt), *Hexaméron* Variations, *Ständchen* (Schubert/Liszt), *Réminiscences de "Robert le Diable"* (Meyerbeer/Liszt), Choral Fantasy (Beethoven).

Seventeenth programme [2 March]: Overture to *Coriolan* (Beethoven), Piano Concerto in C minor (Beethoven), *Oberons Zauberhorn* (Hummel), *Réminiscences de "Don Juan"* (Mozart/Liszt), *Ave Maria* and *Erlkönig* (Schubert/Liszt).

Eighteenth programme [late February]: ?

Nineteenth programme [late February]: ? *Grand Galop chromatique* (Liszt).

Twentieth programme [late February]: Symphony No. 5 in C minor (Beethoven), Overture to Spontini's *Olympia*, conducted by Liszt, Meyerbeer's *Le Moine*, accompanied by Liszt, &c.

Twenty-first programme [3 March]: ?

283 Verses in homage to Liszt published in the *Berliner Modenspiegel* on 15 January 1842

Postlude
to Liszt's Concert on 27 December 1841.

Who lent thee, o magus, who lent thee thy power over
 music?
Who lent thee that priestly power, higher and mightier yet?

Amazed, the mind bows low to thee, o conqueror of strings,
With dizzying speed it scales the heights and plumbs the
 depths of art. –
Withal to thee, o conqueror of *souls*, the *soul* itself bows
 low,
Enthralled it follows after thee, in blissful joy exulting,
And, borne aloft on sempiternal love's seraphic wings,
It soars above with thee to enter realms of heavenly light. –
For thou, o spirit ruler, sit'st enthroned above the clouds,
Guiding the listening world where'er thy fancy taketh thee.
'Mid flashes of refulgent lightning thou unleashest blind
Demonic powers from which we hastily avert our eyes,
Rolling thunder rages at thy bidding, storms and tempests
 roar,
The very ocean depths do quail and tremble at thy might.
Once more thou wav'st thy magic wand and peace returns to
 earth,
Dispersing storms and heralding the rosy-fingered dawn
Which tempts the blushing sunbeams into bloom, while
 playful winds
Caress and flirt with meadow flowers, the ocean billows
 kissing.
A flood of joy o'erwhelms the world, and blessed angels
 tune
Their heavenly harps to feast the enraptured ear! –
Thus from ecstasy to pain, and thus from pain to ecstasy
Our souls by thee are torn and drawn along etherial paths,
And whither thou wouldst lead them, be it Hell or be it
 Heaven,
They follow at thy bidding as though it were a god's decree,
For only thus can genius hold sway o'er kindred souls.

284, 285 Two reports on Liszt's final days in Berlin in March 1842

(Berlin, 2 March.) Liszt is leaving us tomorrow. A prince could not leave us in more brilliant style! It is not his virtuosity but the noble ends to which he puts it, and the artist's generous, worthy and truly aristocratic cast of mind, which have earned these expressions of interest. Today's newspapers once again reported that the sum of 1794 thalers had been distributed, representing the proceeds of the artist's latest charity concert. Of this sum, 500 thalers went to the Infants' Day Nursery, an act of generosity which this morning gave rise to a touching scene. A hundred of these children, all of them under the age of six, appeared together with their supervisors at the Hôtel de Russie, where Liszt is staying, and congregated in the main hall. Informed of their presence by a deputation of principals, Liszt came down from his room. The children greeted him with a chorus of thanks, *Praise the Lord, ye youthful choirs*, and four of their number strewed flowers at their benefactor's feet. The amiable artist was most profoundly moved and touched; he was unable to speak, but lifted up the children in his joy and kissed them most cordially. This evening is his grand farewell concert, the eighteenth occasion on which he will have performed in public during the last two months. Tomorrow lunchtime, immediately before his departure, he will be playing again, at his hotel, this time for the benefit of the poorer students. In return, the University is preparing a festive send-off for him of a kind never before seen here. Together with thirty coaches driven four in hand, and with students wearing academic dress, he will be accompanied to the village of Friedrichsfeld, a mile outside the city, where the wealthy local landowner, Herr von Treskow, has invited all the students to dine with him. Thus Liszt leaves us, truly a prince among artists.

(Berlin, 3 March.) Liszt left Berlin today in truly royal fashion. Having been dismissed yesterday from his twentieth public concert with scenes of indescribable jubilation and acclaim, he gave a further concert today for poor students. Packed though the hall of the Hôtel de Russie was, it was empty compared with the crowded street outside, where thousands of people had gathered from 12 o'clock onwards. By half past one it was almost impossible to force one's way through the crowds, and the knot of carriages could disentangle itself only with difficulty. Passing from one embrace to the next, Liszt was all but carried to his carriage. This latter was drawn by six white stallions; the senior students took their place beside him. In order to break free from the crowd, the carriage began by taking a detour, driving past the Armoury to Unter den Linden, before turning round, crossing the Schloßbrücke and Schloßplatz, and taking the road to the city gate. The townspeople had turned out in force; the roads were lined with people until far out beyond the gate; indeed, even in Friedrichsfeld there were a hundred or so private carriages, and the whole village was crowded with people. The students were received here in the hall of the private residence of Herr von Treskow. After a song had been sung by all those present to the tune of the Hungarian National March, Liszt was accorded three rousing cheers, to which, deeply moved, he replied with a few words of thanks. After about an hour's break, he took his leave of the young men, who, standing in rows in the hall, touched glasses with him individually and shook his hand in turn. A single shout of "Hurrah" rang out as he left the hall, looking forward, no doubt, to the days ahead and a period which, if far less turbulent than his time in Berlin, may none the less be beneficial for the rest which it may bring him and which he most assuredly deserves.

286, 287 Occasional verses written as tributes to Liszt's charity concerts in Berlin and St Petersburg

To Franz Liszt,
following his concert
for the Cologne Cathedral Building Fund.
The prince of German rivers is the Rhine,
Cologne Cathedral is its princely crown.
A Rhineland son gives thanks to thee and thine
For adding stone on stone to its renown.
From music's magisterial throne shall shine
The glory of a name which shall go down
In history; for thou hast built so fair
A monument which time will ne'er impair.

In days to come when none is left to hear
Those sounds with which the ear e'en now imparts
Ecstatic joy to ravished soul, that ear
Which trembles at the tempest and its smarts,
It will be said of Liszt the mage and seer
Who once breathed fire into our frozen hearts,
Of him whose name is writ throughout Cologne:
"Liszt built this glorious pile with German stone."
Berlin, 10 January 1842.   Philipp Kaufmann.

To Franz Liszt.
Reports of Hamburg's baleful fire
Had scarce had time to spread from shire to shire
And cross the River Neva, where they reached thine ear,
When, weeping for Hammonia's hapless plight,
Thy heart, with incandescent pity dight,
Was seared by white-hot flames of love which fear
Could never quench; the moment such a thought
Found lodging in thine heart, the deed was wrought.

Thou worthy master! First to hear the call
For help and first to ope the sacred hall
Of art in succour of thy fellow men.
As once thou toil'dst for us in foreign land,
So now thou offerest a kindly hand
To Germany, prime mover now as then.
In honour of thy name, thy work shall be
An everlasting monument to thee.

That noble muse to whom thou art in thrall
Hath never brought thee such acclaim in all
Thy life as when inspired by charity:
True benediction now attends thine art,
Which ne'er shall play a finer, nobler part
Nor yet attain to greater dignity.
No fairer garland could adorn thy brow
Than these same thanks we offer to thee now!
14 June 1842.

288, 289 Two further reports of Liszt's donation to the Berlin Day Nursery
A surprise morning call for Franz Liszt.
Among the many demonstrations of respect and gratitude which were accorded the celebrated artist during almost three months here, none can have left a more gratifying impression upon his sympathetic heart than the one which he received yesterday. Led by Major von Plehwe representing the directors of the various day nurseries in whose benefit Herr Liszt had given a concert, *one hundred* children, of whom not one was more than six years old, were taken to see him in order to express their thanks in person in the name of a thousand other beneficiaries. A number of boys from the Malmène School had similarly appeared, accompanied by their teachers. The landlord of the Hôtel de Russie, Herr Roth, had been kind enough to open up his ballroom for the children, and it was here that they took up their positions in a semicircle. A deputation of principals then went up to see Herr Liszt and to ask him to accept the children's thanks. On entering the ballroom he was greeted with the anthem, *Praise the Lord, ye youthful choirs*. Major von Plehwe then said a few words of thanks in the name of the Society of Day Nurseries, and Herr Borchardt expressed his especial thanks for the donation received by Institution No. 1. Four of the children now stepped forward, recited a little poem, and "scattered flowers upon their benefactor's path through life." All who were present, and especially the artist himself, were so deeply moved by this touching scene that he could find no other way to reply than by kissing the children tenderly and lovingly. One of the boys from the Malmène School now delivered a short speech of thanks, similarly couched in verse, whereupon the other children recited several of their commemorative verses, thereby giving rise to much hilarity, more especially when a thousand little fingers were raised playfully in the air with the words "these were given us to play with." An amusing concert without instruments but fully orchestrated by the boys from the Malmène School brought the occasion to a close. Repeatedly assuring his visitors that their surprise morning call had given him the sincerest pleasure, the philanthropic artist took his leave of the assembled company, whose blessings accompany him on his way.

Acknowledgements.
The virtuoso Herr Liszt
has furnished a further demonstration of his untiring love of charity through the donation of
100 thalers
which he has made to the Malmène Children's Home out of the proceeds of the charity concert given in the Royal Opera House. It is with all the more sincere joy that we offer this benevolent virtuoso our most heartfelt thanks in that the dear children from the Home have recently found difficulty in providing for their own maintenance. May God's blessing go with this donation!
Several friends of the boys
from the Malmène Children's Home.

290 Report of Liszt's visit to Königsberg in March 1842, where he was awarded the honorary degree of Doctor of Philosophy
Königsberg, 20 March. (Private communication.) Liszt has left us, after the most universal admiration was shown him here as elsewhere, not only for his unsurpassed accomplishments but also for the rare qualities of his heart and mind. We believe that we may earn the gratitude of the great master's many friends and admirers, both near and far, if we communicate the following letter which is circulating here in Königsberg and which he addressed to the Faculty of Philosophy of the town's University.
"Most esteemed and learned gentlemen,
"I should attempt in vain to express the deep and heartfelt emotion occasioned me by the rare mark of honour which you have accorded me. A doctorate conferred on me by a Faculty like yours, in which there are men of European standing, is a source of much happiness to me, and would be a source of pride as well if I were not also conscious of the spirit in which it was conferred. I repeat that in assuming the honourable name of a teacher of music (and I would note here that I accept the word *music* only in its great, full, *classical* meaning) with which you, my esteemed Sirs, have favoured me I am fully aware of having assumed the obligation attendant upon uninterrupted learning and unremitting labour. In constant fulfilment of this duty to keep the doctorship *docte* and *dignified* and, by word and deed, to disseminate what little technique I am able to learn as the *form* and *means* by which to reveal what is *true* and *godlike* in music: in constant fulfilment of this duty and with whatever success it may yet be granted to me to enjoy, I shall always retain a vivid memory of your good will and of the touching way in which a famous member of your Faculty informed me of it. Most learned Sirs, please accept this expression of my most grateful respect and utmost veneration. Königsberg, the 14th of March 1842. F. Liszt."

291 Report from the *Leipziger Allgemeine Zeitung* of July 1842
Königsberg, 9 July. In view of the total silence which Russian journals have been observing on all matters even remotely connected with the imperial family, it comes as no surprise that rumours concerning those relations have found their way into general circulation with all the greater frequency. Thus the rumour has again been put about for some time past that the sudden departure from Petersburg of a famous virtuoso was the result of his having been sent into exile. It is said that during a concert, while a fairly loud conversation was taking place in the imperial box, he kept on turning round to face the direction from which it was coming and, since he remained unheeded, thereupon stopped playing. In consequence of this, he is said to have received instructions the very next day to withdraw from Petersburg and the confines of the Russian Empire without any further delay.

313 Review from the *Allgemeine Musikalische Zeitung* of 12 September 1845
The evening concert again brought only works by Beethoven, viz.: (1) The C minor Symphony, conducted by Herr Liszt in his free and easy manner, since the improvised conductor describes the traditional way of conducting an orchestra as "rococo." Indeed, the orchestra, which already knows this glorious work by heart, played it on the whole just as admirably as if a rococo conductor had been standing on the podium; it refused to be put off by the untoward antics of its present director. (2) The E flat major Concerto for Pianoforte, performed by Herr Liszt with unusual repose and level-headedness. Although other experts were not in agreement and were right to complain, among other things, of a flagrant flirtatiousness with *pianissimo* effects which, in view of the size of the hall, ought rather to have been avoided, the present reviewer is grateful to Herr Liszt for having exercised self-control on this occasion. (3) The Seraph's Aria from *Christus am Ölberg*, sung by Mlle Tuczek with more pious fervour than theatrical bravura. The effect was profoundly moving. (4) *Coriolan* Overture. (5) Canon Quartet from *Fidelio*, a piece unsuited to the occasion. Even less suited was (6), the String Quartet in E flat major, op. 10, performed by the Cologne Quartet. What can four string instruments hope to achieve in so large a space, when they are not accustomed to playing in even a small room with adequate strength or to representing a small orchestra? – Irony! Finally, (7) the finale to Act II of *Fidelio*, conducted by Liszt. This, too, was an unsuitable choice, in addition to which the mediocre performances of some of the soloists could only engender a feeling of boredom. Whereas this day's events brought little pleasure to the great number of informed listeners, the following and final day of the festival was to prove even more dismal in every respect, undermining the good and praiseworthy achievements that had gone before and transforming into indignation the memories we took away with us.

316 Report from the *Großherzoglich Hessische Zeitung* of 6 October 1845
Franz Liszt
Darmstadt's art lovers can look forward to a pleasure which has been withheld from them for far too long; they will be able to admire the king of all virtuosos. Franz Liszt has arrived, and will give us a taste of his talents. When one reads the superlatives which mercenary journalists nowadays lavish on mediocrity, one finds oneself in a real dilemma, not knowing which expressions to use to advertise the arrival of a European celebrity, the performance of a world-famous genius. For such a man is Franz Liszt – and the enthusiasm which has everywhere accompanied his artistic revelations has assumed the most extraordinary forms in an attempt to celebrate the highly talented artist in a fashion worthy of his name: orders, titles, appointments, doctorates, diplomas, ceremonial swords, triumphal processions have characterized his progress from his native Hungary to seething Spain, from wealthy Petersburg and ecstatic Berlin to oversated Paris and glittering London; like his achievements, his successes too remain unequalled and unique. Faced with the picture of such an artist, envy is branded as folly, as the Beethoven Festival in Bonn clearly showed, and caricature becomes a compliment, as we saw when the Paris sculptor and wit Jean-Pierre Dantan produced a statuette of Liszt with ten fingers on each hand. And Liszt triumphs on an instrument which we see all around us, from the salon to the garret, played by young and old, rich and poor, filling the world *ad nauseam* and spreading terror in the concert hall; but it is not on the pianoforte than Liszt is so brilliant. Beneath his hands an orchestra comes to life: his eye does not merely rest upon two times fives lines of music, but his spirit roams through whole orchestral scores; he does not play but becomes a poet, living through sound. This keyboard, so often a feeble instrument of tedium, becomes a source of admiration beneath his masterly hands; even the blasé listener is filled with wonderment and ecstasy; and the thrill of beauty passes through his soul when Liszt's genius speaks to him so powerfully, shatteringly, and enthrallingly through such an imperfect and everyday instrument. His playing cannot be described: it must be heard, comprehended, and felt; it is immeasurably greater than anything we have previously heard by way of instrumental virtuosity. Even as an eleven-year-old boy, Liszt had already thought through all of Beethoven's composi-

tions and could reproduce them with the most perfect technique; as a young man, inspired by the accomplishments and successes of Paganini, Liszt resolved to be like him, and he has kept his word: in terms of technical mastery he may even stand higher than Paganini, and he certainly surpasses him in compositional talent and imagination. His rendition of a piece is never merely mechanical, but is a composition in the truest sense of the word, an autonomous artistic creation reborn from within through fire and suffering. Every piece that he plays he regards in general as a theme on which to improvise, almost always re-creating something wonderful and at the same time revealing a truly inspired tendency to free his art increasingly from all formal and alarming fetters and, with real enthusiasm and irrespective of all external and constraining rules, to reconstruct what his inner eye has seen. – That Liszt is the most brilliant and, at the same time, the most interesting of all living virtuosos and the most remarkable of leading artists has been universally acknowledged; that his achievements may more readily be understood, we should like to add only that he is a "child of our time" in the finest sense of the term. A genius equipped with the most brilliant abilities and with an all-round education; a mind which, by virtue of an astonishing force of sympathy, has been associated and intimate with all the great, glorious, and novel achievements that our highly progressive age can show in art and life. That his titanic power to create and re-create may be expected to produce not the quietly self-satisfied fancies and polished affectations of a previous age but the impetuous storm of the present period's intellectual movement will be readily guessed by all who can grasp the importance of our age and its reflection in the soul of a great artist. With his mind and with his art Liszt is a noble son of that age: his life story and the jubilant acclaim which rings out on every side bear witness to this fact; but he is no less noble in his feeling heart – and what the simple artist has done for poverty, for aspiring young artists and for charitable institutions, and in encouraging others to act in a truly magnanimous spirit has ensured that it is not only the artist who has been awarded the palm, but that as a human being, too, his grateful contemporaries have offered him the citizen's crown.

317 Review of Liszt's concert in Darmstadt on 8 October 1845

Franz Liszt's Concert

Liszt gave his concert on the 8th in the Hall of the United Society, where he performed to a large and glittering audience. We are pleased above all that this is *not* the only concert which the brilliant maestro is performing here, but that the public will have a further pleasurable opportunity within the next few days to admire him in the theatre. – Breathless attention followed each inspired flight on the part of a virtuoso whose achievements have reached that pitch of perfection from which no further advance can conceivably be made, since the instrument's exhausted mechanism forms a delimiting barrier. But a genius like Liszt knows no limitation in his inspired and constant urge to advance: he is the Archimedes of art, seeking only the place to which he may transfer his latest creations. We are therefore not surprised to discover that he is currently toying with the inventive idea of developing the mechanism of his instrument in order to gain new terrain for performing what he feels within himself. We heard Liszt in seven numbers, only one of which, a Mazurka by Chopin, was not by him, for the Overture to *William Tell* and the delightful *Tarantella*, although sprung from Rossini's genius, have been so transformed by Liszt's incomparable and exuberant transcription for the pianoforte as to become as much his property as Rossini's. In our previous article we drew attention to a certain aspect which will certainly have impressed and convinced all his listeners: beneath Liszt's hands an orchestra comes to life, nay, more than that, through the power of the whole one hears and feels the silvery sound of singing. An astonishing impression was made by the Fantasy on themes from *Norma* and by the highly original *Chromatic Galop*. These are works whose execution, as demonstrated here – and taking account of the flood of sound, the tempo, clarity, and imaginative embellishment – bordered upon the fantastic. Virtuosity has reached the pinnacle of its achievements in Liszt: that he maintains his position here, forever active in new and affecting ways, while others wear themselves out and fall asleep after one or two years of fame is the most cogent proof of his great musical genius in general, a genius which would have enabled him, like a certain Greek artist, to have become a great figure in art even without any hands. – It is impossible to write any other report of a concert by Liszt except to say: Go and hear for yourselves! Berlin and Vienna, overwhelmed by a surfeit of artistic celebrities, have not grown tired of jostling for space at each of the twelve concerts which he has given there or of listening to him when his fingers, like ten steel hammers, force the sharpest or driest tone from the instrument or, like violin bows, coax forth the gentlest of sounds, while always revealing the fullness of an abundant spirit. As for his next concert at the theatre, we hear that the stage is to be specially built out over the orchestra pit and the instrument placed as far out into the auditorium as possible, thus ensuring that none of its notes escapes the audience and that, under *his* hands, the pianoforte will certainly seem to fill the hall.

368 The opening section of Liszt's article on *Lohengrin*, originally published in the Leipzig *Illustirte Zeitung* of 12 April 1851

However varied may be the views that are held on the degree of admiration, interest, or approbation to which Richard Wagner's musical achievements may justifiably lay claim, not even his avowed enemies and critics can deny the brilliant richness of his harmonies and his intelligent handling of the orchestra, nor the immense amount of work and the meticulous studies to which those achievements bear witness. Each of his works is deeply thought through and knowledgeably worked out. Their style is sublime, utterly remote from all vulgarity. The subject matter is poetical, and he knows how to use its effectiveness to the best advantage. If his operas remain little known even today, and if theatre managements hesitate to stage them, then the reason is certainly not to be sought in any material difficulties involved in performing them – for these difficulties would be soon overcome! – but, rather, must be found in the far more significant obstacles which lie in our path and prevent us from introducing a wholly new system into the art of dramatic composition. Among these obstacles are the circumstance that the art of dramatic composition demands more imperiously than any other the patronage of a public which has always striven obstinately to resist all innovations. Among the many ideas which Wagner has set forth in his writings on art and on the future of art (and which we do not propose to repeat here in their manifold ramifications), his conception of drama under as yet untried conditions is the one which has most directly influenced the direction taken by his genius. For far too long we have been content to allow stage performances to derive their principal interest from the one-sided deployment of a *single* art, while the other arts were used as non-essential attributes; thus, for example, we were satisfied with all too mediocre music in the entr'actes of tragedies; we demanded only a scant degree of truth and poetry in operatic texts, placed little weight upon singers' acting and gestures, and so forth. Rare exceptions in which the ancillary arts were raised to a pitch of greater perfection were appreciated by audiences, who however did not see sufficient reason to censure the standards to which they were accustomed. – There emerged, however, a towering genius, a coruscating spirit who, destined to wear the double crown of fire and gold, boldly dreamed, as poets are wont to do, of setting himself a goal so high that it could be reached by art and acknowledged by society – if ever – only when audiences no longer comprised that vacillating, bored, distracted, ignorant, and arrogant mass which nowadays comes to the theatre, sitting in judgement and dictating laws whose powers even the boldest among us scarcely seeks to check. Wagner, the passionate artist whom we may praise not just for the conscientiousness of his love of beauty – for he is consumed by the noble, inwardly searing wound of artistic *fanaticism*; Wagner, whose inborn abilities and lofty culture have rendered him equally sensible to the charms of every art, and whose heart beats with the selfsame fire for Euripides' Iphigenia as it does for Gluck's: Wagner overcame our ancient traditions and customs. Offended by that fragmentation which prevented the most important element of the entire presentation from appearing in its highest beauty, he believed it was merely a question of *willing* into existence a drama which would embrace in equal perfection all the arts involved in the theatre. He convinced himself that if such a drama were to come into being it must necessarily involve the disappearance of that practice which consisted of favouring each privileged art in turn by enlisting the help of several others, each of which served merely as an ancillary art intended not to develop independently but to throw into greater prominence that particular art which the author himself preferred. Wagner recognized the possibility of linking together in a single bond the arts associated with the spoken *word*, the musical *sound*, and the mimic *gesture*, together with those others branches of art which are employed on the stage, combining them indissolubly and weaving them together in intimate association. To his way of thinking, each of these arts should contribute to the effect which all are destined to create through their wondrously harmonious interplay.

Far be it from us to judge the substance of those arguments which have already aroused widespread passions across the length and breadth of Germany's musical world, for it is not our aim to attack or defend this presentiment of so comprehensive a conquest for the brilliant manifestations of art. Wagner's idea is bold but beautiful; his goal is daring and would be worthy of a great artist even if it were unattainable. Where such endeavours reveal themselves, and where they are supported by genius, it would be just as superfluous to praise them on drily rational grounds as to contest them, even if they were to prove to be aberrations. Does not the splendid goal which they seek to attain bear adequate witness in their own defence? Will they not have a hard enough struggle against the facts and natural obstacles which they will encounter on their way? If fate has assured their triumph – and who, after so many unforeseen victories, could deny this prospect? – why seek to impede the progress of so glorious a triumphal chariot? It is therefore certainly not our intention to re-examine here everything that could be said for or against Wagner's system. There are enough people who will set about this task with fevered and passionate partiality – a partiality which we forswear in this discussion, although it may perhaps be necessary if all the advantages and errors of any system are to be seen in their proper light. We have felt obliged to offer this summary survey of the ideas of the poet of *Tannhäuser* as they relate to the drama, since his latest work, *Lohengrin*, recently performed for the first time in Weimar, is the one in which these ideas are most decisively set forth, a work which appears to be imbued with the most heartfelt and vivid sensations, and which is therefore the clearest reflection of the noblest features of Wagner's individuality. For that reason it cannot be fairly judged if the listener tries to find in it the old kind of opera with its traditional arrangement of vocal numbers, its accepted distribution of arias, romances, solos, and ensembles – in a word, the whole of the present system of showing off the singers and tunes in an arbitrary relationship which tends to favour the former. Wagner solemnly abjures all consideration for the demands of a *prima donna* or a *basso cantante*. In his view there are no *parts*, only *roles*, and he finds it entirely natural to leave a leading singer completely silent throughout an entire act where her presence, actually necessary for the truth of the scene, is evident only through a dumbshow which would not only be disdained with an air of superiority by every Italian *diva* but which would also be far beyond her powers. One should not expect to hear cabalettas here, or encounter those little pieces which belong on the music stands of dilettanti; it would be more than difficult to remove one part of so perfectly compact a unity without impairing the whole. The unity which these operas share derives from the effectiveness of a style which inhabits regions hitherto unexplored and which is almost as far removed from simple recitative as it is from the phrases of our grand operatic arias with their cadenza-like decorations. On the contrary, one must be prepared to see human beings who are far too full of their passions to while away their time with trills and runs, and for whom singing, like verse in tragedy, becomes a natural language, a language which, far from impeding the course of the drama, makes it all the more effective. And while they declaim with a simplicity that tends towards the sublime, the music in Wagner's orchestra finds its limits much expanded. For it is in the orchestra that he causes the souls, the passions, the feelings, the slightest sensations of his characters to be reflected so that they might be revealed to us. With Wagner the orchestra is like an echo, transformed, as it were, into a gossamer garment that allows us to see every palpitation of the characters' hearts: they beat, one might say, beneath this veneer, and through these diaphanous diaphragms of sound we perceive their slightest stirrings and their most violent agitations. Then we hear the cry of hatred, the fury of revenge, the tenderness of love, the rapture of devotion! The most secret dreams are depicted in dissolving shadows, the proudest schemes are painted in brilliant colours.

Whatever fate the future holds in store for Wagner's system, we believe there can be no doubt that, sooner or later, the knowledge of his achievements will lead operatic composers to a more eloquent orchestration, more closely connected than heretofore with the nature of their material, and, more especially, to a choice of libretti whose texture will offer some serious and lasting interest and whose poetry will display a fascination that is independent of the musical rhythms. When one sees the finest tragedies of every age mercilessly mutilated and reduced to formless masses of pitiful verse where the goal should, rather, be to translate into the realm of music both the expression of those passions which such tragedies represent and the dramatic momentum behind the situations which bring them about, then one can feel only the liveliest pleasure that there is finally some hope of seeing an end to the intolerable implausibilities, the ridiculous rhymes, the crude motivations, in a word the most inferior imaginative products which so long have been thought an adequate basis for the most admirable masterpieces of musical genius. Is it not time that composers refused to accept libretti of this sort, libretti which Voltaire once denounced in a bitterly scornful but witty remark which has so often, and so deservedly, been repeated: "What is too silly to be said should be sung!" – As far as we ourselves are concerned, we believe that if it came to the worst and we had to choose between two evils the lesser of the two would be simply to use speech for what is unworthy of the higher expression of music.

The libretto of *Lohengrin* is, as I say, a work of dramatic art in itself and one which contains beauties of the first order. To understand the course of the action in the theatre and to grasp the entire import and range of the music from the first bars of the Prelude onwards, it is perhaps necessary to know the secret on which the entire action depends. This secret rests upon those accounts of the Holy Grail which are found in courtly romances and which occupy so important a position in the works of Wolfram von Eschenbach and a number of his contemporaries. The story of *Lohengrin* draws upon those traditions and, in its account of the principal events, departs from them only where required to do so by the structure of the drama. But with what poetry has Wagner furnished it! And what are the events related here? the manifestations of fate. How tedious it would be to relate the calamities which befall the characters on a journey whose progress is just as rough and just as uneven for some as it is for others! If events inspire any interest it is because of the feelings of sympathy, pain, or joy they arouse in the human heart, and because of the poetic significance which lies behind them. – Let us see how things stand in this regard with the present subject.

As Wagner has shown in his *Nibelungen* [recte: *Wibelungen*], the myth of the Holy Grail is the heir and successor of the Nibelung hoard. This latter was too closely related to a specifically Germanic paganism for it to be able to merge with Christianity, and so it was turned into a fictional tale devoid of all deep meaning, whereupon the legend of the Holy Grail, whose original Provençal nucleus could be readily associated with related Judaic and, hence, with Christian Biblical views, entered the world as a symbol of all that the people of that time thought worth striving for. The chalice in which Joseph of Arimathea caught the blood that flowed from the wound in the Redeemer's side was guarded as a sacred relic, tended by a chosen body of knights, whose members gained strength from the sight of the relic and who remained ever free from mortal sin. This power was renewed every Good Friday by a sacred wafer placed in the Grail by a dove. The knights enjoyed earthly happiness and heavenly bliss. Only he who was chosen by God to serve the Grail could find the temple in the midst of a forest of cypress trees: built of gold, precious stones, and sweet-smelling aloe: it remained unattainable to everyone else. Once the hoard had become identified with the Grail, and more especially after the impetuous Emperor Frederick Barbarossa had met his death by drowning while on a Crusade, this mysterious goal of all mythical striving (a striving which found its historical justification in the Crusades, just as the Grail Temple is said to have been located in the Orient) became associated with the equally mysterious legend of the Swan Knight, who must needs depart whence he came if, in defiance of his prohibition, questions are asked of him. From this there arose that glorious legend in which we must see the tragic conflict of faith and love, as Wagner has indicated in his poem. Lohengrin, the son of Parzival, the "Lord of the Grail" and himself a Knight of the Grail, after restoring the good name of the young and gravely defamed Duchess of Brabant by fighting a duel on her behalf, forbids her to enquire as to his nature and, in accordance with the Grail's decree, makes this ban a condition of his remaining there. When love makes it ineluctably necessary for her to know who her lover is, she ventures to ask the fatal question, and he has to abandon her. – This tale is dealt with in greatest detail in a poem which dates from the time of the minnesingers and which, according to the chronicles, Wolfram von Eschenbach, the true representative of a religiously visionary faith, is said to have sung, at the request of the Landgrave of Thuringia, in the presence of the assembled ladies of the court, and to have sung, moreover, on the very day when his present enemy, Klingsohr, tempting him into evil ways and striving to awaken his envy by expounding a science superior to his own, addressed to him all manner of questions which, although they were intended to confuse and confound him, he was able to answer with surprising ease and apt simplicity, so that, thanks to the help of the Blessed Virgin, it was in fact his adversary who was thrown into utter confusion.

386 Liszt's open letter to Richard Pohl of 5 November 1853

In the various reports on the Karlsruhe Music Festival which have come to my attention I have found but a single point on which there is any real agreement: it is the *inadequacy* of my abilities as a conductor.

Setting aside the degree of intentional *prejudice* which has contributed to this opinion – indeed, without wishing to enquire to what extent this view has resulted from the simple fact that the choice of conductor fell on me after the Kapellmeisters of Karlsruhe, Darmstadt, and Mannheim had all been passed over – I should regard it as inappropriate to make any claims that contradicted the assertion which others are at pains to make if that assertion were based in fact or in some way justified. It is, however, precisely this which I must most categorically dispute.

To begin with the *facts* of the matter, no one seems able to deny that the entire programme received an outstanding performance, and that the balance and sonority of the instruments, arranged with due regard for the chosen venue, must be called satisfactory and even admirable. All of this is naively admitted with the qualification that it is truly surprising that the whole thing turned out so well "in spite of" the inadequacy of my conducting.

I am far from wishing to claim credit for the achievements of the orchestras from Karlsruhe, Mannheim, and Darmstadt; indeed, I am more than anyone inclined to do justice to their outstandingly talented individual members; yet I must regard it as having been proved by the testimony of my opponents themselves that the performance turned out to be sometimes surprisingly good and, on the whole, far better *than one felt entitled to expect in view of my conducting*.

Once this *fact* has been admitted, it only remains left to examine whether I really am as thoroughly alien to this task as people are fond of claiming, and to ask why an orchestral conductor is placed on public trial in this way even though his orchestra performed satisfactorily, the more so when one considers that the pieces offered were new to almost all the performers. As was amply recognized in Karlsruhe, apart from the movement by Berlioz, which only a *section* of the Karlsruhe orchestra had performed in Baden under the composer's own direction, the Ninth Symphony, together with the works by Wagner, Berlioz, Schumann, *et al.*, was thoroughly known only to me, never having been performed before in these places.

In turning to the *fairness* of the above charge, I would ask my critics whether, faced with these facts, they can, in good conscience and with their perfect knowledge of the subject, reproach me for being an inadequate, inexperienced, and uncertain conductor?

Without wishing to defend myself – which I do not believe I need do towards those people who have taken the trouble to understand me – I may perhaps be permitted a remark which goes to the very heart of the matter. The majority of the works which I publicly admit to admiring and preferring are among those which conductors who are more or less famous, and more especially those said to be "competent," rarely if ever find worthy of their personal sympathy, so that for them to organize a performance of one of these pieces would indeed be a novelty.

These works are among those which are generally described as being "in the style of Beethoven's last period," a style which until quite recently was declared, with considerable lack of respect, to derive from Beethoven's "deafness" and "mental confusion" (!). In my own judgement, they demand of the players who perform them a level of skill which we now appear to be approaching, but which is still far from being realized in every quarter: what is required is advancing skill in accentuation, in rhythm, in the detailed way of phrasing and declaiming certain passages, and in distributing light and shade across the whole; in a word, *in the style of the performance* itself. In this way a bond is forged between the musicians at their desks and the musician placed in charge of them, but a bond unlike that which is struck by imperturbable time-beaters. For there are certain passages where simply to maintain the beat and each individual part of the beat | 1, 2, 3, 4 | 1, 2, 3, 4 | very much runs counter to a meaningful and intelligible form of expression. Here, as elsewhere, *the letter kills the spirit* – a death sentence which I would never sign, however malicious in their feigned impartiality the attacks may be to which I am subjected.

For the works of Beethoven, Berlioz, and the great composers who are related to them, I see less than ever the advantages (which even elsewhere I would in fact dispute) of having a conductor assume the function of a windmill, seeking by the sweat of his brow to communicate the warmth of his enthusiasm to the players in his charge.

For when it is a question of understanding and feeling, of a firm intellectual grasp, and of inflaming hearts in a spiritual communion intended for the enjoyment of all that is beautiful, great, and true in art and poetry, the *self-sufficiency* and basic skills of ordinary conductors can no longer *suffice*, and may even conflict with the dignity and sublime freedom of art! And – with the permission of my kind critics – I shall, on every further occasion, content myself with my own "insufficiences" and "inadequacy" as a conductor, and I shall do so, moreover, on principle and in obedience to an inner conviction which will never allow me to sink to the level of a time-keeper, a role which 25 years of experience, study, and genuine enthusiasm for art have most certainly made me ill equipped to play.

Notwithstanding the respect which I owe to many of my colleagues, and my readiness to acknowledge the excellent services which they have rendered and will continue to render to art, I do not believe myself obliged to imitate their example on every point, either in my choice of the works to be performed or in the manner of their interpretation and conducting.

I believe I have already expressed my opinion that the conductor's true task is to make himself *ostensibly superfluous* and if possible to disappear with his function. *We are steersmen, not oarsmen.*

Even if this assertion were to meet with yet greater opposition from certain individuals, I am incapable of altering an opinion which I am bound to consider just. As far as the Weimar orchestra is concerned, the application of this principle has already produced outstanding results – results which even some of my present critics have in the past had occasion to praise. And so I shall continue, undiscouraged, without false modesty, to dedicate my services to art in the way I consider best – which, after all, is no doubt the best course of action for me to take. –

Let us therefore calmly and unconcernedly take up the gauntlet that has been thrown down at us in the form of a nightcap, and let us persist in the consciousness of our right – and of our future.

Weimar, 5 November 1853. *F. Liszt.*

403 Part of Liszt's Open Letter of 26 March 1857, analysing his Piano Concerto No. 1 in E flat major

The fourth movement of the concerto, from the *Allegro marziale* [music example], corresponds to the second movement, *Adagio* [music example]; it is merely a condensed recapitulation of what was heard earlier, involving fresh and livelier rhythms, but containing *no* new motif, as will immediately become clear to you when you peruse the orchestral score. This way of drawing *together* a piece and rounding it off at the end is something virtually unique to me, although it can be thoroughly defended and justified from the standpoint of musical form.

The trombones and basses [music example] take up the second part of the motif from the *Adagio* (B major): [music example]. The piano figuration which follows [music example] is none other than a repeat of the motif first heard in the *Adagio* on flute and clarinet [musical example], just as the final section is a major-key variant and intensification of the motif from the Scherzo [music example], until finally the first motif [music example] enters on the pedal of the dominant *B flat* accompanied by trilled figurations [music example] and brings the whole piece to an end. –

The E flat minor Scherzo from the entry of the triangle I intended by way of a conciliatory contrast [music example]. As far as the triangle is concerned, I make no secret of the fact that it may cause offence, especially if struck too hard and imprecisely. There is a preconceived dislike and objection to the use of percussion instruments, an objection which is not unreasonable considering how often they are misused. Few conductors are circumspect enough to show off these instruments to their best advantage in compositions where they are used with due care, having regard for the composer's aim to introduce a rhythmic element without the crude addition of clumsy noise. In the majority of cases, the dynamic and rhythmic spice and intensity which percussion instruments are capable of producing could be achieved far more effectively through careful rehearsal and balancing of such entries and additions. But musicians who wish to appear serious and respectable prefer to treat percussion instruments as though they were pariahs which did not deserve to be found in the decent company of a symphony orchestra. These people sincerely regret that Beethoven allowed himself to be seduced into using a bass drum and a triangle in the finale of his

Choral Symphony. The use of such instruments by Berlioz, Wagner, and my own poor self should come as no surprise, for "birds of a feather flock together," and since we are treated as impotent pariahs among musicians it is entirely natural that we should get on so well with the pariahs among musical instruments. Be that as it may, the right thing to do here is to find the harmonious golden mean and then hold firmly to it. In the face of so sagacious a sentence of excommunication as that delivered by my doctrinaire critics, however, I shall have to continue to use percussion instruments for some time to come, and devise a few more unfamiliar effects from them.

459 Anna Liszt's letter to her son of 4 May 1865

Paris 4 May 1865

My dear child,

People often talk of things at such great length that they finally happen, and so it is with your present change of status. There have been frequent reports in the *journeaux* here that you had chosen clerical status, but I have vigorously contradicted them whenever they were mentioned. And so your letter of the 27th of April, which I received yesterday, upset me deeply, and I burst into tears. Forgive me; I really was not prepared for such news from you. But after reflection (they say the night brings *conseil*), I bowed to your will and His, and grew calmer; for all good ideas come from God, and this decision which you have now taken is no *vulgaire* decision. May God grant you the grace to fulfil it to His satisfaction. It is a great undertaking, but you have been preparing yourself for it on the Monte Mario for some time now. I have noticed it in your letters to me for some time past: they were so beautiful, so *religieuse*, that I was often very moved and shed the occasional tear *en lisant*. And now in this latest one, my child, *tu me demande pardon – oh!* I have nothing to forgive, your good qualities have far, far outweighed your youthful failings. You have always been strict in fulfilling your duties in every respect, and in that way you have accustomed me to peace and joy. That I can live in peace and free from worry is something I owe to you alone. So live happily, my dear child, and if the blessing of a feeble old mother can achieve aught with the Almighty, then I bless you a thousand times. *Ollivier est touchée de ta resolution et tu dis quelques lignes si amicale a lui dans mon lettre, aussi, lui il restera toujours le même pour toi.*

Baron Larrey came to see me yesterday. He had read about you in the *journeaux*. He wanted to know if it were true, *il me chargea des Compliements et d'amietiée sincere pour toi*. Reményi *aussi* came to find out the truth. I expect I shall now have many *visites* because of this *évenement*. *Adieu*, my dear child; you give me hope that I may see you here this year; I pray to God that this promise is, or may be, fulfilled.

I commend you to our dear lord and remain

Your
faithful mother
Anna Liszt.

When you write to me, use black ink and a better quill; my eyes are becoming very weak.

462 A review of the first performance of *Die Legende von der Heiligen Elisabeth* from the Leipzig *Illustrirte Zeitung* of 16 September 1865

Franz Liszt conducts the first
Music and Choral Festival in Pest.

R. – On 15 August the 25th anniversary of the founding of the Pest-Ofen Conservatoire was celebrated with a music festival on the grandest scale. Franz Liszt, the darling of the nation and the country's leading musical light, was the soul of this festival, a festival which had been brought into being by a committee presided over by Baron von Orczy. Just as the attention and admiration of the country has constantly been drawn to Liszt from the moment when, as a nine-year-old boy, he played his first concert number in public, to that instant when, moved by dreams of ambition, the artist sought refuge beneath the mantle of renunciation, so there were extraordinary scenes of jubilation when, on the 15th of August, Liszt stepped up to the conductor's podium to direct the first performance of his oratorio *Saint Elisabeth of Hungary* in the festive Redoutensaal. The composer, whom we have been accustomed to seeing storming irrepressibly ahead with his Symphonic Poems, keeps the musical reins much more firmly under control in this oratorio. It is a work of magnificent conception and holds the attention by its colourful instrumentation. At the festival concert on the 17th of August, the first part of Liszt's *Dante Symphony* was performed, in addition to which Robert Wolkmann, General Music Director Franz Erkel, and Mosonyi had all provided new compositions, which won much applause, for this first Hungarian music festival. On Sunday, the 20th, the Feast of Saint Stephen, the patron saint of Hungary, the 50 choral societies gathered here undertook an excursion to woodlands outside the city; bands of musicians played on every side, alternating with the singing of the thousand-strong chorus. Bonfires lit up the woodlands, and not until late in the evening did the endless crowds of revellers make their way back home.

503 Copy in Liszt's hand of Wagner's letter to him of 18 May 1872

My very dear friend,

Cosima maintains that you would not come even if I were to invite you. That is something we should have to endure, as we have had to endure so much else! But I cannot forbear to invite you. And what is it that I call out to you when I say "Come"? You entered my life as the greatest man to whom I have ever been able to address myself on terms of intimate friendship; you slowly moved away from me, perhaps because I had become less close to you than you were to me. In your place there came your innermost being, born anew, and it was she who fulfilled my yearning desire to know you close to me.

Thus you live before me and within me in perfect beauty, and we are as one beyond the grave itself. You were the first man to ennoble me through his love; I am now wedded to a second, higher self through her, and can achieve what I could never have achieved alone. Thus you could be everything to me, whereas I could only ever be so very little to you: what a tremendous advantage I have over you!

If I now say to you: "Come," what I mean by this is: "Come to yourself!" For you will find yourself here. – Whatever your decision, you have my blessing and my love!

Your old friend
Richard.

Bayreuth, 18 May
1872.

504 Draft of Liszt's reply to Wagner's letter

My dear, exalted friend,

Deeply stirred by your letter, I cannot reply in words. But I hope with all my heart that every shadow of a consideration that keeps me fettered far away will disappear, and that we shall shortly see each other once again. Then you, too, will see quite clearly how inseparable from the two of you my soul remains, inwardly reborn in your "second, higher life, where you can achieve what you could not have achieved alone." Herein lies Heaven's forgiveness.

May God's blessing be with you both, together with all my love.

20 May 72 Weimar. FL

535 Hanslick's review of Liszt's *"Gran" Mass* and *Loreley*, from the *Neue Freie Presse* of 10 April 1879

It was at Hellmesberger's last quartet evening that Liszt came into the room, unobserved, during the E flat major Trio by Schubert. Modestly, he remained in the background until the end of the piece, before passing along the rows of listeners and taking his seat in the *"cercle."* The audience's attention, which had already begun to waver considerably during the Schubert finale, was now directed exclusively at the famous new arrival, giving way to such a mood of elation that, as though at a given sign, the assembled company began to applaud, and continued to do so until Liszt stepped forward and bowed in gratitude. It was a delightful, unforgettable moment. We know of no other instance when an artist has entered a concert hall, neither as a composer nor as a performer but as a mere listener, and been welcomed as loudly and as unanimously by the entire assembly. If Bismarck and Gambetta, Richard Wagner and Verdi, the youngest and prettiest *prima donna* and the oldest virtuoso were to appear at a concert or in the theatre, they could none of them boast of such a scene. No one in the whole of Europe could, indeed except for Liszt. The feeling that flared up instinctively in the majority of the listeners, that it was right to welcome Liszt, was transmitted as though by electric cable, until almost simultaneously the entire hall erupted in thunderous acclaim. A deeply felt, amiable impulse which does our public much credit, just as it honours the object of their acclaim. This general sympathy, directed not merely at the artist but, in equal measure, at the man, is always evinced on every occasion when Liszt is present. What magic still surrounds the elderly man! If he himself conducts one of his compositions, not only are the well-known sounds of opposition silenced (as of course befits a well-bred public): no, the very opposition itself, the inner resistance felt by many listeners towards Liszt's works, falls gently silent when the old spitfire raises his head and gazes at them with a face alight with genius and benevolence, so that his music speaks to us, as it were, through Liszt's own lips. Yesterday's performance of the Gran Festival Mass in the large Musikvereinssaal offered the latest proof of this striking phenomenon. The Festival Mass, which in any case is Liszt's most substantial work, was of course first performed in Vienna in March 1858: the fact that during the ensuing 21 years not one of our secular or spiritual musical bodies has thought of repeating the work shows how slight was the pressure to do so here in Vienna. Even today, it is doubtful whether the public would attend in adequate numbers were it not for the lure of Liszt's personal appearance. The Gesellschaft der Musikfreunde [Society of Friends of Music] had wisely assured itself of this talisman, and he did not fail them. For my own part, I find it painful to admit that I received the same impression of this work on this occasion as I did twenty years ago, however honest my attempts to find any pleasure in it. This work has no doubt lost a number of its thornier aspects over the years, but no roses have grown in their place. Musically we have experienced much, and suffered much, during these twenty years – many of its more outlandishly formless, violent, and discordant aspects no longer have their former power to provoke and to irritate. After twenty years the "Gran Mass" has found us more mellow, but has not made us any the happier. From whichever of its two aspects we look at this piece of church music, the ecclesiastical or the musical, it offers us stimuli but no further satisfaction. We do not doubt for a moment in the composer's individual piety and religion, but for our own part we cannot find any of the transfigured peace and healing power of prayer in a type of music which stirs up the whole turmoil of human passions, a drama of earthly unrest and inner conflict. Interesting for its numerous intelligent features and its penetrating musical exegesis, impressive in the seriousness and greatness of its aims, and remarkable, finally, as the creation of a phenomenally gifted and brilliant man, the "Gran Mass" none the less remains a thoroughly unedifying, unhealthy, and oversophisticated work, in which the striving for religious expression and the invincible tendency to strain after theatrical effect struggle constantly for supremacy. Like Mahomet's coffin, Liszt's Festival Mass hovers, homelessly, between heaven and earth. The performance of the "Gran Mass" provided a remarkable sight – it was in any case of first importance that the audience should *see* what was going on. Liszt stood on a raised conductor's dais, wearing his long black abbé's dress from the topmost buttonholes of which a long, heavy bundle of miniature orders hung, like a cluster of the choicest Malaga grapes. Numerous garlands of flowers and bay had been hung from the podium or placed on the ground around it, forming a kind of miniature bower from whose dark green background Liszt's imposing white head stood out effectively. Liszt conducted, if one can describe as conducting the few sketchy hand movements which he made. "The conductor should be a steersman, not an oarsman," runs a well-known saying of Liszt's. And when one is fortunate in having two excellent "oarsmen" working away at one's side, little can go wrong of course if the steersman puts his hands in his pockets every once in a while. Herr Kremser, who had most carefully prepared the whole performance, conducted with a baton, Herr Hellmesberger similarly with his violin bow; above them both, in a general sort of way, hovered the Holy Ghost in the form of Franz Liszt. When he stretched out his hands from time to time over the singers and musicians, he seemed not so much to be conducting them as blessing them. Yet whatever he does makes him appear a distinguished and significant figure, enabling him to exercise that well-known magic charm on young and old that half a century has not diminished in potency. On the soloists, too, this charm was not without its effect: they sang their difficult parts with truly apostolic commitment.

Liszt was also accorded the liveliest interest at the final Philharmonic Concert, when Frau Pauline Lucca – no doubt in honour of the composer, who was himself present – sang two of his Lieder, *Mignon* and *Loreley*. Of all Liszt's compositions, his songs – of which there are fifty or more – are the least known and performed. The most widely known and most popular is certainly *Es muß ein Wunderbares sein*, one of the few songs by Liszt whose tender, unified mood is never forcibly broken and which can offer pure enjoyment. All of these songs are notable as highly individual expressions of an interesting personality who tends, however, to behave in a highly cavalier way when faced by the majority of poetic texts.

595 Report on the Weimar *Tonkünstlerversamlung* of 1884
Music of course has its factions almost as much as politics. Who has not heard of the war of the Gluckists and the Piccinists? In much the same way in our own day, the friends of the old confront the adherents of the new, the admirers of Liszt, Wagner, Berlioz. The new of course itself becomes old with the passage of time, and what was initially violently resisted is finally found acceptable. The Allgemeiner Deutscher Musikverein [General German Music Society] was founded in 1859 at a *Tonkünstlerversammlung* [meeting of musicians] held in Leipzig. The aim of the meeting was to celebrate the twenty-fifth anniversary of the *Neue Zeitschrift für Musik*, founded by Robert Schumann and at that time edited by the distinguished music historian Franz Brendel. Just as this journal had always supported the new, so this celebration was attended almost exclusively by like-minded spirits. At its centre was Franz Liszt, who had been active for a number of years as Court Kapellmeister at the Court Theatre in Weimar. *Lohengrin* had received its first performance in Berlin that same year. If even this work had met with such lively resistance, it is not hard to imagine what must have happened when the introduction to *Tristan and Isolde* was played for the first time in Leipzig or when Franz Liszt's "Gran Festival Mass" received its first performance. But adversity brings friends together, and thus it was that the Allgemeiner Deutscher Musikverein was founded. The art-loving Grand Duke of Saxe-Weimar, Carl Alexander, assumed the role of patron, and it was at his official residence that the first music festival of the new society took place the following year. Twenty festivals have been held since then, and everywhere attempts have been made, as far as possible, to give the present age its due and to allow aspiring young artists to be heard in public. As a memorial on the centenary of Beethoven's birth, a Beethoven Foundation was summoned into existence with the aim of supporting musicians in much the same way that the Schiller Foundation supports writers. The Allgemeiner Deutscher Musikverein can look back with satisfaction on its 25-year history. Its number of members continues to grow; and not only musicians form part of its membership. For the paltry sum of 6 marks annually, all who love music can do something to serve the ends of art and at the same time gain admission to the music festivals which take place every year, each time in a different place, thereby ensuring themselves a wealth of musical pleasures.

The Society celebrated its 25th jubilee in Weimar between 23 and 28 May, returning to its proper home, the town where even today Liszt spends the summer months each year, in the circle of his pupils of both sexes. Much has changed in the last 25 years, and many who then looked forward with optimism to their future lives have now passed to their final resting-place. Public taste has changed, moreover. What was condemned in 1859 is now admired. An enthusiastic audience listened to the *"Gran" Mass*; and *Saint Elisabeth* – another of Liszt's oratorio compositions which initially people did not wish to know about, even in the concert hall – now finds such an audience in a staged performance in the theatre. The Society alone remains loyal to its principles: the jubilee was distinguished by the presentation of a whole series of new or rarely heard compositions. And Liszt is still the same. Of course, as our picture shows, the hair that flutters around his temples is now as white as snow. But there are still the same unforgettable, characteristic features. The aged master is still aglow with the same enthusiasm for all that is great and beautiful, the same self-sacrificial willingness to defend those virtues; his creative powers are undiminished, and when, in the festival play by Adolf Stern performed in honour of the day, he was compared with Goethe as an old man, it was a comparison which suggested itself almost without prompting. Liszt is honorary president of the Society, its actual chairman being Professor Karl Riedel of Leipzig, a man as widely known as a composer as he is as a musicologist and as the conductor of an excellent choral society whose performances won universal admiration this winter in Berlin. Liszt and Riedel are the distinctive personalities at these meetings. But there is no shortage of well-known names elsewhere; they take pleasure in the up-and-coming generation and in aspiring talents, and they guarantee that art in our German fatherland will not lie fallow but will always be cultivated and encouraged. The Dresden-born Felix Draeseke, whose portrait we have also included here, belongs, as it were, to the middle generation, since his name was already encountered at the earliest festivals. Since then he has worked unremittingly at improving himself: a symphony of Draeseke's, which was played in Weimar, is of such translucent beauty that it has met with recognition in every musical camp. The extremes are gradually levelled out. August Klughardt, at present Court Kapellmeister in Dessau, is the author of a quartet which may be said to represent just such a conciliatory standpoint. Klughardt's instrumental compositions are of great melodic charm and formal accomplishment; he has been less fortunate in the field of opera, for which he appears to lack the great dramatic sweep that is necessary here. None the less, he may be reckoned among the most significant of younger composers. Of younger ones, but not the youngest. The youngest must, rather, be Felix Weingartner, born in Zara in Dalmatia in 1863, who in spite of being only in his twenty-first year, has already written both text and music of a grand opera in the Wagnerian style, *Sakuntala*. It goes without saying that such a work bears numerous traces of youthful inexperience; indeed, it would be wrong if this were not the case, for how else might the artist develop? That Weingartner will indeed develop we have every reason to hope, not least because he is a musician through and through: this is not only proved by the wonderful skill which he displays as a composer, but it was also felt in the admirable way he conducted his own opera to mark the end of the festival. At all events, Weingartner is proof of Goethe's remark that fresh young blood continues to circulate. And so let us hope that this is also true of the Society but, most of all, that its honorary president, Franz Liszt, will continue to serve as its leading light!

638 and 639 Local press reports announcing Liszt's death

Special Supplement
to the Oberfränkische Zeitung.

Bayreuth, 1 August. Scarcely has one pillar of the first Bayreuth Festivals collapsed in the figure of Scaria, when death has now snatched away Wagner's most trusted friend, a man who supported his works in their most difficult days. The Abbé Dr Franz Liszt, born in Reiding near Ödenburg (Hungary) on 22 October 1811 as the son of an accountant, died yesterday evening at 11.30 at the age of 75.

The leading pianist in the world, an important composer, a man who worked enthusiastically for his ideals, a dependable friend and great benefactor of incomparable goodness has left us in the person of Liszt.

Liszt spent long periods in almost every great European artistic centre, including Vienna, London, Rome, and Pest, and, more recently, in Weimar, where on 16 February 1849 *he gave the first performance outside Dresden* of *Tannhäuser*, that pioneering work by Richard Wagner, who was later to become his son-in-law, following it on 28 August 1850 with the *very first* performance of *Lohengrin*. The University of Königsberg, through its Faculty of Philosophy, conferred the title of Doctor of Music on Liszt in 1842, and in 1865 Pope Pius IX invested him with the title of Abbate.

A number of well-to-do Hungarian Counts, including Amadé and Szapáry, had provided the means that enabled Liszt to study in Vienna with Czerny and Salieri, and then at the Paris Conservatoire. He received the title of Court Kapellmeister in Weimar as early as 1844, willingly discharging its functions from 1848 to 1859, in which latter year he was appointed Chamberlain to the Grand Duke. He entered the clergy in 1865 and later, during the 1870s, was elected Court Canon of San Albano.

Bayreuther Tagblatt.

In the midst of the joy and enthusiasm aroused by the happy, nay resplendent, course of the Festival, we received the sad news yesterday evening that Franz Liszt, the great composer whose fame has filled the whole of the civilized world, Liszt, the intimate friend and supporter of Wagner, Liszt, the father of Wagner's wife, had departed this life at half past eleven on Saturday evening.

For all that we were prepared for the catastrophe by the fact that the revered composer had fallen ill some few days earlier and that, in view of his advanced age, the most serious consequences were to be expected from its very onset, it was believed until the last two days that the end was not so close, so that the news of his death was all the more painful for the assembled visitors and the inhabitants of the entire town.

Our deepest sympathy is extended first and foremost to the Wagner family and more especially to the sorely tried Frau Wagner, who, in the midst of the Festival and of the difficult task of running the performances which she has taken upon herself, has been afflicted by this heavy blow of fate, a blow which must needs strike the heart of a loving daughter with all the greater force. All who know the great composer's true love for his relations will feel the immensity of the loss suffered by the highly revered Wagner family, and they may be assured, in their grief, of the most heartfelt sympathy of us all.

Today, in the first awareness of our deepest grief, we are unable to offer an exhaustive account of the great man's life, a life whose merits will be assessed by more worthy pens than our own; we restrict ourselves therefore to some general facts:

Franz Liszt was born on 22 October 1811 in the Hungarian village of Raiding, the son of an accountant with Prince Esterházy. At an early age he revealed an outstanding gift for music. It was at the age of nine that Liszt first performed in public on the keyboard and aroused universal astonishment. With financial support from Counts Amadé and Szapáry, Liszt's father took his talented son to Vienna, where he had lessons with Czerny and Salieri. After eighteen months of lessons Liszt appeared in Vienna and enjoyed a brilliant success. Soon after that Liszt turned his attention to Paris, where, in spite of much hostility, fomented by Cherubini, his outstanding talent soon broke through, irresistibly, and met with the greatest triumphs. Liszt quickly became the darling of the Parisian world. He then turned his attention to England, where he achieved the same degree of success. In 1827 there followed a foray to Switzerland, from where Liszt returned to England; but his ailing health soon obliged him to repair to the baths at Boulogne. It was here that Liszt's father died, whereupon the young man returned to Paris. In 1831 he heard Paganini, an experience which affected the whole future course of his life. From 1833 to 1835 Liszt lived in Geneva in relative seclusion, but he then returned to Paris, where he and Thalberg became rivals; in 1837 he betook himself to Italy and remained there until the end of 1839.

In 1848 Liszt gave up his career of an itinerant virtuoso and turned his attention to Weimar. From now on he was active there as Court Kapellmeister in Extraordinary Service, becoming the centre of a circle of adherents and pupils which propagated not only the ideas and products of Richard Wagner and Berlioz, but also the aims derived from them. In 1859 Liszt was appointed Chamberlain to the Grand Duke of Weimar, and in the same year he went to Rome and was received into the Church, living henceforth as an abbé. More recently he spent part of his time in Pest, where he was active as President of the newly founded Royal Hungarian Academy of Music. At the Bayreuth Festival Liszt was a constant visitor; he attended every performance, and through the participation of his illustrious presence he contributed in no small part to the success and the frequency of the great undertaking.

What Liszt achieved as a virtuoso and as a hero of music we leave to the pens of more competent writers to describe, contenting ourselves here with listing only his most important compositions:

Of symphonic poems Liszt composed: *Tasso*, *Die Hunnenschlacht*, *Faust*, *Die Ideale*, *Orpheus*, *Promotheus* [sic], then

Church music: a large-scale Mass, then the oratorios *Saint Elisabeth*, *Christus*, etc. Also noted as a gifted writer, Liszt contributed monographs and articles to the leading journals of the day.

As for the details of Liszt's illness, we have received the following communication from a private quarter:

Liszt had attended the wedding celebrations of his granddaughter on 4 June with his health unimpaired, and the following day had set off on a journey to Luxembourg. Here he caught a series of chills and in consequence contracted bronchial catarrh, which he was still suffering from when he arrived here for the Festival performances on 21 June [recte: July]. However, the resultant cough which had been tormenting him had improved in the mean time, and Liszt was able to attend the first two performances; it was granted to him to be present at the premiere of *Tristan*, and to witness and experience the magnificent success of this musical child of suffering, the offspring of Wagner's muse. During the night of 25/26 July there was cause for considerable anxiety, and Dr Landgraf Senior, who was treating Liszt, diagnosed the presence of a fever when he visited the following morning, giving it as his opinion that the right lung was threatened by an inflammation. The patient was no longer allowed to leave his bed, and the strictest rest was prescribed; Professor Fleischer of Erlangen University, a medical practitioner on friendly terms with the more immediate acquaintances of the Wagner family, was called in to give a second opinion. Initially the symptoms did not appear to be dangerous, but they gradually grew worse, and on Saturday, the 31st of July, the whole of the right lung proved to be infected. The patient's strength and his heartbeat, which the doctors treating him had hoped from the outset would be maintained, had remained satisfactory until then; he remained conscious, moreover, even if he was frequently delirious. That a crisis was at hand was evident, but it was hoped that it would end favourably, when, at around 8 o'clock in the evening, the first signs of an imminent collapse appeared, and cardiac activity grew noticeably weaker. Both doctors mustered all their resources to improve the heartbeat, using the most powerful stimulants, but without success. Towards half past eleven that night breathing and heartbeat ceased, and the patient passed away peacefully, just as his subjective condition during the whole of his illness had been notable for its absence of any particular pain.

Liszt will be buried – according to his own express wish – in the local cemetery on Tuesday morning at 10 o'clock. (See latest news.)

641 Report of Liszt's burial from the *Oberfränkische Zeitung* of 4 August 1886

Bayreuth, 3 August. (Burial of Franz Liszt. Conclusion.) The procession included all the *great figures from the world of music and art* who are at present staying here, in particular almost all the *participants* in the stage festival, representatives of the town, the imperial government and military, and numerous friends and local inhabitants from every class of society. Black flags fluttered from many of the houses along the streets.

The funeral carriage with its sombre decorations was the work of Herr Eysser (Dammallee). The funeral procession reached the cemetery at half past ten, and, followed by the cortège, a number of men from the Bayreuth Choral Society carried the black metal coffin, with its gilt corners and fine lace covering, from the mortuary to the tomb some hundred feet to the northwest of the corner of the church.

Here Herr Korzendorfer of the church council concluded the ecclesiastical part of the ceremony, and the large party of mourners was overcome by the deepest emotion when they heard him offer up moving prayers of supplication for the Abbé Franz Liszt and call down the Church's benediction on him. Rarely if ever can a cemetery have witnessed a gathering which brought together more outstanding celebrities from the world of art.

Expensive wreaths from near and far had already been laid beside the coffin, and the deceased's numerous decorations were arranged on a velvet cushion.

The mayor, Herr Muncker, now stepped up to the grave and, in a sonorous voice shaking with emotion, spoke the following moving words:

"Dear mourners,

"When our great master, whom we have here laid to rest, lingered on that last occasion with his family in the temple of art over there on the heights above our town, the words that he heard there as a baleful prophecy addressed to Tristan the hero, 'Death-devoted head, death-devoted heart,' we now cry out in our grief as a bitter lamentation at his graveside.

"For his head is bowed, that head before whose exalted greatness we stand in admiration. And his heart is given up to death, that heart whose fervent devotion we learned to know and understand at its best and at its finest in the circle of his daughter's family.

"Happy is he! – and we say this also to console ourselves – happy is the weary traveller who, surrounded here by his grandchildren, was fated to breathe his last in the arms of his loving daughter.

"Now it is night in the house, but the torch of his fame will never be quenched. Liszt, the brilliant virtuoso and master musician, will live for ever.

"Him, too, we lay to rest in Bayreuth soil, as years ago we buried our dear departed Master. May he find it a peaceful resting-place!

"The place where he sleeps will be hallowed in our memory. To the most intimate friend and great benefactor of our late Master, Wagner, and of his works we owe, now and hereafter, our warmest and most reverent thanks.''

(After placing a wreath from the City of Bayreuth on the grave:)

"Accept this final gift of our love, dear departed one! rest with us here in peace! may the choirs of angels – among whom is the redeemed soul soaring aloft to Paradise in your last great tone-painting – may they guide thee, too, into the other world!''

Mayor Muncker placed a second wreath on the grave, this one in the name, and at the request, of the City of Vienna, which had always been loyal to the deceased. He was followed by Kapellmeister Reuß of Karlsruhe, who offered up a wreath in the name of Liszt's *pupils* with words of the deepest gratitude to their fatherly friend who, as no other, had been filled with goodness of heart. After him came Herr Krause with a like votive offering, in the name of the Leipzig Liszt Society. His voice choked by sobs, the deceased's friend of long standing, Court Councillor Dr Gille of Jena, called out his final words of farewell; then the various ladies and gentlemen among the illus-

trious party of mourners – including Frau Cosima Wagner and her children, all of whom were reduced to a state of deepest distress – followed the example of Mayor Muncker and all the members of the Festival Committee, throwing consecrated earth into the grave of their great and dear departed friend. Thus Liszt's burial came to an end; most of those present left the place of mourning with tear-stained eyes. *Ave anima pia!*

At the graveside, meanwhile, more and more wreaths had been placed in position, including a truly remarkable tribute from the German Crown Prince, five from the Grand Duke's family in Weimar, others from Princess Hatzfeld, and Prince Hohenlohe, two from Count and Countess Wolkenstein, a wonderful wreath of edelweiss from Sophie Menter, two enormous wreaths from the orchestra and the theatre personnel, and so forth. Who can name all those who came?

Not until after midday did the last of the mourners leave this place, solemn beneath which lies one of the greatest of artists and one of the best of men. God rest his soul!

SOURCE REFERENCES

The biographical information is taken from all the currently available letters to and from Liszt, together with previously unpublished letters in various archives or in the present author's private collection. Concert dates were established by retracing Liszt's footsteps across Europe and by researching original programmes and reviews in contemporary newspapers.

Among the biographies of Liszt which I have consulted by way of comparison, pride of place must go to Lina Ramann's *Franz Liszt. Als Künstler und Mensch* (2 volumes in 3, pub. 1880 [Vol. I], 1887 [Vol. II], and 1894 [Vol. III]). The author was almost fanatical in her admiration for Liszt, and her achievement in writing this first biography of the composer is undeniable, even if the text no longer stands up to critical scrutiny. Lina Ramann knew Liszt personally for thirteen years and must have received much of her information from the composer himself, which makes the first volume of her biography, published six years before Liszt's death, especially important. In her second volume the reader misses a sense of completeness and reliable dating, while Volume III, dealing with the period 1848–86, is scarcely biographical in character any longer, the author's concern here being Liszt's works, which she treats in a not especially enlightening way.

The best documentation to date relating to Liszt is without doubt Peter Raabe's biography, first published in 1931 and reissued in 1968. Volume I, *Liszts Leben*, includes a short biographical sketch of the composer, together with a convincing psychological study. The work-list included in Volume II, *Liszts Schaffen*, is a well-researched piece of scholarship which is bound to remain authoritative. Dr Felix Raabe, who was closely involved in his father's researches, kindly allowed me to use those findings as the basis for the work-list in the present volume; the work-list has been revised and supplemented, and additionally includes works discovered or published since 1968, together with others which are now believed lost. For the English edition, the entire work-list has been thoroughly revised by Leslie Howard (London).

Alan Walker's *Franz Liszt. The Virtuoso Years 1811–47*, first published in 1983 (second, revised edition 1987) offers probably the most important documentation since Raabe for this period in Liszt's life. It includes a wealth of hitherto unrecorded detail, and also deals with figures and events outside Liszt's immediate circle. Walker's exact source references are especially valuable. Equally indispensable are the writings of the outstanding Liszt scholar Dezsö Legány, whose findings are virtually unassailable. Mention may be made finally of Lina Ramann's *Lisztiana*, a collection of reminiscences from the final years of Liszt's life, edited in 1983 by Friedrich Schnapp and the present writer; the volume also contains Liszt's own corrections to Volume I of Ramann's biography.

The most important volumes of letters (with year of publication in brackets) are:

Franz Liszt's letters:
Vol. I: *Von Paris bis Rom* (1893)
Vol. II: *Von Rom bis ans Ende* (1893)
Vol. III: *Briefe an eine Freundin* (1894)
Vol. IV: *Briefe an die Fürstin Wittgenstein* (1899)
Vol. V: *Briefe an die Fürstin Wittgenstein* (1900)
Vol. VI: *Briefe an die Fürstin Wittgenstein* (1902)
Vol. VII: *Briefe an die Fürstin Wittgenstein* (1902)
Vol. VIII: *Briefe 1823–1886. Neue Folge zu Bd. I und II* (1905)

Correspondance de Liszt et de la Comtesse d'Agoult:
Vol. I: 1833–1840 (1933)
Vol. II: 1840–1864 (1934)
(A German translation of Vol. I was published in 1933)

Briefe hervorragender Zeitgenossen an Franz Liszt:
Vol. I: 1824–1854 (1895)
Vol. II: 1855–1881 (1895)
Vol. III: 1836–1886 (1904)

Briefwechsel zwischen Wagner und Liszt, 2 vols. ed. Erich Kloss (3rd ed., Leipzig 1910); English trans. by Francis Hueffer, revised by William Ashton Ellis (New York 1897, repr. 1973), based on Hueffer's incomplete German edition of 1887
Briefwechsel zwischen Franz Liszt und Hans von Bülow, ed. La Mara (Leipzig 1898); also published in French (Leipzig 1899)
Briefwechsel zwischen Franz Liszt und Carl Alexander, Großherzog von Sachsen, ed. La Mara (Leipzig 1909)

Franz Liszts Briefe an Carl Gille, ed. Adolf Stern (Leipzig 1903)
Franz Liszts Briefe an Baron Anton Augusz, ed. Wilhelm von Csapó (Budapest 1911)
Franz Liszts Briefe an seine Mutter, trans. from the French, ed. La Mara (Leipzig 1918)
Franz Liszt. Briefe aus ungarischen Sammlungen 1835–1886, ed. Margit Prahács (Kassel 1966)

The Letters of Franz Liszt to Olga von Meyendorff 1871–1886, trans. William R. Tyler (Washington, D.C., 1979)
The Letters of Franz Liszt to Marie zu Sayn-Wittgenstein, trans. Howard Hugo (Cambridge, Mass., 1953)
119 római Liszt dokumentum, ed. László Eösze (Budapest 1980)
Correspondance de Liszt et sa fille Madame Émile Ollivier 1842–1862 (Paris 1936)
Letters of Franz Liszt, 2 vols., trans. Constance Bache (London 1894)

Franz Liszt: Correspondance, ed. Pierre-Antoine Huré and Claude Knepper (Paris 1987)

Franz Liszts Gesammelte Schriften (6 vols. in 7), ed. Lina Ramann (Leipzig 1880–83)

Abbreviations of frequently cited sources:
Br. = *Liszts Briefe*
Corr. = *Correspondance Liszt/Marie d'Agoult*
Ges. Schr. = *Franz Liszts Gesammelte Schriften*
Roman numerals indicate volume numbers, arabic numerals page numbers.

The notes that follow are cued to superscript numbers in the main text, chronology, work-list, and picture captions.

Notes

1 *Franz Liszts Briefe an seine Mutter* (Leipzig 1918), p. 69.
2 In his book *Franz Liszt. Eine Studie auf der Grundlage der bekannten Quellen, Biographien und zeitgenössischen Darstellungen* (Eisenstadt 1978), Emmerich Karl Horvath has brought together a number of anecdotal details from Liszt's early years.
3 *Briefe aus ungarischen Sammlungen* (Kassel 1966), p. 239; letter to Géza Zichy of 4 March 1881.
4 *Br.* I,219; letter to Dionys Pruckner of 17 March 1856.
5 Ramann/Schnapp, *Lisztiana* (Mainz 1983), p. 389.
6 Horvath (see note 2 above) mentions (p. 94) a concert in Preßburg on 27 March 1823: "[. . .] From Pest he went to Preßburg via Eisenstadt, where his father said goodbye to his friends. His son gave a concert here on 27 May (not 17) [. . .]." I have been unable to find any evidence for this concert appearance. Although the itinerary Pest–Eisenstadt–Preßburg (rather than Pest–Preßburg–Eisenstadt) appears unusual, a concert could well have been fitted in on the way back from Pest, where Liszt performed on 24 May 1823.
7 *Ges. Schr.* II,31–2. *On the Conservatoire*.
8 Ramann/Schnapp, *Lisztiana* (Mainz 1983), p. 119.
9 In his article "Die Autorschaft der literarischen Werke Franz Liszts" in *Ungarische Jahrbücher*, xx (Berlin 1940/41), the distinguished Liszt scholar Émile Haraszti mentions "Préludes et Exercices de Muzio Clementi, corrigés et marqués au métronome par le jeune Liszt suivi de douze de ses études chez Dufaut et Dubois à Paris (1826)." I have been unable to find any trace of this edition.
10 Charles Salaman, *Pianists of the Past* (London 1901).
11 *Aus Moscheles' Leben. Nach Briefen und Tagebüchern herausgegeben von seiner Frau* (Leipzig 1872), I,138.
12 *Franz Liszts Briefe an seine Mutter* (note 1 above), p. 9; letter of 24 August 1827.

13 Janka Wohl, *Franz Liszt. Erinnerungen einer Landsmännin* (Jena 1887), pp. 191–2.
14 *Ges. Schr.* II,128. *To George Sand (January 1837)*.
15 Wilhelm von Lenz, *Die großen Pianofortevirtuosen unserer Zeit* (Berlin 1872).
16 *Ges. Schr.* II,127. *To George Sand (January 1837)*.
17 *Ges. Schr.* II,128. *To George Sand (January 1837)*.
18 *Ges. Schr.* IV,102. *Berlioz and his "Harold" Symphony*.
19 *Ges. Schr.* IV,4. *Berlioz and his "Harold" Symphony*.
20 *Ges. Schr.* IV,61. *Berlioz and his "Harold" Symphony*.
21 Berlioz on Liszt in *Gazette musicale*, No. 24, 12 June 1836.
22 *Frédéric Chopin. Briefe* (Berlin 1983), p. 129; letter to Tytus Woyciechowski of 12 December 1831.
23 *Frédéric Chopin. Briefe*, p. 134; letter to Józef Elsner of 14 December 1831.
24 Alan Walker, *Franz Liszt. The Virtuoso Years* (London 1983), p. 116.
25 Auguste Boissier, *Liszt pédagogue: Leçons de piano données par Liszt à Mlle. Valérie Boissier en 1832* (Paris 1927); German trans. *Franz Liszt als Lehrer* (Berlin/Vienna/Leipzig 1930), p. 15.
26 *Br.* I,7–8; letter to Pierre Wolff of 2 May 1832.
27 *Ges. Schr.* II,112. *Paganini: An Obituary (1840)*.
28 Ramann/Schnapp, *Lisztiana* (note 5), p. 406.
29 *Ges. Schr.* I,155–6. *To Adolphe Pictet (September 1837)*.
30 *Br.* I,382; letter to Otto Leßmann of 5 September 1885.
31 Auguste Boissier, *Liszt pédagogue* (note 25), German trans. p. 10.
32 *Frédéric Chopin. Briefe* (note 22), p. 140; letter to Józef Nowakowski of 15 April 1832.
33 *Br.* I,7; letter to Pierre Wolff of 2 May 1832.
34 *Corr.* I,358; letter to Liszt of 18 January 1840.
35 All the books on Liszt which mention this incident transfer the setting to Marlioz during the whole of the winter of 1832/33. However, Liszt played a series of concerts in Paris on 19 January, 2, 19, and 23 March 1833, so he cannot have spent "the whole of the winter" at the castle in the Swiss Alps "cut off from the outside world by snowdrifts." Although he could have been at Marlioz in February, there is no documentary evidence to support this. On the other hand, there is a letter from Liszt to his mother written from Marlioz on 9 January 1831; other letters of 12 February 1831 and May 1831 were written from the neighbouring town of Geneva. The winter visit to Marlioz may therefore have taken place

from January to mid-February 1831 or possibly also from mid-February to the end of April 1831, the more so in that there is no evidence during this period for Liszt's presence in Paris. Not until the spring of 1831 did he supposedly return to the French capital.

36 *Frédéric Chopin. Briefe* (note 22), p. 135; letter to Tytus Woyciechowski of 25 December 1831. [*Translator's note*: Chopin's reference to "the fourth floor" is translated – as throughout this book – in the British sense; in American usage this would be "the fifth floor."]

37 *Frédéric Chopin. Briefe*, pp. 145–6; letter to Ferdinand Hiller of 20 June 1833.

38 Marie d'Agoult, *Mémoires 1833–54* (Paris 1927); German trans. *Memoiren* (Dresden 1928), I,35–6.

39 In her edition of *Franz Liszts Briefe an seine Mutter* (pp. 10, 11, 12) La Mara dates this visit to Carentono "1832 or 1833." It is clear from a letter from Liszt to Marie d'Agoult that the correct date should be 1834.

40 Émile Haraszti states that Liszt's *Lélio* Fantasy for piano and orchestra received its first performance on 24 November 1834. I have been unable to find any evidence in Paris reviews of the period to support Haraszti's claim.

41 In his article "Liszt's *Lyon*: Music and the Social Conscience" in *19th-Century Music*, Spring 1981, pp. 228–43, Alexander Main advances the view that the fragmentary *Harmonies poétiques et religieuses* had already been composed between 16 May and 30 October 1833, and that *Lyon* was not written until between 19 December 1837 and 31 January 1838.

42 *Corr*. I,109; letter to Marie d'Agoult of 25 August 1834.

43 *Br*. I,12; letter to Félicité de Lamennais of 14 January 1835.

44 *Br*. VIII,8; letter to George Sand of spring 1836.

45 Cf. Aldobrandino Malvezzi, *La Principessa Christina Belgiojoso*, and H. Remsen Whitehouse, *A Revolutionary Princess: Christina Belgiojoso-Trivulzio, Her Life and Times, 1808–1871* (New York 1906).

46 See previous note.

47 *Corr*. I,414; letter to Marie d'Agoult of 20 March 1840.

48 *Ges. Schr*. II,208–9. *To Lambert Massart (April/May 1838)*.

49 *Ges. Schr*. II,210–11. *To Lambert Massart (April/May 1838)*.

50 *Ges. Schr*. II,151. *To Adolphe Pictet (September 1837)*.

51 *Corr*. I,223; letter to Marie d'Agoult of 28 April 1838.

52 Marie d'Agoult, *Mémoires* (note 38), German trans. II,145.

53 *Br*. II,132; letter to Professor S. Lebert of 2 December 1868.

54 *Corr*. I,234–5; letter to Liszt of 25 June 1838.

55 *Br*. I,25; letter to Princess Christina Belgiojoso of 4 June 1839.

56 *Br*. I,30–31; letter to the Beethoven Committee in Bonn of 3 October 1839.

57 *Corr*. II,155; letter to Liszt of 13 June 1841.

58 *Ges. Schr*. II,254. *To Hector Berlioz (2 October 1839)*.

59 *Une Correspondance Romantique* (Paris 1947), p. 127; letter to Henri Lehmann of 20 September 1840.

60 *Ges. Schr*. II,253. *To Hector Berlioz (2 October 1839)*.

61 *Corr*. I,262–3; letter to Liszt of 23 October 1839.

62 *Corr*. I,264; letter to Marie d'Agoult of 25 October 1839.

63 *Corr*. I,308; letter to Marie d'Agoult of 4 December 1839.

64 *Corr*. I,313; letter to Marie d'Agoult of 6 December 1839.

65 In her edition of *Franz Liszt. Briefe aus ungarischen Sammlungen* (p. 457), the normally reliable Liszt scholar Margit Prahács gives "18 to 24 December" as the duration of Liszt's stay in Preßburg. That Liszt was already in Pest on the 23rd is clear from (1) *Allgemeine Theaterzeitung* of 28 December 1839; (2) *Corr*. I,342; (3) the title page of the poem reproduced in Illus. 227.

66 *Br*. I,32–3; letter to Clara Wieck of 25 December 1839.

67 *Corr*. I,364; letter to Marie d'Agoult of 23 January 1840.

68 *Corr*. I,342; letter to Marie d'Agoult of 25 December 1839.

69 *Robert und Clara Schumann. Briefe einer Liebe* (Königstein 1982), pp. 269, 270, 271, 275.

70 *Corr*. I,217; letter to Marie d'Agoult of 13 April 1838.

71 *Ges. Schr*. III,129. *Pauline Viardot-Garcia (1859)*.

72 *Ges. Schr*. IV,192, 193, 194, 195–6. *Clara Schumann (1855)*.

73 *Briefe aus ungarischen Sammlungen* (note 3), p. 50; letter to Leo Festetics of 20 June 1840.

74 *Robert und Clara Schumann. Briefe einer Liebe* (note 69), p. 270.

75 Eduard Hanslick, *Concerte, Componisten und Virtuosen, 1870–1885* (Berlin 1886), p. 122.

76 *Frédéric Chopin. Briefe* (note 22), p. 126; letter to Tytus Woyciechowski of 12 December 1831.

77 The present drawing was formerly owned by Louis de Ronchaud (1816–1887), a friend of Liszt's and Marie d'Agoult's; recognizing the talent of the artist Théodore Chassériau (1819–1856) at an early date, she supported Chassériau and encouraged him.

78 Ramann/Schnapp, *Lisztiana* (note 5), p. 400.

79 Karl August Varnhagen von Ense, *Tagebücher*, 2 vols. (Berlin 1863).

80 Reproduced from Vol. II of Lina Ramann's biography (Leipzig 1887).

81 Ludwig Rellstab, *Franz Liszt* (Berlin 1842), p. I.

82 Vladimir Stasov, *Selected Essays on Music*, trans. Florence Jonas (London 1968); German ed. *Liszt, Schumann und Berlioz in Rußland* (St Petersburg 1896).

83 The majority of these reports appeared in the *Leipziger Allgemeine Zeitung* of 1842.

84 Varnhagen von Ense, *Tagebücher* (note 79).

85 Ramann/Schnapp, *Lisztiana* (note 5), p. 401.

86 *Corr*. II,332; letter to Marie d'Agoult of 18 February 1844.

87 Adelheid von Schorn, *Zwei Menschenalter* (Stuttgart 1923), p. 133.

88 Cf. Alan Walker, *Franz Liszt. The Virtuoso Years* (note 24), pp. 392–6.

89 *O Patriota*, 24 January 1845.

90 Henry F. Chorley, *Modern German Music* (London 1854).

91 *Br*. VIII,44; letter to Professor Christian Lobe of 25 August 1845.

92 Adelheid von Schorn, *Zwei Menschenalter* (note 87), pp. 191–2.

93 *Corr*. II,379; letter to Marie d'Agoult of 1 May 1847.

94 *Corr*. II,347–8; letter to Marie d'Agoult of 2 February 1846.

95 The original of this daguerreotype was formerly in the possession of Lina Ramann, who evidently presented it to the Liszt Museum in Weimar. It now appears to be missing: neither Friedrich Schnapp nor the present writer has succeeded in locating it. The daguerreotype reproduced here is a contemporary copy in the author's private collection. Cf Ramann/Schnapp, *Lisztiana* (note 5), pp. 328, 329, 460.

96 *Br*. VIII,50–51; letter to Erard, Paris, probably July 1847.

97 *Br*. II,328; letter to Henriette von Liszt of 8 February 1884.

98 *Br*. VIII,163; letter to Julius Schuberth of 5 September 1863.

99 A letter from Liszt to Marie d'Agoult said to be written from Weimar (!) on 29 April 1848 is evidently incorrectly dated by the editor; cf. *Corr*. II,395.

100 *Richard Wagner. Gesammelte Schriften und Dichtungen* (Leipzig 1887/88), IV,340.

101 Cf. John Deathridge and Carl Dahlhaus, *The New Grove Wagner* (London 1984), pp. 34–6.

102 *Briefwechsel zwischen Franz Liszt und Carl Alexander* (Leipzig 1909), pp. 33–4.

103 *Hans von Bülow. Briefe und Schriften* (Leipzig 1895), I,172.

104 Review by H. Uhde, quoted in *Musica sacra* for 1910, No. 11, p. 131.

105 *Hans von Bülow. Briefe und Schriften* (note 103), I,386.

106 *Hans von Bülow. Briefe und Schriften*, I,483.

107 *Peter Cornelius. Literarische Werke* (Leipzig 1904), I,236–7.

108 *Briefe hervorragender Zeitgenossen an Franz Liszt* (Leipzig 1895), I,43 and 45.

109 Eduard Devrient, *Geschichte der deutschen Schauspielkunst* (Leipzig 1848–74, Zurich 1929).

110 *Briefe hervorragender Zeitgenossen an Franz Liszt* (note 108), I,113–14.

111 *Niederrheinische Musikzeitung* 1853, p. 139ff.

112 *Richard Wagner. Sämtliche Briefe*, ed. Hans-Joachim Bauer and Johannes Forner, vol. VI (Leipzig 1986), 249; letter dated 7(?) October 1854; translation from *Selected Letters of Richard Wagner*, ed. Stewart Spencer and Barry Millington (London 1987), p. 319.

113 *Br*. VII,313; letter to Carolyne von Sayn-Wittgenstein of 2 April 1881.

114 *Briefwechsel zwischen Wagner und Liszt* (3rd ed., Leipzig 1910), II,65; letter of 5 April 1855; English trans. in *Selected Letters of Richard Wagner* (note 112), p. 337.

115 In the table of contents to *Ges. Schr*. III,2, this essay is incorrectly dated "1859," whereas the correct date (as given in the chapter itself) is 1854; cf. *Richard Wagner. Sämtliche Briefe* (note 112) VI,142 and 249, and *Briefwechsel zwischen Wagner und Liszt* (note 114), II,27–8, where Liszt's letter of 20 April 1854 is wrongly dated "20 May 1854."

116 *Briefwechsel zwischen Wagner und Liszt*, II,66; letter of 2 May 1855.

117 *Br*. I,273ff; letter to Eduard Liszt of 26 March 1857.

118 *Briefe hervorragender Zeitgenossen an Franz Liszt* (note 108), I,63.

119 Fanny Lewald, *Zwölf Bilder nach dem Leben* (1888).

120 *Briefwechsel zwischen Wagner und Liszt* (note 114), II,141; letter of 16 December 1856.

121 *Br*. IV,217; letter to Carolyne von Sayn-Wittgenstein of 1855.

122 Franz von Milde, *Ein ideales Künstlerpaar*,

Rosa und Feodor von Milde, ihre Kunst und ihre Zeit (Leipzig 1918), I,26.

123 *Br*. III,35–6; letter to Agnes Street-Klindworth of 21 July 1855.

124 *Briefwechsel zwischen Wagner und Liszt* (note 114), II,200; letter of 18 May 1858.

125 *Briefwechsel zwischen Wagner und Liszt*, II,203–4; letter of 2 July 1858.

126 *Briefwechsel zwischen Wagner und Liszt*, II,208; letter of 8 July 1858.

127 *Br*. VI,306; letter to Carolyne von Sayn-Wittgenstein of 1871.

128 See note 114.

129 From a letter dated 17 December 1858 from Cornelius to his sister Susanne.

130 *Briefwechsel zwischen Franz Liszt und Carl Alexander* (note 102), p. 87ff; letter of 6 February 1860.

131 *Briefwechsel zwischen Wagner und Liszt* (note 114), II,155; letter of 19 April 1857.

132 *Br*. V,209–10; letter to Carolyne von Sayn-Wittgenstein of 12 August 1861.

133 *Br*. V,198; letter to Carolyne von Sayn-Wittgenstein of 29 June 1861.

134 *Briefwechsel zwischen Franz Liszt und Carl Alexander* (note 102), p. 95; letter of 19 August 1860.

135 Thuringian State Archives.

136 Ferdinand Gregorovius, *Römische Tagebücher* (Stuttgart 1892), p. 320.

137 *Br*. II,16; letter to Franz Brendel of 12 July 1862.

138 *Br*. II,26; letter to Franz Brendel of 8 November 1862.

139 Eugen d'Albert in *Der Merker*, second October issue 1911.

140 *Br*. II,35–6; letter to Breitkopf & Härtel of 26 March 1863.

141 *Br*. II,60; letter to Franz Brendel of 11 November 1863.

142 *Franz Liszts Briefe an Carl Gille* (Leipzig 1903), pp. 11–12; letter of 10 September 1863.

143 The dating "Mad. del Rosario, 27 dec. 1866" in *Br*. VI,128 is either a mistake or evidence of an otherwise unrecorded visit to the Oratorio della Madonna del Rosario at this time.

144 *Franz Liszts Briefe an seine Mutter* (note 1), p. 148; letter of 25 July 1863.

145 August Stradal, *Erinnerungen an Franz Liszt* (Berne/Leipzig 1929), p. 127.

146 *Br*. II,64; letter to Franz Brendel of 22 January 1864.

147 *Br*. II,66; letter to Franz Brendel of 28 May 1864.

148 *Corr*. II,411; letter to Marie d'Agoult of 15 November 1844.

149 Kurd von Schlözer, *Römische Briefe* (Berlin/Leipzig 1926), p. 71ff.

150 *Franz Liszts Briefe an Carl Gille* (Leipzig 1903), p. 14; letter of 27 January 1864.

151 *Br*. II,76; letter to Breitkopf & Härtel of 14 September 1864.

152 *Briefe aus ungarischen Sammlungen* (note 3), p. 119; letter to Mihály Mosonyi of 4 January 1865.

153 *Briefe aus ungarischen Sammlungen*, p. 122; letter to Johann Nepomuk Dunkl of 29 September 1865.

154 *Br*. II,81; letter to Prince Konstantin von Hohenzollern-Hechingen of 11 May 1865.

155 *Br*. VIII,170; letter to an unknown recipient of 20 May 1865.

156 *Franz Liszts Briefe an Carl Gille* (note 150), p. 26; letter of 23 October 1866.

157 Kurd von Schlözer, *Römische Briefe* (note 149), p. 73.

158 *Br*. VI,110–11; letter to Carolyne von Sayn-Wittgenstein of 13 April 1866.

159 Marie d'Agoult, *Mémoires* (note 38), p. 174.

160 *Br*. II,107–8; letter to Eduard von Liszt of 20 October 1867.

161 A copy of the manuscript was given to me in Paris in 1976. Unfortunately, the name of the owner of the original manuscript cannot be credited here, since it is no longer known to me.

162 *Br.* VI,158; letter to Carolyne von Sayn-Wittgenstein of 3 October 1867.

163 Cf Ludwig Kusche, *Franz Liszt. Porträt eines Übermenschen* (Munich 1961), pp. 61–2.

164 *Br.* II,118; letter to Franz Brendel of 31 March 1868.

165 *Franz Liszts Briefe an Carl Gille* (note 150), p. 33; letter of 12 July 1868.

166 *Br.* VII,73; letter to Carolyne von Sayn-Wittgenstein of 14 June 1874.

167 *Franz Liszts Briefe an Carl Gille* (note 150), p. 41; letter of 17 November 1869.

168 *Briefe aus ungarischen Sammlungen* (note 3), p. 219; letter to Kornél von Abrányi of 15 September 1879.

169 On p. 159 of *Franz Liszts Briefe an Baron Anton Augusz* (Budapest 1911) a letter from Liszt is dated ''Horpács, 19 January 1870.'' In all likelihood the correct date should be ''19 January 1874.''

170 ''Über Franz Liszt's Symphonische Dichtungen. Brief an M.W.'' in *Richard Wagner. Gesammelte Schriften und Dichtungen* (note 100), V,182–98, esp. 197.

171 Cf. *Briefwechsel zwischen Wagner und Liszt* (note 114), II,234, 226, 29–30, 37.

172 *Cosima Wagner und Houston Stewart Chamberlain im Briefwechsel 1888–1908* (Leipzig 1934), p. 99.

173 *Franz Liszt. Ein Gedenkblatt von seiner Tochter* (Munich 1911), pp. 118–19.

174 Berthold Kellermann, *Ein Künstlerleben* (Erlenbach-Zurich 1932), pp. 31–2. Kellermann (1853–1926) was introduced to Liszt ca. 1871 and studied with him from 1873 to 1879. He later became a tireless advocate of Liszt's works. In 1878, on Liszt's recommendation, he became piano teacher to Wagner's children. From 1882 to 1921 he was Professor of Piano and the History of Music at the Königliche Musikschule in Munich.

175 *Cosima Wagner. Die Tagebücher*, ed. Martin Gregor-Dellin and Dietrich Mack, 2 vols. (Munich/Zurich 1976/77), I,581; entry of 17 October 1872; English trans. by Geoffrey Skelton (London/New York 1978–80), I,542.

176 Eduard Hanslick, *Concerte, Componisten und Virtuosen* (note 75), p. 78ff.

177 *Br.* VII,56; letter to Carolyne von Sayn-Wittgenstein of 8 February 1874.

178 *Franz Liszt. Ein Gedenkblatt von seiner Tochter* (note 173), p. 121.

179 Count Albert Apponyi, *Erlebnisse und Ergebnisse* (Berlin 1933), pp. 69–70.

180 Eduard Hanslick, *Concerte, Componisten und Virtuosen* (note 75), p. 123ff; English trans. adapted from *Vienna's Golden Years of Music 1850–1900*, trans. Henry Pleasants III (London 1951), pp. 113–15.

181 *Br.* VII,91; letter to Carolyne von Sayn-Wittgenstein of 16 March 1875.

182 *The Letters of Franz Liszt to Olga von Meyendorff* (Cambridge, Mass., 1978) contains a letter from Liszt dated ''Hanover, 30 August 1875'' with a reference to Liszt's forthcoming visit to the Castle at Loo. Since Liszt was in Weimar on 30 August 1875 but in Hanover on 30 April 1875 and in Loo on 2 May 1875, the correct dating is presumably ''Hanover, 30 April 1875.''

183 *Br.* VIII,301; letter to Julius Schuberth of 4 December 1875.

184 Count Albert Apponyi, *Erlebnisse und Ergebnisse* (note 179), p. 83ff.

185 Lina Ramann (*Lisztiana* [note 5], p. 100) dates this visit of Liszt's ''4–6 October 1876.'' Liszt's letters to Baroness Meyendorff (Hanover, 5 October 1876, and Nuremberg, 9 October 1876) and to Carolyne von Sayn-Wittgenstein (Nuremberg, 7 October 1876) suggest that Lina Ramann is in error here.

186 *Br.* VII,133; letter to Carolyne von Sayn-Wittgenstein of 8 April 1876.

187 *Franz Liszts Briefe an Carl Gille* (note 150), p. 63; letter of 17 December 1877.

188 *Br.* II,280; letter to Ludwig Bösendorfer of 19 February 1879.

189 *Br.* VII,131; letter to Carolyne von Sayn-Wittgenstein of 14 March 1876.

190 Berthold Litzmann, *Clara Schumann. Ein Künstlerleben* (Leipzig 1909), p. 334.

191 *Robert und Clara Schumann. Briefe einer Liebe* (note 74), p. 269.

192 *Robert und Clara Schumann. Briefe einer Liebe*, p. 272.

193 Johannes Brahms to friends, ca. 1890.

194 Quoted by Arthur Friedheim, *Life and Liszt* (New York 1961).

195 *Br.* VIII,394; letter to Johannes Brahms of mid-April 1882.

196 Malwida von Meysenbug, *Memoiren einer Idealistin und ihr Nachtrag: Der Lebensabend einer Idealistin* (Stuttgart 1927), II,267ff.

197 *Franz Liszt: Correspondance*, ed. Pierre-Antoine Huré and Claude Knepper (Paris 1987), p. 213; wrongly dated 1853 in *Franz Liszts Briefe an seine Mutter* (note 1), p. 101. ''Princess G.'' = ''Princess Gagarine.''

198 In *Br.* VII,179 a letter from Liszt is dated ''Hanover, 16 March 1877.'' The month is definitely incorrect and should probably read ''16 May 1877.''

199 *Cosima Wagner. Die Tagebücher* (note 175), I,1041; English trans. I,956.

200 Eduard Hanslick, *Concerte, Componisten und Virtuosen* (note 75), pp. 202–3.

201 *Br.* VII,202; letter to Carolyne von Sayn-Wittgenstein of 23 September 1877.

202 *Cosima Wagner. Die Tagebücher* (note 175), II,164; entry of 21 August 1877; English trans. II,138.

203 *The Letters of Franz Liszt to Olga von Meyendorff* (note 182), p. 344.

204 *Br.* VI,362; letter to Carolyne von Sayn-Wittgenstein of 9 October 1872.

205 *Br.* II,290; letter to Frau Reisenauer-Pauly of 30 January 1880.

206 *Br.* VII,305; letter to Carolyne von Sayn-Wittgenstein of 26 December 1880.

207 *Br.* II,306; letter to Dionys von Pazmandy of 15 February 1881.

208 Janka Wohl, *Franz Liszt. Erinnerungen einer Landsmännin* (note 13), pp. 173–4.

209 *Br.* II,40; letter to Eduard Liszt of 22 May 1863.

210 *Br.* VI,320; letter to Carolyne von Sayn-Wittgenstein of 27 December 1871.

211 *Br.* VI,175; letter to Carolyne von Sayn-Wittgenstein of 23 July 1868.

212 *Br.* II,316; letter to Camille Saint-Saëns of 6 December 1881.

213 August Stradal, *Erinnerungen an Franz Liszt* (note 145), p. 99.

214 Janka Wohl, *Franz Liszt. Erinnerungen einer Landsmännin* (note 13), pp. 177–8.

215 Janka Wohl, *Franz Liszt. Erinnerungen einer Landsmännin*, p. 176.

216 Hans von Wolzogen, *Erinnerungen an Richard Wagner* (Vienna 1883).

217 Cf. Géza Zichy, *Aus meinem Leben. Erinnerungen und Fragmente* (Stuttgart 1920), III.

218 *Br.* I,75; letter to Gaëtano Belloni of 14 May 1849.

219 *Br.* VII,408; letter to Carolyne von Sayn-Wittgenstein of 24 July 1884.

220 *Br.* VII,353; letter to Carolyne von Sayn-Wittgenstein of 6 August 1882.

221 *Ges. Schr.* III,2, pp. 175–6. *Wagner's Fliegender Holländer (1854).*

222 August Stradal, *Erinnerungen an Franz Liszt* (note 145), pp. 168–9.

223 August Stradal, *Erinnerungen an Franz Liszt*, p. 103.

224 *Franz Liszts Briefe an Carl Gille* (note 150), p. 73; letter of 2 February 1884.

225 *The Letters of Franz Liszt to Olga von Meyendorff* (note 182), pp. 459–60.

226 J. Zichy, *Erinnerungen an Franz Liszt, Muzsika* (Budapest 1929), I,14–15.

227 Count Géza Zichy, *Franz Liszt*, feature article of ca. 1911.

228 The *Csárdás obstiné* is generally dated 1884, but a letter of 26 February 1885 to Baroness von Meyendorff (*The Letters of Franz Liszt to Olga von Meyendorff* [note 182]) might suggest that the piece was not written until February 1885. This later reference may, however, be to an (untraceable) piano duet version which August Göllerich mentions in his 1908 book on Liszt (p. 305).

229 Quoted in Alexander Siloti, ''Meine Erinnerungen an Franz Liszt'' in *Zeitschrift der Internationalen Musikgesellschaft*, Vol. 14, 1912/13.

230 James Huneker, *Franz Liszt* (New York 1911); German trans. (Munich 1922).

231 August Stradal, *Erinnerungen an Franz Liszt* (note 145), pp. 66–7.

232 Ramann/Schnapp, *Lisztiana* (note 5), p. 298.

233 *Ges. Schr.* II,233–4. *On the Position of Music in Italy (1838).*

234 *Ges. Schr.* IV,147. *Robert Schumann (1855).*

235 *Br.* II,262; letter to Jules de Zarembski of 13 December 1877.

236 *Ges. Schr.* III,115. *Donizetti's ''La Favorita'' (1854).*

237 *Br.* I,73; letter to Carl Reinecke of 25 March 1849.

238 *Ges. Schr.* IV,129–30. *Robert Schumann (1855).*

239 *Ges. Schr.* II,233. *On the Position of Music in Italy (1838).*

240 August Stradal, *Erinnerungen an Franz Liszt* (note 145), p. 112.

241 *Liszts Briefe an Baron Anton Augusz* (note 169), p. 13.

242 *Franz Liszt. Ein Gedenkblatt von seiner Tochter* (note 173), p. 121.

243 *Br.* II,226; letter to Lina Ramann of 28 September 1875.

244 Peter Raabe, *Liszts Schaffen* (Stuttgart/Berlin 1931), p. 63.

245 *Br.* II,389; letter to Walter Bache of 11 February 1886.

246 *Br.* II,348; letter to Lina Ramann of 22 February 1883.

247 *Franz Liszt. Ein Gedenkblatt von seiner Tochter* (note 173), pp. 50–51.

248 The most reliable account of the events that followed Liszt's death is that of Julius Kapp. The section *Post Mortem* has therefore been taken over, with minor modifications, from Kapp's *Franz Liszt* (Berlin 1911), pp. 298–9.

Picture Acknowledgements

Many of the illustrations and documents reproduced here are previously unpublished, and the important documents are all published for the first time in colour. I am grateful to the following photographers: Günter and Eva von Voithenberg and Juliane Zilz (Munich), Eberhard and Renate Renno (Weimar), Patrick Thönnessen (Geneva), Guarmathy (Budapest), Schächter (Pottendorf), Mercier (Geneva), Giraudon and Bulloz (Paris).

The following list of collections is arranged according to the number of illustrations made available. In a few cases the owners could not be located or did not wish to be named. The numbers refer to the picture captions in the main text.

All rights of reproduction are reserved by the individual collections.

Ernst Burger, Munich: 4, 5, 6, 7, 9, 10, 11, 15, 16, 18, 19, 20, 22, 25, 26, 27, 29, 30, 31, 32, 35, 37, 38, 44, 46, 47, 48, 49, 51, 52, 53, 54, 55, 57, 61, 63, 64, 68, 70, 74, 75, 79, 82, 83, 86, 94, 96, 97, 100, 101, 102, 105, 106, 108, 111, 112, 115, 117, 124, 126, 127, 128, 129, 131, 154, 156, 157, 159, 160, 161, 164, 172, 173, 176, 177, 178, 179, 181, 182, 185, 188, 190, 192, 193, 194, 195, 196, 197, 198, 200, 203, 208, 209, 210, 212, 215, 216, 217, 218, 224, 225, 226, 227, 235, 238, 239, 245, 246, 247, 248, 249, 250, 253, 254, 256, 260, 261, 262, 263, 264, 265, 267, 268, 270, 272, 273, 274, 283, 284, 285, 286, 287, 288, 289, 290, 291, 292, 295, 297, 304, 305, 312, 313, 314, 315, 316, 317, 320, 321, 323, 324, 325, 326, 327, 328, 330, 332, 334, 335, 341, 348, 349, 353, 354, 361, 362, 363, 367, 368, 373, 375, 385, 386, 387, 389, 401, 403, 404, 405, 408, 412, 416, 417, 418, 419, 426, 427, 430, 431, 432, 434, 436, 439, 440, 442, 443, 444, 446, 449, 450, 451, 453, 454, 455, 457, 458, 461, 462, 463, 464, 465, 466, 467, 469, 470, 471, 472, 473, 474, 477, 478, 479, 481, 484, 485, 488, 489, 490, 491, 492, 496, 497, 499, 500, 501, 502, 507, 509, 510, 511, 512, 514, 516, 520, 521, 522, 523, 524, 525, 526, 531, 533, 534, 535, 538, 541, 542, 543, 549, 550, 552, 556, 557, 558, 577, 578, 581, 582, 583, 585, 586, 587, 588, 589, 590, 591, 592, 593, 594, 595, 596, 597, 598, 599, 600, 601, 602, 603, 605, 606, 607, 608, 609, 610, 614, 615, 616, 617, 618, 619, 620, 621, 622, 623, 624, 625, 626, 629, 630, 631, 633, 635, 636, 637, 640, 641, 642, 643, 644, 645, 646, 647, 648, 649.

Nationalarchiv der Richard-Wagner-Stiftung/Richard-Wagner-Gedenkstätte, Bayreuth: 56, 71, 119, 120, 121, 141, 142, 158, 180, 183, 231, 232, 234, 251, 258, 269, 318, 338, 350, 352, 356, 357, 364, 366, 372, 374, 376, 379, 380, 407, 422, 423, 428, 441, 445, 448, 468, 498, 503, 504, 515, 518, 519, 530, 546, 551, 559, 562, 563, 573, 574, 575, 579, 580, 632, 638, 639, 650.

Nationale Forschungs- und Gedenkstätten der klassischen deutschen Literatur in Weimar: 14, 67, 92, 93, 99, 113, 137, 143, 144, 149, 166, 184, 191, 201, 204, 228, 336, 339, 340, 343, 344, 345, 347, 351, 382, 384, 394, 398, 400, 406, 409, 420, 425, 433, 435, 447, 459, 475, 480, 540, 544, 545, 547, 560, 561, 565, 571.

Former collection of Robert Bory, Coppet: 3, 36, 59, 69, 139, 148, 219, 236, 237, 275, 276, 277, 278, 279, 280, 281, 282, 377, 460, 493, 528, 529, 536, 553, 554, 555, 567, 568, 628.

Bayerische Staatsbibliothek, Munich: 17, 39, 40, 41, 42, 45, 62, 81, 103, 110, 152, 199, 293, 294, 298, 299, 300, 301, 309, 311, 399, 413, 414.

Liszt Museum of the Budapest Academy of Music: 13, 107, 252, 255, 271, 378, 392, 393, 395, 396, 415, 424, 456, 482, 527, 584, 611, 612, 613.

Musée Carnavalet, Paris. Photo Giraudon: 85, 91, 104, 168, 175. Photo Bulloz: 88, 116, 125, 207, 319, 360.

Source References

Gesellschaft der Musikfreunde, Vienna: 189, 213, 214, 322, 505, 508, 513, 517, 532, 537.

Bibliothèque nationale, Paris: 50, 65, 66, 84, 98, 155, 257.

Archiv mesta, Bratislava: 23, 24, 220, 221, 222, 223.

Hungarian National Museum, Budapest: 2, 230, 233, 342, 437, 438.

Kunsthistorisches Museum, Vienna: 241, 242, 243, 244, 391.

Munich City Museum: 43, 302, 303, 383.

Széchényi Library, Budapest: 21, 33, 34, 358.

Geneva Conservatory of Music: 76, 130, 133, 138.

Musée La Châtre, Nohant: 123, 150, 174.

Archives de la Maison Erard, Paris: 58, 60, 163.

Gerry Keeling, San Gabriel: 494, 495, 548.

Collection of Ollivier de Prevaux, Paris: 1, 80. Photo Schächter, Pottendorf: 12, 28. Wagner family, Bayreuth: 167, 205. Wolfgang Dömling, Hamburg: 259, 333. Museum of History, Budapest: 145, 146. Gemeentemuseum, The Hague: 569, 634. Kurt Hofmann, Hamburg: 388, 390. Lisbon State Museum: 307, 308. Margarita Höhenrieder, Munich: 134, 135. Eleonore Recher, Munich: 452, 572. Musée du Louvre, Paris: 95, 266. St Gall Municipal Archives: 410, 411.

Royal College of Music, London: 72. J. Bory, Coppet: 87. Jean-René Bory, Coppet: 89. Richard-Wagner-Museum, Eisenach: 114. De la Garde de Saignes, Paris: 118. George Eastman House, Rochester, New York: 122. Archives d'État, Geneva: 132. S. André-Maurois: 147. Bibliothèque de l'Institut de France, Paris: 151. Musée du Petit Palais, Paris: 153. Ary-Scheffer-Museum, Dordrecht: 165. Hamburg Kunsthalle: 169. Private collection of Alfred Cortot, Lausanne: 170. Berne Kunstmuseum: 206. Brera, Milan: 211. Ernst Collection, Budapest: 229. Picture Archive of Preußischer Kulturbesitz, Berlin: 240. Musée Condé, Chantilly: 296. Bayerische Verwaltung der staatlichen Schlösser, Gärten und Seen, Schloß Nymphenburg: 306. University of Pécs: 329. Hungarian National Gallery, Budapest, Corvina Archives (Photo Schiller): 331. Vittoriale, Gardone: 346. Schackgalerie, Munich, Joachim Blauel-Artothek: 359. Edme Jeanson, Paris: 369, 370. Bovet Collection: 381. Museo della Scala, Milan: 397. Greville Rothon, Munich: 402. Suermondt Museum, Aachen: 421. Longfellow House, Cambridge, Mass.: 483. Newberry Library, Chicago: 487. Lenbach Museum, Munich: 564. Toronto Conservatory of Music: 570. Richard-Wagner-Museum, Tribschen: 576. Musée de l'Opéra de Paris: 604.

Private collections: 8, 73, 77, 78, 90, 109, 136, 140, 162, 171, 186, 187, 310, 337, 365, 476, 486, 506, 539, 566, 627.

Lost: 202, 355, 371, 429.

INDEX

INDEX OF LISZT'S WORKS

The numbers in parentheses refer to Humphrey Searle's catalogue of Liszt's works as used by *The New Grove* and revised by Sharon Winklhofer. The names in parentheses indicate transcriptions of works by the named composers.

Index of Franz Liszt's Works